RUSSIA

POSSIBLE FUTURES SERIES

Series Editor: Craig Calhoun

In 2008, the World Public Forum convened a group of researchers and statesmen in Vienna to take stock of major global challenges. The magnitude of the global financial crisis was only just becoming clear, but the neoliberalism and market fundamentalism of the post–Cold War years had already taken a toll of their own.

Austrian Prime Minister Alfred Gusenbauer opened the meeting with a call to make sure the urgent attention the financial crisis demanded was not just short-term and superficial but included consideration of deeper geopolitical issues and governance challenges facing the global community.

In this spirit, several of the researchers present envisioned a project to bring together the analyses of leading scholars from a range of different countries, assessing not only the financial crisis but shifts in relations among major powers, trends in political economy, and the possible futures these opened. The group sought insight into emerging issues; it did not indulge the fantasy that the future could be predicted in detail.

The World Public Forum, created to facilitate a dialogue of civilizations rather than a clash, saw value in bringing high quality research to bear on public issues and possible futures. It provided financial support to the project including opportunities for many of the researchers to gather at its annual meetings on the island of Rhodes. This initial support was crucial to inaugurating the present important series of books.

VOLUME I
Business as Usual: The Roots of the Global Financial Meltdown
Edited by Craig Calhoun and Georgi Derluguian

VOLUME II
The Deepening Crisis: Governance Challenges after Neoliberalism
Edited by Craig Calhoun and Georgi Derluguian

VOLUME III
Aftermath: A New Global Economic Order?
Edited by Craig Calhoun and Georgi Derluguian

ALSO IN THE POSSIBLE FUTURES SERIES
Russia: The Challenges of Transformation
Edited by Piotr Dutkiewicz and Dmitri Trenin

Russia

THE CHALLENGES OF TRANSFORMATION

Edited by Piotr Dutkiewicz and Dmitri Trenin
Foreword by Craig Calhoun
Afterword by Vladimir I. Yakunin

A joint publication of the Social Science Research Council
and New York University Press

NEW YORK UNIVERSITY PRESS
New York and London
www.nyupress.org

© 2011 by Social Science Research Council
All rights reserved

Library of Congress Cataloging-in-Publication Data

Russia : the challenges of transformation / edited by Piotr Dutkiewicz
and Dmitri Trenin ; foreword by Craig Calhoun.
    p. cm. — (Possible futures series ; v. 4)
  "A co publication with the Social Science Research Council."
  Includes bibliographical references and index.
  ISBN 978-0-8147-8500-3 (cl : alk. paper) — ISBN 978-0-8147-8501-0
(e-book : alk. paper)
    1. Russia (Federation) — Economic conditions — 1991– 2. Russia
(Federation) — Economic policy — 1991– 3. Russia (Federation) — Politics
and government — 1991– 4. Post-communism — Russia (Federation)
  I. Dutkiewicz, Piotr. II. Trenin, Dmitrii.

HC336.27.R87 2011
330.947—dc22

2010052312

New York University Press books are printed on acid-free paper,
and their binding materials are chosen for strength and durability.

Printed in the United States of America
10 9 8 7 6 5 4 3 2 1

References to Internet websites (URLs) were accurate at the time of writing.
Neither the author nor New York University Press is responsible for URLs
that may have expired or changed since the manuscript was prepared.

All references to dollars in this volume are to U.S. dollars.

Contents

Abbreviations   vii

Acknowledgments   ix

Foreword   xi
Craig Calhoun

Introduction   1
Piotr Dutkiewicz and Dmitri Trenin

1   Missing in Translation: Re-conceptualizing Russia's Developmental State   9
Piotr Dutkiewicz

2   The Long Road to Normalcy: Where Russia Now Stands   41
Vladimir Popov

3   The Sovereign Bureaucracy in Russia's Modernizations   73
Georgi Derluguian

4   The Changing Dynamics of Russian Politics   87
Richard Sakwa

5   Leadership and the Politics of Modernization   115
Timothy J. Colton

6   The Sociology of Post-reform Russia   145
Mikhail K. Gorshkov

7   Elites: The Choice for Modernization   191
    Leonid Grigoriev

8   Education for an Innovative Russia   225
    Nur Kirabaev

9   Health and Healthcare in Russia Today and Tomorrow   245
    Oleg Atkov and Guzel Ulumbekova

10 The Imaginary Curtain   271
    Roderic Lyne

11 What Kind of a Europe for What Kind of Russia   301
    Alexander Rahr

12 The Obama Administration's "Reset Button" for Russia   343
    Andrew C. Kuchins

13 Russia: The Eastern Dimension   383
    Bobo Lo

14 Russia and the Newly Independent States
    of Central Asia: Relations Transformed   403
    Rustem Zhangozha

15 Of Power and Greatness   407
    Dmitri Trenin

AFTERWORD
Russia and the West: Toward Understanding   433
Vladimir I. Yakunin

About the Contributors   459

Index   463

Abbreviations

APEC	Asia-Pacific Economic Cooperation grouping
ARF	ASEAN Regional Forum
ASEAN	Association of Southeast Asian Nations
ASMOK	Association of Medical Societies for Quality
BTC	Baku-Tbilissi-Ceyhan
CAC	Central Asia—Center
CFE	Conventional Forces in Europe Treaty
CIS	Commonwealth of Independent States
CNPC	China National Petroleum Company
COMECON	Council for Mutual Economic Assistance
CSTO	Collective Security Treaty Organization
CTBT	Comprehensive Test-Ban Treaty
DPRK	Democratic People's Republic of Korea
EurAsEC	Eurasian Economic Community
FIGs	Financial Industrial Groups
FMCT	Fissile Material Cut-off Treaty
KSOR	Collective Rapid Reaction Force
INSOR	Institute of Contemporary Development
IMEMO	Institute of World Economy and International Relations
LDPR	Liberal-Democratic Party of Russia
MKNT	Moscow Committee for Science and Technology
OECD	Organization for Economic Cooperation and Development

OIC	Organization of Islamic Conference
OSCE	Organization for Security and Co-operation in Europe
PNP	Priority National Project
RFE	Russian Far East
Rosstat	Russian Federal Statistics Service
RF	Russian Federation
VTsIOM	Russian Public Opinion Research Center
SCO	Shanghai Cooperation Organization
START	Strategic Arms Reduction Treaty
WHO	World Health Organization

Acknowledgments

Many people and organizations contributed to this book. Above all, we are all grateful to the World Public Forum "Dialogue of Civilization" for its unwavering support for this project, the generous funding that permitted us to meet in Rhodes (in October 2009) to discuss the first draft of this book, and support in editing and translating several of the chapters. We are in particular grateful to Dr. V. I. Yakunin for his strategic decision to support the presentation of divergent views on Russia in this volume in a true spirit of dialogue of cultures. Many thanks go to Dr. V. Kulikov, who has been the manager of this project from its inception, responsible for its smooth development. Thanks go to O. Y. Atkov for his critical but always supportive oversight. Words of thanks to Kinross Gold (Toronto) and MDS (Montreal) for key support toward this publication during a particularly difficult launch period. Craig Calhoun was always on hand to help with wise advice. Siriol Hugh-Jones's translation of some chapters is very much appreciated. Piotr Dutkiewicz is grateful to Vincent Della Sala from Trento University (Italy) for his hospitality, which allowed him to review the first draft of this volume for a few weeks at Trento, distracted only by the beauty of the Trentino region and its famous grappa. D. Trenin and P. Dutkiewicz thank their families (Vera, Ewa, and Jan) for their time and encouragement when it was very much needed. Finally, thanks to those numerous colleagues and friends who read our chapters and gave us many useful comments.

Foreword

Craig Calhoun

For seventy years, Western policy makers and social scientists obsessed anxiously over the Soviet threat. For twenty years after the collapse of the USSR they have underestimated the importance of Russia. It is time to move past both exaggerated anxiety and relative neglect. Likewise, since the collapse of the Soviet Union Russian intellectuals themselves have vacillated between overstated assertions of the country's power and importance, and insecure catalogs of unfavorable international comparisons highlighting its weaknesses and problems. Again, understanding Russia today demands moving beyond these misleading extremes. And understanding Russia is crucial to understanding what sorts of futures are open on a global scale.

Russia is a major power. Its territory and its natural resources are huge. Though its military was disrupted and damaged during the post-communist transition—not least as equipment was stolen and sold abroad—it remains a nuclear power. After a wrenching transformation from communism to capitalism, Russia's economy is extremely uneven; massive profits haven't translated into either widespread economic opportunity or enough investment in new technology and other long-term sources of growth. But the Russian economy is nonetheless one of the world's largest—and larger in purchasing power parity than nominal values would suggest. It has great growth potential. The Russian state is beleaguered by its own transitional problems but has achieved considerable stability. Some leaders call for modernization and others for a new nationalism, but there is little doubt that most share a commitment to economic development led by a strong state. Russia still faces enormous challenges in achieving stable economic growth, in delivering social services, in maintaining security throughout an ethnically diverse and far-flung territory. But how Russia faces these challenges is not just a local question, it is a question of global significance.

This makes the current book both timely and important. In it, a group of leading Russian intellectuals and social scientists join with front-rank researchers from around the world to examine processes of social, political, and economic transformation in Russia. Some of these processes are pursued as an active project, often under the label of "modernization." This is sometimes articulated as a more scientific and internationally oriented counterpart to nationalism. The two are not sharply opposed, however, and the authors here show how political challenges and ambitions interact with agendas for institutional reform and economic growth. At the same time, the chapters make clear that neither politics nor economics alone holds the key to Russia's future, since questions of social inequality and participation, and more generally of social reproduction, will also be decisive. Part of the contribution of the book is, indeed, to show how these three dimensions are inextricably interconnected. At the same time, the authors do not shy away from critical perspectives on challenges facing Russia, both in its domestic policies and in its international relations. Indeed, there is no likely future in which Russia's global context will not be a basic factor in its domestic affairs. Likewise, Russia's domestic successes and failure's will inform what kind of international actor it is and whether it will be a force for stability or disruption on a global scale. It is appropriate that this book is published as part of the Possible Futures series in which distinguished social scientists explore factors that shape ways in which global order—or disorder—may develop over the coming decades.

The Return of Geopolitics

Russia is one of a small number of states that will play leading roles in an increasingly multilateral—or more worryingly, multipolar—world. U.S. hegemony is in decline, and with it five centuries of EuroAmerican global domination. But neither the United States nor Europe will fade from global power. Indeed, the United States remains the world's leading power. Its hegemony may decline slowly or more precipitously; in either case, the precise way in which it adapts to a less dominating role will be crucial. How much European countries will act in concert and how much as separate nation-states also remains to be seen. The experiment in European unity is echoed in other regional blocks; at the same time, countries distant from each other are developing new models for cooperation, both in international organizations and in bilateral relationships. If the end of hegemony is not to be the beginning of chaos, cooperation among major powers will be vital. Along with the United States, Russia, China, India, Brazil, and Turkey are all likely to be leaders, perhaps along with Iran, South Africa, and others.

Those not part of this big country club will not be irrelevant or unilaterally dependent. Some small countries wield disproportionate financial clout; some have remarkable natural resources. Europe is not the only region trying to achieve greater strength or security or market standing by regional integration. This is likely to be important to South America, Africa, and Asia (whether of a larger or a subregional scale). Russia itself will act not only as an individual nation-state but also as the hegemonic power in its region. And beyond spatially compact regions, religions and solidarities of language or culture will bind otherwise diverse countries. Western Christendom and the Orthodox world may or may not overcome long-standing divisions to unify Christendom, but both will matter. Likewise, the Umma Islam will contend with its own schismatic tendencies but also keep extending and renewing long-distance links.

Crucially, geopolitics may well return to center stage. It never became irrelevant, even though it was pushed into the background during the eras of global European empires, capitalist integration of the modern world system, and enormous but asymmetric expansion in technological capacities. There was a fantasy of air travel and electronic communications linking the whole into a synchronous whole, but this was never altogether achieved. Today, both unequal development and economic crises limit capitalist unity, and for all the remarkable speed of global communications, these are used as much to mobilize people on lines of cultural difference as to overcome such difference. The political geography of the near-term future may look in some ways like the eras of empires past.

One of the pioneers of modern geography, Sir Halford Mackinder, saw the center of the Eurasian landmass as "the pivot of history." Politicians between the World Wars were impressed by his notion that Germany and Russia needed to be separated by an East European buffer lest they be joined by force or diplomacy and come to dominate the world. But Mackinder also worried about a new Asian empire integrating Russia with China and Japan. And indeed, something like this was the project of "Eurasianists" a century ago—and of Eurasianists like Alexander Dugin today, even if they command only a tiny political following. If Mackinder's specific political predictions don't arouse the fears they once did, his broader arguments about the literal centrality of Central Asia may gain renewed currency. Traffic across and along the coasts of the great Eurasian landmass is once again linking the political economies and cultures of the supercontinent. Russia is of pivotal importance.

At the same time, the future of Russia is inextricably bound up with the future of the modern world system. This is true partly because of the disproportionate importance of energy and other natural resource exports to the Russian economy. Trade requires markets. But as the current unusually hot summer is reminding policy makers, Russia is an importer too. And the issues are not just net trade balances but specific relationships, especially with other countries throughout Asia and the Middle East. Politics and economics cannot be fully separated. The modern world system organizes capitalist production and trade on the basis of a division of labor with unequal returns. Resource trade gives Russia an advantage, but to gain a position in the relatively advantaged upper tier of the world system depends on complementing extractive industry with higher value-added production and developing more openness to entrepreneurial innovation. And this Russia does in competition with other countries—and in recent years, it has been at a disadvantage both directly because of institutions that were slow to change and indirectly because opportunities elsewhere led to brain drain. Russians have founded capitalist businesses that lead the world—most famously, Google—but not in Russia.

Politics and Social Reproduction

Here economic challenges are entangled with social and political ones. Economic activity in Russia remains marked by the wrenching transformation from communism, the rapid but strikingly inequitable privatization of many assets, and the challenges of transforming Soviet-era industries into effective capitalist ones. It has begun to develop a financial infrastructure, but this is heavily dependent on both the state and global capital markets. The crisis of 2008 hit hard, particularly because Russia had invested heavily in dollar-denominated securities and more generally accepted a good deal of Western economic advice. The financial crisis, and the weakness of the global financial regulatory system, shocked many. Some responded with renewed nationalism and calls for a romantic withdrawal from global integration; others responded with calls for further modernization, but with greater controls to protect Russian interests.

As neoliberalism was discredited globally, more than a few Russians felt confirmation for what they already knew. Russian leaders already thought an anti-state liberalism was bankrupt not just intuitively but because of the social chaos of Russia's go-go years in the 1990s. The shock therapy recommended by the IMF and American economists like Jeffrey Sachs had indeed produced a transition to markets, but with little fairness, attention to the public interest, protection for ordinary citizens, or development of state capacity. Radical market reforms with weak institutional supports had produced hyperinflation and then the Russian financial crisis of 1998. Millions were plunged into poverty. At the same time, wealth became extremely concentrated, producing an extravagant class of the new rich. Corruption not only became endemic but also took on a large-scale organized character in the combination of criminal economic activity in Russia and heavy reliance on offshore havens for unregulated and untaxed business.

Many of the policies of the Putin years that followed were a response. They reestablished some level of state control and sought to reduce the independent power of the new super-rich "oligarchs." Critics contend that corruption remains widespread and that insiders close to the government are still able to accumulate huge fortunes. They argue that democratic freedoms and human rights have been curtailed along with economic liberalism. Even if the critics are right, the government achieved much greater macro-economic stability—before the shock of the global crisis— and simply much more control. The need for this was felt not only because of economic chaos but also because of major security challenges—not least as fighting in Chechnya and Central Asia more generally was linked to terrorist incidents in Moscow.

Russia is a reminder that we need to shake ourselves free of the illusion that states are fading from the forefront of global affairs. For twenty years after the fall of the Soviet Union, the right wing and much of mainstream academic economics celebrated an illusory neoliberal vision not just of free trade but of reduced roles for state policy and regulation, and, in too many cases, striking elimination of public services, including those hard won by generations of workers' struggles (themselves shaken by the disappearance of the global alternative suggested by the USSR). The financial crisis that came to a head in 2008 brought a renewal of Keynesianism with enormous financial bailouts and stimulus packages. Some economists argue the Keynesian policies haven't been strong enough; others criticize the extent to which they were organized to benefit corporate elites, investors, and especially the financial industry more than ordinary citizens. But in any case, both the policies and the debates signal much wider recognition of the importance of states to economic stability and long-term productivity and prosperity. This is not just an issue of right-wing thought, however, since during the same period that neo-Hayekians and monetarists promoted economic liberalism an antiauthoritarian left was equally suspicious of states. Proper stress on the importance of civil society, social movements, and international organizations too often slipped into imagining that they could somehow substitute for the work of states. At an international level, the idea spread that globalization would somehow bring in its wake not just a rich array of international connections but "cosmopolitan democracy," or at least new forms of governance that would dramatically reduce the importance of states—and do this not only in the interest of capitalist corporations, but of ordinary people.

Russian disillusionment with neoliberal globalization is now shared by a variety of movements and politicians elsewhere. As deeply as China is committed to globalization, it is also strongly nationalistic at the level of both government policy and popular sentiment. The so-called new nationalisms of Latin America have brought forward critiques and alternative policies. And indeed there are critics in the United States and Europe, though generally not among central policy makers. The point is not that all these different critics of neoliberalism now want to follow the same path. It is rather that observers should be clear that states and state interests, sometimes bolstered by strong nationalist identities, are pivotal to political and economic affairs.

But the issues faced by states are not only matters of political power or economic growth. They are matters of social reproduction. Here again, Russia exemplifies the broader pattern. Enormous wealth is concentrated in a narrow class. Too much of this wealth flows offshore and too little into productive investments at home. Too few jobs and opportunities for economic mobility are created. The government attempts to deal with some of the issues by regulatory means, but much depends on social development.

"Modernization" is a code word with many meanings, including updating technology and making government bureaucracies more efficient. But it also necessarily means attempting to build or rebuild institutions that deliver public services and thereby use national wealth in ways that benefit a wider range of citizens and strengthen social solidarity. Nationalist ideology by itself is a weak substitute for policies that ensure that all citizens share in economic benefits and have opportunities for social, economic, and political participation—though it can be a support for such policies. And if modernization and nationalism are currently evocative terms, we shouldn't imagine they exhaust the conceptual frameworks for possible futures. Where, we might ask, does religion fit into Russia's future, as religious practice grows both within the Russian Orthodox Church and outside of it? Where does concern for the environment fit in? Environmental challenges are becoming increasingly important and also pose basic questions about the conditions under which social life can be reproduced—and in some cases, the costs of reproducing environmentally unsustainable social systems.

In Russia's case, many older institutions inherited from the Soviet Union were allowed to deteriorate through years of underfunding and poor management. Compared to other countries of comparable economic standing, Russia still has a highly educated population, but it has suffered sharply from both brain drain and neglect of its educational institutions. The Soviet scientific establishment that was world-leading in many fields simply has not been reproduced, and the same is true at many levels of the educational system. Russians with mathematical skills have been exported to become economists or MBAs in the United States. Health care has suffered in similar ways, and the effects are evident very directly in life expectancy. In each case, there are private alternatives for some, but not for most of the population.

Communism offered an approach to social reproduction, to making sure that the benefits of industrialization and economic growth were distributed widely and became the bases for improvements in both the condition of social life and the capacity of citizens to contribute to social life. Different approaches were developed in capitalist countries during the late nineteenth and twentieth centuries, from public education systems to welfare states. Some of the innovations came specifically in response to crises like the Great Depression and were accompanied by expansion of economic regulations to try to minimize such crises and the damage they do to social reproduction. It is not likely that Russia will return to communism. And in many of the world's capitalist countries, there is a massive curtailment of public services now underway as a result of fiscal stringencies. In a sense, debt-burdened countries of the rich world are being asked to impose "structural adjustment" on themselves—as they, through the IMF, asked it of poorer countries in the 1980s. In the West as in Russia, however, the question of social reproduction is not likely to vanish. On the contrary, it is moving to the forefront, becoming a challenge as basic as economic growth and macro-economic stability or national security.

Russia is in crisis today partly because of specific Russian circumstances, but partly because the world itself is in crisis. Conversely, the continuing transformation of Russia is of central importance to efforts to build a new world order today as well as to efforts to create a flourishing national future. This book is published alongside a series of efforts to look globally at the "possible futures" that are open as the world deals with financial crisis, declining U.S. hegemony, rapid growth in Asia, and a range of other challenges, from environmental degradation to infectious diseases. Russia is a vital shaping influence on these possible futures. This book is a good place to start giving Russia the intellectual attention it deserves.

Introduction

Piotr Dutkiewicz and Dmitri Trenin

This book seeks to "re-think Russia." Over the past years, there has been a tendency, in the global academic community but even more widely in the world media, to focus on Russia's failure to transit from communism to democracy. The verdict reads, sternly, "lost in transition." A countertendency, actively propagated within Russia, has extolled the virtues of the country's stabilization after the tempest and tumult of the 1980s and 1990s. The motto of this group proudly states, "Russia has risen from its knees." From that perspective, it is the outside world's responsibility to be more objective toward Russia.

Both arguments were superseded by the world economic crisis, which did not spare Russia as a safe haven, as some of its leaders had hoped. In fact, Russia turned out to be among the world's worst-hit economies. The recovery has been slow. The crisis, however, also has laid bare the flaws in the economic, social, and political systems of North America, Europe, and Japan, which had been touted as models for the rest of the world, including Russia. Thus, the debate along the familiar lines of the mimicry of the "Western model" is now definitely over, and a new round of thinking is about to begin.

In Russia, the buzzword is "modernization." President Medvedev's "Go, Russia!" article, first posted in September 2009, set the tone for a wide-ranging debate. There is a broad realization that unless the country curbs its runaway corruption, diversifies its economy, thus diminishing its dependence on energy exports, and builds a knowledge industry, Russia's future might be bleak. The alternative to modernization is marginalization. However, while the shining image of an "ideal Russia" finds few contestants, there is a lot of confusion and vigorous discussion about how to proceed toward that goal.

The problem, of course, is deeper than the size of the GDP or even its structure, the rate of growth and its quality, or the share of innovation technology. A country's economy is inseparable from the people who work in it, and this raises a whole range of issues dealing with society. Russia's has been very resilient. It absorbed a series of incredibly hard blows that came with the passing of the *ancien régime* and the advent of new, often harsh realities. It survived, but it—inevitably—mutated. Once reputedly collectivist, today's Russia has gone private. It is a country of consumers but not—at least not yet—citizens; it is also a state in search of a nation. As Yevgeny Yassin, a former cabinet minister and the informal dean of Russian liberal economists, wryly observed, "There is no drive behind the modernization slogan."

Russian modernizations, however, traditionally came in a top-down fashion. Suffice it to recall Peter the Great and Alexander II; Stolypin, Stalin, and Gorbachev. Would the twenty-first century be different? It might well be: entrepreneurial spirit, in the age of globalization, trumps mobilization directives. The bigger problem is, can modernization succeed in the economic realm, while the system of government remains a closed and well-protected area? Liberal critics of the authorities are quick to quip that it is hard to change anything without changing anything.

The dilemma that the Russian authorities face is, indeed, very serious. Those who sincerely want to modernize the country—if only to keep it in one piece and earn a decent ranking in the global pecking order—have the image of the hapless Mr. Gorbachev before their eyes. He, too, genuinely tried to make the country more modern, but, in the end, lost his bid and the country with it. Those, on the other hand, who lay emphasis on regime stability as the highest value—if only to protect their own vested interests—need to have the image of the hapless last tsar who lost the country and his entire family to the waves of popular discontent. Thus, the channel of Russian modernization seems to pass somewhere between the Scylla of Gorbachevian ill-informed enthusiasm and the Charybdis of Nicholas's stubborn reaction.

Despite the usual fog prevailing in the channel, Russia is hardly doomed. Both the elites and the ordinary people have learned a lot from history. There are fewer illusions of any kind. Cure-all solutions are not in high demand. There is more appreciation of the results achieved so far, however modest, and deep reluctance to gamble with them. Popular discontent is more targeted and government control more limited. With borders much more transparent, there is a sense that Russia exists in a wider world, and that it may be very special but hardly unique within that world.

The official attempt at "conservative modernization" now under way in Russia is likely to hit its own limitations fairly soon. Take one example: Effectively dealing with corruption is the admission price to any real positive change. However, it is impossible to deal with the scourge by cutting a few odd branches and sparing the trunk and the roots that are organic to the present politico-economic system. The widely publicized reforms of the Ministry of the Interior (police) and the judiciary are a litmus test as to how much is achievable within the present setup. It is likely that the system will fail that test.

This will be a crucial moment in Russia's entire post-communist history. Will there be determined leadership at the top willing to press forward, steadily expanding the "modernization area," even as they will do everything to preserve — and improve — governance? Will this leadership use a meritocratic or a democratic model? Will there be a broad social coalition for modernization, consisting of the bulk of the middle class, which so far has been busy making material gains without thinking much about social responsibility? In other words, will a public space re-emerge in Russia, and will there be enough public agents and advocates to fill it?

As of this writing, these are all moot questions. One reason for this is that the knowledge of present-day Russia is too thin. There is no shortage of strong opinion, of course. However, the notions that people often use in making their points are predominantly rooted in ideological abstractions. It is ironic that, almost three decades after Yuri Andropov's stunning admission (coming from an ex-KGB chief) that "we do not know the country in which we live," one has to confess that the amount of hard knowledge and the degree of understanding of contemporary Russia are insufficient — both within the country and beyond its borders.

The essays in this book take stock of the nearly two decades of Russia's post-communist transformation. They do not compare Russia's achievements and failures to the widely held, though sometimes unreasonable, expectations. Rather, they seek to determine what capacity the country has for modernization, what are the obstacles on its path to success, and, most important, what could be the way forward. The editors are fully aware, of course, of the current lack of interest in the West in modernization as an academic subject, but their own interest here is political rather than academic. While Russia's ultimate success or failure is still an open question, the implications of either are significant enough, and not only for the country's residents. It is time to start thinking out of the box.

The authors of this book, who come from Russia, Britain, Canada, Germany, Ukraine, and the United States, engage in an intense dialog among themselves, based on some new research, and offer novel perspectives on a number of key issues. There is a range of views and a certain amount of disagreement among them. Where they do agree, however, is in the rejection of domestic conservation and international isolation, and the need to bring forward the kind of change that would also better integrate Russian with the international community.

Chapter 1, written by Piotr Dutkiewicz (Carleton University, Ottawa), presents a broad overview of the evolution of the Russian economy and politics since the end of the Soviet era. Professor Dutkiewicz makes a point of present-day Russian realities having been *lost in translation*. His focus is on the experience of the state as the modernizer-in-chief and its chances of continuing to act in that role in the twenty-first century. This chapter presents, in a way, the book's main theme in a nutshell by eliminating the black-and-white view of Russia in favor of a richer, multicolored vision.

Chapter 2, by Vladimir Popov (Higher School of Economics, Moscow), brings the debate to a new level by sifting through a wealth of empirical economic and social data. He begins by asking whether Russia has become a "normal country," proceeds with some very sobering assessments, and concludes that the key to Russia's modernization is the quality of its institutions.

The next two chapters keep their focus on the state, given not merely the traditional dominance of that institution in Russia but also its reformist potential. Where is the state now, in view of the bureaucracy's "sovereignization"? asks Georgi Derluguian (Northwestern University). Evidently, whoever tries to employ the state as an instrument of change will have to deal with the interests of the group that has its own interests. Richard Sakwa (Kent University) takes the discussion a step further by analyzing the duality of the Russian state, composed of what he calls the constitutional regime enshrined in a body of law and the administrative regime, which reflects the realities of group interests. This creates tensions that will immediately emerge if one challenges the existing order.

Timothy Colton (Harvard University) wonders, in chapter 5, whether personalities can act as locomotives of change. He examines the problem of political leadership in Russia, with a particular emphasis on the tandem arrangement involving its present incumbents. He offers a range of scenarios for 2012 and beyond, all highly interesting and relevant to the central issue: are the nominal leaders capable of leading the country into a higher orbit of development?

In chapter 6 Mikhail Gorshkov (Institute of Sociology, Moscow) seeks to paint a portrait of contemporary Russian society, which he finds in a state of permanent transition. He offers to the reader an annotated list of "Russian realities" that should debunk the myths about the motives of Russian people's behavior.

Leonid Grigoriev (Institute of Energy Policy, Moscow) narrows the focus and looks, crucially, at the elites. In chapter 7 he defines the composition of the various elite groups, their evolution and links to the respective Soviet-era groups. Historically, splits within the elites created openings for political and social evolution. Grigoriev reveals relations among the elite groups, looking at who influences/controls whom and who is relatively autonomous. He also studies the relations between the elites and the rest of society, notably the middle classes. He asks the question of whether entry to the elites is blocked now, and how those suppressed middle classes become politically passive or express opposition to the elites.

Acceleration of the economy and innovativeness of the system would be impossible nowadays without a significant contribution from science and the education system. Nur Kirabaev, in chapter 8, (People's Friendship University, Moscow) assesses the transformation of Russian post-secondary education for the last twenty years from that perspective.

Oleg Atkov and Guzel Ulumbekova's chapter 9 deals with a key area of the state of Russian society—its health. This essay displays the complex linkages between the depressed state of health and demographics in Russia and the integrity and security of the Russian social organism.

The chapters toward the end of the volume examine Russia's foreign policy, its relations with neighbors and the major players, such as United States, the European Union, and China. This part of the volume asks the question: where does Russia fit into the wider world? What role can it play vis-à-vis its former provinces and clients? What are the prospects for a pan-European rapprochement, and even integration? Can the reset lead to a sustainable relationship between Russia and the United States? What does the future hold for Sino-Russian relations?

Roderic Lyne, a retired British diplomat who served as UK ambassador to Moscow from 2000 to 2004, offers a candid view of relations between the United States and Europe, on the one hand, and Russia, on the other, in chapter 10. His well-informed reflections on the subject are interspersed with unique personal reminiscences that make his chapter a particularly lively and interesting read.

Where Ambassador Lyne is reserved, occasionally even skeptical, Alexander Rahr of the German Council on Foreign Relations (DGAP) is decidedly positive and enthusiastic in chapter 11. Rahr argues that Russia can and should fit into a wider Europe, and that this will be good for both the Russians themselves and for other Europeans. His chapter concludes with a set of practical recommendations for Russian and European leaders aimed at creating an integral relationship between Russia and the West.

Andrew Kuchins of the Center of Strategic and International Studies in Washington, D.C., looks at U.S.-Russian relations. Kuchins focuses on the Obama administration's Russian policy, popularly summarized by the notion of a "reset." He examines the origins and sources of the reset, its nature and limitations, and its prospects. Written from an American perspective, chapter 12 also contains an in-depth analysis of Russian interests and capabilities.

Bobo Lo, a former deputy chief of mission at the Australian embassy in Moscow and now a London-based academic, is a leading expert on Russo-Chinese relations. Chapter 13 offers a spectacular *tour d'horizon* of Russia's relations with Asian countries. Whereas in the past, Asia served as an area of Russian expansion, today its phenomenal economic dynamism, rapid demographic growth, and increasing political assertiveness present a major challenge to Russia. Alongside America's relative dominance, and Europe's new unity, Asia's rise has dramatically altered the international environment for Russia. How Russia responds to it will in large part determine its future.

Rustem Zhangozha, a Kazakh-born researcher now with the Ukrainian National Academy of Science in Kiev, projects in chapter 14 a view of Russia from its former imperial borderlands in Central Asia. This chapter makes it clear that post-imperial exit is a difficult process for both the core of the former empire and the newly independent states.

Finally, Dmitri Trenin of the Carnegie Moscow Center concludes the long narrative by drawing a line under five centuries of Russian imperial experience. He proceeds in chapter 15 to analyze Russia's soft landing from an empire to a great power. He argues, however, that to become such a great power and not face another collapse, Russia indeed must go through a modernization phase.

CHAPTER ONE

Missing in Translation: Re-conceptualizing Russia's Developmental State

Piotr Dutkiewicz

> Oil is a resource that anesthetizes thought, blurs the vision, corrupts... oil is a fairy tale and, like every fairy tale, is a bit of a lie. Oil fills us with such arrogance that we begin believing we can easily overcome such unyielding obstacles as time.
> —Ryszard Kapuscinski, *Shah of Shahs*

This is a story about power, accumulation, state, bureaucracy, and survival. It draws the contours of Russia's attempt at modernization via etatization.[1] It provides a sketch of Russia's trajectory over the past twenty years, and it is about "politics from above" as a vehicle of social change and its successes and failures. This chapter is also a theoretical vignette within the open-ended story of the possible developmental direction of one of the world's most important subsystems.[2]

Black and White in Colors

In these days, a palette consisting only of black and white has seemed sufficient to paint a picture of Russia (particularly after the war in South Ossetia in August 2008). A sketch of the dominant conceptualization of the last two decades of the country's history looks something like this: The democrat Boris Yeltsin introduced a market system and erected the foundation of a Western model of democracy. This free market and a newly free press effectively overhauled the Russian political system, giving rise to hope for the emergence of a democratic and pro-Western Russia, one that would become a good citizen of the post–cold war rapidly globalizing world order. In 2000, all such hopes were dashed. A new ruling group led by Vladimir Putin (often with a military or KGB background) decided to undertake a coup d'état. Granted, this coup was constitutional, but due to its radical nature it was no less revolutionary. In effect, it moved Russia back to the level of a mega Euro-Chinese gas station. Russia became no more or less than a classic petrostate, albeit one protected by a mighty nuclear arsenal.

Arguments of the most pristine simplicity have been dominant in both the Russian and Western media (I might note here that European policy and media assessments are more nuanced that their U.S. equivalents). Generally, the argument goes as follows. Russia's failure is de facto the failure of its constituent part: Putin's regime. The regime, we read further, is on its way to committing collective seppuku as a result of its own mistaken policies. The talk these days is increasingly about a new authoritarian empire, within which one can already discern the resurrection of the Soviet Union. It threatens not only the rights and freedoms of ordinary Russian citizens but also the former Soviet republics, Eastern and Western Europe, and, in fact—as can be ascertained by the Russian navy docking in Venezuela, Russian strategic bombers' unwelcome visit to the Arctic close to Canada, and Russian subs watching the U.S. East Coast—the entire world.

Many area specialists are now increasingly skeptical about the prospects for a convergence of the "uncivilized" Russia with a united Europe, while others speculate about a return to dictatorship.[3] Economic arguments (particularly after economic crises hit Russia in the fall of 2008) are equally damaging. "Russia markedly stands out from its neighbors in its industrial rate of decline. In Russia, industrial production," write Boris Nemtsov and Vladimir Milov, "fell by 14.8 percent in the first half of 2009—the highest among CIS countries.... But behind that glamorous television image, high popularity ratings, and personality cult stands a deplorable track record. During Putin's years in power, the country lost a complete decade."[4] Anders Aslund, one of the most recognized economists specializing in Eastern Europe, agrees: "The crisis has revealed how little Putin has done for the well-being of the Russian population during his time in office. The high economic growth of the last decade has been driven by market transformation, free capacity, and high oil prices."[5]

Indeed, as Vladimir Popov and I argued in late 2008, the Russian economy is too dependent on oil and gas exports, which account for one-half to two-thirds—depending on world fuel prices—of its total exports.[6] The prosperity of the recent years was mostly based on rising fuel prices. A simple calculation shows the importance of the windfall oil revenues. Russian GDP at the official exchange rate was about $1 trillion in 2007, with the oil and gas sector, which employs less than one million workers, valued at about $500 billion (at world prices of $80 per barrel of oil). When oil was priced at $15 a barrel in 1999, Russian oil and gas output was valued at less than $100 billion. The difference, $400 billion, is profit that literally landed in Russia's lap. Few specialists would have called the USSR a resource economy, but the Russian industrial structure changed a lot during twenty years of transition. Basically, the 1990s were a period of rapid de-industrialization and "resourcialization" of the Russian economy; the growth of world fuel prices since 1999 seems to have reinforced this trend. The share of output of major resource industries (fuel, energy, metals) in total industrial output increased from about 25 percent to over 50 percent by the mid 1990s and has stayed at that level since. The share of mineral products, metals, and diamonds in Russian exports increased from 52 percent in 1990 (USSR) to 67 percent in 1995 and to 81 percent in 2007, whereas the share of machinery and equipment in exports fell from 18 percent in 1990 (USSR) to 10 percent in 1995 and to below 6 percent in 2007. The share of research-and-development spending in GDP amounted to 3.5 percent in the late 1980s in the USSR, but fell to 1.3 percent in Russia today (China: 1.3 percent; U.S., Korea, Japan: 2–3 percent; Finland: 4 percent; Israel: 5 percent). So today Russia really does look like a "normal resource abundant developing country." The government failed to channel the stream of petrodollars to repair the "weakest link" of the national economy—the provision of public goods and investment into non-resource industries. Investment and government consumption amounted to about 50 percent of GDP in the early 1990s, fell to below 30 percent of GDP in 1999 (right after the 1998 currency crisis), and recovered only partially afterwards—to about 40 percent of GDP in 2007. Wages and incomes in recent years have been growing systematically faster than productivity.

These weaknesses were partially concealed by high oil and gas prices in 2003–08, but became evident in mid-2008–early 2009 when oil prices fell. From May to November 2008, Russian stocks (RTS index in dollar terms) lost three-quarters of their value. The decline was driven partly by the global financial crisis and partly by declining world oil prices (from a maximum of nearly $150 per barrel in June 2008 to below $50 by the end of the year). There was an outflow of capital starting from August 2008, so foreign exchange reserves dropped from $600 billion in August 2008 to $400 billion in February 2009. The seasonally adjusted index of industrial output, which had not grown since May 2008, fell by more than 20 percent by mid 2009 as compared to mid-2008.

In short, Russia has been hit by a "double crisis" in 2008, one growing out of its own faults and another created by global processes. Such tectonic shifts cause earthquakes. The obvious question emerges of who will be the main beneficiaries and victims of this upheaval? What kind of societal and political coalitions may emerge as a result? It seems that it is easy and obvious to summarize the arguments presented earlier: Putin's (and, by proxy, Medvedev's) regime is in a deep crisis, clinging to the edge of survival. If so, why do the majority of Russians support him (and his successor)?[7] The crude answer is that this is the result of having to deal with an "accidental society," a foolish mass, unprepared to pass judgment, bamboozled by the media—in short, a society that does not know what is good for itself. The reality is, obviously, more complicated. Putin's Russia is neither a banal authoritarian state nor a soft incarnation of the Soviet Union. It is a continuity of Yeltsin's Russia with an important diversion toward the statist, twenty-first-century incarnation of the developmental state. But such an understanding requires that we add some colors to a hitherto black-and-white etching of the country. The following section is a concise analysis of the past decade in Russian politics in order to build a solid background for the theoretization of "Putin's Developmental State," which comes in the third section of this chapter.

A Neither-Nor Russia

Today's Russia is certainly a challenge for the willing analyst. It is obviously not a liberal democracy, but, given the freedoms available to every Russian citizen, neither can it be labeled an authoritarian regime. Russia does have democratic electoral law, but the electoral mechanism gives considerable influence to the party in power (and the huge bureaucracy that accompanies it). Vladimir Putin is considered by many to be a twenty-first-century incarnation of the tsars, but in reality his power—especially in the regions (mainly due to the "autonomous bureaucracy" that is *de facto* the most powerful socio-economic force on its own)—is seriously constrained (see Derluguian, chap. 3). The Kremlin, even though it fosters an aura of omniscience, continues to base its politics on what might be termed as a timid trial-and-error approach. Russia has a market system (as recognized by the EU and WTO), but the system of accumulation is to a large extent based on nonmarket political access. The media are not "free" per se, but neither are they under total state control (with the exception of state television). The government's rule is seen as strong, but the state's institutions remain fairly weak (as evidenced by the existing corruption and noteworthy lack of accountability and transparency). While the decisions of the Kremlin's elite are seen by many as systemic manipulation—or just a massive PR exercise—many of them are real responses to the needs of the Russian people: strength and weakness in one. Russian politics is becoming increasingly assertive, but its implementation is anything but that. At the moment, there is neither stability nor change. Instead, Russia is experienced a sort of stable stagnation. As observed by a Kremlin insider, such a situation cannot continue for long, as "this is a dead end" for the system.[8] In other words, a neither–nor Russia.

Moreover, while Russian foreign policy may at times seem clear to the West, it is anything but, even for insiders. Russia wants to influence the decisions of other countries and of international institutions, though in reality there is little certainty (in most cases) exactly what her position on many issues is. "What does Russia actually want?" This question is on everyone's minds these days. Is internal stability stable enough to allow Russia to enter a new phase of modernization without suffering serious political and social convulsions? I agree with Krastev that "insecurity goes a long way toward explaining not only the greed and lust for power...but also the regime's curiously ambiguous relationship to authoritarianism as well as democracy."[9]

Just as authoritarian actions do not necessarily equate to a belief in an authoritarian system, a lack of a central governing ideology does not necessarily signify a lack of ideological basis for state governance, a lack of democracy is not synonymous with the absence of freedom, and rejection of Marxism is not a rejection of the historical value of the USSR as this elite's fatherland. It's a classical neither-nor situation dominated by shades and ambiguities, in many cases dressed up for the occasion in boldness, strength, high morality, and, let's admit it, sometimes arrogance and self-righteousness.

But before continuing with this line of analysis, let's step back to the late 1990s.[10] This period deeply shaped the systemic thinking of the Kremlin's ruling group. A sense of humiliation rooted in the all-too-obvious evidence of social and economic collapse, evaporating sovereignty, "pauper-liberalism" pushing Russia away from its "great status"—indeed, a sense of Russia being "driven to its knees"—all contributed to the "deep mental formation" of a current elite.

As many know, production dropped in the 1990s in Russia; however, not everybody knows that this decline was of a magnitude unprecedented in the twentieth century. Neither the First World War along with the revolution of 1917, with the subsequent bloodshed of the civil war, nor the horrors of the Second World War brought about such a dramatic drop in output as was seen in the 1990s. The national income fell by more than 50 percent between 1913 and 1920, but by 1925 had rebounded and surpassed the prewar 1913 level. In 1998, at the lowest point in the transformational recession of the 1990s, Russia's GDP was 55 percent of the pre-crisis peak of 1989. In short, the economic losses from the 1990s recession were exceptional in scale and, importantly, in duration.

Leaving aside the question of the reasons for the recession or how it could have been avoided, I would only point out that such an unprecedented plunge in production caused equally unprecedented tension in society. In the 1990s, real incomes and consumption decreased on average by a minimum of a third, which was less than the drop in production (since the recession was more significant in the defense and investment sectors, while consumer-goods imports grew), but still very substantial. Moreover, due to the immense growth in income inequality, the real incomes of the absolute majority—80 percent of the more-vulnerable members of the population—were approximately cut in half.[11] During privatization, there occurred a massive redistribution of national wealth; in just a few years, somewhere around a third of all state property passed into the hands of a few dozen oligarchs for a song.

Inevitably, the brunt of these hardships was borne by society's most vulnerable groups because they had fewer resources with which to cushion the impact of economic decline and increased insecurity. This was further exacerbated by their limited ability to respond constructively (either through political or economic means) to rapidly changing circumstances and by a lesser capacity to protect their vital interests in the political process. It is difficult to exaggerate the degree of the social and economic collapse of the 1990s.

The transformational recession was brought on not so much by market liberalization as by the virtual collapse of the state.[12] In countries that were successful in keeping government revenues and spending from plunging (Central Europe, for instance), the decline in production was less substantial. By contrast, Russian spending on "ordinary government" (excluding spending on defense, investment and subsidies, and debt servicing) in real terms decreased threefold, so that government functions—from collecting custom duties to law enforcement—were either curtailed or transferred to the private sector.[13]

The shadow economy, estimated at 10 percent–15 percent of GDP under Brezhnev, grew to 50 percent of GDP by the mid-1990s. In 1980–85, the Soviet Union was placed in the middle of a list of fifty-four countries rated on their level of corruption, with a bureaucracy cleaner than that of Italy, Greece, Portugal, South Korea, and practically all the developing countries. In 1996, after the establishment of a market economy and the victory of democracy, Russia came in forty-eighth in the same list, between India and Venezuela.[14]

The regionalization of Russia was happening in leaps and bounds in the first half of the 1990s. In 1990, in an attempt to win the Russian regions over to his side in his battle with the Gorbachev government, Yeltsin promised them as much sovereignty "as they could digest." As a result, the percentage of the regional budgets in the revenues and expenditures of the consolidated budget increased, while the federal government was forced to haggle with the subjects of the federation over the division of powers, including financial jurisdiction. Many of them directly blackmailed the federal government, threatening to withhold money from the federal treasury. In 1992–94, agreements were signed with many regions, establishing different levels of tax contribution to the federal budget in each specific case. Chechnya, for one, virtually left the federation; Dagestan was ready to follow; Bashkhorstan introduced a provision that federal laws could be implemented only with the consent of its parliament.[15] Russia as a federation was on the brink.

The voucher privatization of 1993–94 and the "loans for shares" auctions of 1995–96 led to state property being sold off for a pittance, and this at a time when the state needed money more than ever before. Throughout the eighteen months that the vouchers were valid, they were never quoted at more than $20 a piece, so about 150 million vouchers, issued one per resident, were worth less than $3 billion all told. This amount could have bought out somewhere around a third of all the assets in a country with an annual GDP of more than $500 billion (purchasing power parity). Just imagine the temptation of the oligarchs: if they could have skillfully transferred capital from domestic-based to transnational ownership, they could have bought "Mother Russia" for less than the capitalization of a medium-scale European bank. At "loans for shares" auctions, companies with an annual output of several billion dollars were sold for hundreds of millions. Yes, by and large, the privatization was legitimate, but the fact is that the laws were such that the supply of property was tens of times greater than the solvent demand. Plants, factories, and banks went for simply ridiculous amounts. As a result, anyone who could call himself a least bit well-to-do at the time not only had unlimited opportunity for incredible enrichment but also was able to take partial control of the economy of the former superpower. As many journalists so aptly put it, the country ended up under the thumb of the "seven bankers" ("semibankarschina"), along the lines of the "seven boyars rule" ("semiboyarschina") during the Time of Troubles of the early seventeenth century, the most anarchic period in Russian history. For the elite living without laws and norms, the ability to buy anything and everyone was a delightful experience. The Russian business elite had found joy in the unbearable lightness of living within a weak state.

V. Popov and I argue that an attribute of a modern state is a minimum of three monopolies—a monopoly on force, tax collection, and currency issue. All three monopolies were undermined in the Russia of the 1990s.[16] The unprecedented rise in crime and the notorious assassinations of leading politicians, journalists, and businessmen testified to the bankruptcy of the law-enforcement agencies. The decline in tax revenue resulting from the growth of the shadow economy meant more generally the "privatization" of those revenues by the bureaucracy and the criminal element, which took the place of the state as the "protectors" of business. The increased spread of monetary substitutes (such as bills of exchange of the regional governments) in 1994–96, and the tremendous rise in barter and nonpayment (trade and tax arrears), which peaked in the summer of 1998 (right before the August crisis), virtually stripped the central bank of its power to regulate monetary circulation.

In 1995–98, in the period of macro-economic stabilization, it finally became possible to bridle inflation by linking the exchange rate of the ruble to the dollar, and it seemed that things were going to get better. A small increase of 1 percent in GDP was detected in 1997 after seven years of unabated decline in production; mortality, crime, and suicide rates began to drop.

However, there was no healthy underpinning to this stabilization—the pyramid of government debt and nonpayments continued to grow; the real exchange rate of the ruble rose, undermining the competitiveness of Russian goods; the balance of payments deteriorated; and production slumped once again in 1998 due to the stubborn unwillingness of the authorities to devaluate the ruble. As a result, in 1998 the short-lived stabilization ended in stunning failure after only three years with the August devaluation of the ruble and subsequent default. Real incomes on a month-to-month basis fell by 25 percent in the fall of 1998, only climbing once again to the pre-crisis mark in 2002.

The state crisis had reached its apex: federal-government revenues and spending fell in 1999 to 30 percent of GDP at a time when the GDP itself was almost half of what it had been ten years before. State debt and foreign debt had peaked; the currency reserves had shrunk to $10 billion, less than those of the Czech Republic or Hungary. In August 2000, the top of the Ostankino television tower in Moscow caught fire, and the nuclear submarine Kursk sank. The prevailing feeling was that the federal government was so useless that it might as well just shut down.

In 1997 Russian oligarchs turned up for the first time on *Forbes* magazine's list of the world's billionaires; by 2003 the same list included seventeen names from Russia. With a per capita GDP lagging behind Mauritius and Costa Rica, with life expectancy of sixty-five years (compared to Cuba's seventy-seven), and with 17 percent of the population making an income below the subsistence minimum (about $2.50 a day by the official exchange rate), Russia had outdone all the countries of the world except the United States, Germany, and Japan in its number of billionaires. In May 2004, *Forbes* counted thirty-six billionaires in Russia, which left Japan in the dust and Russia in third place after the United States and Germany.

In its property and control structure, Russia was in the late 1990s somewhere between the developing and the developed world. In 2003, according to a World Bank study, twenty-three oligarchs controlled 35 percent of the industrial output (the state had 25 percent) and 17 percent of the banking system assets (the state had 26 percent). In the United States in the late 1990s, the fifteen richest families controlled around 3 percent of GDP, while in Japan it was 2 percent. On the other hand, the figure was 62 percent in Indonesia, 38 percent in South Korea, and 53 percent in Thailand.[17] However, it is unlikely that there are many countries in which the oligarchs, first of all, started with nothing and became "world leaders" in only ten years and, second, openly pitted themselves against the government, in effect demanding its privatization.

It would be hard to name countries with developmental levels similar to Russia's, where the state lost so much of its independence in its relationship with private capital. A virtual merging of big business and the middle/upper-management levels of the bureaucracy occurred in Russia, and their interests became practically indistinguishable from one other. Neither the civilian ministries nor even the top bureaucracies were able to counter this force; even the "power" agencies, such as the Ministry of the Interior, the army, and the security services began "privatizing." As a result of this process, the state became "capitalist-neo-patrimonial" and to a large extent privatized. In such an environment, the issue of improving equitable policies became irrelevant (as it is almost impossible to implement any kind of policy interventions that might challenge the fusion of such powerful interests). The economic and social collapse served the elite well. It actually "liberalized the elite" from the unpleasantly constraining powers of the state, laws, and regulations.

This crisis of the late 1990s provided Putin with several real challenges: to block the continuing criminalization of the country, to prevent the complete "privatization" of the machinery of government by the oligarchs, to stop the collapse of societal coherence, to halt the weakening of the federal government as a result of the shift of real power to the regions, and to curtail the power struggles between criminal groups, the oligarchs, and the regional governors. In short: to stop Russia from being the "Wild East."

For the first few years the economy was continuing to revive (yes, thanks to a considerable extent to the infusion of tons of petrodollars—about $650 billion between 2000 and 2008): economic growth reached 6 percent in 1999, 10 percent in 2000, and 4 percent to 7 percent annually in 2001–08. Unemployment dropped from 13 percent in 1999 to 6 percent in mid-2008, and inflation shrunk from 84 percent in 1998 to 12 percent to 15 percent in 2003–08. The budget deficit turned into a surplus, and government revenues and expenditures as a percentage of GDP began, ever so slowly, to rise; the foreign debt as a percentage of GDP decreased; poverty decreased. But the important result of the first six or seven years of the new elite in power was probably this: the growth of the economy and the stability of leadership have finally led to increased order and an improvement, albeit an almost imperceptible one, in the social climate.[18] Thus "Stability and Order" became the holy grail of Russia's elite. The number of murders, having hit a sky-high peak in 2002, dropped back down in 2003; the number of suicides has been on the decline; the birth rate, which had sunk to a fifty-year low in 1999, has begun to rise, as has the number of registered marriages (although this is partly a result of the demographic wave of the 1970s); the majority of Russian citizens—as judged by opinion polls over the last seven years—are prepared to forgive Putin his heavy-handed tactics in dealing with the oligarchs and even with entrepreneurs of a lesser stature, his "purges" in Chechnya, and the constraints placed on democracy and freedom of speech, all in the interests of strengthening the role of the state. Exchanging some political freedoms for the freedom of purchasing power and stability seemed like a fair deal to a majority.[19]

To sum up, in the 1990s the Russian state lost its capacity to govern and to manage the tremendous burden of transformational change. The state, facing internal and external pressures, withdrew from its basic functions (protection of its citizens, provision of health care, securing legally bounded transactions, monetary oversight). The accidental elite that took power lacked both coherence and a long-term plan, and so leased the country to a merger of oligarchs (formed by the state's privatization scheme) and the top echelon of Kremlin insiders. The state became engaged in a massive redistribution scheme that gave away state assets and, with them, the dominant power within the system. As state provisions were disappearing, a "parallel state" started to emerge to secure a smooth process of primitive accumulation (based on the state's distributional capacity and de-industrialization) at the regional and federal levels. This mutation of capitalism transformed market relations into a system of complex symbiosis between nominally legal structures and organized crime, which became not only a systemic economic force but also a political actor in its own right. That process led to a massive impoverishment of society with all the associated negative consequences for societal cohesion, health, education, and so on. A process of "commodification of everything and everyone"—including privatization of the state and the commodification of democracy, in fact, an all-embracing commodification of social relations—further eroded Russia to the point that she became a prime candidate for being a "failed state with nukes" by the beginning of the new millennium.

Putin's New Ruling Group started to construct a new edifice—using a mix of old and new bricks—called modern Russia. For that task, they needed not only more power than Yeltsin had as president but—most importantly—a *different kind of power.* The current rulers in the Kremlin are convinced that they needed to restore, at the very core, what was a traditional and central engine of social development in Russian history: the state. In order to accomplish this project, they *had to link the state and accumulation into one undivided whole of social power.* If one looks for a singular explanation of "Putin's Idea," most probably this is the closest we can get.

They also probably felt that along the way they would have to reconstruct the elite in order to control the process of modernization and to "reconcile national and liberal opinion once again; and so create the first government in Russian history to enjoy a broad political consensus" and achieve—at least for some years—as aptly observed by Perry Anderson, a "hegemonic stability."[20] If their long-term task was to reconstruct and modernize Russia—to restructure society and affect the overall development—they had to consider dramatically changing the pattern of accumulation and the structure of power; *indeed, to reshape the political economy of Russia.* The third part of this chapter is an attempt to conceptualize that process by an application of *integrated* notions (models) of the *developmental state and trusteeship.* The "model-matching" process "is the way to get at the shape of reality;"[21] but in our case, model amalgamation also has a creationist effect of shaping a new "model" of Russia's political economy, a model in which the "normal" trajectory of the developmental state led by a "trusted few"—that is generally not democratic—is reshaped (and reinforced) by holding power that is accumulated as capital and secured (so far) by confidence in the obedience of its subjects (citizens).

Accumulation—Power—Modernization

The dominant pattern of Yeltsin's ruling group's accumulation was conditioned by a symbiosis between oligarchs (big, Russian-based business), higher echelons of state (central/regional) bureaucracy, and the Kremlin elite, resulting in a sort of super-amalgamated power structure. The mechanism of accumulation was complex and dynamically changing to reflect the internal political power structure and the changing strength of dominant capital. The main contradictions and changing interests that reflected the dynamic reality of the domestic and international markets between political-cum-bureaucratic power and dominant capital vectored the system's dynamics. In the first phase (in the period before the voucher privatization of 1993–94 and the "loans for shares" auctions of 1995–96), political access was exchanged for profit and the security of spoils (on the trading block were import/export licenses, all kinds of permits, privatization of real estate, quotas, and state contracts). Russian capitalists started to consolidate their position as early as 1992–93 by using an innovative, cross-sectoral merger and acquisition strategy called FIGs (Financial Industrial Groups). They increased their profit simply by not paying taxes, and they secured their gains—in a highly volatile market environment—by sending money abroad and stripping domestic assets of their "real" value.[22] This scheme was significantly modified as new dynamics were introduced by the "loans for shares" auctions—an indigenous invention of the Russian business-cum-political elite that legally, de facto, transferred to the Kremlin's "trusted seven" (plus to the only non-banker, the Kremlin's confidant, Boris Berezovsky) a massive chunk of state property, including the jewels of the Russian economy. The logic of the capital expansion at this stage was nothing short of "to penetrate and alter the nature of the state itself."[23]

They were, however, caught in an existential dilemma—to have a weak state was good for business (no taxes, corrupt officials, etc.), but to have a too-weak state was bad for business. Their main problem was that the state was in fact too weak to secure/protect the gains of the dominant capital and to secure the property rights. In a truly Hegelian spirit, they solved this seemingly deep contradiction by evoking the notion of politics. The oligarchs, then, had to take things into their own hands by engaging in a collective political action. The process of privatization of the state was helped by their overall support for the reelection of the guarantor of their position, Boris Yeltsin (July 1996). The rest was just a matter of socio-technology. By the purchase, tight control, and effective use of the national media, the oligarchs offered a one-dimensional explanation of reality.[24] They took control of the regional bosses and consolidated their position in the security apparatus.

Operation "Privatizing the State" was well underway by the time of the financial collapse in 1998. From the time of the "shares for loans" scheme and the reelection of Yeltsin, politics, while still indispensable, became secondary to capital in the process of accumulation. But, at this point, everything was *not* enough, and as early as the mid-1990s, Russian oligarchs were actively looking for international capital backing. They were seeking, on the one hand, transnational ownership to gain access to international capital (in order to gain more power domestically) and, on the other, to secure their access to safer investment abroad. Having advanced the "privatization of the state," Russian oligarchs were getting ready to make a real deal: to merge with international capital and put the Russian economy on the trading block. Twice in the last fifteen years—in 1994 and 1996—*one could have bought one-third of Russia's assets for $3–4 billion*.[25] Are we still puzzled why Putin's group obsessively put "state sovereignty" at the core of their program? Are we still puzzled why the new power holders organized a "vertical of power"? Are we still puzzled why the Kremlin's planners were besieged by the "threat of unpredictability," "lack of control," and "need for stability"?[26] Are we still puzzled why they re-captured (via state interventions) key money-making industries?

It is time now to try to decipher the political economy of Putin's Russia. A seductively simplistic algorithm of Russia's political economy would look something like this:

Putin's group rule = power + oil/gas + TV
Power = state-based accumulation + presidency (trusteeship)[27]
Oil/gas = principal state/private revenues[28]
TV = relative control of mass opinion
Therefore, Putin's rule + power + oil + TV =
   the Russian developmental state in progress.

In order to make any change, to define new rules and "bring the state back," Putin's Kremlin elite needed more power and new resources in order to avoid becoming trapped in a new dependency cycle by the oligarchs. In fact, power and resources are synonymous with *accumulation*.[29] What they were really looking for was a different mode of accumulation; accumulation that would not differentiate between "economic" and "political" power; where money would not be "separated" from the institutions, law, culture, etc.; accumulation that would be more totalizing in their capture of economy/society; accumulation that would epitomize power; or in Nitzan's and Bichler's terms, "what we deal with here is organized power at large. Numerous power institutions and processes—from ideology, through culture, to organized violence, religion, the law, ethnicity, gender, international conflict, labor relations...all bear the differential level and volatility of earnings.... [T]here is a single process of capital accumulation/state formation, a process of restructuring by which power is accumulated as capital."[30] They attempted to intertwine capital linked to politics, with politics linked to institutions and law, which in turn was linked to ideology, with ideology linked to value systems and culture, with a culture linked to religion, which is linked to almost everything that matters, and, by the end of this logic chain, to turn to power again—*power as confidence in obedience*.[31] However, while the confidence in obedience was quite high (but never taken for granted by the Kremlin) in the first years in power, the current economic crisis may change that quite significantly. As recent opinion polls show, the confidence in the ruling group may evaporate quite fast as Russians expected much more after being obedient for so long.[32]

The relatively easiest and most profitable source of accumulation (and hence power) was oil and gas.[33] With those prices spiking for almost a decade, it gave Putin's group enormous leverage and confidence domestically and internationally.[34] Oil has its vices too, but as a second component of Putin's rule it became indispensable for the project. The third element of the module of power to capture was to take control of television. The Kremlin's staple foods are data from "political technologists," pollsters, and spin doctors. They also know that more that 75 percent of the information absorbed by Russians comes from TV. The press is much less influential due to costs and access. So, to put tighter controls on TV than on any other printed or e-media was the third principal rule of survival in a long-term, strategically thought plan.

The second part of the "algorithm" (Power = state-based accumulation + presidency) is that Putin's group reversed the main vector of accumulation from private to state. The state became the principal agent of accumulation; the state (and the state "hegemonic" bureaucracy and key interest groups related to it) is also its main benefactor. Paraphrasing Joseph Schumpeter's famous conception of capitalism without the capital that led him to the conclusion that the "dynamic characteristics of capitalism arise from non-capitalist sources," we come to the core of Putin's group's base of accumulation: the state.[35] Putin's group is much closer to the ideas of Friedrich List's *National System of Political Economy* than to Adam Smith's *The Wealth of Nations*. It is not the invisible hand of the market but a very visible hand of the state that is to be responsible for "development and progress." List's justification of de facto protectionist approaches through the creation of a constructivist doctrine of national development fits squarely into the "Putin Plan." If we also consider List's moral and spiritual overtones of productive force and his emphasis on the defensive capacity of the state to protect its "integrity," we can add Putin to the list of his hidden admirers.

But to put any plan into motion, you need the implementers, supporters, and at least a slim but trustworthy social base for change. Here enters the need for the presidency—the office, the collective, the institution, the prestige, legitimacy, charisma, and the man himself. There emerges a distinct need to find the ideal individual/collective holder of the trusteeship. Who shall/can lead society in a truly revolutionary time of transformation? Society itself, the idea goes, cannot be trusted entirely as they have lived too long in an entirely different system and so cannot grasp the "goal of the change." Society is also prone—as the 1990s showed—to massive media/political manipulations. Oligarchs and high-level officials were not the best option in 1998 for a ruling group either, as they were engaged in stripping assets and placing them abroad. They were, after all, businesspeople, not interested in the wealth of society or the future of the state. So who was to lead Russia to its revival? From the utopian socialists through the Hegelian principles of development, Marx's debate on the role of the "individual man," the Fabian's Society ideal of correcting the socio-economic change in the British colonies, the League of Nation's institution of trusteeship, the ideas of Sergei Witte, and Lenin's notion of a "vanguard party," theorists and practitioners of all stripes and colors have struggled with the answer to this very question: *Who* is to lead society into development and progress? *Who* can be entrusted to lead the change? Hegel's "spiritless mass" or someone else? In their brilliant book on development, Shenton and Cowan observed that "a 'handful of chosen men' could now assume the mantle of the 'active spirit' to become the inner determination of development," regardless of the system of governance and its ideological dress.[36] This reminds me of the Saint-Simonian ideal that in order to remedy disorder, "Only those who had the 'capacity' to utilize land, labor and capital in the interest of society as a whole should be 'entrusted' with them."[37]

Putin's version of a trusteeship is thus given its philosophical justification. Sociologists are ready to support me with their empirical studies of the configuration of Putin's inner circle.[38] The notion of the trusteeship, I believe, explains a lot about Putin's leadership. It may clarify, for instance, the Kremlin's partial distrust of society (which explains why only very limited change via grassroots social movements was permitted), but also their desperate need to "have society engaged" in the convoluted form of the Social Chamber, among other things, in order to keep the bureaucracy in check. It may also explain some of the reasons for the relative freedom of the parliamentary elections in 2008 and the Kremlin's actions against the "not trustworthy oligarchs" and their anti-bureaucratic outbursts. It can explain an uneasy cohabitation of conservative and liberal ideas that are transformed into policies and institutions by the Kremlin's rulers. It can also—above all—explain their "philosophy of power."

The final part of the algorithm (Putin's rule + power + oil + TV = the Russian developmental state in progress) deals with the longer-term intentional as well as unintentional consequences of ruling Russia for the past ten years. In other words, what was the power for? Today, Russia is a developmental state in progress (being in a state of policy hibernation—or stagnation—for the last three or four years). The recent economic crisis (2008–09) has shown that the painfully accumulated state capacity, both institutional/legal, financial, and moral, to act as a principal agent for change did not result in an economically effective, politically significant, and socially viable transformation of Russia's socio-economic system (or, in the words of Gleb Pavlovsky, one of the Kremlin's chief alchemists, "Medvedev is right, this is a dead end").[39]

The question is: Is it really "a dead end"?

To answer, we should make a small detour to trace the main features of the "developmental state." The idea is not new. The postwar period saw the coming together of statist theories, specific measures of state intervention, and the more general extension of state regulation in critical aspects of the economy. Herein lies the origin of the contemporary developmental state. The idea/practice was first applied in postcolonial Africa, then later—more ambitiously and consistently—to a cluster of rapidly growing economies in East Asia, such as Japan, South Korea, Taiwan, Singapore, Indonesia, and Malaysia. Many argued that their spectacular growth was possibly due to the activist and "market-friendly" state.[40] But not all states can be evaluated as developmental. Adrian Leftwich, one of the key authorities in this area, proposes that only states "whose politics have concentrated sufficient power, autonomy, and capacity at the center to shape, pursue, and encourage the achievement of explicit developmental objectives...can aspire to be the ones."[41] The argument goes that in a developmental state, the state itself becomes the main instrument for the pursuit of both public and private goals. The state comes to define and determine who will be able to make which decision of administrative, political, and economic significance.[42] Political and administrative positions become, obviously, a fruitful means of securing economic resources and opportunities, so it is normal that the state came to be an important avenue for realizing private goals. The claim of the state to define public goals and the legitimate means for pursuing private goals is formally recognized in a notion of "national sovereignty."[43] The expansion of state economic management is justified by the notion of "national development." The state's "capacity for coercion gives the content to these otherwise vacuous concepts."[44] There is, however, a twist to this story. The power arising from the state capacity to allocate resources depends largely on the exclusion of alternative sources of access to capital; hence the tendency of the holders of the trusteeship to organize the provision of services and commodities along monopolistic lines (something that Russian mineral and energy producers know by heart).[45]

From a comparative perspective, the approach taken by Putin and his group is, as a general approach to development, not new. What *is* new is: (a) trivially obvious, the specific historical circumstances in which this project was being launched and, (b) not so trivial, its fundamental understanding of its amalgamated accumulation-as-power and trusteeship-led mode of reproduction of social relations. The Russian ruling group faced a formidable developmental task that required coherent and strategic actions, and the only agency capable of achieving social and economic stability in the given circumstances was, indeed, the state. This, by the way, was in line with the East European political tradition of the state playing a much more dominant role as a principal agent of change.

So far so good, but as the perennial East European question goes (particularly in times of crisis), "If it is so good, why is it so bad?" I offer, as an explanation, two fundamental drawbacks of the model's implementation and sequence. First, the model seems to be based (even if unintentionally) on the "old-fashioned" approach of the first generation of developmental state theorists such as Dudley Seers and Hans Singer, who emphasized the need for a distributional approach to economic growth, with the state's main role being that of principal distributor of wealth. In that sense, the policies based on that notion were emphasizing just one side of the role of the state. What was needed was rather a dual-track, more flexible (more "modern") approach. Contemporary theorists of the developmental state would suggest that the state should be an engine of "liberal" policies and a guarantor of their implementation in the area of economic growth and generation of national income, and simultaneously of the "social and re-distributive" mechanism by giving some developmental opportunities to the poorer section of the population and worse-off regions.

Everyone now is talking about modernization and modernity in Russia.[46] Such talk has become fashionable for radio hosts and newspapers. The problem is that there is no comprehensive economic modernization underway. Whether we like it or not, Russia is today a largely de-industrialized, resource-dependent country with no serious base for technological innovation.[47] Except for the enormously powerful energy sector and high-tech pockets of the military industry, she is not internationally competitive. Is that enough to keep Russia prosperous, stable, and internationally meaningful? Is that adequate for the Russian aspirations? These questions are for the Russians to answer.

A second important point that needs to be made relates to the sequence of the Putin Group Project's implementation. The first six years of the trusteeship-led process of stabilizing the economy, re-creating a state, regrouping power, reshaping politics, diminishing poverty, stopping criminalization of the society, saving oil money, and so on were largely necessary steps. Cumulatively, they formed a strong foundation for the developmental state and, in general, were quite indispensable prerequisites for making the system work again. However, it is quite clear that there was no "second-phase plan" to move from "stabilization" to "accelerated modernization" (ideally from the middle of the first decade). I can only speculate why such a plan did not materialize in 2005–06, when the Kremlin got everything—political power, resources, and high social support at once.[48] The point is that Russia did not enter (having enough resources and power to do so by 2005–06) a second, logical, and fundamentally important phase of fast modernization of industry accompanied by political empowerment of the citizenry. It looks as if groups of busy construction workers suddenly stopped building the road they had so promisingly started, switched off their machines, and went back to patch the holes that were formed while they were busy advancing the construction. (Does this not seem reminiscent of the idea of the National Projects?) In other words, Russia did not capitalize on her wealth to the extent she could have (as her fellow members of BRIC did).[49]

For the above two reasons, the answer to the key question of whether Putin's project has hit a dead end shall at this point be quite ambiguous. Everything depends on the government's/presidency's next steps. The economic crisis finally made it painfully clear that a patchwork approach is not an option. Russia has no choice other than to try to reinvent itself or risk marginalization. There are four basic ways to follow now, and I discuss them in the last section of this chapter, "Do it or lose it."

I cannot end this section without—at least briefly—touching on two of the most contested issues of Putin's presidency: (1) his attitude toward democracy, and (2) the regime's ideology.

1. Democracy as we know it today has many faces. Who does not claim today that democracy is a good thing? Those who have their system labeled as "democratic" are those who are "civilized" by contrast to the noncivilized part (actually the majority) of the world. But a lot depends on the content we put into a word.[50] Popular demand for democratization for the "average person" is in large part a demand for a fairer redistribution of access to health, education, and income. There is nothing wrong with people who are concerned for themselves and their families, and would like to prolong their lives in good health, arrange an education for their children to improve their life opportunities, and worry about the stability of their incomes. On all these fronts, we have witnessed a massive retreat in Russia from 1991 to 2001 and a meager but steady improvement from 2001 to 2008. The unequal participation in "transitional rent" seems to be the main cause of the growing gap between the democratically elected elite and the public and the root cause of the growth of a new breed of radical populism (see Limonov's Party). The main problem of the late 1990s in Russia was that only a few were able to fully take advantage of the fruits of the developing democratic opening created by Yeltsin. What liberalism meant in Russian practice was the liberalization of the narrow business/political elite from any legal or social control. Liberalization of the elite compounded by its (in comparative terms) enormous wealth made it possible for it to commodify democracy. That is to say that "democracy" during the 1990s became a commodity in Russia like anything else (a "thing" that one could buy and sell on the "democratic market"). By buying access to the political process, the redistribution/privatization of property, the media, elections at any level, and decision makers and politicians (in other words, the purchase of civil liberties), a select few were able to become the de facto owners of the state and enjoyers of democracy. Politically speaking, the most profound result of this process was the liberation of the elite, mostly political and business figures, from the state, from the executive

powers that it represents, and from the rest of the population. The Kremlin's reaction was to develop a hybrid of "sovereign democracy."[51] This notion—if deciphered rather than judged—tells us a lot about both the elite's fears and its goals. "Sovereignty," in this approach, means a regime's capacity (economic independence, military strength, and capacity to withstand global pressures and "foreign influence") to be nondependent and thus non-subordinated. "Democracy" means opening for a change, creating a space for the ruling group to govern via reformist strategies; to have some societal support (as most of Russians support the notion of democracy) but not to put too much trust in society; to create an illusion of political pluralism without giving a chance for the development of politics to become a hostage of dominant capital; and, finally, to use it as a tool of legitimization. The regime put a pragmatic spin on the deeply ideological term that "democracy" usually is in order to merge, as Richard Sakwa insightfully observed, this group's simultaneous belief in liberalism and conservative authoritarianism.[52] After all, one of the lessons from the Soviet past that this group learned was that in the final account, people are ruled by ideas and hardly by anything else.

2. So is there any dominant ideology in Russia on which to move forward? In December 2009, the largest political party—United Russia—labeled itself a "conservative party." Such a revival of conservatism in Russia is quite a remarkable development in the home of the Bolshevik Revolution. If you look closely, however, at the behavior of the Russian political elite, particularly over the last decade, it looks as though conservative ideas have indeed served them fairly well in maintaining their hold on both power and wealth. On the surface, the key tenets of classical conservatism fit into United Russia's developmental-state project, with such distinguishing features as a lack of trust in civil society, economic development mandated from above, the central role of the state, distrust in liberal democracy, preservation of social inequalities, the introduction of low taxes, the de facto destruction of welfare provisions, and, above all, trust in the magic effectiveness of vertical power.

There are, however, at least three problems—as seen from a political-economy perspective—with the "conservativeness" of United Russia. First, as Russian citizens seem to be simply the objects of a power game played by the elite, the party is unable to genuinely mass mobilize Russian society; second, conservatives' dislike of change makes it pretty useless as an ideology for the larger-scale goal of modernization; third, conservatives usually react oppressively to any societal upheavals and are thus unable to effectively manage or absorb discontent (which is quite natural in a time of prolonged economic uncertainty). On top of those liabilities, the "official" Russian version of conservatism lacks both coherence and a strategic sense of the future; it is simply a manifestation of the political class's current loyalty to the authorities of the day.

Against this background, President Medvedev's critique of the current state of the federation and his ambitious (but still general) plan to thoroughly modernize the Russian economy, and, as an indispensable part of it, society, seems to be only partially compatible, in the short term, with the socio-economic approach of the dominant Russian party and on a direct collision course, in the long term, with its sense of political management of the country. So far, such a direct collision has been avoided, as the president has adroitly chosen not to seek broader social support for his blueprint and has limited the scope of permitted change to the realm of the economy. This approach can become the nucleus of a *Russian version of progressivism* that is aimed at deep economic and social modernization but still timid in its depth of political restructuring.

Do It or Lose It—The Russian Developmental State in (In)Action

A perennial question among Russia's intelligentsia is, "Chto delat?"—What is to be done?

With an uneasy humbleness, we shall collectively say that we do not know for sure. Based on our best knowledge, we can only point to the best examples known and extrapolate/adjust those experiences into the specific conditions of today's Russia. Crudely, there are at least four basic choices to be made, each with its nationally shaped variations and mutations:

1. The "developmental state way" (as in the East-Asian model)
2. The "conservative modernization" way
3. "deep modernization"
4. The "EU way."

Each "model" has some built-in uncertainties and contradictions; each requires strong political will and policy-implementation capacity. Guaranteed success of any one is anything but certain. My point is, however, that by not making a decision, Russia, willingly or not, will slide down to the junior league of states, regardless of a quite-sure oil price recovery.

1. The developmental-state option: a lot of energy, money, and political capital already have been invested in that strategy for Russia's change. This scenario would unfold (obviously, at this point, *only hypothetically*) as follows: Based on the hitherto achieved pattern of accumulation/power, the Russian ruling group decides to move to the next level of developmental-state evolution—a deep and systemic modernization of the country. But the initial Kremlin-elite-based trusteeship of the stabilization/consolidation period (roughly 2000–05) is no longer enough to move ahead. They prepare a plan that will envision modernization, not narrowly defined (as the need for new technology and equipment) but as an all-embracing, staged process of legal/institutional, economic/social, technological, research/educational, and conscience/ideological change. They set in motion reforms and then move to a clear cluster of priorities in their plan, centered on reconstructing a sophisticated industrial base linked to innovative scientific research/implementation and pushing banks to finance it. Only those who are really competitive get the money. The Kremlin makes special efforts to make rules and procedures as clear as possible for business, and supports these through a strong, corruption-free court system. Corruption at large is at least halted thanks to changes in the regulatory system, punitive actions, and changing social attitudes that no longer accept it. As the Kremlin needs to find a larger pro-modernization consensus and ways to convince/co-opt/neutralize powerful, interest-based opponents, located mainly in the energy sector, they choose to rely on the small middle-class, medium-scale business, and that section of bureaucracy that is dynamic enough to implement new policies. They also are reshaping the "elite," as only a new ruling group will be able to carry on with the enormously complex tasks. At the same time, they launch a mass-media campaign to explain to the different constituencies the benefits of going through a painful and unexpectedly long (five or six years) initial modernization process (and of the danger of not setting off down this path). As the process advances, the Kremlin is peacefully undermining rising social discontent, which is normal as the redistributive

function of the state is being incrementally diminished and increasingly targeted, and is gaining enough support to make the bold move of reforming the resource and energy sectors. In the first stage (one or two years), they will need harsh measures; paradoxically, one of the impediments to the successful implementation of the "developmental-state scenario" was that Putin was "not dictatorial enough." Finally (within three-plus years), they move decisively to the point of democratization of the developmental state. Does this sound like fantasy? Is there any choice other than some form of this fantasy than a comfortable oil-and-gas-cushioned semi-stagnation?

2. The second way is to have a "conservative modernization." Such a scenario embraces at least five components: (a) some transfer of most modern technology—mainly to military industry, as it will be the only sector capable of absorbing it; (b) keeping the budget filled with petrodollars, which will be quite sufficient at $68 to $70 per barrel to fulfill current levels of social and security obligations; (c) strengthening military and security capacity to secure its diminishing economic and social power both domestically and internationally; (d) implementing even more assertive international policies to hide domestic weakness (for instance, in the Arctic); (e) at least a partial renewal of the elite—in key areas of security and higher-end regional/federal bureaucracy—which is capable of moving beyond the "stability-stagnation phase." Within this scenario, the Russian state can go on without any significant change for at least a couple of years. The rhetoric would be changed, however, focused on a more skillful use of the language of modernization, change, and openness. Thorough modernization can be postponed and reconsidered at a later stage. Energy price stability at above $70 per barrel would be very important to this scenario, and Russia should try to support/create a global mechanism for oil and gas price control. The above scenario is socially risky—as the state should contain any political upheavals and continue to block any significant source of opposition—but it is nonetheless doable (at least for a few years). The implementation of this scenario will be very much appreciated by the current politico-economic elite, as it would mean a stabilization of their power/wealth/influence and also would diminish the level of uncertainty related to the implementation of any alternative scenarios. In the long run, it might relegate Russia to the "secondary powers" club for some years and push it toward marginalization, but no state can be sure of its position in

the unpredictable global environment we have entered due to the current economic crisis.

3. The "deep-modernization" scenario differs from the previous one in scale and in the engagement of significant social actors in the process of modernization and, crucially, re-*industrialization of Russia*. It assumes, quite safely, that one cannot modernize the Russian economy without, in time, modernizing the state's governance principles and enabling society to be more empowered. Russia cannot become stronger without strengthening an industrial base that looks like an obsolete and job-losing machine. It also assumes two more things: that any social or economic change requires the presence of political subjects who are willing and capable of supporting the alternative (i.e., modernization), and that "modernization ideology" is only as good as the meaningful societal support it garners. Thus a meaningful modernization in Russia will require significant societal support, as it will be a real struggle to change the key sectors of the economy and reshape well-entrenched habits and structures. It also will require the participation of organized interest groups that will link their future prosperity with a modernized Russia. It can potentially attract followers, particularly among the middle class, small- and mid-size entrepreneurs, and youth.

Even a loose coalition of "deep modernizers" around the president can create the additional political space that could make Russia more hospitable to the *evolutionary change* that eventually will make the country stronger, more prosperous, and more respected. We admit that the actual level and depth of such support is, at present, unknown, and thus it would be quite risky politically and socially to start a wholesale implementation of the "modernization project" without the formation of a "movement for modernization" that eventually (if it is to gain significant support) may take the shape of a new centrist political party. There are, however, significant risks to such development. Two spring immediately to mind: such a "progressivist" movement might be too all-embracing and thus too loose to formalize itself as a coherent political party or even a social movement, and, second, as history tells us, socio-economic modernizations are capable of delivering a deathblow to the existing system—something that nobody in power is likely to welcome.

4. The "EU way" is a fourth possible option. Obviously, I am not advocating transposing a copy of European Union onto Russia or her applying to join the EU or even imitating its legal system. Vladislav Inozemtsev, a well-known Russian economist, made a very good point by saying that "this path doesn't require such a strong developmental state as the first one, but needs a radical political decision to be made...a pro-European policy based on accepting, if not European values, EU practices. If Russia accepts at least part of the EU-wide regulations known as *acqui communitaire*, complies with European ecological, competition, trade, and some social protection standards...the modernization of this country may take another direction."[53] Of course, it would be a revolutionary decision that would shake the whole system. Russia is far away (institutionally/legally and strategically, as far as the state is concerned) from the EU. This also would mean reshaping Russian foreign policy and some portion of the elite's mentality; but as Russian economic interests are located between Europe and Asia, this becoming a "compatible state but not within the same system" might be a sustainable choice. It would give Russia a firm place within the EU quasi-empire, even if it has been dented recently by deep fiscal problems, guarantee its security, offer better access to the EU market, reinforce Russia's position as a European power, and form a natural counterbalance to the "China vector" (see Bobo Lo's chapter in this volume).

In all cases, the ruling group must consider moving from the "trusteeship" mode of ruling Russia to a "social coalitions"–based system. As history has shown, even the most enlightened "trusteeship" cannot reorganize the system (in the long term) without broader societal support. At this moment, the game is not about technology and innovation transfer, as some members of the elite advocate; rather, it is about making Russian society and its economy innovatively oriented, with the state playing a decisive role in that process.

The choice among accelerated continuity, "deep modernization," and "status quo evolution" should be carefully considered, as the future of a huge country is at stake. What is certain is that the lack of real modernization/innovation policies of the last four or five years cannot be continued without serious, negative, long-term consequences. The only good thing about the current crisis is that no one can deny the necessity for accelerated change and the need for a larger societal debate about the future of the country. And this, in and of itself, is a good thing for Russia.

Notes

The epigraph to this chapter is drawn from Ryszard Kapuscinski, *Shah of Shahs* (New York: Vintage Books, 1992), 35.

1. Etatization is defined here as the accumulation of state capacity to develop and implement modernization/"developmental" strategies; it describes the state as the fundamental instrument of accumulation and nationally defined social change. See Piotr Dutkiewicz and Robert Shenton, "Etatization and the Logic of Diminishing Reproduction," *ROAPE* 13, no. 37 (1986): 108–15; and Piotr Dutkiewicz and Gavin Williams, "All the King's Horses and All the King's Men Couldn't Put Humpty Dumpty Together Again," *IDS Bulletin* 18 (1987): 1–6.
2. The primary theoretical argument regarding power and accumulation will be developed in the Accumulation–Power–Modernization section of this chapter.
3. Robert Kagan, "Stand Up to Putin," *Washington Post*, September 15, 2004.
4. Boris Nemtsov and Vladimir Milov, "White Paper," February 20, 2009, www.grani.ru/Politics/Russia/m.147176.html.
5. Anders Aslund, "The Kremlin's Crisis: Will a Shrinking Economy Force Russia to Pursue Reforms?" *Foreign Affairs*, May 20, 2009, http://www.foreignaffairs.com/print/65098.
6. Piotr Dutkiewicz and Vladimir Popov (all data and tables provided by Popov) in *From Putin to Medvedev: Continuity or Change?* ed. J. Larry Back and Michael Johns, Canada-Russia Series, vol. 10 (Manotick, Ontario: Penumbra Press, 2009).
7. The economic crisis has just barely dented the high popularity of Putin and Medvedev in the last eight months (November 2008–June 2009), with 78 percent support for Putin and 72 percent for Medvedev. Although 57 percent of Russians support the idea of having a "strong" opposition, its leaders are at best twelve to fifteen times less popular than the Putin-Medvedev tandem. *RIA Novosti*, August 11, 2009, http://en.rian.ru/russia/20090723.html; and Levada Center, July 28, 2009, http://www.levada.ru/press/2009072802.html.
8. Gleb Pavlovsky, director of the Effective Policy Foundation, interviewed by Boris Mezhuev and Alexander Pavlov, Kreml.org, August 11, 2009.
9. Ivan Krastev, "The Rules of Survival," *Journal of Democracy* 20, no. 2 (April 2009): 74.
10. For a more elaborate account, see Piotr Dutkiewicz and Vladimir Popov, "Ahead or Behind? Lessons from Russia's Post-Communist Reforms" [in Russian], *Sravnitelnoe konstitutsionnoe obozrenie* [Comparative constitutional review] 53, no. 4 (2005): 9–22.
11. For more information, see Vladimir Popov, "Shock Therapy versus Gradualism: The End of the Debate (Explaining the Magnitude of the Transformational Recession),"

    Comparative Economic Studies 42, no. 1 (Spring 2000): 1–57.
12. An excellent account of this process appears in Georgi Derluguian, "Recasting Russia," *New Left Review* 12 (November/December 2001): 26.
13. J. Hellman, G. Jones, D. Kaufmann, "Beyond the 'Grabbing Hand' of Government in Transition: Facing up to 'State Capture' by the Corporate Sector," *Beyond Transition* 11, no. 2 (April 2000): 8–11.
14. See Transparency International, http://www.transparency.org/.
15. As quoted in a lecture by Vadim Volkov, http://polit.ru/lectures/2009/html
16. Piotr Dutkiewicz and Vladimir Popov, "Democracy Without Liberalism" [in Russian], *Politicheskii Journal* [Political Journal] 40, no. 37, October 2004, 2–12.
17. S. Guriev, A. Rachinsky, "Ownership Concentration in Russian Industry" (background paper for Russia CEM 2003), http://www.nes.ru/files/Ownership Concentration March 2004; S. Claessens, S. Djankov, L. Lang, "The Separation of Ownership and Control in East Asian Corporations," *Journal of Financial Economics* 58 (2000): 81–112.
18. From the perspective of a "developmental state," the last four to five years have largely been lost for Russia's modernization process.
19. Thus far, at least; the recent crises have changed social dynamics quite substantially over the past few months.
20. Perry Anderson, "Russia's Managed Democracy," *London Review of Books*, January 25, 2007, 20.
21. Gabriel Almond and Laura Roselle, "Model Fitting in Communist Studies," in *Post-Communist Studies and Political Science*, ed. Frederick J. Fleron and Eric P. Hoffman (Oxford: Westview Press, 1993), 28.
22. One has to admit that Russian new capital was very innovative. The creation of FIGs made it possible not only to cross sectoral boundaries but also to introduce banking-industrial conglomerates that made their activities more profitable. For instance, the bank, as the owner of, let's say, a metallurgical plant, was financing its production (using noninterest loans) to sell its production to its own construction company or other industrial subsidiary that was using the metal plant's products. The profit, which usually would be divided among three or four agents, remained with one owner.
23. Jonathan Nitzan and Shimshon Bichler, *The Global Political Economy of Israel* (London: Pluto Press, 2002), 319–20.
24. As Nitzan and Bichler rightly observe, "The consequence was the end of Russia's free press." Nitzan and Bichler, *Global Political Economy of Israel*, 322.
25. It is shocking to compare that with the U.S. investment bank, Lehman Brothers,

which, when it filed for bankruptcy in September 2008, had assets valued at $639 billion and $619 billion in debt. *Wall Street Journal*, September 5, 2008.

26. For an insightful analysis of the "change versus stability dilemma" of Putin's ruling group, see Clifford G. Gaddy and Andrew C. Kuchins, "Putin's Plan," *Washington Quarterly* 31, no. 2 (Spring 2008): 117–29.

27. In Johann Wolfgang von Goethe's ballad "The Magician's Apprentice," a young magician thinks that his master is too slow, too narrow, and too stagnant. One has same feeling after reading Putin's millennium statement, issued on December 30, on the eve of his assumption of office as acting president. Vladimir V. Putin, "Russia at the Turn of the Millennium" (speech delivered at Moscow, December 30, 1999), reproduced in Vladimir Putin, *First Person: An Astonishingly Frank Self-Portrait by Russia's President Vladimir Putin*, with N. Gevorkyan, N. Timakova, and A. Kolsnikov, trans. C. A. Fitzpatrick (London: Hutchinson, 2000).

28. Nikolai Zlobin, in a radio interview, recalls a conversation held during the Valdai Club meeting in 2007, when the group members were visiting Gazprom headquarters in Moscow: "When we went to this room at Gazprom, somebody asked, 'Where is the button to turn off Ukraine?' and they have showed us. Remember, that was during the crisis with Ukraine. And when we were leaving the room somebody said, 'That's a regime-change room; that's the main office in Russia.'" Nikolai Zlobin, interview by Marshall Goldman, Radio Liberty, Thursday, June 5, 2008 (transcript by Federal News Service, Washington, D.C.).

29. A brilliant approach to this fundamentally important issue is offered by Jonathan Nitzan and Shimshon Bichler in *Capital As Power: A Study of Order and Creorder* (New York: Routledge, 2009), 464.

30. Ibid., 10.

31. "It expresses the certainty of the rulers in the submissiveness of the ruled." Ibid., 17.

32. Levada Center, "Monitoring of the Economic Crises, January–June 2009," available in Russian on http://www.levada.ru.

33. Since there is a large amount of literature on this topic, I highlight some basic facts. By 2007, Russia's GDP had grown approximately 8.1 percent (surpassing the average growth of all other G-8 countries). That growth was primarily driven by energy exports—the oil and gas sector generated more than 65 percent of Russia's export revenues in 2007 and almost 45 percent of total tax revenues. Between 2000 and 2008 Russian energy companies earned in excess of $650

billion, and its flagship company, Gazprom, is the second largest energy company in the world. Russia also became the world's second largest oil exporter.

34. For a detailed account of Russia's oil politics, see Marshall I. Goldman, *Petrostate: Putin, Power, and the New Russia* (Oxford: Oxford University Press, 2008), 256.

35. Quoted in Michael Cowen and Robert Shenton, *Doctrines of Development* (New York: Routledge, 1996), 397.

36. Ibid., 135. Shenton, in correspondence with me on August 19, 2009, wrote, "The basic idea contained within the doctrine of trusteeship is that certain people are incompetent to manage their own affairs and thus need a disinterested party to manage those affairs for them.... Much of the development theory, in general, is rooted in trusteeship, as is social welfare and social work practice."

37. Ibid., 25.

38. See the main works of Olga Kryshtanovskaya. For the composition of the Kremlin's Trusteeship group, see Olga Kryshtanovskaya, "Authoritarian Modernization of Russia in the 2000s" (paper presented at the international symposium "What Does Russia Think?" Russian Institute, Moscow 2009), 15.

39. Gleb Pavlovsky interview, Kreml.org.

40. Authors such as Johnson Chalmers, Dudley Sears, Hans Singer, Gordon White, Gavin Williams, Adrian Leftwich, Mark Robinson, Robert Shenton, Michael Watts, and Robert Wade, to mention just a few, were the most engaged in that debate—some since the early 1970s.

41. Adrian Leftwich, "Bringing Politics Back In," in *Democracy and Development: Theory and Practice* (Cambridge, MA: Polity, 1996), 401.

42. Mark Robinson and Gordon White, eds., *The Democratic Developmental State* (Oxford: Oxford University Press, 1998), 368.

43. As Gordon White put it, "The presence of globalization also threatens to undermine the viability of political systems of any kind—democratic or otherwise, through the challenge they pose to the sovereignty of nation-states and the autonomy of the governments." Robinson and White, *Democratic Developmental State*, 19.

44. Dutkiewicz and Williams, "All the King's Horses and All the King's Men."

45. Consider an example: to build one kilometer of paved road costs three times more in Russia than in the EU.

46. Russian officials sometimes prefer the terms "innovation" and "innovative economy" to strip the term "modernization" from its original link to T. Parsons's "inevitable Westernization" and/or link to roots of "modernization in Europe-

anization." I use this term without such built-in connotations simply as "the modern transformation of social life."

47. The research and development portion of the budget did not change very much from the Soviet period.

48. Maybe the ruling group was afraid of rapid (hence unpredictable) change or of the excessive empowerment of society and business; maybe they were concerned about the political outcome of the presidential elections of 2008, or had too much faith in the never-ending (and constantly growing) flow of petrodollars; or maybe there was a lack of political will for the new cycle of struggles. For one reason or another, and perhaps for all of the above reasons, Russia did not enter a comprehensive "modernization stage."

49. China's and India's GDP growth were consistently higher over the last ten years that Russia's. Brazil, despite its smaller GPD growth, was quite successful in reducing poverty and building innovative sectors of its economy. China, India, and Brazil are coping more effectively with the economic crisis as well; GDP in mid-2009 (compared to the year before) was as follows: China +8 percent, India +5.5 percent, and Russia -7 percent. *Economist*, August 22, 2009, 85.

50. One possible definition, of course, focuses on the guarantees of freedom from arbitrary political power. This approach can lead us in the direction of looking at citizens' rights from the individualistic liberal perspective. I fully recognize how valuable these rights are, in particular, when they are subjected to constraints or become unavailable. Yet there is another serious but under-discussed dimension within the debate about how democracy should be measured, as Immanuel Wallerstein reminds us. It might be that for the majority of the population in Russia—as well as in most transitional societies—the quality of governance and the political process is somehow measured differently. (All the while civil liberties are seen as valuable, desirable, and important—more than 55 percent of Russians declare their support for "democracy.") The primary concerns of most people hit by enormous dislocations, and accordingly their political priorities, are focused predominantly on their and their children's prospects for material well-being (and a fear of the consequences of growing material inequality), corruption, and their chances of becoming equal citizens within the state (by eliminating sources of discrimination based on age, disabilities, gender, ethnicity, etc.). Immanuel Wallerstein, *The Decline of American Power* (New York: New Press, 2003), 150.

51. *Kommersant*, "Vladislav Surkov Divides Democracy," June 29, 2006, http://www.kommersant.com/p686274/r_l.html.

52. Richard Sakwa, *Putin: Russia's Choice* (New York: Routledge, 2007), 97.
53. Vladislav L. Inozemtsev, *Dilemmas of Russia's Modernization* (paper presented at the international symposium What Does Russia Think? Russian Institute, Moscow 2009), 11.

CHAPTER TWO

The Long Road to Normalcy: Where Russia Now Stands

Vladimir Popov

A "Normal" Country?

The world economic recession hit Russia harder than other countries due to the collapse of oil prices, the outflow of capital caused by world recession, and poor policies to cope with the shock. The reduction in GDP in 2009 totaled 7.9 percent, as compared to 2.5 percent in the United States, 4.1 percent in the European Union, and 5.2 percent in Japan. Emerging markets, however, did much better than developed countries. China grew by 8.7 percent, India by 5.7 percent, the Middle East by 2.4 percent, and sub-Saharan Africa by 2.1 percent. Only the economies of Latin America, Eastern Europe, and the former Soviet Union contracted, by 1.8 percent, 3.7 percent, and 6.6 percent, respectively.

From 1989 to 1998, Russia experienced a transformational recession—GDP fell to 55 percent of the pre-recession 1989 level. From 1999 to 2008, the Russian economy was recovering at a rate of about 7 percent a year and barely reached the pre-recession peak of 1989 (fig. 2.1 and fig. 2.2).[1] Now, even with some luck, pre-recession GDP won't be surpassed until 2010–12. In sum, therefore, for two decades there has been no increase in output.

In 2004–05, Andrew Schleifer and Daniel Triesman published an article titled "A Normal Country: Russia after Communism." They compared Russia to Brazil, China, India, Turkey, and other developing countries, and argued that in terms of crime, income inequalities, corruption, macroeconomic instability, and other typical curses of the Third World, Russia is

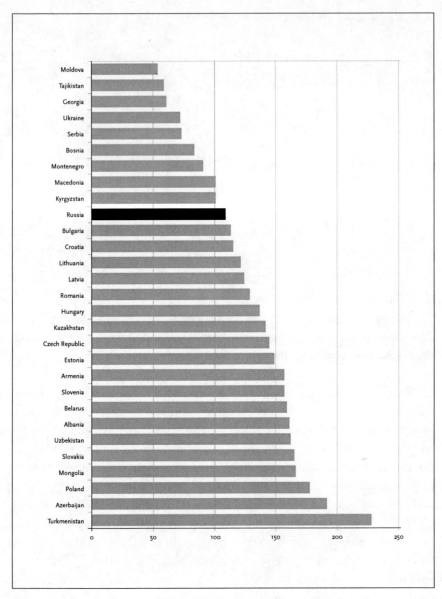

Figure 2.1   2008 GDP as a percentage of 1989 level   [Source: EBRD Transition Report]

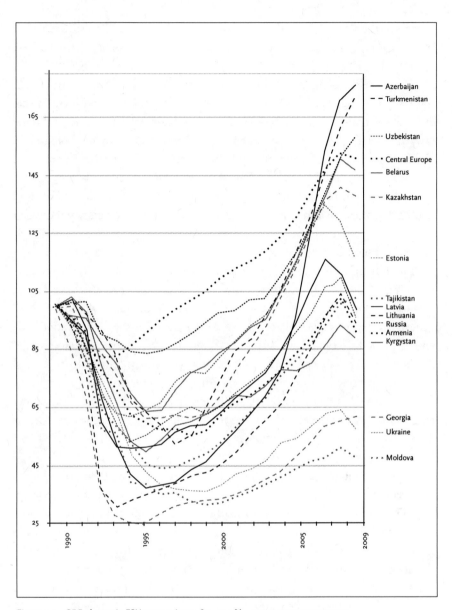

Figure 2.2　GDP change in FSU economies, 1989 = 100%　[Source: EBRD Transition Reports]

by far not the worst—indeed, somewhere in the middle of the list, and better than Nigeria, although worse than China. In short, Russia is a *normal* developing country.

The USSR was an *abnormal* developing country. The Soviet Union put the first man into space and had about twenty Nobel Prize winners in science and literature. Out of about forty living laureates of the Fields Medal (awarded since 1936 and recognized as the "Nobel Prize in mathematics"), eight come from the former Soviet Union, which had less than 5 percent of the world's population. The USSR had universal free health care and education—the best among developing countries—low income inequalities, and relatively low crime and corruption. By 1965 Soviet life expectancy increased to seventy years—only two years below that of the United States, even though per capita income was only 20 percent to 25 percent of the U.S. level.

The transition to a market economy in the 1990s brought about the dismantling of the Soviet state: the provision of all public goods, from health care to law and order, fell dramatically. The shadow economy, which the most generous estimates place at 10 percent to 15 percent of the GDP under Brezhnev, grew to 50 percent of the GDP by the mid-1990s. In 1980–85, the Soviet Union was placed in the middle of a list of fifty-four countries rated according to their level of corruption, with a bureaucracy cleaner than that of Italy, Greece, Portugal, South Korea, and practically all the developing countries. In 1996, after the establishment of a market economy and the victory of democracy, Russia came in forty-eighth in the same list, between India and Venezuela (fig. 2.3).

Income inequalities increased greatly: the Gini coefficient increased from 26 percent in 1986 to 40 percent in 2000, and then to 42 percent in 2007 (fig. 2.4). The decile coefficient—the ratio of the incomes of the wealthiest 10 percent of the population to the incomes of the poorest 10 percent—increased from 8 percent in 1992 to 14 in 2000, and then to 17 in 2007. But the inequalities at the very top increased much faster: in 1995, there was no person in Russia worth over $1 billion; in 2007, according to *Forbes* magazine, Russia had 53 billionaires, which propelled the country to second or third place in the world in this regard after the United States (415) and Germany (55) (see fig. 2.5). Indeed, Russia had two fewer billionaires than Germany, but Russia's billionaires were worth a total of $282 billion ($37 billion more than Germany's richest). In 2008 the number of billionaires in Russia increased to eighty-six, with a total worth of over $500 billion—a full one-third of national GDP.

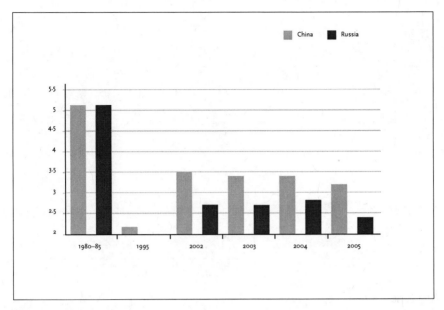

Figure 2.3   Corruption perception indices   [Source: Transparency International]

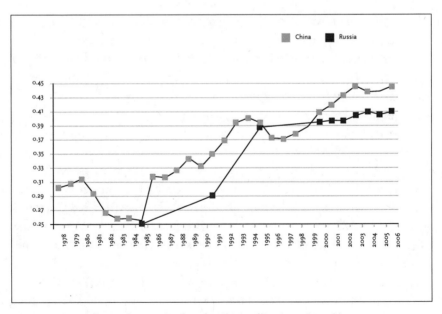

Figure 2.4   Gini coefficient of income distribution in China and Russia, 1978–2006   [Sources: Jiandong Chen, Wenxuan Hou, and Shenwu Jin, "The Effects of Population on Income Disparity in a Dual Society: Evidence from China" (presentation at the 2008 Chinese [UK] Economic Association annual conference at Cambridge, United Kingdom, and at the 2008 Hong Kong Economic Association Fifth Biennial Conference at Chengdu, China); Goskomstat]

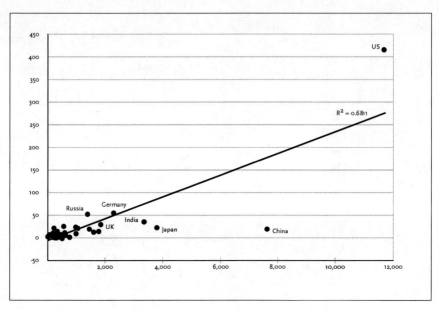

Figure 2.5   Number of billionaires in 2007 and PPP GDP in 2005 (billion $) by country   [Source: Forbes website]

The Soviet Union was abnormal—there were no billionaires at all and very few millionaires (perhaps only a dozen, in the shadow economy).

Worst of all, the criminalization of Russian society grew dramatically in the 1990s. Crime had been rising gradually in the Soviet Union since the mid-1960s, but after the collapse of the USSR there was an unprecedented surge: in just a few years in the early 1990s, crime and murder rates doubled and reached one of the highest levels in the world. By the mid-1990s, the murder rate stood at more than thirty people per 100,000 (fig. 2.6) as compared with one or two people per 100,000 in Western and Eastern Europe, Canada, China, Japan, Mauritius, and Israel. Only two countries in the world (not counting some war-torn, collapsed states), South Africa and Colombia, had higher murder rates, whereas in Brazil and Mexico the rate was half that of Russia. Even the United States' murder rate, the highest in the developed world—six to seven people per 100,000—pales in comparison with Russia's.

The Russian rate of death from external causes (accidents, murders, and suicides) had, by the beginning of the twenty-first century, skyrocketed to 245 people per 100,000. It was higher than in any of the 187 countries covered by

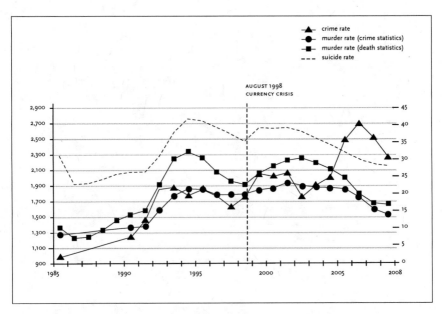

Figure 2.6   Crime rate (left scale), murder rates, and suicide rate (right scale) per 100,000 inhabitants
[Source: Goskomstat]

WHO estimates in 2002—equivalent to 2.45 deaths per 1,000 a year, or 159 per 1,000 over 65 years, which was the average life expectancy in Russia in 2002. Put differently, if these rates were to continue to hold, one out of six Russians born in 2002 would have an "unnatural" death. To be sure, in the 1980s murder, suicide, and accidental death rates were already quite high in Russia, Ukraine, Belarus, Latvia, Estonia, Moldova, and Kazakhstan—several times higher than in other former Soviet republics and in East European countries. However, they were roughly comparable to those of other countries with the same level of development. In the 1990s, these rates rapidly increased, far outstripping those in the rest of the world.

The mortality rate grew from ten people per 1,000 in 1990 to 16 in 1994, and stayed at a level of fourteen to sixteen per 1,000 thereafter. This was a true mortality crisis—a unique case in history, where mortality rates increased by 60 percent in just five years without any wars, epidemics, or volcano eruptions. Russia had never, in the postwar period, had mortality rates as high as those in the 1990s. Even in 1950–53, during the last years of the Stalin's regime, with the high death rates in the labor camps and the consequences of

The Long Road to Normalcy   47

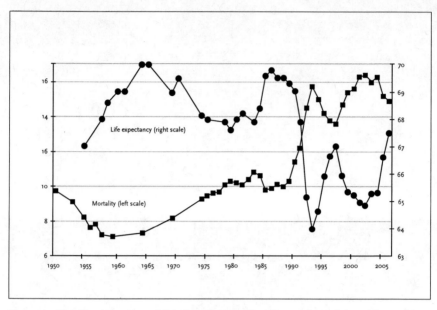

Figure 2.7 Mortality rate (per 1,000, left scale) and average life expectancy (years, right scale)
[Source: Goskomstat]

wartime malnutrition and wounds, the mortality rate was only nine to ten per 1,000, as compared to fourteen to sixteen in 1994–2008 (fig. 2.7).

The Russian Human Development index (computed as the average of indicators of PPP GDP per capita, life expectancy, and educational level calibrated from 0 to 100) did not increase through the 1990s and fell below the level of Cuba and probably that of China (fig. 2.8).

Russia became a typical "petrostate." Few specialists would call the USSR a resource-based economy, but Russia's industrial structure changed considerably after the transition to the market. The 1990s were indeed a period of rapid de-industrialization and "resourcialization" of the Russian economy, and the growth of world fuel prices since 1999 seems to have reinforced this trend. The share of output of the major resource industries (fuel, energy, metals) in total Russian industrial output increased from about 25 percent to over 50 percent by the mid-1990s and stayed at this high level thereafter. This was partly the result of changing price ratios (greater price increases in resource industries), but also that the real growth rates of output were lower in the non-resource sector. The share of mineral products, metals, and diamonds in

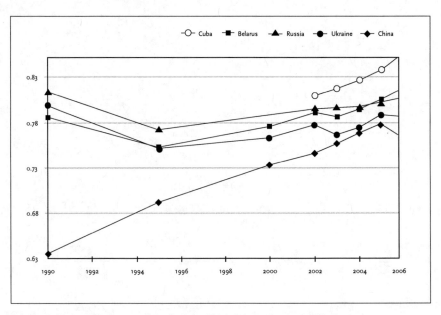

Figure 2.8 Human Development Index for Cuba, China, Belarus, Russia, and Ukraine
[Source: Human Development Report]

Russian exports increased from 52 percent in 1990 (USSR) to 67 percent in 1995, and to 81 percent in 2007, whereas the share of machinery and equipment in exports fell from 18 percent in 1990 (USSR) to 10 percent in 1995, and then to below 6 percent in 2007.

The share of spending in research and development was 3.5 percent of GDP in the late 1980s in the USSR. It has fallen to 1.3 percent in Russia today (compared with China—1.3 percent; United States, Korea, Japan—2 percent to 3 percent; Finland—4 percent; Israel—5 percent). So today's Russia really looks like a "normal" resource-abundant developing country.

Perhaps all these sacrifices were justified by the transition to democracy. But there is not much democracy in Russia today, at least according to the Freedom House. The index of political rights, computed by this institution and ranging from 1 (perfect democracy) to 7 (complete authoritarianism), after decreasing to 3 in 1991–97, returned to the pre-transition level of 6 in 2004–08 (fig. 2.9).

To understand Russia today, one has to evaluate the record of the last twenty years. In the late 1980s, during Gorbachev's perestroika, the Soviet

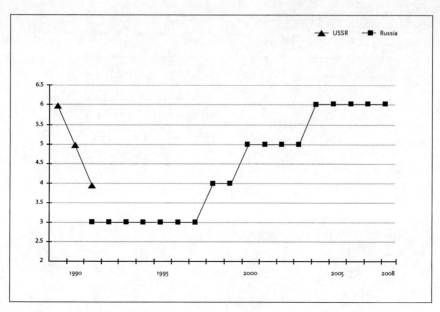

Figure 2.9 Political rights index in the USSR and in Russia, 1989–2008   [Source: Freedom House]

Union was aspiring to join the club of rich democratic nations, but instead degraded in the next decade to a position of *a normal* developing country, which is considered neither democratic nor capable of engineering a growth miracle. For some outsiders, a "normal developing country" may look better than the ominous superpower posing a threat to Western values. But insiders feel differently. Most Russians want to find a way to modernize the country so as to make it prosperous and democratic. However, they also feel that something went very wrong during the transition; the policies and political leaders of the 1990s are totally discredited.

To understand the popularity of Putin in 2000–08—and now the Putin-Medvedev tandem—one has to bear in mind that Putin's policy is the de facto denial of the across-the-board liberalization policies of Yeltsin, his predecessor. It is in essence a modernization project intended to put a halt to the degradation of the 1990s. The actual achievements of 2000–08 may be modest, but they are real: nearly a decade of economic growth; an increase in government revenues and spending; an accumulation of foreign-exchange reserves; a decrease in mortality, murders, and suicides, all thus preventing the disintegration of the country. When Putin was elected president for the first time in 2000, he received 53 percent of the vote. In 2004 he was elected with 71 percent of the vote, and more than 60 percent said they would vote for him in September 2007, never mind that he was not going to run. Even today, in the midst of the economic recession, Putin-Medvedev's policy is receiving a 50 percent-plus approval rate.

Why was Russian performance worse than that of other transition economies? The answer is twofold: the immediate reasons are associated with the collapse of the state institutions that occurred in the late 1980s and 1990s; the deeper reasons (that explain this institutional collapse of the 1990s) are rooted in the three-hundred-year trajectory of Russian institutional development.

Short-term Perspective: Why Russia Did Worse

The debates of the 1990s juxtaposed shock therapy strategy to gradualism. The question of why Russia had to pay a greater price for economic transition was answered differently by those who advocated shock therapy from those who supported gradual piecemeal reforms. Shock therapists argued that much of the costs of the reforms should be attributed to inconsistencies of the policies followed, namely, to slow economic liberalization and to the inability of the governments and the central banks to fight inflation in the first half of the 1990s. Supporters of gradual transition stated exactly the opposite, blaming the attempt to introduce a conventional shock therapy package for all the disasters and misfortunes.

In earlier articles, various explanations of the transformational recession suggest an alternative solution: the collapse of output was caused primarily by several groups of factors.[2] First, by greater distortions in the industrial structure and external trade patterns on the eve of the transition. Second, by the collapse of state and non-state institutions, which occurred in the late 1980s–early 1990s and which resulted in a chaotic transformation through crisis management instead of organized and manageable transition. Third, by poor economic policies, which basically consisted of bad macro-economic policy and import-substitution industrial policy. Finally, fourth, the speed of reforms (economic liberalization) affected performance negatively at the reduction-of-output stage because enterprises were forced to restructure faster than they possibly could (due to limited investment potential), but positively at the recovery stage.

In the first approximation, the economic recession that occurred in former Soviet Union (FSU) states was associated with the need to reallocate resources in order to correct the inefficiencies in industrial structure inherited from a centrally planned economy (CPE). These distortions included over-militarization and over-industrialization; perverted trade flows among former Soviet republics and COMECON countries; and excessively large, and poor specialization of, industrial enterprises and agricultural farms. In most cases, these distortions were more pronounced in Russia than in Eastern Europe, not to mention China and Vietnam; the larger the distortions, the greater the reduction of output. The transformational recession, to put it in economic terms, was caused by adverse supply shock similar to that experienced by Western countries after the oil price hikes in 1973 and 1979 and to postwar recessions caused by conversion of the defense industries.

Figure 2.10 shows that the reduction of output in Russia during the transformational recession was to a large extent structural in nature: industries with the greatest adverse supply shock (deteriorating terms of trade, relative price ratios for outputs and inputs), such as light industry, experienced the largest reduction of output. The evidence for all transition economies is in table 2.1: the reduction of output by country is well explained by the indicator of distortions in industrial structure and trade patterns (it remains statistically significant no matter what control variables are added). The magnitude of distortions, in turn, determines the change in relative prices when they are deregulated.

The nature of the recession was basically an adverse supply shock caused by the change in relative prices. There was a limit to the speed of reallocating capital from noncompetitive to competitive industries, which was determined basically by the net investment/GDP ratio (gross investment minus retirement of capital stock in the competitive industries, since in noncompetitive industries the retiring capital stock should not be replaced anyway). It was unreasonable to wipe away output in noncompetitive industries faster than capital was being transferred to more efficient industries. Market-type reforms in many post-communist economies created exactly this kind of a bottleneck.

Countries that followed the shock-therapy path found themselves in a supply-side recession, which is likely to become a textbook example: an excessive speed of change in relative prices required a magnitude of restructuring that was simply non-achievable with the limited pool of investment. Up to half of their economies was made noncompetitive overnight. Output

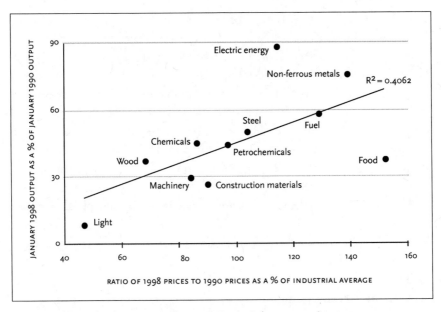

Figure 2.10 Change in relative prices and output in Russian industry, 1990–98

in these noncompetitive industries had been falling for several years and in some cases fell to virtually zero, whereas the growth of output in competitive industries was constrained by, among other factors, the limited investment potential and was not enough to compensate for the output loss in the inefficient sectors.[3]

Hence, at least one general conclusion from the study of the experience of transition economies appears to be relevant for the reform process in all countries: *provided that reforms create a need for restructuring (reallocation of resources), the speed of reforms should be such that the magnitude of required restructuring does not exceed the investment potential of the economy.* In short, the speed of adjustment and restructuring in every economy is limited, if due only to the limited investment potential needed to reallocate capital stock. This is the main rationale for *gradual*, rather than instant, phasing out of tariff and nontariff barriers, of subsidies, and of other forms of government support for particular sectors (it took nearly ten years for the European Economic Community or NAFTA to abolish tariffs). This is a powerful argument against shock therapy, especially when reforms involved result in a sizable reallocation of resources. For Western countries with low trade barriers, low subsidies, low degrees of price controls, etc., even fast, radical reforms are not likely to require restructuring that would exceed the limit of investment potential. But for less developed countries with a lot of distortions in their economies supported by explicit and implicit subsidies, fast removal of these subsidies could easily result in such a need for restructuring, which is beyond the ability of the economy due to investment and other constraints.

However, such a reduction of output due to the inability of the economy to adjust rapidly to new price ratios is by no means inevitable if the deregulation of prices proceeds gradually, or if losses from deteriorating terms of trade for most affected industries are compensated by subsidies. The pace of liberalization had to be no faster than the ability of the economy to move resources from noncompetitive (under the new market price ratios) to competitive industries.

Therefore, it should be expected that there is a negative relationship between performance and the speed of liberalization. It also should be expected that the larger magnitude of distortions in industrial structure and trade patterns would lead to the greater reduction of output during the transformational recession, but would not have much of an impact on performance during the recovery stage (after which the noncompetitive sector would be shut down completely).

The additional reason for the extreme depth of the transformational recession was associated with the institutional collapse. Here differences between EE and FSU countries are striking. The adverse supply shock in this case came from the inability of the state to perform its traditional functions— to collect taxes and to constrain the shadow economy and to ensure property and contract rights and law and order in general. Naturally, the inability to adequately enforce rules and regulations helped create a business climate that was not conducive to growth and resulted in increased costs for companies.

The measure of the institutional strength is the dynamics of government expenditure during transition. This factor seems to have been far more important than the speed of reforms. In Kolodko's words, there "can be no doubt that during the early transition there was a causal relationship between the rapid shrinkage in the size of government and the significant fall in output."[4] Keeping the government big does not guarantee favorable dynamics of output, since government spending has to be efficient as well. However, the sharp decline in government spending, especially for the "ordinary government," is a sure recipe to ensure the collapse of institutions and the fall in output accompanied by the growing social inequalities and populist policies.

When real government expenditures fall by 50 percent and more—as happened in most CIS and Southeast Europe states in just several years—there are practically no chances to compensate the decrease in the volume of financing by the increased efficiency of institutions. As a result, the ability of the state to enforce contracts and property rights, to fight criminalization, and to ensure law and order in general falls dramatically.[5]

Thus, the story of the successes and failures of transition is not really the story of consistent shock therapy and inconsistent gradualism. The major plot of the post-socialist transformation "novel" is the preservation of strong institutions in some countries (very different in other respects, from Central Europe and Estonia to China, Uzbekistan, and Belarus[6]) and the collapse of these institutions in the other countries. At least 90 percent of this story is about the government failure (strength of state institutions), not about the market failure (liberalization).

It is precisely this strong institutional framework that should be held responsible for both—for the success of gradual reforms in China and shock therapy in Vietnam, where strong authoritarian regimes were preserved and CPE institutions were not dismantled before new market institutions were created, and for the relative success of radical reforms in EE countries, especially in Central European countries, where strong democratic regimes and new market institutions emerged quickly. And it is precisely the collapse of a strong state and institutions that started in the USSR in the late 1980s and continued in the successor states in the 1990s, which explains the extreme length, if not the extreme depth of the FSU transformational recession.

To put it differently, Gorbachev's reforms of 1985–91 failed not because they were gradual but because of the weakening of the state institutional capacity leading to the inability of the government to control the flow of events. Similarly, Yeltsin's reforms in Russia, as well as economic reforms in most other FSU states, were so costly not because of the shock therapy but because of the collapse of the institutions needed to enforce law and order and carry out a manageable transition.

It turns out that the FSU transition model (with the partial exemption of Uzbekistan, Belarus, and Estonia) is based on a most unfortunate combination of unfavorable initial conditions, institutional degradation, and inefficient economic policies, such as macro-economic populism and import substitution.

What led to the institutional collapse and could it have been prevented? Using the terminology of political science, it is appropriate to distinguish between strong authoritarian regimes (China and Vietnam and, to an extent, Belarus and Uzbekistan), strong democratic regimes (Central European countries), and weak democratic regimes (most FSU and Balkan states). The former two are politically liberal or liberalizing—i.e., they protect individual rights, including those of property and contracts, and create a framework of law and administration—while the latter regimes, though democratic, are politically not so liberal, since they lack strong institutions and the ability to enforce law and order.[7] This gives rise to the phenomenon of "illiberal democracies"—countries in which competitive elections are introduced before the rule of law is established. While European countries in the nineteenth century and East Asian countries recently moved from first establishing the rule of law to gradually introducing democratic elections (Hong Kong is the most obvious example of the rule of law without democracy), in Latin America, Africa, and now in CIS countries democratic political systems were introduced in societies without a firm rule of law.

Authoritarian regimes (including communist), while gradually building property rights and institutions, were filling the vacuum in the rule of law via authoritarian means. After democratization occurred and illiberal democracies emerged, they found themselves deprived of old authoritarian instruments to ensure law and order, but without the newly developed democratic mechanisms needed to guarantee property rights, contracts, and law and order in general. No surprise, this had a devastating impact on investment climate and output.

There is a clear relationship between the ratio of a rule-of-law index on the eve of transition to a democratization index, on the one hand, and economic performance during transition, on the other. To put it differently, democratization without a strong rule of law, whether one likes acknowledging it or not, usually leads to the collapse of output. There is a price to pay for early democratization—i.e., the introduction of competitive elections under conditions in which fundamental liberal rights (personal freedom and safety, property, contracts, fair trial in court, etc.) are not well established.

Finally, performance was of course affected by economic policy. Given the weak institutional capacity of the state—its inadequate ability to enforce its own regulations—economic policies could hardly be "good." Weak state institutions usually imply populist macro-economic policies (budget deficits resulting in high indebtedness and/or inflation, overvalued exchange rates), which have a devastating impact on output. Conversely, strong institutional capacity does not lead automatically to responsible economic policies. Examples range from the USSR before it collapsed (periodic outbursts of open or hidden inflation) to such post-Soviet states as Uzbekistan and Belarus, which seem to have stronger institutional potential than other FSU states but do not demonstrate higher macro-economic stability.

Regressions tracing the impact of all mentioned factors are reported in table 2.1. Some 80 to 90 percent of the variations in the dynamics of GDP in 1989–96 could be explained by the initial conditions (distortions and initial GDP per capita), institutional capacity of the state (decline in government revenues and rule of law and democracy indices), and macro-economic stability (inflation). If the rule of law and democracy indices are included in the basic regression equation, they have predicted signs (positive impact of the rule of law and negative impact of democracy) and are statistically significant (equation 1), which is consistent with the results obtained for larger sample of countries.[8]

The most powerful explanation, however, is exhibited by the index that is computed as the ratio of the rule-of-law index to the democracy index: 83 percent of all variations in output can be explained by only three factors—pre-transition distortions, inflation, and the rule-of-law-to-democracy index (table 2.1, equation 2). If the liberalization variable is added, it turns out to be statistically insignificant and does not improve the fit (equation 3). At the same time, the ratio of the rule-of-law-to-democracy index and the decline in government revenues are not substitutes, but rather complement each other in characterizing the process of institutional decay. These two variables are not correlated and improve the fit when included together in the same regression: R2 increases to 91 percent (equation 5)—a better result than in regressions with only one of these variables. The liberalization index, when added to the same equation, is not statistically significant and has the "wrong" sign.

To test the robustness of the results, another year for the end of the transformational recession, 1998, was chosen, so the period considered was 1989–98 (by the end of 1998, the absolute bottom was reached in twenty-four of twenty-six countries that experienced the recession). The adjusted

EQUATIONS, NUMBER OF OBSERVATIONS / VARIABLES	1, N=28	2, N=28
Constant	5.3***	5.4***
Distortions, % of GDP[a]	−.005**	−.005**
1987 PPP GDP per capita, % of the US level	−.009**	−.006*
War dummy[b]		
Decline in government revenues as a % of GDP from 1989–91 to 1993–96		
Liberalization index in 1995		
Log (inflation, % a year, 1990–95, geometric average)	−.16***	−.20***
Rule of law index, average for 1989–97, %	.008***	
Democracy index, average for 1990–98, %	−.005***	
Ration of the rule of law to democracy index		.07***
Adjusted R^2, %	82	83

Dependent variable = Log (1996 GDP as a % of 1989 GDP)
For China—all indicators are for the period of 1979–86 or similar

*, **, *** significant at 1, 5 and 10% level respectively

a cumulative measure of distortions as a % of GDP equal to the sum of defense expenditure (minus 3% regarded as the 'normal' level), deviations in industrial structure and trade openness from the 'normal' level, the share of heavily distorted trade (among the FSU republics) and lightly distorted trade (with socialist countries) taken with a 33% weight – see (Popov, 2000) for details.

b equals 1 for Armenia, Azerbaijan, Croatia, Georgia, Macedonia, and Tajikistan and 0 for all other countries

c significant at 13% level

Table 2.1 Regression of change in GDP in 1989–96 on initial conditions, policy factors, and rule of law and democracy indices, robust estimates

3, N=28	4, N=28	5, N=28	6, N=28	7, N=28
5.2***	5.4***	5.4***	5.5***	5.7***
−.003	−.006**	−.007***	−.007***	−.007***
−.007**	−.007**	−.009***	−.008***	−.008***
	−.19c	−.36***	−.37***	−.45***
		−.011***	−.011***	−.011***
.05			−.02	.03
−.18***	−.17***	−.13***	−.13***	−.14***
				−.003**
.07***	.06***	.05***	.05***	
83	85	91	91	90

R2 is slightly lower, but the statistical significance of coefficients remains high (with the exception of the initial GDP per capita). The best equation is shown below:

$$\text{Log}(Y98/89) = 5.8 - .006 DIST - 0.005 Ycap87 - 0.39 WAR - 0.01 GOVREVdecline - 0.17 log INFL - .003 DEM$$

[-2.48]   [-0.09]   [-3.22]   [-2.94]   [-4.60]   [-1.74]

N= 28, Adjusted R2 = 82%, T-statistics in brackets, all variables are shown in the same order as in equation 7 from table 2.1
(liberalization variable is omitted and DEM is democracy index, average for 1990–98, %).

Once again, if the liberalization variable is introduced in this equation, it turns out to be insignificant.

Finally, to deal with the endogeneity problem (liberalization affects performance but is also affected by performance — if output falls, liberalization very likely would be halted) the liberalization variable was used with the democracy-level variable.[9] The results are in table 2.2; the main difference from table 2.1 is that liberalization now affects performance significantly and negatively.

At the recovery stage (1998–2005), the impact of distortions on performance disappears, but the influence of institutions persists, and the impact of the speed of liberalization (the increment increase in the liberalization index) becomes positive and significant.[10] This is very much in line with intuition: after the noncompetitive sector is eradicated at the transformation-recession stage, further liberalization (which inevitably becomes gradual at this point) cannot do much harm, whereas institutional capacity always affects growth.

We end up with the plan that summarizes factors affecting performance during transition: the FSU in general (there are some exceptions) and Russia in particular had poor initial conditions (allocation of resources by industries and regions under central planning was very different from market type; so when prices were deregulated and allowed to govern the allocation of capital and labor, sizable restructuring occurred leading to a recession). To add insult to injury, there was dramatic decline in the institutional capacity of the state.

Long-term: Institutional Continuity

The scheme leaves us with the frustrating conclusion that the bulk of the recession of the 1990s was inevitable (initial conditions and institutions are exogenous, given preceding developments) and economic policy (fast liberalization

EQUATIONS, NUMBER OF OBSERVATIONS / VARIABLES	1, N=28	2, N=28	3, N=17	4, N=17
Constant	6.4***	6.3***	6.0***	6.0***
Pre-transition distortions, % of GDP	−.01***	−.02***		−.004
1987 PPP GDP per capita, % of the US level	−.007**	−.01***		
War dummy[a]	−.45***	−.29[b]		
Liberalization index in 1995	−.18**	−.39*	−.19***	−.19***
Decline in government revenues as a % of GDP from 1989–91 to 1993–96	−.02***	−.02***		
Log (inflation, % a year, 1990–95, geometric average)	−1.7***	−.22***	−.22***	−.19***
Rule of law index, average for 1989–97, %		−.01[c]		
Increase in the share of shadow economy in GDP in 1989–94, p.p.			−.02***	−.015***
R^2, %	86	77	88	90

Dependent variable = Log (1996 GDP as a % of 1989 GDP)
For China—all indicators are for the period of 1979–86 or similar

*, **, *** significant at 1, 5 and 10% level respectively
a equals 1 for Armenia, Azerbaijan, Croatia, Georgia, Macedonia, and Tajikistan and 0 for all other countries
b, c significant at 12 and 16% level respectively

Table 2.2 2SLS robust estimates, regression of change in GDP (1989–96) on initial conditions, institutional capacity, liberalization, and rule of law and democracy indices (liberalization index instrumented with the democracy level variable)

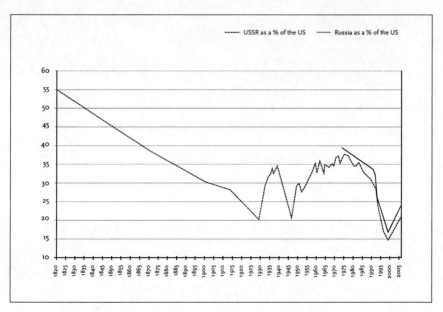

Figure 2.11   PPP GDP per capita in the USSR and Russia, percentage of the U.S. level
[Source: A. Maddison, "Statistics on World Population, GDP and Per Capita GDP, 1-2006 AD, 2008, http://www.ggdc.net/maddison/ Historical_Statistics/horizontal-file_09-2008.xls]

at early stages of development and poor macro-economic policy) more often than not aggravated the recession. Besides, today, after the transformational recession, the prospects for the future seem to depend mostly on institutional capacity, which is the binding constraint of growth. With respect to distortions, gradual liberalization should have facilitated avoiding the collapse of output. But was it possible to preserve strong institutions, as happened in EE and China? This is, in fact, the most crucial question—why some former communist countries retained their strong institutions during reforms; whereas in other countries, institutional capacity, even if it was strong previously, deteriorated?

Soviet catch-up development looked impressive until the 1970s. In fact, from the 1930s to the 1960s, the USSR and Japan were the only two major developing countries that successfully bridged the gap with the West (fig. 2.11).

The highest rates of growth of labor productivity in the Soviet Union were observed not in the 1930s (3 percent annually), but in the 1950s (6 percent). The Total Factor Productivity (TFP) growth rates over decades increased from 0.6 percent annually in the 1930s to 2.8 percent in the 1950s, and then fell steadily, becoming negative in the 1980s (table 2.3). The 1950s were thus the "golden period" of Soviet economic growth (fig. 2.12). The patterns of Soviet growth of the 1950s in terms of growth accounting were very similar to the Japanese growth of the 1950s to 1970s and Korean and Taiwanese growth in the 1960s to 1980s—fast increases in labor productivity counterweighted the decline in capital productivity, such that the TFP increased markedly (table 2.3). However, high Soviet economic growth lasted only a decade; whereas in East Asia it continued for three to four decades, propelling Japan, South Korea, and Taiwan into the ranks of developed countries.

Among many reasons for the decline in the growth rate in the USSR in the 1960s to the 1980s, the inability of a centrally planned economy to ensure an adequate flow of investment into the replacement of retired fixed-capital stock appears to be most crucial.[11] The task of renovating physical capital contradicted the short-term goal of fulfilling planned targets, and Soviet planners therefore preferred to invest in new capacities instead of upgrading old ones. Hence, after the massive investment in the USSR of the 1930s (the "big push"), the highest productivity was achieved after the period equal to the service life of capital stock (about twenty years) before there emerged a need for massive investment into replacing retired stock. Afterwards, capital stock started to age rapidly, sharply reducing capital productivity and lowering labor productivity and the TFP growth rate.

If this explanation is correct, a centrally planned economy is doomed to experience a growth slowdown after three decades of high growth following a "big push." In this respect, the relatively short Chinese experience with the CPE (1949/1959–79) looks superior to the excessively long Soviet experience (1929–91). This is one of the reasons to believe that the transition to a market economy in the Soviet Union would have been more successful if it had started in the 1960s.

The inability to make a timely transition to the market, to shift gears and move the economy away from a planning trajectory leading to a dead end, was perhaps caused by policy mistakes, and the accidental coincidence of events, rather than by an intrinsic evolution of the system. But the result was the slowdown of growth rates, the loss of social dynamism, the bureaucratization of the administrative apparatus, and deterioration of social indicators (increases in the rates of alcoholism, murders, suicides, and mortality). The economy was still growing until the late 1980s but at a constantly declining rate.

COUNTRY/ PERIOD	OUTPUT PER WORKER	CAPITAL PER WORKER	CAPITAL/ OUTPUT RATIO	TPF GROWTH UNIT ELASTICITY OF SUBSTITUTION	TPF GROWTH ASSUMING 0.4 ELASTICITY OF SUBSTITUTION
USSR (1928–39)	2.9	5.7	2.8	0.6	
USSR (1940–49)	1.9	1.5	-0.4	1.3	
USSR (1950–59)	5.8	7.4	1.6	2.8	1.1
USSR (1960–69)	3.0	5.4	2.4	0.8	1.1
USSR (1970–79)	2.1	5.0	2.9	0.1	1.2
USSR (1980–87)	1.4	4.0	2.6	−0.2	1.1
Japan (1950/57/65/–85/88/90)			2.3 – 3.2	1.7 – 2.5	
Korea (1950/60/65–85/88/90)			2.8 – 3.7	1.7 – 2.8	
Taiwan (1950/53/65–85/88/90)			2.6 – 3.1	1.9 – 2.4	

Table 2.3 Growth in the USSR and Asian economies, Western data, 1928–87 (average annual, %)

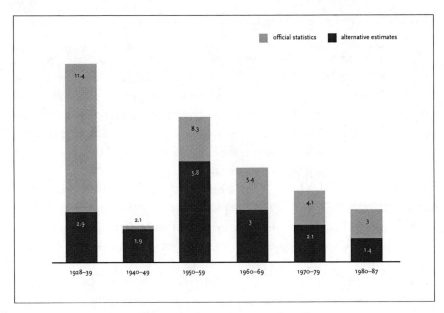

Figure 2.12 Annual average productivity growth rates in Soviet economy, %

However, even if a transition to the market had been carried out in the 1960s, its success was not at all assured. Most likely, it would have produced the same increase in income inequalities and the same weakening of state institutional capacity that occurred three decades later. And the USSR/Russia would look more like Latin America, not like East Asia.

To make a transition to the market economy at the right time is a necessary, but not a sufficient, condition for successful catch-up development. Manufacturing growth is like cooking a good dish—all the necessary ingredients should be in the right proportion; if even one of those ingredients is under- or overrepresented, the "chemistry of growth" will not happen. Fast economic growth can materialize in practice only if several necessary conditions are met simultaneously. Rapid growth requires a number of crucial inputs—infrastructure, human capital, land distribution in agrarian countries, strong state institutions, and economic stimuli, among other things. Rodrik, Hausmann, and Velasco talk about "binding constraints" that hold back economic growth; finding these constraints is a task in "growth diagnostics."[12] In some cases, these constraints are associated with a lack of market liberalization; in others, with a lack of state capacity or human capital or infrastructure.

Part of the answer to the question of why institutions started to weaken during the late-Soviet era and then even more rapidly in the 1990s, during the transition to the market, is associated with the impact of democratization on the quality of institutions. As argued in previous papers,[13] democratization carried out in a poor rule-of-law environment (weak state institutions) is associated with further weakening of institutions and with worsening of macro-economic policy, which has a negative impact on growth and does not facilitate the building of a stable democratic regime, especially in resource-rich countries.[14]

This is only part of the answer, however, because there are a few examples of fast catch-up development under democratic regimes (Japan after the Second World War, Botswana and Mauritius after gaining independence in the 1960s). Besides, democracy is an institution unto itself, and it remains to be explained why some countries adopted it at earlier stages of development, whereas others stayed authoritarian or returned to authoritarianism after short-lived experiments with democracy. And finally, differences in the institutional capacity of the state in countries with authoritarian regimes (for example, China, the USSR, and Russia) are huge and need to be explained.

Yet another reason is the different trajectories of the genesis of the institutions in colonized and non-colonized countries. All countries had traditional community structures in the past; everywhere before Reformation, under the Malthusian growth regime, the law of the land was what we now call "Asian values"—the superiority of the interests of the community over the interests of individuals.

Colonization of sub-Saharan Africa, South America, and, to a lesser extent, South Asia led to complete or near-complete destruction of traditional (community) structures that were only partially replaced by the new Western-style institutions. Among large geographical regions, only East Asia, the Middle East and North Africa (MENA), and, to an extent, South Asia managed to retain traditional community institutions despite colonialism. It could be hypothesized that those countries and regions that preserved traditional institutions in difficult times of colonialism and the imposition of Western values retained a better chance for catch-up development than the less fortunate regions of the world's periphery, where the continuity of the traditional structures was interrupted.[15] Transplantation of institutions is a tricky business that works well only when tailored to the local traditions, such that it does not interrupt the institutional continuity.[16] Otherwise, it leads either to a complete elimination of the local structures (the United States, Canada, Australia) or to a nonviable mixture of old and new institutions that is not very conducive to growth (Latin America, sub-Saharan Africa).

In short, premature dismantling of collectivist institutions, even when allowing to overcome the Malthusian trap, does now allow for healthy growth. It leads to an increase in income inequalities and to a weakening of institutional capacity, defined as the ability of the state to enforce it rules and regulations.[17] "The frequent claim that inequality promotes accumulation and growth does not get much support from history. On the contrary, great economic inequality has always been correlated with extreme concentration of political power, and that power has always been used to widen the income gaps through rent-seeking and rent-keeping, forces that demonstrably retard economic growth."[18]

This explains differences in the long-term development trajectory of institutions in China and Russia. China's 1949 liberation was similar to the Russian Revolution of 1917 not only because communists came to power in both countries but because traditional collectivist institutions, ruined by preceding Westernization, were reestablished and strengthened. However, the Russian communist regime of 1917–91 merely interrupted the process of the transplantation of Western institutions that had been going on at least since the seventeenth century; whereas in China, the liberation of 1949 returned the country to a long-term institutional trajectory that was briefly (and only partly) interrupted after the Opium Wars.

To put it differently, Russia already had been westernized before 1917, and collectivist institutions that were introduced in Russia by the Revolution of 1917 had been largely alien to previous long-term institutional development. If not for the Revolution of 1917, Russia would probably have followed the trajectory of Latin America and sub-Saharan Africa, becoming a "normal" developing country right away. On the other hand, China has aborted an unsuccessful westernization attempt (1840s to 1949) and returned to collectivist (Asian values) institutions. What was a passing episode and a deviation from the trend in Russia was a return to the mainstream development and a restoration of a long-term trend in China. Hence, economic liberalization from 1979 on in China, though accompanied by growing income inequalities and crime and murder rates, has not resulted in institutional collapse.

Conclusions

After allowing for differing initial conditions, it turns out that the fall in output in transition economies was associated mostly with a poor business environment, resulting from institutional collapse. Liberalization alone, when it is not complemented with strong institutions, cannot guarantee good performance. Institutional capacities, in turn, depend to a large extent on the combination of the rule of law and democracy: the data seem to suggest that both authoritarian and democratic regimes can have strong rules of law and can deliver efficient institutions; whereas under a weak rule of law, authoritarian regimes do a better job of maintaining efficient institutions than democracies. To put it more succinctly, the record of illiberal democracies in ensuring institutional capacities is the worst, which predictably has a devastating impact on output.

Why do illiberal democracies emerge? Why did Russia become one of these? It has been argued that the first group of countries that willingly and unwillingly (colonialism) transplanted Western institutions (Latin America, FSU, sub-Saharan Africa) ended up with high income inequalities and an apparent lack of institutional capacity. On the other hand, the second group of developing countries—regions that have never really departed from the collectivist institutions and have preserved institutional continuity (East Asia, India, MENA)—succeeded in maintaining low income and wealth inequalities. This second group of countries may have stayed in the Malthusian growth regime longer than others, but once technical progress allowed them to exit from the Malthusian trap, their starting conditions in terms of institutional capacity turned out to be better than those of the first group.

If this interpretation is correct, Russia unfortunately has fewer reasons to be successful in its catch-up development than other regions of the developing world. After East Asia's impressive breakthrough, the next growth miracles are likely to occur in MENA Islamic countries (Turkey, Iran, Egypt, etc.) and South Asia (India), while Latin America, sub-Saharan Africa, and Russia would be falling behind.

From 1999 to 2008, when oil and gas prices were high, Russia enjoyed relatively fast but not very healthy growth. Windfall fuel profits led to personal consumption, not to investment and public consumption, which were exactly the bottlenecks of the growth process. Personal incomes were growing faster than productivity, while investment, even in 2008, amounted to only 50 percent of the 1989 level, and government spending on infrastructure, education, health care, and research and development as a percentage of GDP did not rebound to the levels of the late USSR.

The weaknesses of the Russian economy—an overvalued exchange rate, a poorly diversified industrial and export structure, low spending for investment and public goods, and high income inequalities—were partially concealed by high oil and gas prices in 2003–08, but were revealed in 2008–09, as world fuel oil prices fell. No wonder, the reduction of output in Russia (GDP fell by 8 percent in 2009) was greater than in all other countries of similar or larger size. The paradox is that the need to deal with these weaknesses becomes more acute exactly at a time when financial resources dried up. If Russia was unable to deal with structural weaknesses during favorable years, there is virtually no hope that investment and public services will be repaired in the lean years. This inability to operate with a longer-term perspective is a sign of poor institutional capacity.

Notes

1. Figure 2.1 is based on GDP indices (2008 as a percentage of 1989) reported in the EBRD Transition Report 2005, whereas figure 2.2 reports chain indices (based on annual growth rates) from the same source. The discrepancies are not that substantial.
2. V. Popov, "Shock Therapy versus Gradualism: The End of the Debate (Explaining the Magnitude of the Transformational Recession)," *Comparative Economic Studies* 42, no. 1 (Spring 2000): 1–57, http://www.nes.ru/%7Evpopov/documents/TR-REC-full.pdf, and "China's Rise, Russia's Fall: Medium Term Perspective" (TIGER working paper no. 99, Warsaw, February 2007), published in *História e Economia Revista Interdisciplinar* 3 (2007): 14–38.
3. Ibid.
4. Grzegorz W. Kolodko, *From Shock to Therapy: Political Economy of Postsocialist Transformation* (Oxford: Oxford University Press, 2003), 259 (my italics).
5. V. Popov, "Lessons from the Transition Economies: Putting the Success Stories of the Postcommunist World into a Broader Perspective" (UNU/WIDER research paper no. 2009/15).

6. Countries like Belarus and Uzbekistan fall into the same category as the central European countries and Estonia, which have experienced a small reduction of state expenditures as a percentage of GDP during transition, good quality of governance, little bribery, a small shadow economy, and a low state capture index; see J. Hellman, G. Jones, D. Kaufmann, "Beyond the 'Grabbing Hand' of Government in Transition: Facing up to 'State Capture' by the Corporate Sector," *Beyond Transition* 11, no. 2 (April 2000). In 2005, Belarus and the Slovak Republic were the only two countries out of twenty-five surveyed in the EE and FSU (BEEPS—Business Environment and Economic Performance Survey) where significant improvement was registered from 2002 to 2005 in all seven areas of economic governance (judiciary, fighting crime and corruption, customs and trade, business licensing and permits, labor regulations, and tax administration). EBRD Transition Report 2005.
7. F. Zakaria, "The Rise of Illiberal Democracies," *Foreign Affairs*, November/December 1997, 22–43.
8. For a larger sample of countries (including all developed and developing countries, not just transition economies), the result is that there is a threshold level of the rule of law index: if it is higher than a certain level, democratization affects growth positively; if lower, then democratization impedes growth. V. Polterovich and V. Popov, "Democratization, Quality of Institutions and Economic Growth," in *Political Institutions and Development: Failed Expectations and Renewed Hopes*, ed. Natalia Dinello and Vladimir Popov (Northampton, MA: Elgar, 2007). For the regressions reported in table 2.1 (changes in output from 1989–96), averages of rule of law and democracy indices were used for the longer period (1989–98) to account for the fact that business agents often anticipate changes in the business climate that are only later captured in experts' estimates.
9. Popov, "China's Rise, Russia's Fall."
10. V. Popov, "Shock Therapy versus Gradualism Reconsidered: Lessons from Transition Economies after 15 Years of Reforms," *Comparative Economic Studies* 49, no. 1 (March 2007): 1–31, http://www.nes.ru/%7Evpopov/documents/Shock%20vs%20grad%20reconsidered%20-15%20years%20after%20-article.pdf.
11. V. Popov, "Life Cycle of the Centrally Planned Economy: Why Soviet Growth Rates Peaked in the 1950s," in *Transition and Beyond*, ed. Saul Estrin, Grzegorz W. Kolodko, and Milica Uvalic (New York: Palgrave Macmillan, 2007).
12. Dani Rodrik, R. Hausmann, and A. Velasco, Growth Diagnostics, 2005, http://ksghome.harvard.edu/~drodrik/barcelonafinalmarch2005.pdf.
13. Polterovich and Popov, "Democratization, Quality of Institutions and Economic Growth"; V. Polterovich, V. Popov, and A. Tonis, "Resource Abundance, Political

Corruption, and Instability of Democracy" (NES working paper no. WP2007/73), http://www.nes.ru/russian/research/pdf/2007/PolterPopovTonisIns.pdf; V. Polterovich, V. Popov, and A. Tonis, "Mechanisms of Resource Curse, Economic Policy and Growth" (NES working paper no. WP/2008/082), http://www.nes.ru/english/research/pdf/2008/Polterivich_Popov.pdf; Zakaria, "Rise of Illiberal Democracies," 22–43.

14. When growth of GDP per capita from 1975–99, y, is regressed on the usual control variables (initial income levels, population growth rates, population density, investment/GDP ratios) and various indicators of institutional quality (share of shadow economy, WB indices of rule of law, government effectiveness, corruption perception indices from Transparency International, investment risk indices) and democratization (increase in democratic ratings from Freedom House), the best result is usually the threshold equation, like the one below:

$$y = \text{CONST.} + \text{CONTR.VAR.} + 0.18\Delta(RL - 0.72),$$

where Δ is democratization (change in index of political rights 1970–2000) and RL is the rule of law index (one of the indicators of the institutional capacity).

15. V. Popov, "Why the West Became Rich before China and Why China Has Been Catching Up with the West since 1949: Another Explanation of the 'Great Divergence' and 'Great Convergence' Stories" (NES/CEFIR working paper no. 132, 2009).

16. V. Polterovich, "Трансплантация экономических институтов" [Transplantation of economic institutions], Экономическая наука современной России [Economics of contemporary Russia], no. 3 (2001): 24–50.

17. V. Popov, "Why the West Became Rich before China."

18. Jeffrey G. Williamson, Branko Milanovic, and Peter H. Lindert, "Pre-Industrial Inequality: An Early Conjectural Map" (working paper, Weatherhead Center for International Affairs, Harvard University, Cambridge, MA, August 23, 2007), http://www.wcfia.harvard.edu/node/2820.

CHAPTER THREE

The Sovereign Bureaucracy in Russia's Modernizations

Georgi Derluguian

Ever since 1553, when the enterprising Englishman Richard Chancellor found Archangelsk, instead of a northern bypass to India, Russia has been described as Europe's eccentric *other*. The familiar tropes of comparison persisted over the centuries: a gigantic frozen realm of fabulous natural riches, a different tradition of Christianity, the subserviently fatalistic populace under mighty autocratic rulers. The stress on *otherness* became a matter of faith for many Russians themselves, from stolid conservatives to messianic subversives and liberal Westernizers appalled by the "Asiatic" backwardness of their native land. Today, the focal point is once again on natural resources and authoritarianism associated with Vladimir Putin's push to regain the position of Moscow vis-à-vis its provinces, the near neighbors, and the West. This chapter, however, does not seek to join the debate on Russia's otherness. Its goal is rather to situate the cumulative cycle of democratizations and de-democratizations in the macro-historical perspective of Russia's long-running modernizing efforts. The exercise is not purely theoretical insofar as it helps to clarify the country's dilemmas at the turn of the new century.

The current Kremlin image-makers sought to excuse the renewed authoritarianism as "sovereign democracy." This expression might be poor propaganda. Nevertheless, it seems to reflect a certain reality. Putin's main achievement was a considerable degree of political sovereignty. The Russian state after 2000 became autonomous from a spate of possible contenders: liberal intelligentsia and domestic private capitalists, middle-class voters and political parties, multinational corporations and foreign "imperialist dictates," let alone the proverbial workers and peasants. This state is, indeed, nobody's servant except its own. *Sovereign bureaucracy* might serve a more realistic definition.

One could stop here, at an indictment verging on satirical caricature. Arguably, this has its own long tradition in the Russian political culture, from the scathing letters of émigré prince Andrei Kurbsky directed to Ivan the Terrible during the infamous *oprichnina* terror in the 1560s to the masterful postmodernist prose of Vladimir Sorokin's *A Day in the Life of an Oprichnik*.

Beyond the polemical élan of Russian intelligentsia, this chapter develops an alternative argument, which in the main derives from the geopolitical and organizational theories of historical macrosociology.[1] In this perspective, Russia appears an uncertain, yet also quite-successful modernizer ever since the unexpected arrival of Richard Chancellor had proven the opportunities as well as dangers of being "discovered" by enterprising (and often smug) Westerners. In the Russian case, centralized despotism, an extreme expression of the state's relative autonomy, has been the traditional strategy of mobilizing resources to remain a serious player in world geopolitics. The strategy of despotic mobilization, however, had been exhausted shortly after 1945 along with the once huge demographic pool of resilient peasants. This historical transformation not once but twice led the ostensibly totalitarian Soviet colossus into democratizations, those of Khrushchev and Gorbachev. The ruinous (albeit perhaps not the worst possible) outcome of Gorbachev's perestroika formed the domestic and international landscape inherited by Putin. If the present recovery of state power becomes a platform for another modernization, in a consequential historical irony Mr. Putin might yet prove a contributor to Russia's future democratization.[2]

At the moment, this prospect seems uncertain. Russian modernizations had a checkered history replete with false starts. In fact, the half-century since the Khrushchev Thaw could be viewed as the single lasting period of faltering attempts to find the formula of robust socioeconomic development minus the terror and coercion that had characterized the past efforts to catch up with contemporary world powers. In a more materialist formulation, that's what is usually called Russia's "damn question." The hope today is that something important could be learned from the past, and this calls for a systematic and theoretically disciplined inquiry rather than circular ideological polemic. This does not mean an Olympian detachment in discussing Russian matters. To the contrary, making good use of macro-historical theory means bringing heftier arguments into the fray. A polemical name-calling is just a slap in the face; a robust theoretical argument made accessible to broader public could deliver a sweeping blow and, hopefully, change the very terms of debate.

The Russian Tradition of Modernizations

The great leaps forward in emulation of best foreign practices have been an intrinsic part of Russian historical dynamics ever since the emergence of the Muscovite state in the late fifteenth century. Emulation in modern times was actually the norm for successful states as well as businesses. Innovation is by definition sporadic and unique, while diffusion is the game in which the rest are catching up as soon as they can on the pain of being pushed to the margins. The pattern of modern geopolitics was in fact the relentless expansion of large territorial states that concentrated all four sources of social power: military, economic, religious/ideological, and the fourth, the quintessentially modern kind of power provided by bureaucratic coordination.[3] In the process, the West has scored a victory of planetary proportions, which is only now being balanced by the resurgence of Asia.[4]

During the last five centuries, Russia was reasonably successful in holding its ground. From the low start in the wake of medieval nomadic devastations, the rulers of Muscovy turned their realm into the rapidly expanding gunpowder empire capable of reversing the secular vector of nomadic raiding and emerging alongside the preeminent powers of its epoch: the post-reconquista Spain, Poland-Lithuania, Ottoman Turkey, the Safavi Iran, and Ming China. At that early stage, the models of success were still found mainly in the East. For Muscovy, this was Ottoman Turkey. The autocracy coalescing in the reign of Ivan the Terrible, complete with a rather developed bureaucracy of *prikazy*, the musketeer army of *streltsy*, the official church, and the *dvoriane* corps of aristocratic cavalrymen, was not at all traditional but rather an adaptation of advanced Ottoman practices.[5] The same, of course, was even truer of Petrine reforms informed by the contemporary examples of Holland and Sweden.

For the sake of brevity, I will limit this historical reconstruction to three observations. First, Russia rose impressively through the sixteenth- and the eighteenth-century rounds of modernization, eventually leaving behind many contemporary states in its class: Poland, Turkey, Iran, China, and even Spain and Austria. This was not a race toward any idealistic evolutionary goal, such as civic modernity, let alone human freedom. Modernization so far meant catching up with the advanced levels of war-making capacity tested in the ongoing geopolitical confrontations with rivals.[6]

Second, tsarist Russia was an explicitly statist, coercion-intensive modernizer. In this, Russia was hardly unique—need one be reminded of Sweden's Gustavus Adolphus, Louis XIV and his *intendants*, Friedrich the Great of Prussia, or Japan's Meiji Restoration? Culturally and geographically, however, Russia stood at a relatively greater distance from the core of emergent capitalism. On the one hand, the distance plus sheer size helped to insulate Russia from geopolitical pressures and unequal economic exchange (which had long plagued the Poles and the Turks). On the other hand, cultural and geographic distance made it difficult to monitor Western advances. The Russian reactions seemed slow. In such phases, the country appeared slumbering to its critics. And then the long overdue change arrived in "rapid bursts of creative destruction," to use Schumpeter's famous expression.

In each instance, Russian modernizations were led by state rulers, not capitalists. And every time, the leap forward began with the ruler creating a new corpus of cadres outside the old established elite, the sovereign weapon of choice. The reforms of Ivan, Peter, and Stalin amounted to revolutions from above that invariably started with the ferocious attacks on established social hierarchies, institutions, classes, and matters of faith. Terror cannot be blamed on psychology alone, because in all three instances madness had a discernible method. Extreme coercion served to undo the domestic sociopolitical obstacles, to wrestle and centralize the material and human resources to feed the modernizing efforts. The human costs to the established elites were horrific, and still greater for commoners.

Last but not least, in all three modernizing cycles there emerged similar patterns of resistance: conservative in the beginning, when peasants, clergy, and older nobilities desperately fought to defend their vanishing worlds; later turning into the progressive variety of criticism escalating into political resistance by the new classes and groups emerging from the modernization itself. This mechanism was already discernible in the seventeenth-century church reformation, which provoked the movement of Old Believers. The most famous examples of progressive resistance, however, emerged with the intelligentsias—both the nineteenth-century noblemen and middle-class *raznochintsy*, and the socialist intelligentsia of specialists produced on a vastly greater scale by the Bolshevik state.

The Short Twentieth Century, 1917–91

Traditions are essentially the practices that have worked more than once. But traditions, for better or for worse, become counterproductive as conditions change. In the middle of the twentieth century, Russia underwent changes no less profound than the rest of Europe or East Asia. Until the 1940s, one could reasonably argue that despite the socialist veneer, it was still the same ever-recognizable imperial Russia, Lermontov's "country of slaves, masters, and the blue uniforms" of secret police. But things obviously changed in the 1950s with the historical passage of peasantry and the emergence of new urban educated classes on a scale of contemporary mass society. The dispositions of Soviet middle classes and proletarians now resembled their Western European counterparts more than their own not-too-distant peasant ancestors. Ever since, the vector of domestic struggles in the USSR pointed toward updating the state structures and social practices according with the vastly increased role of educated specialists. This epochal shift ended the brutal modernizing strategies that had worked for Ivan the Terrible, Peter the Great, and Stalin.

Let me summarize somewhat differently what we all know about the Soviet experience. It is not too surprising that in October 1917, a party of radicalized intelligentsia (which is what the original Bolsheviks were in reality) seized power in a state profoundly shattered by war. It is truly surprising that a year later they were still in power.[7] Unlike the Paris communards, the Bolsheviks survived by building an extensive and ideologically inspiring apparatus of revolutionary dictatorship. They emulated and reinvented the organizational practices borrowed from the leading innovators of the early twentieth century. While their ideological lodestar was Karl Marx, in practice the Leninists followed other Germans: Bismarck, General Lüdendorf, the visionary planner Walter Rathenau, and that most "Germanic" among the American captains of industry, Henry Ford. The resulting Leviathan was what Max Weber himself could not have imagined—a "charismatic bureaucracy."[8]

The Stalinist drive to industrialize and rearm the post-revolutionary state bore resemblance to the ebullient reformism of Peter the Great. The most glaring and puzzling contradiction of the Soviet 1930s is the coexistence of mass terror and mass enthusiasm. The now-prevalent focus on terror and the daily fear that permeated the epoch relegates its apparent enthusiasm to the effects of propagandistic brainwashing. Yet for all its despotic power, Stalinism could never achieve the totalitarian completeness.[9] The mass enthusiasm finds a more robust explanation in the educational élan of intelligentsia and the mass promotion of commoners into the military, industrial, and scientific ranks. Industrialization was rapidly transforming the society along with its physical conditions.

The great test arrived with the Second World War. The splendid fighting machine of the Wehrmacht could not be stopped by Russian climate and piles of dead bodies. It had to be the newly created Soviet industrial base, which overproduced the Third Reich in tanks, warplanes, and munitions. It also had to be the newly acquired technical skills, discipline, and, yes, the ideological determination of Soviet men and women of many different nationalities, who, despite grievous losses, privations, and frightening uncertainty in the first years of war, continued to work and fight. On this count, Russia's third historical modernization must be recognized as a huge and unlikely success.

And then comes another puzzle. Why did the Stalinist state begin to democratize shortly after the death of a dictator? The explanation must be sought in the same profound transformation of Soviet society. Two class interests emerged. First, the nomenklatura bureaucratic elite sought to secure their positions, families, and livelihoods from the scourge of purges and the inhuman work pressures dictated by industrialization and war. Like any oligarchy desiring to enjoy and protect the fruits of power, they envisioned no more than a relaxation. Democratization threatened the elite with new political and economic competitive pressures coming from below. The bulk of nomenklatura could go along, cautiously as any bureaucrats, with denouncing Stalin's cult and reigning in the secret police under the slogan of "socialist legality"—but no further.

This proved, however, enough to unleash growing expectations in the rest of society. Second and more consequentially, the Soviet proletarian workforce, including educated specialists, began displaying attitudes and demands quite unlike those of peasants. Personal apartments and cars, vacations by the seaside, varied and sophisticated consumption, and higher remuneration for higher skills might all seem pretty Philistine urges. In fact, they were denounced as such by official propaganda. Yet these were the manifestations of nascent middle classes whose numerous members would soon also expect more autonomy in cultural expression and a greater say in the formulation of policies and the appointments of bosses at their factories, universities, and the government itself. In the Soviet command economy, middle-class professionals as well as shopkeepers, farmer producers, and artisans were state employees who (at least in official theory) subsisted on wages alone. Ironically, in a very Marxist sense these middle classes were actually proletarians alienated from the means of production. Such groups in various ways sought, in effect, to de-proletarianize in order to become autonomous actors or at least to make their bureaucratic bosses more generous and accountable.

A return to terror was out of the question. This move threatened the newly gained serenity of the officialdom itself. It remained to use coercion selectively and instead to tame the popular expectations with the significantly increased provision of consumer goods and, in general, to keep up appearances. Such a response became exceedingly costly.

During the conservative stabilization of the Brezhnev period, Moscow incurred three kinds of growing costs: geopolitical, administrative, and social. The prestigious arms race against the much wealthier West—plus the growing subsidies to East European allies and the multiplying number of Third World clients—perhaps helped to maintain the ideological impression of world success, yet it was beyond the Soviet's means.[10]

Brezhnev's trademark internal policy of "cadre stability" granted the nomenklatura virtually a life tenure of their positions. This suppressed factionalism and rendered the ruling elite very conformist. At the same time, the central government lost the means to monitor subordinates, punish inefficiencies, and control wastes, let alone introduce any meaningful economic and technological change. The command economy, forgive the tautology, needs a supreme commander. Moscow became instead the supreme site of bureaucratic lobbying and bargaining.[11] The "Center" was losing sovereign power to the mid-ranking bureaucrats.

Last, the paternalistic workplace disbursement of consumer goods (much of them now imported for petrodollars) created a perverse variety of shop-floor bargaining. Workers and specialists, denied the legal right to organize yet no longer subjected to Stalinist coercion, engaged instead in the tacit lowering of work effort. Hence the infamous joke, "They pretend to pay, we pretend to work."

Gorbachev's perestroika, strange as it might seem, is best interpreted in the terms of modified Marxian class analysis. The reform faction at the very summit of Soviet hierarchy allied with the liberal intelligentsia, professionals, educated specialists, and advanced workers against the conservative majority of nomenklatura who paternalistically controlled the masses of lower-skilled workers and rural sub-proletarians. The promotion of public debate through glasnost in effect became a purge of obsolete cadres and practices, the necessary prologue to Schumpeterian "creative destruction" wrought on the state and the state-directed economy. The newly promoted cadres were becoming an alternative lever to the vested interests entrenched in the old apparat. The next stage envisioned the gradual introduction of competitive mechanisms in politics and economic management. This implied the democratization of decision making processes domestically and opening the way to importation of best practices and technologies from abroad.

For the latter reason, Gorbachev's faction sought from the outset another class alliance—primarily with the corporativist, capitalist establishment of continental Europe (rather than the Anglo-American neoliberals), whose technocratic and paternalistic ethos stood the closest to the habitus of Soviet reformers. America still had to be placated with concessions in nuclear arms negotiations and Third World conflicts. The main bargain, however, was offered to Europeans. Historically, continental Europe was a kindred zone of bellicose absolutist states, not unlike the Russian Empire. After 1945, continental Europe became durably divided and pacified. The practice of corporativist bargaining institutionalized within states and supported by the regularized alternation in power between the moderately conservative and social democratic parties ended the destructive class conflicts.[12] Now Gorbachev essentially offered to vastly extend the pan-European bargain in exchange for nullifying the Soviet geopolitical threat, burying ideological tensions, and equitably sharing access to the human and natural resources of the Soviet bloc. The conversion of the Soviet geopolitical-ideological position into socioeconomic European inclusion appeared the only honorable and profitable way out of the long-exhausted state socialist dictatorship of development. In fact, it so remains to this day.

The Political Economy of Collapse

Gorbachev's perestroika ran into the classical pitfall of authoritarian reformers ever since the fateful decision of a French king to convene the Estates General: the promise of reform unleashed the clashes of revolutionary and counterrevolutionary forces that destroyed the center of previous politics.

Not all revolutionary situations, however, lead to revolutionary outcomes. If none of the forces can prevail, the result could be lasting gridlock and state fragmentation fraught with multiple conflicts. This is when bureaucrats, in the most perverse of emancipations, can gain their sovereignty.

Commentators typically blamed the catastrophe on ethnic conflicts, the bickering in newly elected parliaments, the virulent "Russian" mafias, the corrupt barter schemes controlled by regional governors in opposition to free market reforms (read bankruptcies).[13] These were not the causes but, rather, the chaotic consequences of Gorbachev's failure to follow the route of European integration similar to that of Spain after the death of Franco. Admittedly Gorbachev had to deal with a far more complex federal state and less organized civil societies. The Europeans themselves felt too baffled at the scope of troubles that suddenly engulfed their partner in Moscow. Notice by contrast that ethnic irredentist wars were prevented in the former socialist countries of Central Europe and the Baltic republics. There, the mature civil societies that had been continuously organized by oppositionist intelligentsias ever since the symbolic dates of 1956, 1968, and 1980 could offer sustainable bargains to the technocratic factions of national nomenklatura. Critically important, these bargains were secured by the promise of European accession.

The derisive Russian pun "*prihvatizatsia*" (grab-and-run privatization) captures the essence of what happened elsewhere. The networks of nomenklatura entrenched in regional administrations and economic enterprises, often acting in opportunistic alliances with various interlopers, hastened to build safe landing strips by deploying the newly legitimate ideologies of nationalism and market reforms. The luckier among them privatized the assets that they had already controlled by bureaucratic appointment. National republics thus became independent states under the semi-authoritarian presidents; the enterprises with exportable assets (above all, primary commodities) offered the best opportunities for turning their bosses into billionaires. This kind of transition was facilitated by the inherently corrupt and unstable collusion bargains that Weberian scholars call neopatrimonialism—the private appropriation of ostensibly public offices.

The results proved disastrous at all levels. The former Soviet edifice simply fell apart along the lines of bureaucratic control. In the absence of functioning legal guarantees, the short-term concerns and most predatory practices acquired limited rationality. The locus of accumulation shifted abruptly from public production to haphazardly privatized exchange. Social inequalities grew to the levels of South America. The nascent civil societies became numb along with the abruptly marginalized intelligentsia, workers, and technical professionals (especially in state-supported health care, science, and higher education). Instead of joining Europe, the majority of former Soviet republics in the 1990s recoiled to the world's periphery.

From Nadir to Another Rise?

Yeltsin's presidency went successively through three phases that all ended in debacles. In 1991–93, the near-messianic hopes vested in the neoliberal shock therapy delivered instead demoralizing and destructive hyperinflation. The subsequent shift to neoimperial grandeur in the absence of a functioning state soon led to the humiliating defeat in Chechnya. Beginning with the reelection campaign of 1996, Yeltsin became hostage to financial oligarchs whom he himself had created. In its turn, the reign of oligarchs ended in the financial meltdown of 1998 and the concerted bid for power by regional governors that threatened Russia with further fragmentation.

A countervailing tendency emerged in the early 2000s from the elite factions who became losers in the previous decade because their assets could not be profitably privatized. On the one hand, they were the former ideologists who banded into the formidable but hopelessly oppositionist Communist Party of the Russian Federation (KPRF). On the other hand, consider the plight of public servants whose status and skills are nullified without a strong state (the diplomats, old-school bureaucrats, professional educators), the managers of state monopolies (such as those vitally important for Russia railways and the suppliers of urban utilities), and especially the cadres of former KGB—an organization that in privatized mode degenerates into organized crime.

Their return to power amounted to a bloodless coup (except, tragically, in Chechnya). The new regime, centered on the unexpectedly charismatic Colonel Putin, marginalized oppositional parties, bought over the fabulously corrupt governors, exiled or imprisoned the more assertive economic oligarchs, and wrestled control of their business and media empires. Against the background of "colored" revolutions in Ukraine and Georgia, the Russian state restorationists then clamped down on NGOs that harbored the remaining nuclei of radical intelligentsia. Less noticed was the fact that since approximately 2003–04, the once-infamous Russian criminality has significantly subsided.[14]

The revanche of state centralizers has indeed amounted to a massive de-democratization. One should soberly ask, however, what the social character and vector of Russian electoral democratization was in the previous decade. And then one might try to evaluate the present dilemmas and future prospects in the perspective of Russia's past, asking what in it remains alive and what has long been less alive, serving mostly as bogey. This might actually lead us to guarded optimism.

Putin's recovery so far has strengthened the state at the expense of all other claimants to power and its fruits. In a pessimistic scenario, the presently ruling elite could now simply relax to enjoy these fruits at the gargantuan scale of office corruption that became common in the nineties. Yet some indicators point in a different direction. In politics, there is Putin's decision not to become president for life, which would have placed the Russian political system squarely in Central Asia.

Second, Russian social indicators show a recovery since the nadir of 1998. This appears a largely autonomous demographic and quotidian movement of the people, who have learned, at great price, how to cope with new realities. Nonetheless, it arguably contributed to the renewed sense of normalization and therefore extended the social time horizon beyond the immediate survival.

Third, the post-depression economic recovery, notwithstanding the huge influx of petrodollars in the early 2000s, was also driven by the return to life of the basic economic sectors, especially those where the investment and technological thresholds were relatively low: agriculture and food processing, home construction, consumer services. The fledgling economic recovery could choke in the world crisis, exhausted by limited growth potential, or, as many economists point out, because the exceptional energy earnings of previous years were allowed to trickle down into consumption rather than being invested in a more conscious and disciplined manner into restoring infrastructure and the provision of public goods.

Still, the result is that today, unlike the 1990s, the majority of Russians have jobs with clearly identifiable owners and managers. The class conflicts of the late-Soviet period died out after 1991 precisely because the wage-earning proletarians so suddenly lost the identifiable subjects to whom they could address their demands. That is no longer so. Any economic downturn now threatens the rulers and owners with social upheaval. Overt coercion for whatever stabilizing or modernizing purposes has been unavailable to Russian rulers ever since the de-Stalinization. What remains is bargaining on multiple fronts, which points again in the direction of continental European patterns of politics and welfare provision.

In a fundamental sense, Putin's restoration brought back the old Soviet dilemmas. If the enormous geopolitical costs of the Cold War and the external empire are now gone, the costs of bureaucratic self-serving inefficiency, paternalistic consumerism, and perverse class bargaining leading to subterfuge and corruption stand as huge as ever. Besides its sheer ongoing material and moral cost, bureaucratic arbitrariness renders futile any innovative economic initiative or an autonomous class organization.

This is now a major obstacle to the next technological modernization. Having re-centralized power, Putin and his successor Medvedev now face the question of what can be done with this power, or even how much power they can effectively deploy for any purposes besides the routine reproduction of bureaucratic privileges. Despite their political demonstrations intended to remind everyone that Russia still matters, as well as the more recent openly critical pronouncements, both so far refrain from serious action. Evidently, they must fear repeating Gorbachev's errors. Yet, whatever their subjective feelings and intuitions, objectively the Russian rulers now face another perestroika that must begin with making the ruling bureaucracy more accountable and thus less sovereign. In the past, concentrations of power at the top served as prologues to great leaps forward. What made it move was the charisma of a great tsar or dictator and his sovereign deployment of terror. In the present, such concentration by itself appears useless unless supported by the alternative charisma of a publicly trusted politician and the institutional strength of a modern publicly accountable state. The state is now back there, but will it move?

Notes

1. Randall Collins, *Weberian Sociological Theory* (New York: Cambridge University Press, 1986).
2. This point was made by Charles Tilly in *Democracy* (New York: Cambridge University Press, 2007).
3. Michael Mann, *The Sources of Social Power*, vol. 1, *A History of Power from the Beginning to A.D. 1760* (Cambridge: Cambridge University Press, 1986).
4. Giovanni Arrighi, *Adam Smith in Beijing: Lineages of the Twenty-First Century* (London: Verso, 2007).
5. Karen Barkey, *The Empire of Difference: The Ottomans in Comparative Perspective* (New York: Cambridge University Press, 2008).
6. Dominic Lieven, *The Russian Empire and Its Rivals* (London: Murray, 2000).
7. James Scott, *Seeing Like a State: How Certain Projects to Improve Humanity Have Failed* (New Haven: Yale University Press, 1998).
8. Stephen Hanson, *Time and Revolution: Marxism and the Design of Soviet Institutions* (Chapel Hill: University of North Carolina Press, 1997), 19.
9. This is well documented in the recent works of social historians. See Lynne Viola, *Peasant Rebels under Stalin* (New York: Oxford University Press, 1996); William Rosenberg and Lewis H. Siegelbaum, eds., *The Social Dimensions of Soviet Industrialization* (Bloomington: Indiana University Press, 1993); Stephen Kotkin, *Magnetic Mountain: Stalinism as a Civilization* (Berkeley: University of California Press, 1995); and Moshe Lewin, *The Soviet Century* (London: Verso, 2005).
10. Valerie Bunce, "The Empire Strikes Back: The Evolution of the Eastern Bloc from a Soviet Asset to a Soviet Liability," *International Organization* 39 (Winter 1985): 1–46.
11. Vladimir Popov and Nikolai Shmelev, *The Turning Point: Revitalizing the Soviet Economy* (London: Tauris, 1990).
12. G. Esping-Andersen, *The Three Worlds of Welfare Capitalism* (Princeton: Princeton University Press, 1990); Michael Mann and Dylan Riley, "Explaining Macro-Regional Trends in Global Income Inequalities, 1950–2000," *Socio-Economic Review* 5 (2007): 81–115.
13. These state-destructive processes are explored in detail in Georgi Derluguian, *Bourdieu's Secret Admirer in the Caucasus* (Chicago: University of Chicago Press, 2005), especially chaps. 6 and 7, "The Nationalization of Provincial Revolutions" and "The Scramble for Soviet Spoils." The book also comments theoretically on the eccentric pattern of Yugoslavia.

14. Vadim Volkov, *Violent Entrepreneurs: The Use of Force in the Making of Russian Capitalism.* Ithaca, NY: Cornell University Press, 2002.

CHAPTER FOUR

The Changing Dynamics of Russian Politics

Richard Sakwa

Following the dissolution of the communist regime in 1991, President Boris Yeltsin was faced with the challenge of establishing a new political order. This involved a twofold project: transformative and adaptive. The transformative element was intended to overcome the Soviet legacy and to introduce elements of the market, and thus in certain respects was reminiscent of the Bolshevik attempt at grandiose social engineering, although in reverse gear. The adaptive element, however, mitigated the Bolshevik features of the new system. Rather than the regime setting its face against what were perceived to be existing patterns of subjectivity and popular aspirations, it began to adapt to them. The tension between the transformative and the adaptive elements has still not been overcome and has imbued post-communist Russian politics with an acute developmental crisis, as the forces for change are stymied by conservative and nativist constituencies and sentiments.

This stalemate is reflected in the emergence of a distinctive type of "dual state." Entrenched social interests (notably, the bureaucracy and the security apparatus) are expressed in the form of an *administrative regime*, while the attempt to institutionalize the normative values of the post-communist experiment in liberal democracy is represented by the *constitutional state*.[1] The two pillars of the dual state give rise to a distinctive type of hybrid regime, in which a type of "mixed constitution" has emerged, combining two types of governmentality: the legal-rational proceduralism, and open political contestation and pluralism of the constitutional state, balanced by the shadowy and arbitrary factional politics based on informal networks in the administrative regime. By the time of Vladimir Putin's second presidential term in 2004, it was clear that the two subsystems had become locked into stalemate, inhibiting further movements toward consolidating the democratic pluralist gains achieved in the early 1990s, but also blocking full-scale regression to a consolidated authoritarian regime. The boundaries between the two systems are blurred, yet they act as distinctive poles in Russian politics. The dualism of the system is reflected in contrasting evaluations of the system that has taken shape in Russia and in differing views over appropriate paths of development.

"Failed Democratization" versus "Democratic Evolutionism"

When in the first decade of the twenty-first century the regime began to reassert the assumed prerogatives of the state, it did so in a distinctive way. On the one hand, it appealed to the spirit of the constitution and the rule of law, a theme taken up by Putin in his early speeches in 2000 stressing the "dictatorship of law" and by President Dmitry Medvedev in his condemnation of "legal nihilism" and cautious program of political modernization. Combined with administrative reforms, this entailed the *reconstitution* of the state, based on a return to ordered governance and legal norms to strengthen the constitutional state. At the same time, by establishing a strong "vertical" concentration of power and numerous control mechanisms over business and society, the process was accompanied by *reconcentration*, which only reinforced dualism because of the failure to limit the arbitrariness of the administrative regime. The logic of reconcentration was intended to overcome the institutional nihilism of the earlier period, but in practice it reproduced and intensified that nihilism in new forms.

The dualism *of* the system is reflected in bifurcated views *about* the system. In rather simplified terms, we can divide mainstream views on the changing dynamics of Russian politics into two mains schools.[2] On the one side, there are those who assert that democracy in Russia has failed. As in 1917, Russia has not been able to live up to the challenge of transforming itself into a modern state governed by a responsible government and law-bound polity. The *failed democratization* camp points to the legacy of the Soviet system, its personnel (above all in the security agencies), and its spirit. Notable landmarks in the failure of democracy in Russia from this perspective include the violent confrontation between parliament and president in September-October

1993, the foisting of a super-presidential constitution on a cowed people in a flawed referendum in December 1993, and the deeply divisive events of the 1990s, including the "shock therapy" that robbed people of their savings (thus undermining popular trust in the new order), the wild "privatization" of state property by a small group of so-called oligarchs, the massive growth in social inequality, and a pattern of elections that may well have been free but were certainly far from fair.[3]

These negative trends were allegedly accentuated by Putin, including attacks on media freedom and the undermining of judicial independence and property rights, notably in the Yukos case, in which the oil company saw its assets effectively expropriated by the regime. In the associated trial of the company's former chief executive Mikhail Khodorkovsky, in a process dubbed "Basmanny justice" (from the Moscow district where Khodorkovsky's prosecution was masterminded), the country once again saw the reemergence of "telephone law," whereby the authorities make sure that they get the verdict they want.[4] Above all, human rights abuses in Chechnya and the questionable juridical grounds for waging the first war (1994–96) and the refusal to negotiate in the second (1999–2003), accompanied by some unresolved questions over the apartment bombings in Moscow and elsewhere in September 1999, are seen by the failed-democratization school as fostering the emergence of a self-seeking, secretive elite interested only in maintaining its own power, using the levers of the state to enrich itself at a time of abundant energy rents. Increased incumbent capacity exploited authoritarian state power, elite organization, and the technical skill of manipulating elections to maintain ruling elites in power while keeping allies in line and depriving rivals of resources.[5] The result, according to Stephen Fish, is that democracy has been "derailed" in Russia: "By the time of Vladimir Putin's reelection as president of Russia in 2004," he argues, "Russia's experiment with open politics was over."[6]

A second school of thought rejects the view that Russia has become an "undemocracy," to use Charles Tilly's term,[7] and maintains a guarded optimism about the potential of the existing constitutional order to evolve into a more pluralistic and accountable democratic polity.[8] The *democratic evolutionist* camp argues that an evolutionary outcome to the present stalemate is not only possible but essential, since a revolutionary or catastrophic breakdown of the present order would not only challenge the administrative regime but would also destroy the achievements of the constitutional state.

While Russian democracy may be in crisis, it is not yet terminal—the train may be derailed, but it can be put back on track. Democratic evolutionists do not deny that Russia's post-communist trajectory has been characterized by severe breaches of generally recognized democratic standards, but that this has to be seen in context. The "new evolutionists" suggest that the gulf between what an ideal transition to democracy should look like and the bitter realities of Russia's transformation emerges out of the tough choices facing its leadership in the post-communist era. The violence of September-October 1993 reflected not only poor leadership but the sheer scale of the institutional-design questions facing the country.[9] Everything was contested: the balance between executive and legislative power, federal relations, the shape of the representative and electoral systems, and perhaps above all, how the new elite and leadership structure would be formed.

Democratic evolutionists argue that it is unrealistic to believe that Russia could rapidly become a splendidly functioning liberal democracy. It would take decades for the spirit of reason, tolerance, public service, and rule subordination to develop. As late as 1969, for example, Ralf Dahrendorf was extremely skeptical about whether German society had internalized the values of democracy, and this was twenty-four years after the end of the war, whereas Russia has had only two decades to transform every aspect of its social existence.[10] Civil society takes time to develop, and the habits of societal pluralism need to be rooted in real autonomous social subjects.[11] This is taking place in contemporary Russia, although perhaps not at the pace or in the way radical liberals would like.[12] For the evolutionists, in comparative terms Russia is probably no worse than a number of other countries but is singled out for criticism because of its geopolitical autonomy, a point that the Russian authorities often make in pointing out the double standards of its critics.[13] Evolutionists observe that many of the criticisms made of Russia today are based on traditional Cold War and Russophobic reactions of part of the Western elite, fearing its re-emergence as an autonomous great power as a separate and independent pole in the international system.[14] Why is China, which has a far worse human rights record than Russia, regarded relatively benignly, whereas Russia, which retains at least a rhetorical and institutional commitment to democracy, is singled out for relentless criticism? Why are its legitimate interests in the post-Soviet space discounted?

The failed democratization school, in the view of the democratic evolutionists, ascribes far too much coherence and unity to the political system.

The "dual state" nature of Russian politics imbues it with far greater opportunities for competition, however constrained, between factions, groups, and autonomous institutions, as well as imbuing the whole system with the potential for democratic renewal and geopolitical rapprochement, but at its own pace and on its own terms. From this perspective, the taming of the "oligarchs," regional barons, and "irresponsible" party leaders, while reasserting Russia's perceived interests and voice in international politics, is no more than what any state worth its salt would do. The methods may have been robust, but for the evolutionists the reassertion of the prerogatives of the state does not preclude the country's further democratic development.[15] As long as the renewed state retains its dual character, we cannot speak of the consolidation of an administrative regime, let alone of an authoritarian state. Yevgeny Yasin, the former presidential economic advisor and a professor at the Higher School of Economics, notes that the present system contains most of the elements for democratic development, and thus there are no systemic obstacles to evolution in that direction.[16] This is the theoretical framework in which Medvedev sponsored a gradualist program of political deconcentration and economic modernization.

The Dual State in Russia

In many respects, the Soviet regime had stopped being the old regime in most essential ways long before it fell. An inner transcendence had taken place, recognized by Mikhail Gorbachev, which transformed the system before it finally dissolved. By the end of 1990, the Soviet Union had become a proto-democracy, with relatively free elections (indeed, the elections in Russia in March 1990 were among the freest and fairest held in the country to date), with a nascent multiparty system and vigorous societal pluralism. However, the Soviet "administrative-command" system, although extensively modified, above all through the abolition of the "leading role" of the Communist Party, remained in place. Equally, the proto-democracy lacked constitutional consolidation and coexisted with a powerful autonomous political regime that still retained considerable powers, especially over the force ministries, the media, and the economy. Elements of this duality continue to this day, although the "party-state" has given way to a type of "regime state." The governmental system as a whole is not effectively subordinated and constrained by the constitutional state, and the weakness of accountability mechanisms allows the administrative regime to exercise certain prerogative powers.

Russia is a classic example of a hybrid regime combining democratic and authoritarian features.[17] Dimitry Furman gives the hybridity specific content when he describes many of the states in post-Soviet Eurasia as "imitation democracies," a "combination of democratic constitutional forms with a reality of authoritarian rule." Such systems emerge "when conditions in a given society are not ripe for democracy, and yet there is no ideological alternative to it." This is the classic situation of what Antonio Gramsci called a passive revolution, defined as "an abortive or incomplete transformation of society." This can take a number of forms, including one where an external force provokes change but lacks a sufficiently strong domestic constituency and runs into the resistance of entrenched interests. When the forces are equally balanced, a stalemate emerges, giving rise to a situation of "revolution/restoration."[18]

The post-communist leadership in Russia remains committed to a moderate state-led modernization process, accompanied by a constrained liberal democratization project, but lacks the resources or the will to achieve either full-scale Thermidorean reaction or breakthrough into unconstrained liberal democracy. The regime under Putin maintained the transformative revolution in property and power begun in the late Gorbachev years, but its rhetoric of antirevolution strengthened adaptive processes and restored some systemic elements of the previous regime. Promoted as the ideology of reconciliation, the inconclusive nature of the system takes the form of a dual state, with all of its accompanying contradictions.

In the dual state, the normative/legal system based on constitutional order is challenged by the shadowy arbitrary arrangements of the administrative regime, populated by various conflicting factions. The tension between the two is the defining feature of contemporary Russian politics. Neither can predominate over the other, but the relationship between the two is the critical area in which politics is conducted. The two subsystems not only interact but also constrain the behavior of the other. The bifurcated political order gives rise to distinct political processes, but neither is hermetically sealed from the other. At the same time, both the administrative regime and the constitutional state contain elements of adaptation and transformation.

The double dualism—in which the transformative agenda is countered by adaptive processes and the formal procedures of the constitutional state are undermined by the administrative regime—is the matrix through which the contemporary Russian political landscape can be understood. Indeed, the transformative agenda from the outset reinforced the administrative features of governance, as Yeltsin drove through a program of what he hoped would be capitalist modernization. Later, Putin rationalized the administrative regime to become a self-sustaining system, and despite attempts to insulate itself from the new socio-economic realities created by the transformation, the power of his regime was derived from adapting to the new order—and thus by the end, his presidency had lost much of its transformative drive. While all states are hybrids containing elements of the dualism suggested above, in Russia this was a *hybridity of stasis*, reflecting the evenly balanced forces locked in stalemate that lie at the basis of the contemporary dual state.

The tension between evolutionary and revolutionary approaches to overcoming the crisis in Russian democracy is the natural corollary of such a hybrid system. As noted, the democratic evolutionists argue that only a gradual process will permit the arbitrary state to be tempered by the constitutional order, whereas a revolutionary rupture is likely to perpetuate the existing duality in new forms and to undermine even the existing hesitant development of constitutionalism. Although the development of genuine constitutionalism and transparent political pluralism is debilitated at present, the normative and political resources of the existing constitutional state are far from exhausted. For radical critics of the stultifying effects of the administrative system, standing, as it were, outside and above the law and political processes, only systemic change could break the stalemate. Instead of conceptualizing the present equilibrium as relatively benign and offering a "breathing space" (*peredyshka*), critics stress the need to restore a transformative dynamic to Russian politics that could curb some of the excesses of the corrupt adaptation that is now depressing socio-economic renewal and vitality. As before the Russian revolution of 1917, the country is faced with an epochal choice.

Even these two opposed strategies (although accompanied by innumerable shades of gray in between) are equally balanced, contributing to the overall pattern of systemic stalemate. The fundamental argument of this chapter is that as long as the arbitrariness of the regime is accompanied by recognition of the normative constraints of the constitutional order, the system retains elements of dualism, and it would be premature to talk of the full-scale construction of an authoritarian system. Indeed, the normative resources of the constitutional state act as a power reserve for those who seek to limit the arbitrariness of the prerogative system, including, apparently,

Medvedev himself. Whether the "choice" can be indefinitely finessed in this way depends to a degree on external challenges and the capacity of the regime to maintain internal coherence and popular support.

Dual State, Dual Society, and Factions

There is a large amount of literature, in Russia and abroad, arguing that post-communist consolidation in the first decade of the twenty-first century fits into a traditional pattern of Russian state-society relations, which was perpetuated in new forms in the Soviet era. Robert Tucker argues that irrespective of changes in political regime, a certain view of the state has been relatively constant. He calls this the image of dual Russia: on the one side, *vlast'* (power) or the state (*gosudarstvo*), encompassing autocratic power and bureaucratic officialdom; while on the other side, there is the population at large, society (*obshchestvo*), and the people (*narod*). The division is more than descriptive; it is fundamentally evaluative, with state power seen as something profoundly alien and hostile, with the implication, moreover, that it is of questionable legitimacy, to be tolerated at best, but not something belonging to the people.

The creation of a centralized autocracy from the sixteenth century was in part a response to security threats, and the link remains between relatively autonomous state power at home and geopolitical challenges abroad. As Tucker notes, Russia expanded from 15,000 square miles in 1462 to one-fifth of the world's land surface in 1917, placing a premium on military strength.[19] With Peter the Great, this alienation between *vlast'* and *obshchestvo* was reinforced by the imposition of a Western-inspired modernization model, with the state seen as a type of occupying force, and by 1917 it had few supporters left. A type of inner decay eroded support for the regime and undermined self-belief, a process paralleled at the end of the Soviet system. The Bolshevik revolution destroyed the old state; but in its place a much more savage and dictatorial system was built that nullified "sixty years of Russian history in emancipating society from the aegis of the state."[20] Under Joseph Stalin, *gosudarstvo* once again waxed strong, although the legacy of the estrangement of power and people in the late-Soviet era took distinctive forms. Alexei Yurchak argues that the fundamental values, ideals, and realities of the communist order were genuinely important for many Soviet citizens, although they routinely transgressed and reinterpreted the norms and rules of the socialist state.[21] This attitudinal and behavioral dualism has been perpetuated in new forms into the post-communist era. This is reflected in popular attitudes, with 51 percent in 2005 supporting the view that Russia needs a president to exert a "firm hand" to govern the country, while 44 percent favor a leader who "strictly observed the constitution."[22] Society began to be emancipated from state tutelage; but in reaction to the "anarcho-democracy" of the 1990s, the first decade of the twenty-first century brought a return to the consolidation of bureaucratic statism, this time in a democratic guise, accompanied by the suffocation of independent civic self-organization of society and the stunted development of the individual as an autonomous citizen. A new tutelary regime was in the making.

The presidency is at the heart of the administrative regime but is not limited to it. These forces come together in informal factions, notably in the form of two meta-groups conventionally labeled the "*siloviki*" and the "liberal-technocrats," which can then be subdivided into at least six other identifiable spheres of interest, if not into interest groups in the traditional meaning of the term.[23] However, the administrative regime is more than personalized leadership, certainly more than the presidency on its own, and broader even than the executive writ large, but it is much less than an institutionalized law-governed system. The development of the dual-state model is an attempt to provide a more developed theoretical framework to understand the operation of regime politics.

The presidency retains considerable autonomy, although it is constrained by both the constitutional state and the administrative regime. There is an element of Bonapartism in contemporary Russia; but this is of a mild form, since the presidency lacks a social base of its own (for example, the military), and although Putin relied on the *siloviki*, he also ensured strong representation by liberals to avoid the presidency becoming hostage, or even "captured," by any single faction. The presidency acts as the balancing force mediating between the politico-bureaucratic groups that populate the Russian political system.

Factions act as informal mechanisms to prevent elite defection, binding individuals to a power system by ties of informal loyalty and reward while eschewing more demanding indicators of group membership. Factions are not the same as clientelistic groups, which tend to be vertically integrated, leadership-based associations built on the exchange of services between patron and client, typically support and loyalty to the patron in exchange for office and promotion.[24] Regional ethnic-based patronage networks in Central Asia and elsewhere ultimately hollowed out Soviet power, allowing the effective fusion of economic and political power in conditions of scarcity, and contributed to the fall of the communist order.[25] They remain to this day the core of Central Asian power systems and fostered monocratic power systems, whereas Russia remains a dual state.

Factions are coalescences (coalitions would be too strong a term) united not so much on the principle of loyalty to a patron but on the basis of instrumental goals. These coalescences are unstable and formed in an ad hoc manner in response to specific circumstances, but the long period of Putinite stabilization from 2000 endowed them with an enduring quality that was not an inherent characteristic. While the notion of "competitive clientalism" [sic] has been identified as one of the pathologies besetting contemporary democracies,[26] contemporary Russian politics is characterized more by "competitive factionalism," although competition between them is constrained by the constitutional pillar of the dual state and by the convention of an "informal constitution" that prevents factional struggle becoming overt warfare. Formal institutions and strong political leaders have to date inhibited the rampant overspill of factionalism into state institutions. This is also why it is a mistake in Russia to identify factions with networks of fiefdoms and rackets. A faction has network elements, but it is more than just an opportunistic network focused on self-enrichment.

The nonpolitical aggregations that we call factions coexist with the formal associational life of political parties. The two systems operate in parallel, imbuing Russia's hybrid system with a permanent tension. Parties in Russia fulfill few of the classical functions of such organizations. Parties have limited political reach and fail to provide the framework for the institutionalization of political competition or the integration of regional and national politics.[27] They are not the source of governmental formation, personnel appointments, or policy generation, and neither are they, more broadly, "system-forming," in the sense of providing the framework for political order. Although parties are the main actors in parliamentary elections, even there they are at best accessories to processes taking place within the regime. The regime's monopoly over political resources and its control over the distribution of rents were systematically reinforced by Putin, resulting in the marginalization of other actors and institutions, to the degree that the very term "opposition" can only be used conditionally.[28]

Henry Hale has advanced the idea of party substitutes. He examines the question in terms of a political market in which voters and political elites are seen as consumers sought by suppliers of various types. Hale argues that Russian political parties were unable to close out the electoral market, and various non-party alternatives such as factions, cliques, and other informal aggregations as well as corporate groups were able to take on quasi-party functions to offer alternative paths to power. Parties in his view organize on the basis of two types of capital: ideational, drawing on issues of identity and values that attract people to the party, and administrative, which includes offices and power that can attract ambitious politicians. Russian parties have not been able to establish a monopoly on these sources of political capital and thus are challenged by non-party alternatives. Although parties do perform important functions, including structuring electoral competition, they have not been able to establish dominance over the political system. There are institutional reasons for this, above all the strong presidency, which undermines incentives for party affiliation; but the political condition of duality and stalemate also marginalizes formal actors, and instead personal patronage and informal networks bypass the party system. Hale accepts that parties have the potential to dominate the electoral market, and in his view United Russia is beginning to develop as a programmatic party and is thus transcending its roots as a patronage-based group.[29]

Para-constitutionalism and Para-politics

The regime is at the center of a shifting constellation of forces that operates not according to the legal precepts of the normative state but applies para-political stratagems to advance its goals. A government established on the basis of a formally negotiated *coalition* is political, whereas the loose factional *coalescences* of post-communist Russia are para-political. Equally, the characteristic feature of the operation of the administrative regime is the creation of a number of para-constitutional institutions that undermine the spirit of the 1993 constitution but provide important integrative functions. We use the term "para-constitutional" deliberately, because the political regime and its factions do not repudiate the formal constitutional framework but operate within its formal constraints while subverting much of its spirit.

Para-constitutional bodies include the seven federal districts, the State Council, the Public Chamber (*Obshchestvennaya Palata*), and the Presidential

Council for the Implementation of the National Projects, established in autumn 2005 to advance the four national projects in housing, education, health, and agriculture announced in September of that year, but bypassing the cabinet of ministers. The history of the Public Chamber reflects the ambiguities of the hybridity that is at the heart of the dual state. In his speech of September 13, 2004, which announced a whole raft of measures in the wake of the Beslan hostage crisis, Putin argued that a Public Chamber would act as a platform for broad dialogue, to allow civic initiatives to be discussed, state decisions to be analyzed, and draft laws to be scrutinized. It would act as a bridge between civil society and the state.[30] The chamber monitors draft legislation and the work of parliament, reviews the work of federal and regional administrations, offers nonbinding recommendations to parliament and the government on domestic issues, investigates possible breaches of the law, and requests information from state agencies.[31]

The Public Chamber introduced a new channel of public accountability against overbearing officialdom, and thus usurped what should have been one of parliament's key roles. Work that should properly have been the preserve of the State Duma was transferred to this new body, a type of nonpolitical parliament. It acted as a type of "collective ombudsman," operating as a feedback mechanism since formal channels were blocked. It also allows steam to be let off before conflicts take on a regime-threatening character, acting as a "lightning rod," designed not just to legitimize the existing order and to mobilize support but also "to elicit but also to contain popular initiatives that contribute to the effective governance of Russian society."[32] The existence of the Public Chamber could not but diminish the role of parliament, which democratic theory suggests should act as the primary tribune for the expression of popular concerns. The creation of this social corporatist body of managed representation harks back to the era of fascism in the 1930s, as well as to Soviet-style controlled participatory mechanisms. Nevertheless, it provides an important forum for the consideration of social problems and allows some of its prominent members to engage in the resolution of political conflicts.

Para-constitutional accretions to the constitution are designed to enhance efficacy but in practice undermine the development of a self-sustaining constitutional order, the emergence of a vibrant civic culture and civil society, and, above all, weaken the supremacy of the normative state. The spirit of constitutionalism is eroded by the failure of sections of the Russian political class to subordinate themselves to the constitution. Formal hierarchical structures are unable to generate adequate ordering mechanisms, while the lack of development of intermediate political structures opens up a gulf between state and society. This threatens to both isolate the state and marginalize social forces. The creation of para-constitutional agencies is an attempt to fill the gap by manual means, reflecting neither spontaneous social development nor the formal provisions of constitutional law while not repudiating those provisions. The political analyst and former political adviser Sergei Kurginyan analyzes this politics behind the scenes, which he calls *parapolitika*, or "under the carpet" politics.[33]

Para-constitutional innovations are accompanied by the luxuriant development of what may be termed para-political practices. These are forms of political activism not envisaged by the constitution—notably, formal party politics and pluralistic elections—and instead are forms of politics that are hidden and factional. By contrast with public politics, para-politics focuses on intra-elite intrigues and the mobilization not of popular constituencies and open interests but of organizational and situational capital. The regime devised para-political operative rules on political life that deprive it of the grounded antagonistic competition, which is an inherent feature of a genuinely open political process. A whole series of techniques is devised to manage political competition, dubbed "virtual politics" by Andrew Wilson.[34] This rendered the 2007–08 electoral cycle, for example, a sterile arena for the enactment of decisions made elsewhere. The performance, however, was not deprived of a certain legitimating logic, and thus a degree of genuine engagement remained and was reflected in a relatively high turnout. The regime on the whole did not need to have recourse to overt coercion, and its undoubted reliance on administrative resources to ensure popular participation was more in the nature of an insurance policy. Even without this intervention, the regime would have achieved its goals—a strong parliamentary majority and the election of the appropriate successor, a testament to the success of Putin's adaptive strategy.

The institutions of democracy remain central to political practice and democracy remains the legitimating ideology of the regime, but politics operate at two levels, the formal constitutional (the normative state), and the nominal para-constitutional and para-political (the administrative regime). The persistence of a strong constitutional level is reflected in the agonism that is much in evidence in the discourse of the public sphere, where intellectuals, scholars, journalists, and politicians conduct a vigorous debate about the nature of the Russian system, tolerated by the regime as long as this does not take structured independent political form. It is precisely the tension between the two levels that gives ample scope, as we have seen, for democratic evolutionists and failed transitionists to put forward their arguments with some credibility. The two levels have their own institutional logic and legitimating discourses. It is this that gives Russian politics its permanent sense of a double bottom.

Depoliticization and the "Democracy Paradox"

A characteristic feature of "dual Russia" is the politicization of much of social life, while "the political," that is, the sphere of public contestation and formal choice, remains at best stunted. Post-communist Russian governance has been characterized by a tendency toward depoliticization, with a technocratic logic of administrative management predominant. There are good reasons for this, since clearly the period of 1991–93, when parliament and president were in almost permanent conflict accompanied by increasingly intense street politics, was reminiscent of the invasion of the political sphere by society that Carl Schmitt characterized as the core problem of the Weimar Republic. In the first decade of the twenty-first century, the fear of oligarch power and of various types of extremism, including right-wing Russian nationalism, once again put the premium on depoliticization. The effect of this, however, is to create a tutelary regime standing over society, which is considered not to be trusted to manage its own affairs, and by the same token, society is infantilized. Thus the logic of tutelary politics reproduces in new forms the isolation of *vlast'* from the autonomous operation of free political contestation and debate that was typical of the Soviet period. A ruling regime considers that it is entrusted with a public good that stands higher than democracy, although democracy in the post-communist era is not entirely negated and remains the legitimating ideology of the system.

Post-communist Russian leadership has relied on a technocratic apprehension of depoliticized leadership creating the conditions from the outside, as it were, for democracy. The dilemma of a system in which democracy is unable to create the conditions for its own existence without destroying the state in which democracy is being established was resolved by the Putinite gambit of formalizing the existence of a regime managing democratic and other political processes. The maintenance of the dual state is a way of finessing what is perceived to be the "democracy paradox," whereby a people given free choice elect a group that repudiates the premises of the system through which they were chosen. This allegedly was the case with the election of FIS in Algeria in 1992, Hamas in Palestine in January 2006, and would have been the case in the 1996 presidential election in Russia if the elites had not rallied around Yeltsin to guarantee his reelection by fair means or foul, thus defeating the communist challenge. In this model, democracy cannot be trusted to come up with the correct result, and thus some tutelary force intervenes: domestically in the form of a regime-type system; or internationally, in the form of nonrecognition, the imposition of sanctions, or outright intervention.

The fear that a Russian nationalist-populist movement would surge to power if free and fair elections were held may well have been exaggerated, but the political elite perceived the threat as real. This provoked the tutelary politics whereby the constitutional state was considered in need of protection from powerful social actors (the so-called oligarchs, regional bosses, and criminal networks). All this ensured that the dual state in Russia both shielded and undermined democracy, simultaneously insulating the democratic order from the dangers of the "democracy paradox," while operating a constrained electoralism that legitimated its own power. However, by depriving democratic politics of open-ended contestation (within recognized limits) characteristic of contemporary liberal democratic orders, the tension between the two pillars of the state was exacerbated. The attempt to both succor and emasculate democracy as part of the governing equilibrium effectively managed the "democracy paradox" in Russia but could not be a long-term strategy for development.

While Putin's regime insulated itself relatively effectively from political movements and civic associations, it became prey to two processes: the importation into the regime, in the form of factionalism, of the political pluralism that it suppressed in society, and the "economization" of its transactions. This economization at the most basic level took the form of venal corruption, which eroded the administrative system; but it was also accompanied by metacorruption, where the logic of the market undermined the autonomy of politics. This was the sting in the tail of the depoliticization strategy, but it also reflected a broader process in mature capitalist democracies. The global hegemony of neoliberalism in the early post-communist years was accompanied by the retreat of the state from earlier levels of social protection and public service, accompanied by what Cox identified as loss in "confidence in the integrity and competency of the political class": "Political corruption is inherent in the transformation of public goods into marketable commodities."[35]

Putin took a strictly instrumental and pragmatic view of the political process. As far as he was concerned, what works is best, and thus his thinking adopted a technocratic approach to society and lacked a dynamic sense of autonomous civic development. The political domain was to act as a relatively hermetic sphere of decision making insulated from what he perceived to be the untoward influence of social forces, irrespective of whether this took the form of the so-called oligarchs, regional bosses, or civic leaders. This was a classic attempt to combine power and knowledge to resolve modernization challenges from above. Makarychev calls this "metapolitics," defined as "a form of politics that legitimizes itself by means of a direct reference to rational knowledge and the concept of effectiveness."[36] Putin's elite may well have been devoured by venal corruption, but in its own self-assessment it was leading a developmental strategy that would bring Russia to its rightful place in the ranks of the great powers. This metapolitical developmental strategy, however, became prey to the metacorruption that is inherent in a dual state, where the political prerogatives claimed by the regime undermine the autonomy of legal and constitutional processes. As far as the leadership was concerned, however, the administrative regime was managing a relatively benign remodernization project that fostered the development of the socioeconomic foundations on which, in due course, a robust normative state could come into its own. This is a classic instance in which the "sacred tomorrow" displaces the inadequate present.

The Political Economy of Dualism

The operation of the free market is constrained by statist imperatives that transcend the logic of the market. The practices of neoliberalism are combined with a continued loyalty to neopatrimonial traditions. In strategic branches, notably in the energy sector, the state moved beyond its role as regulator and became an active player, which provoked the creation of what Hanson has called a "dual economy."[37] This is reflected in factional alignment, with the *siloviki* favoring a strong *dirigiste* system, whereas the liberal-technocrats are concerned with the extra scope that such an approach gives the bureaucracy to enlarge its powers and to generate rents in the form of corruption.

The border between politics and economics remains porous, despite early rhetoric about "equi-distancing" the oligarchs and the assault against Yukos, which was in part a repudiation of the claims of the nascent economic bourgeoisie to have a share in decision making at the level of the regime, while promoting the autonomy of civil and political society. Makarychev argues that "the restored central state was functionally unable to stay within the self-constructed boundaries that were supposed to both delimit and secure the political domain," and in the end, "politics divorced from business and mass media began to imitate and replicate the norms embedded in those sectors."[38] A reverse process took place, whereby "business practices sometimes spilled into the political sphere," which in Makarychev's view gave rise to the "marketization of the state."[39] This was a type of internal blowback in which the regime not only assumed the role of the main driver in the political realm but also of the main arbiter in economic life.

Gerald Easter has called this a "concessions economy," whereby the most valuable assets of the old command society became state concessions, and the system as a whole became an "upstairs-downstairs economy," with strategic industries and the large state service corporations on the top floor, while the mass retail and consumer sectors were downstairs.[40] In the wake of the Yukos affair, between 2003 and 2007, the proportion of state-owned shares on the Russian stock market rose from 20 percent to 35 percent. The politicization of hydrocarbons, moreover, fueled notions of Russia becoming an "energy superpower" and provided the grounds for inflated rhetoric about "sovereign democracy."[41] Instead of capitalist development fostering liberal democracy, a hybrid system emerged. Equally, in China it has been argued that instead of the development of a market economy transforming political relations in a more liberal direction, a type of "crony communism" has been created in which economic entrepreneurs have become partners on the Communist Party in maintaining the existing political system.[42]

The New Evolutionism in Practice

Although there are some structural similarities between the Soviet regime and the post-communist administration, above all the technocratic rationality of supra-democratic governance, there is a fundamental difference. The option of the communist regime adapting to society was foreclosed, since that would have meant the self-liquidation of the system. When Gorbachev tried to achieve this adaptation in the late perestroika years, this entailed the dissolution of the communist order accompanied by the accidental disintegration of the country. The situation today is very different, and the adaptive strategy by the regime only increased its popular legitimacy, although it was not at all clear that it also enhanced its efficacy and ability to modernize the economy and society.

The tension between the two faces of the dual state is constantly apparent. The raid on the St. Petersburg offices of the Memorial for human rights and historical association on December 4, 2008, for example, was conducted by masked men from the Investigative Committee of the General Prosecutor's Office. Having forced their way in with truncheons, they confiscated the association's entire archive, consisting of databases with biographical information on more than fifty thousand victims of Soviet repression, burial sites in the St. Petersburg region, personal documentation about the terror and the gulag, as well as all the materials of the Virtual Gulag Museum. However, the appeal against the raid on January 20, 2009, was upheld by the Dzerzhinsky district court, noting the procedural irregularities with which the raid had been conducted, and an order was issued that all of the confiscated materials should be returned to Memorial. Typical of the lack of finality in the Russian justice system, this decision was overturned by the St. Petersburg city court following an appeal by the Procuracy; but on further appeal on May 6, the city court ruled that the raid was justified but illegal due to gross procedural violations. This represented only a partial legal victory since Memorial had sought to have the raid declared unjustified, but the recognition of gross violations was accompanied by the order to return the confiscated hard drives. This decision was as final as Russian justice allows, and the material was returned to Memorial.

Fear of giving dualism political form was evident when the initial idea of running two approved candidates against each other in the presidential election of March 2, 2008, (Medvedev and Sergei Ivanov) was abandoned. Equally, the idea of allowing the two approved regime parties, Just Russia and United Russia, to compete on equal terms in the parliamentary ballot of December 2, 2007, was dropped also. From the regime's perspective, allowing even this degree of managed competition would have entailed the risk of the protagonists aligning with the cleavage of the normative state versus the administrative regime, which would not only have been fundamentally destabilizing but risked giving this constitutional tension political form. There was evidence of precisely such a development in the regional elections held in 2007 and early

2008 until the regime made clear that its preferences lay with United Russia, and thus the threat of damaging splits in regional elites was averted.

The fear that para-politics, where the key decisions are made through a process of factional contestation within the administrative regime, would spill over into genuine competitive politics reinforces the depoliticization and economization of contemporary Russian politics. In part, this was institutionalized in the division of power within the regime, with a political presidency and a depoliticized government headed by a politically neutral prime minister, a feature inherited from the Soviet regime and, in a different way, from the constitutional-monarchy period of late tsarism. This bivalency is in part internalized in individual behavior, as the neodissident "homme double" has once again emerged, divided between an internal and informal life, and public dissembling. Political dualism, as in the Soviet era, gives rise to behavioral dissembling. Post-communist Russian leadership has relied on a technocratic apprehension of depoliticized leadership creating the conditions from the outside, as it were, for democracy; but this has profound social effects.

At the same time, it would be misleading to identify the two leaders in the "tandem system" from 2008 as heads of the respective pillars of the dual state. Putin's political personality includes a liberal element, while Medvedev has shown himself to be open to a hard line in foreign policy and a cautious reformer at home. If Putin's goal had been to consolidate the administrative regime (in a *silovik* or patriotic guise), he could have selected any number of other individuals as his successor. Instead, he chose the lawyer Medvedev, whose opposition to the Yukos affair and the term "sovereign democracy" was well known.

Russia is indeed engaged in a complex process of social and political reconstitution, but only an approach rooted in a structural analysis of actual political forces and the competition between them allows us to understand the dynamics of contemporary development. The crisis of Russian democracy is real, but the situation remains open-ended, and Russia remains committed ultimately to an adaptive type of democratization project. Politics, too, remains constrained by the tension between the two aspects of the dual state, with the constitutional framework limiting the arbitrariness of the administrative regime. Another revolutionary overthrow of the existing regime, as advocated by "Leninist liberals" such as Garri Kasparov and the United Civic Front (OGF), would only reinforce political voluntarism and return Russia to yet another cycle of transformative politics and its associated arbitrariness.

The complacency and metacorruption of the administrative regime may well be challenged most effectively by gradually extending the scope of the normative state, and thus reducing the pernicious effects of contemporary dualism.

This certainly is the view of the democratic evolutionists on the ground, since the position is not just an academic one but is rooted in the realities of contemporary Russian politics. The Institute of Contemporary Development (INSOR), a liberal body created under Medvedev's sponsorship that sought to generate ideas for the new leadership, acted as the programmatic forum to give Medvedev's presidency its own identity and to develop strategies to strengthen the constitutional state. One of INSOR's first reports, "Democracy: Developing the Russian Model," criticized Russia's political system, notably the lamentable condition of Russia's political parties, a weak and servile parliament, limits on party competition, excessive hierarchical centralization, and an electoral system that delivered neither free nor fair elections. Russia had focused more on modernization than democratization, which froze institution-building and restricted pluralism, but the "hands-on" style of political management, in the report's view, had exhausted its potential. While a strongly presidential system should be retained, the country needed a "top-down liberalization of Russian politics."[43]

A later report developed a model for post-crisis modernization and stressed that socio-economic development could be achieved only if the political system was modernized as well. The basic argument was that sovereign democracy should give way to a competitive democracy to allow the development of a flexible civil society responsive to new challenges. This was still a top-down model of democratization, considered a function of the modernization process itself, based on elites learning how to compete democratically between themselves, with the fear of a popular revolution weighing heavily on the minds of the Medvedevites, as it did on the Putinites.[44] This generation of post-communist leaders across the former Soviet Union has an aversion to mass politics, even when institutionalized in political movements. Tutelary politics remained, but Medvedev was beginning to carve out a defined program of controlled democratization. Medvedev's latent liberalism now took the form of a "silent war" with the Putinite administrative regime.[45]

This was reflected in Medvedev's programmatic article "Forward, Russia!," published on a liberal Web site (Gazeta.ru) in September 2009.[46] Although the form was original, the style resembled Putin's lengthy question-and-answer sessions with domestic and foreign media. Both allowed the leader to communicate in a relatively free format while retaining control of the agenda and were thus another type of para-political behavior. The article reflected the Kremlin's growing perception that continued political drift was no longer an option, but it also suggested uncertainly over what was to be done. The article was presented as a discussion document for the president's annual state of the nation address to the Federal Assembly, but the harshly critical tone went beyond what would be acceptable on such a formal occasion.[47] He characterized Russian social life as a semi-Soviet social system, one that unfortunately combines all the shortcomings of the Soviet system and all the difficulties of contemporary life."[48] Underlying the article was the view that the rent-extraction model of Russian political economy was unsustainable in the long run. The fundamental question was whether Russia, with its "primitive economy" and "chronic corruption," has a future? Medvedev attacked not Putin but the system that Putin represented, a balancing act that blunted his message.

The article listed a devastating series of Russian problems, although it was weaker on suggesting ways in which the situation could be remedied. First, Medvedev argued that the country was economically backward and distorted by dependence on extractive industries. Who would act as the modernizing force, however, was not clear: the state or private enterprise? Second, corruption had long been one of Medvedev's bugbears, and here he once again condemned the phenomenon. It would require a wholly impartial and independent judiciary to achieve a breakthrough; yet as the endless cases of judges working closely with business "raiders" demonstrated, little progress had been made in the Medvedev years. Third, Medvedev condemned the "paternalist mind-set" prevalent in Russian society. A similar charge could be made against most advanced democracies, where a widespread political passivity has set in; but in Russia, a society that underwent at least two revolutions in the twentieth century, the charge could be seen as misleading. However, there was a noticeable rise in social paternalism, reflected in the most desirable careers for young people shifting from business to administration, indicating a return to a "quasi-Soviet social contract."[49]

With businesses under attack from bureaucrats, it was safer to join the latter. Basically, Medvedev sought to break away from neo-Soviet attitudes, viewing innovation, democracy, and freedom as the responsibility of the individual; but he recognized that entrenched interests stymied popular initiative. More broadly, it was all very well blaming the elite for having driven Russia up a dead end, but that same elite retained its full powers, and it would take an act of political courage from above or a revolution from below to remove its grasp on power. It was precisely a revolutionary approach that Medvedev rejected in his article, but that only placed a greater weight of expectation on changes from above. The fundamental weakness of Medvedev's reform program was its failure to devise a process of modernization from the middle, mobilizing not a centrist political coalition (that was Putin's constituency) but social forces that could provide substance to the ground between the two pillars of the dual state, and thus to establish a dynamic to transcend the division.

Conclusion

We have characterized contemporary Russian politics as a struggle between two systems: the formal constitutional order, what we call the *normative state*, and the second world of factional conflict and para-constitutional political practices, termed the *administrative regime*. Much of politics takes place in the charged zone between the two pillars of the dual state. Therefore, it would be incorrect to label contemporary Russia as an authoritarian regime *tout court*. Not only does it remain formally committed to constitutional democracy and liberal capitalism—and this remains the source of its political legitimacy—but these commitments moderate its behavior and allow the formal constitutional framework to structure and influence the conduct of politics. Although many of the regime's actions are authoritarian in spirit, the formal niceties of a constitutional democracy remain preeminent and the legitimating framework for the system as a whole.

The technocratic managerialism that characterizes the system blurs functional differentiation between the various branches of government, but does not repudiate the distinct logics on which executive, legislative, and judicial authority is based. Key constitutional principles are not sustained by political practices; but the constitution still constrains behavior and acts as a normative boundary-setter for the system as a whole (although when it comes to executive powers, the borders, admittedly, are set rather wide, but in formal terms remain within accepted democratic limits). Russia's administrative regime operates according to a tutelary logic, standing as a force above competitive politics, but does not repudiate the logic of political pluralism, the rule of law, and the autonomy of the normative state. The Putinist gambit may in the end, paradoxically, allow the constitutional state to come into its own and gradually diminish the role of the administrative regime to the sort of proportions typically found in liberal democracies.

A fundamental feature of our model of the dual state is the potential for existing institutions and processes to become autonomous in their own right. Just as the Soviet system nurtured institutions, notably union republics based on a titular nationality, which emerged as independent actors when the regime, seized by a democratizing impulse, weakened in the late 1980s, so today there remains a powerful latent potential in the formal institutions of post-communist Russian democracy.[50] Parties, parliament, the judiciary, and the whole juridico-constitutional system established in the early 1990s have potential to evolve within the existing system. The federal system under Putin lost its autonomous character, but federal institutions have been preserved and could come to life in different circumstances. The tension between constitutional federalism and unitary political practices, as in the Soviet system, provokes a permanent contradiction. In this sphere and in others, there is a conflict between the latent and the actual. It is for this reason that evolutionary gradualism in contemporary Russia could achieve the most profound revolutionary transformation in social relations and ultimately transform the quality of democracy. In the Russian context, there is nothing more revolutionary than evolutionary politics.

Notes

1. The model of the dual state is drawn from the experience of Germany described by Ernst Fraenkel in *The Dual State: A Contribution to the Theory of Dictatorship*, trans. E. A. Shils, in collaboration with Edith Lowenstein and Klaus Knorr (New York: Oxford University Press, 1941; repr., Clark, NJ: Lawbook Exchange, 2006).
2. This section draws on Richard Sakwa, "Two Camps? The Struggle to Understand Contemporary Russia," *Comparative Politics* 40, no. 4 (July 2008): 481–99.
3. Many of the "failed democratization" arguments were summed up in the Independent Task Force Report no. 57, chaired by John Edwards and Jack Kemp, with Stephen Sestanovich as project director, published as *Russia's Wrong Direction: What the United States Can and Should Do* (New York: Council on Foreign Relations, 2006).
4. Richard Sakwa, *The Quality of Freedom: Khodorkovsky, Putin and the Yukos Affair*

(Oxford: Oxford University Press, 2009), chap. 6.
5. Lucan A. Way, "Authoritarian State Building and the Sources of Regime Competitiveness in the Fourth Wave: The Cases of Belarus, Moldova, Russia, and Ukraine," *World Politics* 57 (January 2005): 234–35.
6. M. Steven Fish, *Democracy Derailed in Russia: The Failure of Open Politics* (New York: Cambridge University Press, 2005), 1
7. For the list of Russian failings, drawing on Fish, see Charles Tilly, *Democracy* (Cambridge: Cambridge University Press, 2007), 47.
8. For an exemplary positive study of one region and its dilemmas, see Nicolai Petro, *Crafting Democracy: How Novgorod Has Coped with Rapid Social Change* (Ithaca, NY: Cornell University Press, 2004).
9. This argument is stressed, inter alia, by Michael McFaul in *Russia's Unfinished Revolution: Political Change from Gorbachev to Putin* (Ithaca, NY: Cornell University Press, 2001).
10. Ralf Dahrendorf, *Society and Democracy in Germany* (New York: Doubleday Anchor, 1969).
11. For one of the best overviews, see Alfred B. Evans Jr., Laura A. Henry, and Lisa McIntosh Sundstrom, eds., *Russian Civil Society: A Critical Assessment* (Armonk, NY: Sharpe, 2005).
12. Elena Chebankova, "The Evolution of Russia's Civil Society under Vladimir Putin: A Cause for Concern or Grounds for Optimism?" *Perspectives on European Politics and Society* 10, no. 3 (September 2009): 394–416.
13. For a Russian statement on this view, and a vigorous assertion of how Russia should respond, see I. N. Panarin, *Informatsionnaya voina i geopolitika* (Moscow: Pokolenie, 2006).
14. Cf. Andrew Hurrell, "Hegemony, Liberalism and Global Order: What Space for Would-be Great Powers?" *International Affairs* 82, no. 1 (2006): 4, 5, 12–13.
15. M. N. Afanas'ev, *Nevynosimaya slabost' gosudarstva* (Moscow: Rosspen, 2006); Sergei Glaz'ev, *Vybor budushchego* (Moscow: Algoritm, 2005).
16. Yevgeny Yasin, *Prizhivetsya li demokratiya v Rossii?* (Moscow: Novoe izdatel'stvo, 2005).
17. Lilia Shevtsova, "Russia's Hybrid Regime," *Journal of Democracy* 12, no. 4 (October 2001): 65–70. For a discussion, see Larry Diamond, "Thinking About Hybrid Regimes," *Journal of Democracy* 13, no. 2 (2002): 21–35.
18. Robert W. Cox, "Civil Society at the Turn of the Millennium: Prospects for an Alternative World Order," *Review of International Studies* 25 (1999): 16.
19. R. C. Tucker, "The Image of Dual Russia," in *The Soviet Political Mind* (London:

Allen and Unwin, 1972), 121–42, at 123.
20. Ibid., 132.
21. Alexei Yurchak, *Everything Was Forever, Until It Was No More: The Last Soviet Generation* (Princeton: Princeton University Press, 2005).
22. Poll taken October 14–17, 2005, with 1,600 representative respondents in forty-six regions. Levada Center, November 9, 2005, http://www.levada.ru/press/2005 110901.html.
23. The six interest groups are the aforementioned *siloviki* (and various subfactions) and the liberal-technocrats, with four other factions acting as poles of influence: (1) the neo-oligarch interest, sometimes called the old Muscovites, which favors the development of an independent bourgeoisie; (2) democratic statists of the Vladislav Surkov type, propounding earlier the idea of "sovereign democracy"; (3) the big business lobby, ready to work in a subaltern relationship with the state, sometimes known as "state oligarchs" of the Oleg Deripaska and Roman Abramovich sort; and (4) the residual influence of the regional grandees, notably the "city boss" in Moscow and the titular presidents of the Volga republics (joined by the "Chechenized" leadership of the previously insurgent republic).
24. For a historical and political study of clientelism and Russian state development, see M. N. Afanas'ev, *Klientizm i rossiiskaya gosudarstvennost*, 2nd ed. (Moscow: MONF, 2000).
25. Gregory Gleason, "Fealty and Loyalty: Informal Authority Structures in Soviet Asia," *Soviet Studies* 43, no. 4 (1991): 613–28.
26. Ellen Lust-Okar, "Competitive Clientalism," in *Global Democracy and Its Difficulties*, ed. Anthony J. Langlois and Karol Edward Soltan (London: Routledge, 2008), chap. 9.
27. Kathryn Stoner-Weiss, *Resisting the State: Reform and Retrenchment in Post-Soviet Russia* (Cambridge: Cambridge University Press, 2006), 111–46.
28. For informative discussions on the fate of the opposition in Russia, held under the aegis of the Panorama Center, see E. Mikhailovskii, ed., *Rossiya Putina: Ruiny i rostki oppozitsii*, Managed Democracy Series (Moscow: Panorama, 2005).
29. Henry E. Hale, *Why Not Parties in Russia? Democracy, Federalism and the State* (Cambridge: Cambridge University Press, 2006).
30. "Ob Obshchestvennoi Palate Rossiiskoi Federatii," http://document.kremlin.ru/index.asp. Official documents and other material can be found on the Web site of the Public Chamber, www.oprf.ru/ru/interaction/.
31. For details, see James Richter, "Putin and the Public Chamber," *Post-Soviet Affairs* 25, no. 1 (January–March 2009): 39–65.

32. Ibid., 61.
33. Sergei Kurginyan, *Kacheli: Konflikt elit–ili razval Rossii?* (Moscow: Eksperimental'nyi tvorcheskii tsentr, 2008).
34. Andrew Wilson, *Virtual Politics: Faking Democracy in the Post-Soviet World* (New Haven: Yale University Press, 2005).
35. Cox, "Civil Society at the Turn of the Millennium," 12.
36. Andrey S. Makarychev, "Politics, the State, and De-Politicization: Putin's Project Reassessed," *Problems of Post-Communism* 55, no. 5 (September/October 2008): 66.
37. Philip Hanson, "The Russian Economic Puzzle: Going Forwards, Backwards or Sideways?" *International Affairs* 83, no. 5 (September/October 2007): 869–89.
38. Ibid., 62–63.
39. Ibid., 64
40. Gerald M. Easter, "The Russian State in the Time of Putin," *Post-Soviet Affairs* 24, no. 3, (July–September 2008): 212.
41. For a critical analysis of this concept, see Peter Rutland, "Russia as an Energy Superpower," *New Political Economy* 13, no. 2 (2008): 203–10.
42. Bruce J. Dickson, *Wealth into Power: The Communist Party's Embrace of China's Private Sector* (Cambridge: Cambridge University Press, 2009).
43. The report, published as *Demokratiya: Razvitie rossiiskoi modeli* (Moscow: Ekon-Inform, 2008), was commissioned from the Center for Political Technologies, headed by Igor Bunin and Boris Makarenko.
44. *Rossiya XXI veka: obraz zhelaemogo zavtra* (Moscow: Insor, 2009); with commentary by Elina Bilevskaya and Aleksandra Samarina in "Suverennuyu demokratiyu zamenyat sostyazatel'noi," *Nezavisimaya gazeta* 30 (September 2009): 4.
45. Aleksandr Ryklin, "Medvedev Requires Opposition Tolerance" [in Russian], *Ezhednevny zhurnal*, July 22, 2008; reprinted in *Johnson's Russia List (JRL)*, no. 136, 2008, item 17.
46. Dmitrii Medvedev, "Rossiya, vpered!" *Gazeta.ru*, September 9, 2009, http://www.gazeta.ru/comments/2009/09/10_a_3258568.shtml.
47. Medvedev admitted this in his meeting with the Valdai Club, when he argued that "the actual Address is of course a much more conservative document." "Beginning of Meeting with Valdai International Club Participants," September 15, 2009, http://eng.kremlin.ru/speeches/2009/09/15/1647_type82914type84779_21667.shtml.
48. Ibid.
49. Andrei Kortunov, "The New Russia," event summary, Kennan Institute, February 5, 2009; reprinted in *JRL*, no. 71, 2008, item 10.

50. Cf. Valerie Bunce, *Subversive Institutions: The Design and the Destruction of Socialism and the State* (Cambridge: Cambridge University Press, 1999).

CHAPTER FIVE

Leadership and the Politics of Modernization

Timothy J. Colton

> All nations have rulers. This fact is almost a truism. It is simply the way things are.... Whether countries happen to be democracies or dictatorships, the people eventually want one person at the helm whom they can identify as their leader.
> —Arnold M. Ludwig, *King of the Mountain: The Nature of Political Leadership*, 2002

If a country has ever fit this near-truism to a "T," it has been the Russia seemingly designed by nature for one-man rule. That being so, the presence today of a pair of ostensible captains of the ship, Vladimir Putin joined by Dmitrii Medvedev, is a novel and puzzling sight. Speculation about a rekindling of Russian modernization would be hollow at the core without a look at this anomaly and the circumstances behind it, at leadership in general, and at its place in promoting or retarding change.

The Web of Leadership

Comparative studies of leadership have long struggled to escape the shadow of reductionist, Victorian-era notions of "the great man in history." The critics, who see impersonal factors of broader scope as the drivers of politics and policy, tend not only to rebut leader-oriented theories but to caricature them. Every now and then, somebody comes out with the contrary point, rediscovering individual agency as if it were some long-lost treasure and reproaching the structuralists for neglecting it.

I am inclined toward the middle ground captured in the epigraph. Disproportionate power and influence in the hands of the acknowledged leader is the norm in political life—across continents, cultures, stages of modernization, and regime types. Typically, the leader exerts or has the potential to exert far more of an impact on events than any other single actor. That is not to say that this human being is omnipotent or 100 percent independent. He or she is in varying modalities and degrees constrained by institutions, elites, and social forces, and cannot be effective without compliance and a minimum of cooperation from them.

Leadership in politics is multifaceted. Mainstream research on it asks three overarching questions: about who, how, and what.

The first addresses who the leader is. If an earlier age might have stressed innate talents and quirks or the Oedipus complex, a behavioral approach would scrutinize the way leaders are made rather than born, as comes about through an incremental learning and skill-building process or through crystallizing experiences. A reply to the "who" question may be framed by biography, developmental psychology, or psychiatry.

The second big question is about how leaders do their work. Answers here are best structured by social psychology, sociology, or micro-political economy. In an authoritarian or totalitarian political system, the strongman may lead primarily through brute force.[1] In democratic and semi-democratic systems, the means available boil down to a triad: constructing and managing coalitions at the elite and state-institutional level; cultivation of a mass constituency below, which entails some willingness to take its preferences into account (to follow one's followers, so to say); and molding the agenda of political debate.[2]

Question three has to do with what the leader accomplishes in the grand scheme of things—the outcome as opposed to the origins or phenomenology of his or her statecraft. History and the macro branches of the social sciences are the germane disciplines here. Leadership scholars need to make allowance for the intricacy of the agent's motivation. A typology fruitful in the study of American presidents parses goals into three classes: power, which is intrinsically prized and also a prerequisite for attaining other goals; achievement, the urge to shape and reshape society in accord with a set of values; and affiliation, the pleasure taken in friendly relations with persons and groups.[3]

I would round these out with a fourth goal: avarice, the desire to milk public office for private gain. Once the goals of a leader have been identified, the brief is to assess how efficacious the subject has been in attaining them, and at the end of the day how much of a say she or he has had in comparison with other presences on the scene.

Even to categorize the particulars of political leadership is a thorny exercise, and they are interconnected in myriad ways. Furthermore, the particulars are embedded in a shared context that contains political-cultural, institutional, sociological, and developmental (path-dependent) dimensions, among others. The context has a volatility to it that, as Machiavelli memorably explained through his parable of the river in flood, generates opportunities for the would-be prince either to make his mark or to fall short.

In light of its multifaceted, interconnected, and embedded nature, political leadership should be envisaged as operating in a web or network. The leadership web is one where everything hooks up with everything else, losers massively outnumber winners, and the winners prevail against forbidding odds.[4]

Russia's Search for a Model of Leadership

Discourse about Russia's web of leadership feeds on history and a stylized image of it. "We have a center, the supreme power we call the Kremlin," intoned one pundit in 2009. "There is a throne up above, over all of us."[5] Such pronouncements are not without merit: numerous aspects of politics in Russia's successive incarnations as absolute monarchy, communist dictatorship, proto-democracy, and now authoritarian-democratic hybrid have indeed been highly centralized and personalized.

Scratch beneath the surface and we find more complex patterns. Some historians of Muscovy and the pre–World War I empire recount a byzantine high politics in which royal prerogative was often a façade, and clans and courtiers jostled for advancement under a cloak of "hermetic silence."[6] In the Soviet period, Communist Party agitprop both enshrined collective decision making and glorified the general secretary, as if the two versions could be equally true. In the new, post-Soviet Russia, Putin and the early Yeltsin come across as forceful leaders; but the late Yeltsin and the early Medvedev, as paper tigers.

One reason for these discrepancies is that the Russian state for most of its existence has not possessed a consensual and stable model of top political leadership. Instead, it has been engaged in an inconclusive hunt for one, continuing to this day. With rare exceptions, there has been unanimity about having a single throne and a single individual to occupy it.[7] Agreement, however, has not carried over onto the tangible powers, responsibilities, and purposes of that individual. Excluding intervals of extreme arbitrariness when the question was moot, the darkest of them the Stalinist purges of the twentieth century, the claim holds up pretty well.

The idiom of government has reflected that ongoing lack of clarity. The pre-1917 tsar was *gosudar'* ("sovereign") of the realm. Familiar stuff from the European doctrine of the divine right of kings, this was an elastic marker that left ample room for secularization and the evolution of the autocracy, and could have been adapted, via constitutionalism, to democracy, as it was in Britain and Scandinavia. In the 1920s, the quasi-religious "cult" of the martyred originator of Bolshevism, Lenin, was transferred to the living Stalin, uninhibited by serious institutional checks and balances, and rendered in the extravagant expression *vozhd'*, Russian for "the Leader" or "the Supreme Leader." For most of the 1930s, but not after that, the party and state saluted mini-*vozhdi* in every remote corner of the USSR. Stalin worship was downplayed during World War II, then revived for his seventieth birthday celebration in 1949. Declassified archives reveal that many Soviets rejected the cult and some were not afraid to say so.[8]

The mantle of *vozhd'* died with Stalin in 1953, and the number one in the regime, under the watchful eyes of his Politburo peers, was downgraded terminologically to a *rukovoditel'*. This exquisitely bureaucratic word computes only when the leader's decision domain is specified. Someone could be the authorized *rukovoditel'* of a work unit or, as Khrushchev and Brezhnev were portrayed, *rukovoditel' partii* ("leader of the party"), but he could not be the *rukovoditel'* of the Soviet Union in some undifferentiated sense. On the ground, the person giving orders, as under Stalin, was in everyday parlance the *nachal'nik* or "boss." The iron-fisted *nachal'nik* issued commands pertaining to specialized matters and answered to higher-ups, without fulfilling a more strategic function.[9]

Transition

Mikhail Gorbachev and his *perestroika* threw the Soviet leadership web into disarray in the 1980s. Discretionary promotions and demotions escalated into wholesale replacement as the environment turned revolutionary and the old system began to fracture. The locus for choosing political personnel shifted from the selectorate within a hegemonic party to the electorate. Boris Yeltsin triumphed over his fellow apparatchik, Gorbachev, and outlasted the Soviet Union because he grasped how to ride the democratizing wave, first as a rebel within the ruling party and then as populist leader of the opposition and elected head of the nascent Russian state. Millions of ordinary people identified with him for having shared their sufferings, for promising to accelerate social change, and for his apparent ability to keep their tormentors in check—"a boss for the bosses" *(nachal'nik dlya nachal'nikov)*, in a turn of phrase from his maiden election campaign in 1989.

In power as the founding president of post-communist Russia, Yeltsin in the early 1990s stitched together coalitions of elite groupings and organizations, enchanted and mobilized the masses, and reworked the agenda of politics. His free-market thrust, "shock therapy," brought the honeymoon with society to an abrupt end. It steered Russia toward capitalism and prosperity in the long run; in the short run, it was traumatic and impoverishing to the majority. The cynics held that Yeltsin was motivated by nothing more than power lust and avarice (no one felt he was after only affiliation). Actually, he mostly pursued achievement, in the sense of putting Russia foursquare on a Westernizing trajectory. Like most achievement-obsessed leaders, he left office frustrated by his inability to make good on promises, apologizing to compatriots in his retirement speech for putting them through an "agonizingly difficult" ordeal. Despite the problems and the backlash against the disorder he unleashed, Yeltsin and his messy reforms changed Russia forever.[10]

It has been alleged that a fluid political context is more conducive to strong leadership than a settled context.[11] Transitional Russia illustrates that uncertainty cuts both ways. Yeltsin's ambitions soared, and he was free to harness popular yearnings and ride roughshod over discredited Soviet-era structures. At the same time, the protean environment deprived him of the knowledge, institutional levers, and societal allies indispensable to executing his program as initially outlined. To salvage some of his reforms, he sought the company of the nouveau riche business moguls ("the oligarchs"), social conservatives, and non-democrats in the bureaucracy and security services.

In the rough-and-tumble of it all, scant thought went to characterizing top political leadership in Russia. Yeltsin spoke of himself merely as *prezident,* "the president"—a foreign borrowing that demarcated an office pure and simple, not a role. The constitution adopted in 1993 endowed the position with vast powers, warranting that the president was its "guarantor" and that he and only he "determines the basic directions of the domestic and foreign policy of the state." Overall, the document reinforced the executive against the legislative branch and provided a legal foundation for the de-democratizing acts of his successor.

In the wider reaches of politics, Yeltsin shied away from crafting the one tool—a political party dedicated to bolstering him as president and his reforms—that would have been most helpful in realizing his program and perpetuating it after him. The time to do so would have been his first term; in the second, to which he was narrowly elected in 1996, he was plagued by sickness and abysmal ratings, and could not have done much to assist a new party. A capable pro-Kremlin electoral bloc, Unity, was born only in 1999, finishing a close second to the neo-communists in that December's election of the State Duma (the lower house of parliament). Yeltsin kept his distance, wary of giving it the kiss of death. The decisive boost for Unity was endorsement by the man who had emerged out of obscurity to become Yeltsin's last prime minister and designated heir—Vladimir Putin.

Restoration

Yeltsin left the presidential suite in Kremlin Building No. 1 on December 31, 1999, eight months before the expiry of his mandate, and in a final decree before giving up his job appointed Putin the acting president. Putin had been assigned to quell the latest round of fighting in Chechnya and the North Caucasus and to deal with a rash of terrorist incidents in the Russian heartland. He immediately struck a chord with the electorate, as Yeltsin had counted on, and was elected president in March with a first-round majority.

Born in 1952, Putin was an age bracket younger than his benefactor and in good health. Working his way up the career ladder in the Soviet security organs, the St. Petersburg municipality (as lieutenant of a well-known democrat of the day, Mayor Anatolii Sobchak), and the Kremlin bureaucracy, he was known for his businesslike demeanor and reliability. In the words of Yeltsin's daughter Tatyana, Yeltsin "liked his pithy reports, his argumentation, his calm and restrained approach to severe problems," and his faithfulness to Sobchak, who fled the country after losing a reelection contest in 1996 and undergoing investigation for corruption.[12] The intuitivist Yeltsin was convinced—erroneously, on the whole—that only a person with Putin's toughness and composite background could consolidate the transformations he had started: "Society needed a new quality in the state, a steel backbone that would strengthen the political structure of authority. We needed a person who was thoughtful, democratic, and innovative yet steadfast in the military manner."[13]

Vladimir Putin was not bashful about his concerns. On the eve of his takeover as interim president, he posted on the Internet a "Millennium Manifesto," a trumpet call for the rebuilding of state authority and capacity. Democracy, legality, and personal liberties were all to be protected, he said, but Russia was doomed without "the appropriate restoration of the guiding and regulating role of the state," in harmony with enduring national traditions.

Putin, who had never run for election until 2000 and did not conceal his distaste for retail politics, stood the philosophy of democracy on its head. Beginning with ownership of a potent state position, handed to him unasked by Yeltsin, he then worked to garner support for an action program that was first and foremost about fixing the state, his starting point. The point of overlap with democratic norms was that he had to secure a modicum of mass assent through elections. It would be approached through a statist prism, as Putin's first election campaign gave a foretaste. The screws were tightened in 2000 on the media and on state officials who had backed various parties for the Duma. It was reminiscent of the contests for attainment of production quotas staged in Soviet days. Among the regional leaders, for instance, "A peculiar sort of 'socialist competition' was spurred...for who could support the acting president best and loudest. Any form of neutrality, to say nothing of opposition, was made out to threaten unpleasant post-election consequences."[14]

Although lacking the flair of Yeltsin in his heyday, Putin did reach out to the citizenry. He closely monitored the polls, lavished funds on public relations, and each year conducted a much-awaited open-line telecast with the rank-and-file. It was his good fortune to preside over a roaring economy fueled by record oil prices, the delayed benefits of the Yeltsin reforms, and prudent fiscal and monetary policy. Consumer income grew at double-digit rates, the budget deficit was erased, and national financial reserves swelled. With this wind in his sails, the president in 2004 was reelected to a second term with 71 percent of the popular vote. And United Russia, the disciplined "party of power" made out of the Unity bloc and several collaborators, won a solid majority in the 2003 Duma election.

State restorationism did not preclude some liberal economic and judicial reforms and upgrades to public administration, such as prompt payment of social allowances and government wages, rigorous tax collection, and anti-corruption regulations. In social policy, Putin in 2005 launched four "national projects" for pumping the budgetary surplus into health, education, housing, and agriculture. In 2006 he commissioned German Gref, author of the Millennium Manifesto and now economics minister, to write a long-range plan. The "Concept of the Long-Term Socioeconomic Development of the Russian Federation," published in September 2007, sketched a raft of targets for Russia in 2020—such as making it the fifth-largest economy in the world, a high-tech industry twice the size of the petroleum sector, good housing and cars for all, and public-health indices at West European levels. Drawn up before the global financial meltdown of 2008, the Gref plan made rosy assumptions about continuation of the gush of petrodollars and of the boom. The other postulate was that the top-heavy system for state management of society was not to be questioned. Russia, Putin said, had to uphold a "manual" or "hands-on" regime until it could safely be lifted for an "automatic" regime of unfettered markets and democracy. The time frame he recommended was "approximately fifteen to twenty years" more of the same.[15]

If economic and social Putinism had progressive and futuristic pieces to it, the paradigm in politics was largely regressive and soft-authoritarian. A tone was set in his first term by the occupation of Chechnya; the reining in of the governors and republic presidents; the rescinding of many media freedoms; and a crackdown on the oligarchs, the wealthiest of whom, Mikhail Khodorkovskii, was arrested in 2003 and later sent to a Siberian prison colony for economic crimes. While a few of these actions were defensible from a democracy perspective, as correctives to the fecklessness of the previous decade, the same cannot be said of Putin's second term. Highlights (or lowlights, depending on your point of view) were the de facto de-federalization of Russia; electoral laws and practices that screened out small parties and were advantageous to United Russia; onerous restrictions on nongovernmental organizations and their cooption into state-minded "public chambers"; and, after the Orange Revolution in Ukraine in 2004–05, the stigmatization of anti-system opposition as foreign inspired. In the first year or two, political Putinism was often dubbed "managed democracy." Beginning in 2005,

Vladislav Surkov, Putin's chief political aide, encapsulated it in the slogan "sovereign democracy," lumping together the domestic trend and Russian self-sufficiency and self-assertiveness in the international arena.

In eight years, Putin rewrote the political agenda and wooed a mass following, albeit a passive one. The manipulation of public opinion and the stifling of electoral competition notwithstanding, there was genuine support for his policies in almost every quarter of society, an association in people's minds of Putin with "a core set of principles" including the attachments to national unity, stability, and growth in a mixed economy.[16] Putin also put together a workable elite coalition. At its heart were the so-called *siloviki*, his comrades from law enforcement and the security services and natives of his hometown St. Petersburg. Yeltsin, who died in 2007, frowned on many of Putin's changes, although he refused to speak out against them. All the same, technocrats and elective politicians whose careers flourished on the first president's watch pragmatically threw in their lot with the second. A subset of the oligarchs was granted privileged access in exchange for loyalty, while United Russia lengthened the ruling group's reach to regional and local officialdom.

Putin as president was no less motivated than Yeltsin by achievement goals, although power ranked higher for him, seeing as enhancing the capacity of the state was the principal result he sought. He succeeded in doing much of what he set out to do, but nowhere near everything—unrelieved corruption and the lack of economic diversification are conspicuous failures. In the fullness of time, history will take him to task for them and for diverting Russia away from democratic governance.

Staying the Course

The current indeterminate state of affairs with Russian leadership was triggered by an obscure clause in the constitution of 1993. Hardly noted at the time, Article 81(3) stipulates that a president can serve no more than two four-year terms consecutively. Had it never been written, there is not a shred of doubt that Putin would still be in Building No. 1 today. But it was a fait accompli, in black and white, and it obliged Putin to vacate office by May 7, 2008, at the crest of his popularity and in the prime of life. The article says nothing about what comes next.

The only legitimate way to prolong Putin's tenure was to amend the constitution, not a letter of which had been tampered with since 1993. By late in his first term, with the Duma, the Federation Council (upper house of the Federal Assembly), and most of the regions firmly in the president's camp, passage of an amendment bill in almost any area was a foregone conclusion.[17]

Two specific constitutional fixes would have circumvented the roadblock. The more drastic would have been to change the form of government wholesale and institute a parliamentary republic, whereby a prime minister would serve for as long as he held a legislative majority, without limit of time, and the presidency would be abolished or downgraded into a ceremonial position. Mikhail Kas'yanov, Putin's first-term prime minister, has testified in a memoir that as early as April 2003 the Kremlin administration wrote into the draft of Putin's annual state-of-the nation address a proposal to parliamentarize Russia in the near future, and that it was withdrawn only at the last minute. According to Kas'yanov, the plan "was not about a parliamentary republic per se but about creating a mechanism for retaining power." Kas'yanov, an unfriendly witness who broke with Putin in 2004, does not say Putin was personally in on the proposal or why it was discarded.[18]

An openly discussed and milder remedy for the year 2008 problem would have concentrated on Article 81(3). Sergei Mironov, the chairman of the Federation Council, had spoken in favor of moving to a three-term limit since 2001, well before the trial balloon on a parliamentary republic, and other Putin stalwarts went so far as to advocate getting rid of the cap altogether. Mironov also called for an increase in the duration of the president's term from four years to between five and seven years.

Grassroots sentiment did not object to a revision along these lines. In a February 2007 poll, 60 percent of the populace wanted Putin to have "the opportunity to occupy the post of president three or four terms in a row," and 59 percent, up from 44 percent in 2005, favored a constitutional amendment on a third term. Another survey, in July 2007, disclosed that Putin would be handily reelected if allowed on the ballot. Fifty-five percent of all eligibles, and 71 percent of decided voters (the same as in the 2004 election), would have supported him for president; no one else attracted 5 percent.[19] In elite circles, sympathy among winners from the Putin era was more robust. Many of those who were dubious about its excesses feared a sudden termination—better the devil you know than the devil you don't. There were also misgivings about a redistribution of property and squabbling among the *siloviki* and presidential entourage once the chief was gone, as had started to materialize in 2006–07. Below and above, extension of the Putin presidency was backed by a broad coalition of the passionate, the acquiescent, and the insecure Until ready to tip his hand, Putin confined his remarks to two themes, one negative and one affirmative. The negative one was that he was unalterably against a change in the term-limit rule and was going to leave the presidency on schedule. "Staying for a third term was never a lure for me," he was to profess a bit piously at his farewell press conference. "If God gave me the good fortune to work for my country...I should be grateful for the opportunity, which is its own best reward. It is offensive to seek further reward or to get it in your head that once you are in the top post you have the right to stay there until they lay you in your grave."[20] Besides the impropriety of it, Putin insisted that any tailor-made amendment would open up an institutional Pandora's box. "If each new head of state modifies the constitution to suit him," he said in 2005, "before long there will be nothing left of the state."[21] Left unsaid was that many world leaders would have disapproved. Sophisticated Russians would have thought clinging to power through an insincere rule change a travesty in a European country.[22]

As for what he would do affirmatively as ex-president, I saw Putin field question after question about his plans at the annual meetings of the Kremlin-sponsored Valdai Discussion Club. The line he stuck with was that he would be "leaving the Kremlin" in 2008 but not "leaving Russia," and increasingly he insinuated that his next act would have political content. He began to drop public hints to this effect in 2006. During his phone-in that October, a truck driver from the Urals asked Putin to explain "what will come of us and the country" after he honored his commitment to step down. Putin was adamant that he would hold on to "the most important thing for any politician, your trust." With that as the basis, "You and I will find a way to influence the life of our country and see to it that it sticks with a consistent path of development."[23] Putin, in other words, was gesturing toward a substantive *role* in politics, divorced from the exact *position* of president. Most Russians foresaw—correctly—that such a post-presidential role would be found. In an opinion survey taken in August of 2007, seven respondents in ten thought he would somehow "remain in politics" and just as many were warm to the idea.[24]

One technique for preserving Putin's power, repeatedly bruited in 2007, would have cast him as an elder statesman, reliant on his moral authority only, along the lines of Lee Kwan Yew in Singapore or Deng Xiaoping in China. An intriguing proposal was made in an open letter by a Chechen operative for United Russia named Abdul-Khakim Sultygov. The term for "leader" he put forward—*lider*—had entered circulation in Russia only in the 1990s, most frequently in commercial applications such as "brand X is the *lider* in detergent" or "rock singer Y is the *lider* in the ratings among teenagers." It sounded trendy and had neither the pomposity of the Stalinist *vozhd'* nor the dryly administrative ring of *rukovoditel'*. Sultygov demanded that an extra-parliamentary Civic Assembly of the Russian People be convened forthwith, recognize Putin as "national leader" *(natsional'nyi lider)*, and swear a solemn oath of allegiance to him, after which Putin would act as a final court of appeal on disputes and periodically send "messages" to the nation. The Sultygov letter went unmentioned by Putin and was speedily disowned by allies.[25] Inasmuch as Russia does not have a Confucian heritage, Putin is middle aged, and United Russia is not as institutionalized as its East Asian counterparts, a carbon copy of Lee or Deng was impractical.

With all these ideas hanging in the air, Putin and his confidantes resolved his conundrum ad hoc. The three-part solution they came up with would keep him in the thick of the political game but play it by the rulebook constitutionally. Simultaneously, (1) a trusted client on the Putin team would be put forward for president; (2) the patron, Putin, would migrate to the constitutionally inferior but still meaty job of prime minister; and (3) while he was at it, Putin would take over leadership of United Russia as an insurance policy. The client picked for president, to the consternation of many, was Dmitrii Medvedev, the forty-two-year-old first deputy prime minister accountable for the national projects. Medvedev was an alumnus of the same St. Petersburg (Leningrad) law school as Putin, taught there for a decade, and was an adviser to Anatolii Sobchak. He worked under Putin's supervision part-time for five years in St. Petersburg and after 1999 in Moscow as full-time campaign manager, deputy chief and chief of staff, and first deputy head of government. Medvedev was to be the first Russian leader of middle-class origins (both his parents were academics) and the first to have made money in private business, and he had never served in the KGB.[26]

Putin started the process by announcing on October 1, 2007, that for the first time he would head up the United Russia slate of candidates in the forthcoming Duma election and that in the national interest he was willing to relocate to the premier's office if Russians elected as president "a decent, able, and efficient person with whom I could work in a pair."[27] The mechanics went like clockwork. United Russia carried the Duma election in a landslide on December 2. Putin publicized his choice of Medvedev on December 10; Medvedev took one day later to reciprocate that Putin would be his prime minister. On March 2 Medvedev rode Putin's coattails to an electoral win, tallying a fraction of a percentage point less than Putin's 2004 vote share. Putin was chosen chairman of United Russia in mid-April, and he and Medvedev were inducted into their new state positions on May 7 and 8.

The principle of the succession was stability in the leadership web. In his speech accepting Medvedev's invitation, Putin told a United Russia convention in December that the reshuffling of positions would go through smoothly, "without changing the distribution of powers between the president and the government." Medvedev for his part vowed solidarity with "the program proposed by President Putin"—"I intend to be guided by [it] in my future work" if elected president. More than that, he was "persuaded that full implementation of this strategy is doable only together with its author," with whom he would work hand in hand. Putin, Medvedev added, would do anything but fade away: "Vladimir Vladimirovich will go on utilizing his huge political and professional assets and his influence in our society and all over the world."[28] These were all prescient comments.

And Then There Were Two

It has been somewhat of a cliché to classify Russia's political order as "super-presidential" or "hyper-presidential." If the issue is about the imbalance between the branches of government and about ultimate control being vested in the executive, the cliché is accurate.

It overlooks, though, the formality that the Russian constitutional formula is, in lawyer's parlance, "semi-presidential," a label with very different connotations from "super" or "hyper" presidentialism. The French scholar Maurice Duverger, who coined the concept of semi-presidentialism in the 1970s, saw it as an up-and-coming alternative to classic, U.S.-type presidentialism. Its central attributes were three: a president elected by universal suffrage, consignment to him of "quite considerable powers" superior to those of a chief minister answerable to parliament, and a prime minister and cabinet "who possess executive and governmental power and can stay in office only if the parliament does not show its opposition to them" via a vote of no-confidence.[29] If Duverger's second criterion is applied strictly, the number of semi-presidential systems has risen from several in the 1950s to twenty to twenty-five worldwide in 2010; if not, and if countries with elected but weak presidents are counted, the figure is about double that. Semi-presidentialism is predominant in the fifteen post-Soviet states, found everywhere but in the parliamentary Baltic republics (Estonia, Latvia, and Lithuania, a borderline case) and Moldova, which renounced semi-presidentialism in 2000.

In post-communist Russia, a bifurcated executive was present from the outset and survived the constitutional watershed of 1993.[30] Presidents always had the whip hand and changed premiers at will (Yeltsin six times, Putin two). But institutional dualism had a flexibility that made it a vehicle for Putin's makeshift solution in 2007–08: it could furnish a dignified platform to a second heavyweight player in national politics, in addition to the president.

While the Medvedev-Putin tandem was politically expedient, it was obviously awkward for a paramount leader to turn over his job to a protégé and then not get out of the way to let him govern. And it was obvious that the allocation of peak offices was incongruous with the stature of the two principals. Putin, the country's longtime strongman, was relegated to the junior job; Medvedev, hitherto a politico of middling reputation, held the senior job, and only by sufferance of his mentor.

One of the ironies is that Putin as president, much more than Yeltsin before him, had kept his prime ministers on a short leash and barred them from developing an independent political persona. Putin's first premier, Kas'yanov, believes that his having been "far removed from public politics" until then, as a financial expert, improved his chances for recruitment. Putin directed him to focus on economic and social policy and not interfere in national security or in "internal politics," that is, elections and parties, civil society, government-business relations, and federalism. It transpired that arms exports and the Gazprom gas monopoly, the motor of the Russian economy, "and practically everything connected with it," were also off limits to him.[31] Putin's second and third chief ministers, the veteran functionaries Mikhail Fradkov and Viktor Zubkov, faced similar boundaries and were less in the news than Kas'yanov.

Although the precise division of labor between President Medvedev and Prime Minister Putin is a closely guarded secret, we know for sure that it has little in common with that of 2000 to 2008. The official distribution of powers has not been touched, as Putin pledged in 2007; unofficial norms and behavior have changed.

Medvedev has tended to the vital powers allotted the president in the constitution, making the headlines on Georgia and Ukraine, arms control negotiations with Washington, the administration of justice, and so forth. He has also embarked on a sweeping verbal crusade to expose shortcomings in Russian society.

But it is Putin, not Medvedev, who has been the government's firefighter on the disastrous economic slump and who has inserted himself routinely in energy policy, foreign economic affairs, federalism, and mass politics. He keeps up a frenzied travel schedule. In 2009 Putin visited fourteen foreign countries, to the president's twenty-six; seven of Medvedev's trips abroad were to multilateral diplomatic events. At home, Putin toured thirty-six of Russia's eighty-three federal regions, or ten regions *more* than Medvedev.[32] Wearing his United Russia hat, he has leverage over elections and parliament. Where protocol could stand in the way, the party opens doors. "Putin reception offices," to hear the grievances of disaffected citizens, were opened by United Russia countrywide in the summer of 2008. As prime minister, Putin also has continued his presidential practice of the annual televised phone-in. The first "Conversation with Vladimir Putin" was held in December 2008 under the auspices of the party and its reception offices. Putin was in fine fettle over the three hours, noted an observer. "Like in the old days, Putin demonstrated that it is he who is prepared to talk with the people one-on-one and he who understands the interests of our citizens."[33] The four-hour broadcast in 2009, his longest ever, was paid for by the prime minister's office. By choice or of necessity, Medvedev has organized no such colloquy with his constituents. The closest thing is the videoblog he set up in October 2008, which reaches the well-educated urbanites who frequent the Internet in Russia and not the plebes who ask most of the questions in the Putin "Conversations."

The blurring of roles has put on hold the discourse on leadership doctrine in Russia. There is no talk just now of a national *lider*. Medvedev describes himself as *rukovoditel' gosudarstva* ("leader of the state"), officialese for kingpin of the apparatus of government but not of the country. The public Putin is incarnated as often as not as the nation's *nachal'nik*, the fixer and issuer of edicts who keeps the wheels turning. His bravura performance in the small town of Pikalevo, near St. Petersburg, on June 4, 2009, where with television cameras grinding he commanded businessmen and local officials to sign an agreement on resuming production at three idle factories, is emblematic. A target of his fury was Oleg Deripaska, the billionaire proprietor of one of the factories. "Putin compared the three plant owners (including Deripaska) to cockroaches, and accused them of greed. He then threw his pen on his desk and ordered Deripaska to approach and sign an agreement on raw material supplies intended to help restart the Pikalevo factories. Putin decried the inability of the board members to make the necessary decisions without his intervention. Adding to Deripaska's complete humiliation, following the signing of the contract Putin told him, 'Do not forget to return my pen.'"[34] Putin sounded the same note when he looked back on the Pikalevo incident a half-year later, during his question-and-answer marathon: "I had the feeling that far from every leader in the regions and municipalities, and for that matter in the government of the Russian Federation, appreciated the scale [of the crisis we faced]. I thought it correct and proper to send a signal to society and to leaders at all levels that they have to answer for what is going on." He did not spare a word for Deripaska.[35]

Stylistically, gritty episodes like this might be thought a comedown from the Olympian Putin of 2000–08; but in their own way, they telegraph his persistent mastery of the landscape. No politically attuned Russian with whom I have spoken questions that he in the final analysis lingers as the real leader of the country, regardless of constitutional niceties. *Forbes* magazine echoed the in-country conventional wisdom in late 2009 when it ranked him the third most powerful person *in the world,* behind only Barack Obama and President Hu Jintao of China. Medvedev was put in forty-third place. Putin, *Forbes* wrote with some hyperbole, "might as well be known as tsar, emperor, and Autocrat of all the Russians" and is "vastly more powerful than his handpicked head of state."[36]

If it is the former president who is at the helm, if he continues to ride high in the public's esteem, and if his regime's hammerlock on political communications is not relaxed, then in effect contemporary Russia may be in a strange regency period — a hiatus separating long periods of direct rule by the king. There is no legal barrier whatsoever to his reinstatement as president. Whereas the Twenty-Second Amendment to the U.S. Constitution (passed by Congress in 1947 and ratified in 1951) provides that nobody may ever be elected president more than twice, Article 81(3) of the Yeltsin constitution sets no lifetime ceiling. Now that he has been out of office for a time, Putin could go back when Medvedev's four-year term concludes in 2012, or earlier if Medvedev were to resign prematurely. Conjecture is all we have to go on until Medvedev and Putin tell us what was said between them when they negotiated their entente in 2007. It is entirely credible to suppose that they agreed at the time to an eventual Putin comeback. A straw in the wind is that six months into his administration Medvedev introduced the first amendment ever to the 1993 constitution, a decision unthinkable without Putin's encouragement. The change, which sailed through in weeks, is to Article 81(1) and elongates the presidential term henceforth to six years from four. Should Putin once again be elected in the spring of 2012, when he will be only fifty-nine years old, he will be eligible to stand one more time in 2018 and serve as president until 2024, twenty-five years after he supplanted Yeltsin. All Putin will say for now—and it is not trivial—is that he is keeping his options for 2012 open. He has pointedly declined to state his support for Medvedev's reelection beforehand. Asked during his 2009 "Conversation" if he might soon leave politics, he replied, "Don't hold your breath." Might he run for president again? "I will think it over. There is plenty of time for that." Words and body language signal that he feels entitled to make the call.[37]

Staying the course, followed by Putin's triumphant return, therefore represents the best-bet prediction for leadership in the next three to five years, with all that would ensue. And yet, it would be unwise to ignore the chance of disruption. If students of Russia and Eurasia have erred in their forecasts over the last generation, it has been on the side of underestimating the potential for change.

In this connection, the duumvirs have never denied that they will not agree on each and every policy question they face in the course of their duties. In a fit of candor at his last presidential press conference, Putin said he would respect Medvedev's right to make decisions as chief executive, but, "I naturally have the right to express my views." He conceded that differences could perchance crop up between them and that third parties could try to drive a wedge. "Dmitrii Anatol'evich and I are well aware that attacks will be made along personal, political, and economic lines. There will be constant attempts to find differences in our approaches. There are always differences, I have to say, but over our more than fifteen years of working together we have gotten accustomed to listening to each other."[38]

Moreover, under the right conditions conflict could be stimulated by the very constitutional blueprint that was instrumental to setting up the Russian duumvirate. Semi-presidentialism has been known elsewhere to be conducive to dissension within the executive household. Where executive power is divided:

The constitutional tensions are structural and...there is always the potential for warring executives....Something as simple as personality differences between the president and the prime minister may lead to disagreements over policy and over who should direct government, even if the president and prime minister share the same policy program. Or, perhaps, a president's particular beliefs about his leadership role and his own popular, direct legitimacy, as opposed to the prime minister's indirect legitimacy, may lead him to completely dominate his prime minister, who, in turn, might resist this domination, setting off a spiral of backbiting and mutual recriminations.[39]

Warfare between president and prime minister was the narrative of politics in neighboring Ukraine from 2005 to 2010. Were such hostilities to erupt in Russia, or take place in a muted form more like the interludes of presidential–prime ministerial "cohabitation" in France, they would be much harder to suppress, since the political mentality in Russia is so intolerant of ambiguity over supreme authority in the state. So long as Medvedev and Putin are on the same wavelength, elite and mass opinion will accommodate itself to some vagueness. If the relationship dissolves in rancor, there will be enormous pressure on each of them to go all-out for victory, with explosive spillover effects.[40]

The Measure of Medvedev

What might plausibly push the Putin-Medvedev relationship in such an apocalyptic direction? Intimate associations rupture in politics, as in marriage and business, all the time. One would guess that Putin and Medvedev, knowing one another well for so many years, would not fall out on petty personal grounds. But the personal can coalesce with the political in unpredictable and incendiary ways, especially when naked ambition is involved. Putin may aim to reclaim the Russian presidency; Medvedev may crave the power and perquisites of an office he holds in theory but has never disposed of in reality. In so delicate a situation, displays of individualism on the part of the recently elevated junior partner can easily be taken by the senior partner as aggression or ingratitude, and avuncular advice from the older man can be construed by the younger as meddling.

Listen to the Russian rumor mill nowadays and you will hear about irritants between Putin and Medvedev. Friction between their publicists and policy staffs is an open secret in Moscow. Listen also to Medvedev on December 3, 2009, in Rome, when a journalist interrogated him about Putin's statement in his "Conversation" that he may run for election in 2012: "Premier Putin said he doesn't rule out this possibility, and I also don't rule out this possibility." One political Web site called it "a long-range polemic."[41] Such jousting can acquire a life of its own.

If we think about ambition in a longer horizon, Putin already has his guaranteed niche in the national pantheon; Medvedev has none. What he wants in his heart of hearts remains a mystery. Is it to go down in history as a footnote, a placeholder between Putin's first and second comings as leader, or as an individual who made a difference? The three leaders who set politics in motion in Russia from the mid-1980s to 2008—Gorbachev, Yeltsin, and Putin—answered that they wanted to make a difference. Hypothetically, Dmitrii Medvedev may yet join their company.

Given his multitudinous ties, organizational and surely emotional, to Putin, it is most improbable that Medvedev will throw down the gantlet to him without a larger, values-based rationale. This rationale might conceivably flow from Medvedev's diagnosis of Russia's present-day ills, which is an extraordinary phenomenon in its own right. After a slow start, Medvedev has been a veritable criticism machine. In presidential speeches, interviews, and his videoblog, he has found fault with virtually every one of the new Russia's fundamentals. In "Go, Russia!," an essay published in the liberal online newspaper gazeta.ru in September 2009, he condemned "a primitive raw-materials economy, chronic corruption, the inveterate habit of looking to the government, to foreigners, to some kind of invincible doctrine, to anything or anyone—as long as it is not to ourselves—to solve our problems." Russia, as Medvedev tells it, is being held back by "legal nihilism," technological backwardness, apathy and poor self-organization, parasitism on the physical assets of the Soviet past, demographic decline, bureaucratic contempt for citizen rights, and whitewashing of Stalinism.[42]

Some rhetorical divergence between Medvedev and Putin was inescapable and was almost certainly part of Putin's plan in 2007. If Putin had wanted a clone as successor, he would have chosen a member of the KGB fraternity and not Medvedev. It stands to reason that he all along intended Medvedev to make some modest emendations and adaptations to the inherited state of affairs. Still, it has to be asked how much will be enough from Putin's vantage point, and when the reformist verbiage of Medvedev is to be interpreted as veiled censure of Putin and his policies. "Go, Russia!" may have crossed such a line when it cited the severity of the 2008–09 recession in Russia as proof "that we did not do all we ought to have in recent years, and that far from all of what we did was done correctly."[43]

As we take his measure at the halfway mark of his 2008–12 term, the finding has to be that Medvedev has offered mostly talk about what is wrong. What, one might ask, would it take for him to lessen the yawning gap between word and deed? He would have to have the ego strength to want to be his own man, to take charge—to be *the* leader. He would move to forge a distinctive elite coalition, energize a mass audience, and reshape the national agenda. He would know how to amass power resources and use them as a device for achievement.

Thus far, none of these conditions has really been met. Temperament is one of the reasons. As Medvedev confessed in a series of interviews before his inauguration with the TV journalists Nikolai and Marina Svanidze, this former law-school lecturer has had difficulty leaving the professorial mode behind. Getting across his ideas in politically actionable form "is not always so simple" for him, he said to the Svanidzes. "When I formulate such things, I often do it as if I were giving a lecture." "One gets the impression," they wrote with some empathy, "that Medvedev the scholar takes precedence over Medvedev the politician."[44]

The trouble is that political leadership, all the more in so hard and unforgiving a culture as Russia's, is not a game for the scholar. Medvedev has the qualities of mind to perceive and declare that Russia must change, but he may not have the qualities of character to put this vision into effect. Character aside, too much of the political wherewithal is still in the grip of Putin, and Medvedev invariably will be constrained by elite composition, Russian institutions, and the spoken and unspoken understandings between state and society—all of them heavily influenced by Putin's past actions.

One standard mark of a new leader's clout is his success in making personnel changes in the machinery of government. Be it for lack of motive or ability, Medvedev has made astonishingly few changes in the most sensitive state positions. He has replaced only about one-quarter of the regional governors. While a few of his appointees have varied the Putin mold, most have not. In the central establishment, there has been continuity in most major seats in the Council of Ministers. Medvedev's own executive office is populated almost totally by holdovers from the old team, including Vladislav Surkov,

Putin's political eminence grise. The cadres who have not stayed behind in the Kremlin inner sanctum have journeyed to analogous posts in the Moscow White House, the governmental office tower on the banks of the Moskva River where Putin holds court.[45]

Nevertheless, it is worth reminding ourselves that the institutional capital of an incumbent president of Russia, which Medvedev is, is formidable. Putin cannot literally force Medvedev to bow out of the 2012 election or do anything else. In the Russian setup, the president has symbolic primacy, an almost unlimited range for decree-making, and the power (dormant until now) to hire and fire thousands of officials. The artillery most applicable is the president's right under Articles 111 and 117 of the constitution to dismiss the prime minister at will and nominate someone who pleases him better. If the Duma spurns his nominee for the premiership three times, the president selects an acting prime minister unilaterally, whereupon the Duma disbands, and a parliamentary election is held. In any showdown with Putin, Medvedev would have to contend with the United Russia majority in the Duma and with laws that make formation of any new party a long ordeal, so that some liberalization of registration procedures would be crucial to success. He could be optimistic about some United Russia deputies defecting to him over the issue and many officeholders worrying more about going with the winner than about supporting either one of them.

Under the best of circumstances, a frontal assault on Putin would be a risky business. Medvedev has shown absolutely no stomach for taking risks. This applies to *modernizatsiya* of the country—a word that is now a Medvedev mantra—as well as to dealings with Putin and the political class. And too, Medvedev has been excruciatingly slow to modify major institutions and government policies. In his first year in the Kremlin, Russian politics became more undemocratic than it had been in Putin's second term. Only in year two was there "an even partial loosening of the previously tightened screws, so far on the micro-political level only."[46] The president, for example, championed legislation reducing the membership minimum for a registered political party from 50,000 to 45,000 members and seating several representatives from registered parties that fall between 5 percent and the 7 percent threshold in a State Duma election. He has lately voiced support for elimination of signature requirements for candidates and parties, a more meaningful change. Regional elections in the spring of 2010, in contrast to those in 2008 and 2009, were not marred by widespread falsification of turnout and pro-government votes, although non-approved candidates were filtered out in many districts, and media coverage of the campaign was strongly biased. Medvedev has announced a series of anti-corruption initiatives, one of them making bribery of foreign officials a crime. In the area of rights, he has condemned the Stalinist terror, met with independent journalists, and forced through an end to pretrial detention for defendants who are accused of economic offenses. He also has committed the government to construction of an R&D park for nanotechnologies outside Moscow; it will raise funds on international capital markets, recruit foreign engineers, and have special provisions for taxation and policing.

To date, these are all emendations within the house that Putin built. They leave its essential architecture intact. In the words of one analyst of the Medvedev presidency, his reforms "do not threaten managed democracy and do not exceed the limits of 'freedom for your own,'" jealously guarding entry into the center ring of national affairs.[47]

This gingerly approach to change can be imputed in part to Medvedev's co-leader. What we see today may well be the gist of what Putin had in mind in selecting Medvedev in the first place. Medvedev diagnoses the patient. Surgery, if any, is to be done only with Putin's blessing and participation.

I would give equal credence to internal recoil against radicalism. This attitude likely stays Medvedev's hand as much as any external restraint applied by Putin and the prevailing institutional and factional arrangements. For all the boldness of his critique of the Russian status quo, he propounds gradualism in correcting it and maintains that the social fabric will shred if it is done in haste. As he put it in the Svanidze interviews, "What I want is for us to develop a new civilizational model but develop it calmly and in evolutionary fashion. The main thing is to avoid shocks or turns in the wrong direction. We still have a fragile civil society and generally a fragile state." Medvedev told the Svanidzes he looked upon the words *radikal* and *radikalizm* with distaste and that "poor management on the part of the authorities" is to blame for radicalism in any country.[48] He went back to this credo in "Go, Russia!"—change in the Russian political system had been tortuous, he admitted, but was better that than "permanent revolution":

> Not everyone is satisfied with the rate at which we are moving....They talk about the need to force the pace of change in the political system and sometimes about going back to the "democratic" 1990s. No, it is inexcusable to return

to paralysis of the state. I have to disappoint the supporters of permanent revolution. We are not going to rush. Hasty and ill-considered political reforms have more than once in our history led to tragic consequences and pushed Russia to the brink of collapse. We can't jeopardize social stability or the safety of our citizens for the sake of any kind of abstract theory. We have no right to sacrifice a stable life, even for the highest of goals.... Changes will come, but they will be steady, well-conceived, and step by step.[49]

Outlook

Russia needs political reform. It is an end in and of itself and a means to facilitate other changes needed for the country to resume its stalled march toward modernity. Political change is clearly not the highest priority for Dmitrii Medvedev, let alone for Vladimir Putin, whose opinion counts for more. It would be naïve to hold out for any dramatic breakthrough in this sphere in the short term. But the leaders may back willy-nilly into a more moderate sequence of reforms because it will help them make headway on goals that matter to them more. They understand that Russia cannot do without a diversified, dynamic economic base and that little progress has been made since the unraveling of communism toward assembling one. For it to be constructed, the burden of corruption must be lightened, small and medium-size businesses must thrive, and foreign capital and know-how must pour in. It will be difficult if not impossible for these good things to come to pass unless the system of government acquires or reacquires elements of the competitiveness, transparency, and feedback that have been methodically designed out of it.

If the gauge is who is articulating noble intentions, the best hope for a turn toward democracy in Russia is for Medvedev, still a cipher, to wrest control of the political leadership web as soon as possible. Even at that, the most he promises, as a Medvedev adviser informed me in late 2009, is "change in small doses" *(peremeny dozirovaniyem)*. The continuation of Putin in a preponderate role for an indefinite period of time would make the doses smaller than they would otherwise be. Having Putin or anybody else in charge for a whole generation—"until they lay you in your grave," as he said scornfully in 2008—would be a recipe for ossification and decay. It would be bad for Russia even if it were headed in an unreservedly authoritarian direction.

Comparative studies show that successful autocracies, the most proficient at supplying public goods, are by and large those that have higher leadership turnover.[50]

Unless Putin's health gives way or Medvedev pulls off the unlikely feat of overthrowing him or challenging him in the 2012 election, it will be Putin who decides voluntarily on when and how he will relinquish control. His return to the Kremlin is a better than a fifty-fifty proposition. However, it is not inevitable; and if it does occur, it will not inevitably put Russia into a political deep freeze.

The Medvedev-Putin tandem has created a precedent for parallel roles and power sharing that will have reverberations in the future. If Putin rules again after 2012, it may be in a condominium where he is not as dominant as he was before 2008. He could appoint a fresh face as prime minister and dispatch Medvedev, who has been eloquent on Russia's deficit of rule of law, to head the Constitutional Court. Conveniently and maybe not accidentally, the chair of the court was made subject to presidential appointment by a law enacted in 2009.[51] Putin could in principle flip positions a second time and make Medvedev his prime minister, having already accepted this demotion himself in 2008 with grace. Or, not to be discounted, he could consent to continuation of Medvedev—a known quantity in whom Putin has invested much—in the presidency. If so, it is doubtful that Putin would carry on as head of government, but there would be other acceptable permutations and combinations. In particular, he could relinquish the premier's post to yet another disciple while holding on to the rudder of United Russia, thereby converting the duumvirate into a triumvirate. This solution would let Putin divest himself of day-to-day control over the bureaucracy but safeguard his veto rights and, if he desired, make his way slowly toward the tutelary function that was deemed premature in 2007, or even toward the exits. Sooner or later, Putin will have to go. Sometimes the mark of a statesman, like an athlete, is to know when to leave and to find a moment of his choosing.

Whichever scenario materializes, we should follow it closely, not be fooled by appearances, and expect to be surprised. If there is any chance of Russia being reinvented as a normal modern country, we can rest assured that the leadership factor will be a key.

Notes

1. James MacGregor Burns has made the moral case that individuals who limit themselves to such methods must be seen as dominators, not true leaders. See especially his *Transforming Leadership: A New Pursuit of Happiness* (New York: Atlantic Monthly Press, 2003). Whatever box we put them in, such people need to be studied. In any event, pure dominators are few and far between. Even Hitler and Stalin used supplementary methods.
2. See especially Bryan D. Jones, ed., *Leadership and Politics: New Perspectives in Political Science* (Lawrence: University Press of Kansas, 1989), especially the chapter by Morris P. Fiorina and Kenneth A. Shepsle, "Formal Theories of Leadership: Agents, Agenda Setters, and Entrepreneurs," 17–40; Robert C. Tucker, *Politics as Leadership* (Columbia: University of Missouri Press, 1995); and Richard J. Samuels, *Machiavelli's Children: Leaders and Their Legacies in Italy and Japan* (Ithaca, NY: Cornell University Press, 2003).
3. The original statement was by David G. Winter, "Leader Appeal, Leader Performance, and the Motive Profiles of Leaders and Followers: A Study of American Presidents and Elections," *Journal of Personality and Social Psychology* 52 (January 1987): 196–202.
4. Think only of the chances of any American citizen being elected president of the United States. The odds are one in tens of millions, whereas in any given election a person's likelihood of voting for the Republican or Democratic party is about one in two.
5. Olga Kryshtanovskaya, quoted in Aleksandra Samarina, "Medvedev mezhdu proshlym i budushchem" [Medvedev between past and future], *Nezavisimaya gazeta*, September 22, 2009.
6. See especially Edward L. Keenan, "Muscovite Political Folkways," *Russian Review* 45 (April 1986): 115–81, and the discussion that followed in later issues of this journal.
7. The main exception before 1917 dates back to the seventeenth century. When the tsar died without an heir in 1682, the feeble-minded Ivan Romanov and his stepbrother Peter were proclaimed co-tsars and a special double-seated throne was built for them. Their sister Sophia governed as regent until 1689, when Peter deposed her and imprisoned her in a convent. Ivan died in 1696, after which Peter ruled unimpeded as Peter I (Peter the Great) until 1725. In the Soviet period, Nikita Khrushchev and Georgii Malenkov shared supreme power for six months in 1953. For several years after Khrushchev's removal in 1964, there was a semblance of parity between Leonid Brezhnev, the Communist Party general secretary, and Aleksei Kosygin, the

chairman of the Soviet government. Brezhnev soon imposed his authority, although Kosygin kept his job until 1980.

8. "Although the official cult discourse was employed on certain occasions, it was also ignored, misinterpreted, rejected, criticized, and subverted in various ways. Its messages did not always get through, or did so in a distorted form, either because of the inefficacy of the agitprop, or because people deliberately chose to ignore or misinterpret it. However, there were individuals who were only too well aware of the cult's omnipresence, and criticized it directly, or attacked it in other ways, which included subverting its gravity and sense of hierarchy and permanence." Sarah Davies, *Popular Opinion in Stalin's Russia: Terror, Propaganda, and Dissent, 1934–1941* (Cambridge: Cambridge University Press, 1997), 168.

9. Informally, some bosses (e.g., party first secretaries in regions) were referred to as *khozyain*, which in its most common meaning in Russian refers to the head of an extended household.

10. See Timothy J. Colton, *Yeltsin: A Life* (New York: Basic Books, 2008).

11. "In times of tremendous change, individuals often assume greater importance. Individuals, in contrast to large bureaucracies or unwieldy parliaments, can act decisively and purposefully. There was a good reason why the Roman Republic transferred the powers of the Senate to a dictator in times of crisis: A single person can react quickly to rapidly unfolding events, seizing opportunities and fending off calamities." Daniel L. Bymant and Kenneth M. Pollack, "Let Us Now Praise Great Men: Bringing the Statesmen Back In," *International Security* 25 (Spring 2001): 142.

12. Tatyana Yumasheva blog, December 23, 2009, http://t-yumasheva.livejournal.com/3609.html. See also Colton, *Yeltsin*, 431–35, which relies on interviews with Yumasheva and others. Sobchak returned to Russia in June 1999, after two years in France. He died in February 2000.

13. Boris Yel'tsin, *Prezidentskii marafon* [Presidential marathon] (Moscow: AST, 2000), 254.

14. Rostislav Turovskii, "Regional'nyye strategii kandidatov" [Regional strategies of the candidates], in *Rossiya v izbiratel'nom tsikle 1999–2000 godov* [Russia in the 1999–2000 electoral cycle], ed. Michael McFaul, Nikolai Petrov, and Andrei Ryabov, 498 (Moscow: Moscow Carnegie Center, 2000). Only one of eighty-odd provincial governors did not endorse Putin.

15. Vladimir Putin, statement to journalists, October 18, 2007, at http://kremlin.ru/appears/2007/10/18/1647_type63380_148675.shtml.

16. Timothy J. Colton and Henry E. Hale, "The Putin Vote: Presidential Electorates in a Hybrid Regime," *Slavic Review* 68 (Fall 2009): 473. See also Richard Rose, "The

Impact of President Putin on Popular Support for Russia's Regime," *Post-Soviet Affairs* 23 (April–June 2007): 97–117.

17. For most chapters of the 1993 constitution, amendment required approval by the president, two-thirds of the Duma deputies, three-quarters of the members of the Federation Council, and the legislatures of two-thirds of the territorial units of the federation. United Russia had the required majority in the Duma by the end of 2003. The Federation Council, previously dominated by governors and republic presidents, would have been as amenable by this time. Resistance from the regions was conceivable only in a few parts of the country and would not have been enough to forestall an amendment.

18. Mikhail Kas'yanov, *Bez Putina: politicheskiye dialogi s Yevgeniyem Kiselevym* [Without Putin: political dialogues with Yevgenii Kiselev] (Moscow: Novaya gazeta, 2009), 208–9. Kas'yanov states that the paragraph about a parliamentary republic had been revised but was still in the draft less than an hour before Putin delivered the speech. He does not quote the texts directly.

19. Levada Center, http://www.levada.ru/srok.html; Public Opinion Foundation, "Ratings," July 26, 2007, http://bd.english.fom.ru/report/cat/policy/services/government2/government_putin/putin/putin_summ/attitud_2007/ed073001.

20. Presidential press conference of February 14, 2008, transcript at http://kremlin.ru/appears/2008/02/14/1327_type63380type82634_160108.shtml.

21. Statement to Dutch journalists, October 31, 2005, http://kremlin.ru/appears/2005/10/31/1836_type63379_96446.shtml.

22. A Kremlin staffer told me off the record in 2004 that an amendment to give Putin extra terms would be a sign that Russia was trending in an African rather than a European direction. As he was aware, a number of African countries have abolished rulers' term limits, although in some countries (such as Nigeria and Zambia) attempts to do so have been defeated. A case closer to home for Russia is Turkmenistan, in post-Soviet central Asia, where a president for life, Saparmurat Niyazov, served from 1990 until his death in 2006.

23. Transcript of broadcast, October 25, 2006, http://www.kremlin.ru/appears/2006/10/25/1303_type82634type146434_112959.shtml.

24. Public Opinion Foundation, "Vladimir Putin After 2008: Predictions," August 9, 2007, http://bd.english.fom.ru/report/whatsnew/ed073220.

25. The letter was posted November 6, 2007, on the front page of the United Russia Web site. Partial text and commentary may be found at http://www.zaks.ru/new/archive/view/35853; and in Dmitrii Kamyshev, "I. o. tsarya" [Acting tsar], *Vlast'*, November 12, 2007. Boris Gryzlov, the party's senior official, used the term "national leader" from

the summer of 2007 until early 2008, and then quietly abandoned it.

26. In 1990 Medvedev was co-founder, with university classmates, of a small, government-controlled company in St. Petersburg called Uran. Several years later, the same group set up a consultancy group, Balfort. From 1993 to 1999 (until 1996 he was mainly employed by the city government), Medvedev was chief legal officer of Ilim Pulp, a paper-processing company based in St. Petersburg, and owned a significant proportion of its shares through a holding company. Although he never served in the security organs, "He used a connection to former KGB and military intelligence officers to help fight off a hostile takeover attempt of the lumber company." Medvedev was also associated with the Bratsk Forestry Complex and the Rus insurance company. Quotations are from *Russia Profile*, Who's Who database, s.v. "Medvedev, Dmitry Anatolyevich," http://www.russiaprofile.org/resources/whoiswho/alphabet/m/medvedev.wbp#4.

27. Vladimir Putin, October 1, 2007, http://kremlin.ru/appears/2007/10/01/1924_type63374type63376type63378type82634_146477.shtml.

28. Dmitrii Medvedev, December 17, 2007, http://kremlin.ru/appears/2007/12/17/2041_type63374type63376type82634_154550.shtml.

29. Maurice Duverger, "A New Political System Model: Semi-Presidential Government," *European Journal of Political Research* 8 (June 1980): 166.

30. Strictly speaking, the governmental chief is the "chairman of the government," but the colloquial alias "prime minister," *prem'er ministr,* has been universal except in official documents and speeches. Russia also had an elected vice president from 1991 to 1993.

31. Kas'yanov, *Bez Putina,* 124, 128, 136.

32. See prime minister's and president's Web sites.

33. Mikhail Vinogradov, quoted in Yelizaveta Surnacheva and Aleksandr Artem'ev, "Tratit' ogromnyye den'gi na govoril'nyu koshchustvenno" [It is blasphemy to spend this kind of money on a talk show], *Gazeta.ru,* December 4, 2008, http://gazeta.ru/politics/2008/12/04_a_2904095.shtml. In the past, all Russian television channels broadcast the Putin program. In 2008 and 2009 only one network and a news channel did so, and the production was less lavish.

34. Yuri Zarakhovich, "Putin Resolves Protest in Pikalevo," Jamestown Foundation, *Eurasia Daily Monitor,* June 9, 2009.

35. Transcript posted at the vesti.ru Web site. Pikalevo was one of seven localities from which Putin accepted calls during the broadcast.

36. *Forbes,* "The World's Most Powerful People," http://www.forbes.com/lists/2009/20/power-09_Vladimir-Putin_KNJM.html. *Forbes* ranked Igor Sechin, Putin's deputy

premier for industrial and energy policy, forty-second on its world list, one spot ahead of Medvedev.

37. This was the gist of Putin's comments to the Valdai Club, meeting at his Novo-Ogarevo residence on September 11, 2009. He said all the correct things about sitting down with Medvedev to work things out, but also got across that he intends to be the final authority.

38. Presidential press conference, February 14, 2008.

39. Cindy Skach, "The 'Newest' Separation of Powers: Semipresidentialism," *International Journal of Constitutional Law* 5 (January 2007): 97–98.

40. A clue may come here from the brief experience with a vice president, Aleksandr Rutskoi. The former general fell out with Yeltsin over economic and constitutional issues. Yeltsin dismissed him by decree in 1993 and wrote the office out of his new constitution. Amazingly few people, even in the anti-Yeltsin opposition, took Rutskoi's side.

41. Ivan Yartsev, "Tandem pritersya loktyami" [The tandem elbowed each other], December 4, 2009, http://politcom.ru/9245.html.

42. Dmitrii Medvedev, "Rossiya, vpered!" [Go, Russia!], September 10, 2009, http://www.kremlin.ru/news/5413.

43. Ibid.

44. Nikolai Svanidze and Marina Svanidze, *Medvedev* (St. Petersburg: Amfora, 2008), 16, 49.

45. For example, Igor Shuvalov and Igor Sechin, who were responsible for economic coordination, industrial policy, and energy on the presidential staff, now tend to the same issues as deputy prime ministers.

46. Dmitrii Kamyshev, "Kremlevskii polusrochnik" [The Kremlin's half-term man], *Vlast'*, May 10, 2010.

47. Ibid.

48. Svanidze and Svanidze, *Medvedev*, 24, 68.

49. Medvedev, "Rossiya, vpered!"

50. See especially Timothy Besley and Masayuki Kudamatsu, "Making Autocracy Work" (research paper no. 6371, Centre for Economic Policy Research, London, June 2007). The title of the paper is a pun on Robert Putnam's well-known book *Making Democracy Work*.

51. Until then, the Constitutional Court was entitled to select its own leaders. Under the new law, proposed by Medvedev, the president of Russia will nominate the chairman and two deputy chairmen, and they will need to be confirmed only by the Federation Council, where presidential suggestions are rarely flouted.

CHAPTER SIX

The Sociology of Post-reform Russia

Mikhail K. Gorshkov

Translated by Siriol Hugh-Jones

Introduction

Russian society is frequently accused of being secretive and of not lending itself to sociological analysis. It is said that it is too strange and incomprehensible for the West to understand. This is no coincidence. It is perfectly obvious that compared with most Western countries, there are certain peculiarities about Russia that complicate any analysis, assessment, or forecast of the direction of socio-economic and political change there, past and present.

Life in Russia has changed considerably in the last decade. Contemporary Russian society can be described as a relatively integrated system containing elements both of nascent capitalism and substantial remnants of the Soviet system. Is Russia a society in which the values of democracy, private ownership, market economics, and the institutions of civil society predominate? In many respects it is not. Though a constitutional republic, Russia is evidently still a long way from being a democracy: the party and parliamentary systems are not stable and the country's power division is a unique combination of a one-party state and federalism.

Although a significant portion of production resources are not state-owned, the state and the economy are closely intertwined. Enterprises remain largely dependent on the state, while various types of non-cash transactions play a huge role. Russia's place within the global economy is primarily as a raw-materials appendage. Income is created not out of any value added through manufacturing but through trade. The Russian economy is largely privatized;

markets do exist within the country. Nevertheless, Russia is yet to become either a modern market economy or a European-type consumer society.

Russian society therefore finds itself in a state of permanent transition; at the same time, no one knows exactly where it is going or how fast society is changing. Consequently, the question of Russia's future remains open on many issues. What can the current work provide to discussions about Russian identity, norms, and attitudes in this uncertain period? Quantitative sociological research can provide us with a snapshot of Russian society in the contemporary age.

First, it can show us how, amid the variegated processes associated with Russia's ongoing social, economic, and political transformations, Russian society is transforming into a more complex organism: a proliferation of social categories is now visible. Some of these groups will be more successful than others in adapting to new social and economic challenges and increasing their quality of life, while others will remain vulnerable.

Second, it can provide us with a picture of the prevalent attitudes and norms held by these groups, individuals, and society as a whole in Russia amid such transformations. It is our contention that such attitudes and norms are not predetermined by a Russian cultural archetype. Instead, degrees of both social consensus and disagreement can be witnessed in Russia's post-reform age.

Abundant empirical and quantitative figures provided here enable us to present a series of indicators for determining contemporary Russian views on a number of salient questions about the profound social, political, and economic transformations associated with post-reform Russia. These can contribute a more nuanced understanding to the more general qualitative questions of Russian identity, norms, and attitudes. Relying on the results of nationwide research conducted between 2001 and 2009 by the Institute of Sociology, Russian Academy of Sciences (IS RAS),[1] this chapter seeks to answer the following questions:

1. How does modern Russia really see itself?
2. With whom do its citizens most commonly identify themselves?
3. What do Russia's current social structure and class model represent?
4. What does it mean to be a poor, low-income, or rich Russian?
5. What are the attitudes of Russians to private ownership and their position regarding state intervention in the country's economy?

6. Does Russia have a middle class and, if so, what is it like?
7. What are the social inequalities that most concern Russians?
8. What are their values in life?
9. How has the country's political life changed over the past decade?
10. How do Russians view democracy?
11. What do they see as its shortcomings and what, in their opinions, is needed to improve the workings of democratic institutions?
12. In the conditions Russia is in today, what are the reasons for the evident decline in political engagement?
13. What are the specific foreign policy aspects of Russian identity?

There are no straightforward and simplistic associations between the modernizing components of Russia's transformation (broadly understood as nascent capitalist and democratic institutions), the more conventionally Russian statist elements, and Russian norms. Survey data confirms a more complex picture in which Russians increasingly accept some of these tendencies while rejecting others. The real social processes and attitudes of post-reform Russia suggest an open-ended state of "permanent transition" for Russia, in which the future of democratic institutions remains uncertain. We endeavor to display these in depth with quantitative figures and corresponding analysis.

The ongoing transformation entails a mixture of *real social changes* on the one hand: for example, an emerging, dynamic middle class, whose attitudes often resemble those of Western counterparts; the prevalence of vulnerable and precarious groups who, in spite of seeing a quantitative increase in certain material indicators, have not witnessed qualitative benefits—the attainment of greater degrees of social stability. It entails *attitudinal changes:* for example, the acceptance of the normative aspects of democracy while displaying cynicism to its accomplishments in practice—the acceptance of the inalienable right to own property and increasing attribution of crises to foreign decisions. It also entails *the reproduction of attitudes and norms prevalent in previous eras:* for example, dissatisfaction with the inequities in income and property distribution, and the belief in the overarching role of the state in determining economic priorities so as to ensure the interests of society as a whole.

It is in this light that the identity project associated with post-reform Russia may be understood. Appeals to a strong state and a great power resonate with a Russian populace that had been accustomed to a period of anomie and uncertainty during the 1990s, a period in which the very question of "What is Russia?" provided no simple answers. Rather than select elements to make categorical statements about the suitability or unsuitability of the Russian character to democratic and free-market transformations, we instead present our data to answer the questions listed earlier. In so doing, we hope to capture the complex nature of post-reform Russia as well as the persistent uncertainties of its future. This is based not only on the aforementioned norms that are perhaps peculiar to the Russian case, but also on the more tangible criteria of the extent of Russian society's dissatisfaction with the current system's ability to improve standards of living. The challenges faced by Russia's political system in ameliorating social conditions amid the contemporary economic crisis may tell us more about the future of democracy in Russia than appeals to innate qualities of Russia's identity.

Russia's Identity Quest

Prior to providing our quantitative figures and corresponding analysis, we consider the elusive nature of the Russian identity quest in the transitional age. Studies on Russia's identity quest, initiated in both Russia and the West, are largely influenced by the eye of the beholder.[2] Assessments of Russia's national identity often vary considerably according to subjective elements and whether the author is pessimistic or optimistic about Russia being able to successfully endure and adapt during its prolonged period of transformation. It is our intent to provide a portrayal of national consciousness, identity, and associated values in Russia as being subject to the complex processes of social, economic, and political transformation. Such a portrayal would emphasize the degree to which individual and group responses may vary (e.g., according to different socio-economic and age categories), as well as the prospect for broad degrees of social cohesion with the reproduction of general norms. While noting the potential for a reoccurrence of traditional values, such an analysis rejects timeless archetypes and stereotypes of a Russian mentality. Instead, insofar as these occur, they are subjected to sociological scrutiny.

It is important to stress that in the 1990s, Russians were confronted with the need to redefine themselves within a nation rather than empire, and within a transitional and unsettled political and economic structure. President Yeltsin's initial strategy was to articulate a Russian national identity through openly identifying himself and his economic policies with democracy while negating the lingering presence of Soviet institutions.[3] And yet it was far from a foregone conclusion that a democratic and civic definition of the Russian nation would emerge at that time. This was reflected in Russian intellectual debates, in which multiple conceptions of the Russian nation were forwarded: *a union identity*, in which Russians are deemed as an imperial people with the mission to create a supranational state; a nation of *all eastern Slavs*, who are united by common origin and culture; a *language-based definition* of the Russian nation, in which all Russian speakers are deemed part of the Russian nation irrespective of ethnic origin, *a racial* understanding of the Russian nation; and a *civic Russian (rossiiskaya) nation*, the members of which are all citizens of the Russian Federation, regardless of ethnic and cultural background, united by loyalty to the newly emerging political institutions.[4] The period of stability witnessed in the past seven to eight years has given an opportunity for this once-fledgling civic identity to emerge.

The general systemic crisis in the 1990s compromised the possibilities for any consolidation of national identity around a liberal and democratic pole. Both Russian and Western scholars have stressed the collapse of state institutions and the general state of lawlessness in Russia in the transition period.[5] In the absence of effective state institutions, a condition that in the minds of some constituted a "privatization" of the state by narrow economic forces, the development of social consensus and solidarity proved elusive.[6] To borrow a phrase from David Lane, Russia's early transitional, post-socialist political economy may be considered as a "chaotic social formation," wherein institutional coordination, governing institutions, and social cohesiveness are lacking.[7]

Amid such a period of transition, systemic crisis, and uncertainty, it is important to stress that new practices, norms, and consciousness—those that comprise identity at both the macro and micro level—would take time to become routine, habitual, and consonant with national political objectives. The liberal economic transition initiated under Yeltsin could not initially be met with a corresponding social consciousness to ensure its broad acceptance and success.[8] Indeed, the profound impoverishment and anomie experienced by much of the Russian population during "shock therapy" hardly provided fertile ground upon which a positive social consensus could emerge.[9]

The transitional period in Russia involves both the formal rewriting of rules in a political or social system as well as the processes of the transformation of social norms and attitudes. In other words, the normative and cognitive aspects of the post-Soviet social order warrant as much consideration as do formal institutional developments. Life had to be relearned. Some

Western scholars have been eager to investigate the intricacies of the micro-level sociological phenomena associated with the complexities of transitional economics, including the challenges surrounding the internalization of fiscal responsibility in "autonomous, formally free and calculative actors,"[10] or the broader project of developing and institutionalizing the norms, values, and knowledge consistent with the shift from planning to marketing.[11] Historical institutionalist arguments also are helpful, introducing the prospect for national variation in transitions, questioning the assumptions about the applicability of liberal economic laws in the Russian case due to the propensity for institutions to reproduce themselves.[12]

The reality of the need for profound social adaptation of Russian citizens and corresponding developments in Russian society may be juxtaposed against approaches that assert the timeless quality of the Russian identity. The classic Western statement of Russian cultural path dependence emphasizes Russians' preference for stability and centralization; their conservative and risk-averse tendencies; their desire for order, security, and aversion to chaos; and their overly pessimistic and cynical view of political man, among other things.[13] Exemplifying this tradition, Richard Pipes uses survey data to assert that Russians' contemporary values reflect an inherently conservative mind-set and above all a craving for stability and great power status. Such a mentality influences a "flight from freedom" and imperils the chances for democratic institutions in the country.[14] These arguments proceed from the position that there is something inherent in the Russian national character inimical to the pursuit of democracy and associated norms and attitudes. Our argument is that Russian attitudes will vary considerably on such questions, particularly amid profound transitions. For example, "modernist" and "traditionalist" attitudes, both of which are discussed in greater detail later, may be witnessed in significant numbers in contemporary Russian society.

Furthermore, that some Russians reject democratic processes is largely the result of their views of how effective these are at solving social problems and increasing their own personal well-being. Such variation does not preclude the possibility, however, of a resurgence of traditional norms and attitudes with respect to the role of the state. The relative prevalence or absence of these attitudes and norms are best demonstrated by survey data and corresponding analysis.

The Russian state would play a crucial role in the nation-building project and the consolidation of Russian national identity. This trajectory in Russia's transition was evident in the "Millennium Speech," wherein Vladimir Putin stipulated the need to reconcile Russian particularities and "traditional values"—patriotism (pride in Russia's accomplishments as a great power), "statism," and "social solidarity"—with "supranational universal values," including peace, security, a law-based society, and market relations.[15] Scholars have noted Putin's success in creating a Russian national identity in the process that combines elements of the Soviet past as well as contemporary elements. Putin is considered in the line of Russian liberal statists (*gosudarstvenniki*) who presented a Russian identity that incorporated notions of a strong state, "Great Power" Russia, order, and patriotism with liberal components. From the onset of his first administration, Putin also pursued a corresponding foreign policy that insisted upon Russian autonomy and an integrative form of patriotism predicated on Russian diversity and statism.[16] In this regard, he has been successful in focusing on the public's desire for stability and great power status after the chaotic and distressing period of the 1990s. The re-traditionalizing of Russian norms may be partly explained by these tendencies witnessed throughout the Putin era. While this has provided some grounds for social consensus, the prevailing attitudes are far more complex and must be investigated within the context of the concrete social processes evident in the post-reform age.

Ten Realities of Russia's Post-Reform Transition

THE FIRST REALITY

Having overcome the systemic crisis of the 1990s, a crisis dangerous for its ability to spread throughout and affect all aspects of society, Russia has, it seems, emerged onto a consistent trajectory and course of development. This is despite the world economic and financial crisis and, against that background, Russians' clearly deteriorating assessments of their lives (as recorded by sociologists at the beginning of 2009), the increasing numbers of Russians experiencing anxiety and shame at the country's current situation, who feel they are helpless and unable to influence what is happening around them, and who also regard the situation in the country as one of crisis (67 percent) or catastrophe (14 percent). Regardless of such trends, Russia has generally moved over the past twenty years of change, and in particular over the last ten years, from a country of reform to one of post-reform, with relatively established (and relatively consolidated) state, political, and social institutions.

We should not deny the obvious problems: the Russian economy's reliance on raw materials; the way Russia ignores the needs of consumers; the fact that its manufactured goods are extremely uncompetitive; the decline in production during the current crisis, which was relatively large in comparison with other national economies; those problems that limit Russia's enormous potential for influencing global economic processes; its weak democracy and feeble civil society; negative democratic tendencies and "neo-Soviet" social sectors; the existence of corruption leading to abuse of power; and, finally, the lack of freedom and justice. The significance of all of this is acknowledged today not just by scholars but also by the wider public and representatives of political circles. Nevertheless, we see that modern Russia "is no longer the semi-paralyzed semi-state it was ten years ago."[17]

Following the logic of arguments by Kant and Hegel, it is necessary here to differentiate what "should be" from what "is," "what should be done," and "what is actually being done"—in other words, the ideal and reality, the real practice of everyday relations. The latter is such that it allows the current period of Russian history to be evaluated as one of the quietest and most stable, inspiring certainty in the advantages of allowing reforms to evolve gradually.

The clearest examples of the spiritual, moral, and psychological renewal of Russian society are expressed in the results of an analysis of how Russians see themselves. Recent research shows that currently most of the population see themselves individually (the "I-identifier") as first and foremost Russian or Russian citizens (almost 60 percent). Identification with a particular locality or as the "representative of a specific nationality" lags far behind. We would add to this that, as concerns the wider "we-identification," more than 80 percent of the country's population feel "part of the Russian community" more or less frequently. These results indicate Russian's society's relatively high—and growing—internal integration and even the possibility within the foreseeable future of the formation of a civil nation within Russia.

Even in the early 1990s, many people did not understand what country they were living in after the collapse of the USSR. To the question, "What is Russia?" they could not give a clear answer. Now they can. From the point of view of sociology and political analysis, one term for this would be "the restoration of a great power," as we alluded to earlier. Another indicative—and notable—result is the fact that in the time it has taken for the systemic crisis to be overcome, there has been a radical rethinking of status among the population. The share of Russians who are satisfied with their social position has begun to predominate over the share of those not satisfied with it by a ratio of four to one. Today it is possible to contend that the social structure of Russian society, determined on the basis of the public's own assessments of their place within society, is approaching the model typical of countries enjoying stable development.

Sociological analysis shows that, over the past seven or eight years, the changes in people's own feelings about their positions in society have been enormous. And what they demonstrate is a significant reduction in the number of those who regard themselves as "social outsiders" and, at the same time, growth in the number of those who see themselves as middle class. This, of course, reinforces Russian social stability. Beginning with 2001–02, the results of monitoring research conducted by IS RAS show a gradual increase in those with a positive outlook due to reduced social unease and an increase in the level of adaptation by the population to conditions of social transformation. This was reflected in the reduced numbers of extremely negative and worrying assessments, not only of the overall conditions in the country but also of people's own daily lives, to the benefit of Russians' certainty in their future.

THE SECOND REALITY

Crucially, qualitative characteristics and quantitative indicators used to describe the profundity of the changes to social layering allow us to conclude that over the reform years, a new social reality has come into being in Russian society. Specifically, research results show that, in post-reform Russian society, ten social strata have replaced the Soviet Union's working class, collective farm workers, and national intelligentsia.[18] They have their own long-standing and unique interests, and the standard and quality of life of each is radically different.

An obvious nuance of Russian society is that in current conditions, the level of education or professional position held does not always determine income level or social status. This forces Russian researchers to adopt different approaches to social stratification, one of which uses standard-of-living criteria and was developed by the IS RAS. Using this approach, society can be divided into different strata on the basis of criteria relating to consumer opportunities, or the so-called standard of living index. This takes into account the wide range not only of financial but also other economic resources available to the public (in terms of personal property, where they live, etc.), and also the degree to which its members can afford to satisfy their demands in non-product-linked areas (recreation, entertainment, health care, personal development, communications, etc.). The basic theory behind the construction of the index was the suggestion that the Russian population is divided not just in terms of what families have but also what they do not have. Thus, an examination of the real standard of living includes not only an assessment of the prosperity level but also an assessment of the level of deprivation—hardships suffered and constrictions vis-à-vis common consumer benefits.[19]

Within the scope of the identified social stratification models, on the basis of the approach described earlier, the first two bottom strata comprise the sector of the population that falls below the poverty level, consisting of 16 percent of Russians. The third and fourth strata are composed of the low-income population, in which two subgroups can be identified. The third stratum is the first subgroup of those with limited, short-term income and covers Russians on the borderline of poverty (16 percent). The country's fourth stratum is the second subgroup of those with low incomes. It covers that sector of the Russian population living at what might be described as the "classic" low-income level—for Russia, the most typical level, comprising more than a quarter of the country's population (27 percent). This sector of the population can therefore be described as having low personal income.

The fifth to eighth strata, which include at least a third of the country's population, represent the middle layers of Russian society. Although there are significant differences between them, they can be regarded as relatively well-off in the general context of Russia. The same applies to those within the ninth and tenth strata, relating, at least in terms of popular opinion, to the category of the rich, but belonging, by the standards of leading Western countries, to the upper middle class (6 percent to 8 percent). Those within the fifth to tenth strata together represent the well-off among the country's population.

So, what is the outcome?

It turns out that at the beginning of 2009, 59 percent of the Russian population could be described using three standard-of-living measurements: "below the poverty level," "on the borderline of poverty," and having "low-income," while 41 percent were classed as relatively well-off (see fig. 6.1). The results obtained by sociologists are also confirmed by official data. Thus, according to the Federal State Statistics Service, in the first quarter of 2009, 17.4 percent of Russians had incomes below the minimum subsistence level

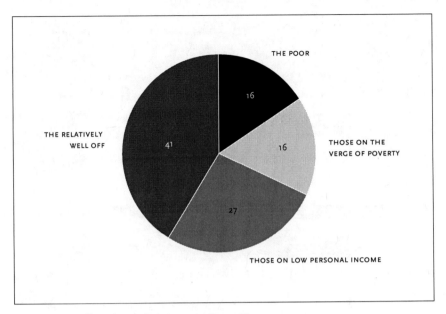

Figure 6.1   The different layers of Russian society (2009, %)

of Ruble 5,083 per person ($148.60[20]) per month.[21] This corresponds with the 16 percent of the population belonging to the two lowest strata of Russian society, below the poverty level. Moreover, the minimum wage at the time was fixed at RUB 4,330 ($126.60), or 78 percent of the minimum subsistence level for the working-age population. Despite the clear upward trend in the average monthly wage level (as of September 2009, it came to RUB 18,702 [$606.20[22]] and exceeded the September 2008 level by 4.9 percent), actual disposable income (income after deduction of mandatory payments, adjusted by the consumer price index) was 1.1 percent lower in January and September 2009 than in the same period in 2008.

THE THIRD REALITY

Among all social problems evident in Russian society today, of greatest concern are those of the poorest groups among the population. Moreover, a particular worry is not so much the number of the poor but rather the reasons for their descent into poverty. This is an indicator of both the inadequacy of state social policy and the unhealthy employment situation.

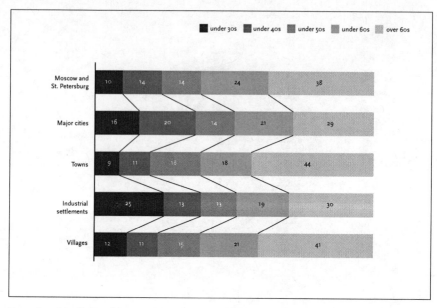

Figure 6.2   Distribution of poor among age groups in different location categories (2006, %)

From a sociological perspective, what are these problems?

First of all are the nuances of Russian poverty that relate to where people live and with their ages (see fig. 6.2), with each category having its own "set of risks."

Russian poverty is made up of specific features that together comprise an overall picture. The attributes are as follows: First, up to 40 percent of the Russian poor come from groups in the over-sixty age group. Second, poverty is concentrated in the Russian "periphery" (small towns and villages); in major cities 11 percent to 13 percent of residents are extremely poor, but in small towns and villages real poverty affects 20 percent to 30 percent of the population. As it pertains to age and location, however, the situation is reversed for those at risk of poverty (who constitute 10 percent to 15 percent of the population): the young and those in early middle age (under forty) account for more than one-third of the at-risk group. Moreover, the larger the location, the higher its share of those at risk (for example, in large cities, the share of those under forty who are "at risk" of poverty is 54 percent of respondents). Among the first to fall into the poverty trap are those with low

SOCIAL/PROFESSIONAL GROUPS	THE POOR	THOSE ON THE VERGE OF POVERTY	THOSE ON LOW INCOMES	THE WELL-OFF
1. Entrepreneurs and the self-employed	0	2	2	4
2. Managers at all levels	0	3	4	10
3. Qualified specialists/professionals (including the officer class)	13	20	22	30
4. Office workers	10	9	11	11
5. Shop workers and those working in the field of consumer services	14	22	17	12
6. Factory workers and laborers	63	44	44	33
6.1 Highly skilled workers	11	14	15	17
6.2 Skilled workers	36	24	24	13
6.3 Semi-skilled and unskilled workers	16	7	5	4

Table 6.1 Social and professional make-up of different social strata (2008, % among them who work)

levels of education and qualifications. One in four of the poor did not finish school and only one in ten has a higher-education diploma.

The social and professional structure of the working population falling below the poverty level has a series of specific features (see table 6.1).

For example, very few of these workers are qualified specialists or professionals, and a significant majority are workers in jobs requiring few qualifications. There is also a relatively high risk of poverty among lower-level workers in the service and retail sectors. Thus, it would be wrong to pretend that poverty affects only those among the Russian population who are unemployed or unable to earn an adequate level of income because of their age (pensioners) or ill-health (the disabled) and those in villages. Poverty has affected many working Russians, albeit to varying degrees, regardless of their age and place of residence. Thus, Russia faces "working poverty."

No less significant, and a phenomenon that has arisen in recent years, is the way the problem of poverty has become one of an "underclass," that of social exclusion and the formation within Russian society of a subculture of the poor, which has a particularly negative effect on young people. This trend

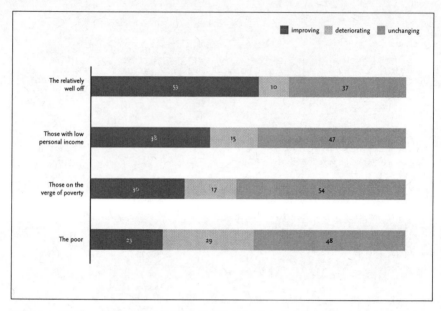

Figure 6.3   Assessment by members of different social strata of how their lives will progress in the future (2008, %)

is all the more dangerous because the poor themselves do not see any way out of their predicament (see fig. 6.3).

The poor, particularly those who have become destitute, suffer not only from a lack of money but also from an inability to meet their own most basic human needs—adequate food, clothing, and housing. Moreover, research shows that the poor lose hope and resign themselves to living without many of the essentials they can no longer afford.

THE FOURTH REALITY

The existence in the country of a great many people on low incomes, a significant number of whom are on the borderline of poverty, is a serious challenge to national social and economic policy. In conditions of slower economic growth, these people could easily slide into poverty because they have no reserves—i.e., sufficient (material or financial) resources that they could sell in order to compensate for any unexpected deterioration in their situation, such as a decline in the health of the main breadwinner. Table 6.2 provides a breakdown of average monthly incomes among different strata.

	THE POOR	THOSE ON LOW INCOMES, INCLUDING THOSE ON THE VERGE OF POVERTY	RELATIVELY WELL-OFF SECTIONS OF THE POPULATION
Monthly average per person	4,449 ($154*)	5,789 ($201)	10,279 ($357)
Personal income (wages, pension entitlement, etc.)	5,338 ($185)	7,624 ($265)	13,005 ($452)

* 1 US dollar = RUR 28.80

Table 6.2 Average monthly incomes per family member at different levels of Russian society (2008, in RUR and USD)

However, the main differences between these groups' economic situations are less evident at the income level than in terms of living standards and quality of life. The first measure of this is the level of material prosperity, which is extremely modest among these sectors of the population. For example, 45 percent of Russians on the borderline of poverty have no meaningful real estate beyond the apartment or house they live in; among the rest of the low-income population, 40 percent have no real estate other than their apartments; only 2 percent of those on the borderline of poverty and 7 percent of other low-income groups have an apartment, a car, and a dacha, the items that denote a relatively high standard of living in Russia; one in five of those on the borderline of poverty and 9 percent of those on low incomes have neither housing nor a car nor a dacha.

In terms of the living conditions of those on low incomes, 15 percent don't have their own separate housing but live in hostels and rented or communal apartments. A third of those in these sectors of society have restricted or no access to utilities (central heating, electricity, plumbing, and a bath or shower). Furthermore, 50 percent of Russians on low incomes live in housing that is below the accepted social minimum size of eighteen square

	THOSE ON THE VERGE OF POVERTY		THOSE WITH LOW PERSONAL INCOME	
	2003	2008	2003	2008
Apartment or house	69	74	75	85
Dacha or kitchen garden with house	23	15	31	21
Kitchen garden with no house	23	11	20	11
Land	12	11	13	13
Livestock	10	5	0	6
Garage or reserved place in a parking lot	18	3	26	15

Table 6.3 Property owned by Russians on low incomes and those on the verge of poverty (2003/2008, %)

meters (174 sq. ft.) per person. These people's conditions are made worse because they have gradually had to dip into their reserves, selling what property they previously had—dachas, plots of land, garages, reserved spots in parking lots—for the sake of maintaining their current standard of living (see table 6.3).

Whatever income they do earn has noticeably increased over the last six years (the same also being true of other sectors of the population). But despite the growth in income, a large proportion (43 percent) of low-income Russians believe their situation has remained unchanged over the last six years. A further 40 percent insist that it has improved. (However, the proportion of those convinced of data is but a fraction of that among the better-off sectors of the population.) Seventeen percent of those on low incomes (the overwhelming majority of whom belong to the oldest age groups) are sure that their situation has deteriorated over the past five years.

A certain increase in income, more positive assessments of specific aspects of their own lives, and an increase in the number owning durable goods indicate significant *quantitative* changes over recent years in the lives

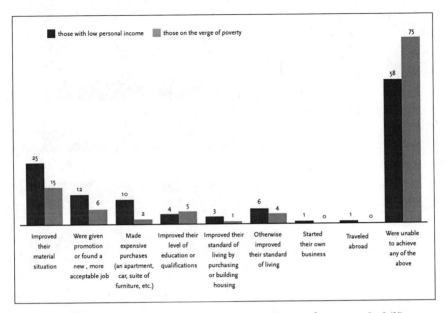

Figure 6.4   Achievements by low-income Russians and those on the verge of poverty, 2006–08 (%)

of low-income Russians. But how do things stand in regard to qualitative changes? The data we have obtained confirms that three-quarters of those on the borderline of poverty and more than half of low-income Russians have been unable to achieve any significant *qualitative* changes in their lives over recent years (see fig. 6.4).

It is clear that the material circumstances of low-income Russians have generally improved, but the change has not improved the quality of their lives as a whole. Thus, the condition of these sectors of the population remains at a level no higher than "relatively stable survival." This suggests that any progress in the state of low-income sectors of the population is inconsistent. On the one hand, their incomes have gone up, as has their access to the cheapest durable goods. On the other hand, the level of ownership of genuinely valuable real estate (at least by their standards) has fallen. By any genuinely meaningful standard-of-living parameters, their situation over recent years has indeed deteriorated.

In addition, low-income Russians use paid amenities relatively rarely—i.e., they do not invest in themselves or their children, and over recent years their

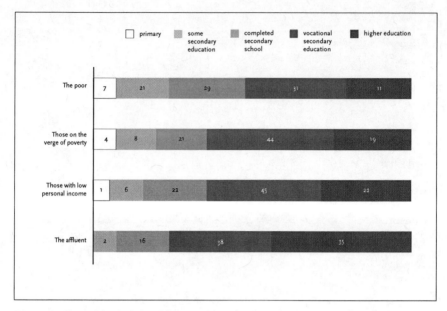

Figure 6.5   Education levels among different social sectors (2008, %)

use of such amenities has declined even further. This is a severe impediment to improving employment opportunities and life skills. The relatively low use of paid amenities by low-income Russians can be explained by the fact that they are in the worst position at the outset: they grow up in families with little education, largely in small towns and villages. As a result, their education level is lower than that of better-off sectors of the population (see fig. 6.5). And even when their education level is, objectively speaking, equal, they have fewer life skills—a most important resource, helping those who have them gain relative success.

Socially and professionally, the low-income sectors of the population in Russia today are quite disparate. Thus, 44 percent of those on low incomes are workers, two-thirds of whom should be treated as having only very basic or intermediate qualifications. About a quarter of those in this sector are highly qualified, while the rest work in retail or the service sectors. A feature of most of the manufacturing positions occupied by low-income Russians is their instability. Almost a third of rank-and-file workers in retail and services are worried about losing their employment as a result of stiff competition for the jobs they occupy, caused, among other things, by intensive migration into a country with a large unskilled workforce.

Among the working population, 67 percent of those with low personal incomes and 75 percent of those on the borderline of poverty are concentrated in small towns and villages, despite the fact that only 60 percent of the working population live in small towns and villages. Thus, those in Russia on low incomes are today concentrated not so much in social sectors distinguished by the level of their qualifications as in the Russian provinces, with their narrow and depressed labor markets in which people are forced to agree to whatever work and wage is offered and where there is, as yet, no significant demand for skilled workers.

A large proportion of low-income city-dwellers are able to "keep their heads above water" and not slide into poverty thanks to their having second occupations. However, were there to be any recurrence of economic crisis, they could end up on the borderline of poverty or poor (as happened with the last crisis). This is an indication of the lack of stability among the population, even in major and medium-sized towns and cities.

Among other factors leading to low-income levels, socio-demographic inequality plays a major role, and this has further increased its influence over the last six years. Such inequalities are primarily associated with age (the older a sector of the Russian population is, the larger its share of poor and those on low incomes) and health (any deterioration of which leads to an increased risk of falling into poverty or the low-income bracket). It is therefore not surprising that the most vulnerable group among the Russian population is pensioners, half of whom fall into the low-income bracket and a further 30 percent of whom are poor (see fig. 6.6).

Apart from people's individual characteristics such as age or state of health, their family status also influences the risk of their falling into poverty or the low-income bracket. Financial problems are most easily resolved by those who are not married and who, as a rule, have none of the burdens associated with dependants.

Another important risk factor for those on low incomes concerns the nature of regional socio-economic development. Whereas regions classed as "zones of economic growth" have a higher proportion of the relatively affluent among their population, others are divided into two groups. The first is identifiable by its high proportion of people on low incomes; the second by its high proportion of the poor. Evidently, social policies adopted by the regions

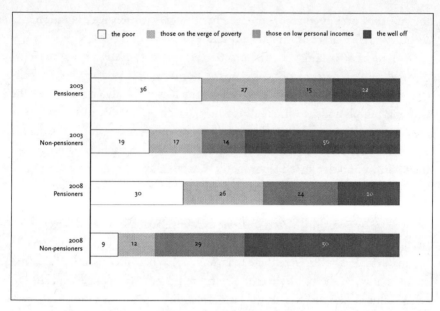

Figure 6.6 Different social sectors divided into pensioners and non-pensioners (2003/2008, %)

to solve problems of poverty and low incomes vary in degrees of effectiveness, and this can affect the social structure of those regions.

Overall, many social groups are underprivileged as an indirect result of the institutional conditions of Russians' lives, as well as of mistakes in health care reform and pension-fund policy. Inadequate provision for the elderly and restrictions on certain population groups' access to the employment market as a whole, and certain sectors in particular, are reflections of these mistakes.

THE FIFTH REALITY

A large middle class has developed in Russia over the reform years, which, though similar to the general population in terms of its principal features, places particular emphasis on achievement. This means that all resources are devoted to continuing professional development, leading ultimately to professional success. Sociologically speaking, the modern Russian middle class is made up of those who have been able to adapt successfully to the new social reality, are rightly proud of this, and, unlike the lower classes, feel in charge of their own destinies.

The four main approaches used to distinguish the middle class are:

1. The *marketing approach*, which considers the middle class as that large social grouping characterized primarily by a relatively high standard of living and level of consumption, whose members are distinguished by the level of their per capita income and/or existence of a certain range of valuable assets.
2. The *subjective approach*, which emphasizes how individual members see themselves and assess their social status. According to this approach, nearly 48 percent of Russian citizens identify themselves as middle class.
3. The *resource-based approach*, which takes into account not only movable and immovable property but also details of the volume, type, and structure of the assets (or resources) the middle class has at its disposal. It also considers their life skills and the nature of their employment (whether they are blue- or white-collar workers).
4. The *integrated approach*, the most common approach in both Russia and the world in general, is based on the indicators listed above (professional characteristics, education, property, and income levels and how they see themselves).

However, there is no consensus in Russia on just how this group of indicators should be applied in any definition of the middle class. Consequently, the use of different methods and indicators to define the middle class gives rise to a tenfold variation in the numbers of the middle class in contemporary Russian society—from 2.1 percent[23] to about a fifth of the population.[24]

Taking into account the nature of social and professional status (white-collar employment criteria), education (having at least a secondary-school vocational education), level of affluence (average per capita incomes no lower than the median for that class of population or the number of those owning durable goods valued no lower than the median value for the population as a whole), and how people see themselves (people's own integrated assessment of their social position on a scale of one to ten of from five upwards), we can see that by the end of 2008 no less than 30 percent of the population was middle class.

In the pre-crisis period, the middle class expanded rapidly thanks to its borderline members (those who met all but one of the criteria for membership of the middle class). Despite the numbers of borderline members of the

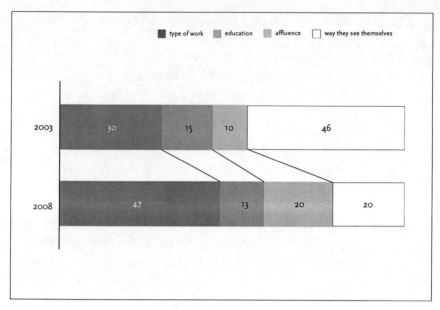

Figure 6.7 Criteria that representatives of the border-line middle class "did not meet" (2003/2008, %)

middle class (reflected in fig. 6.7), unless Russian society is modernized, the scope for any further increase in this social grouping is limited in practical terms, and its numbers in the next few years will vary between 30 percent and 35 percent of the country's working population. Moreover, the trend toward middle-class expansion was also disrupted by the 2009 crisis. Judging by the results of research, by spring 2009 the overall numbers of the middle class as a share of the population had declined from a third to a quarter (26 percent) and the share of middle-class members of the working population had declined from more than 40 percent to 30 percent.

Research shows that the Russian middle class's standard of living is relatively modest (see table 6.4), which casts doubt on its ability to resolve its immediate social problems on its own (acquisition of housing, covering increased costs of housing and public utilities, payment for health care and education, etc.) when such problems occur all at once.

In terms of property ownership, the middle class differs from other large sectors of the Russian population (see fig. 6.8), although the difference is more quantitative than qualitative and not particularly great.

	SOCIAL STRATUM LEVEL 5	SOCIAL STRATUM LEVEL 6	SOCIAL STRATUM LEVEL 7	SOCIAL STRATUM LEVEL 8
Average monthly earning per capita	6,994* $243	8,203 $285	9,712 $337	11,786 $409

*1 US dollar = RUR 28.80

Table 6.4 Monthly incomes within the Russian middle classes calculated per family member (2009, in RUR and USD)

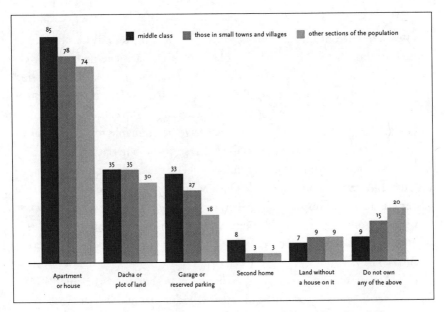

Figure 6.8 Property owned by the middle class and other sections of the population (2006, %)

As far as possession of durable goods is concerned, the difference between the real standard of living of the middle class and that of the rest of the population is very obvious.

In terms of household goods, the main difference between the middle class's standard of living and that of other population sectors is the enormous number of hi-tech goods owned by the middle class—computers, video cameras, and digital equipment. This is true regardless of age: even among those aged fifty-one to sixty, more than half have a home computer, whereas only 15 percent of Russians in this age group who are not middle class have a computer at home.

A major feature of everyday middle-class behavior that distinguishes it from the rest of the Russian population is the active use of paid amenities. Given that paid education, health care and medical, and other services are essentially an investment in the development of human potential and life skills, we can say that the middle class actively invests in itself and its children. This is reflected in the different opportunities those in the Russian middle class have in life, which suggests that they have realistic chances of improving their lives. Thus, if one looks at how real achievements in different areas of activity vary between different population groups for the period 2006–08, the middle class's typically positive assessment (in 2008) of its present and future turn out to be fully justified (see fig. 6.9).

Overall, 28 percent of the middle class have been unable to achieve any of the items listed in fig. 6.9, whereas for the rest of the population it is 67 percent. Thus, there is a positive dynamic typical of the middle class that manifests itself in concrete and tangible ways, while most of those in other social classes are unable to improve their lives in this way. The Russian middle class stands out from the rest of the population by its living standards, and this difference is reflected in the level of demand among members of different social classes.

IS RAS's numerous sociological measurements show that the middle class does not act as one. On top of the differences within the middle class itself, there also are significant differences between the cities and the provinces, such that Moscow, for example, is closer to Western capitals in terms of its standard of living, employment structure, and mentality. There also have been significant changes in recent years in the social and professional makeup of the Russian middle class. Some of these changes are associated with the general growth in the Russian economy and the corresponding expansion of the middle class, while others concern a

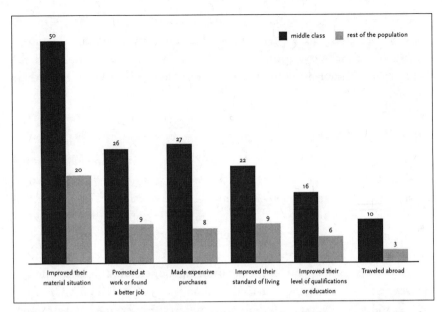

Figure 6.9 Share of those who in 2006–08 were able to make significant improvements to their lives of one kind or another, divided by social group (% of those among them making these improvements)

change of situation on the employment market, allowing public-sector workers to improve their situations relatively quickly. Others still are linked to the growth in importance of professional practices and ability, regardless of position held.[25]

Many Russians are prepared to adopt a broad-minded approach to "the wealthy," considered here not the elite of society—from whom most are far removed and who are more readily associated with the terms "power" (*vlast*) and "riches"—but, rather, the upper middle class, who most Russians think of as being securely provided for in material terms. Results of research indicate that Russians' *images* of the rich are of someone with a per capita monthly income of about $3,000–$4,000 in the provinces and $5,000 in Moscow and St. Petersburg. At first glance, the low threshold of the definition of "rich" may be surprising. One should not forget, though, that the income level at which wealth begins, the decisive influence on Russians' perceptions is their own, extremely unenviable, material position. The rich are, in modern Russia, made up primarily of relatively young entrepreneurs. Whereas the average age of the middle class is forty-two, the average age of the rich is thirty-three.

As the rich themselves would agree, the main differences between their lives and the lives of all other sectors of society are a much higher standard of living, the ability to acquire a good education, the spending of holidays abroad, the availability to them of high-quality medical services, and the ability their children have to achieve a great deal more in life than others their age.

THE SIXTH REALITY

Russians' greatest dissatisfaction is caused by the extreme inequality in the distribution of property and income. Moreover, it is not only their personal interests that determine people's position on the question of the fairness of one or the other inequality, but also general ideas of social justice as being a social and cultural norm, typifying Russian society at the current stage of its development. The public response to social inequality in Russia today stems from Russians' basic moral and social outlook. Concretely, this is manifested as discontentment with the social and economic conditions laid down in Russia over the reform years, including how property and income are distributed (see fig. 6.10). Moreover, individual-level protests spread to the macro level, mutating from individuals' dissatisfaction with their own positions to general dissatisfaction with the new social system as a whole.

Next in the scale of injustices comes inequality in the field of medical care, which only 33 percent of Russians consider to be fair. Russians regard the remaining inequalities as legitimate. These relate to inequality in the pension level taking previous salary into account, inequality in living standards, and inequality in the ability to give one's children a better education. Thus, one can conclude that Russians are relatively tolerant of most "day-to-day" social inequalities, with the exception of inequalities in the provision of medical care.

Does this mean that Russian citizens are committed opponents of private ownership? No, not at all. Suffice it to say that around 90 percent of Russians agree that private ownership should be an inalienable right for everyone. The problem is not one of Russians' negative attitudes about private ownership in general, but about the legitimacy of how it is distributed throughout society when all the national wealth created through the labor of many generations and the country's "God-given" natural resources have, literally overnight, been concentrated in the hands of a small group of large property-owners.

Research has shown that property is one of the most important aspects of social inequality in Russians' everyday lives. About 60 percent of the

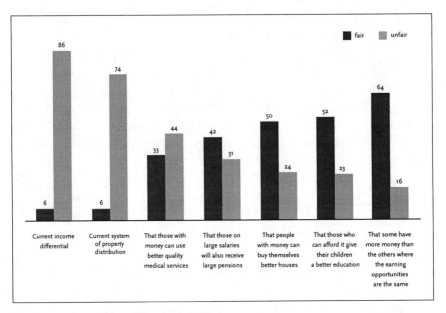

Figure 6.10 Russians' ideas of fairness (2008, %)

country's population have neither property—apart from the housing they live in (which in most cases is of very poor quality)—nor savings. Half of them have debts of one sort or another. At the same time, the social inequalities existing in post-reform Russian society cannot be reduced merely to inequality of income. Rather, they are apparent in the varying quality of different aspects of life: differing positions from a social, psychological, and health point of view, as well as the availability of both opportunities and ways of adapting to the new system.

The results of research in 2009 suggest that 18 percent of Russians believe their lives are going well, 12 percent that they are going badly, and 70 percent deem their lives "satisfactory." Thus, Russians' positive assessments of their lives currently outweigh negative assessments. However, compared with 2008 these assessments are considerably worse. A year ago, 30 percent of the population thought their lives were going well and only 7 percent thought they were going badly. In the period from 1994 to 2000, negative evaluations of their lives exceeded positive evaluations. In 2001 this relationship changed, and over the years since then the share of positive evaluations has exceeded the negative. However, it is likely that the negative trend that appeared in 2009 under the influence of the crisis will persist.

THE SEVENTH REALITY

Despite the radical nature of the social and economic changes that have occurred in the country, the socio-cultural stereotypes that determine Russian citizens' overall consciousness are evolving relatively smoothly, while Russian society continues to pass on its basic values.

IS RAS research indicates that attitudes about the meaning of life prevalent in the general consciousness show the typical Russian to be someone prepared for unexpected developments, well able to adapt, inclined to act autonomously and to regard the purpose of life less as the accrual of material comforts as the attempt to live as he or she pleases, deriving maximum moral satisfaction in the process. It is no coincidence that two-thirds of the Russian population define freedom as the ability to take control of their own lives.

For Russians, family is the most important aspect of their lives (see table 6.5). What is more, family has enormous significance for all population groups, irrespective of worldview, age, or income.

In post-reform Russia those with traditional, paternalist views coexist with those for whom ideas of personal responsibility, initiative, and personal freedom take precedence—i.e., those with a modernist outlook. There is also a third sector of the population, which can be described as representing an "interim" state of mind, combining elements of traditionalism and modernism. In recent years, the number of modernists has slightly fallen while that of traditionalists has grown; the frequency of those with an "interim" outlook has remained virtually unchanged (see fig. 6.11). This trend has affected all age groups—even those under twenty-five (where the percentage of modernists has fallen from 37 percent to 27 percent compared with 2004, and the percentage of traditionalists has grown from 29 percent to 39 percent).

What do these results indicate? It would seem that despite the influence of transition processes, traditional values are reestablishing their influence over society. Thus, the values and ideas that are crucial to the Russian mentality continue to demonstrate remarkable resilience.

The worldview of each group leads to a particular set of social ideals. Particularly interesting in this respect are the largely polarized positions of the modernists and traditionalists. These groups have profound disagreements over the country's history, which era they would like to live in, the nature of

	VERY IMPORTANT	RELATIVELY IMPORTANT	RELATIVELY UNIMPORTANT	NOT IMPORTANT AT ALL
FAMILY	91	8	1	0
FRIENDS	58	35	7	0
FREE TIME	46	40	12	1
POLITICS	10	26	46	18
WORK	64	28	5	2
RELIGION	18	36	32	13

Table 6.5 Russians' opinions on the importance to them of certain aspects of their social and personal lives (2007, %)

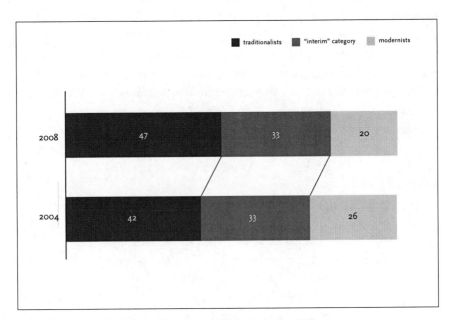

Figure 6.11 Russians divided into categories by world view (2004/2008, %)

reforms, which social forces enable development and which prevent it, and, most importantly, the place of an all-powerful state and the freedom of the individual. Whereas modernists place importance on personal freedom and accept the Western model of development, along with its values, as perfectly applicable to Russia, traditionalists as well as those in the interim group deem this unacceptable. Instead, they favor Russia's traditional, state-led model of development based on an all-powerful state, which serves primarily as an expression of common interests and aims at protecting both the individual citizen and society as a whole.

Furthermore, the Soviet paradigm, which was disrupted in the first half of the 1990s, demonstrates surprising resilience in the contemporary period. Consequently, despite existing variations in the ways different generations and regions experienced Russian history, the overwhelming majority of Russians continue to regard the events and achievements of the Soviet era as major sources of national pride, ruling out any possibility of Russian society being divided in terms of its values.

THE EIGHTH REALITY

The past twenty years of modern Russian history have been marked by profound changes in the country's political life. But despite the extent of these changes, post-communist Russia can still be described as a society "in transition," the prospects for the democratic evolution of which are by no means certain. Among the main obstacles to the development of democracy in Russia, the finger is pointed not only at the country's leaders but also at society itself, which has apparently been disappointed in democracy. Research over recent years by a number of different sociological centers indicates that the situation concerning democracy in Russia and its acceptance by the country's population is not as straightforward, unequivocal, or hopeless as is sometimes imagined.

First of all, it should be remembered that Russians have no particular problem understanding what does and does not constitute democracy. This understanding was established as early as Gorbachev's "perestroika" period and, overall, differs little from how the world in general understands democracy. A significant number of Russians adhere to many democratic values and institutions: the electability of those in authority; freedom of speech and of the press; freedom of movement, including freedom to travel abroad; and freedom of enterprise. What's more, Russian attitudes toward these values and institutions have remained largely unchanged over the last ten years (table 6.6).

Rather more complicated are Russian attitudes toward the party system—only just over a third of those asked (36 percent) acknowledge its importance, while 43 percent believe they can do without it. Fundamental to the current social condition are, so Russians believe, those criteria and elements that make an efficient democratic system possible. These include the equality of all before the law; an independent judiciary and political pluralism; free elections, including the election of heads of state; and no excessive social or property divide. Moreover, the results of IS RAS research indicate that over the past decade social and political practice has, to an extent, changed Russians' ideas regarding the importance of the various components of democracy.

Throughout the period, the legal basis of democratic government and an independent judiciary remained extremely topical, and their importance even grew over these years. On the other hand, other items have become less topical. These are, primarily, freedom of the press and the ability to voice one's political opinions freely. While accepting that elections are relevant as an essential instrument to legitimize those in power, noticeably fewer respondents suggest they find it difficult to envisage democracy without political competition or the presence of an opposition. This is a particularly worrying symptom, evidence of certain "backward trends," including some the public is conscious of—the preservation of formal elections procedures but with less freedom to represent alternative points of view in the press and with political parties not being given equal treatment.

It is a sociological point of principle that Russians clearly distinguish normative ideas on democracy (how and what it should be) from what is actually happening in Russia. The main claim against the version of democracy being implemented in Russia is its lack of effectiveness—above all as concerns those institutions whose function it is to express and protect the public's interests. Research has exposed a paradox—it is those very institutions that by their nature and purpose should "play on society's side," so to speak, and express and represent people's interests that enjoy less support than the authorities, including the *siloviki*. As is clear from the data set out below (see fig. 6.12), Russians are least of all inclined to trust political parties, the judicial system, the militia (police), trade unions, the State Duma (lower house of parliament), the press—both in printed and electronic form—and social services. Only human rights, women's, war veterans', and environmental

	1997	2000	2003	2007
MULTI-PARTY SYSTEM				
Important	39	26	29	36
Not important	36	50	50	43
Not sure	25	24	21	21
THE EXISTENCE OF REPRESENTATIVE AUTHORITIES (THE FEDERATION COUNCIL, STATE DUMA ETC.)				
Important	50	39	50	50
Not important	20	33	25	28
Not sure	30	29	26	22
FREEDOM OF ENTERPRISE				
Important	63	57	62	58
Not important	16	22	19	23
Not sure	22	21	19	19
FREEDOM OF SPEECH AND OF THE PRESS				
Important	86	77	75	70
Not important	5	10	12	17
Not sure	9	13	14	13
FREEDOM TO TRAVEL ABROAD				
Important	68	52	56	60
Not important	17	30	30	25
Not sure	15	18	15	15
ELECTABILITY OF AUTHORITIES				
Important	76	64	77	70
Not important	9	15	10	15
Not sure	15	21	13	15

Table 6.6 Russian citizens' ideas of what is important and what is not important to them in modern Russian society (%; one answer was permitted for each item)

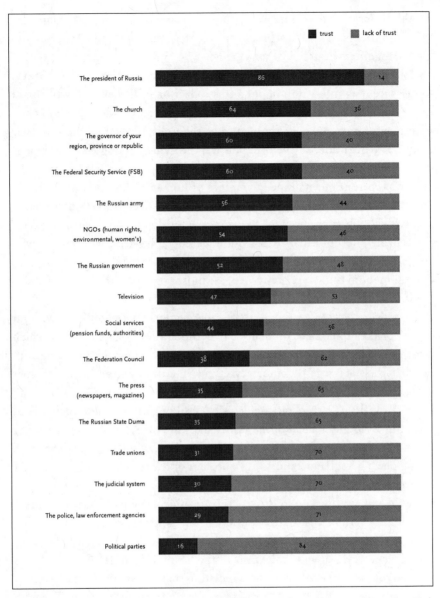

Figure 6.12 Level of trust/lack of trust in state and social institutions (2007, %; one answer was permitted for each item)

organizations and the church enjoy public support. The highest degree of trust is in the "power vertical"—the president, government, and regional governors, together with the FSB and army.

When we talk of the effectiveness of democracy, it is important not just to measure it as an institution but also a reflection of the level of public trust in the authorities and social institutions. This is a much wider phenomenon with many more variables: the nature of the political regime, the influence democratic institutions have over politics, the dynamics of growth and quality of life, the level of social protection given to those in employment, the extent of corruption, genuine guarantees of human rights and civil liberties, and the like. Together, these have long been relatively successfully identified within public opinion as "the workings of democracy." Most Russians (72 percent) are not satisfied with how democracy works, while those who are satisfied represent a mere 28 percent. The successful sector of society, those for whom things are going well, are most satisfied with the way Russia's model of democracy works.

It is clear that we are seeing that stable democracy cannot exist without a level of economic development that permits a level of prosperity, which most people regard as acceptable. At the same time, it would not be right to say that Russians regard democracy exclusively through the "prism of their purse." They simply want a government that calls itself democratic to do all it can to "fulfill" its democratic reforms by resolving key social problems. And since this is not done in all of the places all of the time, it is hardly surprising that a significant number of Russian citizens refuse to call the transformation taking place here democratic. Only 5 percent of those asked believe that over the last fifteen years a democracy that fully meets their conceptions of what it should be has grown up in Russia. Twenty-nine percent of Russians believe that despite serious costs, Russian democracy is nevertheless close to being optimal. However, 43 percent are convinced that Russia today is as far away from democracy as it was in the time of the Soviet Union (see fig. 6.13).

The young, active sector of the population that represents the backbone of the group described as "modernist" agrees more frequently than others with the point of view that "Russia is already a democratic country" or "on the way there." The opposite view is more frequently held by elderly Russians and by those living in the Russian provinces—i.e., by those generally described as traditionalists. But both groups are relatively restrained in their assessments and judgments of the type of democracy achievable for Russia.

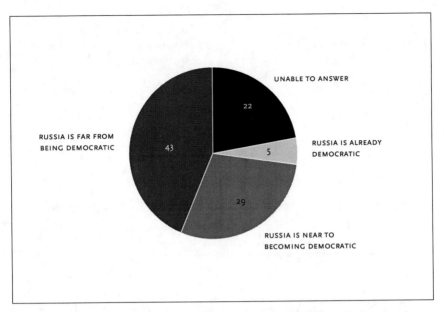

Figure 6.13 The opinion of Russian citizens on how far Russia has progressed over the years since the collapse of the USSR in terms of building democracy (2007, %; one answer only was permitted)

The research results indicate that the Russian perception of the normative model of democracy and its basic values differs little from what is the case in so-called developed democracies. At the same time, the positive attitude to the values of democracy is generally mixed with skepticism regarding its practical potential. This in turn means that democratic values do not yet affect the behavior and attitudes of the majority of the population. Many Russians, while acknowledging the priority and relevance of such values, also believe that in the conditions affecting Russia today, such values can for various reasons be ignored in order to allow people to achieve their aims in life or adapt to the new order. Russian democracy is thus implemented primarily as a "normative model" but does not expand into a "democracy of participation," while most of the public continue to regard it with "well-meaning skepticism."[26]

In Russia, there is an ingrained opinion that social and political participation is of little use. Over the last two decades, an entire generation has grown up that expects nothing from the authorities or from social institutions, preferring to take care of themselves. Generally, they channel their energy into fields far removed from politics. Since 2001 the share of Russians taking an

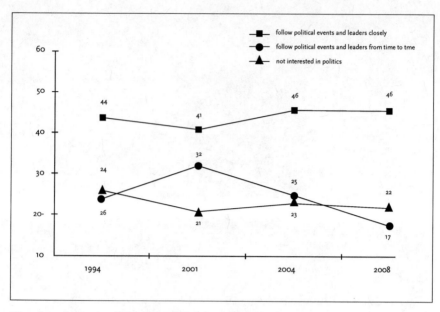

Figure 6.14 Are Russians interested in politics? (1994–2008, %)

active interest in politics has fallen (see fig. 6.14). Most Russian citizens take an interest in politics from time to time, mainly upon the occurrence of significant events in the life of the country.

Research results suggest that on this issue, the main difference is age: the younger the respondent, the less frequently he or she takes an interest in political events.

The evident decline in political engagement over the last ten years is objectively predetermined by a whole series of reasons and circumstances associated both with the authorities and with the evolution of Russian society itself. The latter has ceased to require that its citizens be proactive within the community or that professional success be conditional upon their participation in the life of the community. Consequently, the overwhelming majority of Russians make the "sensible choice": if social or political engagement brings no direct material or career advantages and no social advancement, people will channel their energies into other fields—work, education, family, children, their close circles, creativity, religion, leisure activities, and so forth. Russians now have private lives and the freedom to choose whether to participate or not. Judging by the current level of political engagement, many have taken full advantage of the right of nonparticipation.

Russians believe that the best policy in life is the organization of social and economic niches within their own immediate circles—niches in which people feel at home. In other words, the emphasis is on themselves or their close circles—family, friends, work mates, etc.—whereas the relationship between the state and society is increasingly along the lines of "you leave us alone and we'll leave you alone."

THE NINTH REALITY

One of the most important objects of public attention for Russians—in a sense indicative of the way they perceive the world—is the place and role of the state in the economy and society. Russians mainly support state domination of the economy and administration of property.

Does this mean that a majority of the population advocates re-nationalization of absolutely everything and in particular a transition to a planned economy? Again, no, not so.

According to the results of IS RAS research, this is, first of all, because Russians have no objection to a market economy as such, although most of them reject the particular model that currently exists in Russia. This is not only because they themselves have lost out in the process of its establishment but also because, as far as they are concerned, it damages the interests of the state and society as a whole.

Second, despite the fact that Russians believe that all strategic sectors (the electricity energy, mining industry, transport, etc.) should be state-run, there is a series of nonstrategic sectors, particularly associated with everyday consumer items, in which most people would allow a mixed economy to prevail. This includes the construction and maintenance of housing, the media, road building, the financial sector, telecommunications, and the food industry. Although Russians do not allow the private sector to dominate any field, even the older generation prefers to see a mixed economy in Russia where the state sector co-exists with the private sector in a series of nonstrategic fields under overall state control, with the state having to align private-sector interests with the interests of the state as a whole. This means that most Russians expect the government to implement a model of state capitalism appropriate for an economically developed country.

Typical of the national consciousness in post-reform Russia is a sharp increase in the specific weight that public opinion gives to assessing the direction of foreign policy. The Russian public's attention to international events and processes affecting Russia's interests now almost matches that usually given to events and processes within the domestic arena.

In terms of sociological interpretation, it is worth noting how rare it is for the population to be almost as interested in the foreign-policy aspects of governmental activity as it is in its domestic policy. There are reasons for this. By the mid 1990s, many Russians had gradually become convinced that however tempting the Western approach to development (which Russia had already had a taste of), it was not acceptable to Russia. Consequently, Russian society's cultural and historical uniqueness began to be interpreted as an immutable fundamental value. Under the new paradigm, the relationship between "us" and "them" began to be reassessed, including in terms of the state's foreign-policy aims. This mentality has been reinforced by recent events. For example, a nationwide poll by IS RAS in September 2008 on the subject of "Phobias and threats in the Russian popular consciousness" showed that the reaction of Western countries to Russia's response to Georgia's attack on South Ossetia only reinforced the Russian public's anti-Western stance.[27]

We see that the West appears in various incarnations within the Russian consciousness. These alternate depending on the specific context. In terms of the main subject of international relations, it is represented by various political, military/political, and economic structures, the most problematic of which for Russians is NATO, the Russian public's attitude to which has been persistently negative for some years. Thus, according to these polls, the very word "NATO" arouses negative emotions among almost 80 percent of those questioned. Similarly, in the public consciousness, a stream of negative associations also accompanies the image of the United States and American politics. Whereas in 1995 more than 77 percent of respondents were favorably disposed to any reference to the United States, by the beginning of the twenty-first century that share had fallen to 37 percent, and after the five-day war in the Caucasus (in August 2008) the level of Russian sympathy toward any reference to the United States dropped to 14 percent.

When explaining Russian public opinion on Russia's place in the world, we cannot ignore the question of the public attitude toward the various processes that dictate how the modern world operates. Here it is worth noting that Russian attitudes toward various transnational structures are very cautious. For example, on the question of their attitude toward the IMF and the WTO, Russians were virtually evenly divided (50 percent to 52 percent gave them a positive assessment overall, while 46 percent to 47 percent were put off by them). The word "globalization" currently carries predominantly negative associations (in the case of 58 percent of respondents, it arouses negative feelings and only 40 percent view it positively), while "anti-globalists" have the sympathies of virtually two-thirds of the Russian public.

What do Russians think of the prospects for Russian integration into the EU? In 2002, the number of "Euro-optimists" linking Russia's future with its entry into a united Europe noticeably exceeded the number who saw no particular point in this (the "Euroskeptics") by 42 percent to 30 percent. By the beginning of 2009, it was an entirely different picture: opponents of union with the European Union made up 50 percent while only 30 percent of Russians were Euro-optimists.

Does this data mean that most Russians are outspoken adversaries of any rapprochement between Russia and Europe? No, not at all. This is not so even where Russian popular psychology and culture, as well as the specific foreign-policy situation, impose a whole series of limitations on any rapprochement. Unlike any other aspect of foreign policy, greater integration with Europe would not subject Russian society to any unwelcome psychological tensions and would not provoke any significant religious differences. Figuratively speaking, the implementation of a sensible policy of rapprochement with Europe would not require Russians to compromise themselves. And that in itself is quite important. Ultimately, the European way can be accepted by all the mainstream social-democrat groups and sectors of the population with no particular internal resistance (though with certain provisos). Of course, this would be subject to the condition that a movement in this direction would not cause Russians any obvious or painful disappointment, which depends not just on Russia but on its partners.

Conclusions: The Next Stage in Russia's Transition

Analysis of the dynamics of the public national consciousness shows that post-reform Russia is not only on its feet but indeed capable of self-determination and self-affirmation. Over the past seven or eight years, Russia has succeeded in taking control of itself and has turned into a country with an independent destiny and its own plans for the future.

Of course, there is still a significant amount of work to do to construct a new, free, thriving, strong Russia. The possibilities for improving the social situation are today determined both by the current financial and economic crisis—which, at the end of 2008/beginning of 2009, evolved from being a virtual crisis, manifest in people's moods, of concern and even panic—to a real crisis. The overwhelming majority of the population have begun to feel its negative effects to varying degrees, whether directly (through the loss of jobs or reduced salaries) or indirectly (price hikes, particularly on imports). A particular type of at-risk group has come into being, making up about 15 percent of Russians, whose losses from the crisis are, according to their own estimates, extremely substantial.

Against this background, the public attitude to the surrounding social reality is changing. Instead of confidence that Russia is a successful country with a lengthy period of gradual economic and social development ahead of it and increasing prosperity among the population, there is a feeling of uncertainty. Nonetheless, stability is maintained amid conditions of crisis, as only about a quarter of Russians attribute responsibility for the crisis to the government and other authorities. Most of those questioned thought that the main reason for the crisis was the economic policies of leading Western countries, primarily the United States.

Overall, those Russians questioned did not anticipate any serious political upheavals, revolutions, or even significant changes to those in government as a result of the crisis. In their opinion, it was fairly likely there would be mass social protests demanding changes in economic policy. However, only 5 percent of the population were definitely prepared to participate in such acts of protest, which is little different from the pre-crisis period. This is due to the lack of any political culture of protest and ineffective trade unions, which are fearful of relinquishing even those few guarantees of which the population is assured.

Most Russians believe the crisis will be relatively long term, possibly lasting for two or three years. They are not yet prepared, however, to make radical changes to their lives, to retrain, or to move from their homes. As a result of the economic crisis, the ratings of those at the top of the government began to fall, particularly compared with when they enjoyed greatest support—in spring/summer 2008. The drop in ratings has been gradual and spread evenly across virtually all social and age groups. The "power duumvirate" of Putin-Medvedev has not yet elicited great opposition or charges of ineffectiveness. The main political victims of the crisis are the regional and local authorities. As the elections held in a number of regions at the beginning of March 2009 showed, there is obvious dissatisfaction in the country with the acting heads of municipalities, and the elections themselves were more fiercely contested than in the recent past.

The crisis has not increased the level of trust in political parties, including the opposition. This means that the transformation of the political system is more likely to be linked to the political resuscitation of other social institutions, perhaps the trade unions or municipalities, while the party system as it exists now remains relatively unchanged.

The crisis has shown not only the potential for political stability but also the inertia within Russian society and the economy, the inability to adopt and follow imaginative decisions, change economic policy, or construct new social mechanisms. This creates the risk of certain features of the crisis stagnating in the medium to long term and gradually turning an economic crisis into a systemic crisis of government.

Evidently, the way out of this situation should not just be an economic one, envisaging an "intelligent" solution, capable of producing proprietary knowledge, importing the newest technology, and results of innovatory economic activity, but also modernization of the social system as a whole. This would, albeit gradually, resolve many of the most difficult questions—including such as how to withstand the global crisis and the challenges of competition, modernize the army, and govern a country that is both enormous and complicated in its national and cultural makeup. In the process, the country's democratic institutions would be strengthened and its stability ensured.

Notes

1. Research materials are contained in the following publications: M. K. Gorshkov, *Rosiiskoe obshchestvo v usloviyakh transformatsii: mify i realnost (sotsiologicheskii analiz)* [Russian society and the conditions of transformation: myths and reality (a sociological analysis)] (Moscow: ROSSPEN, 2003); M. K. Gorshkov and N. E.

Tikhonova, eds., *Izmenyayushchaya Rossiya v zerkale sotsiologii* [Changing Russia in the mirror of sociology] (Moscow: Letnii Sad, 2004); M. K. Gorshkov and N. E. Tikhonova, eds., *Rossiya—novaya sotsialnaya realnost: Bogatye. Bednye. Srednii klass* [Russia—the new social reality. The rich. The poor. The middle class] (Moscow: Nauka Science, 2004); M. K. Gorshkov and N. E. Tikhonova, eds., *Rossiiskaya identichnost v usloviyakh transformatsii: opyt sotsiologicheskogo analiza* [Russian identity in conditions of transformation: experience from sociological analysis] (Moscow: Nauka, 2005); M. K. Gorshkov, N. E. Tikonova, and A. Y. Chepurenko, eds., *Sobstvennost i biznes v zhizni i vospriyatii rossiyan* [Property and business in the life and perception of Russians] (Moscow: Nauka, 2006); M. K. Gorshkov "Rossiiskoe obshchestvo kak novaya sotsialnaya realnost" [Russian society as a new social reality], *Rossiya reformiruyushchaya* [Reforming Russia] 6 (2007); E. P. Dobrynina and M. K. Gorshkov, "Svoboda. Neravenstvo. Bratstvo: Sotsiologicheskii portret sovremennoi Rossii" [Freedom, Inequality, Brotherhood: a sociological portrait of contemporary Russia], *Rossiiskaya gazeta*, 2007; V. A. Medvedev, M. K. Gorshkov, and Y. A. Krasin, eds., *Sotsialnoe neravenstvo i publichnaya politika* [Social inequality and public policy] (Moscow: Kulturnaya revolyutsiya, 2007); "Dinamika sotsialno-ekonomicheskogo polozheniya naseleniya Rossii" [The dynamics of the socio-economic situation of Russia's population], based on "Rossiiskogo monitoringa ekonomicheskogo polozheniya i zdorovya naseleniya 1992–2006" [Russian Monitoring of the Economic Situation and Health of the Population 1992–2006], *Informatsionno-analiticheskii byulleten' IS RAS* [IS RAS information and analytical bulletin] 2 (2008); "Maloobespechennye v Rossii: Kto oni? Kak zhivut? K chemu stremyatsya? [Those on low incomes in Russia: Who are they? How do they live? What do they strive for?] *Informatsionno-analiticheskii byulleten' IS RAS* [IS RAS information and analytical bulletin] 5 (2008); M. K. Gorshkov and N. E. Tikhonova, eds., *Sotsialnoe neraventsvo i sotsialnaya politika v sovremennoi Rossii* [Social inequality and social policy in modern Russia] (Moscow: Nauka, 2008); M. K. Gorshkov, R. Krumm, and V. V. Petukhov, eds., *Rossiya na novom perelome: strakhi i trevogi* [Russia at a new turning-point: fears and anxieties] (Moscow: Alfa-M, 2009); and N. E. Tikhonova and S. V. Mareeva, *Srednii klass: teoriya i realnost* [The middle class: theory and reality] (Moscow: Alfa-M, 2009).

2. V. Zubok, "Russia's Identity Quest," *Orbis* (Winter 2005): 183–93.
3. M. L. Bruner, *Strategies of Remembrance: The Rhetorical Dimensions of National Identity Construction*, (Columbia: University of South Carolina Press, 2002).
4. V. Tolz, "Forging the Nation: National Identity and National Building in Post-Communist Russia," *Europe-Asia Studies* 50, no. 6 (1998): 993–1022.

5. V. Popov, "Shock Therapy versus Gradualism: The End of the Debate (Explaining the Magnitude of the Transformational Recession," *Comparative Economic Studies* 42, no. 1 (2000): 1–51; V. Popov, "Russia: Inconsistent Shock Therapy with Weakening Institutions," in *Transition and Institutions: The Experience of Gradual and Late Reformers*, ed. G. A. Cornia and V. Popov, 29–54 (Oxford: Oxford University Press, 2001); V. Popov, "Russia Redux," *New Left Review* 44 (2000): 36–52; V. Shlapentokh, "Hobbes and Locke At Odds in Putin's Russia," *Europe-Asia Studies* 55, no. 7 (2003): 981–1007.

6. P. Dutkiewicz and V. Popov, "Ahead or Behind? Lessons from Russia's Postcommunist Transformation," in *Turning Points in the Transformations of the Global Scene*, ed. A. Kuklinski and B. Skuza, 233–51 (Warsaw: The Polish Association of the Club of Rome, 2006).

7. D. Lane, "What Kind of Capitalism for Russia? A Comparative Analysis," *Communist and Post-Communist Studies* 33 (2000): 485–504.

8. R. Sakwa, "Subjectivity, Politics and Order in Russian Political Evolution," *Slavic Review* 54, no. 1 (1995): 943–64.

9. See Atkov and Ulumbekova (chap. 9) in this volume.

10. S. J. Collier, "Budgets and Biopolitics," in *Global Assemblages: Technology, Politics, and Ethics as Anthropological Problems*, ed. A. Ong and S. J. Collier, 373–90 (Malden, MA: Blackwell Publishing, 2005).

11. J. K. Hass, "The Great Transition: The Dynamics of Market Transitions and the Case of Russia, 1991–1995," *Theory and Society* 28 (1999): 383–424.

12. S. Hedlund, "Such a Beautiful Dream: How Russia Did Not Become a Market Economy," *Russian Review* 67 (2008): 187–208, and "Rents, Rights, and Service: Boyar Economics and the Putin Transition," *Problems of Post-Communism* 55, no. 4 (2008): 29–41.

13. E. Keenan, "Muscovite Political Folkways," *Russian Review* 45 (1986): 115–81.

14. R. Pipes, "Flight from Freedom: What Russians Think and Want," *Foreign Affairs* 83, no. 3 (2004).

15. V. Putin, "The Modern Russia: Economic and Social Problems," *Vital Speeches of the Day* 66, no. 8 (2000): 231–36.

16. See J. Godzimirski, "Putin and Post-Soviet Identity: Building Blocks and Buzzwords," *Problems of Post-Communism* 55, no. 5 (2008): 14–27; A. Tsygankov, "Vladimir Putin's Vision of Russia as a Normal Great Power," *Post-Soviet Affairs* 21, no. 2 (2005): 132–58; A. B. Evans Jr, "Putin's Legacy and Russia's Identity," *Europe-Asia Studies* 60, no. 6 (2008): 899–912; and R. Sakwa, *Putin: Russia's Choice*, 2nd ed. (New York: Routledge, 2008).

17. D. Medvedev "Rossiya, vpered!" [Russia, ahead!], *Rossiiskaya gazeta*, September 11, 2009, federal issue no. 4995 (171).
18. Here and elsewhere we refer to the results of the following research projects: "Novaya Rossiya: desyat let reform" [New Russia: ten years of reform] (Institute of Complex Social Research, 2001); "Evropa i Germaniya glazami rossiyan" [Europe and Germany through Russian eyes) (Institute of Complex Social Research, 2002); "Bogatye i bednye v sovremennoi Rossii" [The rich and the poor in modern Russia] (Institute of Complex Social Research, RAS, 2003); "Sotsialnoe neravenstvo v sotsiologicheskom izmerenii" [Social inequality in the sociological dimension] (RAS Institute of Sociology, 2006); "Gorosdkoi srednii klass v sovremennoi Rossii" [The municipal middle class in modern Russia] (RAS Institute of Sociology, 2006); "Rossiiskaya identichnost v sotsiologicheskom izmerenii" [Russian identity in the sociological dimension] (RAS Institute of Sociology 2007); "Maloobespechennye v Rossii: Kto oni? Kak zhivut? K chemu stremyatsya?" [Those on low incomes in Russia: Who are they? How do they live? What do they strive for?] (RAS Institute of Sociology, 2008); "Chego opasayutsya rossiyane?" [What makes Russians apprehensive?] (RAS Institute of Sociology, 2009); "Rossiiskaya povsednevnost v usloviyakh krizisa: [Russian everyday life in conditions of crisis: the sociologists' view] (RAS Institute of Sociology, 2009).
19. The index is calculated using the following group of indicators: (1) subjective assessments of the existence of the more significant forms of deprivation, (2) material prosperity, (3) real estate owned, (4) quality of life, (5) existence of savings, (6) use of paid amenities, and (7) leisure opportunities entailing additional expenditure. For details, see M. K. Gorshkov, R. Krumm, and N. E. Tikhonova, *Rossiiskaya povsednevnost v usloviyakh krizisa* [Russian daily life in conditions of crisis] (Moscow: Alfa-M, 2009), 272.
20. 1 U.S. dollar = RUB 34.20.
21. Here and elsewhere, when dealing with official statistics we use data provided on the Federal State Statistics Service's Web site, in the "Population" section (subsection "Employment and Wages" and "Standard of Living"). See http://www.gks.ru.
22. 1 U.S. dollar = RUB 30.85.
23. O. I. Shkaratan, V. A. Bondarenko, Y. M. Krelberg, and N. V. Sergeev, "Sotsialnoe rassloenie i ego vosproizvodstvo v sovremennoi Rossii" [Social layering and its reproduction in contemporary Russia] (preprint WP7/2003/06, Moscow Higher School of Economics, 2003).
24. See, for example, L. A. Belyaeva, *Sotsialnaya stratifikatsia i srednii klass v Rossii: 10 let postsovetskogo razvitiya* [Social stratification and the middle class in Russia: ten years of post-Soviet development] (Moscow: Academia, 2001); E. M. Avramova, M.

V. Mikhailyuk, L. I. Nivorozhkina, T. M. Maleeva and others, *Srednie klassy v Rossii: ekonomicheskie i sotsialnye strategii* [The middle classes in Russia: economic and social strategies] (Moscow: Gendalf, 2003).

25. For details, see Tikhonova and Mareeva, "Srednii klass" [The middle class].
26. For details, see V. V. Petukhov, *Demokratiya uchastiya i politicheskaya transformatsiya Rossii* [The democracy of participation and political transformation in Russia] (Moscow: Academia, 2007).
27. For details, see Gorshkov, Krumm, and Petukhov, *Rossiya na novom* [Russia at the new turning-point].

CHAPTER SEVEN

Elites: The Choice for Modernization

Leonid Grigoriev

Translated by Siriol Hugh-Jones

Every country—Russia is no exception—"acquires" a new functioning elite—be it political, financial, or intellectual—as a result of revolution or a change of regime. The old elite may lose control and depart or, with luck, may merge into the new formation of social strata existing in that particular country. The composition and structure of elites are country-specific and reflect that country's history. The removal of the old power elite—particularly the Communist elite—has been no easy matter. In Russia, transition has been extremely complicated, primarily because the change of power elites occurred within a superpower during peace time.[1]

In this chapter, we concentrate on a few important issues of the theory and practice in the transformation of elites. In the case of Russia, we are dealing with a country that has changed its political elite twice within three generations.[2] The tsarist political elite's inability at the beginning of the twentieth century to adapt to transformation, to reach a timely accommodation with the new bourgeoisie, or to implement "perestroika" within the conditions of a severe external conflict proved P. N. Durnovo's woeful prediction that, "Russia will be flung into hopeless anarchy, the outcome of which cannot be foreseen."[3] We proceed from the assumption that until the Russian Revolution of 1917, the protracted coexistence (since 1861) of the feudal political elite and the business elite remained an obstacle to modernization through peaceful regional development. The pre-revolutionary political and financial elites were destroyed in 1917–22 and again during the Stalinist repressions of the

1930s. Subsequently, the intellectual elite was replenished, but it again suffered heavy losses during World War II and as a result of the economic emigration of the 1990s.

Who is this chapter about? Who makes up the Russian elite?

Regarding Russia's elites, we can begin with O. V. Gaman-Golutvina's clear categorization of four basic elite groups: political, economic, intellectual, and professional. She defines them as the economic elite, which includes "those who own or control the largest volume of economic resources"; the intellectual elite, who "dictate society's 'spiritual' agenda"; and the professional elite, which "covers all those who have reached the top of their field of professional activity."[4] I would like to propose a different approach, by which the professional elite will be included as part of the intellectual elite, and we will add (for historical reasons) the crucially important military and Orthodox Church elites. Thus we set out the following categorization:

> The *political elite* is the country's leadership of the government and the main ministries, including those of the security forces and law enforcement; the leading parties; the upper part of the state business sector; the regional authorities; and a few from official and unofficial think tanks, including part of the government's public relations machine. Most political analysts would probably agree that the political elite is made up of Kremlin figures (including the executive), key members of the government and of the Duma, key figures from political parties and some public organizations, key figures in security, plus regional governors.

> The *business elite* comprise the principal owners and top management of Russian big business (including its foreign and mixed Russian-foreign elements) in both the nonfinancial and financial sectors. In terms of their actual economic power, they are able to influence not just economic but political decisions. Quantitative analysis in this case is more complicated: it is not quite clear who is inside Russia and who is outside. Huge amounts of capital are hidden in all sorts of foreign funds. In 2009 there were sixty-two billionaires in Russia, as well as other nouveaux riches and top managers, together making up a business elite of between one thousand and two thousand.

> The *military elite* are the generals of the armed forces and the heads of key enterprises within the military-industrial complex. According to the

Ministry of Defense's Web site, in 2006 the Russian military included twelve hundred generals of varying ranks.

The *religious elite* is mostly the senior leadership of the Russian Orthodox Church, but also the top people of the organizations of the other major faiths. We are not familiar with Islamic structures in Russia. The site of the Moscow Patriarchy lists 161 important figures within the Orthodox Church, including 118 bishops and archbishops.

The *intellectual elite* is a combination of the "branch" elites, including leaders within the professions as well as recognized leaders in the sciences, arts, and the media—somewhat broader than the definition of Gaman-Golutvina: "Intellectual Elite is formatting the philosophic ('soul') agenda of the society."

Normally students of a country's politics and history want to know the size of its elite, who is influential, and preferably their names. Here, we adopt a general approach that should be verified against special studies (which are now extremely rare). There has been an attempt to build a special Web site (www.viperson.ru) dedicated to numbering the VIPs in Russia. The site currently lists nearly five thousand people.

Another problem is the fact that we would underline the quite substantial difference between the elite and the "inner circle" of each country's decision makers, and this is especially relevant in the case of Russia. The less mature democracies may also have a less developed political elite than that of the established democratic societies. There is a huge difference between the groups in power and the groups whose interests must be taken into account. Each specific elite may have factions, different interests, or positions on major issues such as property rights, the military, or legal reform. In other words, the Russian elite is fairly fragmented.

Elites—Emerging from the Lather of Transformation

The first issue (particularly important for Russia) is the origin of the elite at a time when society is undergoing radical transformation. Most of the literature focuses on the old, long-established elites. They can be regarded as the normative elite on the grounds of longevity and their capacity for self-renewal.

The transformational process at the end of the twentieth/beginning of the twenty-first centuries entails the collapse of old elites and the formation of new ones. Of course, for a new power elite the immediate problem is one of legitimacy, the search for "roots" (including ancestors—the nobility, academics, generals, etc., ideally "pre-1917") to justify inclusion in the elite and the attempt to create systems of power retention. The struggle within the elite ultimately reveals the group (or clan) that develops the dominant paradigm and is able to impose this on all the others. Those who achieve this ultimately become the permanent elite. They govern the country and own the property. Gradually, they acquire the nature of a normative, traditional elite, providing, of course, that they are able to fulfill the strategic functions of protecting and promoting the national interests. If we adopt Yuri Levada's definition, then the new elite possesses a "unique resource"—through force, it endeavors to realize its cultural potential for the creation and upkeep of "symbolic structures"; it also tries to shore up its position and ensure its self-renewal from one generation to the next.[5] The second and third steps toward self-affirmation are complicated and require time, effective action, and interaction with other social forces. In cases of dramatic, profound social transformation, the new elite is all the more likely to face a prolonged period of struggle for acceptance of its dominant role.

We are dealing not with an isolated process of transformation of an elite or elites but with the transformation of the whole of society. The ranks of the middle class and the elite are undergoing changes that, though simultaneous, are not identical. The old elites are disappearing and new elites appearing, though the process by which this occurs varies from one elite to another. The formation of a middle class in the transition from a planned to a market economy does not occur in a vacuum, but emerges from what is left of those old social strata that can be regarded as the "proto" middle class. We need to distinguish between the structure of society as a whole and the position of the elite vis-à-vis a strong middle class in developed democracies or a weak middle class, as in Latin America. When transformation occurs, the question of social inequality and the approach to income distribution offer two completely different environments for the formation or positioning of the new elite. In the former COMECON countries of Central Europe, the middle class has developed fairly quickly over the past two decades, while in Russia it has lagged behind. This makes the conditions in which new elites are formed and operate materially different. In most cases, including in Russia, we also have to take into account a most important factor—that of the additional layer of *regional* elites, with their substantial interests.

Not to be forgotten is the external factor in elite formation—influence from abroad, particularly where the interests of particular elites are translated into "the national interest." The new elite will naturally seek acceptance from its peers, both at home and abroad. Domestically, the position of the middle class vis-à-vis the elites and the poor is difficult in general, let alone in the case of serious inequality and conflict with the underprivileged or where there is a clear socio-economic crisis. Rifts between elites and between the elite and the bulk of the middle classes are what cause revolutions. Where the new elite takes over as the ruling class, there is an assumption that they and their interests are compatible with the interests of the middle class, including where the elite's interest and style of behavior vis-à-vis their middle class counterparts (the officer classes, the clergy, and the intelligentsia) is concerned.

As far as the new composition of elites is concerned, we can generally see that elements of the old Soviet elites have a tendency to survive. This is most evident in the political and military elites, not only in terms of personnel but also in the imitation of statist approaches (table 7.1). The church elite remain basically the same as they were. The business elite are naturally being pulled in opposite directions as their self-interest encounters the growing role of the state in the economy (particularly in light of the recession of 2008–09). The intellectual elite is also torn between its traditional independence and dependence on public funding.

In the case of Russia, it is not just the Soviet political elite that needs to be borne in mind. Just as the societies of Central and Eastern Europe remember, so too should we remember the lost political and (much-prized) intellectual elite of the old Russia. Some of the Russian Empire's intellectual and even its military elite accepted the 1917 revolution and ended up on the opposite side of the barricades from the "White" political elite and the fragile business elite. Later, they all succumbed to the Stalinist terror. The political and business elite emigrated (some of the latter taking their financial assets with them), as did members of the army. The church elite and clergy (the middle class) were unable to leave their congregations and endured the most terrible persecution. The split in the Russian Orthodox Church was overcome only in the twenty-first century, and the merger of the two parts of this elite will clearly take some time. At the beginning of the twentieth century, the new anti-elite came

	ORIGINS WITHIN SOVIET SOCIETY	RELATIONSHIP WITH THE WORLD PRE-TRANSFOR-MATION	RELATIONSHIP WITH THE WORLD NOW	SEARCH FOR BELIEFS AND PROBLEMS
POLITICAL	Second tier	Domestic isolation inside "socialist camp"	Initial respect and recognition	Russia as a great power
CHURCH	Traditional	Conflict	Unique	Stability of the church and its role
MILITARY	Tradition	Conflict	Danger of losing status in the world	Risks encirclement and falling behind
NEW FINANCIAL	From the "proto" middle	The virtual underground of commerce	Integration in the world	Recognition via overseas assets
THE LEADING RANKS OF THE TECHNICAL INTELLIGENTSIA	Dependence on the state	Isolation and prestige	Emigration thanks to the loss of working conditions	Hope of recapturing status
ARTS INTELLIGENTSIA	Difficult history	Moderate liberalism	Attempt to integrate	Finding themselves again
OLD INDUSTRY	Directors	Isolation	Offshore	Income from privatisation

Table 7.1   Origins of the elite and their relationship with the outside world (before and after 1991 collapse)

from "the bottom" and destroyed its political and ideological adversaries: the nobility, the bourgeoisie, the army, and the church. It did not hold back and, influenced by ideological paranoia, largely destroyed (or exiled) the intellectual elite, including even natural scientists and technical experts: the heaviest blow was delivered to the ranks of the middle class who had suffered losses during World War I and the Russian Civil War (as did the nation as a whole, of course) and who had played a huge part in the run-up to the revolution.

The repressions of the 1920s and 1930s exposed the internal clan wars of the new elite itself, with the destruction of part of this new elite. The winning clan imposed modernization by force, at unthinkable human cost (largely to the new middle class). In fact, the change of elite and jockeying for position within it continued until 1956 or even 1964, when Khrushchev was pushed out. The purges of 1930–53 prevented the formation and consolidation of a stable elite and made it harder for elite positions to be passed down within families. In the 1950s and 1960s, the cessation of mass repressions and the considerable stability of the regime after World War II had two important consequences. First, the rules for recruitment of the nomenklatura were finally laid down, based on the renewal of the political elite, without further repressions (and with the army and "authorities" being subject to party control). Second, in practice, there was a convenient compromise between the political and intellectual elite, with the situation being divided into an emphasis on natural sciences (while maintaining ideological "correctness") and the domination of the party ideology in social sciences, despite covert intellectual opposition. Subject to certain provisos, one could say that the Soviet political elite maintained a "stable regime" for less than forty years—from 1953 to the beginning of the 1990s.

The sector of the intellectual elite that we refer to as the "science and technology elite" easily survived the disappearance of communist ideology, but two decades of transformation and crisis with no financing of essential scientific and defense projects have severely weakened it. Its privileged position in Soviet society (just behind the political and military elites) has been threatened. For understandable reasons, the arts and social sciences are rather more difficult to transform. The renewal of these elites must occur eventually, even if under a completely different regime and with some resultant loss of specialist knowledge.

Contemporary Russia is emerging from two decades of transition in which it has undergone three transformations—from a planned to a market economy, from the Soviet system to democracy, and from the USSR to the Russian Federation. The process is ongoing. During the transformation at the beginning of the 1990s, the replacement of the nomenklatura with the new elites followed several courses. Ultimately, the Russian power elite represents a complicated conglomeration of members of the old Soviet elite, regional elites, and the new bourgeoisie, the latter having the most disparate origins. To the formation of the new power elite they have brought their experience and customs, from both the Soviet period and the difficult struggle for power and ownership in the 1990s.

An analysis of the process of mutual infiltration and gradual "accommodation" between the strata of the power and business elites is beyond the scope of this chapter. The period when the post-privatization oligarchs dominated the politics of the second half of the 1990s, and the "revenge" of the political elite at the beginning of the first decade of the twenty-first century, gave rise to a complicated process of struggle over modernization programs, and their lack of conclusion and compromise thus far is reminiscent of the early twentieth century As Olga Kryshtanovskaya emphasizes, a most important part in the formation of the financial elite was played by the old elite's own, perfectly natural, program of adapting to the new conditions by privatizing assets to suit their own interests. She has shown that in many cases the old nomenklatura used the more versatile, younger generation (the "Komsomol"[6] members) as their "authorized representatives" during privatization.[7] The old elite, along with the directors of Soviet enterprises and new businessmen, were to an extent able to join both the country's new political and the business elite. The old "senior" elite were confined to acting as "hidden stakeholders" via the next generation of "future nomenklatura" and, to an extent, via relatives and clans, including regional clans. Voucher privatization presented ample opportunities for directors to turn their management into rights of ownership (sometimes via offshore companies). Where levels of property ownership were highest, the right to dispose of and use assets was secured through the right of possession. The deliberate relaxation of procedural requirements and of owners' qualifications (for the sake of speeding up the process and making it politically irreversible) opened up the possibility for anyone to own property—from simple entrepreneurs to illegal "underground" commercial traders. The privatization scheme essentially enabled ownership of assets to be concentrated and excluded the bulk of the middle class from becoming shareholders and property owners. This seriously weakened the position of the intelligentsia in the future transformation of society. In turn, the public perception of this privatization as having very little legitimacy also weakened the position of large-scale private business vis-à-vis the state bureaucracy.[8]

The crisis in the Soviet economic and political system freed some of the intellectual elite from the domination of party ideology, gave national proto-elites a sense of opportunity, and caused a rift within the nomenklatura (party elite) over how to adapt to the altered situation. The transformation process reflected Russia's preexisting problems, in particular the opposition between two models of modernization—the bureaucratic and the intellectual. The absence of consensus over how to transform society at the end of the 1980s led to the stripping away of the elite's traditional control over the middle strata of society, who saw no prospect of a way out of the socio-economic crisis. The old elite was bankrupted by its failure to lead the country (society) effectively in conditions of global competition and to maintain internal unity or achieve compromise in order to contain socio-political risks and thus ensure its own survival. Even within families, the renewal of the political elite was rendered extremely difficult, for specific reasons: the violence of the struggle kept pushing its members (the active party members) to make the eminently sensible decision to transfer their children out of harm's way to the intellectual elite (i.e., to positions where they received nomenklatura income without taking political risks). But this gave the new Soviet politicians ample room for growth. It was only through transformation and privatization that elements of the political elite acquired (with varying degrees of success) the opportunity to "retreat" to the business elite.

The old nomenklatura retreated much more easily and with less resistance than many observers expected after the August 1991 putsch. No small part was played by the rift within the nomenklatura, some of whom had supported transformation and won the battle to enter the new elite. Society was spared an extended civil conflict with uncertain consequences.[9] But they thereby preserved better opportunities for their own integration into a post-transformation society. Of less concern is the problem of the threat of "communist revenge," which was actively discussed throughout the 1990s. Property ownership has been undergoing rapid transformation, and the old elite have found channels of integration into the market economy, in particular via the second echelon of the young Soviet nomenklatura "in waiting." The professional elites adapted relatively easily and the church began to plan its revival.

Those politicians who found themselves at the helm after the change of regime faced an unprecedented economic crisis, the disintegration of the country into fifteen sovereign parts and the need to resolve the problems of transition. The crisis decade of the 1990s was largely responsible for the loss of that bedrock of transformation, the middle class, some of whom emigrated while others were reduced to poverty. The middle class's new businessmen had to find their feet against the backdrop of a 43 percent fall in the country's GDP. Initially, the legitimacy of the new political and financial elite looked perfectly valid compared to the collapses of the Soviet period, but it was soon called into question. An important part of this process was the distorted nature of privatization and the segregation of the financial oligarchy, together with the mass distribution of voucher shares. From a quasi-egalitarian Soviet society, citizens instantly found themselves in a society with an Anglo-Saxon income distribution and the wealth distribution of Latin America. A small but very new wealthy elite and the impoverishment of the educated population are conditions that make the formation of a stable society difficult. And the formation of the character and structure of the elite erred, like the social structure as a whole, toward Latin America rather than Europe.

In these conditions, the measure of the elite's success was the surmounting of the economic crisis and the country's ability to reclaim its status as a great power. Economic growth between 2000 and 2008 provided a basis for success both for the population at large and some among the elites. The power groups of the 1990s and the financial elite were, for one reason or another, unable to demonstrate comparable success. For the middle and lower classes, the immediate results of market transformation are associated primarily with the crisis and a highly controversial privatization. However, the restoration of GDP volume and stable growth in real consumer income of 11 percent a year from 2000 to 2008 are serious indicators of success for the incumbent political elite, which, of course, demanded greater influence in economic management.

The Russian power and financial elites have survived the shock of transformation and the crisis of transition. They are new, and seek acceptance and stability at home and abroad. They have not yet demonstrated either a capacity for self-renewal or the ability to resolve national issues. The restoration of growth and the achievement of stabilization (based on oil revenues) was an unconditional success, but primarily for President V. V. Putin personally and the bureaucracy, rather than for the elites in the broad sense of the word. The success of the current modernization of society, the government, and the economy within the democratic process will be the criterion for the success and viability of the new power force (the *silovniki*), changing the configuration of the political and business elite. We note that in Russia's case, one must always take into account the country's self-perception as a natural "great power." Unlike many countries undergoing transformation, Russia is unique in that its new political and financial elite judge it by the standards of great powers and tie themselves to a promise to Russian society of modernization matching that status—indeed a heavy burden and enormous responsibility! Such a program requires unity among the elites and between elites and society—particularly with the middle class—in relation to the aims and methods of modernization.

The Structure of the Elite

The issue of the makeup and behavior of the elites is widely discussed in the literature of political analysis—and of course, generally in the context of the political elite and at times its interaction with the financial elite.[10] The financial elite and its role are widely discussed in a series of economic statements or discourses—from control over the economy and society to questions of corporate control and inheritance tax, social equality, and privatization.

The discussion continues in academic literature as to what is the correct approach to the elite—"normative" (the "real" elite) or "functional" (i.e., those who carry out the functions of the elite and aspire to become the "normative" elite).[11] Any elite that bases its position and claims on traditions and qualities needs to have a certain history of successful service of its country, society, and people. We agree with V. Ledyaev that "today the structural or functional approach has essentially become widely accepted ('mainstream') in political science and there seems little prospect of political scientists being 're-educated' into understanding the elite otherwise. The convention which has grown up is relatively durable and works explicitly against normative approaches."[12]

Of course, we sympathize with all those who would like to see in the Russian elite (whether political or not) a fully commendable, normative elite. For example, M. Afanasiev, in his critique of the contemporary Russian political elite, provided this emotional definition: "the legitimate elite is nothing other than a by-product of adherence to general rules."[13] This reflects the intelligentsia's disappointed hopes of decent behavior by the political and financial elites within the bounds of middle-class morality.

Russia has had its oligarchy period, but the financial crisis of 1998 and the advent of the political elite removed big business's virtually total control over the government. To many observers this elite has been unable to demonstrate the necessary responsibility and concern for the country's development.

We see the particular difficulty for the elite of a new state and society (after an extremely difficult social revolution) of immediately acquiring normative status, respect, and traditional acceptance. This is usually possible where there have been revolutions of liberation or where certain large national issues have been resolved by social revolution; even in those cases, it is achievable only for a small group and is rarely quick or immediately stable. Moreover, the difficulty of achieving the superior status of a "genuine elite" relates to Russia's rather unsuccessful and, in many respects, painful transformation, both in the 1990s and the first decade of the twenty-first century.

The assortment of elite factions may, to a degree, reflect both the country's idiosyncrasies and the composition of the middle class.[14] We are dealing here primarily with a more exact separation of the political and intellectual elite from the professional elite. And this of course means we are dealing with the army and the church. Professional elites as a phenomenon are, again, beyond the focus of this chapter, although their mutual relations with the corresponding ranks of the middle class may be important for the study of society's transformation. We suggest that the elite is unable to "lose touch" with society as a whole—however great its importance and power—but has relatively important ties with other social strata that not only have to accept it but support it. As is evident from the experience of pre-revolutionary Russia, a rift between the political elite and the intellectual ranks of the middle class can be extremely dangerous to social stability and to the elite itself. In fact, what we have before us is a kind of social matrix in which the perspectives of the elite and the corresponding ranks of the middle class more or less interrelate, although, of course, the elites use their own methods and means to influence the whole of society.

When discussing the Russian elite we have to consider the age factor. The ranks of political elites who come to power with their leader are almost all around fifty or older. In the case of Russia, it is important that those under fifteen never lived in the USSR and that in the course of a generation, the post-transformation generations will be the age of the junior elite. Today's political elite has pretty much reached the age of forty-five to sixty. But that

	SENIOR LEADERSHIP	PARLIAMEN-TARY ELITE	GOVERN-MENT	REGIONAL ELITE	OVERALL BY TEAM
Brezhnev's team	61.8	41.9	61.0	59.0	55.9
Gorbachev's team	54.0	44.0	56.2	52.0	51.6
Yeltsin's team	53.1	46.5	52.0	49.0	50.2
Putin's team	52.0	48.9*	48.9	53.6	50.9

Research data from the RAS Institute of Sociology's department for the study of the elite, 1989–2001. Each elite team (that of Brezhnev, Gorbachev, Yeltsin, and Putin) was examined during the second year its leader was in power. (* Kommersant-vlast, January 25, 2000.)

Table 7.2 Average age of elite groups (yrs)

does not mean that it has ample time to implement its program, particularly as the business elite as a whole is younger still.

The way to the top of the business elite is now closed following the end of privatization and given the huge challenges to the growth of private enterprise in Russia. The exceptions are bureaucrats in state companies (as in the "French approach") and corporate raiders, who invade private business by any means, even force. It is highly likely that the country will continue to be governed by the current power elite, just as it is influenced by the church and military elites, for a prolonged period. The difference in the intellectual elite is that the struggle for the "Soviet inheritance" continues and, with the exception of the media, it is not yet clear how in fact the old normative elite and the new functioning elite will combine to create a really high-class, genuine, intellectual elite of the future. Attempts by the power elite to create its own integrated intellectual elite could be successful, but this will depend on its potential for social innovation and political and intellectual freedom. There can either be an obedient nonelite or a free elite—historically, the choice is limited but clear (table 7.2).

The tentative conclusions regarding the origins of the Russian elites are relatively straightforward. The political elite has largely emerged from the second and third tiers of Soviet society. But at the beginning of the twenty-first century, it was increasingly replenished specifically from the intelligence and security services. This largely determines its mentality, regardless of current political opinions. In the post-reform Russia of 1990–2000, there was no blanket ban on political activity by the core group of Communist Party members, unlike in some Central European countries. To a degree, this allowed the old elite to regenerate itself, with generational adjustments. This was largely as a result of the particular type of political transformation that occurred under Boris Yeltsin, whose power group included a series of factions from the old bureaucratic and regional elites, which dominated behind the façade of the liberal intelligentsia.

By the first decade of the twenty-first century, the political elite had already significantly reinforced its position among the middle class by making large-scale additions to the ranks of the bureaucracy. Given the political leaders' high levels of popularity, continued economic recovery, and demonstrable foreign-policy successes, the elite as a whole have gained domestic legitimacy. Recognition from abroad is more difficult to come by but here, too, great-power status, a nuclear arsenal, and energy resources certainly help. The outside world has no choice but to recognize the political elite of a great power, whatever its colors. Opportunities to replace an elite are few and far between, and extremely difficult to exploit. The "color revolutions" did not, after all, extend beyond a few relatively small countries but were regarded, by the elites of many other countries, as a real threat. The question of whether such a revolution could happen in Russia was at least discussed: "The technology of 'velvet revolutions,' developed in the 1980s in the course of genuine revolutions in Eastern Europe, was cloned in the twenty-first century for the needs of regime changes which left virtually untouched the social makeup and the group of world powers steering regime change."[15]

In Russia, all professional elites from the sciences and public life can be included within one or other subdivision of the intellectual elite, just as groups from the different fields of the middle-class intelligentsia may be combined into one elite body. But this is where two important exceptions arise that require separate treatment—the army and the church. The enormous historical importance of these two organizations; their complicated internal structures, traditions, social influence, independent hierarchies, and methods of selecting the acting elite; a certain independence from other factions of the elite; and their own traditional agendas—these are all sufficient grounds for setting them apart, in Russia at least, from the political, financial, and intellectual elites. At the same time, we regard the intelligence services, and in particular counterintelligence and the police, as being more on the side of the state and the administrative apparatus.

The Russian Orthodox Church has, virtually alone among the country's institutions, preserved its elite through the post-Soviet transition. Its adaptability allows its elite to concentrate on the country's domestic issues, on adapting to the twenty-first century, and on the core historical tasks of consolidating its role in society, relations with the Vatican, and counteracting break-away divisions of the church, particularly in Ukraine.

The Russian army is gradually recovering from the crisis of the 1990s and the psychological aftermath of the first Chechen war. There have been some signs of recovery, particularly since the conflict of August 2008 in South Ossetia. Psychological stability depends on the country's financial potential. The change of professional elite is, in this case, an important part of the revival of the army's traditional place in society. The Russian Federation's military spending is, objectively speaking, relatively low, military reform is far from complete, and problems remain critical. But defending the country's borders and interests make the military elite and the defense industry (with its multibillion-dollar exports) part of that segment of the political elite that aims to reinforce the state and prioritize its needs. Of course, the army has an interest in research and innovation, but they are used to it coming from "closed" state institutes, not from small hi-tech companies. Only these two elites—the army and the church—have no need of domestic or foreign legitimacy: it has either been preserved or basically restored.

The position of the intellectual elite remains the most problematic. It is not united and the interests of its component parts remain diverse. The return to state financing has reinvigorated certain segments of the old elite, particularly those connected with the natural sciences (and part of the military-industrial complex). In these circumstances, the desire to consolidate the role of the state reduces the scope for individual, modernizing initiatives. Other complications leave the arts and social sciences elite in a state of unrest. In the sphere of economics, there is not the faintest glimmer of any consolidation of theories and economic policy. The latter remains an area of pragmatic decisions. The possibility is beginning to emerge of funding serious research, but generally within academic structures and a few universities. Here the question of the elite remains open. As we reach the twentieth anniversary of the beginning of the transition period, there are growing disputes about the country's future path. This places serious obstacles in the way of any consolidation of opinion and the selection of a normative elite. In this vital sphere, there is an important bridge between the intellectual and the business elites: overall, the new market economists have greater faith in the potential for business to modernize the country.

Russia's business and financial elites have been well researched by O. Kryshtanovskaya, Y. Pappe, and others.[16] The definitions of the Russian business elite are relatively close to Wright Mills's definition cited above, but with one important amendment: W.Mills argues that the elite are in charge, whereas in Russia the elite find themselves in permanent competition with the bureaucracy. The formation and evolution of the business elite over the past two decades has reflected the instability of ownership rights and the fact that privatization is not yet over. Each successive generation of the political elite attempts to reinforce its position by infiltrating the financial elite in one way or another. In the regions, elements of the local bureaucracy emulate their senior colleagues in their attempts to become co-stakeholders in the revenues of medium-sized business.[17] But in Russia, even the business elite is anything but homogeneous, and this is not just in terms of the apparent division between private and state business. The interests of the manufacturing industry, the financial or energy sectors, and the military-industrial complex do not always coincide.

The financial crisis of 1998 weakened the oligarchs. In effect, the political elite were able to significantly limit the role of big businessmen. The current composition of the elite as it existed in 2008–09 appears largely stable, although the global financial crisis has brought fresh tension. The growing "Petersburg contingent" within the federal government makes the political elite increasingly homogeneous.[18] The political elite has not yet existed long enough for us to talk seriously about its renewal.[19] The political elite is replenished through the appointment of technocrats as ministers, governors, and leaders of nationalized companies. Despite the domination of the political elite, the big business elite remains rather more stable than many observers claim. It holds enormous assets abroad and, whereas restrictions can be placed on its domestic business dealings, it is extremely difficult to deprive the elite of its offshore assets.[20]

Ultimately, a conglomeration of elements from the executive elite, all with different origins, was faced with the problem of the survival of a country with a great past through a terrible crisis. They were unprepared for such a responsible role. It is understandable that they fought, more often than not, for power and ownership—i.e., for rights without responsibility. These days, these members of the elite have to meet the monumental challenge of Russia's revival.

The Elite and the Middle Class

If political analysts are to be believed, power elites are doomed to play quite a definite role vis-à-vis the rest of society. Russian society has undergone the deepest economic and social crisis. Hopes for transformation from the Soviet state and planned economy proved vain. Instead, there was deep crisis for a decade, mass impoverishment, and social inequality of Latin American proportions. The initial combination of elites during the 1990s was undermined by the financial crisis of 1998, which brought back some from the former Soviet echelons.[21] Bureaucracy with growing Soviet elements started to make a comeback against the oligarchs. Politics and new wealth were discredited to a certain extent, and this brought about certain turnarounds during 1998–99, ending in the emergence of a new political leader, Vladimir Putin, in 2000. Elites were to be transformed while the rest of a society could do little to influence this process.

Inequality and the continuous attempts on the part of the political elite to ensure social stability and strengthen its positions led to further efforts to limit the potential for the development of a strong opposition. The rapid economic recovery of 2000–07 provided resources (real retail sales grew by an average of 11 percent) for consolidating the state's ability to influence the political process. Weak civil society was the natural result of the limited middle class (generally estimated at 20 percent to 25 percent of population).

Vertical mobility in the labor market has been more or less adequate in recent years., but entry into the elites has become a different matter altogether. Business or privatization in or since 2000 has been unable to match the wealth accrued in the 1990s. One exception has been the ability of the state to interfere in the process of wealth re-allocation—e.g., in cracking down on corporate raiders that had at one time become a serious threat to owners of assets. Privatization and reprivatization have been going for a considerable time. The political elite has continued to recruit from its established base, with limited entry from outsiders. Recruitment of the intellectual elite has remained more traditional, while the choice of the political elites for more loyal intellectuals has been clear. The actual relations between the elites and the middle classes are key to the interaction between the elites and society. The upper middle class is the natural source of recruitment into the elites, but so far the processes have not been studied in sufficient depth.

In most works on the elites, the middle class remains in the background or appears on the periphery, just as the elites remain in the shadows in works on the middle class.[22] The ranks of the middle class—the intelligentsia, bureaucrats, and small business—match those of the corresponding elites and are the sources of the replenishment and renewal of those elites. In this work, we deal with five elite factions. We also have five ranks of the middle class: the bureaucracy, management of large companies, intelligentsia (in education, the sciences, health care, etc.), and small businesses in manufacturing and sales. The political elite have to base their supremacy on their reflection of the interests of other elites and all ranks of the middle class and the poor. Their function is to serve the nation, although frequently the nation is forced to adopt the elite's values.

During the period of transformation, the intellectual elite was influenced by two factors—by the change of ideology and form of government and by the economic crisis. It is important to take into account the role of the latter, which forced out part of the normative elite and up-and-coming tiers of its potential recruits, up to and including its young people abroad. It would be unfair to accuse those elements of the elite and of the middle class who chose to emigrate of lacking patriotism: the crisis was simply too long and too difficult. For more than a decade, talented people were faced with difficult choices: individuals' personal ambitions were, as was the case for the country and society as a whole, centered on ensuring the survival of their families and being able to continue with their creative work, rather than on achieving elite status.

The question of the regeneration of Russia's scientific elites is important to the discussion and to other factions of the elite: "The identification of the scientific elite as a social and professional unit is based on a system of social, cultural, and socio-psychological criteria. For the regeneration of the elite it is critical that its individual members achieve the highest results in their professional work. Therefore, the scientific elite is, by its very nature, small. Its 'uniqueness' is confirmed by the responsibility imposed on the scientific elite for specific types of activity (for example, leadership in the sciences) and by its particular status and high level of social prestige. Aware of its particular mission, the elite claims power, influence, the right to form scientific (and education) policy, and it could reasonably be described as the catalyst of the social system. If the level of the elite's productivity falls below a certain 'critical mass,' social development is blocked."[23]

We have not found any definition of "intellectual elite" developed in the context of Russia's transformation over the last twenty years. The term, as it traditionally appears in the language of Western sociology, needs to be used in association with real events. In this case, we proceed from the basis that, in the reality of a large country with a rich intellectual history, the functioning intellectual elite inevitably stands out. Assuming there is a structure of elite factions unique to the country, then in the case of Russia there are (in practice) three subsections within the intellectual elite: the natural sciences, social sciences (particularly economics), and literature and art.

The social and institutional requirement for the intellectual elite in contemporary Russian society is dictated, according to Russian scholars, analysts, and social activists, by both tradition and ambition. The domination of American culture, particularly pop culture, has long been regarded as a threat in Europe. With the dramatic decline in natural sciences, the undermining of the status of Marxist social sciences, and the crisis in the country's cultural sphere, this same threat has affected Russia. It is perfectly possible that Russia will adopt the global intellectual elites as its own gurus (which, in certain areas, would be no bad thing). In the course of the crisis and emigration of part of the elite, the Russian (normative) elite could disappear altogether from the world stage, leaving only the memories of scholars and poets. In every country, the functioning elite occupy a relatively high position in their fields, in particular insisting that they merit their superior titles and roles. This problem persists even in these days. What we need is not a reliable demonstration of new individual works of art (or the recovery of out-dated military-industrial-complex inventions).

As the Soviet stereotypes disintegrated, the old social sciences elites found themselves under enormous pressure from hard realities during the transformation. They coped in ways that are all too familiar: some left public life (sometimes for education) while others changed their ideology or simply lost it among slogans advocating freedom from the pressure and control of the political elites of Soviet times. The latter was typical both of the natural sciences and of culture and the arts. The majority, as with other factions, preferred to say goodbye to ideology rather than to their positions in society.

In the most diverse fields, we nevertheless see a perfectly predictable symbiosis of the old functioning elite (which were also the normative elite under the old standards) with the new groups. The functioning elite of old are flexible enough to concede their positions to the aggressive new elements, although they don't hurry to do so, offering what is essentially a compromise: maximum preservation of their positions of command in exchange for recognition of elements of the new political elite and the latter's absorption into their own ranks. Of course, the transfer of elements of the political elite into the ranks of the functioning intellectual elite does not make them normative, recognized, or respected, but not everyone realizes this. Historically, the "new bourgeois" have usually been unable to tell the difference between "a bit of a bling" and a genius. The huge numbers of businessmen pursuing PhDs and the demand for qualifications and positions reflect this early and very particular stage of transformation.

Ultimately, the intellectual elite has to demonstrate that it includes groups and participants who have produced paradigm shifts in different intellectual fields, where possible on a global scale. Of course, every country has its intellectual elite. The ambition of great cultural powers is to have a world-class international, intellectual elite. Such an elite cannot be appointed; it has to be nurtured. This requires considerable intellectual freedom for the creative individual, a demand for ideas, and substantial resources. This situation also gives an indication of the diversity of the functions of the intellectual elite in its immediate social effect on other factions and as a source of high-quality intellectual production, competitive globally and inspiring near-universal recognition at home.

For groups and individuals, the difficulty of immediate or gradual recognition by the normative elite renders their inclusion in the functioning elite a long-term aspiration. Without being one of the functioning elite, the way into the normative elite from the depths of the middle class was, and remains, extremely difficult. Of course, some of the creative elite find their way to the summit, but often late and at great cost. There they are met by the nomenklatura. Admittedly, inclusion in the functioning elite only creates the illusion of belonging to the normative elite, although it is less controversial than in Soviet times (with the possible exception of the natural sciences). One or another group's (or individual's) identification of themselves as an element of the intellectual elite has to be tested to determine how realistic such pretensions are. Other factions may accept this claim on the basis of the group's long standing, but the group's effectiveness will nevertheless be tested by counter-elites, by the middle class, and by external challenges. Remaining within the *normative* elite is difficult, even if the position of members of the *functioning* elite is secure.

In contemporary society, the intellectual elite keep a certain distance from politics in order to retain their independence. The financial elite and bureaucracy have significant influence through the funding and sponsoring of research and arts projects. Within conditions of social transformation, the intellectual elite turn out to be a natural source of recruitment into the political elite thanks to their social position and independence from the previous regime. Where restrictions exist on the activity of the former political and ideological elite in many Central and Eastern European countries, the relevant ranks of the functioning elite — and thus possibly their political and intellectual positions — have been filled from the intellectual middle class — in effect, the (active or passive) opposition. The role of the intellectual elite and the middle class as a reserve was remarkable even at the initial stage of Russia's transformation. Admittedly, society's and the middle class's skepticism about this period and those active in it made it much more difficult for them to secure their positions. In conditions of extreme crisis and dissatisfaction among an impoverished population, the second and third tiers of Soviet bureaucracy found their way up. Big business took on recruits from among directors, criminal "underground" traders, and the intelligentsia. The specific nature of privatization painted such a bright picture of the new business elite that it felt no need to unite for the sake of shared long-term interests. It preferred to concentrate on simply maximizing the proceeds of privatization and keeping its assets liquid.

In the current conditions, the historical struggle between the bureaucratic and intellectual approaches to modernization acquired new meaning: "top-down" modernization by force using state and quasi-state instruments, or "bottom-up" modernization through innovation on the basis of individual creativity and the development of civil society. These two approaches produce completely different outcomes in terms of relations between the elites and the middle class.

The distinction between the interests of the ranks of the middle class and the elites is relatively noticeable even at this level. The financial elite may, of course, rely on middle-class management but struggle to gain the sympathy of small business. Without getting into the nuances of the behavior of groups and factions, we would point out, for example, the tax systems imposing different conditions on big and small business, and also directly setting off the business middle class against recipients of taxes from the budget: the bureaucracy and the intelligentsia. There are still serious differences between the latter two groups regarding the purpose of funding from the public budget. Finally, bureaucracy and other groups fundamentally disagree on the problem of corruption.

The middle class is the anchor that ensures social stability through the de facto recognition of elites and their exclusive role in the formulation of the country's aims and administration, both through its main social institutions and its assets. Contemporary democracy has its limitations, but rather than undermining the position of the elites, it has created channels for recruiting members of the elites (from the "people's tribunes") and for calculating the public mood (the middle class again) and the role of civil society. The traditional elites, having long since achieved recognition and success, are interested in keeping the gates open for some exchange of the gene pool with the middle class—a little but not a lot. Vertical migration in a functioning society is important not only at the bottom but further up—right up to the possibility of entry into the elite on the grounds of engagement and merit.

Traditionally, Russia has been wont to emphasize the role of the intelligentsia, but emigration and the difficult financial situation in the 1990s and the first decade of the twenty-first century weakened its role and position in society, which, at the end of the 1980s and early 1990s, had seemed so active and promising. The increase in the role of business at the expense of intellectuals was to be expected in the earlier stages of transformation, but over the last five years we have seen the strengthening of officialdom, often working in opposition to business and in support of the political and particularly the bureaucratic elite. The weakness of the middle class and civil society is vital as a matter of principle—particularly in contrast to the countries of Central and Eastern Europe and the OECD. This strengthens the role of the elites and personalities in stabilizing the situation in the country and choosing the path of development. The intellectual elite is also not homogeneous, and traditionally some of its branches are linked much more closely to the government than is the case in many free-market democracies.

The Fight for Modernization

The duality of the elite's objectives—self-preservation on the one hand and the task of acting as leaders of the country and society on the other—requires it to unite around the goals of economic and social development, and the means to these goals—basically providing an institutional setting for society, the economy, and the state. Post-transformation and -crisis modernization is the key to the future of the country. The success of modernization is recognized as an ultimate objective, while the dispute as to ways and means, even goals, persists. Elites all have their ways, but the political elites are trying to take control, particularly over the financial elites and the media. Nevertheless, it can be said that the new business class and groups of intellectuals (themselves, essentially elements of the elite) retain a certain degree of independence, while enjoying rather limited support from civil society or the middle class.

For contemporary Russia, one essential aspect is the question of whether the country's power elite is sufficiently united to achieve its goals. It is probably accurate to say that there has been significant consolidation among the political elite, although there is some internal discussion on the approaches to modernizing the country. In terms of the broader scope of the elite, it is certainly less homogeneous than it was, particularly where the business elite is concerned. It is gradually becoming more difficult for business and the middle class to develop civil society. In any case, the country's leaders have all but admitted that corruption is a key problem, rendering economic policy much less effective. It follows from this that the crucial question is which of the elites will determine the country's long-term interests and on which criteria. To what extent are national interests determined by the urge to modernize, compete, and integrate the country in the global community, and to what extent by the issue of legitimizing and protecting the new elite's positions? In established democracies, the basic parameters are usually set, so the struggle is over narrower, more specific aims, or over the set of instruments used to achieve such aims.

Russia's business and financial elite was made up of the old directors and Komsomol entrepreneurs. There is an active process of integration between these groups, particularly under pressure from those bureaucratic elements who themselves would like to become part of the financial elite. The new post-reform business groups in Russia are fairly weak, politically cautious, and threatened by the Privatization Bureau. Overall, this elite is far from consolidated and too dependent on the state to undertake any active defense of its own interests.

In public life, there are clear attempts on the part of the political elite to create elements of the intellectual elite to suit it, in coordination with sympathetic organizations within civil society. There is a manifest attempt, using the media, to have elements of the new nomenklatura recognized as the normative intellectual elite. This is not particularly successful given the skepticism of the Russian intelligentsia regarding any new "propaganda guru." The intellectual milieu may provide criticism of the country's policies or suggest new horizons, but what it cannot do is itself stimulate a political discussion process. The circle is closing—the intellectual elite is able to maintain its common sense and internal independence from the political elite, but, apart from sermonizing, it has no instruments at its disposal with which to reform the political elite. The other way of influencing the country's choice of approach—via the financial elite—is just as limited and ineffective. Although intellectuals active in public life and the economy traditionally appeal to business, the latter has, over the first decade of transformation, proved weak and preoccupied with the immediate problem of shoring up its position.

There is no simple solution to the interaction of the two key factions of the elite. In countries where private business has traditionally dominated, the political elite has been very much influenced by (and recruited from) the business circle with its role in the selection of political upstarts. Populist leaders and movements have usually been part of the internal structure of the political elite, extending their base within the middle class and creating an additional outlet during periods of severe crisis and serious social inequality. Rather more complicated is the process of re-creating the business elite in statist conditions, starting from state ownership and planned economies, in countries where the state has been historically dominant. We see the difficulty of China's evolutionary path, but Russia itself has undergone an extremely vexed twenty years in this regard. In conditions of great crisis, the new owners have had very little time in which to carry out their role and acquire the image of responsible and effective managers of the country's economy. They also have had to satisfy the country's long-suffering population immediately, in particular, a critical middle class, that they were the "elite." Of vital importance here is that only with extensive, resilient small and medium business, involving the middle class and a more developed civil society, will the instant financial elite be able to develop any stability and gain recognition at home and abroad. To a large extent, big business has turned out to be incapable of coordinating this, and has been rather more occupied with retaining and protecting control of assets through the withdrawal of capital or the securing of offshore asset-ownership rights. Business stability was based on specific external insurance mechanisms rather than the business elite's control of its situation, and on compromises with disgruntled elements in society, business, and the government.

Essentially, big business undertook a risky endeavor in the 1990s. Its aim was to take overall control of a small group of bankers and the state apparatus and political process, and give itself freedom of action and post-privatization security (despite an obvious lack of legitimacy). Major financial groups emerged where there was no widespread share ownership and the middle classes became impoverished and frequently emigrated. This affected potentially innovative small business and the intelligentsia. The social basis of the business elite remained extremely narrow. The political elite subsequently took steps to maintain its monopoly on power. As at the beginning of the twentieth century, business has been unable to find a way either of consolidating itself or of becoming economically independent of the government. Rather, the reverse has been true, with elements of the bureaucracy infiltrating business and extending their control, both directly and indirectly. The symbiosis does not benefit private business, but produces a neo-state model of business. This means the entrenchment of behavior supporting unearned income versus the maximization of profit—a constraint on innovation.

After two decades of transformation, the elite factions are, in current conditions, far from well balanced. The business elite missed its chance (if it ever had one) of gaining support from the middle class and creating its own system for the formation of the overall elite. The political elite turned out to be capable of consolidation on the basis of the traditional levers of Russian government: the fight against external threats and separatism, and the country's restoration and international respect. However, an economic crisis arrived once again in 2008–09 and brought to a halt the option of top-down modernization by force using state instruments and companies.

Just as big business had, by the beginning of the crisis in 2008, failed to demonstrate, either to the political elite or to the public, any ability or willingness to lead the country along the path of innovation, so the political elite has not yet shown it knows *how* to do so either. The challenge of restoring the country's 1989 GDP was only met in 2007–08 on the basis of an influx of oil dollars and prior to an 8 percent fall in GDP in 2009. For years, there has been public support for modernization, but the elites have been unable to embark effectively on one or other approach. Thus, the successes of the first economic resurgence turned out to be successes of the political elite. The business elite, though unable to offer its own approach to modernization, received enormous dividends thanks to the rise in the value of assets.

The 2008 economic crisis unfolded in conditions of uncertainty and a struggle over the choice of approach to modernization. The business elite is under pressure from the political elite and elements of the bureaucracy to hang onto property, in which they have only very weak support from the middle class. The government and the political elite are trying to carry out traditional top-down modernization with inadequate resources, both in terms of manpower and finances. The most difficult issue in the relations between the elites and the middle class is that of corruption (of course, some of the middle class is also caught up in this). But, in principle, the business and intellectual elite and the main ranks of the middle class have an interest in the country being open and in having normal relations with the outside world, and this too encourages the political elite to broaden cooperation. To date, we have to admit that after two decades of transformation, there are material differences in the interests and positions of the elites on an array of important issues. This is not an immediate threat to stability, particularly given that the most severe phase of the crisis is over, but it certainly threatens the country's long-term development and modernization.

In Russia, within the power elites and their intellectual milieu, there is a struggle for the very interpretation of the essence of Russian modernization. In their attempts to understand Russia's future, all sides, the elite groups *and* the middle class, argue for modernization and adopt this as an aim—but the difference is in their approaches to achieving it. This is a choice between technocratic modernization from above and modernization of the state, civil society, and the economy on the basis of engagement on the part of the individual in innovation. The first approach is state-led (or rather, led by officials, despite corruption remaining a problem) and involves a chain of spontaneous decisions from above relating to problems of socio-economic development. This approach enjoys support (albeit not universal support) among the political elite and part of the bureaucracy, extending into the middle class.

This approach also offers the permanent subjugation of business to the state and the nationalization of all the country's available resources. It has support both from the military-industrial complex and among the intellectual elite. Any real or supposed complications in the outside world provoke an instinctive revival of the tendency to use force. А natural component of this approach is a strengthened bureaucracy and business's fragile rights of ownership, a weak civil society, and limited democratic processes. Modernization problems and the considerable amount of time (two decades) already lost in the transition period spur the political elite to search for quick and simple solutions. Coalitions for forced, top-down modernization come naturally to Russia, but the chances of their success in genuine modernization are quite low (table 7.3).

The second approach involves difficult institutional reforms and combining sensible (limited and predictable) state regulation with maximizing social engagement and business activity, the rule of law, and stable property laws. The interminable waves of nationalization and re-privatization have to come to an end. Both programs envisage—or rather, look for— a great future for Russia in the twenty-first century, despite enormous obstacles in terms of demographics, lost time, and human capital. But the intelligentsia is just one rank of the middle class and a small part of the intellectual elite ("Moscow intellectuals"). The weakness of the political process overall and the civil society of a country that has only recently survived an economic catastrophe, and a business elite attempting to adapt to the political situation, make it difficult to develop an active coalition for modernization. The lack of potential for social modernization within the political elite has been highlighted by Lev Gudkov and Boris Dubin: "Three quarters of representatives of the Russian elite see no alternative political approaches, whether based on catastrophe or reform, to that selected by the country's leaders."[24]

Intellectuals (experts) surrounding the power elite are constantly attempting to persuade the top authorities to opt for broader socio-economic and political modernization. The functioning intellectual elites find themselves in an ambivalent position. They are capable of leading their own field but are forever competing for state resources against other branches of the elite and are consequently dependent on the political elite. This discussion on the potential for modernization has its optimists, who argue that there is a "development elite" who have turned away from state-run capitalism to genuine capitalism: the rule of law and competition.[25] In these surveys, only the *siloviki* appear retrograde, although the actions of many categories of the

M. AFANASIEV 2009	L. GUDKOV, B. DUBININ 2007
DEVELOPMENT ELITES	**SUPPORTERS OF MODERNIZATION**
Enterprise management	Large and medium-sized private business
Mass media and public appraisal	Leaders of regional mass media and professors from local universities; "Moscow intellectuals"
Regional officials	Top regional politicians (deputies from regional legislative assemblies, among whom there are increasing numbers of local businessmen)
Siloviki — military officers	
Others: the law, science and education, health care	
GOVERNMENT ELITES	**OPPONENTS OF MODERNIZATION**
Siloviki — "KGB"	*Siloviki* (both in the army, the Interior Ministry and elsewhere and in structures reinstated under Putin) — high-ranking army officers and officers of the security forces (interior ministry)
Heads of large corporations	Directors of large state enterprises
Federal officials — the "oligarchy" of senior members of the government	Officials (from the executive authorities at federal, regional, and local level) are high-ranking representatives of executive authorities on the ground, deputy governors, and the leadership of the federal districts ("okrugs")

Table 7.3 Positions of the elite on modernization, from surveys conducted between 2007 and 2009
[Sources: M. N. Afanasiev, *Rossijskie elity razvitiya: Zapros na novij kurs* (The Russian development elite: The demand for a new way) (Moscow: Liberalnaya Missiya Fund, 2009); and L. Gudkov and B. Dubinin, "Illyuziya modernizatsii: Rossijskaya byurokratiya v roli 'elity'" (The illusion of modernization: Russian bureaucracy in the role of the elite), *Pro et contra*, no. 3 (May–June 2007): 76–77]

political class demonstrate a clear preference for paternalism, the domination of state-owned business, and the state having extensive powers. There can be little doubt about business's preferences for stable ownership rights or those of intellectuals for the liberalization of public life. In practice, the realization of such policies is much more complicated. A personal preference for freedom does not mean a willingness to oppose corruption and support the genuine independence of the courts.

Of note here is "Koalitsii dlya budushchego" (*Coalition for the Future*), 2007–08, by the Institute of Contemporary Development (INSOR) as an example of the search for such an approach. Acknowledging the peculiarities of the new power elite and the weakness of business and civil society, the experts usually proceed on the basis of agreed goals: the struggle against the country's marginalization as a raw-materials power, the search for ways to revive or reinforce (depending on the evaluation of the situation) Russia's status as a great power in the future. In fact, this involves a strategic re-convincing of the political elite on the question of its national role. Rather than regenerating the country through bureaucracy, there is a need for political liberalization to curb corruption and increase the efficiency of the executive and legislature. The supremacy of law is not required as a symbol per se but as a guarantee of the position of the political and business elite within a society that has undergone a transformation toward democracy. The reinforcement of rights of ownership is required specifically to encourage innovation — so that the active business class and those working in social and scientific innovation can apply their ideas at home instead of exporting them for commercial application abroad.

The global recession has cut short attempts to introduce forced, top-down modernization. Although the worst of the crisis is over, the effects will be felt for some time. The world economy, financial system, and the energy industry are beginning a transformation. The country's adaptation to new dynamic conditions and global competition for the next generation cannot be carried out on a purely technical basis: by guessing the trend and hopefully making the right decision. This time the question of modernization is determined at the very top as a matter of the Russia's survival.[26] This goes to the heart of the country's status as a great power and of the "political elite of a great power." But in that case, we should be discussing developing the potential of the country's creative class (i.e., its intellectuals and active business elements) as the bases of modernization and the business and political elite's consolidation of its position. There is a push to convince the national elites of the need to turn their attention from their functioning roles (and income) to their strategic responsibility for the fate of the country: "the old belief in the power of enlightened people, who are morally and intellectually capable of influencing the nation and the authorities is being revived virtually as a matter of course among the educated part of the Russian population."[27]

In this relation, there is an important aspect to the internal-expert discussion that has not yet been fully developed—the possibility of preventing the country from sliding into a nonintellectual version of development through forced, top-down modernization, which is costly in terms of time and resources. The message to the power elites is relatively simple and may be summarized in a few points:

> Continued struggle for property rights—problems over ownership in large and small business paralyze investments and innovation
>
> Corruption curtails the possibility of technocratic "top-to-bottom" modernization success
>
> The struggle within the political class may lead to erroneous decisions, given that it suggests a coalition not based on modernization principles but just to gain "allies"
>
> In the long term, resilience and the ability of the power elites to establish systems to reproduce themselves depend on their willingness to look beyond the short-term horizon of high incomes. Extensive social modernization promises much more to the elites as well as to the public at large.

Of course, there is nothing to guarantee the success of experts "preaching uphill" outside the regular political process. The report of the Institute for Modern Development has provided a certain impulse to debates on the future of the country.[28] Socio-political apathy among the public after the shocks of the 1990s and the sudden abundance of oil revenues in the first decade of the twenty-first century will not disappear in the course of the crisis, but neither will it last forever. The question is whether the current system of modernization is capable of delivering palpable results in terms of innovation. The demographic composition of the country is changing in one important direction—those under thirty-five only experienced the USSR as children. They are already incapable of remembering life at the time, but neither do they automatically accept the nomenklatura elite and the norms of Soviet society. Where there is economic stability and powerful propaganda, most of the public can be convinced of their own material well-being, but two problems still remain. One is the comparison with countries with high growth rates. Given the free exchange of information, it does not matter whether these are far away or nearby. The demonstrable effects of a consumer society brought socialism to an end without the Internet or any large-scale diaspora. Nowadays, the effect of comparison may relate to innovation and the prevailing conditions of life and business, low levels of corruption, and the efficiency and self-control of the authorities. We would emphasize that without people being able to act freely and without reliable rights of ownership, it is impossible to achieve a flow of innovations, and modernization will be restricted to capital-intensive projects.

There are historical precedents for modernization enforced from above, but it is virtually impossible to implement in conditions of widespread corruption, since some decisions would not necessarily be implemented, and there would be an enormous waste of resources. Social engagement allows the middle class to be contained—the intelligentsia, officialdom, and small and medium business all have an objective interest in extensive modernization, even if they are not prepared to participate in the political process. The middle class will, however, decide the success or failure of the elite. The policy of modernization is binding also because, according to the view from above, it is possible to attempt to reduce it to a technological achievement and the imposition of order. But the middle class patiently awaits more far-reaching results. Without acceptance on the part of the middle class and the public as a whole, neither the existing political elite nor the business elites will be able to establish themselves as a genuinely recognized and legitimate elite. Russia's eventful history once more waits for modernization, and this depends on unity among the national elites and on the ability of their leadership to govern.

Notes

The author would like to thank Alla Salmina, a postgraduate student at Russia's Higher School of Economics and an expert at the Institute for Energy and Finance, for her assistance in the preparation of this chapter.

1. The theme of political elites formation and configuration has been noticeably developed in recent decades due to interest in the role of elites in the transformation of social and political structure and especially new elites in countries in transition. Before going into Russian specifics, we need to stress the importance of at least a few major works in the field: Mattei Dogan and John Higley, eds., *Elites, Crises, and the Origins of Regimes* (Lanham, MD: Rowman & Littlefield, 1998); Mattei Dogan, ed., *Elite Configurations at the Apex of Power* (Leiden: Bril, 2003); John Higley and Michael Burton, *Elite Foundations of Liberal Democracy* (Lanham, MD: Rowman & Littlefield, 2006); Jeff Faux, *The Global Class War* (Hoboken, NJ: Wiley & Sons, 2006).

2. The theory and history of this issue in Russia are set out in the excellent work by O. Gaman-Golutvina, "Gruppy interesov: retrospektiva" [Groups of interests: a retrospective], *Politiya* 4, no. 18 (Winter 2000/2001): 38–49, and "Elites Studies in Russia: Main Directions, Results, and Challenges," in *Social and Political Transformation in Europe* (Berlin: Не мог найти, 2010), http://www.mgimo.ru/publish/document145812.phtml.

3. P. Durnovo, "The Future Anglo-German War Will Be Transformed into an Armed Conflict between Two Groups of Powers" (memorandum, February 1914).

4. O. Gaman-Golutvina, "Rossijskie elity kak predmet nauchnogo analiza" [The Russian elite as the subject of scholarly analysis], *Society and Economics* (Общество и экономика), no. 3, April 2008, 175–96.

5. See Yu. Levada, "Esche raz o probleme sotsialnoj elity" [Once again on the problem of the social elite], in *Ot mnenij k ponimaniyu. Sotsiologicheskie ocherki. 1993–2000* [From opinion to understanding. Sociological studies. 1993–2000] (Moscow: Moscow School of Political Research, 2000), 269.

6. The Komsomol was the youth wing of the Communist Party. Its members were the first (in the late 1980s) to set up private commercial enterprises. They had knowledge, commercial ability, and, crucially, connections in power. The best example is the former head of Yukos, Mikhail Khodorkovsky.

7. O. Kryshtanovskaya, "Transformatsiya biznes-elity Rossii: 1998–2002" [The transformation of Russia's business elite: 1998–2002], *Sotsiologicheskie Issledovaniya* 8 (2002): 17–29; and O. Kryshtanovskaya, *Anatomiya rossijskoj elity* [An anatomy of the Russian

elite] (Moscow: Zakharov, 2005).

8. R. Kapelyushnikov, "Sobstvennost bez legitimnosti?" [Ownership without legitimacy?], in *Prava sobstvennosti, privatizatsiya i natsionalizatsiya v Rossii* [The right of ownership, privatization and nationalization in Russia), sec. 5.2, and "Liberalnaya missiya," *New Literature Review* (2009); L. Grigoriev, "Problemy privatizatsii" [Problems of privatization], in *Ekonomika perekhodnykh protsessov* [The economy of transition processes] (Moscow: MUM Publishing House, 2010), vol. 1, sec. 2.

9. The Russian Civil War and the purges of the 1930s left such an impression on families and on society (the main one being the impossibility of surviving a civil conflict in Russia) that it helped prevent events from taking a turn for the worse at the beginning of the 1990s. Similarly, memories of the civil war in Spain in the 1930s helped the Spanish find their way in the post-Franco transformation.

10. "In principle, the term elite is not an empirical one but, to use the familiar terminology of M. Weber, an 'ideal-typical' category, i.e., a construction used for research purposes." Y. A. Levada, "Elitarnye struktury v sovetskoj i postsovetskoj situatsii" [Elite structures in Soviet and post-Soviet conditions], in *Obshchestvennye nauki i sovremennost*, no. 6 (2007): 5–15.

11. See, for example, A. Chirikova, "O teoriyakh elit" [On Theories of the Elites], 2008; R. K. Simonyan, "Elita ili vse-taki nomenklatura? (Rasmyshleniya o rossijskom pravyashchem sloe)" [An elite or a nomenklatura after all? (Thoughts on the Russian governing class)], 2009; and L. N. Vasilieva, "Elita ili erzats-elita: politicheskoe budushchee Rossii" [An Elite or an Ersatz Elite: Russia's political future].

12. V. Ledyaev, "Kogo otnosit k elite?" [Who falls within the elite?], *Obshchestvo i ekonomika*, no. 3 (April 2008): 121–29.

13. M. Afanasiev, *Rossijskie elity razvitiya: zapros na novyj kurs* [The Russian development elite: the demand for a new way] (Moscow: Liberalnaya missiya, 2009), 16.

14. See L. Grigoriev and A. Salmina, "Struktura srednogo klassa v Rossii: gipotez i predvaritelnyj analiz" [The structure of the middle class in Russia: a hypothesis and initial analysis], in *Rossijskij srednij klass: analiz struktury i finansovogo povedeniya* [The Russian middle class: an analysis of its structure and financial behavior] (Moscow: INSOR, Ekon-Inform, 2009).

15. A. Shubin, *Rossiya—2020: budushchee strany v usloviyakh globalnykh peremen* [Russia—2020: the future of the country in conditions of global change], and *Rossiya i mir v 2020 godu. Doklad Natsionalnogo razvedyvatelnogo soveta SShA "Mapping the Global Future"* [Russia and the world in 2020.   A report by the U.S. National Intelligence Council. "Mapping the Global Future"] (Moscow: Evropa, 2005), 184.

16. O. Kryshtanovskaya, "Transformatsiya biznes-elity Rossii."

17. See I. Busygina and M. Filippov, "Problema vynuzhdennoj federalizatsii" [Problems of compulsory federalization], *Pro et contra* (May–August 2009): 125–38.
18. In Soviet times, too, there were few Muscovites among the top political nomenklatura, but they accounted for a large share of the professional elite and major officials.
19. In the future it may be possible to assess the stability of the elite by the degree of integration of subsequent generations into the power elite. The "Soviet version" also cannot be ruled out: the first generation takes risks in the struggle and takes up positions in the political and business elite in order to send its children and revenues abroad or into the intellectual elite, where they will be further removed from the risks of power and business struggles.
20. The term "quasi-undisclosed owner," refers to the actual owner of major assets whose ownership is legally hidden via offshore accounts. This is one of the (private) business elite's most important abilities. See "Problemy sobstvennosti: ot perestroyki do peredela" [Problems of ownership: from restructuring to redistributing], in *Puti Rossii: dvadtsat let peremen* [Russia's ways: twenty years of change] (Moscow: MSSES, 2005).
21. See O. Gaman-Golutvina, *Political Elites of Russia* (Moscow: Rospen, 2006), 338.
22. See L.Grigoriev and A.Salmina, "Struktura srednogo klassa v Rossii," in *Possijskij srednij klass*.
23. Quoted by V. M. Firsov, "Vosproizvodstvo nauchnoj elity" [The reproduction of the scientific elite], in *Problemy i perspektivy obshchestvennogo razvitiya* [Problems and perspectives for social development], 1998, http://www.nir.ru/sj/sj/1firsov.htm.
24. L. Gudkov and B. Dubin, "Illyuziya modernizatsii: rossijskaya byurokratiya v roli 'elity'" [The illusion of modernization: Russian bureaucracy in the role of the "elite"], *Pro et contra*, no. 3 (May/June 2007): 94.
25. M. Afanasiev, *Rossijskie elity razvitiya: zapros na novyj kurs* [The Russian development elite: the demand for a new way] (Moscow: Liberalnaya missiya, 2009), 95ff.
26. D. A. Medvedev, 2009.
27. Gudkov and Dubin, "Illyuziya modernizatsii" [The illusion of modernization], 73.
28. E. Gontmaher, L. Grigoriev, I. Yurgens, and others, *Russia in the 21st Century: Vision for the Future* (Moscow: INSOR, 2010).

CHAPTER EIGHT

Education for an Innovative Russia

Nur Kirabaev

Translated by Siriol Hugh-Jones

These days, Russia is, statistically speaking, a world leader in the field of education, with 630 students for every 10,000 members of the population. Bearing in mind that 88 percent of Russian citizens regard higher education as extremely desirable for their children, it is obvious that post-secondary education is playing an important role in constructing Russia's future role within the world system.

Nowadays, the fate of Russian education arouses deep concern not only regarding the development of the quality of education for its own sake but also in its capacity as the fundamental basis of Russia's modernization as a whole. This is not just a matter of education as a social issue but of those systemic challenges that science faces in the modern era to create a more competitive, innovative economy.

This chapter analyzes the state of post-secondary education in Russia in the context of its capacity to meet the challenges of required innovation within the socio-economic system.

Pros and Cons of Education in the USSR

In the 1950s, an education model was developed which, at the time, had significant potential as a developmental tool. The main principle for the training of professionals was a thorough and systematic grounding in the relevant subject, based on the assumption that education was required not just for the practical needs of a specific profession but in order to develop creative abilities to be applied to scientific problems. The general level of secondary-school leavers was relatively high. To this should be added that an education network was created that allowed talent to be supported and nurtured. This was particularly true of the high-profile specialist physics and mathematics schools.

History tells us that it was after World War II that Russian education began to be particularly highly regarded by the rest of the world. Even then, the main difference between the Soviet Union's education system and that of other countries was the emphasis not just on higher education but on higher *vocational* education. It was no coincidence that American experts attributed the USSR's main achievements in the 1950s and 1960s to the high level of Soviet vocational higher education. This assessment was based on the launch in 1957 of the world's first artificial satellite to orbit Earth and also on the creation and development of nuclear power stations, nuclear-powered vessels, and Soviet jet aviation. Of course, this did not apply to all areas of the Russian education system but primarily to the natural sciences, mathematics, and technology. Traditionally, the level of professional training in the fields of medicine, languages, oriental studies, archaeology, psychology, and the like was very strong. As far as social sciences were concerned, the situation was more complicated, given that this discipline was based exclusively on the Soviet development model and did not take sufficient account of developments elsewhere in the humanities.

By the mid-1960s, the transition in the USSR to universal secondary education was complete, and one in eight citizens of the USSR had a university/college degree. This was reflected in the population's social and cultural profile. Although it was still possible to talk of the existence of a certain degree of inequality in education, the reasons were more ideological than social. In the case of a series of non-science professions involving work abroad or within the ideological system, for example, recommendations were required from district committees or the regional committee of the Komsomol or Communist Party.

The end of the 1960s/beginning of the 1970s saw the onset of the period commonly known as the "stagnation," which was naturally reflected in the education system. Despite the fact that education had become one of society's key values, the command economy remained geared to the requirements of the country's insular agricultural complex.

The sources of the current modernization of Russia's higher education system have their beginnings in the era of Gorbachev's so-called "perestroika."

Faced with sharp criticism of ideological dogmatism, the authorities were no longer able to restrain the enormous public enthusiasm for democratization and the humanization of education. It was in this period that concepts of public and private management initiatives (*gosudarstvenno-obshchestvenno upravlenie*) and variation in education programs were introduced into many higher-education institutions, and there began to be considerable support for the idea of higher-education institutions having increased autonomy. The first multicandidate, democratic elections for provost of Lomonosov Moscow State University and the victory of V. A. Sadovnichii, who enjoyed wide support from the university community, as well as the defeat of the candidate recommended by the "powers-that-be," were evidence of the real role of the Russian Federation's academic and teaching community. This meant that the Russian Council of University provosts acquired a considerable role and authority, independent of the influences of the administration. However, the expectation heralded by the new Russian law on education (adopted in 1992) was unfortunately not met. On the one hand, with the beginning of market reforms, education was financed on the "remainder" principle and higher-education institutions encountered severe difficulties when it came to paying teaching staff's salaries and utility charges, maintaining buildings, and purchasing teaching equipment. All this was an indication that the government itself was unable to offer the education community a definite strategy or tactics for the development of Russian education. Instead, public psychology and the public mood turned increasingly to conservative models in an attempt to preserve the Soviet education system. The creation of myths around the achievements and quality of Soviet science and education became a leitmotif in the widespread resistance to all attempts at reform "from above." At the same time, under the new conditions of mass education, adherence to the Soviet education standard (which in fact only offered a genuinely elite training at a few dozen colleges or universities) required the adoption of new approaches to the introduction of a unified educational space and new requirements for the training of future scientists, teachers, and arts graduates, together with the training of employees in the broad range of subjects required for the country's economy as a whole.

The Post-Soviet Education Philosophy

Following the collapse of the Soviet Union, the system of higher education in Russia was supposed to provide a solution to at least four major problems in the context of sharp political confrontation between the pro-communist Duma and Yeltsin's team of liberals. First, there was the question of the new strategy of development in education in connection with the change to the social and economic setup. The new education strategy should have been based on the requirements and challenges of the structural rebuilding of the economy, taking into account the prevalent new trend for "mass education." Second, Russia's new politics raised the question of the need to enter the international sphere of education as a consequence of the Russian Federation's strategy for political development. Third, in the conditions of the systemic and structural crisis of the transition period, a solution had to be found to the question of financing the education system as a whole. At the same time, a state monopoly existed in the field of education throughout the Soviet period, and therefore the state bore subsidiary responsibility that, according to the new strategy, it was to share with nascent private enterprise. Fourth, there was the particularly pressing problem of retraining those teachers who in Soviet times had taught the "ideological disciplines": scientific communism, the history of the Communist Party of the Soviet Union, Marxist-Leninist philosophy, and political economy.

For at least the first ten years of the new Russia's existence, the strategy for the development of education remained undecided. Nevertheless, within the scope of structural rebuilding in the field of education, the autonomy of higher-education institutions substantially expanded. It became possible for state universities and institutes to obtain funding from multiple sources; the first private higher-education institutions appeared in the country; in 1995 the first state standard for higher professional education was adopted with the aim of restoring a unified education system on the one hand and the introduction, at the discretion of higher-education institutions, of a two-tier system of preparation for entry into the international education space. And if this signaled the restoration of a single education system, then the introduction of the new state standard did not lead to the widespread adoption of the "bachelor and masters degree" system. Unfortunately, higher-education institutions have regarded the opportunity to enter the international education space merely as an attempt to copy the Western education system and thus relinquish the best traditions of Russian higher education.

The education system was ultimately funded under the remainder principle; it led to the destruction of the infrastructure of higher-education institutions and to a sharp fall in the living standards of teachers and professors.

Within the framework of the retraining of teachers of the so-called ideological disciplines in the mid-1990s, courses were organized and run on a systemic basis in which tens of thousands of teachers participated.

Indeed, it was in the first decade of the new Russia that the priorities of the political parties became clear in the field of education, and these generally remained unchanged in subsequent years. Whereas in 1990 the party of power, Our Home is Russia, generally promoted the government's policy in the field of education, the Communist Party defended the Soviet model of education in its policy documents, demonstrations, and manifestos. Yabloko (Russian United Democratic Party) adopted a more liberal position in the field of education, its position being linked to demands for a review of the structural rebuilding of the economy and a review of Western education models. All the main parties, including the liberal-democratic party of Russia (LDPR), regarded keeping the system of free higher education as a strategic priority. Moreover, even taking into account the current political policy documents of parties such as United Russia, A Just Russia, the liberal democratic party of Russia, Yabloko, and the Union of Right Forces, it is difficult to discern any new strategy of development for the domestic higher-education system. These days, virtually all the parties believe it is essential that the best traditions of Russian education be kept and declare the need for serious investment in personnel and targeted support for innovative structuring of higher-education institutions.

There remains, however, the unsolved problem of adequate funding for the higher-education system in the context of the challenges of the modern world. By the end of the 1990s, federal spending on education was less than 1 percent of the country's GDP. Shock therapy had—and still has—severe consequences on education and science. For the first time in many years, the country was divided into rich and poor, and the thread of the tradition of one generation being replaced by the next was broken. Working at a university or college or one of the institutes of the Academy of Sciences was no longer a matter of prestige since the salaries they paid their scientists and teaching staff were barely enough to cover the costs of food. The teaching and science professions ceased to be regarded as belonging to the area of social engagement, where young people could effectively realize themselves and their potential while also having a rewarding career.

The difficult financial and economic situation consolidated the education community and the anti-Yeltsin mood in protest against the neoliberal wave of putting market priorities ahead of the interests of education.[1]

An article in *MOST* (2001) stated, "As a result, at the beginning of the twenty-first century, Russia's overall potential had, according to UN calculations, fallen to a thirty-year low."[2] Thus, Russian education met the era of globalization in conditions of systemic crisis. In fact, it was only with the appointment of Yevgeny Primakov to the post of prime minister of the Russian Federation in 1998 and the election of Vladimir Putin as president of the Russian Federation that questions were raised regarding national education policy. In 2001 the government of the Russian Federation adopted the idea of modernizing Russian education by 2010, and a system of measures to improve the quality and competitiveness of education services was set out in the "Priority Areas of Development" of the Russian Federation's education system, approved by the government in 2004.

Beginning in 2005 a special, targeted, federal educational-development program emerged. Education was included in a series of other national projects, among which the priority national project "Obrazovanie" (Education) is worth particular mention. Under the auspices of this program, RUB 30 billion were allocated and spent between 2006 and 2008 on the development of innovative programs at fifty-seven higher-education institutions in the Russian Federation.[3] The purpose of state support was to improve the quality of education and research by financing new equipment, textbooks, programs, and the retraining of teachers.

Under the auspices of this program, higher-education institutions have developed more than six hundred bachelor's programs and about eight hundred master's and PhD programs, in addition to a record number of new-generation textbooks and teaching materials. This breakthrough occurred largely thanks to the implementation of programs retraining teaching staff. In the course of three years, about forty thousand teachers underwent retraining. Closer links were established between colleges and the employment markets.

The development of modern infrastructure for higher-education institutions has become a priority area. Universities have set up scientific research centers, training and innovation complexes, center's where multiple users share equipment, joint laboratories and basic business-incubation programs, student incubator programs, and technology parks. The number of units implemented within higher-education institutions using partner organizations has trebled, the number of student business-incubation programs has grown 1.5 times, and the number of multi-user centers has grown by 60 percent.[4]

Aware of the importance of Russian education's ability to compete, the government in 2006 created two universities of a new kind, the Siberian and Southern Federal universities. They were founded with the aim of resolving the geopolitical task of guaranteeing social and economic development in those regions. Their job entailed effectively developing integration between education and science by involving leading Russian and foreign academics, and also of improving the ratio of students and postgraduates within the framework of a mobility program.

In 2008 two national research universities were founded on the basis of two of the country's existing institutes—the Moscow Engineering Physics Institute and the Moscow Institute of Steel and Alloys (MISiS). The purpose of this was to improve the teaching and research potential of the hi-tech sectors of the domestic economy in the priority areas of science and technology. In 2009 another twelve higher-education institutions were selected. Finally, in 2009, a law was adopted regarding the particular status of Lomonosov Moscow State University and the St. Petersburg State University. These universities have been given particular status as "unique science and education complexes, the country's oldest higher-education institutions, having enormous significance for the development of the Russian community."

After ten destructive years, the further development of Russian education within the framework of state social policy is now relatively clearly demarcated. However, the consequences of the previous period were so negative that the tasks we face today involve not just modernization but restoration. This also goes for the restoration and improvement of higher-education institutions' material and technical base, the social and financial status of teachers and academics, and the introduction of younger staff.

In Russia, one of the most important trends linked to ensuring education remains competitive and develops consistently is the new role of the state in developing strategy and policy for education development, as well as the creation of the necessary incentives and favorable conditions for the modernization of education. A second trend is linked to the changing structure of the higher-education system and transition to multi-tier training of professionals. The third trend tracks the development of internationalization and integration of education spaces, which for Russia means development within the framework of the Bologna Process and participation in the creation of a unified European area for education and science.

Among the basic problems of education development in Russia are those of ensuring equal access to education, the quality of education, internationalization and the export of education services, and new teaching technologies.

Ensuring equal access to education ("education for all") in current conditions means the resolution of all those quality-related problems in conditions dominated by the trend toward mass education. The reverse side of this problem is that of maintaining and developing the so-called elite: vocational higher education when state funding is being cut and the negative social consequences of commercialization are affecting higher education.

Given the significant increase in the value of knowledge to the economy, we cannot ignore the fact that over the last twenty years higher education in Russia has ceased to be the privilege of the few most able students in the fields of science and education. Of course, mass higher education is a slightly different kind of education from that traditionally provided in classical universities, which base themselves on the Humboldt model, with its emphasis on teaching and research. Whereas in 1990 there were 514 state higher-education institutions with 2,824,500 students and private higher-education institutions did not exist, in 2007 there were 1,108 higher-education institutions with 7,461,300 students, of which 450 were private institutions. At the same time, one must bear in mind that of those 7,461,300 students, only 3,571,300 were studying on campus. In 1990, 583,900 students enrolled at higher-education institutions; in 2007 this figure was 1,384,000—and that in conditions of demographic decline.[5]

One of the negative consequences of the perestroika era for the education system was the sharp decline in the standard of education and in quality control. In 1995 the first State Educational Standard in higher vocational education was prepared and adopted. The purpose of this was to re-create a unified educational arena and vocational training requirements, taking into account other countries' experiences and the national tradition. Within the framework of this document, keeping the international market in education services in mind, higher-education institutions were allowed the freedom to opt for a multi-tier system (BA followed by MA) or to keep the single five-year course. This option was retained following the adoption of the second generation of state education standards in 2000. Unfortunately, most higher-education institutions did not take advantage of the multi-tier option and continued to gear themselves to the requirements of the Russian employment market. After Russia joined the Bologna Process in 2003, the process of transition to a multi-tier education system became an irreversible trend.

One of the aspects of the development of mass education is the reduction in course lengths, but for the education community this process turned out to be extremely painful given the potential decline in the quality of teaching, national tradition, and the thorough and systematic grounding given to professionals as part of their training. This was a hotly debated issue not only in the education community but also among the wider public. It was no coincidence that the term "Bolognization" of education appeared, meaning the devaluation of knowledge and quality of education, and of the degrees awarded to graduates.

Over the last five years, there has been active discussion of the problems of the third state standard. The particular idea behind this document is based on emphasis being placed less on the process and more on the results of education, which should allow education to be gradually brought into line with the specific requirements of the country's social and economic development. This "competency-building approach" should be geared to the rapidly changing employment market and society as a whole.

Particularly critical today is the question of adequate funding for education. The experience of the last twenty years, during which private higher-education institutions have gained a certain standing, has shown the validity of obtaining funding from multiple sources: from the state, from the commercial sector, and from savings and investments by private individuals. This question is particularly important given that the market reforms of the Yeltsin era doomed education to chronic underfunding, thereby substantially undermining the social prestige of those who had gone through higher education, which in Russia was traditionally fairly high.

The main source of funding for education has been various levels of the public budget. After a significant reduction in 1998–2000, the ratio of education spending as part of the Russian Federation's consolidated budget has tended to grow. Whereas in 2000 this figure was 11 percent, in 2005 it was 13.3 percent. Nevertheless, the dynamic of state funding for education as a share of GDP has been extremely inconsistent. In 1997 this figure reached its highest point of 4.8 percent; it slumped to its lowest in 2000 at 2.9 percent. In 2005 the ratio of spending on education came to 3.7 percent, of which 0.6 percent of GDP went to higher education.[6] If we examine the number of students at higher-education institutions by their sources of funding, students at state and municipal higher-education institutions whose studies are paid for from the public purse made up 86.9 percent of the total number of students in the 1995–96 academic year, while in 2004–05 they accounted for 43.6 percent. The private sector is particularly prominent in higher vocational education: in the mid-1990s it made up 5 percent; in the 2004–05 academic year it represented 15 percent.[7]

One of the problems of the "relevancy of higher education" is linked to the emphasis on people having access to higher education irrespective of their future employment. Even today, many graduates from higher-education institutions do not work in their field of expertise. This obviously suggests that the absence of any assessment of the economy's requirements results in overproduction of certain categories of professionals with degrees. At the same time, the popularity of professions in the fields of economics, business management, and law means that today there is hardly a higher-education institution that does not offer qualifications in these fields. That said, this trend has led to a sharp fall in the standard of education in these areas. In 2008 the question of the quality of training for lawyers was discussed even at the presidential level. This was primarily as a result of mass higher education with a decline in the standard of teaching. There were plenty of graduates with legal degrees but very few good lawyers.

State higher-education institutions have introduced a practice of offering different types of paid services as a way of diversifying their sources of funding. In 2005 only 6 percent of higher-education institutions offered courses completely free of charge. Twenty percent of higher-education institutions charge for supplementary subjects not included in the basic education curriculum. Eighty-eight percent of all students in higher-education institutions pay for their courses in full. Today, almost a third of higher-education institutions operate on commercial principles. Thus, of 1.4 million students accepted in 2005, more than 800,000 were allocated fee-paying placements at state institutions or paid courses at commercial institutions. Only 600,000 were given publicly funded placements. This data reflects a positive trend in the development of state higher-education institutions that are partly funded by students. It must be noted, however, that there is no system for stimulating the development of private higher-education institutions with guaranteed state funding, which allows us to conclude that public officials do not understand the role and place of private-education institutions, which in developed countries enjoy a traditionally high status. Private higher-education institutions in Russia have no real support either as regards being able to participate in competitions to attract state-funded students, or in terms of support for technology parks and business incubators, or for student hostels and other aspects of the social lives of those students who are self-financing or financed by their parents. Despite the fact that in recent years scientific discoveries have begun to be registered to private higher-education institutions, V. Zernov, chair of the board of the Association of Russia's Private Higher Education Institutions, points out that not a single private higher-education institution was among the winners in the competition for innovative higher-education institutions. In a country in which 85 percent of GDP is generated in the private sector of the economy, private higher-education institutions are left with no support from the state in terms of resources. But, for the sake of argument, if the government had not stepped in to help private banks, what would have happened to the Russian banking system?

These days, Russia has about 1.5 million students at private higher-education institutions, a fifth of the total number of students at Russia's higher-education institutions, and there are more than 470 accredited private higher-education institutions. The private-education sector was only just beginning to get established when it was hit by the financial crisis, and a demographic crisis is already underway (whereas in 2006 there were 1.2 million students who came out of the Russian school system having completed all eleven grades, in 2010 the figure was 900,000, and in 2012 it will be only 740,000). It is understandable that in this situation, the primary victims are the private higher-education institutions, to which graduates turn as a last resort when they have not been given a state grant.

In the opinion of O. Smolin, a deputy chair of the State Duma's education committee and head of an expert commission on private education, discrimination against the private sector is discrimination against a segment of Russia's children and young people. What's more, there are no such things as "private" children or students: thus the government should ensure that quality education is available, and that means education for all. These days, 95 percent of private-education institutions provide arts education while technical education remains the "privilege" of the state. But Russian industry is in private hands. Why prepare employees for plant owners at the expense of the taxpayer?

The demand from private higher-education institutions that public funding be allocated throughout the education system—not by type of institution but by performance—is already reflected in the government's conceptual documents. As noted by G. Safaraliev, a deputy chair of the State Duma's education committee, the concept adopted for the long-term development of Russia to 2020 refers to the equal allocation of public funding in education irrespective of the form of ownership of higher-education institutions. But whether this position will ever be put into practice is a big question. It may well go the way of one of the decisions the State Council made long ago regarding equal access to public funding: it was never implemented.

When looking at the role and influence socio-cultural factors have on trends in the development of mass higher education, we have to acknowledge the legacy of the "Soviet mentality," which regarded higher education as an essential condition to the achievement of success both professionally and in life. Although in the Soviet era graduates from higher-education institutions benefited very little financially, they nevertheless enjoyed social status and the prestige of being a graduate. In recent years, however, financial considerations also have come into play. The term "successful professional career" is gaining currency, which many interpret as meaning having a degree in law or economics. Thus, the emphasis on higher education has become a widely accepted norm, virtually regardless of the social class of those involved. According to the results of polls conducted by VTsIOM (the Russian Public Opinion Research Center), the demand for higher education is set to grow.[8] In spring 2003, in answer to the question of what level of education people considered adequate for their children/grandchildren, 70 percent of those questioned said that completion of higher vocational education was essential.

Pros and Cons of Mass Higher Education

In Soviet times the state established higher-education institutions as a way of meeting the needs of the national economy, yet over the last twenty years new higher-education institutions have appeared under the influence of market processes. Furthermore, the dynamic of development of mass higher education has led to the modernization of traditional higher-education institutions and the emergence of private higher-education institutions. Unfortunately, there is no competition evident between state and private higher-education institutions, although as a rule the latter are more flexible and less restricted when it comes to making decisions on the opening of new departments and updating teaching plans. That said, most private higher-education institutions are not yet competitive and produce poor-quality students.

The process of developing mass higher education has raised the particularly vexing question of education quality, since traditionally it was thought that the advantage of the Russian education model was based on the idea of its providing a thorough, systematic grounding.[9]

The trend toward the development of higher education could perhaps lead to a general decline in the image of the quality of education traditionally provided by the country's leading higher-education institutions. The question that remains is the price of such decline in quality. It is no coincidence that there has been talk in recent years of the need for state support for 250 to 300 higher-education institutions and of those, 20 to 30 being selected for the provision of elite training in return for additional state funding. Unfortunately, the state is not yet providing any serious incentives within the framework of small- and large-business legislation for the development of education and science, even bearing in mind Federal Law No 217 of August 2, 2009, "On the introduction of changes to individual legislative acts of the Russian Federation on questions of the creation of business entities using publicly funded science and education institutions for the purpose of the practical application (implementation) of the results of intellectual endeavor."

That said, the academic and higher-education community is concerned by the context in which reforms are being carried out: the critical situation regarding staff in education, science, and manufacturing; the decline in the status of academics and teachers; the aging of the scientific and teaching population; the reduction in the share of public funding in higher-education institution budgets; and a decline in Russia's international competitiveness.

Among these risks, we could include the fact that the shadow economy in education is expanding, from preparation for entry into higher-education institutions to the simple purchase of diplomas. The result is that poor-quality higher education is relatively accessible to the public at large. The opportunity to obtain an education giving future professionals a high standard of vocational training is, for most of the population, clearly becoming more remote. Even in the case of publicly funded education, the cost of living in the large cities—where most of the elite higher-education institutions are located—acts as a financial barrier for a significant portion of secondary school graduates from the provinces. The highest education fee levels in Russia (from $4,000 to $9,000 a year) apply at the most prestigious higher-education institutions in Moscow, a degree from which is highly prized on the employment market. Overall, this poses the crucial question of the accessibility of higher education, in particular, publicly funded higher education, and the possibility of social conflicts being exacerbated.

According to the results of numerous research projects, 42 percent of Russian citizens (practically all social groups) are willing to pay for higher education unconditionally. This concerns not just direct spending on education but also incidental costs—books, textbooks, living costs in a city away from home, and so forth. In family budgets (of families with children in their last years at school or who are at college/university), spending on education consistently emerges as one of the three major areas of expenditure.

At the same time, taking into account the traditionally high status of qualified professionals, many Russians are geared to obtaining a higher-education degree regardless of the type of degree. A smaller proportion choose their higher-education institution based on the institution's "brand" or reputation, and very few actually compare the opportunities at different higher-education institutions or assess the opportunities for their further career and professional progress.

In Russia, it has historically been the case that serious scientific study and research has largely occurred beyond the confines of the higher-education system. As early as the 1930s, there was a significant expansion in the importance of the role of the Academy of Sciences, which had previously, under a project of Peter the Great, occupied a position inferior to that of university education. In Soviet times, as, incidentally, is true today, science for many higher-education institutions in Russia ceased to be university science. Current reforms in higher education are being carried out in the context of creating an academic science network operating independently of the higher-education system. Still, the development of scientific research is, in a group of leading higher-education institutions, largely guided by the interests of the defense industry, since this allows them fairly reliable funding for scientific research and for design and experimentation.

Higher-education institutions are not the only losers from the separation of science and education—academic science has lost out too, deprived of ongoing, repeated experiments by academic staff. Even the elite training of personnel for the science departments of Russia's leading higher-education institutions is today unable to meet the demands of academic research and development departments.

Furthermore, given new technologies, the science that has been virtually isolated from education is unable on its own to produce personnel capable of applying intellectual achievements commercially and thereby developing not just the economy but the knowledge economy. Therefore, the question of realizing the scientific potential of higher-education institutions (which employ about 80 percent of the country's doctors of science) is particularly acute, both as concerns the application of the results of basic research in the education process and the fundamentalization of education. Of course, this does not affect higher-education institutions that encourage widespread demand for mass education but those continuing Russian traditions of providing professionals with a sound academic training, allowing them to develop academic and strategic positions in their research. Currently, the government is attempting to overcome this trend toward the separation of science and education by defining the priorities of innovative development in the Russian economy: energy efficiency and energy supply, nuclear technology, space technology, technology in the field of medicine, and strategic IT.

The time has come to make decisions of principle (which, most importantly, can be verified) concerning the genuine modernization of, and development of innovation in, the economy. The crux of this decision has long been known. Where education and science are concerned, it is the transition from centralized funding of science in general to support for specific projects and teams of scientists. This approach is a global trend arising from global political and economic change.[10]

The Development of Higher Vocational Education via the Bologna Process

Modern, competitive higher education poses the particularly vexing question of the need for thorough training of professionals in multidisciplinary projects. It is no coincidence that the national program for the development of nanotechnology raised the question of the training of qualified professionals for the nano industry. From 2004 to 2007, the volume of the global nano market almost trebled, reaching $1.4 trillion. It is forecast that by 2015 it should grow to about $4 trillion. The Russian share in that market to date is only 0.07 percent. Changing this situation and increasing this figure to 3 percent by 2015 will be no easy task.[11]

In the 1960s the terminology of biophysics, biochemistry, and other such disciplines was unfamiliar, yet present-day modern economic development demands that professionals are trained in interdisciplinary areas. For the education system, this poses the task of developing new forms and techniques, and also of a transition from qualifications to skills, permitting, first and foremost, the development of an ability to make effective, sensible decisions in rapidly changing conditions of employment and professional operations. It is within the framework of a discussion of the Bologna Process that the question is raised of changing the emphasis from the process to the results of study. This was the strategy at the heart of the ideology behind the new education standards. This is not just a question of paying lip service to fashion. As mentioned earlier, in 2003 Russia became a signatory to the Bologna declaration, which provides for the building of a unified European educational arena (involving, among other things, the introduction of separate BA and MA programs rather than the single five-year course traditional in Russia and the introduction of a credits-based system). Over the last five years, this has been a hotly debated subject in which participants have expressed diametrically opposing views. First of all, for Russia this does not involve the copying of any European education system or the fulfillment of any specific obligations regarding the implementation of Bologna Process provisions. Second, Russia's entry into a unified European educational arena gives it the opportunity, in conjunction with European countries, to work out common rules governing the operation of this system on the basis of a comparable legal framework and as concerns specific mechanisms for the implementation of the Bologna Process documents. Third, this makes it possible to take account of basic trends in the internationalization of education and, broadly speaking, to participate in the European education-services market. Fourth, the Bologna Process is a timely opportunity to make sense of and attempt to reform the national system of higher vocational education so as to train competitive professionals for the modern employment market and the demands of the country's social and economic development.[12]

More than anything else, a multi-tier higher-education system meets the demands of a market economy, in which the employment market has particular requirements regarding the flexibility of the workforce. There has to be a flexible combination and a convergence between the study and work processes, increased mobility of the workforce, flexible approaches to the length and makeup of working hours and study time, and to the forms of study and work.

Higher education in Russia will become increasingly prestigious. Under the influence, in particular, of opportunities to find well-paid work in Europe in their areas of expertise, young people will be given an additional incentive to study at higher-education institutions. Furthermore, while participating in mobility programs allowing them to study at higher-education institutions in Europe, Russian students will get used to the real conditions of life and work in the West, which will greatly assist them should they then decide to seek work abroad.

Russia's entry into the Bologna Process may have a positive effect on the state of Russian science—by strengthening the research potential of higher-education institutions and through their planned participation in joint research projects with European universities.

The weakest aspect of the activities of higher-education institutions is the commercial application of intellectual achievements. Thus, for example, in 2006 there were 6,836 patents awarded in Moscow. By comparison, IBM made 3,415 patent applications; overall, 796 companies in the world receive more than a hundred patents and evidence of intellectual property (IP) rights every three years. Of 800 Russian organizations examined, according to the Moscow Committee for Science and Technology (MKNT), the highest number of patents any one of them had was 26. But this is not just a matter of absolute figures. The percentage breakdown of the owners of the 6,836 patent applications is as follows: Moscow higher-education institutions, 7.5 percent; organizations within the Russian Academy of Sciences, 1.875 percent; the Russian Academy of Medical Sciences, 2.31 percent; and the Russian Academy of Agricultural Sciences, 1.35 percent.

We should point out that 22 percent of all the country's scientists are concentrated in Moscow. It seems that this has led to the country having a "shadow" economy in intellectual property rights: over the last three or four years in Moscow, for example, not a single patent license or other licensing agreement for the use of intellectual property (know-how, trademarks, design inventions) has been registered. Consequently, in 2006 the Russian Federation occupied forty-second place in the world in terms of patent activity: it lagged behind Jamaica and the Antilles. Only on August 2, 2009, was the long-debated law No. 217-FZ adopted. The passage of this law was regarded as a political gesture in support of small, innovative business. Time will tell how long it will survive. However, this affects applied science, which is capable of generating profit and not just covering its costs. Items of intellectual property are the basis for innovation in industry. For example, hi-tech manufacturing, the world market for which is worth

$2.3 trillion, is largely dominated by the following countries: the United States accounts for $700 billion, or 30.4 percent; Germany at $530 billion, or 23 percent; and Japan at $400 billion, or 17.4 percent. In Russia, on the other hand, the figure is $7 billion, or 0.3 percent of global hi-tech production.[13]

Finally, there is one more important consideration. As a full member of the Bologna Process, Russia can in turn actively influence higher education in Europe: the voices of more than a thousand Russian higher-education institutions cannot but be heard when decisions are made on education.

Thanks to the Bologna Process, the European university will probably acquire greater autonomy in the new, broader sense of the word. The Magna Charta of European Universities (1988) confirms that "the university is an autonomous institution at the heart of societies." Moreover, for the Soviet education system, just as is the case in the modern Russian system, higher-education institutions are generally largely dependent on the Ministry of Education, which determines the key parameters of their existence. By contrast, autonomy in the Bologna sense means minimal dependence by higher-education institutions on officials and a much greater degree of public trust in these institutions, their teachers, and their students.

So far, we have to be satisfied that a competence-based approach is gradually taking over as the new paradigm for vocational education. An analysis of the modern employment market in Russia also reveals that the wider the area of expertise, the easier it is for graduates of higher-education institutions to adapt to their new places of work and carry out their work effectively.

Problems, Quests, and Prospects of Current Modernization

Today as never before, it is clear that when talking about the modernization of education we have to discuss the changes that will permit the systemic development of Russian higher education.

The following should be counted among the positive changes in the development of higher education to date: the increase in public funding from RUB 71.8 billion in 2004 to RUB 161.7 billion in 2006; the new practice of diversifying sources of funding; support for the best higher-education institutions via the priority national project "Education 2006–2008" (RUB 37 billion shared between fifty-seven higher education institutions); equal access to education and measures to combat corruption based on a single state examination (which should, of course, be improved, taking into account all the constructive criticism of recent years); the adoption of a law on a two-tier higher-education structure (BA and MA) in the context of compliance with the Bologna Process, which allows us to talk about individual educational trajectories and widens the opportunity for training competitive professionals for the employment market; and the involvement of business associations in setting out the requirements they have of graduates.

These are the main problems that need to be resolved in the light of global economic development. First of all, there is a lack of time—restructuring within the economy requires new qualified personnel. It is already clear that there is a gulf between the quality of education and growth in the necessary skills levels of professionals, meaning that new technical skills need to be acquired. Workers are needed for the "new" economy.

Then, there is the problem of the social responsibility of education and the requirements for the adoption of necessary measures to reduce the negative consequences of the commercialization of higher education and the danger of its becoming fully governed by market mechanisms and corresponding policies and funding.

Third, there is the sudden growth in high-quality international education programs, which render the requirements of national quality and technology standards even tougher (for example, the role of the Internet and information and communications technology in the modern teaching process).

Fourth, there is the problem of demographic decline and the increase in the average age of academic and teaching staff at higher-education institutions (in 2008, about 40 percent were over 65).[14]

Finally, there is the need for a "revival" of science in higher-education institutions and the effective solution of problems associated with the commercial application of intellectual achievements.

Notes

1. A. L. Andreev, *Rossiiskoe obrazovanie* [Russian education] (Moscow: Nauka Science, 2008), 256.
2. O. Lebedev and M. Shabelnik, "Dukhovnye i intellektualnye potentsialy" [Spiritual and intellectual potential], *MOST*, no. 46 (2001).
3. *Poisk* (Search) no. 6, February 6, 2009.
4. Ibid.
5. *Obrazovanie v Rossii*—2007. *Statisticheskii byulleten* [Education in Russia—2007. A statistical bulletin] (Moscow: MGUPI, 2008), 405.
6. Materials from the scientific and practical conference "The Economics of Education—the Results of Monitoring" (Higher School of Economics, October 6, 2006).
7. See http://upr.1september.ru/2005/14/8.htm.
8. "Monitoring ekonomiki obrazovaniya: Analiz vzaimosvyazi sistemy obrazovaniya i rynka truda v Rossii" [Monitoring the economics of education: An analysis of the mutual links between the education system and the employment market in Russia] (Higher School of Economics' Information Bulletin, Moscow, 2005).
9. See *Obrazovanie, kotoroe my mozhem poteryat* [The education we may lose] (Moscow: Moscow State University, 2003).
10. See http://www.ng.ru/editorial/2009-08-10/2_red.html.
11. *Poisk* (Search) no. 5, January 30, 2009.
12. *"Myagkii Put" vkhozhdeniya rossiiskii vuzov v Bolonskii protsess* ["The Gentle Way" of Russian higher education institutions' entry into the Bologna Process] (Moscow: Olma-Press, 2005).
13. See http://www.ng.ru/science/2008-02-13/18_innovations.html.
14. In 2006 there were 1.3 million secondary school leavers; in 2007, 1.1 million; in 2010 there will be 952,000; and in 2012, 740,000.

CHAPTER NINE

Health and Health Care in Russia Today and Tomorrow

Oleg Atkov and Guzel Ulumbekova

Translated by Siriol Hugh-Jones

Introduction

This chapter discusses some of the demographic challenges faced by the Russian government since the fall of communism. It then analyzes the government's attempts to address those challenges and proposes several steps aimed at improving the overall performance of the Russian health care system.

In 2006, then president Vladimir Putin referred to the demographic crisis as the most serious problem facing Russia.[1] Some scholars adopted a very pessimistic view about Russia's future, predicting a population decline of more than 30 percent over the next fifty years (from 143 million in 2003).[2] Indeed, the fall of communism and the liberal economic reforms did result in a rapid decline in population. This, together with the fact that the population was aging and its health was deteriorating, posed serious economic and security problems for the Russian state. In addition, medical services at the state-run polyclinics and hospitals were rapidly degrading. Despite a large number of hospitals and numerous health care personnel, the health care system had been unable to provide an acceptable level of medical services and was faced with many problems, including lack of public expenditures, outdated medical and technical equipment, and inefficient management.

Section 1 of this chapter presents some population and health statistics for the Russian Federation (RF). Section 2 examines some factors that influenced the deterioration in the health of the Russian population. Section 3 discusses problems in the RF health care system that affect the quality and availability of medical and preventive care. Section 4 evaluates the challenges that the system will face till 2020 and the expectations of the parties concerned. In Section 5 the authors present their recommendations for the development of a health care strategy to improve the health status of the Russian population according to the guidelines set by the RF government for the year 2020.

Section 1: Population Health Status in the Russian Federation

Here we look at an analysis of demography and population health status in Russia from 1980 to 2008 compared with the European Union (EU) countries.[3] Almost all indicators in the Russian Federation are worse than the corresponding indices in "new" or "old" EU countries, and even worse than in the USSR in the years from 1985 to 1990. The most serious demographic and health problems in the RF are the high mortality rate of the employable population due to preventable causes (cardiovascular diseases, external causes of mortality, and cancer), the low birth rate, the growing number of senior citizens, a high morbidity rate, and the inequality in health indicators between inhabitants of different regions as well as between rural and urban populations. Such health issues require urgent measures from the RF government, employers, and the citizens.

If no steps are taken to decrease the current mortality rate and increase the birth rate, a pessimistic scenario of the Russian Federal Statistics Service (Rosstat) predicts a reduction in the RF population in 2031 by 12 percent (from 141 million to 127.4 million people). Such de-population of the vast territories of Russia would present a serious security problem as it could provoke instability and trigger problems in managing the country, due to reduced numbers of the employable population and men of draftable age; it could also destabilize families as a result of the imbalance in the numbers of men and women.

POPULATION SIZE AND COMPOSITION

According to Rosstat, in 2009 the population of the RF stood at 141,904,000 people: 63 percent were employable; 16 percent were children between 0 and 15 years old; and 21 percent were at retirement age. Starting in 1992 the country's population began to decrease—from 1998 to 2005 by about 700,000 people annually. In 2006–08, however, the average rate of reduction slowed to 1.5 and 3.5 times accordingly.

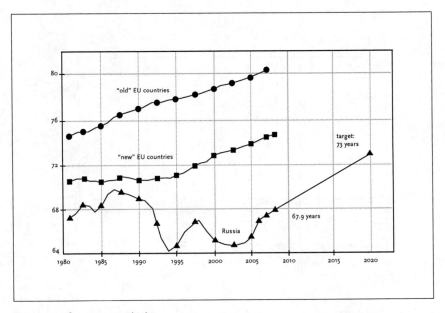

Figure 9.1 Life expectancy at birth

LIFE EXPECTANCY

Starting in 2006 life expectancy in Russia grew and reached 67.9 years in 2008 (see fig. 9.1). Still, it remains low: 7 years lower than in the "new" EU countries and 12.5 years lower than in the "old" EU countries.[4] The difference in the life expectancy of men and women in Russia is 12.4 years, which is the highest index in the world. The key role in the low life expectancy of the Russian population is played by the increased mortality of the employable population, most of which are men.

MORTALITY RATE AND CAUSE-SPECIFIC MORTALITY

In 2008 the crude death rate in Russia, defined as the total number of deaths per year per 1,000 persons, was 14.6. Despite the declining trend it is still 1.3 times higher than in the "new" EU countries and 1.6 times higher than in the "old" EU countries. The infant mortality rate, the total number of deaths under one year old per 1,000 live births, has been steadily improving; it has decreased to the level of 8.5 deaths per 1,000 live newborns,

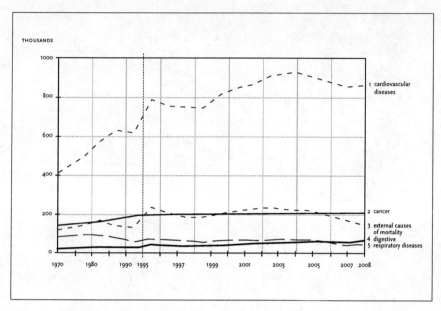

Figure 9.2 Main causes of death in the Russian Federation since 1990 per 100,000 population

although it is still 1.2 times higher than in the "new" EU countries and 2.2 times greater than in the "old" EU countries.

Figure 9.2 illustrates the main causes of death per 100,000 people in the RF since 1970. Cardiovascular diseases (1) were the main cause of mortality increase in Russia (1.3 times over the last fifteen years). Other causes of death include: cancer (2), external causes of mortality (3), and digestive (4) and respiratory diseases (5). Figure 9.2 shows that the death rate started to improve only in 2005.

In 2008, deaths in Russia were caused mostly by non-infectious diseases, including those of the circulatory system (57 percent), cancer (13.9 percent), external causes (11.8 percent), and digestive (4.3 percent) and respiratory diseases (3.8 percent).

Life expectancy at birth varies across the regions of the Russian Federation. For example, in the Amur and Sakhalin regions the death rates are lower than the average level in the RF by 3.5–4.5 years. In other regions, such as Tver, Smolensk, Tula, and Ivanovo, the death rates exceed the average value in the RF by 1.4 times. Furthermore, the life expectancy of the rural population is lower than that in the urban centers by 2.6 years, while the mortality rate for the rural population is almost 20 percent higher.

BIRTHRATE AND AGEING

The demographic problems in the Russian Federation are aggravated by the decline in the crude birthrate. Specifically, between 1987 and 1999, the birthrate dropped by more than half, from 17.2 to 8.3. However, in 2007 and 2008, it increased and reached 11.3 and 12.1, respectively, surpassing the birthrates in the EU countries. This positive dynamic is attributed to the implementation of Priority National Project (PNP) "Health" and an increase in the number of women of childbearing age.[5] Yet the demographic problem remains. In particular, in 2008 the total fertility rate, defined as the average number of children that would be born alive to one woman throughout her reproductive period (fifteen to forty-nine years), was 1.5. For comparison, in the "old" EU countries the total fertility rate on average is 1.56, and in the "new" ones 1.3. In order to secure the reproduction of a population, the total fertility rate needs to be 2.14. Efficient demographic policy has allowed the rise in this indicator to 2 in France and 2.1 in the United States, while in Russia it is still lagging.

The number of abortions in the RF among women aged fifteen to forty-nine years decreased by half since 1995. However, it remains too high: for example, in 2008 there were 36 abortions per 1,000 women of childbearing age, which amounted to 1,386,000 abortions per year; this is roughly comparable to the number of births during the same year (1,714,000).

The age structure in the Russian population is characterized by a decrease in the number of young people and an increase in the number of people aged sixty and older. The reason is obvious: the low birth rate for the past fifteen years, especially in comparison with the higher figures in the 1970s and 1980s. Twenty years ago children up to fifteen years of age comprised 25 percent of the Russian population, whereas presently they constitute only 16 percent; meanwhile, the share of persons in the age group sixty years and over increased from 18 to 21 percent.

NATURAL INCREASE RATE

Figure 9.3 illustrates indicators of the natural increase rate in Russia. Annual natural loss in the RF averages 0.28 percent of the total population. In 2000–06 immigration influx compensated for no more than 10–20 percent

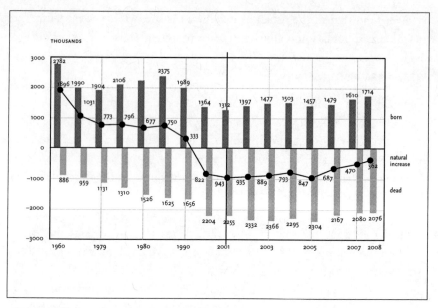

Figure 9.3 Indicators of natural increase rate in Russia

of population loss in the RF. The situation turned for the better in 2007 and 2008 due to annual migration increases to 240,000 people, which slowed down de-population in Russia.

MORBIDITY

The total morbidity of the Russian population has persistently increased over the last sixteen years. On the one hand, this trend resulted from the increase in the number of senior citizens and the more efficient detection of diseases due to the adoption of new diagnostic methods; on the other hand, it reflects the degradation of the health care system in the RF. For example, in 1990 there were only 158.3 million documented disease cases, while in 2008 this number increased by 40 percent to 221.7 million cases. The recalculation per 100,000 population reveals an increase in morbidity of 46 percent; the number of cardiovascular diseases doubled during this period, and oncologic diseases increased by 60 percent. The rise in morbidity closely correlates with the death rate in Russia over the same period.

After 1990 there was a dramatic increase in the number of children either born ill or succumbing to a disease in the neonatal period; this negative dynamic has remained unchanged; almost 40 percent of all newborns in 2000–08 had health problems.

From 1990 until 2008 the documented number of new cases of tuberculosis increased by 2.2 times, and one-third of those with lung TB had it in advanced form. The registered number of new cases of syphilis has been declining since 1995, but it still remains twelve times higher than in 1990 and almost three times greater than in 1980. Increased prevalence of these diseases testifies to severe socioeconomic problems in the society and to inefficient preventive measures.

OCCUPATIONAL HEALTH

Occupational traumatism in the Russian Federation has steadily declined since 1990, and in 2008 it decreased to 2.5 cases per 1,000 employees.[6] However, the total number of fatalities caused by industrial accidents has remained relatively high, reaching 0.109 per 1,000 workers (or 1.8 per 100,000 population), which exceeds similar indicators in the "old" EU countries by 1.6 times and in the "new" EU countries by 1.2 times.[7]

Section 2: Basic Factors Affecting the Health Status of the Russian Population

Fundamentally, the poor state of health of the Russian population since 1990 is attributable to: (1) unhealthy lifestyle, including alcoholism, tobacco smoking, and drug abuse; (2) unsatisfactory labor conditions; (3) lack of an efficient state policy for health care; (4) and underfinancing of the public health care system (details of the RF health care system are presented in Section 3).

LIFESTYLES AND BEHAVIORS IN RUSSIA

According to World Health Organization (WHO) statistics in 2002, four factors were responsible for 87.5 percent of all mortality cases and for 58.5 percent of all disability incidents in the RF: high blood pressure, high level of blood cholesterol, tobacco smoking, and excessive alcohol consumption. According to expert assessments, these relative indicators did not significantly change over the last six years.

Of these four factors, alcohol abuse represents the most acute problem for population health. According to Rospotrebnadzor (the Russian Trade and Sanitary Inspectorate), the average annual alcohol consumption among adults is eighteen liters of pure alcohol per capita.[8] In OECD countries the average consumption of alcohol is lower; although still relatively high, it is not accompanied by abnormally high death rates. The consumption of drinks with high alcohol content is considered one of the main reasons for high mortality rates among employable men in Russia. According to A. Nemtsov, alcohol consumption has an enormous impact on the number of deaths resulting from external causes (59 percent for men and 43 percent for women).[9]

Another cause of high mortality rates in Russia is smoking; tobacco consumption increased by 87 percent in the period between 1985 and 2006, mostly among females and adolescents. The annual increase in the number of smokers in Russia is 1.5–2 percent. Over forty million people are regular smokers: 63 percent of men, 30 percent of women, 40 percent of teenage boys, and 7 percent of teenage girls. The percentage of adult smokers in Russia is one of the highest in the world—twice as large as in OECD countries on the average.

Drug use also has had an impact on health in the RF. Since 1995 the number of people registered as illicit drug users in medical and drug prevention institutions increased by five times and reached 356,000 in 2008. Every year nearly thirty thousand people are registered as first-time drug users, and 700 of them are children and teenagers. Current assessments of the actual number of people addicted to various types of drugs in Russia can exceed the official data by five times.

The WHO states that about one-third of all cardiovascular diseases are caused by improper nutrition. Although per capita consumption of fruits and vegetables in Russia grew by 27 percent between 1995 and 2007, it is still much lower than in Italy and France (the two countries with low levels of mortality from cardiovascular diseases). Obesity is another cause of premature death and long-term disability. Indeed, the life expectancy of obese people is five to twenty years shorter than that of an average Russian citizen. According to the Nutrition Institute of the Russian Academy of Medical Sciences, 47–54 percent of Russian men and 42–60 percent of Russian women between twenty-five and sixty-four years of age are overweight, and 15–20 percent of these people are obese. More than one million people are officially registered as obese, which is 0.7 percent of the whole population, but the real levels of obesity and excessive weight are even higher.

HEALTH PROTECTION PROGRAMS

The RF has taken no serious steps in the health protection area since the anti-alcohol campaign in 1984–87. That campaign, despite certain organizational drawbacks, proved to be highly successful. Within those three years real alcohol consumption in Russia declined by almost 27 percent, which increased life expectancy for men and women by 3.1 and 1.3 years, respectively. Taking into consideration this relatively successful experiment in the past, in November 2008 President Dmitry Medvedev announced his decision to launch a massive anti-alcohol campaign. The main points of this endeavor were formulated in the "Strategy of Long-Term Social-Economic Development of the Russian Federation till 2020."

HEALTH CARE FUNDING

Figure 9.4 shows gross domestic product (GDP) and public health care expenditures (in constant currency, with the year of 1995 taken for 100 percent). In 1998 and 2007 the mean annual GDP increment was 7 percent (in prices comparable to the previous year). The annual rate of growth for health care expenditures for the same period lagged behind the GDP growth by almost twice. Thus economic improvements in the country were not converted into a steady growth of public health care spending. Only in 2006, following the launch of the PNP "Health," did the rate of growth of public health care expenditures start to exceed the growth rate of GDP.

ENVIRONMENTAL FACTORS AND WORKPLACE CONDITIONS

The contraction of industrial output in Russia resulted in better overall environmental conditions during the period between 1990 and 2008, including reduced levels of industrial waste and less pollution of the atmosphere and water supplies. At the same time, a significant part of the Russian population in industrial urban regions still lives under poor environmental conditions. In 2008 Rosstat listed ninety towns characterized by the most unfavorable environmental conditions caused by annual atmospheric pollution exceeding 1,000 tons of industrial waste. Several towns (e.g., Novokuznetsk, Cherepovets, Lipetsk, Norilsk) showed some of the highest rates of atmospheric

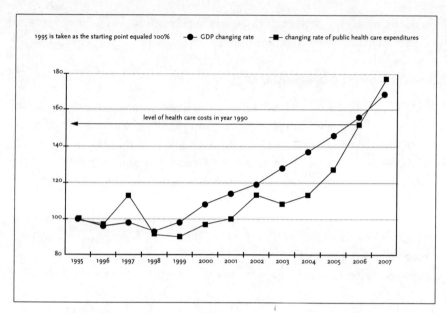

Figure 9.4 Changing rates of GDP and public healthcare expenditures (in constant prices)

pollution (more than 100,000 tons of industrial waste). In fact, Norilsk is one of the three most polluted towns in the world.

Another factor influencing the health of the employable population in Russia is unhygienic working conditions. According to Rosstat, the number of employees working under such conditions in the industrial sector increased by 1.3–2 times from 1990 to 2008, including every third worker in the mining industry and every fourth worker in the energy and processing industries.

Section 3: The Health Care System

The main problem responsible for the limited access to and the poor quality of health care in Russia is the shortage of public health care resources. Medical care requirements went up by at least 46 percent in the period from 1990 to 2008, while the degree of medical care guaranteed by the government remained at the old "Soviet" level. The problem is further aggravated by the uneven distribution of budget funds between regions and between the urban and rural areas, resulting in low accessibility to health care services for populations in relatively poor regions and rural areas.

Another important problem for the RF health care system is the non-optimal structure of the medical workforce: there is an abundance of medical specialists and a lack of general practitioners. Low salaries of health workers (30 percent below average throughout the country) explain the lack of motivated staff. The number and distribution of hospital beds are also far from favorable; there are twice as many beds as needed in intensive care units, while there are not enough rehabilitation and long-term beds.

Since 1990, the Russian health care system has lost some of the best institutional qualities of Soviet times, such as prevention, access to primary health care services, availability of industrial and school health care, and close coordination of services by primary care physicians. In addition to the problems reported earlier, there is a lack of public reimbursement for prescription drugs. This leads to an increase in neglected cases and inefficient use of more expensive hospital care.

Ineffective health care management manifests itself in the lack of strategic planning and responsibility by health care managers for the effectiveness and efficiency of the system.

ORGANIZATIONAL STRUCTURE

Starting in 1924 the USSR employed a health care model built on the principles of N. Semashko (the first RSFSR Health Care People's Commissar).[10] The model was based on many efficient measures, including the distribution of health care facilities by area,[11] structured medical care for adults and children, the integration of primary care doctors and specialists in the outpatient clinics, and a strict health care process for patients. Particular attention was given to prevention, health improvement, and industrial health care. The system at that time was rigorously vertical in relation to subordination of the municipal health care subsystem, first to regional and then to federal medical agencies, which ensured the integrity of financing, resource support, and management.

The Soviet system did have its drawbacks: extensive concentration of resources (number of doctors and beds) without taking into consideration the quality of care; slow implementation of high technologies into medical practice; and an administrative-command style of management, which degraded the efficiency of the overall health care system. However, with the collapse of the Soviet Union, a number of attractive features of the health care system were lost: prevention was neglected, access to primary health care facilities became dramatically unequal, and the capacity of industrial and school health care systems was drastically reduced.[12] The liberal economic reforms had a dramatic impact on financing for the public health care system. In order to increase funds for health care, the decision was made in 1991 to develop compulsory health insurance. Although a federal law "On Medical Insurance for Citizens in the Russian Federation" was approved, it did not secure an adequate level of financing.[13]

In 2003–04 the public health care system was divided into municipal, regional, and federal levels with financial responsibilities correspondingly divided.[14] This resulted in the degradation of the system as medical care in different areas became dependent on local and regional budgets.

Presently the public health care system in Russia looks as follows: (1) in financing, a mixed budget and compulsory insurance model; (2) in organization structure, there are still some features of the Semashko model; (3) in management, three levels—the federal, regional, and municipal; (4) medical providers are of three types—public (federal and regional), municipal, and private. Industry-sponsored medical services either remained within the federal system (for instance, the medical service of the Defense Ministry) or became private due to a change in type (for example, the medical service of Joint-Stock Company "Russian Railways" [JSC "RZD"] is now the largest industry-sponsored health care system in the RF).

The private health care system is presented by private insurance companies (involved in the implementation of the compulsory health insurance program and, partially, voluntary medical insurance), and the network of private providers (their share is around 11 percent).[15] The state does not use enough private medical providers. For instance, the well-equipped and highly qualified health care operation of JSC "RZD" could be more actively involved in the program of state guarantees and would bring a notable improvement in the quality of and access to medical care. However, there are already positive examples of public/private partnership in health care, with JSC "RZD" health care centers offering medical and diagnostic services in twenty Russian regions.

POPULATION HEALTH STATUS AND PUBLIC HEALTH FINANCING

The RF system of public health care is financed by the government[16] and by non-governmental (private) contributors.[17] In 2008 the public share was 66 percent of all expenditures, which is lower than the average OECD figure (73 percent). Overall, public expenditures on health care constitute only 3.4 percent of Russia's GDP, which is half of that in OECD countries (6.6 percent GDP on the average). In absolute figures public expenditures in Russia in 2008 were 635 $PPP (Purchasing Power Parity) per capita, less than one-third the average of OECD countries (2,184 $PPP).

Underfinancing of public health results in low access to medical care, inability to provide care according to modern standards, and a high level of private health spending (34 percent of total health expenditures). There is a close correlation between life expectancy, crude mortality rate, and annual per capita spending for public health in the range from 0 to 1,500 $PPP. Figure 9.5 shows the dependence of the crude mortality rate on spending for public health. In order to decrease the crude mortality rate in Russia to 10.0–11.0, public spending for health care must be not less than 1,200 $PPP per capita. In other words, the amount of spending for public health care would need to be double that in 2008.

HUMAN RESOURCES[18]

In 2008 there were 3.68 million health care workers in Russia.[19] The number of physicians was 704,000, or 5 per 1,000 population. Without taking into account sanitary-epidemiological specialists and dentists (for better comparison with other countries), the number of physicians per 1,000 population was 4.3, which is 1.4 times higher than in OECD countries (3.1 doctors per 1,000 population).[20] However, morbidity and mortality in Russia are higher than in OECD countries; therefore it would not be correct to say that there are too many doctors in Russia. The number of practicing nurses in Russia exceeds that in OECD countries by 13 percent (10.1 and 8.9 per 1,000 population, respectively).[21] In rural areas the number of doctors and nurses is much smaller than the average level in Russia: for doctors it is almost four times lower (1.2 per 1,000 rural population), and for nurses it is twice as low (5.5 per 1,000 rural population).

The public health care system in the RF is characterized by a pronounced imbalance in the ratio between GPs and specialists (1:6),[22] which is significantly higher than in OECD countries (1:2). This results in notably reduced access to primary health care services and causes long lines in the outpatient clinics.

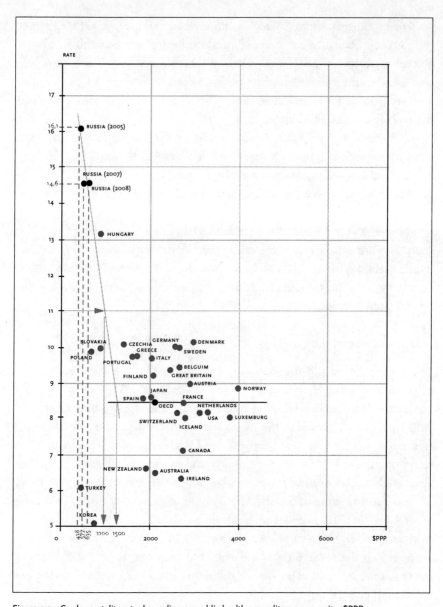

Figure 9.5   Crude mortality rate depending on public health expenditures per capita, $PPP

Today, the work of doctors, nurses, paramedics, and medical researchers is rated among the least prestigious in Russia, primarily because of low salaries on the one hand and the greater workload and level of responsibility on the other. For example, in 2008 the basic monthly salary of a medical worker was 13,000 rubles (840 $PPP), 1.3 times lower than the average salary in the RF, 2.5 times lower than the average wage in the raw-material industry, and 1.6 times lower than in the state agencies (in the Soviet Union the salary of medical workers was near the country's average level).

PHYSICAL RESOURCES

In 2008 the number of hospital beds in Russia was 9.8 per 1,000 population. This number included beds in the intensive care units: 7.8 per 1,000 population, the highest in the world—in OECD countries the average is 3.8 per 1,000 population.[23] On the other hand, Russia is undersupplied with rehabilitation beds—only 0.35 per 1,000 population. Long-term beds for senile citizens and disabled persons are also lacking—approximately 4 beds per 1,000 population versus 8 beds in OECD countries on the average. Furthermore, hospital beds are not used efficiently: in the RF, patients stay in hospital for 10.5 days on the average, which is 1.6 times longer than in the OECD countries. Indicators of re-admissions and admissions of patients who could have been treated in outpatient clinics are also rather high (30 percent).

Russian hospitals are in great need of modern equipment. Capital investment in hospitals often does not consider the long-term needs of the population in medical care, the efficient use of equipment, or availability of qualified personnel. As a result, certain regions in the RF have abundant resources, while others experience serious shortages.

HEALTH CARE REGULATION AND MANAGEMENT

In an attempt to address all the problems mentioned above, the government in 1997 designed the "Strategy of the Health Care and Medical Science Development in the Russian Federation" (RF Government Enactment No. 1387 of November 5, 1997). The program, however, was never realized due to the absence of mechanisms for its implementation.

The most intense legislative activity to improve the health care system took place almost sixteen years ago. Today, the health care system is regulated mostly by federal laws of indirect action, which do not reflect the current vital needs. In many ways this situation, which impeded the development of the Russian health care system over the last decade, resulted from the absence of any long-term strategy and insufficient demand by professional and civil communities for the changes.

Management suffers from the lack of any comprehensive analysis of various regional experiences in their attempts to improve public health care, as well as the absence of detailed evaluation reports on the efficiency of the health care system. The quality of medical care is not assessed on the basis of internationally approved indicators. The emphasis in state programs is mostly placed on construction and the purchase of expensive equipment, which sometimes leads to inefficient use of available resources, instead of investing in health care personnel, qualified medical workers, and pharmaceutical reimbursement.

Section 4: Challenges and Expectations

Major factors influencing the Russian health care system in the RF were analyzed on the basis of existing Rosstat forecasts until 2020. The main challenges will be as follows: the low birth rate, reduction in the employable population, a rapidly aging population, labor shortages, and the necessity to address these challenges by increasing the retirement age. Future health care policy should also take into account cross-regional financial and demographic differences, as well as unfavorable environmental conditions. Health care policy makers should keep in mind that the Russian population awaits noticeable improvements in the quality of medical services. As for Russian medical workers, their main expectations are salary growth and better working conditions.

DEMOGRAPHIC CHALLENGES

In 2008 Rosstat presented three possible demographic forecasts for the period until 2020. The pessimistic scenario was based on the extrapolation of current demographic trends into the future; the medium scenario took into consideration the partial implementation of various governmental demographic policies; and the optimistic scenario reflected the goals set out in state strategic planning documents.

In all three scenarios (pessimistic, medium, and optimistic), the working population declined by no less than 11 million, whereas the number of retired population increased by 5 to 7 million. As a result, it was calculated that over this period, the share of the working population will drop from 63 percent to 55–57 percent. The share of the population over age sixty will increase from 21 percent to 25–26 percent. As for life expectancy, there would be no change in the pessimistic version, whereas in the optimistic version the average life expectancy would rise to almost seventy-three years. Note here that the birth rate in the optimistic scenario would increase merely by 2.5 percent. This insignificant increase is explained by the decline in the number of Russian women of childbearing age. To be precise: in 2008 the number of women between fifteen and nineteen and forty to forty-four years of age was 33.4 million; in 2018 this figure will not exceed 28.4 million (without considering the death rate), which is 15 percent less than in 2008. As for the morbidity structure, the prevalence of chronic noninfectious diseases would be at least the same or will grow due to the increase in the number of senior citizens.

ECONOMIC CHALLENGES

Rosstat also forecast that annual growth of GDP, initially expected to reach 6 percent to 2020, will slow down in 2010–13 because of the economic crisis. The decline in the number of employable population, together with high levels of morbidity and mortality in this group, may create a labor force deficiency. Proposals to prolong the retirement age are indeed reasonable, but they cannot be implemented, since presently less than 50 percent of men live to age sixty-five. Provided the life expectancy increases by five years, 60 percent of men would live to age sixty-five. Therefore, the most important prerequisite conditions for extending the retirement age is an increased life expectancy and health improvement among the men of employable age. It should be noted that the GDP reduction accompanied by increased governmental social expenses (pension payments are planned to be increased in 2010–11) would trigger dramatic competition among the budget-receiving agencies. It would be difficult to maintain adequate financing for the health care system in that period.

SOCIAL CHALLENGES

Social inequality and regional differences in access to medical services were predicted to intensify during the economic crisis. During this period, one would also expect an increase in the number of medical complaints and growing needs for medical services. The situation can be further aggravated by the lessened ability of citizens to pay for medical services, especially in the depressed regions of the RF. Increased demand for and impeded access to medical services accompanied by growing inequality among the population in the access to medical aid could potentially provoke tension in society.

TECHNOLOGICAL CHALLENGES

The public health care system in Russia strongly needs the development of a national health information technology program, including elaboration of unified standards for storing and exchanging information, all of which should be harmonized with the European community. There is also a shortage of educational information resources, including electronic medical libraries, distance learning technologies, and so on. These standards should be introduced immediately—their development and implementation does not require large investment but can greatly enhance efficiency of the health care system and the quality of delivered medical services.

ENVIRONMENTAL CHALLENGES

Urbanization, industrial pollution, expansion of environmentally critical territories, and outdated utilities, such as water supply systems, will continue to deteriorate the health of the population.

EXPECTATIONS OF THE PARTIES CONCERNED

Patients expect better quality of medical services, better access to medical care, and affordable prices for medical services and pharmaceuticals. Inhabitants of remote and rural areas expect better access to specialized medical services.

Medical workers expect to be paid adequately to get proper compensation for their comprehensive, highly technological, and often dangerous work. They want their salaries to be increased at least by two to three times and to be free from humiliating dependence on their patients. They also await differentiated approaches to wages depending on the complexity, intensity, and quality of the work. They expect protection during court proceedings, improved labor conditions, and respect from in the society.

Pharmaceutical companies and medical equipment manufacturers are interested in promoting their products in the market, and the health care system should set regulations to allow on the market only effective pharmaceuticals with optimal price/quality ratios.

Private providers expect equal access to implementation of the Program of State Guarantees. Participation of private providers may result in more efficient spending of resources. For instance, public capital investment funds (aimed at building the modern infrastructure) could be reallocated to provide better financing of medical care in existing public and private practices. That in itself may shorten the waiting lists for all types of medical services for the population. In some regions, such successful cooperation has already been effected between JSC "RZD" and the municipal health care systems.

Section 5: Basic Directions for Health Care Strategy

Based on the analyses carried out in sections 1–4, we can formulate recommendations for modernizing the health care system in Russia in order to improve population health. This cannot be achieved without elaboration and implementation of a comprehensive development strategy authorized by the state and based on pronounced increase of public spending for health care. This section contains the basic principles and goals of the strategy, together with its main tasks, divided into five groups: (1) increase in health care financing; (2) provision of material and human resources; (3) reformation of the organizational structure; (4) improving the efficiency of health care management; and (5) implementation of comprehensive prevention programs. The implementation of this strategy will also stabilize social conditions and improve the economy in the country.

The strategy's basic principles are the following: solidarity; equality; total coverage; fairness; honesty and high competence of the managers at all levels of the system; transparency of decisions; and parity in responsibility between the state, employers, and the citizens in the maintenance and improvement of health.

The aims to improve population health by 2020 were already set in the RF government statements, which specify an increase in life expectancy to seventy-three to seventy-five years, reduction of the crude mortality rate to 11.0 (per 1,000 population), and a decrease in the infant mortality rate to 5 per 1,000 newborns.

According to WHO recommendations, some other important goals are also specified: enhancement of public satisfaction with the quality of and the access to medical services to 70 percent (from the present level of 31 percent), and fair distribution of the expenses for medical care between the poor and rich groups of the society (which can be achieved through a progressive taxation scale and modernization of health care insurance system dues).

BASIC GOALS OF THE STRATEGY TO INCREASE HEALTH CARE FINANCING

1. Double government spending for health care within the next five years (to 1,200 $PPP or at least to 6 percent of GDP) by adopting a progressive taxation scale, increasing excise taxes on tobacco and alcohol by two to three times, and rate fixing of regional health funding (based, for example, on a share of GDP or regional consolidated budget). The state should cover up to 80 percent of all health care expenditures.
2. Organize the system of a single payer for state health care guarantees by concentrating the sources of income in a federal fund for compulsory health insurance (CHI).
3. Improve the mechanism of federal transfers to the regions by adopting new principles for distribution taking into account the morbidity and the age and sex structure of the population.
4. Increase efficiency of the medical care system by purchasing services according to quality-based competition between providers regardless of their type. Expand the autonomy of governmental and municipal providers (accompanied by rigorous control over the quality of medical services and liabilities of the subsidiary companies).
5. Specify the detailed list of guaranteed medical services and pharmaceuticals.
6. Discontinue unofficial payments in medical institutions by doubling (at least) the salaries of health care workers and by improving the work of ethics committees.

BASIC GOALS OF THE STRATEGY FOR PROVIDING MATERIAL AND HUMAN RESOURCES

1. Improve the quality of medical education at the undergraduate and postgraduate levels; develop a system of continuing medical education; update the scientific and technological bases in Russian universities and centers of medical education, including expansion of electronic medical libraries and launching an online professional dialogue among specialists.

2. Develop an environment for telemedicine communication with the goal of raising the quality of care in the most remote regions of the RF.
3. Create an effective and adequate system of incentives, in which the wages of medical personnel would depend on the quality and difficulty of their work.
4. Reform the existing workforce structure by doubling the number of general practitioners, diversifying the number of specialists in various fields of medicine, and harmonizing the ratio between doctors and nurses to one to three.
5. Create a national program of health infrastructure development until 2020 based on updated standards and long-term population needs in medical care.
6. Invest in medical science by increasing the financing of medical research up to 0.3 percent of GDP, placing R&D orders on a competitive basis, and improving the quality of expert assessments.
7. Develop a mutual cooperation plan to 2020 of the health care system with the pharmaceutical and medical industries in order to enlarge the share of local manufacturers in state procurements.

BASIC GOALS OF THE STRATEGY FOR IMPROVING ORGANIZATIONAL STRUCTURE

1. Reform the existing system of health care provision by re-establishing the most important elements of the Soviet model: availability of industrial and school health care and prevention services; responsibility of GPs for delivered medical services (the latter is possible only if there are sufficient numbers of GPs in the regions).
2. Improve the accessibility of medical care in rural areas by drawing physicians and nurses to these regions with higher salaries and subsidized housing.
3. Improve the quality and organization of emergency services by additional re-equipment and provision of modern information systems; optimization of managerial technologies; and the development of updated rules and standards.
4. Improve hospital care by optimizing the distribution of hospital beds between intensive care, rehabilitation, and long-term care departments. Their approximate proportion should be about 30:30:40. Develop updated standards for personnel, equipment, and expenses in order to provide

hospitals with beds according to international experience. The corresponding expenses should be approximately 2:1.5:1.
5. Increase public subsidies for prescribed pharmaceuticals by at least three times. Public reimbursement for prescribed medicines per capita is less than one-fifth that in OECD countries (annual per capita figures are 45 $PPP and 230 $PPP, respectively). This could be organized through special funds in the CHI system.
6. Improve the quality of medical care offered to patients with AIDS, TB, and other infectious diseases; intensify the preventive component in the treatment of these patients.
7. Introduce the quality management system over medical care by developing the indicators and rules of quality of medical care (QMC) at all levels of health care according to international standards; introduce a compulsory accreditation system for providers; and introduce annual reporting on QMC at the national level.
8. Continue implemention of the current specialized long-term programs, and develop new programs in the priority fields of health care, such as child health. Implementation of these programs should be concentrated on training medical personnel and applying new standards of care.

BASIC GOALS OF THE STRATEGY FOR INCREASING EFFICIENCY OF HEALTH CARE MANAGEMENT

1. Develop the health care strategy with specified tasks, health indicators, and implementation mechanisms. Assign qualified managers for implementation of this strategy. Organize an intersectoral health care commission subordinated to the president of the Russian Federation.
2. Improve educational programs for managers and introduce an objective assessment system of managerial efficiency.
3. Implement market mechanisms in health care by competition between providers of medical services, differentiated systems of labor payment, autonomy of medical care providers, and introduction of regulations for public/private partnerships.
4. Combat risks of corruption; increase transparency of decisions by introducing national reference prices for services, equipment, and pharmaceuticals; and improve control over state procurements. Use the method of complex assessments of medical technologies as expertise for decision-making in state procurements.

GROUP OF PARTICIPANTS	EXPECTED BENEFITS
POPULATION	Get access to medical services of better quality in more favorable environment. Cut private expenditures for medical care. Avoid chronic diseases, premature mortality and get higher income.
STATE	Save lives and improve health of citizens. Get powerful boost to develop economy and additional contribution to GDP. Profitability of additional investment in healthcare will be up to 200%. Preserve political stability in the country. Create conditions for long-term national security.
HEALTH CARE PERSONNEL	Get higher salaries and additional social respect, free access to modern information resources at work. Improve qualifications with constant encouragement through conferences, exhibitions and access to distance learning systems.
MEDICAL PROVIDERS	Get larger orders from the state to provide medical care; openly compete for state orders (in exchange for better quality). State and municipal agencies will provide their resources more freely and make their operations more efficient.
MANUFACTURERS OF MEDICAL EQUIPMENT AND PHARMACEUTICALS	Get larger orders for their products, transparent procurement market, and equal competitive conditions, as well as ability to plan the scope of production according to state orders (in exchange to state price control and centralized planning of procurements).

Table 9.1

5. Maintain the health care normative and legislative basis at the modern level; develop and approve a number of federal laws with norms for direct action, such as "On health care"; "On state guarantees," "On compulsory health insurance," and the like.

BASIC GOALS OF THE STRATEGY IN ACTUALIZATION OF PREVENTION PROGRAMS

1. Enhance responsibility of the population and employers for maintaining and improving health; introduce a differentiated (relative to adhering to a healthy life style) system of co-payments to CHI and voluntary health insurance; and strengthen the control over employers in the matter of labor protection according to international standards.
2. Motivate RF citizens to lead a healthy lifestyle. Implement state anti-tobacco, anti-alcohol, and anti-drug programs. Improve the sanitary-epidemiological surveillance in the country. Secure integration and coordination of the prevention programs at the level of the health care ministry.

The above proposals would lead to expected benefits shown in table 9.1.

Notes

1. Steven Eke, "Russia Faces Demographic Disaster," *BBC News,* June 7, 2006, http://news.bbc.co.uk/2/hi/europe/5056672.stm, accessed July 20, 2010.
2. World Bank, *Dying Too Young* (Washington, DC: World Bank, 2005).
3. Russian Federal Statistics Service (Rosstat) data 2003–09. See Rosstat, *Demographic Annual Book of Russia, 2009: Statistics Digest* (Moscow: Rosstat, 2009), 557; Rosstat, *Envisaged Strengths of the RF Population until 2025: Statistical Bulletin* (Moscow: Rosstat, 2008), 235; Rosstat, *Envisaged Strength of the RF Population until 2030: Statistical Bulletin* (Moscow: Federal Service of State Statistics, 2009), 235; Rosstat, *Russian Statistical Annual Book, 2009: Statistics Digest* (Moscow: Rosstat, 2009), 847; Rosstat, *Russia and Countries of the World, 2008: Statistics Digest* (Moscow: Rosstat, 2009), 361; WHO statistics database, http://data.euro.who.int/hfadb/index.php; and OECD, *OECD in Figures* 2008 (Paris: OECD, 2008), 92.

4. Hereafter, data on "old" EU countries refers to 2007, and data on "new" EU countries refers to 2008.
5. See A. Vishnevsky and C. Bobylev, "Russia in the Face of Demographic Challenges" (report on development of human potential in the Russian Federation, Moscow, 2008), 257.
6. Comparisons of cumulative industrial traumatism in different countries are difficult due to different record-keeping systems; comparison of the number of fatalities caused by industrial accidents provides a more objective picture.
7. These traumatism indicators are used by the WHO.
8. Federal service—supervision in the field of the defense of rights for users and the prosperity of men.
9. A. Nemtsov, *Alcoholic History of Russia: Contemporary Period* (Moscow: Librokom, 2009), 320.
10. RSFSR stands for Russian Social Federal Soviet Republic.
11. The provision of medical care was based on a territorial principle of location of medical facilities: in a rural area, an agricultural medical center and hospital as well as a central and regional hospital; in a town, an out-patient clinic, a town hospital, and a specialized hospital. Each level provided different medical technologies: primary, specialized, and advanced.
12. With the exception of a number of industry-sponsored medical services.
13. Federal law no. 1499-1, June 28, 1991.
14. See the following federal laws: *On General Principles of Organizing Local Self-Government in the Russian Federation*, no. 131 FL, October 6, 2003; *On Introducing Changes into Legal Acts of the Russian Federation and Recognizing as Becoming Inoperative Certain Legal Acts of the Russian Federation Due to Approval of Federal Laws, On Introducing Changes and Amendments into the Federal Law, On General Principles of Organizing Legislative (Representative) and Executive Bodies of the State Power in Russian Federation Subjects*, and *On General Principles of Organizing Local Self-Government in the Russian Federation*, no. 122 FL, August 22, 2004; and *On Introducing Changes in Certain Legal Acts of the Russian Federation Due to Improvement of Authority Delineation*, no. 258 FL, December 29, 2006.
15. There are about 15,600 ambulatory and outpatient organizations (separate, as well as those belonging to other organizations) in the RF; 16 percent of them are private. Of the 6,500 hospital medical organizations, 1.8 percent are private. The total number of private medical providers is 2,500, out of 22,100 hospital, ambulatory, and outpatient institutions in the RF. Rosstat, *Statistical Bulletin*, 235.

16. Here, "public" health care funds (from centralized taxes or compulsory medical insurance) mean the same as "state" funds, since funds for compulsory medical insurance come from uniform social taxes and the budgets of those regional bodies responsible for health care. After 2010 uniform social taxes will be substituted by insurance payments, but since the means will be directed to state non-budget funds, the term "state" is also quite proper.
17. Rosstat 2008 data was used for this section, as well as data from OECD 2008 and reports on the implementation of the program of state guarantees to provide free medical help to RF citizens in 2006, 2007, and 2008.
18. Rosstat 2008 and 2009 data was used for this section.
19. Without taking into consideration those engaged in social services, veterinary activity, and the production of pharmaceuticals and medical equipment.
20. Provision is calculated as the number of people (medical workers) divided by the number of people served in the area (territory) and multiplied by 10,000 — calculation for 10,000 inhabitants. International practice usually makes comparisons for 1,000 people.
21. Without taking into consideration laboratory workers and dentists.
22. The primary link in the state and municipal health care system employs 73,400 doctors, according to Roszdravnadzor.
23. Intensive care beds imply around-the-clock medical care.

CHAPTER TEN

The Imaginary Curtain

Roderic Lyne

In Moscow, on July 6, 2009, President Obama stated that he and President Medvedev were "committed to leaving behind the suspicion and rivalry of the past so that we can advance the interests that we hold in common."[1] On September 10 (in his article "Go, Russia!"), President Medvedev declared that "resentment, arrogance, various complexes, mistrust and especially hostility should be excluded from the relations between Russia and the leading democratic countries."[2]

How often have we heard these words over the past twenty years? How often, indeed, have many of us uttered them?

The Berlin Wall parted on November 9, 1989. That was the end of the "Iron Curtain." On July 1, 1991, the Warsaw Pact declared itself "non-existent," and on December 25 of that year the USSR ceased to exist. The Cold War was over. In their Founding Act of May 27, 1997, NATO and the Russian Federation declared that they "do not consider each other as adversaries."[3] They bound themselves to a "shared commitment to build a stable, peaceful, and undivided Europe, whole and free, to the benefit of all its peoples." Likewise the European Union declared its intention to "build a genuine strategic partnership, founded on common interests and shared values." The 1994 EU-Russia Partnership and Cooperation Agreement proposed "to provide an appropriate framework for the gradual integration between Russia and a wider area of cooperation in Europe."[4]

But twenty years after the fall of the wall, there is still a curtain in the imagination of the peoples of Russia and the United States and Western and Central Europe. It is not tangible like the Iron Curtain, through which I passed on many occasions; but a dividing line is clearly perceived, and reflected in language.

When people talk of "Europe," they do not use the term to include Russia, the most populous country in geographical Europe. NATO is still generally seen in Russia as an adversary. On the eve of President Obama's visit to Moscow, the chairman of the International Affairs Committee of the Federation Council, Mikhail Margelov, argued that "decision makers in Washington still see Russia as a potential enemy";[5] while the president's adviser, Michael McFaul, said that "if you look at Russian public opinion, what Russian elites say,...the United States is considered an adversary." Obama himself said that he wanted Prime Minister Putin to understand "that the old cold-war approach to U.S.-Russia relations is outdated." He thought Putin still had "one foot in the old ways of doing business." Putin countered that it was the United States that was still stuck in the Cold War.[6]

Clearly the shadow of the Cold War, the old "enemy image," still affects the way that Russia and the West view each other.

The Cold War Experience

I am a child of the Cold War.

I was born in 1948, as it was beginning. My father was an officer in the Royal Air Force who flew Spitfires against the Luftwaffe as a twenty-year-old. He spent the last thirty years of his career in a NATO air force geared to defend Western Europe from the Red Army. In August 1961, when my father was serving as defense attaché in Moscow, I stood on Gorky Street to watch the second cosmonaut, German Titov, parade down to Red Square after circling the earth for twenty-five hours. In October of the following year, my parents and my future parents-in-law lived through the Cuban missile crisis in the Soviet capital, wondering if they were going to be obliterated by their own side's nuclear weapons. When my wife and I visited her parents in Prague in 1970 (my father-in-law was ambassador there, before going back to Moscow in 1977), we observed Soviet tanks in the woods around the city, keeping a watchful eye on their Socialist comrades.

In May 1972, as a junior diplomat in the British Embassy, I saw the beginnings of détente, when Richard Nixon became the first U.S. president to visit Moscow and signed the Strategic Arms Limitation Treaty (SALT I). At the time the British were not at the détente party: we were vying with the Chinese People's Republic for the status of Public Enemy Number One, and enduring the coldest of Cold War treatment in retaliation for the British government's temerity in expelling 105 Soviet intelligence officers from London in 1971.

In the late 1980s, I found myself serving again in Moscow as the Cold War gradually came to an end: the most riveting experience of my diplomatic career. During Gorbachev's first year in power, the West remained highly suspicious of perestroika. In 1985 the (London) *Times* forecast that "the Gromyko-Ponomarev line in foreign policy will continue at Geneva and other East-West negotiations."[7] The *New York Times* said that "whatever his ambitions, Mr. Gorbachev is unlikely soon to make waves."[8] Western governments did not initially take Gorbachev at face value. They saw him as trying to make the Soviet system stronger—and therefore *more* threatening—by modernizing it. (In a way they were right. He wanted to improve socialism and the Soviet Union, not abolish them.) When I published an article in *International Affairs* as late as the spring of 1987 arguing that Gorbachev had taken us into a different ball game, I was told I had contradicted the foreign secretary's official line.[9] But for the next four years, as a result of the revolution initiated by Gorbachev, we awoke almost every day to events that I, for one, had never expected to see in my lifetime.

For all of us who in some small way were engaged in it, the Cold War was a powerful experience. It shaped our outlook. Some of my generation, wherever they live, have found it difficult to shake off the experience. Some have a certain nostalgia for the predictability, the clear lines of demarcation, and the written or unwritten rules of the age of two competing superpowers—not to mention for the status of superpower. They don't want the Cold War back, but they cannot quite believe it is over—especially when they see recrudescences of Cold War language and behavior on the other side of what is now an imaginary curtain. The imagination is a powerful instrument.

My own reaction, which I think is more typical, is that I regret that the Cold War happened, because it was a negative, wasteful, and painful process; but I do not regret in the slightest degree what my country did during the Cold War, because it was necessary and right. When Reagan described the Soviet Union as an "evil empire," he did not speak wisely in terms of the effect of his remarks, but he spoke the truth. He did not call the peoples of the Soviet Union evil: it was the system that was evil, because of the cruel suffering it imposed on millions. Those millions were the biggest winners from the collapse of Communist dictatorship and the end of the Cold War.

Now we are in a different situation and, one hopes, moving toward a different era, though the transition is an uneven process with a very long way still to go. For old Cold Warriors, such as myself, there is now at least the possibility to do constructive things, rather than simply to be a defender or a passive observer. I am someone who wishes Russia well. I do so partly for personal reasons: I have many friends there, and have spent more than half of my adult life working on Russian affairs. Partly also for reasons of the best interests of my country and region. I am in no doubt that a prosperous, stable, secure, harmonious, and well-governed Russian Federation, a Russia that fulfilled its potential to be one of the advanced countries of the world (my definition of a genuinely "strong" Russia) would be greatly to the benefit of the global system and of the continent of Europe—a continent of which Russia is part.

A Russian journalist asked me, soon after my arrival in Moscow as British ambassador in January 2000, what my hopes were for the period of my tenure. I said that I looked forward to the day when Russia had "normal" relations with my country, with Europe, and with the West (however defined). Relations similar to those we enjoyed with other partners—where one might have heated family quarrels but without threatening the relationship as a whole.

We have not yet achieved this happy state of normality. Over the past six years, we have moved farther away from it. In the rest of this chapter, I ask what it is that still keeps us apart. My answer divides into four parts: the burden of the historical legacy; uncertainty about Russia's direction; strategic divergence over European security and the "post-Soviet space"; and the argument between Russia and the West over "values." Finally, I ask what we should do about our differences. Are we doomed to remain at odds? Or can Russia and the West realistically hope to move closer together in the first half of the twenty-first century?

The Burdensome Legacy of History

Are Russia and the West "enemies"? Self-evidently not. During the Cold War, we opposed each other at every step of the way. We threatened each other with nuclear weapons; we promoted conflicting ideologies; we fought proxy wars. Now we compete in various ways, as is normal between states, but we do not threaten each other.

The defining characteristic of the Cold War was fear. Fear, at a state level, of what we might do to each other (and nearly did, during the Cuban missile crisis). Fear, at a personal level, of subversion. Fear, within the Soviet system, of the all-pervasive organs of security. Visiting Moscow as a teenager in Khrushchev's time, and working there as a young diplomat in the Brezhnev era, I sensed this fear. It was an eerie feeling to live in a country and want to get to know its people, but to be unable to have normal human contact with them. A Russian friend later told me how she had walked past the house I lived in every day on her way to school. Her mother had made her walk on the opposite side of the street: proximity to foreigners was dangerous. In Stalin's time, innocent or even accidental unauthorized contact with foreigners had landed people in the gulag. Such contacts (except with dissidents and refuseniks, who were prepared bravely to defy the system) were still off-limits until the late 1980s. Until the Soviet Union ended, 90 percent of its territory was closed to visits by foreigners.

Over the past decade, I have encountered thousands of Russians, from the highest in the land to some of the poorest, in more than thirty of the country's regions. I have met a huge amount of friendship and very few incidents of personal hostility. I recall one encounter with a group of youngsters who vented their anger with the West, in particular over Yugoslavia: this sticks in the mind precisely because it was an isolated incident. In my official dealings, I came across the cold and deep-rooted enmity toward my country of some former KGB officers, now serving in the internal security organs. Given the history of the KGB and of our relations with it, this was no surprise. It did not so much reflect the general attitude of the people of the country as the inward-looking nature of the security services and their need for external enemies to justify their existence.

Although the fear has largely gone, the long years and dark deeds of the Cold War (and the brutal events of the previous three decades) have left an inevitable legacy of mistrust and bitterness. It should surprise no one that history has left some of the deepest scars in the Baltic states, Poland, and other parts of Central and Eastern Europe. There is no need to spell out why this is so. Experience has shown that when empires dissolve, it takes not years but generations for the scars to heal. After the partition of Ireland in 1922, it took something like seven decades to establish a normal relationship between the Republic of Ireland and the former metropolitan power, the UK, and some would argue that the process is still not complete. Strong feelings have been raised about war memorials in Ireland (as happened also in Tallinn) and about differing interpretations of history. Much the same could be said about Britain's post-imperial relations with many other countries or, say, France and Algeria, or Japan's relations with South Korea and China (which have been complicated by another war memorial, the Yasukuni shrine, as well as by what is written in history books) or Turkey and Armenia, or a host of other examples. As a Russian speaker put it at a recent conference, present-day relations are afflicted by Eastern European paranoia about Russia, and Russian paranoia about the United States. Against the background of twentieth-century history, the paranoia is not hard to understand.

The past is a psychological impediment, and we see this most strongly when old suspicions are reawakened—as happened when NATO bombed Yugoslavia in 1999; or during the Russo-Georgian conflict of 2008; or when tensions have arisen between Russia and other ex-Soviet neighbors; or with the unsolved murders of Anna Politkovskaya, Alexander Litvinenko, and others; or the two Khodorkovsky trials, to name just a few examples.

There are also important differences of perception both about the Second World War (or, to Russians, the Great Patriotic War) and about Stalin. With much justification, Russians argue that the West has tended to underplay the huge sacrifices made by the Soviet peoples and the significance of Hitler's defeat on the Eastern Front. The Western view is colored by Stalin's pact with Hitler from 1939 to 1941, and by his occupation of Central and Eastern Europe from 1945 on. More generally, Russia and the West are deeply divided in their assessment of Stalin. The prevailing, though not universal, view in Russia seems to be that Stalin's achievements in defeating Nazi Germany and in developing the Soviet Union into a great military and industrial power override the brutal excesses of his behavior. The prevailing view in the West is that—through the Ukrainian famine, the purges and the gulag, the mass deportations of peoples and cruelly repressive policies imposed by the NKVD (subsequently KGB) and their acolytes throughout the Soviet Union and the Warsaw Pact—Stalin was responsible for the death and enslavement of millions of people and thereby ranks alongside Hitler and Mao Tse-tung.[10] The process of de-Stalinization begun by Khrushchev was brief and limited. A further process took place after the collapse of the USSR, including a state-sponsored investigation into the archives by a commission under the late Alexander Yakovlev and efforts by nongovernmental organizations such as Memorial; but the official efforts have disappeared from sight, the unofficial efforts have come under pressure, textbooks have been rewritten to convey a benign view of the Stalinist period, and an ominous-sounding Commission to Counter the Falsification of History has been announced. In any nation, coming to terms with dark periods in history is difficult and painful; but justification, let alone glorification, of Stalin (or, for that matter, Dzerzhinsky[11]) is as irreconcilable with the value systems of the West as would be justification in Germany of Hitler and Himmler. Where this occurs, it creates a sharply negative resonance. It is particularly worrying if members of the younger, post-Soviet generation are seen to be taking a heroic view of Stalin.

Russia's Uncertain Direction

The search for Russia's identity, and the debate over the country's future direction, will inevitably determine the quality of Russia's external relationships. You cannot form a lasting partnership unless you know whom you are partnering with and have some confidence that your values and aspirations, as well as your interests, align.

There was a sense in the early 1990s, and again between 2000 and 2003, that Russia and the West were on broadly convergent courses. As I have noted, the EU-Russia Partnership and Cooperation Agreement set the objective of a "gradual integration between Russia and a wider area of cooperation in Europe." It also declared that "the full implementation of partnership presupposes the continuation and accomplishment of Russia's political and economic reforms." The Russian government repeatedly committed itself to goals of democracy; the rule of law; independent judicial systems; respect for fundamental freedoms, including free and independent media; and full integration in the international economic and trading system. These were the building blocks of partnership.

This sense of convergence was palpable when I returned to live in Russia for a fourth time at the beginning of 2000. There was hope in the air. Russia was recovering well from the 1998 crash. I had expected to find the country in a distressed state after the tumult of the 1990s. Instead, what was striking was how rapidly (albeit unevenly) life had advanced in less than a decade; how quickly people had learned to live in the new conditions; how much had been achieved in the face of huge difficulties and much disorder. For millions of Russians (though not for all), the standard of living was already far ahead of their Soviet lifestyle. Political debate, between parties and individuals and in the media and across regions, was free and lively. Meeting students, not only in the capital but in universities across the country, I could see no difference in their tastes, their dress, and their ambitions from those of their counterparts in the western half of our shared continent. Most importantly, during the next two or three years I met many talented young Russian professionals who had acquired qualifications and experience in the West and had chosen to return to their homeland because they saw more attractive prospects in Russia: faster promotion, more exciting opportunities, and a comfortable lifestyle. They had voted with their feet, and were a scarce resource essential to the future.

What would-be Western partners now see is a Russia divided about its future course. When oil prices were high and national wealth peaked, it was constantly asserted that Russia was "strong again," would reassert its rightful place as an independent Great Power, and did not need to heed or concede to outside opinion. Powerful voices, notably that of the late patriarch of the Russian Orthodox Church, inveighed against the intrusion of Western values.[12] Russian nationalism became much more assertive. Convergence with Western Europe was replaced by divergence. Now, with the end of the boom, the mood has changed again. Young professionals who returned are once more talking about leaving. The optimism of the early part of this decade has melted away. The president's speeches point in one direction; the actions, or inaction, of the administrative machine in another. Debate over Russia's identity and future character has been renewed.

It is too simplistic to see this as simply a replay of the nineteenth-century debate between Slavophiles and Westerners. Many of the protagonists of conservative nationalism are very actively engaged in business with the West. The modernizers, in my experience, are no less patriotic than their opponents (although this accusation is thrown at them): they simply take a different view of the best way of advancing Russia's interests. There is universal pride in Russian culture and in its impact on the wider world, but I also do not see any mass rejection of Western culture—indeed quite the opposite.

At base, there seem to be two fault lines. One concerns the addiction to a concept of Russian "greatness" rooted deep in history and reinforced by the superpower status acquired through the Great Patriotic War and the subsequent development of nuclear weapons. This approach dictates that Russia must maintain large armed forces, project power over its neighbors, use natural resources as an instrument of state policy, and reject relationships, whether geopolitical or commercial, which might constrain Russia's "independence." Accepting help from outside is seen as humiliation. Concessions or a "win/win" approach are weakness. Foreign investment can be useful, but the investor must be kept in a junior position. Russia is to be respected and feared by other nations, but will deal as an equal only with the United States and perhaps China.

There are those in Russia, on the other hand, who see the obsession with "greatness" as a nineteenth-century concept of little relevance in the current age—a barrier between Russia and the complex, interdependent outside world: a world in which most problems are transnational, markets are global, and even the United States is heavily constrained and unable simply to impose its power. They argue that it risks marginalizing Russia, and preventing the country from developing its potential. Their preference is that Russia should seek to become a "normal" country and part of the community of the most advanced nations, rather than bank everything on remaining "exceptional."

The second fault line, and to me the key determinant of Russia's future, is over economic policy, but in a wide sense that embraces the political economy, including governance, institutions, and social policy.

In the period after the 1998 crash, the Russian authorities took a series of important steps to restructure the economy. The economy's rebound coincided with a rapid rise in world oil prices. In their celebrated BRIC (Brazil, Russia, India, China) report of 2003, the Goldman Sachs research team saw potential for Russia to overtake Britain, France, and Germany in GDP by 2028, and in per capita income to be one of the world's half-dozen richest large countries by 2050.[13] But they added an important qualification: "the key assumption underlying our projections is that the BRICs maintain policies and develop institutions that are supportive of growth."

As Russia became richer, the momentum to continue with such policies dissipated. The modernizing trend stalled. Modernization, institution building, diversification, and innovation became no more than popular buzzwords, and few steps were taken to enact them. A golden opportunity to tackle underlying problems and lay the foundations of long-term growth was lost. Stagnation and statism became embedded in the permafrost of a self-interested status quo, and ambitious hopes to overtake the GDP per head of Portugal (which remained almost twice that of Russia in 2008) seemed to vanish in the mist. By 2008 Russia was even more dependent on hydrocarbon exports than in 1997 (68 percent of all exports by value, compared to 44 percent in 1997).

Since late 2008, the end of the Russian boom and the deep effects of the global crisis on Russia have reinvigorated the internal debate. Conservative defenders of the status quo have argued that Russia has come through the crisis without severe damage. There has been a partial recovery in the oil price; the ruble has stabilized, after a prolonged slide; the stock market has rebounded; discontent in the worst-affected regions has been contained; and the state's reserves have been used to prop up ailing industries (such as the Avtovaz car plant) and to boost social security (with pensions rising by 30 percent in 2009 and due to go up by another 45 percent in 2010). Conservatives maintain that there is no need for fundamental changes, which might threaten social stability.

On the other side, advocates of modernization see reliance on a return to higher commodity prices as wholly inadequate to the task. They point out that, far from being a "safe haven" during the crisis, in 2009 Russia has been the worst-performing of all the world's large economies, developed or emerging, with GDP having shrunk by about 8 percent. Far from being out of crisis, they fear that the worst may be yet to come, with unemployment threatening to rise to acute levels in the single-industry towns. With the budget running into deficit and a risk of capital outflow, the state will not be able to continue throwing public money at the problem indefinitely. This could lead to a crunch within two or three years. Even if that can be avoided (with the help of rising prices for hydrocarbons and raw materials), the modernizers argue that Russia faces a very slow recovery and a future trend rate of growth nearer to 3.5 percent than the 6.5 percent of the past decade. From a still relatively low baseline, this would neither enable Russia to match the more dynamic growth of countries like China, India, Brazil, Indonesia, and several in Eastern Europe, nor would it close the gap on the advanced OECD economies. The crisis has reinforced the argument propounded by modernizers for several years that deep-seated institutional changes are needed if Russia is to become a competitive, advanced country—let alone to achieve Deputy Prime Minister Shuvalov's dream (March 2009) of becoming by 2020 the most desirable place in the world to live,[14] or Finance Minister Kudrin's vision (September 2009) of Russia as "a major locomotive of the world's economy."[15]

In his "Go, Russia!" article, President Medvedev appeared to lean in the direction of the modernizers. "Should a primitive economy based on raw materials and endemic corruption accompany us into the future?" he asked. Russia had not escaped from "its humiliating dependence on raw materials," and its finished products were "plagued by their extremely low competitiveness." This was why production had declined much more than in other economies during the crisis. Civil society was weak and the levels of self-organization and self-government were low. He called for economic modernization based on scientific and technological progress, which was "inextricably linked with the progress of political systems." Russia should have a democratic system based on parliamentary parties that would be "open, flexible, and internally complex"; and modern, efficient judicial and law enforcement organizations. However, he also struck a note of caution: "We will not rush.... We cannot risk our social stability and endanger the safety of our citizens for the sake of abstract theories. We are not entitled to sacrifice stable life, even for the highest goals."

Logically, the case for modernization appears irrefutable. The economic crisis has exposed the fragility of the existing model, and has borne out the warnings and arguments put forward for a decade by modernizers. The case is so strong that even opponents of change are now cloaking themselves in the language of modernization. But, while the balance of the argument points one way, the decision-making power continues to defend the status quo. It is not hard to see why. Modernization requires institutional change—indeed the development of a range of independent institutions and of the rule of law, and the curtailing of the power and privileges of the bureaucracy and of gigantic, inefficient, subsidized, and anticompetitive state corporations. This would threaten the personal interests of those who currently wield power. They will inevitably resist change for as long as it is possible to do so. As the old saying has it, turkeys do not vote for Christmas.

The Arc of Mistrust: The "Post-Soviet Space" and Europe's Security Architecture

During the Cold War, the Soviet Union and the West were in competition for strategic dominance around the globe. They lined up on opposite sides in almost every regional conflict—in the Far East, Central Asia, the Middle East, Africa, Latin America, and the Caribbean. I recall going to a camp in Baluchistan in 1980 with the then British foreign secretary when we were encouraging and materially assisting Afghan mujahideen in their resistance to the Soviet invasion: an instinctive, knee-jerk reaction on the part of the West, but one which has had unforeseen consequences for us today.

Almost all of this has changed. The interests of Russia, the EU, and the United States are of course not identical, but they broadly align at a strategic level. Afghanistan is a prime example: Russia has supported NATO's efforts to suppress Al-Qaeda and the Taliban, and is providing supply routes for NATO. There are almost no *strategic* issues that divide us. As President Medvedev has noted, "Epidemics, technological disasters, social instability, extremism, terrorism, illegal immigration, piracy, organized crime...these problems are a threat to everyone without exception."[16] We are working together on nuclear proliferation and on the Arab/Israel dispute. We shall both benefit from the stabilization of Iraq, whatever our tactical differences there. We have been affected in common by the global financial crisis, and have a common interest in economic recovery and the revival of world trade. We both have large parts to play in combating and dealing with climate change. Russia, Western Europe, and the United States are all having to adjust to changes in the balance of world power, especially as a result of the rise of China. Our interests diverged sharply in the Balkans, but this is now receding into the past.

However, there remains one area of the globe where there is strategic disagreement and a risk of conflict between Russia and the West: the area closest to Russia—an arc from the Arctic through the Baltic states, Belarus, Ukraine and Moldova, across the Black Sea, the Caucasus and the Caspian, and into Central Asia. I once labeled this "the arc of mistrust." Foreign Minister Lavrov objected to the term, but I stand by it. President Medvedev has asserted that Russia has "privileged interests" in this area; Lavrov has developed the term "historically conditioned mutually privileged relations";[17] other leading figures, including the defense minister, have spoken baldly of Russia's right to a "zone of influence." To Russians, it is the "near abroad" or the "post-Soviet space." To the EU, these are the "new neighbors" or the "Eastern partners." Whatever one calls it, this is the area where the sharpest and most dangerous tensions have arisen over the past decade and thus risk recurring in the future.

The origins of the strategic disagreement are easy enough to discern.

When the Soviet Union collapsed, only fourteen "new" states were born. Russia did not regard itself, and was not seen by others, as a "new" country. It was treated in international law as the "successor state" of the Soviet Union—with the full agreement of the Western powers, which were fearful of possible instability and conflict in the area of the former USSR. (I well recall some of the nightmarish possible scenarios that I fed into our contingency planning as the head of the Eastern Department of the Foreign Office at the time—provoking one senior official to say that the only answer was to go home with a case of whisky and drink it under the bedclothes.) Russia retained the nuclear weapons, the permanent membership on the UN Security Council, and the outlook of the metropolitan state—but without its satrapies. It could not instantly adjust to thinking of former "Soviet republics," previously ruled and micromanaged from Moscow, as sovereign equals. Historically, lacking secure land boundaries and having been invaded from both East and West, Russia had protected itself through buffer zones. Now, without warning or preparation, zones within Russia's former security perimeter were independent and no longer under control (even though NATO ministers, including the U.S. secretary of state, had given verbal assurances that they did not intend to encroach). Russia's economy was umbilically linked to these states—and vice versa. Ethnic Russians lived in them in large numbers, and still do—and vice versa. For Moscow to assert a *droit de regard* over its former domains, as it did from the outset, frequently praying the Monroe Doctrine in aid, was hardly surprising.

The West's overriding concern, as I have indicated, was for stability. Indeed, as recently published documents have shown, Margaret Thatcher was so worried about this that in 1989 she appeared to encourage Mikhail Gorbachev to keep the Warsaw Pact in being.[18] As the fears of destabilization receded, Europe seemed to be moving rapidly toward an era of harmony and cooperation (the famous "end of history" notion popularized by Francis Fukuyama).

Some have argued that, at this point in the early 1990s, a so-called golden opportunity existed to incorporate Russia rapidly into the institutions of Western Europe, thereby ending the division of the continent forever; but that the West was insufficiently generous and far-sighted to grasp this historic opening. I have heard Russian liberals assert that in this time of weakness, Russia would have accepted an invitation to join the European Union, which in turn would have locked the country irrevocably into democracy, the rule of law, and a fairly regulated market economy. Others, not only of a liberal persuasion, have pointed out that in the Yeltsin period leading figures (including even Vice President Alexander Rutskoi[19]) spoke positively of the possibility of joining NATO; and that President Putin hinted at openness to this idea during his first term. A more general thesis has been developed in Moscow that, instead of helping Russia in the 1990s, the West rejected Russia's overtures and took advantage of its weakness.

A different interpretation, not surprisingly, tends to be heard on the Western side. The West thought that it did a great deal to assist Russia's transition to democracy and a market economy. In the heady days of the early 1990s, it provided financial help, rescheduled debt, and offered widespread transfer of knowledge and political support. Bankers, businessmen, and advisers of every kind poured into Russia. Much closer links were developed between the Russian Federation and Western institutions. Russia became a member of the IMF and was given a seat on its executive board. The EU repeatedly invited President Yeltsin to consultations during its council meetings, usually at a specially organized dinner, and began to negotiate the Russia-EU Partnership and Cooperation Agreement. NATO, as mentioned earlier, adopted the Founding Act in 1997, set up a council with Russia, and agreed to exchange military and civilian representatives. The G-7 began to ask the Russian president to special consultations at its summits, and then invited Russia to become the eighth member of the group.

With the benefits of hindsight, how is it that this rapid coming together became a falling apart, that growing trust reverted to mistrust, that two such divergent interpretations of the same period of history can now be held?

I think it is clear that neither side understood the other. Both were naïve. In the euphoria at the end of the Cold War, expectations far outran what might realistically have been achievable. The intentions were benign, but the naïveté foiled them. Western leaders had been steeped in the Soviet Union. Post-Soviet Russia was completely unknown territory for them—the dark side of the moon, as it were. They had very little understanding of the complexities of the situation and the feelings of the Russian people. False analogies were drawn: with the postwar transformation of Japan and Germany; with the post-Franco transformation of Spain; and, especially, with the fast pace of transformation in Central and Eastern Europe. Russia was different though. It had not been defeated; it retained its global status as a leading power; it was a much larger country, with a different social composition; it had been run as a command economy throughout the adult lifetime of all of its inhabitants; and, most crucially, it did not or could not summon up an alternative ruling elite. For the most part, the old elite stayed in power, some changing their labels, and are still in power. All of this meant that in Russia, in contrast to the other countries mentioned, there were limits to the leadership's tolerance of outside advice or interference and to the ability of a conservative population of 140 million souls spread over eleven time zones to reinvent themselves within a very short period.

Equally, on the Russian side the long isolation had left the leadership (even those who had worked as undercover intelligence officers in the West) with inadequate understanding of Western institutions and ways of doing business. The notion that Russia should have to apply for membership to an organization like NATO, rather than simply be invited in, or should be treated as an associate by the EU, rather than as a full member, was seen as inappropriate to Russia's Great Power status. I have several times heard Russian ministers complain about finding themselves around a table (e.g., at NATO) where much smaller countries were represented, when their interest was only in speaking to the big players. The biggest stumbling block was a lack of comprehension of what in practical terms would be required for Russia to become a member of NATO or the EU, or even an assumption that these organizations would be ready to transform themselves (or in NATO's case to dissolve) in order to accommodate Russia. In fact, EU membership entails acceptance of an "acquis" of policy and legislation accumulated over many years, and of the pooling of sovereignty within a supranational union. This has not proved easy for many existing EU members (as has most recently been shown by resistance to the Maastricht, Nice, and Lisbon Treaties in several EU countries). Whenever I have asked Russian advocates of accession to the EU whether they could imagine their government imposing EU directives on internal policy against its own wishes, having been outvoted in Brussels, the answer has always been that this would be inconceivable.

In reality, the golden opportunity was no more than a dream in the 1990s; well-intentioned on both sides but something that could only be achieved over decades. What happened in practice was that events (or, as Russians are wont to put it, "life itself") took over and drove Russia and the West apart. Two events (or series of events) in particular undermined trust: conflict in the Balkans and the enlargement of NATO. With the wisdom of hindsight,

NATO should have taken a strategic approach to enlargement. It did not. NATO had changed its doctrine. It was no longer Moscow's opponent and was in a dialogue with Russia. Countries that met both democratic and military criteria applied, ad hoc, for membership. They were accepted, ad hoc, on their merits. From NATO's point of view, there was no reason why Russia should feel threatened by this; but that was not the Russian perspective. Thus an unplanned process was set in train—with the unintended consequence that the combination of NATO's bombing of Belgrade in 1999 and the creeping accession to NATO of former Warsaw Pact members began to appear to Moscow as deliberate and threatening encroachment.

The turning point was 1999. Since then, the conflicting positions have hardened. The Russian leadership has inveighed against NATO "encirclement" (although no such intention exists among NATO's leaders), and chose to interpret the 2003 Rose Revolution in Georgia and, especially, the 2004 Orange Revolution in Ukraine as attempts by the United States and other NATO partners to "tear away" these countries from Russia. NATO has admitted three former Soviet republics (although many NATO members had never formally recognized the forcible incorporation of the three Baltic states in the USSR), and contemplated the possibility of accepting applications from Ukraine and Georgia at some unspecified time in the future. Russia has asserted its claim to a zone of influence much more stridently, and in its relations with its neighbors has moved from words to coercive deeds. The West has reacted by reinforcing its support for the independent sovereignty of the "new neighbors"; and major Western leaders, including President Obama, have emphasized that their refusal to acquiesce in a Russian "zone of influence," a second Yalta, is nonnegotiable. Hence the impasse. Is this to be a lasting confrontation, or can it be resolved?

The Argument over "Values"

Few things arouse greater ire on the part of Russian officials than Westerners preaching about values.

In his annual address to the federal assembly in 2005, Vladimir Putin protested that Russia shared and had helped to develop European values: "Achieved through much suffering by European culture, the ideals of freedom, human rights, justice, and democracy have for many centuries been our society's determining values."[20]

Any discussion of this subject quickly leads to the accusation that the West applies "double standards": Westerners are critical of Russian failings, blind to their own, and treat Russia more harshly than other countries—China, say, or Saudi Arabia—where the West has important strategic and economic interests. Statements made by former U.S. Vice President Cheney in his speech in Vilnius in 2006, praising democracy in Kazakhstan and Georgia while criticizing Russia, are frequently cited.

There is force in this argument. Western governments and commentators have certainly been guilty of inconsistency. Neither China nor Saudi Arabia (to pick up the two examples mentioned) has escaped criticism. There were very strong reactions to China's violent suppression of protestors in Tienanmen Square, in Tibet, and, most recently, in Xinjiang province. However, over the years concern about human rights has arguably played a larger part in Western relations with Russia than with other countries with comparable records. Why is this so? Part of the answer lies once again in the legacy of the Cold War. But I think there is a second reason. Russia, unlike many of the other countries one might name in this connection, has declared its adherence to "European" values (including the precepts and traditions of Christianity) and has become a party to the European Convention on Human Rights and the Council of Europe. These are the standards by which Russia itself has chosen to be judged.

A second argument is also made—sometimes in the West, and not infrequently in Russia. It is an argument based on realpolitik, that states should not concern themselves with each other's internal affairs and that their relations should be governed by interests, not values. Writing in 2007, Lavrov declared that "the Westphalian system...has placed differences in values beyond the scope of intergovernmental relations."[21] This argument can be sustained up to a point. Day in and day out, states with widely different or conflicting values cooperate in their common interests. Without such cooperation, the global system would be unworkable. However, the world has moved far beyond the Westphalian system, which established the principles of the sovereign state more than 350 years ago. The economics, communications, and indeed problems of the twenty-first century transcend the boundaries of the Westphalian state. International relations are no longer the exclusive preserve of governments and diplomats. Citizens, organizations of many kinds, all that is embraced by the term "public opinion," play a very large part; and public opinion is influenced and exercised by values in a way that governments cannot ignore. Values and interests are entwined. Values, in the globalized world, are an interest.

This is particularly relevant to the question of Russia's "gradual integration" with a "wider area of cooperation in Europe." The institutions of Western Europe, notably the EU (which includes the European Parliament and the European Court of Justice), the Council of Europe, and NATO, stand on foundations of values held in common. The EU is a union of democracies in which the rule of law, including adherence to the laws of the union, is a core value. Spain, Portugal, and Greece were not admitted to the EEC (the EU's forerunner) until they had embraced democracy and the rule of law. Questions about Turkey's alignment with the values of the EU have been at the center of the debate about Turkish membership.

What Is to Be Done: Do Russia and the West Want to Engage?

Defining the problem is the easy part. If only it was just a matter of pressing a "reset button"! With the benefit of hindsight, there is much in the last two decades that we might have done better or differently, though we should not forget that many good things have been done, and in some areas significant progress has been made. What we now need to do is to take the situation as it is, not as we might wish it to be in an ideal world, and to draw the right lessons from our past experiences.

There are those who take an irredeemably pessimistic view. I recall, for example, a letter that appeared in the *Economist* in September 2007 from a former Sovietologist and deputy director of intelligence for the U.S. Navy. On his retirement in 1994, the chief of naval operations had asked him what would become of Russia: "I answered that I did not know exactly, but I was sure that in about ten years it would again be an authoritarian state. Not a hard prediction of course. Any scholar of Russia knows that Russian history revolves around long periods of authoritarian rule, broken only by brief periods of chaotic liberalization before a new kind of authoritarian regime comes to power to exploit the nationalistic anti-Western xenophobia of the Russian people."[22]

It is not hard to find people inside and outside the Russian Federation who pursue a similar line of argument, but to me it is a negative and defeatist approach. Nor is it necessarily accurate. Before the Great War of 1914–18, Russia was industrializing, had become the fourth wealthiest country on earth, and was beginning to develop representative institutions.[23] Had the war—a pointless and avoidable conflict—not broken out, who knows what would have happened to Russia? It is highly unlikely that there would have been a Bolshevik Revolution (just as Germany would probably have avoided Fascism), and Russia would have been spared seven decades of arrested development, backwardness, and isolation under communism. I would be the last to deny the influence of history in shaping a country, but history is not a straitjacket, and it is only one among many influences. Geography, climate, religion, and culture all have their effects. So do the advancement of science, economic competition, and individual aspirations. Living, as we do, in a world where information is communicated instantaneously around the globe, and travel has become cheap and rapid, the external environment has an immensely powerful influence on any country. For the first time in history, the citizens of one country can benchmark their living standards and personal freedoms against those of other countries. Controlling information was one of the most valuable instruments of both the tsarist and communist regimes. It was one of the reasons why the tsars delayed the introduction of the railway to Russia, a country made for the railway like no other. I remember brief conversations (all that was ever possible) with ordinary Russians on park benches in the 1970s, some thinking that I came from a Socialist country rather than the West, in which they told me with complete sincerity how much better their housing was than that of the average Westerner. It is no longer possible to keep a country in that depth of ignorance.

Evidence about the aspirations of the Russian people is contradictory. There is no shortage of nationalism (nor is there in most Western countries). There is an ingrained belief that Russia should be respected as a great and independent power. Many Russians struggle to come to terms with the independence of Ukraine and Belarus, and have bought into a view that the West is encroaching and wants Russia to be weak. To many, the status quo of an imperfect authoritarianism is preferable to destabilizing change or the risks and chaos that they associate with "liberalism."

But does that mean that the Russians want to be stuck forever in the same groove? There is plenty of evidence—from polls and other manifestations of public opinion, as well as from personal observation—that they are not content with the status quo. They would like to have the more effective and more just system of law and order that the leadership has promised but not yet delivered. Hardened though they are, from the Soviet period, to corruption and the abuse of authority by anyone who has it, they are nevertheless angry at the levels that corruption and personal enrichment by state officials from traffic cops on up have now reached (and which Putin described five years ago as being without precedent)—and they see corruption extending its tentacles into areas that were once almost untainted, such as the educational system. I do not believe that Russian citizens are in principle against representative government. Some polls, at least, have shown that they would like to be allowed to elect their regional governors again. They give high approval ratings to the two leading personalities at the top (though alternative leaders are of course not an option), but simultaneously and paradoxically give very low marks to the government's performance. And their attitudes toward the West by no means all go in the same direction. Here Russian opinion polls have been at their most contradictory (so much depends on the way a question is asked). However, the broad picture that emerges is that the majority of Russians, while wishing to remain distinctively "Russian," associate themselves with "Europeans"; would like their country to move closer to Europe, not isolate itself; aspire to a Western European standard of living; and look with some envy upon Western values. They want to be received on their own terms, not forced to accept conditions set by others; but a European orientation seems to be the direction in which they ideally would wish to travel, even though they do not know how and when this might become possible.

From a Western viewpoint, there is in any case nothing to be said for a policy of isolating Russia. Isolation would cut off the enlightened, entrench in power the most backward-looking and most authoritarian forces, damage Russia's development—and simultaneously damage Western interests of every kind. If a test laboratory is required, one need look no farther than Cuba. An unconvincing attempt was made a few years ago by certain elements, mainly in the United States, to argue for a general Western policy of the "neocontainment" of Russia. If and when Russia encroaches on or attacks the legitimate interests of sovereign states, it must be opposed and contained. But unless Russia were again to reject the international status quo and pose a general threat to the West, as did the Soviet Union (an improbable contingency), "neocontainment" would make no sense. It is not hard to understand why twenty-two well-known figures in Eastern and Central Europe, including the widely admired Vaclav Havel and Lech Walesa, should have signed an open letter to President Obama after his Moscow visit, urging him to stand up to "revisionist Russia";[24] but in present circumstances (which are of course conditional on the Russian government's actions), no Western government has concluded that "neocontainment" would be the right approach.

So there is effectively a broad Western consensus on the need to engage with Russia, even if opinion in the ruling elite in Russia is more sharply divided on engagement with the West. (Moscow-based commentator Ivan Safranchuk, for example, opined in July 2009 that "Russia does not want to fight with America, but it is not prepared to make concessions to America either. Moscow's general policy is one of disengagement."[25]) This begs an important question: What sort of engagement?

The Gateway to Partnership

The central issue determining Russia's place in the world of the twenty-first century, as I have suggested earlier in this chapter, is the country's direction of travel. Will it be isolationist or integrationist? Modernizing or regressively conservative? An economy dependent on raw materials, or a diversified and competitive producer with an accent on technology and added value?

These questions can be answered only within Russia. Outside advice, however well-intentioned, is not needed, not wanted, and will not affect the outcome. Everything hinges on what sort of a future the Russian people want for themselves, and whether they are prepared to make the considerable effort to achieve it.

My own belief is that it is not a question of whether Russia will modernize, but when. Russia is going through a phase of inertia after a period of bewildering change; but Russia is not immobile, and its elites cannot afford to fall too far behind the pace of development elsewhere in the world or to postpone forever the task of tackling deep underlying problems. A modernizing trend will at some point return. Rationality, and the pride and ambitions of the Russian people, surely point this way.

Simply to dismiss the possibility of change because, over the past six years, Russia appears to have reverted to type is to invite a self-fulfilling prophecy. If people within Russia cease working and pressing to modernize their own country, if people outside cease trying to work constructively with Russia where it is possible to do so, if collectively we abandon hope because times are difficult, change will be much slower to come.

When Russia begins to develop in the way mapped out, for example, by President Medvedev in "Go, Russia!" the West should be ready to respond.

The steps that he and many others have proposed—to build a range of democratic institutions (in place of the existing single institution of the vertical of power transmitted through the bureaucracy and the security organs), to generate a "political culture of free, secure, critical thinking, self-confident people," to "cultivate a taste for the rule of law" including among the law enforcement agencies themselves, and to use an independent judiciary to "cleanse the country of corruption"—would establish the foundation of common values that is currently lacking. As part of this approach, Medvedev has shown recognition of the need to tackle the legacy of history: "Nostalgia should not guide our foreign policy.... We must look clearly at our past and see our great victories, our tragic mistakes, our role models, and the manifestations of the best features of our national character." Without mentioning Stalin by name, he observed that the legacy of the "modernizations" of Peter the Great and the Soviet period "unleashed ruin, humiliation and resulted in the deaths of millions of our countrymen." The next modernization, the "transition to the next, higher stage of civilization" should be accomplished through nonviolent methods—"not by coercion, but by persuasion."[26]

Change in this direction, if it could be accomplished (notwithstanding past disappointments and much skepticism within Russia), would be the gateway to an East-West partnership not between personalities, which are transient, but between democratic systems: a reliable and lasting partnership. However, as Medvedev made clear, these large changes cannot happen overnight and are being resisted by "those who are completely satisfied with the status quo.... Those who are afraid and do not want change." The test will be deeds rather than words.

Tackling European Security

If we are ever to achieve a partnership, we need to address our strategic differences in the "arc of mistrust." The tensions in this area are too dangerous to be ignored.

Since the low point of August 2008, fears of renewed conflict between Russia and Georgia have not so far come to pass, and there have been few steps toward a resolution of their differences. NATO enlargement and theater missile defense are less immediate issues, although they still feature in the Kremlin's rhetoric. NATO and Russia are quietly groping toward a more constructive relationship.

The process needs to go much wider in two respects. First, it is surely time that the Russian leadership audited the profits and losses of the use of coercive diplomacy as a means of conducting relations with neighboring states. Perhaps this is what President Medvedev had in mind when he spoke of the dangerous "path of confrontation, self-isolation, mutual insults and recrimination." Has Russia gained from the use of economic and other measures against Ukraine, the Baltic states, Belarus, Moldova, Georgia, and Turkmenistan? Has coercion benefited Russia's interests? Has it made these countries more or less willing to work with Russia? What effect has it had on Russia's wider international reputation? For several years many Russian experts on international affairs have been arguing for a policy of attraction rather than coercion. Russia has large economic assets at its disposal. Their argument is that a benign Russia, developing two-way trade and investment and other relations on a voluntary basis, would achieve greater influence than a menacing Russia cutting off trade.

Second, NATO and EU members, with a few exceptions, have shown far too little interest in the sources of tension and potential conflict in the former Soviet area, and need to review their dismissive attitude toward Russian concerns about their country's exclusion from European security arrangements. Western skepticism about President Medvedev's proposals for a new security architecture in Europe inevitably deepened when Russian forces crossed Georgia's boundaries and remained in occupation of part of that country's internationally recognized territory. The Russian government has not thus far couched its suggested treaty on European security in a form that will win the support of Western governments. Nevertheless there is a genuine need for a serious debate on the plethora of issues—most, though not all, in the "post-Soviet space"—that challenge the security and stability of the European continent. This debate should involve all of the countries concerned, as sovereign and independent states, and the relevant organizations. It should embrace all of the issues that threaten to divide these countries, including the so-called frozen conflicts. It should seek a way of diminishing Russia's sense of exclusion—consultation on NATO's "New Strategic Concept" is one obvious entry point—and also of knocking down the false perception that Russia and the West must endlessly be engaged in a zero-sum contest in Eastern Europe.

To take perhaps the most important example, Ukraine does not have to "choose" between its Eastern and Western neighbors. For reasons of geography, security, history, ethnicity, culture, religion, economics, and communications, Ukraine should naturally and perpetually have a very close relationship with Russia—to the benefit of both countries. There is no reason why this need prevent Ukraine from also developing close ties, perhaps leading to eventual membership, with the EU. Its relations with Russia will improve to the extent that Russia respects Ukrainian sovereignty and does not seek to dictate how it should conduct its own affairs. To suggest that the West is trying to tear Ukraine away from Russia flies in the face of the reality that Western countries, and the EU collectively, have invested too little rather than too much effort in Ukraine. If anything is likely to push Ukraine away from Russia, it is Russia's own actions.

Weaving the Fabric of Engagement

Engagement is a long-term approach, not a Grand Design. It is not realpolitik and does not require values to be traded for interests. Rather it is a business of working together in those areas where it is possible to work together; of progressively dismantling ignorance, establishing channels of communication, combating misperceptions, and building confidence and trust. Engagement means connecting threads that in time can be woven together into a larger fabric. It works best from the bottom up rather than the top down.

Engagement between Russia and the West has been growing for the last twenty years, through good times and bad and often in contrast to political moods at the upper levels. There have been many setbacks (one sad example I saw at first hand was the onslaught by Russian security organs against the UK's cultural and educational agency, the British Council, which led to the closure of most of the council's libraries and resource centers in Russia's regions); but there have also been successes, which tend to attract less publicity.

At a high political level, engagement can mean joint work to try to dissuade Iran or North Korea from developing nuclear weapons—something that is clearly in the common interest. In the economy, it embraces massively important trade and investment, which has created a mutuality of interest between Russia and the European Union that constrains political disputes between them. However, we should not discount the importance of humbler day-to-day endeavors involving hundreds of thousands of people. To pluck a few examples out of many, I have met Russians and Britons working together and exchanging experience in dealing with HIV and tuberculosis,

Down syndrome, domestic violence, physical disablement, and the causes of early mortality. I have heard from the education authorities in Krasnoyarsk how they modeled certain changes in their school system on techniques that had been trialed in Britain. I have observed British and Russian universities introducing each other to companies interested in the commercial uses of technology; and I have seen the benefits to both countries of hundreds of educational exchanges. I met some of the twenty thousand Russian officers who graduated from courses to equip them with qualifications for jobs in civilian life, courses that were run in a partnership between the Russian and British governments. These were officers who had joined the Red Army to oppose NATO, many with combat experience from Afghanistan or parts of Africa, and who to their surprise and pleasure ended up working with, rather than against, the British military. I was welcomed into the shipyard at Severodvinsk, which builds and repairs nuclear submarines—because my government was part of a G-8 program to dismantle redundant nuclear vessels. Since my retirement from diplomacy I have worked side by side with Russian colleagues in several businesses, nongovernmental organizations, and educational institutions in both the UK and Russia.

This is a list that I could continue for many pages, and which counterparts from other countries could multiply many times over. The point is simple. These are people-to-people contacts. Only a tiny percentage of these contacts were taking place twenty years ago. They educate us all and change perceptions. This is engagement in action. It is a slow business, but over time it will create a much larger pool of mutual comprehension and appreciation.

Conclusion: What Sort of Partnership?

The Cold War was an unpleasant and tense experience, but for more than four decades nuclear deterrence produced a long period of stability in interstate relations in Europe. The end of the Cold War brought instability and interstate conflict in the Balkans and the Caucasus. More widely, we are living through a period in which the international status quo is being reshaped. History did not "end" in 1991, but we are experiencing a new phase of history in which changes in the global economy, the dramatic acceleration of technology, the challenges of international terrorism and nuclear proliferation, climate change, the competition for resources, and migratory flows are reordering the globe. One manifestation of this change, among many, has been

China's emergence from isolation, becoming an economic powerhouse that is playing an increasingly influential role in international affairs. The instruments that made the Soviet Union a superpower in the late twentieth century—above all the ability to project military power around the globe—are of declining relevance in this new world order. The zero-sum thinking and the lexicon of the Cold War—the language of "peaceful coexistence" and "détente"—are as outmoded as ZIL limousines and Bakelite wireless sets.

The critical factor in the twenty-first century will be not so much how powers compete as how they interact. Interaction in tackling the economic crisis (which inter alia has led to the appearance of the G-20 as a significant force) is a recent example. Russia clearly aspires to play an important role in the new international status quo. This will place a premium on Russia's ability to deploy economic and intellectual capital and to forge effective relationships with other key actors.

Within this spectrum, Russia's relationships with the European Union and the United States will not be the only determinant (the relationship with China will be of great importance), but they represent an opportunity. Glorious isolation does not look like the recipe for future success. The potential benefits of much closer involvement with the rest of the European continent and of a more stable, productive, and trusting relationship with the West appear self-evident.

We need to be clear about what sort of relationship is possible. Amid the exaggerated expectations of the 1990s, the term "strategic partnership" was bandied about with little thought as to its meaning and enshrined in many a diplomatic document and speech. The intentions were benign, but the proclamation was wildly premature. This devalued and discredited the term, and contributed to a mood of bitter public skepticism.

I would distinguish between three levels of agreement between states. The first is when two or more states form a pact or treaty or alliance for a specific purpose (and often for a defined period), based on a specific interest held in common. It is the most common form of relationship between states. Second, a genuinely "strategic partnership" is a relationship at a much deeper level. It does not exclude the possibility of states competing with each other or disagreeing vigorously over tactical issues (one could cite disagreements between NATO members over the correct way of dealing with Iraq; or between the United States and the EU over preferential trade in bananas, which led to the Clinton administration threatening economic sanctions against the British cashmere industry at a time when British and U.S. forces were operating side by side in the Balkans and Iraq). It has to reflect not only a commonality of interests but also of values—and a sense that, when the chips are down and there is a serious threat, the partners can rely on each other to be on the same side. It is a partnership not just between governments but between peoples. It is founded much more on trust than on formal documents. If two parties require a legally binding document to create a "strategic partnership," they almost certainly do not have such a partnership: it should come from the bottom up and be self-evident and self-enforcing. A third, and yet deeper, level is where states voluntarily agree to pool sovereignty. In agreeing to place national forces under a common military command, NATO members pooled sovereignty in a limited area. A much wider pooling of sovereignty has taken place within the European Union, which developed from the initial customs union into a values-based community with the ambitious goal of an "ever-closer union," with supranational institutions at its center.

At the present time, the Russo-Western relationships clearly belong in the first of these categories. Many agreements of the kind described already exist between Russia and Western countries, and more are under negotiation. Equally clearly, anything resembling a genuine "strategic partnership" between either Russia and the United States or Russia and the EU does not yet exist because of strategic differences over the sovereignty of the post-Soviet states, and because of the lack of a solid foundation of common values and the trust this engenders. A relationship that entailed the pooling of sovereignty would be a big step beyond that, and it is not something that at the moment either side would contemplate; although a specially tailored agreement bridging the Russian and EU economies without the obligations and constrictions of full membership would not be beyond the bounds of possibility.

This suggests certain obvious conclusions. We should refrain from declaring that we have a "strategic partnership" until this is genuinely the case. Otherwise we fool ourselves: it is no good pretending that the situation is better than it is. The *idea* of a strategic partnership is a worthy goal but will require time, effort, and evolution. With that evolution in mind, we should focus on the steps necessary to stabilize and develop the existing relationship—to move upward from where we now are. This means talking frankly about our differences, while trying to avoid exacerbating them. It also means building up and facilitating—not constricting—the networks of engagement described above.

Can we really leave behind the suspicion of the past? Not rapidly: there are too many mental and physical scars. Can we live with these memories but not be governed by them? Yes, so long as we don't bring them back to life. Is "gradual integration between Russia and a wider area of cooperation in Europe" a feasible concept? In a rational appraisal of Russia's interests, strengths, and potential, certainly: Russia's interests point toward modernization. Over time, practical engagement, generated naturally between citizens and organizations with shared interests of every kind, is the way that we shall increase trust and overcome the unnatural separation imposed by the Soviet Union's long years of isolation.

Notes

1. President Obama's statement in Moscow, reported by the *Financial Times* on July 7, 2009.
2. Dmitry Medvedev. "Rossiya, vpered!" [Go, Russia!], www.eng.kremlin.ru\1534_type 104017_221527.shtml.
3. Founding Act on Mutual Relations, Cooperation, and Security between NATO and the Russian Federation, signed in Paris on May 27, 1997, www.nato-russian-council.info/HTML/EN/documents27may97.shtml.
4. The Partnership and Cooperation Agreement between the European Union and the Russian Federation, signed at Corfu in 1994.
5. *Financial Times*, July 3, 2009.
6. Ibid.
7. *Times* (London), March 12, 1985.
8. Editorial, *New York Times*, reprinted by the *International Herald Tribune*, March 13, 1985.
9. Roderic Lyne, "Making Waves: Mr. Gorbachev's Public Diplomacy," *International Affairs* 63, no. 2 (2010).
10. Anyone inclined to question Mao's place in this list need look no farther than the authoritative biography by Jung Chan and Jon Halliday, *Mao: The Unknown Story* (London: Jonathan Cape, 2005).
11. Felix Dzerzhinsky was the first head of the Extraordinary Commission to Fight Counter-Revolution, the forerunner of the NKVD and later the KGB (1917–26).

12. Alexy II, patriarch of Moscow and All Russias (1990–2008).
13. "Dreaming with BRICs: The Path to 2050" (Goldman Sachs global economics paper no. 99, October 1, 2003).
14. Reported by several Moscow newspapers on March 25, 2009.
15. *Moscow Times*, September 15, 2009.
16. President Medvedev's speech at the international conference in Yarovslavl, September 14, 2009.
17. See Sergei Lavrov, "Russian Foreign Policy and a New Quality of the Geopolitical Situation," *Diplomatic Yearbook* 2008, http://www.mid.ru/brp_4.nsf/e78a48070f128a7b43256999005bcbb3/19e7b14202191e4ac3257525003e5de7?OpenDocument.
18. Archive documents from 1989 published by the UK Foreign and Commonwealth Office on September 11, 2009.
19. Rutskoy served as vice president of Russia from 1991 to 1993.
20. President Putin's address to the federal assembly of the Russian Federation, April 25, 2005, http://eng.kremlin.ru/speeches/2005/04/25/2031_type70029type82912_87086.shtml.
21. Sergei Lavrov, "The Present and the Future of Global Politics," *Russia in Global Affairs*, no. 2 (April–June 2007).
22. William Manthorpe, letter to the editor, *Economist*, September 8, 2007.
23. Estimates of GDP in 1913, derived from Angus Maddison, *The World Economy: Historical Statistics* (Paris: OECD, 2003): (1) United States (19.1 percent of global GDP); (2) China (8.9 percent); (3) Germany (8.8 percent); (4) Russia (8.6 percent); (5) UK (8.3 percent); (6) British India (7.6 percent); (7) France (5.3 percent). Based on IMF figures, the comparable list for 2008 would read: (1) United States (23.5 percent); (2) Japan (8.1 percent); (3) China (7.2 percent); (4) Germany (6.0 percent); (5) France (4.7 percent); (6) UK (4.4 percent); (7) Italy (3.8 percent); and (8) Russia (2.8 percent).
24. Open letter to President Obama by twenty-two intellectuals and former policy makers from central and eastern Europe, July 15, 2009.
25. Quoted in the *Economist*, July 11 2009.
26. Dmitry Medvedev, "Rossiya, vpered!" [Go, Russia!].

CHAPTER ELEVEN

What Kind of a Europe for What Kind of Russia

Alexander Rahr

This chapter examines what went wrong in the relations between Russia and the West over the first two decades after the end of the Cold War and how the idea of an alliance can be repaired in the coming decades.

Instead of tackling common threats and seeking a basic agreement about the future European architecture, NATO, the EU, and Russia are at loggerheads over so many issues that some observers have concluded that the Cold War has returned. The areas of conflict can be easily named: human rights; rule of law; press freedom; free elections; NATO enlargement; missile defense; dependencies on Russian gas; Russian treatment of former Soviet republics; and Russian military support for Iran, Venezuela, and Syria. The West favors relations with Russia that would be based on a community of liberal values. Russia, instead, wants a partnership with the West based on purely pragmatic interests. Given these deep and serious misunderstandings, it remains open whether Russia and the West will reach a consensus, which has become more difficult than it was a decade ago because "the West" is no longer a united entity. The West has had to deal with two different Russias. The first was Boris Yeltsin's neodemocratic, post-communist Russia, which played the role of a "junior partner" of the West. The second is Vladimir Putin's post-imperial Russia, which wants to become a key power in the European "global concert of nations." To become a global player in the future and successfully compete against increasing rivalry from Asia, the EU has no choice but to align itself with Russia. The same common sense dictates that Russia must manage its modernization in the context of a European architecture.

Conflicts, Different Perceptions, and Initiatives

The breakup of the Soviet Union almost two decades ago opened the possibility of a period of freedom for Europe that the continent had never witnessed before. The two main positive elements of this new order were the inclusion of almost thirty states in a joint European Union and the emergence of a new cooperative, non-totalitarian Russia. Russia chose to open itself up and eventually ally itself with the West. The EU became Russia's main trading partner, and Russia emerged as the EU's main energy supplier. President Yeltsin and his foreign minister, Andrei Kozyrev, suggested creating a joint democratic system in the North consisting of Russia, the United States, the EU, and Japan.[1] They thought this was the only way to protect Russian civilization from challenges from the South.[2] During an early state visit to Poland, Yeltsin officially stated that Russia did not object to Poland's membership in NATO. The West took great advantage of the dramatic changes in Russia in the 1990s. It welcomed Russia's revolution and the end of communism. The Cold War ended peacefully, and the United States and the EU supported Russia with financial credits and other assistance out of fear that a weak Russia might collapse and throw Europe into chaos.

But after Putin's rise in 1999, they became increasingly worried about a strong Russia that took on anti-Western traits and was more difficult for the West to influence.[3] Like Yeltsin, Putin also first embraced the EU and NATO. At the beginning of his presidency he proposed elevating the existing partnership with the EU from a purely economic to a more strategic level, including a security dialogue. Speaking in Berlin in 2001, Putin suggested that the energy-resource-rich space of Siberia and the Far East be merged with the technologically rich space of Western Europe. He obviously wanted to foster a further reunification of the European continent—with Russia inside Europe—via the energy factor.[4] The events of 9/11 provided Putin with the unique chance to integrate with the West on a security agenda. He could portray his country as an indispensable ally for the United States in fighting the new global threats. Through security and intelligence cooperation with the United States, Putin in 2001–02 secured a free hand in the war against Islamic extremism in Chechnya. A new Russian-

American alliance unseen since World War II was unfolding on the world political stage.

America, however, was not interested in increasing its partnership with Russia as long as the Russian economy lacked clearly defined rules. The United States also did not seek a real alliance with Russia in the struggle against Islamic extremism. The George W. Bush administration signaled to Putin that it was basically interested in Russia's cooperation in containing Iran's nuclear program. The United States was reluctant to discuss elements of a future world order with Russia, which was increasingly perceived by Washington as the loser of the Cold War, and focused instead on China as a possible future main strategic partner in shaping the world. In 2001 the United States had renounced the Anti-Ballistic Missile (ABM) Treaty and, despite assurances that it did not intend to build a full-scale national defense directed against Russia, started in 2007 to develop a limited missile defense system in Central Europe to fend off Iranian missiles. In response to that, Russia suspended implementation of the Conventional Forces in Europe (CFE) Treaty, which was essential for regulating conventional armed forces in Europe after the end of the Cold War. At the end of the presidential terms of Bush and Putin, relations between Russia and the West became tense. The United States enhanced its plans to develop a missile defense system in Central Europe and sought to expand NATO to include Ukraine and Georgia.

Although no real partnership relations developed between the United States and Russia, there were initial hopes of a strategic partnership between Russia and the EU. Both sides agreed in 2003 to form so-called common spaces—in the economic, cultural, informational, and security areas—which could substitute for Russian EU membership. But the EU was so focused on protecting its liberal value system vis-à-vis Russia that it failed to create even a free trade zone with Russia. Russia, in turn, began to ignore Western companies' investor's rights, erected trade barriers, and demonstrated to the West that it was inclined to use its energy resources as a foreign policy instrument to reinforce its strategic interests in Europe. Russian authorities started deliberately to rewrite the conditions for foreign companies' engagement in Russia's energy sector. The authorities in Moscow were using murky environmental pretexts in order to change conditions in the Russian energy production sphere. From the Russian point of view, Western companies had received unjustified privileges in the Russian energy sector in the 1990s, when the country really needed Western technologies and investments. Russian efforts at creating major state-controlled energy companies and Russian politicians' proclamations to restore dominance by using energy supplies as a lever led to a defensive counterreaction from the EU, which started to de-monopolize its domestic energy markets and close the doors to Russian downstream investments.

Consequently, the EU concentrated its policy on accomplishing the historical reunification of the West with most of the countries of Eastern Europe. The entrance of the former Warsaw Pact states and the three Baltic republics into the EU and NATO in 2002–04 made the general Western attitude toward Russia more critical. The "new" member states, in contrast to the "old" EU nations, had not reconciled with post-communist Russia, and Russia had not forgiven them their drive toward the West. Slovakia and Bulgaria remained more faithful to cooperation with Russia until the gas crisis of 2009, which literally froze them. The EU expansion, which began with the widening of the Schengen Area deep into Eastern Europe, was perceived by Russia as harmful to its interests because Moscow had lost its traditional markets in Eastern Europe. Russia's perception about itself strongly differed from the West's perception. Russia regarded itself as a re-emerging great power, which followed its own geopolitical ambitions in global affairs. Russian elites largely underestimated the political significance of the new EU.

Moscow was irritated when, after expanding into the territory of Central Eastern Europe, a politically stronger EU began to focus its new foreign and defense policies on the Western members of the Commonwealth of Independent States (CIS) and the South Caucasus, calling these former soviet republics the EU's "new abroad." Geopolitics—a term that had been labeled as outdated because the modern world had distanced itself from the notion of "spheres of influence"—re-emerged in the European continent's new architecture after the EU proclaimed its "neighboring policy" toward the countries of the post-Soviet space. This strategy was set to assist democracy and economic reform, prevent instabilities, and help to resolve conflicts in its broader neighborhood, especially in regions that were seen as transit routes, raw material bases, or potential markets for the EU. Countries like Ukraine, Georgia, and even Belarus were promised some sort of EU association should they succeed in reforming their economic and political systems.

In the 1990s, Russia had learned to deal with the EU as an economic power. Now, when the EU started to develop its own common security policy, criticize Russia from its Brussels headquarters, and keep the visa barrier along Russia's western borders, it began to fear that the EU was working on a new European architecture from which it would be excluded. Russia tried hard to develop its own reintegration model for the post-Soviet space, which was perceived by the EU as a hostile attempt to rebuild the lost hemisphere. Since the beginning of the twenty-first century, Russia's foreign policy followed two contradictory goals: on the one hand, Russia intended to closely engage itself with Europe; on the other hand, Putin sought to revive Russia's great power status by using the country's new energy export potentials.

Russian policy collided with Western interests. In 2003, without consultations with the West, Russia developed the so-called Kozak Plan for stability in Moldova, which stipulated the transfer of Moldova into a confederation. The separatist Transdniester autonomous republic would have received a veto right over the politics of Chisinau. Of course, the hidden agenda of Russian diplomacy was to keep Moldova, which was orienting itself toward the EU and NATO, in Moscow's sphere of influence. The plan was blocked by the EU and the United States. In November of the same year, a huge popular protest movement against a manipulation of parliamentary elections in Georgia swept away the corrupt regime of Eduard Shevardnadze. As a result of the accession to power of pro-Western forces under Mikhail Saakashvili, Russia was over night deprived of all its traditional leverage over Georgia and the Southern Caucasus. Saakashvili immediately proclaimed a policy of reunifying Georgia with its breakaway republics and got involved in a heavy political conflict with Russia over Moscow's continuing support of separatists in Abkhazia and South Ossetia.

In 2004 Russia and the West came into conflict over another country in Eastern Europe. Moscow's support of Viktor Yanukovich's electoral manipulations in the Ukrainian presidential race led the EU to defend the opposition forces under Viktor Yushchenko. The Orange Revolution swept away the old regime and changed Ukrainian foreign political orientations. Several weeks after coming to power, Yushchenko was already heavily knocking at the doors of NATO and the EU, and the West made clear that it would contain Russia, should the latter try to rebuild its empire by force.[5] Russia had underestimated the desire of the elites of its neighboring states to become part of the West and escape Russia's dominance once and for all.

Attempts by Moscow to reorganize the CIS into anything more than a forum for the peaceful settlement of the former soviet republic divorce did not materialize. The economic dependencies of the newly independent states were gradually reduced. Neither Putin nor his predecessor Yeltsin succeeded in forging a reunification with pro-Russian Belarus. A collective defense treaty was supported by only half of the former Soviet republics and in time lost its significance. All Russian efforts to construct new oil and gas alliances in the Caspian region and prevent the emergence of alternative communication, transportation, and trade patterns were in the end unsuccessful. The United States, the EU, and China became active players in the resource-rich Caspian region and Russia's competitors for influence in the whole post-Soviet space.

At that particular moment, the West needed a proper discussion of joint threat perceptions and common strategies, because some of the newcomers from Central East Europe behaved as if they had joined not renewed NATO and EU institutions but the old organizations of the Cold War. Poland, Romania, the Czech Republic, and the Baltic states seemed to perceive NATO and the EU as instruments of containment against Russia. In 2006 they developed the ideas of an "Energy NATO," a "frontline for freedom," and a "union of transit states."[6] Most of their rhetoric was clearly directed toward attracting special security arrangements with the United States, which the countries of the so-called old West found irritating.

The EU faced a severe split on the question of how to deal with Russia. Its previous Russia agenda, which included such issues as human rights abuses in Chechnya, limitations on media freedom, manipulation of elections, and the destruction of Yukos (2004), became even more negatively oriented as a result of relations of the new EU member states with Russia. The agenda now included quarrels over such issues as visas for Russian travelers between Russia and the intra-EU enclave Kaliningrad; the diversification of energy pipeline routes; new geopolitical rivalries in the post-Soviet space; "frozen conflicts," which some Central East European states regarded as a threat against them; and Russia's opposition to the U.S.-led war in Iraq. Russia's participation in the creation of the so-called Berlin-Paris-Moscow axis, which, in the view of many observers, almost split up the transatlantic alliance (2003), also spoiled the relationship. Soon, rifts emerged between the new EU countries' and Russia's perception of the history of World War II. The West tended to see Hitler and Stalin as similar criminals, whereas Russia, whose historical identity and state legitimacy as a great power were shaped from its victory in World War II and the Yalta world order, opposed such views. These rifts brought Europe and Russia into another contretemps, especially during the sixtieth anniversary of the end of World War II (2005) and the seventieth anniversary of the beginning of the war (2009).

Overall relations between the EU and Russia further soured when the West became worried about the reliability of future energy deliveries from Russia. The gas conflict between Russia and Ukraine demonstrated that Moscow was willing to use gas exports as a political tool to pressure neighboring countries. The EU took the side of Ukraine in the conflict between Moscow and Kiev, and reconsidered its energy strategy toward Russia. Fearful of becoming subject to political blackmail, the EU decided to diversify and reduce its dependence on gas imports from Russia.[7] The EU failed to properly analyze the real causes of the Russian-Ukrainian gas conflict. It ignored the fact that Kiev had made it appear that it had become a "victim of Russian imperialism" in the hope that provoking Russia would boost its chances of getting "protection" from the West. Ukraine openly blackmailed Russia by using its transit monopoly.

Values or Interests

A true partnership between the West and Russia could not rest on such propositions as described above. Obviously, from the beginning the EU and Russia had misperceptions of their new relationship. After the end of the Cold War, the EU transformed itself into an institution of common liberal values and expected Russia to seek to become a democracy. Russia's idea of integration with the EU was a purely practical one: Russia saw the EU primarily as the source for economic modernization and not as a tutor on democracy. Russia looked mainly for economic cooperation with the West, never thought of becoming part of modern European liberal civilization, and never imagined giving up its own sovereignty rights to Brussels. Russia agreed to play according to common established rules, but rules that were co-developed with Moscow.[8]

Given these misunderstandings, it was not surprising that the Russian move toward Europe did not succeed. Russia got stuck halfway in its process of democratization. The first decade after the escape from communism—the 1990s—were perceived by most ordinary Russians as an economic as well as a moral collapse of society and state. When Russian economic life started to recover at the beginning of the twenty-first century, the Russian population began to think that prosperity and global integration could be attained without adopting liberal values.

As of today, nearly twenty years after the breakup of the Soviet Union, Russia finds itself in a serious dilemma. Geopolitically, it is being surrounded by an enlarging NATO. The two main pillars on which the new European architecture after the end of the Cold War has been built are the EU and NATO. Russia is not a member of either and has no intention of joining them in the foreseeable future. Russia views the enlargement of NATO as an infringement on its national security interests. However, without being a member of NATO or the EU, Russia cannot participate in the decision making on Europe's future. The consequence of not being anchored in the all-European institutions is a seriously felt isolation from the future economic and security architecture of the Occident—to which Russia historically belongs. Russia risks being cut off from the integration processes in Europe, which carries the danger of it losing any interest in democratizing itself. The issue of Russia's fate in future Europe is the last unanswered question of the Cold War. Only if the Russian problem is solved, can a stable Europe of the twenty-first century be established.

The Russian-Georgian War in August 2008 became an unfortunate expression of the "small" Cold War that shook Europe twenty years after the end of the previous East-West conflict. Russia had warned the West that any attempt to proclaim the sovereignty of Kosovo would lead to the application of the same secession rights for the non-recognized separatist republics in the post-Soviet space.[9] Some observers thought that the quick recognition of South Ossetia and Abkhazia by Moscow in the Russian-Georgian War was a kind of response to Western recognition of Kosovo's independence. The positive aspect of the war was that it forced the West and Russia to make a "tabula rasa decision": either start redirecting military arsenals against each other or press the so-called reset button and forget the mutual conflicts of the past few years. In other words, the West could either treat Russia as the disturber of international peace and contain it with Cold War tools or it could accept the incompatibility of some Russian and Western strategic interests and nevertheless return to a strategic partnership with the idea of incorporating Russia in a joint alliance against the "real" challenges faced by mankind, such as dealing with international terrorism and crime, climate change, nonproliferation, energy security, new global trade, regional conflict resolution, poverty, and illegal migration.

The Reset

The rise to power of the more liberal-minded Dmitri Medvedev helped to improve the atmosphere between Russia and the West. The West gave Medvedev a chance to restore trust in international relations. The NATO Russian Council was revived, and the installation of U.S. missile defenses in Poland and the Czech Republic were suspended. The West discussed with Medvedev new ideas of cooperation on reforming international organizations such as the G-8, and there were signs of new setups of "coalitions against international terrorism," such as the NATO-Shanghai Organization for Cooperation. Russia showed willingness to more closely cooperate with NATO in stabilizing Afghanistan. It had been the French EU presidency that made intensive diplomatic efforts to reconcile Russia and the West after the Georgian War.[10] If another EU member state such as Poland had held the presidency, it would probably have initiated a different approach toward Russia.

The Czech Republic and Sweden, which assumed the EU Council presidency in 2009, distanced themselves from the Russia-first approach of France, and their "Eastern partnership" policy focused on assisting former Soviet republics, such as Belarus, Ukraine, Moldavia, Armenia, Azerbaijan, and Georgia, to more closely approach the EU institutions.[11] Given the way the Eastern partnership was designed, it could easily be interpreted as an attempt to return to the policy of containment of Russia. The partnership also included a new EU energy security package for all neighboring states that were dependent on Russia. The idea of the so-called Nabucco pipeline, which would carry Central Asian gas to the European markets in circumvention of Russian territory, suddenly received greater priority in the EU than the Nord Stream pipeline. The latter was initiated by Germany and Russia in the beginning of Putin's presidency with the goal of circumventing Ukraine as the main transit route for Russian gas exports to Europe.

In the end it was German Chancellor Angela Merkel who ensured the continuity of partnership between the West and Russia. Germany probably became the Western country that went the farthest in establishing close links with Russia. Strong lobbyists in the German elites, which historically look more favorably on Russia than the elites of most of the other European countries, were the first to develop a more interest-driven than value-driven approach toward Russia. This would help overcome many of the dilemmas in the Western-Russian relationship, which until now had been based on too many misperceptions and expectations. Therefore, it is important to look at the German-Russian relationship as a special chapter in the overall analysis of Russian–Western cooperation.

Germany as Russia's Advocate in Europe

Russia and Germany are for historical reasons doomed to a "special" relationship. For several years, Germany, of all foreign nations, enjoyed the most sympathy among Russians. Opinion polls conducted in Russia in recent years indicate that the Russian elites regard Germany as their advocate in the West. Germany is a non-nuclear state and is not considered a geopolitical rival in the post-Soviet space as, for instance, is the United States. Germany remains Russia's most important foreign trade partner.[12] By the same token, German elites enjoy seeing their country in the role of advocate for all-European interests vis-à-vis Russia, particularly in the economic field. German Social Democrats seriously wished to play the role of mediator between Russia and the United States.

As curious as it might appear, Germany and Russia had already closely cooperated during the Cold War, when the governments of Willy Brandt and later Helmut Schmidt conducted the so-called Ostpolitik (eastern policy) with the USSR.[13] West Germany at that time aimed at having a maximum influence on the GDR that was possible only through better relations with Moscow. Thanks to the deepening of economic relations, trust was established on both sides. The process led to West German technology and capital transfer into the Soviet Union and the GDR. West Germany in turn received energy supply from the East. Ostpolitik was a big monetary investment for Germany, but it opened doors to German companies in the Soviet energy market.[14] The famous German pipeline deal was the foundation on which the later energy alliance between the EU and Russia was built.

The success of the Ostpolitik helped later to foster the reconciliation between former foes of World War II after the Cold War. The significance of this reconciliation for post–Cold War Europe has yet to be properly understood by other EU countries, which are suspicious of the Berlin-Moscow "special" relationship. While Germany's eastern neighbors will still need to overcome their trauma of the forty-five-year-long Soviet occupation, the German elites enthusiastically applauded the constructive role played by the last Soviet leader Mikhail Gorbachev and first Russian president Boris Yeltsin in the crucial years of Germany's reunification (1989–93). In the Western debate about the reasons for the demise of the Soviet Union—whether the collapse occurred due to military and economic pressure from the United States, or because Germany timely started a consistent Ostpolitik of "engagement" that helped to change the Soviet Union from within—many Germans favor the latter explanation.

After successfully negotiating with Gorbachev and Yeltsin a smooth national reunification for his own country, Chancellor Helmut Kohl in 1990 realized that Germany should take the lead in tackling the issue of Russia's role in future Europe. Germany's Russia policy for the next twenty years was always designed toward an incorporation of Russia into the larger European architecture. Kohl took the role of being Russia's advocate quite seriously and showed reluctance to accept a too fast inclusion of the Baltic states into NATO, fearing Russian isolation from Europe. Subsequently, Germany became the strongest supporter of Russia's inclusion in the G-8 and the WTO. When the post-Soviet Russian economy showed signs of collapse in the mid-1990s, Kohl personally secured the necessary financial support for ailing Russia. Kohl's Russia policy helped to maintain a positive picture of Germany in Russia during the latter's renunciation of the "romantic phase" of open policy toward the West in the mid-1990s. For the eastern enlargement of NATO, Moscow blamed the United States not Germany. The Russian elites associated the intrusion of Western geopolitics in the post-Soviet space not with Germany but with the foreign policy of the United States. This again intensified the German role as a Russian advocate.

Together with France, its main European ally, Kohl initiated regular German-French-Russian troika summits.[15] These meetings were aimed at creating a trilateral strategic partnership on European economic and security issues in a time when other European states were not ready for strategic cooperation with Russia. The troika meetings were designed to make Moscow feel that although not a member of the EU or NATO, Russians were not excluded from decision making in Europe. The troika was attacked in Central Eastern Europe as an anti-U.S. "axis" at the beginning of the war in Iraq in 2003. Some former Warsaw Pact countries were shocked by the closeness of ranks between Berlin, Moscow, and Paris.

With Putin's speech in the Bundestag in September 2001—a few days after the events of September 11—which he held in German, Russia reaffirmed its adherence to a common democratic European civilization, as had been previously stipulated by Gorbachev and Yeltsin in the 1990s. In the aftermath, Chancellor Gerhard Schröder forgave Russia six billion euros of its debts, which Moscow owed from the former GDR. Like no other EU country, Germany stood up for the energy alliance with Moscow and for the easement of existing visa barriers with Russia. In turn, Putin allowed Germany to be the first NATO state to transport military supplies to Afghanistan through Russian territory. Putin also invited Germany to cooperate in the economic reconstruction of the Northern Caucasus. Putin met with no other Western politician as often as with Schröder. The two statesmen even visited each other with their families. Putin helped Schröder adopt two Russian orphans, which symbolizes Schröder's emotional bond with Russia.

In 2003 Russia established, together with Germany and France, an opposition to the United States and Great Britain in the Iraq war. That "antiwar coalition" of Berlin-Paris-Moscow may have been the beginning of a new European order—something unthinkable during the Cold War. Germany and France indirectly promoted Russia to become a player of its own in European security policy. In 2004 Schröder firmly sided with Putin in the Yukos affair. To advance the energy alliance with Russia, Schröder personally held negotiations with international energy companies. As a result of his effort, a bank consortium was created that helped finance Russo-German projects within the energy sector. To secure Russia's integration into the world economy, Schröder gave the German chair for the G-8 summit in 2006 to Russia. The German chancellor hinted that he could well imagine Russia's accession to NATO and the EU in a long-term perspective. Schröder never tired of stressing that although he saw Russian internal developments as contradictory and not free from setbacks, he was nevertheless certain that stability in Russia would strengthen European security and prosperity. The West would not need to worry about a collapsing Russia or spend billions to stabilize it as in the 1990s. Schröder's strategic partnership approach to Russia could have become an important element of the future European order. With this, Berlin fulfilled its historical self-imposed role as an advocate for the integration of Russia into the West. In turn, this reassured Russia in its belief that for the achievement of its own objectives in Europe special relationships with Berlin and Paris had to be sustained.

Schröder's Russia policy and the Berlin-Paris-Moscow troika summits were heavily opposed by the former Warsaw Pact countries and also by the Bush administration. In 2005 Schröder proposed to connect Russia and

Germany via a new gas pipeline through the Baltic Sea, which would turn Germany into the chief distributor of Russian gas in Western Europe; the idea provoked an outcry in the United States and Central Eastern Europe. The latter feared diminishing Ukraine's existing gas transport monopoly. The lack of coherence among the EU member-states regarding Germany's positive approach to Russia confronted Berlin with an unpleasant dilemma between fostering a pragmatic partnership with Russia and supporting the critical approach of the Central East European states toward Russia. In the debate over the next round of NATO enlargement, which took place throughout 2008, Germany and France spoke against it.

Chancellor Merkel, after coming to power in 2005, kept Germany's Russia policy on the same course as her predecessors Kohl and Schröder. Although taking a slightly more critical approach on human right issues in Russia, she remained committed to the "strategic partnership" between Germany and Russia, particularly in energy questions. In 2006 two major German energy companies—E.ON and BASF—gained gas exploration rights directly on Russian territory.[16] Merkel, who grew up in East Germany during the Soviet occupation, remained skeptical about Russia's path toward democracy, but she fully understood the opportunities that German and European businesses faced in the fast-growing Russian economic market. However, she stopped conducting the Berlin-Paris-Moscow summits so as not to annoy the new EU and NATO members.

The German business lobby enthusiastically applauded the new opportunities in the Russian market.[17] During the 1990s, German companies considered the business climate in Russia as critical and expressed their worries about the Russian mafia. The lack of law and order was seen as the biggest problem. Against this background, German companies followed Putin's advancement very carefully. After his takeover, economic relations became the flagship of the partnership. Germany rose to the most important trading partner of Russia from which it imported almost 40 percent of its gas and over 30 percent of its oil. The trade balance between both countries rose by 20 percent in 2008 and reached 68 billion euros. Germany was the first country allowed to invest directly in Russian oil production.

For the German economy, East Europe became the biggest growth market (17 percent of all German foreign trade; the United States accounts for only 6.5 percent of German trade, and China 5 percent). The German consumer and food industries benefited most from the improved business climate. East European shops became packed with German products. Major German retail firms started their expansion course toward the East. Germany today delivers one-third of all machinery and equipment going to Russia.

At present, Germany is the main foreign investor in Russia. Before the financial crisis, Germany had directly invested $17.4 billion in the Russian economy. German industrialists believed that Germany could become Russia's main modernization partner, but they also welcomed the strengthening of the role of the state in Russia, because this would lead to more law and order and less criminality and corruption. German companies had traditionally conducted business with the Kremlin and through the state apparatus since the 1970s and not—like the U.S. firms in the 1990s—through the private business structures of the new oligarchs. Germany and Russia developed a unique cooperation in the industrial-technological sphere. Whereas before the financial crisis, German politicians rejected any kind of larger Russian investments in the German economy due to Russia's often non-transparent behavior, by 2009 they began to welcome Russian capital flow into "strategic" companies like the Wadan shipyards, Opel, and Infineon.[18]

In the 2009 federal election campaign in Germany, the once-critical Russian factor no longer existed. A remarkable consensus appeared in all leading parties for the boost of a strategic economic partnership with Moscow. Official Berlin forgave the Russian military intrusion into Georgia. A new alliance between Berlin and Moscow was unfolding itself as in the best days of Kohl and Schröder. Merkel revived the idea of a strategic partnership with Russia with the dual goal of ensuring long-term security for Russian energy deliveries to the West through additional pipelines and providing Russia with Western technologies for the long overdue modernization of its industry. Germany did not give up the idea to develop between the EU and Russia a plan for modernizing Siberia as a practical tool for achieving the objectives of the energy alliance. This plan would not only promote economic cooperation but also codify the strategic value of Russian resources for Europe's future prosperity.

The positive relations between Germany and Russia, on a pragmatic rather than value-based approach, could become a model for the improvement of relationships between Russia and the entire EU. If Russia becomes tempted to try to further divide the EU by picking up individual states for bilateral partnerships, then the EU's internal rifts on the question of how to deal with Russia will deepen. In order to prevent a further division of Europe on that basic question, Germany should engage itself in convincing its eastern neighbors of the benefits of engaging Russia "pragmatically." Unfortunately, the energy security issue has become highly politicized in the West and Russia, while energy policy could in theory become the best link connecting Russia with Europe.

Energy: Russia's Link with Europe

The Russia-EU energy alliance could have reached the historic status of the Franco-German coal and steel community, the predecessor of the European Economic Community and, not least, the European Union. Germany thought to foster that, but due to its specific gas policy toward Russia, Berlin has the questionable reputation of being too friendly toward Moscow, for exchanging human rights for gas. The majority of European states ask on what common principles could an energy alliance with Russia work, given the dissonance between a state-owned energy sector in Russia and a predominantly market-driven sector in the EU. Gazprom, not surprisingly, is against the competitive approach of the EU, while the latter does not want to depend largely on long-term contracts with a monopoly like Gazprom. Russia's wish to be the only provider of gas to Europe from the post-Soviet space and Gazprom's strategy of trying to thwart all alternative routes that bypass Russia deeply irritate consumers in the West.

During the 1990s, Russia appeared to embrace the liberal political and economic system of the West. Had this prevailed, the United States and the EU would have sealed an open energy partnership with Russia, and Western energy companies would have acquired large stakes in the privatized oil and gas market. Russia would have established itself as a reliable supplier of raw materials, and doors would have opened for comprehensive technology transfer from the West. With Putin's rise to power, the current Kremlin administration considered the consolidation of state power and regaining great power status more important than democracy and a market economy. Russia transformed itself from a weak country, financially dependent on Western institutions, to a strong, inconvenient, and globally noticed actor that pursued its own national interests. Germany and other Western European countries became afraid of the Russian dominance and started to develop tools for diversification of their energy imports.

The EU now wants to expand the pan-European pipeline network connecting it to other large energy exporters to create a broader energy alliance than one based only on Russia. The Baku-Tbilissi-Ceyhan (BTC) pipeline, which runs across the South Caucasus and bypasses Russia, already deprives Moscow of its transit monopoly. Western companies also have a stake in convincing Central Asia to diversify their transport routes away from the Russian monopoly through the so-called Nabucco pipeline, which would reach from the seabed of the Caspian over the South Caucasus to the Black Sea and from there to the Balkans. Russia, meanwhile, is well aware of the situation and continues to buy up Central Asian gas, paying global market prices. At the moment, the Russian pipeline monopoly in the south of the CIS would only be endangered if the West decided in favor of a strategic cooperation with the nearby transit country, Iran—which will likely be prevented by the United States.[19]

However, the reality is that the world has entered a new era, in which previously unseen strategic importance is attributed to energy resources. The rules of the game will alter. Today's demand for oil is at its twenty-five-year peak. According to the IEA World Energy Outlook, global primary energy consumption will grow by 50 percent during the period until 2030. Until 2015, it will increase by 25 percent. Developing countries will contribute more than 70 percent to the increase in consumption; China alone will be responsible for 30 percent.[20] Presently, there are no alternative sources of energy having the realistic potential to substitute for fossil fuels. Even more alarming: Due to the increase of global energy demand—in spite of the financial crisis and the ensuing economic recession—the oil price will, most likely, stay at the present high level of $60–$70 per barrel. The question regarding the sources of the European Union's energy supply becomes increasingly urgent. It hardly requires profound analysis to understand that the EU's energy dependence on Russia will rise during the years to come. Considering the fact that within fifteen years' time, the EU will be importing 80 percent of its energy demands, it should not lose sight of cooperation with Russia.

Nevertheless, it is not uncommon to hear political arguments against too close a Western energy alliance with Russia. First, so goes the argument, Russia acts in a truly neoimperialistic fashion: it employs its energy resources as political leverage against its direct neighbors such as Ukraine but also against the West. Second, Russia has re-nationalized and re-monopolized its energy fields, thus hampering investments from the West. Russia is said to play by different rules than those of the market and, therefore, the West would be better advised to distance itself from too close a strategic energy partnership with Moscow. The third reason put forward against an energy alliance is economic: Not only does Russia suffer from the "Dutch disease," its economic growth, fuelled by high energy prices, has proven to be unsustainable in the financial crisis. If Russia fails to fundamentally modernize its energy complex, moreover, it will not be able to meet its export obligations as the oil and gas produced will be needed to satisfy domestic demand. In other words: Why trust Russia if it is running out of energy export capacities?[21]

Those in favor of an energy alliance with Russia, on the other hand, argue in a more pragmatic fashion, focusing on economic and security aspects. According to them, Russia is closest to the European markets. Moreover, for almost forty years, the West has been profiting from Russian reliability as an energy supplier. There are no reasons to suggest that this might change. What is more, in economic terms, it is easier to bind Russia to Europe than the countries of Northern Africa and the Middle East. Besides, the West's dependence on the latter countries would be endangered by the region's instability—state-building failure in Afghanistan and Iraq, the nuclear dispute in Iran, and the situation concerning Israel. In case of massive shortages of energy supplies from the Persian Gulf, Russian and Central Asian oil and gas reserves would constitute the only realistic alternative source.

In 1998 Russia's currency reserves amounted to only $8 billion. Today, Moscow disposes of approximately $400 billion. Russia held almost $600 billion in reserves before the financial crisis. Moscow also repaid all international debts ahead of schedule. Clearly, oil and gas were at the core of the country's revival: today, the energy sector is responsible for 25 percent of GDP. Oil and gas make up two-thirds of Russian exports. The EU's immediate neighbor holds the world's largest gas reserves; in coal and oil, its reserves rank second and eighth, respectively. Russia is the top producer of gas, and more recently, it appears as if it became the top producer of oil as well.

According to Russian geologists, the region of eastern Siberia contains huge energy reserves; however, only a tenth of this area has been explored geologically. Moreover, oil production in the Russian part of the Caspian Sea has only just started. Moscow regards itself as owner of giant strategic oil and gas resources that it plans to put on the global market after the world energy resources start petering out and prices increase dramatically. Only then will technically complex explorations in climatically difficult-to-access areas, for example the Arctic, render themselves economically viable. Russia's overall natural resources wealth is estimated at $40 quintillion, six times larger than the rest of the European continent.

Russia is home to 27 percent of the known global gas reserves, Turkmenistan and Uzbekistan each own 10 percent, and the southern neighbor Iran has 15 percent. It is for this reason that Russia tries to foster a strategic partnership with Iran. Together, Russia, Central Asia, and Iran control more than half of the global gas reserves so that building a powerful gas cartel, in the same vein as OPEC (whose members control more that 75 percent of global oil reserves), becomes a realistic option.

Russia's large gas fields do not lie in western but in eastern Siberia—closer to the Asian doorstep than to the European one. Now, Russia supplies 88 percent of its total gas exports and 58 percent of its oil exports to Europe. In fifteen years though, two-thirds of its gas exports and three-quarters of its oil exports will go not to the EU, but to Asia. Against this background, some experts question Russia's ability to continue to supply the EU, China, and the United States with Siberian energy. Therefore, it will be of strategic importance who will be the first to transfer the necessary technology and capital to Russia to modernize its energy sector. Within the next ten years, investments amounting to 85 billion euros will need to be made to create infrastructural capacity for the targeted doubling of Russia's energy exports to all three markets.

President Medvedev continues to pursue the strategic goal of integrating Russia more deeply with the global economy. With regard to the Russian energy supply, many irritations still need to be eliminated. The aftermath of the East-West conflict and the ensuing defeat of the Soviet empire rendered the West politically and economically strong as never before. During the 1990s, liberal rules leading to economic globalization were not questioned, and the young European Union devised a framework for its future relationship with Russia that, under the current geopolitical circumstances, is no longer sustainable. Russia, on the verge of economic collapse in the 1990s, hardly had any other option than navigating toward the European Union, the more so as its elites were oriented toward the West. The energy dialogue between Russia and the West gave preference to the consumer states, at the expense of the exporters. In this respect, today's ineffective Energy Charter is a good example. The West demanded guarantees for the security of energy supplies, the opening of the Russian energy market for investments, and, not least, joint control over the infrastructure for energy transportation.

With the onset of the twenty-first century, Russia, spurred on by newly gained strength, changed its strategy toward the West. It demanded not only the opening of Western markets to investment by Russian energy companies but also direct access to the European end users for Gazprom. After the financial crisis, Russian corporations are likely to continue expanding into Western markets. While consumers in the West are fretting about secure energy supplies, Russia focuses on the security of demand and the ensuing earnings. Due to its ties to the state, Gazprom makes sure that the Russian state—unlike during the 1990s—remains the principal earner in the Russian energy export business. Russia is rejecting ratification of the Energy Charter because it does not want to lose sovereignty over its transport monopoly. But the West is urging Russia at least to stick to the same rules for energy transfer as Moscow demands from Ukraine and Belarus.

Russia's dirigisme, apparent in the corporate strategy of all enterprises, can become a real problem for the European Union. Indeed, it may not be that European energy security depends exclusively on the Kremlin. On the other hand, the EU is rightly accused of preferential protectionism with regard to its own energy corporations. In line with the liberalization of the European energy market, the European Commission demands guarantees of supplies from the export states, most notably Russia, but without offering guarantees of demand in exchange. For now, the commission seems to have no solution as to how the differences between export and import countries could be settled.

The West and Russia must push the reset button in this important area as soon as possible. Even the usually Russia-critical Central European states understand that, facing the difficulty of the current global situation, there is no way around a strategic partnership with Russia in the realms of global energy supply and security. As long as the relationship between Russia and the EU remains asymmetrical to this extent, a well-functioning energy alliance will not be able to emerge.

Next Steps

In June 2008 Russian President Medvedev suggested a security dialogue on a new "cohabitation" between Russia and the West.[22] But so far, Russia's Western partners are not prepared to sacrifice NATO in favor of another, more explicit, pan-European organization.[23] On the other hand, Russia and the

West understand that they have just escaped the beginning of a new Cold War in the Georgian crisis and need proper mechanisms and new trust building to avoid further crises. There is no real reason to restart the Cold war; there is simply no ideological foundation for it.

Russia and the West are in the midst of new debates on how to improve the institutional framework for future partnership cooperation. By 2008–09 many of the institutions that formed the core of relations between Russia and the West had vanished. Russia quit the CFE Treaty and the Energy Charter, the EU and Russia failed to renegotiate the Partnership and Cooperation Agreement, the West was reluctant to revive the Organization for Security and Co-operation in Europe (OSCE) in its old status (fearing that the OSCE could supplement NATO), Georgia and Lithuania tried to deprive Russia of its mandate in the Council of Europe, and Russia was still not a member either of the WTO or the OECD. Hardly anyone remembers the Paris Charter of 1990, which was supposed to lay the groundwork for a new eternal peace between Russia and the West after the end of the Cold War. Despite all the conflicts of the past years, the chance for a true reconciliation between Russia and the West emerged. That policy might become as important as was détente in the 1970s.

So how could Russia better approach the EU and how could the EU more successfully approach Russia in order to create a twenty-first-century Europe stronger and wealthier with Russia than without? What could be done in the short and medium term help Russia and the West learn from the unsuccessful marriage of the last decade of the twentieth century and start to rediscover each other on a more pragmatic basis? It has become clear that the foundation for a new common European house could not to be laid on romantic dreams, as in the 1990s; but how should the economic and political systems adjust to each other? The West and Russia understood that apart from pressing the reset button in their relations, both sides had to agree on a new platform on which further cooperation could develop. That platform was supposed to constitute the new "cohabitation" between Russia and the rest of Europe and the United States. Proposals turned from the idea of a new revitalized Paris Charter to a new OSCE Security Council, which would incorporate Russia into the European architecture.[24]

Russia and the West need to agree on a common-threat-perception approach in the new international system and find out how divisive issues could develop into common strategies, that is, in the areas of nonproliferation, maritime security, and the fight against international terrorism and organized crime. The institutional structure of security relations in the Euro-Atlantic space should be reviewed in order to identify where Russia could fit into the network of cooperative institutions. The easiest way for Russia to approach the EU and the United States would be to strengthen its internal economic market institutions, make decision making on federal and regional levels more transparent, enhance efforts to combat corruption, and apply WTO rules more quickly in order to accomplish the long-awaited integration into the world economy.[25] Russia could become more attractive for Western business, if it creates its own middle-range business class. Relations in the economic field must be transformed in a manner that increases stability in mutual expectations. This particularly refers to energy security.

The year 2010 seemed to signal a breakthrough in Russian-Western rapprochement. Russian elites finally understood that successful modernization of their economy demanded deeper integration with Western economies — and that only the EU could play a pivotal role in Russia's further modernization and transformation into a country of technological innovation and global energy structure. The financial crisis facilitated the rapprochement. The extension of the START, the beginning of a new thaw in Russian-Polish relations after the tragedy in Smolensk, and the onset of a new historical "partnership of modernization" between the EU and Russia marked an important shift by Russia toward a more multilateral approach to resolving international problems as part of a new rules-based architecture. The Russian government clearly began to invest in a more cooperative relationship with the West. The United States and the EU offered Russia a roadmap on how to move toward achieving these goals and return to more cooperative modes of behavior. In practice, the EU agreed to facilitate the visa regime between the EU and Russia and move in the direction of more cooperation in the high-tech sector. In the end, EU-Russia cooperation started to develop on converging interests. Russia began to see modernization not only in terms of buying technologies from the West but as a "political" means to restructure its society from within. In that respect, Medvedev's plea for modernization resembled Gorbachev's perestroika.

After the rise to power of Yanukovich in Ukraine, energy relations stopped being politicized. Russia and Ukraine even moved in the direction of merging their energy complexes. That opened the way for Russia and the EU to create a pact for securing long-term deliveries from Russia to the West and guaranteeing Russia access to Western technologies for overdue modernization of the Russian energy complex. This complex should in future include the formation of commercial pipeline consortia involving a mixture of governmental and private ownership in order to provide predictability for investors in the context of future energy supply. Russia should accept that supply routes would also pass over non-Russian territory. Finally, Russia and the West could jointly develop a plan for the modernization of Siberia as a practical tool for achieving the goals of the energy alliance. Western criticism that Russia is a difficult partner because it has no market philosophy ignores the fact that Russia still is more democratic and market-oriented than most of the other energy producing states—Algeria, Turkmenistan, Iraq, Venezuela—on which the EU and the United States will have to rely heavily in the future. Russia and the EU could mastermind a joint energy saving program that would help to meet the UN Framework Convention on Climate Change and the Kyoto Protocol.

In terms of closer economic integration, Russia and the West are now going to further dismantle visa barriers, allowing Russia to create human capital with access to worldwide technologies. A free-trade zone between Russia and the EU, similar to the arrangements between Norway and the EU, could be created within the next five years. Joint policy options within the framework of the Kyoto process and in the broader field of climate control would bring the parties closer together. What the EU probably has to do to facilitate positive changes in relations with Russia is to create a mechanism for economic cooperation that will not be dependent upon achieving consensus among all twenty-seven member-states of the present EU. The EU should delegate responsibility for negotiating with Russia to a core group of states in which the old and the new EU countries would be adequately represented. Poland, which turned from a radical critic of Russia to a supporter of the extension of the EU-Russia Partnership and Cooperation Agreement, should join that core group.

Russia will probably never be integrated into the West politically, due to its diverse national interests and different traditions, but the Euro-Atlantic space would largely benefit from its economic integration, especially in the aftermath of the world economic crisis. The Asian economies are going to overtake those of the EU countries very soon. It is in the EU's own interest to forge a strategic alliance with Moscow and confront future challenges together.

When the economic alliance succeeds, and the EU and Russia demonstrate that they are compatible in coping with the global economic crisis, the idea of Russia's integration with the United States and the EU into a future supranational Euro-Atlantic security architecture will eventually be dropped. After the political changes in Ukraine and Russia's new cooperation activities with the West, NATO expansion into the post-Soviet space disappeared from the international agenda. The West can now get engaged in a broader dialogue with Russia on the security of the European continent by looking at ways to make the OSCE, chaired in 2010 by the former Soviet republic of Kazakhstan, more effective and allow it to participate more strongly in international conflict prevention. The OSCE established itself as a regional arrangement under the UN Charter in 1994; it could therefore continue along this path by assuming additional competencies under the mandate of the UN Security Council.

When, after economic cooperation, the political partnership also proves functional, the West could think of opening NATO for Russia's membership. Such a vision seems totally unrealistic for now, but, as everybody knows, the present world and its institutions undergo continuous changes. The response to this action can be seen not only in the West but noticeably in Russia. A good test for the creation of common NATO-Russia politics and trust building is the current cooperation on combating international terrorism in Afghanistan. Russia cannot be interested in U.S. and NATO failure in Afghanistan because that would leave Russia with a renewed international terror regime at its southern borders. It is hard to understand why NATO has so far been reluctant to bind Russia in a more operational manner in the conflict resolution to that regional crisis. It is seemingly difficult to understand why Russia has so vigorously opposed the creation of U.S. military bases in some states of Central Asia. A strong U.S. posting in countries neighboring Afghanistan would diminish the chance for Russia to be forced to send its own troops to fight insurgence from Afghan terrorist groups. The West must alter the Russian security thinking of "encirclement" by U.S. and NATO forces from the West (through NATO enlargement) and the South (bases in Central Asia; military presence in the Middle East), which Moscow perceives as a greater threat than insurgence from the Taliban.

In moving toward practical cooperation in global security issues, the United States and its Western allies must more strongly institutionalize with Russia the struggle against drug production and export from Afghanistan.

That might not work with purely military methods and will take many years, but a first step could be to set up a U.S–Russian anti-drug agency in support of the Kabul government to combat drug trafficking. A second practical step could be closer military consultation mechanisms between NATO and the Collective Security Pact Organization (CSPO) of CIS states. NATO should also conduct negotiations about a more cooperative, constructive involvement of the Shanghai Organization for Cooperation into a peaceful solution for Afghanistan. In this organization, Russia does not hold a dominant position as in the CSPO. This will help to exclude geopolitical rivalries in regard to solving the Afghan problem and open a chapter of joint peace settlement in the entire greater Middle East.

Russia has to understand that it must use the historical chance of renewed cooperation with the United States and the West in general in the greater Middle East, because through this cooperation it could become an indispensable "strategic" and equal ally of the United States and the EU in shaping the future world order. The next years should be spent repairing the relationship and keeping open the chance to rebuild a common European house. The West must stop its habit of trying to teach Russians about democracy. The world economic crisis has demonstrated that the Western liberal economic model must be corrected toward greater control of the state. Russia drew this conclusion at the end of the 1990s. Now the West follows suit. The West needs a partnership of patience with Russia. Moscow, in turn, should be more consistent in collaborating on a modernization partnership with the EU and the United States, because turning to Asia would destroy Russia's roots in European civilization.

Notes

1. See Vera Tolz and Iain Elliot, eds., *The Demise of the USSR* (London: Macmillan, 1995), 269.
2. Andrei Kozyrev made this point in a meeting at the German Council on Foreign Relations, Bonn, in February 1996. He recalled the letter that the leader of the Iranian Revolution, Ayatollah Khomeini, wrote to Gorbachev in 1989, urging the USSR to convert to Islam. See Alexander Rahr, *Russland gibt Gas* (Munich: Hanser, 2008), 25.

3. See Dmitri Trenin, "Russia Redefines Itself and Its Relations with the West," *Washington Quarterly* (Spring 2007): 95; and Heinrich Vogel, "The Putin System," *Internationale Politik* (transatlantic ed.) 3, no. 1 (2002): 3.
4. Vladimir Putin spoke in the German Bundestag on September 25, 2001.
5. See Andrew Wilson, *Ukraine's Orange Revolution* (New Haven: Yale University Press, 2006).
6. See also the analysis and suggestions in the report on Russia and the EU by Mark Leonhard and Nicu Popescu, *A Power Audit of EU-Russia Relations* (London: ECFR, 2007).
7. Tony Barber, "Barroso Races to Prevent Escalation of Ukraine Gas Dispute," *Financial Times*, June 20, 2009.
8. See A. Motyl, B. Ruble, and L. Shevtsova, "Russia's Reintegration into the West: The Challenges Before Russia," in *Russia's Engagement with the West* (New York: Sharpe, 2005), 3ff.
9. Sergei Lavrov, quoted by the Associated Press, February 16, 2007.
10. See, for more analysis, Alexander Rahr, *Putin nach Putin* [Putin after Putin] (München: Universitas Verlag, 2008).
11. Marie-Lena May and Stefan Meister, "The EU's Eastern Partnership—A Misunderstood Offer of Cooperation" [in German], *DGAPstandpunkt*, no. 7 (September 2009).
12. German-Foreign-Policy.com, "The Berlin-Moscow Economic Axis (II)," October 7, 2009, www.german-foreign-policy.com.
13. Alexander Rahr, "Allemagne—Russie: Un partenariat privilégié," *Le courrier des pays de l'Est*, no. 1049 (May/June 2005): 15.
14. Peter Danylow and Ulrich Soénius, *Otto Wolff—Ein Unternehmen zwischen Wirtschaft und Politik* [Otto Wolff—A Company between Economics and Politics] (Munich: Siedler, 2005).
15. See Andrew Felkay, *Yeltsin's Russia and the West* (Santa Barbara, CA: Praeger, 2002).
16. M. K. Bhadrakumar, "Germany, Russia Redraw Europe's Frontiers," *Asia Times*, May 3, 2006.
17. Klaus Mangold, "Russia and German Investors," *Internationale Politik* (transatlantic ed.), no. 3 (2000): 14.
18. John Reed, "Russia's Bold Opel Gambit," *Financial Times*, October 14, 2009.
19. "Europe's Energy Insecurity," *Economist*, July 16, 2009.
20. International Energy Agency, "Executive Summary," *World Energy Outlook 2006* (Paris: IEA, 2006), 1ff., http://www.worldenergyoutlook.org/summaries 2006/German.pdf. All references made are based on the 2006 data.

21. See Fiona Hill, *Energy Empire: Oil, Gas and Russia's Revival* (London: Foreign Policy Centre, 2004).
22. Dmitri Medvedev spoke at a meeting of the Eastern Committee of the German Economic Association in Berlin on June 5, 2008.
23. See *Moscow News*, "When Will the West Answer Medvedev?" June 10, 2008.
24. The idea of a Euro-Atlantic Security Council has been proposed in a recent report of the Aspen European Strategy Forum, *Russia and the West: How to Restart a Constructive Relationship* (Berlin: Aspen Institute Germany, 2009).
25. President Medvedev promised to enhance this policy in his widely discussed article "Rossiya, vperyod!" [Go, Russia!], *Gazeta.ru*, September 10, 2009, www.gazeta.ru/comments/2009/09/10_a_3258568.shtml.

CHAPTER TWELVE

The Obama Administration's "Reset Button" for Russia

Andrew C. Kuchins

Developing and implementing policy toward Russia has proven to be one of the greatest and most controversial challenges for four administrations in Washington since the end of the Cold War nearly twenty years ago. Presidents Bill Clinton and George W. Bush, whose administrations together were responsible for Russia policy for the majority of the period from 1993 to 2009, each devoted a great deal of time and energy to improving ties with Moscow, yet each left office frustrated and disappointed, and with a bilateral relationship in worse condition than at the beginning of their administrations. Given the deep acrimony and near absence of trust between Washington and Moscow when Barack Obama entered office, we can only hope that analysts will not be drawing similar conclusions at the end of his tenure.

With the monumental tasks that Russia was undertaking to simultaneously democratize, develop a market economy, and change from being an empire to a nation-state—the virtually unprecedented "triple transformation" of a great power—it should not be so surprising that the object of Washington policy makers would present a massive challenge requiring a lot of "strategic patience," as Deputy Secretary of State Strobe Talbott put it near the end of the Clinton administration. Russia's precipitous decline in status virtually overnight from superpower to recipient of international humanitarian assistance in 1991–92, and the radical restructuring of the international system from one of bipolar confrontation to unipolar U.S. dominance, presented massive challenges of imagination demanding inordinate wisdom and empathy—all qualities that Washington policy making—and to be fair, Washington is hardly alone—is not renowned for.

This chapter will address the key themes and issues driving Washington's perspective on and policy toward Russia to set the historical background for an examination of the Obama administration's efforts to improve ties with Russia during the past year and the prospects for the relationship. The approach will be explicitly U.S.-centric and will analyze Russian actions principally in the context of how they are perceived and how they influence U.S. policy toward Russia.

Ideas and Reality of Power in U.S. Russia Policy during the 1990s

Analyzing U.S. foreign policy through the international relations theory prism of *idealism* or *liberalism* vs. *realism* helps to illuminate key schools of thought about the assumptions and core goals driving U.S. policy makers.[1] In the best study of U.S. policy toward Russia from the late 1980s to early 2003, James Goldgeier and Michael McFaul describe these two approaches as those of "regime transformers" or "power balancers."[2] Regime transformers tend to more liberal idealist views holding that the nature of a state's domestic order is the most important determinant of its foreign policy orientation. Their worldview derives from Kantian notions of *democratic peace* and Wilsonian liberalism in the U.S. context. This school would emphasize the importance of Russia's domestic transformation to a market democracy as a more powerful determinant of Russian behavior than the structure of the international system or other external factors. For the Clinton administration that sought a "strategic alliance with Russian reform," this was the dominant paradigm.

The preceding Bush I administration, by contrast, was dominated more by power balancers who were skeptical about the capacity of the United States to influence Russian domestic affairs and who identified maintaining the United States' new status as the dominant global power as the most essential goal. The Pentagon paper developed in 1992 under the leadership of then secretary of defense Dick Cheney epitomized this approach.[3] The Bush I team was reluctant to embrace Boris Yeltsin because they feared the potential chaos of a Soviet collapse and also because Soviet leader Mikhail

Gorbachev was supporting Washington's highest priority goals, including defeating Saddam Hussein in Desert Storm and reunifying Germany.

Of course, as Goldgeier and McFaul qualify, all U.S. administrations have included those tending toward both schools, and, in fact, anybody serving in the U.S. government since the Soviet collapse has been guided by the twin goals of promoting Russia's domestic transformation and extending U.S. power and influence. The essence of Goldgeier and McFaul's argument is that people, their ideas about how the world works, and the goals they support matter a great deal in how U.S. foreign policy is developed. As they correctly point out, often realists will describe their policies as based on *interests* rather than *ideas*, but actually all definitions of the national interest are based on a set of assumptions about how the world works that are essentially cognitive frameworks or ideas.

Caveats aside, the best opportunity for the United States to contribute to Russia's domestic transformation was a short window lasting from the fall of 1991 after the failed coup through 1992 until the reformist prime minister Yegor Gaidar was forced to resign in December. If there were a moment for U.S. and Western intervention into Russian domestic economic and political affairs, be it through a massive aid package or strong advice that President Yeltsin immediately call for new parliamentary elections when his popularity was highest, that was it. But as Goldgeier and McFaul assiduously lay out, this was not the inclination of President Bush and his team. Part of it had to do with the realist mind-set of the president and key advisors like National Security Advisor Brent Scowcroft to beware of the risks of intervening in the affairs of others (also borne out by their reluctance to intervene in collapsing Yugoslavia then).[4] The domestic political environment also was a significant constraining factor. The United States was in a deep recession in 1991–92, and there was little enthusiasm in the U.S. public for expensive international projects during a presidential election year.

The irony for the Clinton administration's orientation to engage deeply in supporting Russian reform as a core strategic goal was that the moment had already passed when they took office. Washington did not have anywhere near the leverage over Russian policy that many of its critics in Moscow and the United States asserted. Reading the history of this period, the dominant impression of the Clinton administration was frustration over the lack of leverage and influence on so many Yelstin policies from wars in Chechnya to "loans for shares" to the 1998 default. While the re-election of Boris Yeltsin in 1996 was Washington's desired outcome, it is impossible to prove that U.S. policy was a major contributing factor.

What did become clear to the Clinton administration during its tenure was the gaping asymmetry in power between Washington and Moscow. As Goldgeier and McFaul conclude:

> In foreign affairs, the main story of the 1990s was the breathtaking speed with which Russia declined as a major power. Once this was finally understood, Russia policy became a secondary concern for many U.S. officials. But this tremendous drop of Russia's international power was not fully appreciated by American officials in real time. Perceptions of Russian power changed more slowly than the velocity of decline.[5]

Once their "man in Moscow" was re-elected in 1996, the Clinton administration acted with a freer hand in pursuing policies very unpopular in Russia, such as NATO enlargement, because there was nothing Russia could do to stop it. The Clinton administration would never have gone to war over Kosovo if they believed the Russian Federation had the capacity to vigorously contest the policy beyond rhetorical fulminations. It is interesting to note that while there were several rounds of "Who Lost Russia?" debates during the 1990s, there were few warnings then of a "new Cold War" because Russia was so widely perceived to be incapable of seriously contesting U.S. hegemony. Cries of the new Cold War began to be popular in some circles only in 2007–08 after the unexpected Russian economic recovery, but that is getting ahead of the story.

Although the Bush I administration was initially wary of Boris Yeltsin, eventually both they and their successors in the Clinton administration found Yeltsin's Russia cooperative or at least refraining from obstructing most key U.S. objectives. The analytical problem is explaining conclusively why. For regime transformers it was because Yeltsin himself was more supportive of the liberal transformation/Western integration objectives. For power balancers, the main reason is Russian weakness. The truth is a combination of these factors. An analogous analytical problem for the Russians might have been determining whether the Clinton administration's decision to pursue NATO enlargement was driven by the liberal justifications of "expanding the zone of peace" in Europe or for power-balanced hedging against a potentially revanchist Russia. This was not really an analytical question for Moscow, however, because of their deep skepticism of liberal or idealist motivations in foreign policy.

As the 1990s came to a close, the Clinton policy toward Russia was deeply divisive in Washington, and the U.S.-Russian relationship was at its first post–Cold War nadir. The 1998 financial collapse was both a massive blow for the beleaguered Yeltsin administration as well as crippling for regime transformers in Washington. The Clinton policy founded on building an "alliance with Russian reform" was in tatters. Scandals over the Bank of New York, the Harvard International Institute of Development, and others put Russian corruption and its perceived Western enablers in the spotlight and emerged as a U.S. presidential campaign issue in 2000. The Republican Party sought to tarnish Al Gore's presidential candidacy for his deep involvement with Clinton's Russia policy through the Gore-Chernomyrdin Commission by painting Washington's failure to address endemic corruption in Yeltsin's Russia more as a crime of commission than omission.[6]

The asymmetry in power between the United States and Russia was never greater than in 1999–2000. The financial crisis and devaluation of the ruble left Russia with a GDP in dollar terms of about $200 billion, or about 2 percent that of the United States. Moreover, the drastic contraction of the Russian economy starkly contrasted with the U.S. economic boom in the 1990s fueled at the end of the decade by the "dot. com bubble" that engendered a heady, but ultimately transitory, optimism about the durability of U.S. global dominance. In sum, for power balancers, there was little Russian power to be concerned about, and for regime transformers, a deep pessimism permeated Washington about prospects for Russia's domestic transformation. This and the deep schism between NATO and Russia over the war in Kosovo suggested the Western integration project would likely be the business for another generation of policy makers.

The Bush II Administration

STRUGGLING WITH PUTIN'S THERMIDOR AND RUSSIA'S RESURGENCE

The George W. Bush administration entered office in January 2001 amid expectations that realist "power balancers" would dominate as they did during the George H. W. Bush administration. The new president's closest advisor on foreign policy during the campaign and newly appointed head of the NSC, Stanford professor Condoleezza Rice, had publicly emphasized that the incoming administration would focus more attention on cultivating ties with great powers like Russia and China.[7] This perceived orientation was warmly received by the Russian political elite, which tends to prefer moderate "realist" Republican administrations (i.e., Nixon and Bush I), which they find easier to do business with and less likely to be critical of Russian human rights and domestic political deficiencies. The new Russian president Vladimir Putin pointedly snubbed the Clinton administration's final efforts to cut a bargain over a new arms reductions treaty together with modest revisions of the ABM Treaty in 2000.

Despite a rocky start in the winter/spring of 2000 over spy scandals and some very tough rhetoric on Russia coming from the administration, most notably Secretary of Defense Rumsfeld and Vice President Cheney, Russian hopes for a new approach seemed justified at the first meeting between presidents Bush and Putin in Slovenia that fostered a surprisingly warm personal relationship between these seemingly unlikely partners. President Bush's efforts to cultivate ties with his new "friend Vlad" appeared rewarded when two weeks after 9/11 Putin decided to strongly support the U.S.-led coalition to defeat the Taliban in Afghanistan, including supporting new U.S. bases in Central Asia.[8] Once again, similar to 1991–92, a lot of "happy talk" about the prospects for a new strategic alliance between Russia and the United States came to the fore briefly as Moscow did play a critically important role in assisting the defeat of the Taliban in the fall of 2001.

But such hopes were based on a fundamental miscalculation that resulted in much disappointment in Moscow. For the Russians, the first inklings of the miscalculation came when the Bush administration announced its decision to unilaterally withdraw from the ABM Treaty in December 2001 and also proceeded to support the second round of NATO enlargement including the Baltic states. As with the first round of NATO enlargement and more so with the Kosovo War, Moscow saw Washington taking actions diametrically opposed to their interests despite Russian cooperation on Afghanistan. Moscow's miscalculation may have been founded on the faulty assumption that "realists" are always "power balancers." But the fundamental tenet of realist theory in international relations is the derivation of policy on the basis of judgments about the military balance of power.[9] Bush administration policies, criticized by the Russians and most of the rest of the world as "unilateralist," can most simply be explained as derivations of realist calculations of the balance of power that the United States during the Bush I administration enjoyed a more dominant position in the international system than any great power in modern history. The success of U.S. military intervention in Kosovo and initially in Afghanistan and later Iraq only embellished the view of the dominant inclination of key officials in the Bush administration in the efficacy of U.S. military power and the willingness of Washington to act unilaterally and/or in tandem with "coalitions of the willing" in the absence of broader international approval.

But it would not be long before the Bush administration's confidence was shaken as initial success in Iraq deteriorated while Russia's economic recovery, which began in 1999, really took off in 2003 as the world oil price surged. For Washington, Putin's Russia was doubly frustrating because of simultaneous trends toward growing authoritarianism at home combined with a resurgent foreign policy designed to intimidate and control its near neighbors, especially the former republics of the Soviet Union.[10]

While the Bush administration did not react strongly, the Yukos case in 2003 was a watershed in Vladimir Putin's presidency from the perspective of official and unofficial Washington. Infused with petrodollars, the Russian economy was taking off, and Putin viewed the devolution of power from the state to a group of increasingly powerful oligarchs in the 1990s as threatening, especially that of the most successful of them, Mikhail Khodorkovsky, the CEO of Yukos, Russia's biggest company then. With the arrest and prosecution of Khodorkovsky, the Kremlin destroyed its potentially most powerful adversary and instilled fear in the Russian business community as to who might be next. This measure was accompanied by many others during Putin's tenure as president, amounting to a consistent weakening of Russia's fragile democratic institutions and its replacement with the so-called vertical of power.[11]

Liberal regime transformers had been wary of Putin from the outset because of his KGB background, and these concerns were aggravated by his policies restricting independent media and the brutal conduct of the second Chechen war. As their disappointment grew, many analysts and officials who had supported engagement with Russia in the 1990s increasingly took far more critical positions of attempts to cooperate with Moscow as empowering anti-democratic and anti-Western political groups in Russia.

Most strikingly, the divergence of mainline narratives in Moscow and Washington about the roles of the United States and Russia in the world quickly became a gaping chasm of perception that further eroded trust. On foreign policy, while the Bush administration was disappointed that Putin did not support the war in Iraq, the initial really deep rupture occurred over the Orange Revolution in Ukraine at the end of 2004. The first gas crisis between Russia and Ukraine in January 2006 marked the next big blow that prefaced the disagreements over Kosovo, NATO enlargement, and missile defense that clouded 2007–08.

Over the years of the Putin presidency, Moscow's narrative of its own domestic experience since the collapse of the former Soviet Union and the emergence of a "unipolar world" dominated by the United States was increasingly at odds with Washington's perspective on these events.[12] For Moscow the 1990s were spun as a modern-day Time of Troubles when state authority collapsed and foreigners exercised too much influence over Russian affairs to the detriment of the Russian state and people. Putin's goal was to restore the authority of the state and ultimately Russia's rightful place as a great power in the world.

The linkage between domestic and foreign policy goals was most starkly illustrated in Putin's remarks to the Russian nation after the Beslan tragedy in September 2004 when he referred to foreign interests that sought to weaken Russia and proposed the remedy of further centralization of state power to protect Russia from such threats.[13] The Kremlin, initially through the ideologue of sovereign democracy, Vladislav Surkov, later linked those foreign interests with an alleged "fifth column" of domestic collaborators.[14] The linkage of foreign threats with domestic collaborators marked a return to the traditional Russian justification for central authority that finds its roots deep in Russian history and reached its apogee in Stalin's terror. For Russia's Western-leaning liberals and their supporters in the West, the return of this new/old ideology resonated deeply and was confirmed through a number of high-profile contract killings, including most notably the brave and independent chronicler of the Chechen wars, Anna Politkovskaya, in October 2006.

Political elites in Moscow were also deeply disappointed with the perception that the Bush administration failed to take Russian interests into account after Putin's decision in late September 2001 to fully support U.S.-led international coalition efforts to defeat the Taliban in Afghanistan. The U.S.-Russia cooperation on Afghanistan in 2001 sparked once again discussions about a much broader and deeper security relationship between Moscow and Washington to an extent not heard since the collapse of the Soviet Union a decade before. Ironically, perhaps the international coalition succeeded too quickly in unseating the Taliban to allow for a more institutionalized security relationship to develop. Bush administration decisions later in the fall of 2001 to go through with the second round of NATO enlargement, including the Baltic states, as well as to withdraw from the ABM Treaty, symbolized for the Kremlin that despite Russian cooperation on key security challenges, the United States would continue on a policy path in other areas Moscow long held to be against Russia's interests.

While the U.S.-Russian relationship remained cordial, and President Bush had a successful trip to Russia in May 2002 during which the Treaty on Strategic Offensive Reductions (SORT) was signed, a bitter seed of unreciprocated concessions to the interests of Washington had been planted in the minds of Putin and his colleagues. As the bilateral relationship began to deteriorate after the Iraq War, this bitterness on Moscow's part congealed into a lengthy list of grievances against the Bush administration, which was repeatedly articulated by Kremlin officials and insiders to their American counterparts for the next several years. The expression of deep frustration with America's "arrogant unilateralism" became the dominant pathos from Moscow, especially during the second term of the Bush administration. At this time, especially with the renewed accent on democracy promotion as the fulcrum of its foreign policy, Russian frustration with Washington morphed into a deeper suspicion that the Bush administration was seeking actively to weaken Russia's position in the world.

Regime transformers in Washington experienced a euphoric burst of enthusiasm with the series of "color" revolutions in Eurasia in 2003–05 and the apparent weaknesses of the Putin government in the face of the tragic series of terrorist attacks culminating in the grisly horror of Beslan in September 2004, and then tens of thousands of Russians demonstrating in big cities across the country in opposition to proposed welfare reform. This period marked the high point of Bush administration confidence as U.S. military power appeared triumphant in Afghanistan and Iraq and a new wave of democratization was apparently sweeping across the globe. There was a growing sense in Washington that the weakness of Putin's authoritarian rollback had been exposed, and certainly his government was on the wrong side of history, soon to be consigned to the dustbin. Those, including this author, advocating "realist" constructive engagement with Moscow were in a rapidly shrinking minority.[15]

The moment of optimism regarding regime transformation in Russia and the region proved effervescent as the momentum of color revolutions was derailed in Uzbekistan in May of 2005 with President Islam Karimov's brutal suppression of the uprising in Andijan that was quickly supported by Moscow and Beijing. By the spring of 2006, optimism about Putin's imminent demise was replaced by growing concern about Russia's oil-fueled economic resurgence.[16] Putin's speech in February 2007 at the Werkunde Munich security conference conveyed the notion that the United States, in its quest for unipolar global domination, had overextended itself geopolitically, and the global balance of power was shifting in favor of Russia and other large emerging market economies at the expense of the West.

Probably the most fundamental difference in the narratives of post–Cold War history boils down to this sense of the shift in balance of power, of the international system becoming truly multipolar, and U.S. relative power being on the decline while Russia's was rising. To mix metaphors, the U.S. ship of state was slowly sinking while the Russian phoenix was rising from the ashes. For Moscow this disjuncture in perceptions probably was widest shortly after Dmitri Medvedev was inaugurated as president (May 2008) when the oil price hit its peak in July, and the financial crisis remained mostly confined to the United States. While Washington acknowledged that Russia was resurgent, conventional wisdom held that its longer-term prospects still looked relatively bleak as economic growth remained too dependent on natural commodity prices, demographic and health trends were extremely adverse, and the country's infrastructure was still decaying.[17] Although the Georgia war in August 2008 finds its roots in a long and contentious history, Moscow's tendency to overestimate its strength and Washington's post-Soviet default position to view Russia as a weak but irritating troublemaker contributed to the failure to prevent the war.

In the last year of the Bush administration, U.S.-Russia relations reached their lowest point since the 1980s. Communication between Washington and Moscow had virtually ceased after the war in Georgia, and 2008 amounted to a "perfect storm" as U.S.-Russia relations were fraught with major cleavages over Kosovo's independence, NATO enlargement, and plans for deployment of missile defense "third site" components in the Czech Republic and Poland. But the breakdown in relations in the second half of 2008 was years in the making. The brief honeymoon in the fall of 2001 after 9/11 rapidly eroded with a series of conflictual issues that highlighted both different interests as well as the absence of trust despite the allegedly close personal relationship between presidents Bush and Putin. Perhaps fortunately for the beleaguered U.S.-Russia relationship after the Georgia war, U.S. and world attention was quickly overwhelmed in September 2008 by the global economic crisis, the repercussions of which resulted in the election of Barack Obama as president of the United States.

The Obama Administration's "Reset Button" for Russia

BACK TO PRAGMATIC ENGAGEMENT AND MULTILATERALISM

Barack Obama assumed the presidency in January 2009 facing the greatest challenges of any U.S. president since Franklin Delano Roosevelt during the Great Depression in the 1930s. The global economic system was still in free fall from a financial crisis catalyzed in the United States, a dramatic difference from the last global crisis that began in Asia in 1997 and resulted in the Russian default of 1998. The United States was also mired in two very difficult wars in Afghanistan and Iraq, with security in the former deteriorating rapidly. Putin's view that the unipolar moment was over found many supporters around the world, including in the United States. Barack Obama had promised a return to multilateralism in U.S. foreign policy and assumed the demeanor of a pragmatic and deliberate problem-solver facing some daunting challenges; a striking turn away from the neoconservative instincts of his predecessor.

Whatever one thought about the origins of the Georgia war, a growing consensus in the moderate or pragmatic middle of the U.S. political spectrum on both sides of the aisle viewed this if not as evidence of failure in U.S. policy toward Russia and Eurasia, then at least minimally as something that had gone badly awry and needed to be corrected. Regime transformation looked far from imminent in Russia, and the growing centrist consensus in Washington argued for a more constructive relationship with Russia in order to deal more effectively with growing regional and global challenges.

The interests of the Obama administration in improving ties with Russia, a policy metaphorically first described by Vice President Joe Biden in February 2009 as "pressing the reset button," are principally driven by three goals: (1) heightened urgency of resolving the Iranian nuclear question;

(2) the need for additional transport routes into Afghanistan to support larger U.S. military presence; and (3) a return to a more multilateral approach to ensuring nuclear security and strengthening the nonproliferation regime. Broader global policy goals of the administration including addressing the climate change challenge, energy security, health, and other issues also require heightened cooperation from Russia, but urgency is not as intense as with the first three issues.

Critics on the Left and the Right in Washington argued that Russia was either too weak and/or fundamentally antagonistic to advancing U.S. interests for Obama's anticipated efforts to woo the Russians. The deeper concern has been that the Obama administration might be willing to compromise core values and interests to secure Russian support on the issues mentioned. Russia's near neighbors are particularly sensitive to Washington possibly compromising their interests.[18]

The Washington policy community in the winter and spring of 2009 issued a plethora of reports and analyses calling for improved relations with Russia.[19] Critics of one of the most noteworthy of the reports, the Hart-Hagel report, categorized many of the recommendations for improved ties with Russia as "realist" compromises of American values of liberty and democracy.[20] This kind of critique, however, misses the crux of the reason why East Central European neighbors are especially nervous. The problem, as captured in the recent German Marshall Fund brief, is that Russia is mostly a status quo power globally, but in its neighborhood it is a revisionist power. Russia wants something that no American administration could give it without committing political suicide: an acknowledgement of "privileged relations" or a "sphere of influence" in its neighborhood. If that circle cannot be squared, the future of the "reset button" is likely to be short-lived.

RATIONALE FOR THE "RESET BUTTON"

Despite the overall breakdown of U.S.-Russia relations in the wake of the August 2008 war in Georgia and the last months of the Bush administration, Vladimir Putin and George W. Bush left behind a useful tool from their last bilateral meeting in April 2008 in the Sochi Declaration, which effectively provides the framework for the Obama administration's efforts to "press the reset button" in U.S.-Russia relations.[21]

Nuclear Security and Nonproliferation

THE RETURN OF ARMS CONTROL

Nuclear security and nonproliferation are areas that the Obama and Medvedev administrations should find most amenable to resetting. The Russians would argue that they have been more responsible in this regard over the past eight years than the Bush administration was. Even though Russia became more reliant on its nuclear deterrent due to the deterioration of its conventional forces in the 1990s, the continued aging of its nuclear arsenal leads Moscow to be interested in deeper cuts in strategic weapons.

Although the Russian economy has (until the global financial crisis) rebounded impressively in the past decade, from a strategic military standpoint, Russia remains in decline. Even with its difficulties in Iraq and Afghanistan, to Russia, the United States still looks as though it's on the march—developing missile defenses, outspending Moscow on its military by a ratio of about 10:1, enlarging NATO, and so on. Russian policy makers still perceive stabilizing the strategic competition with Washington and its allies as being in Moscow's interests.

In his speech in Prague in April 2009, President Obama announced that his administration would be committed to making significant progress on the path to "getting to zero" nuclear weapons in the world. This goal has recently garnered international attention since articulated by the "Four Horsemen"—Henry Kissinger, Sam Nunn, William Perry, and George Shultz—in January 2008.[22] President Medvedev endorsed this goal in his speech in Helsinki in the spring of 2009, and he and Obama agreed in London in April that their negotiating teams would quickly convene discussions for a replacement to the START 1 Treaty, which would expire in December 2009, and report their progress when the two presidents were next scheduled to meet in Moscow in early July.

While the two sides were not able conclude the negotiations on the New Start Treaty by the December 2009 deadline, a quite ambitious goal from the outset, Medvedev and Obama did sign the treaty on April 8, 2010, just before the "nuclear summit" in Washington, DC, the following week. Successfully concluding these negotiations marked the most significant achievement since the "reset" was launched in the winter of 2009.

It is also the case that the Obama administration's approach to nuclear arms reductions is more in line with Russian interests than that of the Bush administration. Russian negotiators have pushed for a new, legally binding treaty that would replace START and supersede SORT (the 2002 Moscow Treaty). Moscow wants the new accord to be more detailed than SORT, whose limits they view as inadequate to ensure predictability and parity in the Russian-American strategic balance. Russian representatives have sought to require the United States to eliminate the warheads that are removed from its active stockpile, rather than placing them in storage, as they are concerned that the earlier agreements leave the United States with the ability simply to upload these warheads back onto U.S. strategic systems.

Given the pressing time constraints to negotiate, the START replacement treaty will call for a fairly modest reduction in offensive arms and launchers while maintaining many of the monitoring and verification measures of the original START.[23] Then hopefully the two sides would agree to immediately engage in the next round of negotiations to take the cuts down to at least 1,000 per side. The Russians have indicated that to get to this next level of deeper cuts, there will have to be some agreement about the limitations of ballistic missile defenses as Moscow is concerned that the combination of deep cuts, U.S. developments in missile defenses, as well as powerful conventional weapons with near-nuclear capabilities may upset the strategic balance. Both Moscow and Washington also agree that in order to make greater progress in strategic reductions once they are below a certain level (probably in the 500–1,000 range), the bilateral negotiations will have to become multilateral to include the other nuclear weapons states.

Another lingering nuclear arms control problem is intermediate-range weapons, those with ranges of 500–5,000 kilometers. The 1987 Intermediate-Range Nuclear Forces (INF) Treaty bans the two countries from developing, manufacturing, or deploying ground-launched ballistic and cruise missiles with these ranges. Russian dissatisfaction with the INF Treaty stems in part from how this bilateral agreement uniquely discriminates against Russia and the United States. In October 2007, Putin warned that Moscow would find it difficult to continue complying with the INF Treaty unless other countries ratified the agreement as well. Washington and Moscow subsequently agreed jointly to encourage other countries to join the treaty, but this has fallen on deaf ears. The most serious concern for Moscow in this regard is China, and Russian officials privately express frustration with the lack of transparency in their "strategic partner."

Concluding the New Start negotiations in April 2010 was also timely in providing greater credibility for Moscow and Washington in fulfilling their Nonproliferation Treaty (NPT) Article VI commitment with the 2010 NPT review conference held the following month in May. Given the NPT's call for nuclear weapons states to relinquish their arsenals, many other governments and international security analysts believe that the Russian Federation, the United States, and other nuclear powers must make more drastic reductions—with many calling for total elimination—to meet their NPT obligations. The Obama administration's desire to ratify the Comprehensive Test-Ban Treaty (CTBT) and to engage in negotiations for a Fissile Material Cut-off Treaty (FMCT) should also provide positive momentum for the nonproliferation regime that has been on "life-support" in recent years. The broader nonproliferation regime needs major reworking to endure effectively, but initial measures need to be taken in particular by Russia and the United States as their close partnership in these efforts is essential.

IRAN

The Iranian nuclear and ballistic missile programs have been, along with differences over their shared neighborhood, the most persistent bones of contention between Russia and its Western partners since the collapse of the Soviet Union. In an effort to avert near-term challenges posed by Iran's nuclear program, Russia and European governments continue to urge Tehran to comply with UN Security Council resolutions to suspend its enrichment and reprocessing activities. Although Russia joined with other UN Security Council members in supporting sanctions in 2006 and 2007, Moscow has never been an enthusiastic backer of punitive measures. Russian diplomats often work to weaken proposed sanctions, and, in addition, they have always defended Iran's right to pursue nuclear activities for peaceful purposes. Russian officials have also been especially stubborn in denying that Tehran is currently seeking a nuclear weapon or is developing long-range missile technology (although this may be changing—see the next section on missile defense).[24]

The urgency of resolving the challenge of the Iranian nuclear program is great as Tehran has already demonstrated the capability to enrich uranium, and the capacity to weaponize this material is not far off. Russia's efforts in recent years to serve as an intermediary with Tehran were tacitly supported by the Bush administration, but ultimately they were unsuccessful (that is, the proposal to take back spent fuel to Russian territory). Moscow's leverage with Tehran is very limited, and the Russians have shown signs of being nearly as frustrated with Iran's intransigence on the nuclear question as the Americans and Europeans. The Obama administration has promised a new approach to engage Tehran in direct negotiations. The fallback strategy in event of continued intransigence even in bilateral negotiations is that the Obama administration would probably have more success in then going to their P-5 partners to support much tougher economic sanctions.

THE MISSILE DEFENSE CONNECTION

Along with NATO enlargement, the U.S. plan to deploy theater missile defense system components in Poland and the Czech Republic was a deeply contentious issue in Russia–Transatlantic security relations. This is likely the issue that pushed Putin over the edge when he made his anti-American tirade in Munich in February 2007, having realized in January 2007 that the United States was serious about deploying missile interceptors in Poland and radar in the Czech Republic. Although NATO endorsed the plans, the issue has been highly contentious within Europe, including in the Czech Republic itself. Moscow responded with both carrots and sticks: threatening to target the planned deployments with nuclear weapons as well as reaching out to the United States to offer use of Russian-controlled facilities. The Bush administration engaged the Russians in discussions of these proposals, notably the Gabala radar station in Azerbaijan, but these talks were not successful.

While there has always been a link between the missile defense plans and Iran, the Obama administration made this linkage more explicit to Moscow after taking office in January 2009. This was reportedly a topic in a not-so-secret letter from newly inaugurated President Obama to Russian President Medvedev in February—the less of a threat Iran poses, the less theater missile defense capabilities in Europe will be needed, thus the greater incentive for Moscow to exercise more leverage on Tehran.[25] There is a virtual quality to this so-called grand bargain as both sides may in fact be giving up little. Moscow has little or no leverage over Tehran, and for a variety of reasons, the Obama team is not as enthusiastic as its predecessors about missile defense. For the first eight months after taking office, the issue remained "under review" in the Obama administration, and the Russians rejected various cooperative proposals unless the United States abandoned the plans for Poland and the Czech Republic. As these discussions continued, Moscow has resisted delivery of the S-300 antimissile system to Iran, likely holding this out as a piece of leverage with Washington.

In the second half of September 2009 there was dramatic movement on issues tied to missile defense and the Iranian missile and nuclear threat. First, on September 13, the Obama administration abruptly announced plans from its conclusion of the missile defense review to move away from a system involving the deployment of X-Band Radar in the Czech Republic and ground-based interceptors in Poland to another system, one using sea-based AEGIS deployments in combination with land-based batteries of SM-3 missiles in countries, yet to be specified, geographically closer to Iran. The administration justified this new system configuration on the basis of more rapid development of Iranian short- and medium-range ballistic missiles, the lack of evidence of significant progress in its long-range missiles (ICBMs), technical developments in alternative missile defense components, timeliness of system deployment, and cost factors. President Obama and other officials in his administration emphasized this decision was not made because of Russian objections to the Bush administration's proposal, but they understood that this proposal was likely to be positively received.

The second development concerns the dramatic revelation on September 24 by President Obama, who announced with French president Nicolas Sarkozy and British prime minister Gordon Brown that U.S. intelligence sources confirmed that Iran had built another uranium enrichment facility near the city of Qom, which had not been revealed to the IAEA in a timely manner, thus constituting a clear violation of its obligations to the nonproliferation regime.

On June 9, 2010, the UN Security Council agreed on Resolution 1929 which imposed the most punitive sanctions to date against Iran for its nuclear program. This marked another significant achievement for the Obama administration and especially for its Russia policy. Privately, administration officials applauded the constructive role that the Russian government played in helping to garner Chinese support for Resolution 1929.[26]

Significant progress on both the Iran and missile defense cooperation agendas continued with Russia into the fall of 2010. On October 9, the Russian government announced it would not sell the advanced S-300 anti-air missile to Iran, effectively forgoing about $1 billion in revenue.[27] Obtaining this capability would have significantly improved Iran's ability to withstand an air strike. It is certainly conceivable that delivery of S-300s to Iran was considered *causus belli* by the Israeli government, which lobbied the Russians very hard on this.

Finally, at the NATO Summit in Lisbon where the alliance's new strategic concept was approved, the allies and Russia agreed to re-start their cooperation on theater missile defense exercises as well as explore the possibility of integrating Russian capabilities with the planned deployment of the phased adaptive system which the Obama administration had announced in September 2009. The achievements in Lisbon, where President Medvedev participated in the summit and a separate meeting of the NATO-Russia Council was held, marked a dramatic change for Moscow's relations with NATO from the tense April 2008 alliance summit in Bucharest and the suspension of NATO-Russia ties after the Georgia war in 2008.

AFGHANISTAN AND THE NORTHERN DISTRIBUTION NETWORK

Many Russian government officials as well as non-governmental experts believe that Afghanistan is the most promising area for U.S.-Russia cooperation.[28] Indeed, it was on Afghanistan in the fall of 2001 that U.S.-Russian security and intelligence cooperation probably reached its high point in the post-Soviet period. Renewed U.S. attention to Afghanistan is taking place in the context of the deterioration of the security environment there as well as the reduction of violence in Iraq.

As a presidential candidate in 2008, Barack Obama promised to deploy more U.S. forces to the war in Afghanistan. Because of increasing problems on the Afghanistan-Pakistan border, in the second half of 2008, U.S. Central Command (CentComm) began to explore the possibility of opening a transit corridor from the north into Afghanistan, which came to be termed the northern distribution network (NDN).[29] Even if U.S. force presence would remain stable, opening the NDN would likely be needed, but with the increased troop presence, the required flow of goods and materials to supply the troops is estimated to grow to 2010 by up to three times.[30]

The opening of the NDN increased the attention of U.S. policy makers to Central Asia and the Caspian as well as Russia. As initially conceived, the NDN is to be composed of two transit corridors. The NDN North starts in the port of Riga where goods are loaded into railway container cars for shipment through Russia, Kazakhstan, and down to Heraton on the Uzbek-Kazakh border. The NDN South would come in through the Caspian to either Kazakhstan or Turkmenistan then to Uzbekistan. In the spring of 2009, the NDN rail route from Riga to Afghanistan became operational as trains were making the trip with full support from Russia and Kazakhstan to the Uzbek-Afghan border in only nine days. Privately, U.S. government officials laud Russian cooperation to expedite the trains.

Despite supporting the establishment of the NDN, Russian intentions have been far more questionable on the issue of U.S. access to Manas, the airbase in Kyrgyzstan from which the U.S. military had been transiting troops and goods into Kyrgyzstan since 2001. In early February, Kyrgyz president Kurmanbek Bakiyev announced that the United States would lose access to Manas at virtually the same time that the Russians and Kyrgyz reached agreement on an economic assistance package of $2.25 billion.[31] While the Russian government denied any linkage between the base decision and the loan package, there was widespread speculation that the loan was contingent on Bishkek closing the base to the Americans.

Negotiations with Kyrgyzstan continued into June until Washington and Bishkek finally reached agreement to allow the United States to use Manas as a "transit center," paying more than three times the previous rent. The agreement was reached shortly before Obama's trip to Moscow in early July, but questions remained as to what extent Moscow supported this decision.[32]

In the run-up to the Moscow summit, U.S. government officials were pleasantly surprised when the Russian government raised the idea of reaching agreement for the air transport of lethal materials over Russian airspace.[33] Although not a high-priority desire on the part of the Pentagon at the time, the agreement on transit of lethal materials in Russian airspace was acclaimed in both Washington and Moscow as the most significant achievement of the July meetings in Moscow between Barack Obama and Dmitri Medvedev.

The murky issue of Moscow's influence on Kyrgyz decisions about Manas highlights for U.S. policy makers the question of whether Moscow views supporting allied efforts in Afghanistan as a higher priority than maintaining and extending its own military influence with Central Asian neighbors. Later that summer Moscow lobbied for the Collective Security Treaty Organization (CSTO) to agree to establish a military base in Osh Kyrgyzstan in the volatile Ferghana Valley. Uzbekistan adamantly opposed the establishment of the base under the auspices of the CSTO, so the agreement for the base was reached on a bilateral basis between Bishkek and Moscow. Tashkent views the establishment of this base as a security threat to Uzbekistan, and policy makers there are very skeptical about Russian policy in the region and even whether Moscow would like to see Afghanistan stabilized.[34]

With the decision by the Obama administration in December 2009 to further increase the number of U.S. forces in Afghanistan to about 100,000 in 2010, the role of the NDN increased dramatically to support the surge. The Pentagon and the rest of the U.S. government rightfully regard the development of the NDN as strikingly successful, and particularly the enthusiastic and key role that Russia has played. The NATO summit in Lisbon highlighted further progress with Russia on the NDN as Moscow agreed to expand the definition of "non-lethal" equipment to allow for armored vehicles to cross Russian territory as well as to allow reverse transit of equipment in the future. Other important agreements included the provision of Russian M-17 helicopters to Afghanistan and deeper cooperation in combating drug trafficking. While we should not expect cooperation with Russia in Afghanistan to reach the point of deployment of Russian forces in that theater, both in Washington and in Moscow there are strong hopes for further cooperation to develop regarding the war in Afghanistan.

The Balance Sheet for the "Reset" of U.S.-Russia Relations

Given the terrible state of bilateral relations when the Obama administration entered office in January 2009, the dramatic improvement of ties between Moscow and Washington over the past nearly two years may well be the most successful aspect of U.S. foreign policy to date. Russia has played a key role in advancing U.S. interests on arguably the three highest priorities of the Obama administration: Iran, Afghanistan, and nuclear security. The "reset" has also now extended to Russia-NATO relations. The relationship has broadened and deepened on a number of other fronts, notably economic, not addressed in this chapter.

The depth and breadth of the improvement in ties with Russia have been pleasantly surprising. The momentum of progress dramatically accelerated in the spring of 2010 with the principle landmarks of reaching agreement on the New Start Treaty in April and new UN sanctions against Iran in June. But there were a number of other developments at the time that added data points to concluding that not only U.S.-Russia relations were improving but also Russia's relations with the West more broadly; these include the Russia-Poland reconciliation in April, the border agreement between Norway and Russia over the Barents Sea, and the participation of U.S. and other NATO military personnel for the first time at the May 9 victory celebration in Moscow.

Perhaps most significant was the cooperation between Washington and Moscow beginning in April on the coup and following unrest and instability in Kyrgyzstan. This, combined with the peaceful election of Victor Yanukovich as Ukrainian president in January, is a striking contrast to the massive rift between the Bush and Putin administrations over the "color revolutions" in 2004–05 in Ukraine and Kyrgyzstan. The allaying of Moscow's insecurities over presumed U.S. and Western encroachment in the post-Soviet space has undoubtedly played a subtle but powerful role in facilitating the current rapprochement.

Is the current positive trend irreversible? Of course not. The situation in Georgia remains tense, and the possibility of this or another rift in the post-Soviet space could lead to the unraveling of the relationship once again. Domestic politics in Washington or Moscow could also derail the "reset." The U.S. Congress will likely face another watershed moment in 2011 in finally dealing with the dreaded Jackson-Vanik amendment as part of Russia's prolonged effort to accede to the World Trade Organization. Political uncertainty will grow in Moscow as the 2012 presidential election approaches. Nevertheless, there is reason for cautious optimism in the near term because a positive and constructive bilateral relationship between Washington and Moscow is fundamentally in the national interests of each country.

The Long View

Despite the nearly two-decade tumultuous post–Cold War history in U.S.-Russia relations, one dramatic conclusion is that Russia does not matter nearly as much for Washington's strategic goals today, and the same can be said of the United States for Russia. Russia is no longer a strategic adversary, and Washington's twentieth-century Eurocentric focus is rapidly shifting attention and resources to East Asia and the greater Middle East as well as to global challenges.

The ongoing shift in the global balance of power to a genuinely multipolar structure contrasts the relative strategic decline of Russia, the United States, Europe, and Japan with the dramatic rise of China and, to a lesser extent, India. Russia's strategic decline dates back nearly three decades and is by far the most precipitous despite the boom years of Putin's presidency. The peak of U.S. power may well be marked at some point during the first term of George W. Bush. Fighting wars in Afghanistan and Iraq has proven far more challenging after initial successes, but the most worrisome development for U.S. power in the world is economic in nature; specifically, fiscal irresponsibility on a massive scale. If the U.S. political system does not soon muster the will to decisively address what looks now to be long-term unsustainable deficits, U.S. power may erode more quickly and add considerable stress to the stability of an already fragile global order. Russia, meanwhile, will face gargantuan tasks of modernization to stem its own strategic decline. Perhaps this new environment may facilitate Moscow and Washington finding a more constructive modus vivendi in the challenging years ahead.

Notes

1. For one of the early texts examining this topic, see Robert E. Osgood, *Ideals and Self-Interest in America's Foreign Relations* (Chicago: University of Chicago Press, 1964). For a compelling analysis of the topic from pre-revolutionary days to the end of the nineteenth century, see Robert Kagan, *Dangerous Nation: America's Place in the World from its Earliest Days to the Dawn of the Twentieth Century* (New York: Knopf, 2006).
2. See James M. Goldgeier and Michael McFaul, *Power and Purpose: U.S. Policy toward Russia after the Cold War* (Washington, DC: Brookings Institution, 2003). Easily the best analysis of its kind, Goldgeier and McFaul interviewed the majority of key U.S. policy makers, with the exception of former presidents, to give their thoughtful account a deeper sense of how those developing and implementing U.S. policy viewed Russia, as well as their goals toward it.
3. See Patrick E. Tyler, "U.S. Strategy Plan Calls for Insuring No Rivals Develop," *New York Times*, March 8, 1992.
4. George Bush and Brent Scowcroft, *A World Transformed* (New York: Knopf, 1998).
5. Goldgeier and McFaul, *Power and Purpose*, 359.
6. Representative Christopher Cox in 2000 chaired a congressional study on Russia that resulted in a comprehensive report slamming Clinton policy on Russia and emphasizing Vice President Gore's role. Unlike a similar study on U.S. China policy that Cox chaired in 1998, which focused on espionage and illegal technology trans-

fer, the Russian study group was composed of only Republicans, with the result that the report, despite some substantive strengths, was deeply politicized. See Speaker's Advisory Group on Russia, Christopher Cox, chairman, *Russia's Road to Corruption: How the Clinton Administration Exported Government Instead of Free Enterprise and Failed the Russian People* (Washington, DC: U.S. House of Representatives, 2000).

7. See Condoleezza Rice, "Promoting the National Interest," *Foreign Affairs* 79 (January/February 2000): 45–62. Note that Rice had also been brought to Washington in 1989 to work under the consummate realist Brent Scowcroft on the National Security Council in the Bush I administration.

8. This is the dominant narrative of Putin's historic decision. The reality is murkier. Moscow's initial reaction was to lobby President Karimov in Uzbekistan and President Akaev in Kyrgyzstan to not allow the Americans access to bases. The more accurate interpretation suggests that the central Asian presidents made their own decisions and Putin made a virtue of necessity in laying claim supporting this decision that was later interpreted by Russian elites as a major Russian concession to Washington, which was not reciprocated.

9. The classic text is Hans Morganthau. The next most significant contribution to realism, a fairly Anglo-American-dominated school, is Kenneth Waltz. See Kenneth Waltz, *Theory of International Politics* (New York: McGraw-Hill, 1979).

10. I participated in small, private briefings for Secretary of State Rice in February 2006 and President Bush in June 2006; both expressed the view that they were reasonably satisfied with Russian cooperation on a number of issues including Iran, but that growing authoritarianism at home and Russia's policies in its neighborhood troubled them the most and contributed to growing concern about where Russia was headed.

11. For a concise summary of the recentralization of power in Russia under Putin, see Anders Aslund and Andrew C. Kuchins, "Political Development: From Disorder to Recentralization of Power," in *The Russia Balance Sheet* (Washington, DC: Peterson Institute for International Economics), 25–38.

12. See Clifford Gaddy and Andrew C. Kuchins, "Putin's Plan," *Washington Quarterly* 31, no. 2 (Spring 2008): 117–29.

13. See, for example, Полит.РУ, " 'Это нападение на нашу страну.' Обращение президента России Владимира Путина к нации всвязи с терактом в Беслане ["This is an attack on our country." The address of the Russian president, Vladimir Putin, in connection with the terrorist act in Beslan], September 5, 2010, http://www.polit.ru/dossie/2004/09/04/putin.html.

14. See Лариса КАФТАН, "Заместитель главы администрации Президента РФ Владислав Сурков: Путин укрепляет государство, а не себя" [Deputy Head of

the Presidential Administration of the Russian Federation Vladislav Surkov: Putin is strengthening the state, and not himself], September 29, 2004, http://www.kp.ru/daily/23370/32473/.

15. I was co-author of a joint Russian-American report published by the Carnegie Moscow Center in early 2005. At a report launch meeting in February at the Carnegie Endowment for International Peace, I vividly recall the resounding thud that our report received. The zeitgeist in the Bush administration, and Washington more broadly, was strongly in favor of regime transformation and accentuation of the "values gap" regarding Russia, not pragmatic engagement. See Andrew Kuchins, Vyacheslav Nikonov, and Dmitri Trenin, *U.S.-Russian Relations: The Case for an Upgrade* ([Moscow?]: Carnegie Moscow Center, 2005).

16. For one of the first such assessments in the mainstream press, see Andrew C. Kuchins, "Look Who's Back," *Wall Street Journal* (Europe ed.), May 9, 2006.

17. In a July 2009 interview with the *Wall Street Journal*, Vice President Biden caused quite a stir when he made similar comments about Russia's vulnerabilities and challenges and then suggested this would lead Moscow to more readily support U.S. foreign policy initiatives. See Peter Spiegel, "Biden Says Weakened Russia Will Bend to U.S.," *Wall Street Journal*, July 25, 2009, http://online.wsj.com/article/SB124848246032580581.html.

18. For example, see the policy brief issued by the German Marshall Fund just after the Obama trip to Moscow in July, "Why the Obama Administration Should Not Take Central and Eastern Europe for Granted," July 13, 2009, http://www.gmfus.org/doc/Obama_CEE.pdf.

19. See Commission on U.S. Policy toward Russia, "The Right Direction on U.S. Policy toward Russia" [commonly known as the "Hart-Hagel Report"] (Washington, D.C.: Commission on U.S. Policy toward Russia, March 2009). Reports calling for improved relations with Russia and consulted in Aslund and Kuchins, *Russia Balance Sheet*, include: Steven Pifer, "Reversing the Decline: An Agenda for U.S.-Russian Relations in 2009" (policy paper 10, Brookings Institution, Washington, D.C., January 2009); Stephen Sestanovich, "What Has Moscow Done? Rebuilding U.S.-Russian Relations," *Foreign Affairs* (November/December 2008); Henry A. Kissinger and George P. Shultz, "Building on Common Ground with Russia," *Washington Post*, October 8, 2008; Michael McFaul, "U.S.-Russia Relations in the Aftermath of the Georgia Crisis" (testimony to the House Committee on Foreign Affairs, U.S. Congress, Washington, DC, September 9, 2008; transcript, Carnegie Endowment for International Peace), http://www.carnegieendowment.org/publications/index.cfm?fa=view&id=22157; Rose Gottemoeller, "Russian-American Security Relations

After Georgia" (policy brief, Carnegie Endowment for International Peace, Washington, DC, October 2008); and Dmitry Trenin, "Thinking Strategically About Russia" (policy brief, Carnegie Endowment for International Peace, Washington, DC, October 2008).

20. See, for example, Lev Gudkov, Igor Klyamkin, Georgy Satarov, and Lilia Shevtsova, "False Choices for Russia," *Washington Post*, June 9, 2009, http://www.washingtonpost.com/wp-dyn/content/article/2009/06/08/AR2009060803496.html.

21. Aslund and Kuchins, *Russia Balance Sheet*, 79, 127–28.

22. George P. Shultz, William J. Perry, Henry A. Kissinger, and Sam Nunn, "Toward a Nuclear-Free World," *Wall Street Journal*, January 15, 2008.

23. The limits of strategic offensive arms will be in the range of 500–1,100 for strategic delivery vehicles, and in the range of 1,500–1,675 for their associated warheads, in that seven years after entry force of the treaty and thereafter. See White House, "Joint Understanding," Office of the Press Secretary, July 8, 2009, http://www.whitehouse.gov/the_press_office/The-Joint-Understanding-for-The-Start-Follow-On-Treaty/.

24. In private discussions, Obama Administration officials have confirmed that Iran was the topic that received the most attention in discussions with Medvedev and Putin during the July Moscow meetings.

25. See Peter Baker, "In Secret Letter, Obama Offered Deal to Russia," *New York Times*, March 3, 2009, http://www.nytimes.com/2009/03/03/world/americas/03iht-03prexy.20548331.html.

26. Personal communication between the author and administration officials.

27. Nabi Abdullaev, "Russia: No S-300 Missile Systems for Iran," *Defense News*, October 9, 2010, http://www.defensenews.com/story.php?i=3764075.

28. The author traveled to Moscow four times in 2009 (February, April, June, and July) to consult with government officials as well as non-government experts on Afghanistan and broader U.S.-Russian relations. There was a strong consensus that it is on Afghanistan that U.S. and Russian security interests most coincide.

29. I met with CentComm planners to discuss NDN in May 2009.

30. Ibid. See *The Northern Distribution Network and the Modern Silk Road: Planning for Afghanistan's Future* (Washington, DC: CSIS, 2009).

31. See Clifford Levy, "Kyrgyzstan: At the Crossroad of Empires, a Mouse Struts," *New York Times*, July 25, 2009, http://www.nytimes.com/2009/07/26/weekinreview/26levy.html?_r=1.

32. See "Kyrgyzstan Agreed U.S Base Deal with Russia," *Reuters*, June 24, 2009, http://www.reuters.com/article/latestCrisis/idUSLO894657.

33. The author's private discussions with U.S. officials in Washington and Moscow have

confirmed that this agreement was on Moscow's initiative. The NDN is designed to facilitate the transit of non-lethal goods, which comprise more than 80 percent of what the U.S. forces require, and all the goods shipped are done on a commercial basis.

34. In private discussions with very high-level government officials in Tashkent in July 2009, the view was expressed that Moscow prefers to see Afghanistan remain unstable in order to justify a Russian military presence in central Asia as well as to deny central Asian states access to global markets through southern transit corridors. See Andrew C. Kuchins and Thomas Sanderson, "Northern Exposure in Central Asia," *International Herald Tribune,* August 4, 2009.

CHAPTER THIRTEEN

Russia: The Eastern Dimension

Bobo Lo

The course of Russian foreign policy over the past four hundred years offers up a singular paradox. On the one hand, Russia's eastward expansion during the sixteenth to nineteenth centuries established the physical reality of a state whose territory lies predominantly in Asia. On the other hand, its rulers—in tsarist, communist, and post-Soviet times—have consistently viewed Russia as part of a larger European and Western civilization. The two-headed Romanov eagle on the national coat of arms makes for a nice image, but at no stage has Russia developed an Asian outlook. Central Asia, Eastern Siberia, and the Russian Far East (RFE) acquired specific identities as European outposts, isolated redoubts of civilization in a vast Asian wilderness,[1] and interaction with mainstream Asia was marked by ignorance and a profound sense of alienation.

It is striking, then, that we are witnessing today the rise of the East in Russian foreign policy thinking, barely two decades after the fall of communism and the apparent triumph of the West. While Moscow continues to look principally to the United States and Europe, there has been a distinct process of "Asianization" in recent years. The most visible sign of this is the transformation of the relationship with China into one of the most important in Russian foreign policy. But it is also apparent in other areas—in Moscow's developing ties with Iran and the Muslim world, the reassertion of Russian influence in Central Asia, and multilateral engagement in the Asia-Pacific region. Most of all, there is the dawning realization that the East matters, not simply as an adjunct or counterbalance to the West, but in its own right.

The sheer diversity and complexity of the East presents enormous policy challenges to Russian decision makers. So far, they have been more adept at recognizing Asia's importance than in developing effective strategies for engaging with it. Old stereotypes and ways of thinking exert a disproportionate influence, and Moscow has found it difficult to reconcile the pursuit of Russia's security and economic interests across Asia with a worldview that remains overwhelmingly Westerncentric. The story of Russia's eastern dimension, then, is one of aspiration over achievement. Intellectually, Moscow grasps the need for a more considered, balanced, and long-term strategy toward Asia. In practice, however, pursuit of this goal is undermined by lack of vision, inconsistent policy making, ideological hang-ups, and an anachronistic geopolitical mind-set.

The Key Questions

This chapter analyzes the principal features of Russia's approach toward Asia—its motivations, strengths, weaknesses, and prospects. To this purpose, it addresses five key questions:

1. *How does Moscow conceive of Asia and Russia's place within Asia?* Although it has long been an article of faith that Russia is an Asian as well as a European country, there has been little attempt to define what this means. Mere geographical extent scarcely constitutes proof of Asian credentials, and it is significant that most Asians regard Russia as a European country, albeit one with distinct characteristics. Although the Russian elite is now more committed to engagement with Asia, this does not imply a sense of belonging or willingness to view Russian national identity through an Asian prism.

2. *What are the objectives and instruments of Russia's Asia policies?* Generally speaking, it is easier to establish what Moscow opposes than what it wants. This is especially true in Asia, where its policy options are limited by a lack of standing, weak influence, and brittle self-confidence. Confronted by diverse challenges, the Russian approach has been largely reactive and driven by geopolitical instinct. This reflects a fundamentally defensive outlook, as decision makers grapple with a number of inconvenient realities: the vulnerability of the Russian Far East, a long-term

American presence in Asia, and the rise of China. Moscow has resorted to various mechanisms in its search for solutions, yet the overriding impression of Russian policy is of aimlessness. If there is a vision of Russia in Asia, then it is unsupported by any comprehensive strategy.

3. *How successful is Russia's "Asia project"?* Despite the enhanced importance of the East, the Asianization of Russian foreign policy remains a work in early progress. In Central Asia, Moscow's historical ties with local elites have enabled it to preserve a substantial influence. But in other parts of Asia, notably the Pacific Rim and South Asia, Russia is a peripheral player. History, geographical distance, and cultural alienation have proved significant obstacles to the spread of Russian influence. Yet often the problems are of Moscow's own making: the clumsy instrumentalism of its foreign policy; the fiction of normative convergence with Beijing; and an excessive Sinocentric bias.

4. *How can Russia advance its interests in Asia?* Although it suffers from being regarded as an outsider, Russia possesses several important trumps. As the world's largest oil and gas exporter, it is well placed to service the energy requirements of Northeast Asia. Long-standing ties with Central Asia represent a promising basis for a pivotal role in Eurasian security-building. And as a member of the P-5 (and second nuclear weapons state), it can legitimately aspire to influence issues of WMD non-proliferation and regional conflict resolution. However, none of this potential will be realized without a major change in Russian foreign policy. Only when Moscow fully values engagement with Asia for its own sake, and not as part of some global grand strategy, can Russia emerge as a genuine player on the continent.

5. *How should the West respond to Russia's engagement with Asia?* It has become fashionable to speak of an emerging authoritarian consensus that would challenge the current Western-centered system of "universal" norms.[2] In fact, this so-called consensus is a figment of neoconservative imagination. While some Asian countries, such as China, share Russia's distaste for Western democratic practices, they remain committed to cooperation with the West for compelling economic, political, and security reasons. Instead of being spooked by imaginary threats, America and Europe should understand that they have a vested interest in a more effective Russian engagement in Asia.

Defining Terms

It is essential to define what we mean by Asia and the "East" in the Russian context. For the purposes of this chapter, Asia extends from Iran in the west to the Philippines in the east, and from Japan to Indonesia. The "East" is an even more general, somewhat mystical, term. Here, it will be applied interchangeably with Asia; Russia's eastern dimension is thus broadly synonymous with Russia's overall attitudes and policies toward Asia.

A few points of clarification are needed. First, we have omitted the Middle East from our discussion. Although some Middle Eastern countries are geographically part of Asia, most are not. Moreover, over the past century the Middle East has developed a specific identity as a subregion, separate from the Asian mainstream.

Second, our discussion of Central Asia will center on Afghanistan and multilateral bodies such as the Shanghai Cooperation Organization (SCO), rather than on the former Soviet Central Asian republics. Although these young sovereign states are indubitably Asian, they retain an even stronger identity as part of Russia's "near abroad." This is not to legitimize Russia's patrimonial attitude toward them, but rather to acknowledge that the political, economic, and cultural links between Moscow and the Central Asians remain very strong, and certainly stronger than the latter's ties with the rest of Asia.

Third, we should recognize that Russia's role and policies in Asia, along with other areas of its foreign policy, have been the subject of sometimes vigorous internal debate. It may therefore seem odd to speak of "Russia" or "Moscow" as largely unitary entities in this context. Nevertheless, we have done so. In our view, there exists a general consensus regarding the basic parameters and assumptions of Russia's approach toward Asia. Few Russians, whatever their personal biases, question the need to engage more fully with the continent, or to develop stable and cooperative relations with major Asian powers such as China, Japan, and India.

Generalizing about Russia's approach toward Asia presents enormous challenges when the continent comprises several distinct subregions: West Asia, Central Asia, South Asia, Northeast Asia, Southeast Asia. Given that Russian policy makers have rarely developed a consistent strategy for managing relations with individual Asian countries, it is perhaps unrealistic to expect an overarching approach to Asia as a continent. It may appear absurd to speak of an Asian policy in Moscow, or of a Russian attitude toward Asia. Nevertheless, notwithstanding substantial variations across different regions and countries, there are a number of common features in Russia's handling of Asian affairs. The first task of this essay, then, is to make the case that there is a Russian understanding of Asia that has proved highly influential in the past and that will continue to shape attitudes and policies well into the future.

Understandings of Asia and "Asian-ness"

The most common justification for calling Russia an Asian country is the fact that 75 percent of its territory lies east of the Ural mountain range, the traditional divide between Europe and Asia. A second qualification, one that elicits ambivalent feelings among Russians, is ethnic and racial heritage. Three centuries of Tatar rule in the thirteenth to sixteenth centuries; the effects of tsarist and Soviet imperialism in the Far East, Central Asia, and the Caucasus; and considerable intermarriage among the more than one hundred nationalities that make up today's Russia have resulted in a population that, physically, is in large part Asiatic. A third aspect, frequently cited by Vladimir Putin, is religion. An estimated 15 percent of Russia's population is Muslim, and Islam is the second largest denomination after Orthodox Christianity. Islam is an important part of Russia's Asian, as opposed to European, identity.

Outweighing the case for Russia's "Asian-ness," however, are several considerations that reinforce its image as a predominantly European and Western nation. The first, flagged earlier, is history. The pattern of Russia's development, beginning with the Kievan Rus in the ninth century, has been founded in and shaped by European language, religion, and culture. Second, the worldview of the Russian elite is centered on the West. One of the singular features of the Putin regime is the frequency with which it balances strident criticisms of Western policies with the insistence that Russia is an integral part of European, and therefore Western, civilization. Significantly, it has never made this claim vis-à-vis Asia; Russia may be part of physical Asia, but it is not an Asian *civilization*.

Third, the main centers of Russian political, economic, and cultural life are located in the European part of the country. The impact of Russia's Asianness on government and business decision making is negligible. Links with Asia are minuscule compared to those with Europe and the West more generally. Thus, nearly 50 percent of Russia's foreign trade is with the European

Union, which in turn accounts for over 90 percent of foreign direct investment into Russia. Washington is Moscow's chief interlocutor on security and disarmament matters. The major priorities of the Putin regime are "Western" issues—the United States-Russia "reset," relations with Ukraine, European security, missile defense, energy security. And, on a personal level, the Russian elite send their children to be educated in Europe. The West is said to be in decline, yet in virtually every respect Russians continue to take it as the benchmark.

Russia's sense of its European-ness is matched by Asian views of Russian identity. It is symptomatic that, despite the impressive progress in Sino-Russian relations over the past decade, the Chinese do not view Russians as Asian. There is no sense in Beijing and Shanghai of a common Asian identity to grease the wheels of bilateral cooperation. This is even more apparent in Tokyo, New Delhi, and Southeast Asian capitals. Skepticism about Russia's Asian credentials is strengthened by the fact that until relatively recently, Moscow made little effort to promote Russia as an Asian country with Asian objectives. Even today, there is a widespread belief that Moscow sees Asia either as a default option when Russia-West relations are in difficulty, or as a source of potential threats.

There is, admittedly, a strong orientalist tradition in Russia, one that has invested considerable intellectual effort in understanding Asian civilizations. However, this is not the same as *feeling* Asian. In this respect, the Russian tradition mirrors that of Western countries such as the UK and France, both of which have a long and distinguished history of oriental studies. Similarly, it would be wrong to interpret the Slavophile strand in nineteenth-century Russia as reflecting identification with the East. Slavophilism, based on the triad of *samoderzhavie* (autocracy), *pravoslavie* (Orthodoxy), and *narodnost* (sense of nationhood), rejected what it saw as corrosive influences from the West. But in no way did it advocate replacing these with Asian values. On the contrary, the Slavophiles sought to emphasize Russia's "special" identity, resisting alien influences from wherever they came.

Evolution of Russian Thinking

What has changed over the past twenty years is that Russian attitudes toward Asia have become more nuanced. The original Mongol complex—the existential fear of a modern-day Asian horde[3]—remains in some degree, but there has been a notable "humanization" of Asia and Asians, stimulated by the diplomatic rapprochement between Moscow and Beijing. The isolationist mentality of the Cold War era has given way to a more open stance. There is now recognition, even among China skeptics, that positive engagement with China is not only useful but essential. In the Russian Far East, hostility toward the Chinese has softened, assisted by a considerable increase in cross-border interaction.[4] Diminution of the "China threat," in the direct sense at least, has been accompanied by a more general warming toward Asia, and the understanding that changing global realities demand more active Eastern policies by Moscow.

However, the extent of this change should not be exaggerated. While the Putin regime talks up the shift in global power away from the United States and Europe, its approach to international relations remains predicated on the continuing dominance of the West, even if the latter is under greater challenge than ever before. Crucially, Russia's rulers see its future as existentially bound with the West. They do not want to leave it, but to redefine it. The normative dominance of the "Anglo-Saxon model" of economic development and the EU's *acquis communautaire* would be superseded by a larger, more inclusive sense of belonging to a common historical-civilizational heritage.

Conversely, acknowledgement that Russia must engage more seriously with the East does not imply *joining* Asia. Moscow's game is cooperation, not integration. This is partly a function of Russia's strong sense of European-ness. But it arises, too, from a deep ambivalence toward Asia, China in the first instance. According to some alarmist views, a powerful China may seek one day to regain territories lost to the Russian Empire in the mid-nineteenth century.[5] More realistically, however, the threat is less military or even demographic than strategic: the likelihood of Russia's growing marginalization from decision making in Central Asia, Northeast Asia, and globally. There is already concern that Russia has become little more than a raw materials appendage to a China that has overtaken it in the quality, diversity, and size of its economy. The "humiliation complex" of many Russians toward the perceived superiority of the West could soon be replicated vis-à-vis the East.

But perhaps the most persuasive explanation for Russia's reluctance to identify with Asia is the concern that this could affect its status as a global great power. For Russia regards itself less as part of a larger regional entity than as a great regional entity *unto itself*; it emphatically rejects the notion that it is simply another European or Asian country. Such thinking is reflected in its interpretation of a multipolar world, in which Russia is an "independent" pole at the level of the United States and China, and distinct from Europe.

Consciousness of this independent identity has led Russia to promote itself as a bridge: between East and West, and also between the developed (North) and developing worlds (South). Whereas the American political thinker Samuel Huntington saw Russia as a "torn country,"[6] belonging neither to Europe nor Asia, Russian policy makers and academics claim instead that it is pivotal to the "dialogue between civilizations." Such interpretations promote the notion that Russia's identity is all-transcending. It is not European, Western, Asian, or even Eurasian; rather, it is all those things at the same time. To adapt a well-known aphorism, Russia seeks to be both "in Asia and above Asia."[7]

Russian Objectives—The Primacy of Geopolitics

The Asian continent across its extent is a much more disparate, "anarchic" environment than Europe. It is characterized by constantly shifting relations among great powers, buffer states, and small countries; regional and subregional balances of power; claimed spheres of interests; and tensions between zero-sum and positive-sum approaches to foreign policy. In contrast to Europe, there are multiple major players whose interrelationships are defined as much by rivalry as constructive engagement. Critically, Asia lacks the institutions that have helped ensure stability and prosperity throughout much of Europe.

Such an environment is especially difficult for a Russia struggling to carve out a role for itself. Given its weak footprint in Asia, it is hardly surprising that Moscow should find it more natural—and easier—to frustrate the objectives of others than to pursue an active agenda of its own. It has a messianic vision of Russia as an "independent" pole in a multipolar order, a Eurasian bridge between East and West, and a fully signed-up member of the Asian community. But such ambitious goals are more aspirational than realizable.

In the meantime, by force of circumstances as well as inclination, Russia's objectives in Asia are dominated by geopolitical considerations. Unlike Europe, where economic and civilizational ties are of comparable significance, in Asia geopolitics is king—at least as far as Moscow is concerned. The centrality of geopolitics is evident in its view of the Asian strategic environment, in the challenges and objectives it identifies there, and in its handling of specific issues.

Geopolitical Challenges

Instinctively, Moscow looks first to the challenge posed by U.S. *hegemonism* (and Western encroachment more generally). In one sense, the United States is the primary focus of Russia's eastern dimension, for how Washington behaves determines to a very large extent how Moscow responds. Containing and counterbalancing the United States has become one of the chief raisons d'être of Russian foreign policy everywhere, and Asia is no exception. Part of this is due to a visceral anti-Americanism that became entrenched during the years of the George W. Bush administration (2000–08). But it also derives from a more ancient Cold War mentality and, specifically, the premise that Russia can reassert itself as a global great power only if it is able to limit American influence. To this end, it has devoted considerable effort to drumming up an anti-hegemonic consensus with others thought to be similarly disposed, above all China and India.

It is one of the paradoxes of Russian foreign policy that China, with whom Moscow enjoys perhaps the best (as in trouble free) diplomatic relationship, is also a subject of concern in Moscow. Much of this centers on the fate of the Russian Far East. The prospect of military or demographic invasion has receded in recent years, but the rapid expansion of Chinese economic influence (alongside Moscow's neglect of the RFE) raises serious questions about the future of the region. Beijing's intentions—China's "peaceful development" and the promotion of a "harmonious world"—may be honorable, but the country's extraordinary transformation over the past three decades is establishing new realities, including a long-term *threat of displacement*. It is a similar story in Central Asia, where China emphasizes positive panregionalism, while expanding its influence at Russia's expense.

The issue is not simply one of (a discreet) competition for regional power, but goes to the heart of decision making in an increasingly globalized world. One of the most vivid aspects of the financial crisis has been the ascent of China as the dominant "other" to the United States, and the corresponding marginalization of Russia. Moscow does not want to see a declining America replaced by a rising China. For the underlying point remains the same: the existence of a hegemon—Eastern or Western—is a major constraint on Russia's revival as a global player. In Asia, then, Russia is at once a revisionist and a status quo power. It is revisionist in seeking to enlarge its strategic footprint in Eurasia. But it is a status quo power in that it tacitly supports a continued American military presence in East Asia as a way of restraining Chinese ambition.

The third major challenge facing Russia is managing the *tension between geopolitical and security objectives*. This pertains particularly to Central Asia. While Moscow is eager to roll back American influence, it is also mindful that only the United States has the financial resources, political will, and military capacity to meet the threat posed by Islamic extremism. When Vladimir Putin endorsed the deployment of American troops to the region in 2001, he did so mainly because he saw an opportunity to develop a "special" relationship with Washington. But he also believed that the United States would have far more success than Russia in defeating the Taliban and defusing the threat it presented to regime stability in former Soviet Central Asia. Since 2002–03, however, the balance between security and geopolitical objectives has tilted increasingly toward the latter. Moscow's initial fears about Central Asian security pale into insignificance compared to geopolitical concerns about an entrenched U.S. presence and the corresponding diminution of Russian influence. This concern has been exacerbated by challenges to its regional authority from the former Soviet Central Asian republics: witness Kazakhstan's balancing between Russia, China, and the West; Uzbekistan's erratic switching of loyalties between Moscow and Washington; Turkmenistan's expanding energy cooperation with China; and Kyrgyzstan's decision to renegotiate, rather than terminate, the lease for the American base at Manas.[8]

Moscow retains an ambiguous attitude toward *U.S.-based alliances* in Asia, such as the security treaties with Japan and the Republic of Korea, and Washington's close political and military ties with several Southeast Asian states—Singapore, Thailand, Indonesia, and the Philippines. At one level, such arrangements are anathema because they legitimize a long-term American strategic presence throughout much of Asia. However, they also serve an important purpose in containing Japanese militarism, Chinese power projection, and the escalation of tensions on the Korean peninsula. The U.S. network of alliances and partnerships in Asia is the main guarantor of the status quo in East Asia, including—in a nice irony—reinforcing the security and territorial integrity of the RFE.

The final challenge facing Russian policy makers is *staying out of trouble*. Even today, during a relatively calm period in the continent's history, there are many sources of potential conflict in Asia: between India and Pakistan, Iran and its neighbors, and on the Korean peninsula, to name only the most obvious. To this one may add worsening tensions between China and India, historical fissures between China and Japan, various territorial disputes (including between Russia and Japan), and the spats that flare up from time to time between Washington and Beijing. As one of the lesser players in Asia, Russia has little to gain and much to lose by entangling itself in these imbroglios.

MEANS AND MECHANISMS

Virtually all Russia's geopolitical objectives in Asia are preventative: to contain American hegemonic power and China's rising influence; to maintain former Soviet Central Asia as a sphere of Russian influence; to erode the formal legitimacy of U.S.-led alliances, but without destabilizing East Asia; and to ensure that Russia stays out of intra-Asian conflicts. It is very difficult to discern an activist agenda that would project Russia as a major contributor in the continent's affairs. Its weakness and non-identification with Asia indicate that this could scarcely be otherwise.

CO-OPTION AND BALANCING

Such realities have naturally disposed Moscow to pursue co-option as its main instrument of policy. We referred earlier to its efforts to develop an anti-hegemonic consensus. But the issue goes beyond mere anti-Americanism or finding ways to mitigate Chinese influence. Since tsarist times, policy makers have pursued the idea of Russia as the great regional and global balancer. Today, this is reflected not only in the general idea of Russia as a bridge connecting East and West, but also in more specific balancing between the United States and China (use of the "China card"); Europe and East Asia (energy diplomacy); the United States and Iran; China and Japan; and China and India. At a time when strategic triangularism has become discredited almost everywhere else, Moscow has kept the faith through its renewed advocacy of a Moscow-Beijing-New Delhi "axis"[9] and ongoing efforts to give life to BRICs diplomacy (a sort of Asian trilateralism plus Brazil).

Underpinning these ideas is a dual rationale. First, Russia cannot alone counterbalance the United States in Asia; it must build a regional consensus or "concert" of great powers to that effect. This means developing closer, "strategic" partnerships with China and India, with smaller (but still influential) states such as Iran, and with multilateral organizations. Second, by co-opting others in an enterprise that many see as desirable—namely, the diminution of America's geopolitical and normative influence—it sees an opportunity to boost its Asian credentials. In effect, Russia seeks to portray itself as a good Asian citizen and "responsible stakeholder" in Asian affairs.[10] It would like to present its actions as being motivated not by geopolitical self-interest, but by a more altruistic desire to contribute to a stable and prosperous environment. In some instances this means uniting to oppose the intrusion of Western norms and values; in other cases, it assumes the guise of a mediatory role, as in negotiations over the Iranian and North Korean nuclear programs. It can also acquire more patrimonial forms, as in Russia's relationships with former Soviet Central Asia.

"Strategic Partnerships"

The most important element in Russia's response to the challenges it faces in Asia is its network of self-proclaimed "strategic partnerships": with China principally, but also with India, Iran, and Mongolia. Although the moniker "strategic partnership" has become devalued through overuse, it does point to those relationships that Moscow believes are in sound shape (or better), and where the bilateral atmosphere is relatively cordial.

China is by far Russia's largest and most important partner in Asia. Over the past twenty years, their relationship has been transformed from one of deep hostility to arguably the signal success of Russian foreign policy in the post-Soviet period. It is closer, more diverse, and more stable than at any time in its history, far surpassing the short-lived "unbreakable friendship" of the 1950s. There are no major bilateral disputes, following the formal demarcation of the frontier and tighter regulation of cross-border traffic. Trade has expanded tenfold in the past decade. And Chinese president Hu Jintao is happy to confirm that Moscow and Beijing agree on the core principles of international relations as well as the substance of major policy issues—opposing hegemonism, the need for a new international financial architecture, the evils of missile defense, and so on.

However, Sino-Russian interaction falls well short of the strategic partnership that both sides proclaim at every opportunity. There are critical differences in the way they view the world, their respective places in the international system, and the key priorities of their relationship. The partnership functions on the basis of selected common interests, not shared values. Their supposed convergence—strategic and normative—is superficial at best, and both attach far more importance to the West than they do to each other. Although the passage of time has dulled much of the historical animosity in the relationship, acute contradictions remain. Some Russians view China as a long-term existential threat, while others are concerned by the strategic implications of the growing imbalance in the relationship. For their part, the Chinese are often bemused by what they see as Moscow's gratuitously confrontational approach to international relations, and its unprofessional attitude to commercial cooperation. They are also contemptuous of Russia's failure to reinvent itself as a modern, diversified economy.[11]

India is one of Russia's stranger relationships. Indeed, it exemplifies the major flaw in Russia's approach toward Asia: the disjunction between veneer and substance. India, like China, is prepared to indulge Moscow and participate in public displays of BRIC solidarity, as in the June 2009 summit in Ekaterinburg. On the other hand, the bilateral relationship contains little substance. The last years of the Soviet era and the early 1990s were a period of mutual neglect, while later attempts by the Yeltsin administration to build a new relationship on the basis of a multipolar consensus proved fruitless. Under Putin, there was a brief period of improvement, based on expanded military and nuclear cooperation. But this too has not been sustained. The strategic rapprochement between Washington and New Delhi has overshadowed—and undermined—the modest progress in Russia-India relations, and the last two to three years have seen a slackening of momentum. Putin's efforts to resurrect the idea of a Moscow-Beijing-New Delhi axis have fallen on stony ground.

Iran is one of Moscow's more problematic partners, "strategic" though it purports to be. On the face of things, the relationship serves an important purpose in showcasing Russia as an indispensable regional and global player, the only effective intermediary between Tehran and the West. However, this image has suffered badly because of Moscow's inability to influence Iranian actions and the anti-Americanism that permeates some Russian official attitudes. The Ahmadinejad regime has been able to manipulate the situation at will, using Russia to counter Western pressure to curtail its nuclear program.[12] In the longer term, a strategically assertive Iran could pose a threat to Russia's control over its volatile southern republics and to its influence in Azerbaijan. Russia could find itself the object, rather than instigator, of anti-hegemonic politics.

With *Mongolia*, Russia benefits from the reality that Ulaanbaatar is more apprehensive about Beijing's intentions than it is about Moscow's. Russia finds itself in the useful position of being neither East nor West, a natural fit for Mongolia's "multipillared" foreign policy. It does not pose the threat that China is sometimes seen to present, and is not expected either to bankroll the Mongolians or support them against the Chinese. It can wait discreetly in the semi-background, taking (mainly commercial) opportunities as and when they arise.[13]

Russia's network of strategic partnerships offers certain strategic, political, and economic advantages. A good relationship with China, for instance, reinforces the RFE's territorial integrity. India and Iran are potential growth areas for military, nuclear, and energy cooperation. And Mongolia offers promising commercial possibilities for Russian companies. In the end, though, the most important dividend of such partnerships is symbolic. They are a way of demonstrating that Moscow is not beholden to the United States and Europe, that it has other foreign policy options. It is a matter of only secondary importance to the Putin regime that such alternatives do not actually exist. What is critical is that the West should subscribe to the illusion of Russian strategic choice and modify its behavior accordingly. The best example of the government's use of such leverage is the so-called China card in energy disputes with the West. Although Russia has no intention of diverting gas exports from its primary European markets to the Pacific Rim, raising this specter has spooked some EU member-states into pushing for a more accommodating line with Moscow on political and security (e.g., NATO enlargement) as well as energy issues.

Managing "Difficult States"

The second major component in Russia's approach to Asia is the management of relations with what might be described as "difficult states." These include, for differing reasons, Japan, the Democratic People's Republic of Korea (DPRK), Pakistan, Afghanistan, and the United States.

Attitudes toward *Japan* are highly ambivalent. On the one hand, the political atmosphere is poor, poisoned not only by an intractable territorial dispute,[14] but also by the fact that Japan is the U.S.'s closest ally in Asia. On the other hand, the Russian elite admire Japan, indeed more so than China. In some respects, Japan offers a template for a postmodern Russia. It is no less developed than the advanced Western countries, but retains a distinct national identity; it engages equally with East and West; it is a knowledge-based, technologically driven economy whose goods and services are in demand everywhere; and it possesses considerable international influence. Strategically, Russia would like a good relationship with Japan in order to be less China-dependent. In the real world, however, the territorial dispute impacts adversely every aspect of their interaction. Moscow's policy toward Japan is founded more on hope—that Tokyo will eventually drop its claims to the disputed islands and that this will lead to a flood of Japanese investment—than realism. It is no surprise that it is the least successful of Russia's relationships in Asia.

The *DPRK* is a special case. It is not badly disposed toward Russia, but its unpredictability makes it a nightmare to deal with. Moscow would like to influence Pyongyang and in Putin's first year as president harbored ambitions to this effect.[15] But it realizes that the United States and China are the only powers that have any input into the opaque world of DPRK policy making. Russia retains a formal status within the framework of the UN P-5 and the Korean Six-Party Talks (when these are not suspended), and has attempted to carve out a role as a facilitator—a position of some status yet minimal responsibility. But its evident lack of clout offers little incentive for Pyongyang (and others) to take it seriously in the negotiating process.

Pakistan is a "difficult state" for Russia in two respects. First, it is the major source of international terrorism today. Although the direct threat to Russia is not as acute as during the first and second Chechen wars, Islamic extremism destabilizes Russia's neighborhood in Central Asia. Second, Pakistan is difficult because of its enmity with India. Although the relationship between Moscow and New Delhi lacks substance, and has cooled somewhat following the U.S.-India rapprochement, it remains important to Moscow. Russian policy makers understand that India will become a global actor some time this century, and they are therefore minded to bet on it rather than Pakistan. This preference is reinforced by the notional possibility of using India at some stage to counterbalance China's growing power, as well as by the memory of the Soviet-Indian strategic relationship. For these reasons, Moscow has maintained its distance from Islamabad while, at the same time, hoping that Pakistan's domestic situation and relations with India do not deteriorate to critical levels.

Afghanistan's importance to Russia is indirect. Given the huge Western military and civilian presence in the country, not to mention the lingering effects of the disastrous Soviet occupation of 1979–89, Moscow's influence on the Karzai government and regional warlords is minimal. However, it retains a foothold by virtue of its continuing close ties with the elites of the former Soviet Central Asian states that neighbor Afghanistan. Russia has kept a watching brief, while opportunistically exploiting American difficulties with, for example, Kyrgyzstan over basing rights. The "prize" for Moscow is not influence in Afghanistan per se but the reassertion of Russia's leading role in wider Central Asia, to which the Afghan conflict provides a means to an end.

The *United States* is a problematic partner across the globe rather than in Asia as such. Moscow views its involvement in East Asia as more a plus than a minus. It is a different story in West and South Asia, where the United States and Russia are direct competitors, albeit with hugely different capabilities. For the most part, though, the Putin regime is keen to manage U.S.-Russia tensions. In Central Asia, it has hidden behind regional multilateral organizations such as the SCO and the Collective Security Treaty Organization (CSTO). This contrasts with its much more direct—and vigorous—response to the projection of U.S. influence in Russia's western (Ukraine, Belarus, Baltic states) and southwestern neighborhoods (the Transcaucasus).

Multilateralism and Pseudomultilateralism

Russian foreign policy has traditionally favored bilateral relationships over multilateral institutions. Nevertheless, multilateralism serves an important function by lending legitimacy to bilateral and great power arrangements. In recent years, it has acquired renewed value as a means of putting pressure on the United States, while highlighting Russia's "good international citizenship." In emphasizing the contrast with a "hegemonic" America, Russian policy makers pronounce their allegiance to "the primacy of the United Nations" and the "democratization" of international relations.

Multilateralism is an essential component of Moscow's approach toward Asia. In fact, there is no part of the world where it is more important to Russian objectives. The main reason for this is Russia's weak influence on the continent. Even its strongest relationship, the strategic partnership with

China, compares poorly to Beijing's far more significant ties with the United States. It is therefore logical that Moscow should give greater weight to multilateral institutions there than, say, in Europe, where its influence is much greater and its bilateral relationships are more substantial.

Russia has steadily increased its involvement with Asian multilateral institutions since the end of the Cold War, and especially under Putin. It is a member of the SCO, the CSTO, the Eurasian Economic Community (EurAsEC), the Asia-Pacific Economic Cooperation (APEC) grouping, the ASEAN Regional Forum (ARF), and the Korean Six-Party Talks. It is a dialogue partner of ASEAN (Association of Southeast Asian Nations) and an associate member of the Organization of Islamic Conference (OIC). Its membership in various bodies is important symbolically, promoting the idea that Russia truly belongs in the Asian community of nations.

But old habits die hard. Russia's commitment to multilateralism is more apparent than real. And far from persuading others of the sincerity of its intentions, the performance of senior Russian officials in bodies such as APEC has sometimes achieved the opposite effect, highlighting the "thinness" of Moscow's interest in pan-Asian diplomacy. In this connection, there is a crucial distinction to be made between multilateralism and multipolarity. The former entails collective consultation and decision making by multiple parties, including smaller and weaker states as well as the great powers. Multipolarity, on the other hand, is centered on the notion of a concert of great powers—"poles"—that would effectively be self-appointed guardians of the international system. Moscow's real commitment is to multipolarity, not multilateralism.

We should also distinguish between bona fide multilateralism and what the American conservative commentator Charles Krauthammer termed "pseudomultilateralism."[16] It is no coincidence that Moscow has shown greatest interest in the CSTO, EurAsEC, and the SCO. The first two are essentially pseudomultilateral organizations: they are managed out of Moscow and have an overtly geopolitical agenda. To some extent, they resemble the old Comecon (or Council for Mutual Economic Assistance—CMEA), which was multilateral in form but subjugated to the Soviet Union's prerogatives in Eastern Europe. The members of the CSTO and EurAsEC are not as blindly compliant as Comecon, as shown by their refusal to recognize the independence of Abkhazia and South Ossetia in 2008. But neither are they inclined to challenge Moscow on a regular basis.

Of all the Asian multilateral bodies of which Russia is a member, the SCO has proved the most substantial. Although its achievements are modest, it has shown a capacity to reach a regional consensus on certain issues, such as resisting the intrusion of "alien" (i.e., Western) democratic norms. Most importantly, the SCO operates in a generally collectivist and democratic fashion; while its member-states are scarcely equal, even the smallest of them—Kyrgyzstan and Tajikistan—are able to be heard. The organization's relatively high standing owes much to the perception that its decision making is much more multilateral in practice than that of the CSTO and EurAsEC.

Moscow has in the past attempted to position the SCO as a kind of "anti-NATO." Such ambitions, however, have been scuppered by China's dominant position within the organization. Beijing's primary interest is to use the SCO as cover to legitimize the re-entry of China as a major player in Central Asia. Anxious to avoid any suggestion that the organization's activities are directed against American interests, it promotes panregional cooperation instead: in counterterrorism, reinforcing the Central Asian regimes, and developing trade and economic ties. As China has consolidated its leadership role within the organization, the SCO's utility to Russia has correspondingly diminished. The failure of the 2008 SCO summit in Dushanbe, Tajikistan, to support Moscow's diplomatic recognition of Abkhazia and South Ossetia exposed the limits of Russian influence.

Russia's Asia Project—Aspiration over Achievement

The Asianization of Russian foreign policy has been geographically extensive. Over the past decade, Moscow's relationships with most Asian countries and multilateral institutions have expanded, in some cases considerably. This improvement has been multifaceted, affecting political ties, trade volumes, military cooperation, cultural links, and human contacts. There is a greater awareness, too, of the importance of Asia in global affairs and how it bears on Moscow's conduct of international relations.

Nevertheless, it is difficult to argue that Russia's position across Asia *as a whole* is significantly, if at all, better than it was at the outset of the Putin presidency. Despite the expansion in political and commercial ties with individual Asian nations, Russia continues to be viewed as an outsider. Although it has a role to play in the Korean Six-Party Talks and Afghanistan, this is scarcely because of its Asian credentials. In the former case, Russia's (limited) influence derives not from its location in Northeast Asia, but from its membership in the P-5—in other words, because of its *global* rather than regional importance. Russia's impact in Afghanistan is similarly indirect. It has minimal capacity to influence developments in that country, but can complicate the U.S. coalition's pursuit of the war by pressuring the former Soviet Central Asian states that adjoin Afghanistan. Meanwhile, Moscow's attempts to play the Eurasian card—Russia as a bridge between East and West—are routinely ignored.

Even in the best of circumstances, Russia faces an uphill struggle. History, civilization, political and economic realities, and demographic distribution conspire to ensure that it will never be seen as an Asian country in the same way as China, India, or even the United States (which has been at the heart of Asian affairs for more than a century). At the same time, however, Moscow's attempts to give Russia an Asian face have been undermined by misconceived assumptions and policy miscalculations.

In reviewing Russia's eastern dimension one is struck by three critical contradictions. The first is the disjunction between Moscow's pro-Asian rhetoric and the continuing Westerncentrism of its foreign policy. The second is the tension between ideological and pragmatic considerations. And the third is the conflict between Moscow's Sinocentric bias and its publicly expressed desire to adopt a more geographically balanced approach in Asia. The upshot of these contradictions is that Moscow's eastern ambitions remain substantially unrealized. Russia is not a serious player in the continent's affairs, much less an Asian power.

THE CURSE OF INSTRUMENTALISM

Russia's most damaging failing is a zero-sum instrumentalism. It has often appeared as if Asia is viewed almost entirely through the prism of Russia's global strategy. As such, it is less an area of intrinsic interest than a theater of geopolitical competition with the United States, a strategic and normative counterweight to a still dominant West, and a default option for Russian foreign policy.

The course of the Sino-Russian relationship in the post-Soviet era illustrates this well. Typically, Moscow has amplified the strategic partnership in times when Russia's relations with the United States have been in serious difficulty—in the latter half of the 1990s and especially during Putin's second presidential term (2004–08). Conversely, China has been pushed backstage whenever Moscow has sought to rebuild or develop closer ties with Washington, for example in the aftermath of 9/11. Putin's decision to endorse the U.S. force deployment in Afghanistan and use of bases in former Soviet Central Asia; his ready acquiescence in Washington's withdrawal from the 1972 Anti-Ballistic Missile (ABM) Treaty; the conclusion of the Strategic Offensive Reductions Treaty (SORT) in April 2002; and the establishment of the Russia-NATO Council one month later—highlighted where Moscow's true priorities lay.[17] More recently, the Obama administration's call to "reset" Russia-U.S. relations has rekindled hopes in Moscow that Russia, rather than China, will become America's principal "other" in addressing major global challenges—starting (but not ending) with strategic disarmament, Iran, and the war in Afghanistan.

Russian instrumentalism in Asia is not restricted to employing the China card. It is apparent also in unsuccessful efforts to recruit India in an antihegemonic coalition; transparent attempts to depict Russia as a part of the Islamic world; and propagation of the misguided concept of the BRICs. The reaction of the major Asian powers to Moscow's instrumentalism is revealing. They have not rejected these overtures out of hand, seeing them as occasionally useful in promoting their own agendas. But they have not allowed them to derail their vastly more significant ties with the United States. The last decade has witnessed a boom in U.S.-China and U.S.-India relations that has far outweighed progress in the Sino-Russian and Indo-Russian strategic partnerships. And whereas Beijing and New Delhi identify a continued role for Washington in co-managing the Asian security environment, they have quietly marginalized Russia from their respective subregions. Moscow has no meaningful input into South Asian affairs, and its profile in East Asia is almost as low.

Summing up, the "curse of instrumentalism" is threefold. At the basic human level, it is demeaning to countries whose global importance is increasing rapidly, and whose strategic choices are expanding all the time. It confirms that Moscow still views Asia as less important than the West. Unfortunately, a largely friendless Russia has greater need for China and India than these countries have for Russia. Indeed, Russia's support is sometimes viewed as a mixed blessing. At a time when China, in particular, is striving to show itself as a benign actor, it has found it useful to keep a little distance from a state that has a poor international image.

Second, an overtly instrumental approach offers little incentive to take Russia seriously as a contributor to Asian security and prosperity. Even where it has the potential to be a player, for example in supplying oil and gas to Northeast Asia, its record suggests that it is more interested in geopolitical maneuvering than actual cooperation.[18] The intrusion of ulterior agendas is literally a deal-killer.

Third, by allowing its Asia policies to be contingent on the fluctuations in Russia-West relations, Moscow has earned a well-deserved reputation as an unreliable partner. The twenty-year saga of the East Siberian-Pacific Ocean oil pipeline; the vicissitudes of the territorial dispute with Japan; the on-off sale of the aircraft carrier *Admiral Gorshkov* to India; foot-dragging over construction of the Bushehr nuclear reactors in Iran—are all examples of policies that have undermined Russia's standing on the continent. To many Asians, such cases confirm that its handling of international relations is largely opportunistic, and influenced more by allergy than strategy. A stark illustration of this came in August 2008 with the ill-advised decision to recognize Abkhazia and South Ossetia as sovereign states—a move not supported by a single Asian country.

THE DELUSION OF NORMATIVE CONVERGENCE

The second major impediment to a more effective Asian policy is closely related to the first. In their Westerncentrism, Russian decision makers retain many of the ideological hang-ups of the Cold War period. Although the confrontation between communism and democratic capitalism is long over, there is a new stand-off today between what may loosely be called "Western" norms and values on the one hand, and an authoritarian, nationalistic set of beliefs on the other. This contest between Russia and the West is especially evident in the European "common neighborhood"—Ukraine, Belarus, Moldova, Georgia, and Azerbaijan—but is also apparent in Central Asia and across Eurasia more broadly.

The ideologization of Russia's Asia policy is demonstrated most vividly in its invocations against the "tyranny" of the "Anglo-Saxon" model. Moscow challenges the universalization of Western norms and values and calls for a new normative consensus that would introduce radical changes to regional and global governance, including a central role for Russia.

The chief purpose of such exercises is to promote Russia's return as a great transcontinental power. However, Moscow has overestimated the utility of normative bandwagoning and underestimated the lack of enthusiasm in Asia for a more influential Russian role. In the first case, the normative convergence between Russia and Asian powers such as China is illusory. While both countries reject external, that is, Western, criticisms of their political systems and handling of human rights, there is very little sense within either elite of a shared set of beliefs. The very fact that Russians see themselves as belonging to European civilization disqualifies them ipso facto from partaking of the same philosophical well as China's mix of Confucianism and legalism.[19] Conversely, the Chinese perception of Russia as a Western power with a strongly Westerncentric focus means that they cannot conceive of the Sino-Russian partnership as the kernel of an emerging world order. On the contrary, the growing imbalance between the two countries ensures that Beijing looks at Russia in increasingly instrumental terms: as a useful ally in certain, relatively specific situations, such as emasculating American attempts to introduce harsh sanctions against Iran, a key energy supplier to China.

The fundamental problem with Russia's ideological-normative approach is that it misses the point. Instead of making positive engagement with Asian countries and institutions the centerpiece of its Asia strategy, Moscow has allowed the latter to be hijacked by instrumental and ideological considerations. Ultimately, it is a Westerncentric and Americacentric approach masquerading as an Asia strategy. The contrast with China's pragmatic stance is instructive. Although Beijing blames the United States for the global financial crisis, it has not allowed such criticisms to derail Sino-American cooperation. While it calls for a new financial architecture and reforms to global governance, it continues to funnel billions of dollars into U.S. treasury bonds. And while it talks in bullish terms about China's "inevitable rise," it is only too happy for the United States to assume the burden of global leadership—as indicated by its lukewarm response to the idea of a Sino-American G-2.[20]

The limits of normative convergence are even clearer when one looks at Moscow's attempts to make common cause with other Asian powers. As the world's largest democracy, India has nothing in common with Putin's Russia. At the other end of the normative spectrum, Iranian theocracy could scarcely be more different from Russia's strongly secular form of government. The ideologization of Moscow's approach, embodied in the fantasy of a new world order, is not only irrelevant to contemporary realities, but also inimical to Russia's strategic interests in Asia.

THE SINOCENTRIC BIAS

But nowhere are the shortcomings in Russia's Asian "strategy" as evident as in its handling of the relationship with China. Although Sino-Russian rapprochement has been one of the few successes of post-Soviet foreign policy, one negative consequence is that Russia's *regional* focus in Asia has become increasingly and unhealthily Sinocentric. The China relationship dwarfs Moscow's ties with all the other Asian countries, including major powers such as Japan and India. As the Putin regime has become closer to the Chinese, so it has progressively alienated the Japanese, Indians, and, to some extent, the South Koreans. The implications of Moscow's Sinocentric bias have been magnified in the larger context of Russian foreign policy, in particular the deterioration of Russia-West relations in recent years. Inevitably, and often justifiably, a pro-engagement line with Beijing has been equated with an anti-American choice. In these circumstances, it is hardly surprising that Russia's relations with close U.S. allies such as Japan and the Republic of Korea should lose impetus, or that the much improved atmosphere between Washington and New Delhi should have an adverse effect on Russia-India ties.

Moscow finds itself in something of a Catch-22 situation. In order to expand its political and economic presence in Asia, it must cultivate the relationship with Beijing. However, the more it talks up their partnership, the fewer are the chances for a more broadly based, comprehensive engagement in Asia. In fact, the problem lies less with Russia's China policy than with its approach to international affairs more generally. As long as this is driven by an outmoded sense of strategic entitlement, relations with the United States and the West will not improve substantially. And geopolitical balancing and zero-sum calculus, rather than positive-sum engagement, will continue to determine Russia's policy choices in Asia.

In the end, Russia could end up with the worst of all worlds. There are already signs that the Sino-Russian relationship is losing momentum. Such fig leaves as the June 2009 BRICs summit in Ekaterinburg cannot hide the reality that China engages much more with the West than with Russia. The global financial crisis has accentuated this trend, highlighting the centrality of the United States in the international system; Russia's exceptional vulnerability;[21] and the unfeasibility of an alternative, "multipolar" world order anytime soon. Meanwhile, the remarkable expansion of Chinese economic and now political interests in Central Asia raises serious doubts about Russia's regional leadership. Moscow's difficulties with the West and neglect of ties with other significant Asian players mean that it has little opportunity, even if it felt disposed, to make common strategic cause with Washington, Tokyo, or New Delhi in response to a rising China. The future, then, could be not so much one of "China or bust," but of Russia's strategic bankruptcy. Other powers would continue to pay lip service to its "indispensable" role, but bypass it on the decisions that mattered.

The Way Forward

All this begs the question of whether Russia is doomed to remain an outsider in Asian affairs or whether it can develop an effective and sustainable approach instead. It is tempting to take a fatalist view and resign oneself to the fact that Russia will always be a European civilization, with a necessarily Westerncentric worldview. But with the greater part of its territory—and natural resources—located in Asia, this is not a luxury it can afford. Although the extent of the shift in global power to the East has been exaggerated, there is no question that the twenty-first century will, in many respects, be an Asian century, dominated by emerging superpowers such as China and India, as well as by other, increasingly important regional powers (Indonesia, Pakistan, Iran). If Russia is to have any significant input in international decision making, then it must find ways to improve the quality of its engagement in Asia.

A successful strategy toward Asia cannot be divorced from a sea change in the overall conduct of Russian foreign policy. More than two decades after Mikhail Gorbachev introduced the concept of "new thinking," there is need for a fresh lease on life in Moscow's approach to the world.[22] Although the Cold War is over, Russian foreign policy is scarcely any less geopolitical today than it was then. The methods of projecting power and influence have become more diverse, but the major goals are much the same: assertion of Russia's "destiny" as a great global power; counterbalancing America; and retaining political and economic control over the neighborhood. As long as such objectives remain paramount, there is little likelihood of significant improvement in policy making toward Asia, or of a more welcoming attitude in Asia toward Russian interests.

The obvious way forward for Moscow is to unburden itself of pointless geopolitical and normative baggage (the "multipolar world order," BRICs summitry, etc.) and concentrate instead on developing a positive Asian agenda. Such an agenda would be largely independent of the periodic crises and revivals that characterize Russia-U.S. relations. It would focus on long-term, but tangible, goals: energy cooperation (not just in oil and gas, but also nuclear and electricity); trade in commodities and natural resources (nonferrous metals, timber, and water); and human contacts through cultural diplomacy and tourism. Economic engagement would become the prime engine of Russia's integration into the Asian community.

This process would be gradual, and there would undoubtedly be setbacks along the way. But in the long run, a more depoliticized—and non-ideological—approach would reap major dividends. It would showcase those areas where Russia has much to contribute, while downplaying the elements of its policies that make it an unattractive partner. Moscow would eschew grand geopolitical schemes—obsessing about the distribution of power and influence—in favor of measurable outcomes, such as the rigorous implementation of energy deals.[23] It would contribute to the development of a new financial architecture, not through idle posturing about the ruble as an international reserve currency, but by working modestly but effectively with Asian (and other) countries within the G-20 framework.

In terms of "hard" priorities, constructive Russian engagement in Asia would incorporate greater intelligence sharing in conflict resolution (Korean peninsula, Iran), counterterrorism, WMD nonproliferation, and combating transnational crime. Military and security cooperation would not be restricted to "strategic partners" such as China, but would extend to Asian countries with very different political systems—Japan, South Korea, and India. This would enhance the prospects of a new security consensus, one that brings together all the major players on the continent. In the same spirit, Moscow would also adopt a more calibrated and responsible approach to arms sales in Asia. Instead of resorting to the barely credible justification that Russian arms are exported for solely defensive purposes, Moscow would show greater sensitivity to the security concerns of others.

Of course, it is not easy to envisage such a transformation today. Moscow will continue to view Asia in predominantly geopolitical and instrumental terms as long as Russia-U.S. relations fail to reach a lasting and positive equilibrium. Although the atmosphere between Moscow and Washington has improved over the past year and the START agreement has been negotiated, the two sides disagree fundamentally on many things: how to manage Iran;

influence and engagement in the former Soviet space; the role of NATO; and the nature of a new Euro-Atlantic security architecture. Some of these essentially extraneous issues will cast their shadow over Russia's engagement with Asia for many years to come.

Furthermore, while the changing realities of global power—specifically, the rise of China and India—will force Russian decision makers to pay greater attention to Asian affairs, this does not necessarily mean that Moscow's worldview will become more Asian. Russian foreign policy could become more introspective—in a reversion to Lenin's concept of the "besieged fortress" (*osazhdennaya krepost*)—or turn increasingly to Europe. In the latter connection, it has been suggested that Russia and the EU should work together to ensure that both continue to exercise influence in an international system that would otherwise be dominated by the United States and China. In this event, Russia's worldview would become even more Westerncentric than it is today. Doctrinally, Moscow might continue to speak of a new multipolar order and a multivectored foreign policy. But in practical terms, it would be focused more than ever on engagement with Europe (and the United States), with Asia occupying its customarily secondary role. Russia would remain the perennial outsider in Asian affairs.

What It Means for the West

Some of the Western reaction to Russia's engagement in Asia has verged on the hysterical. Talk about the rise of "authoritarian capitalism" and a Sino-Russian "alliance of autocrats" raises fears of a normative convergence between Moscow, Beijing, and other Asian capitals.[24] Viewed through this lens, the Asianization of Russian foreign policy presages growing tensions with the West and, in time, a tectonic shift whereby Russia aligns itself with the "non-West" in more or less permanent opposition to the United States and Europe.

As noted earlier, such fears are misconceived. First, the Russian elite has no interest in abandoning the West for the East. For all the rhetoric, Moscow takes its external points of reference from the West—political, economic, technological, military, cultural, and normative. Although Asia has become more important in the Russian mind, it continues to be seen as second-rate and certainly alien. There has been no discernible Asianization of Russian values.[25]

Second, in the improbable event that Russia were to go against the grain of its history, traditions, and instincts to become an Asian power one day, there is nothing to suggest that Asia would welcome it into its bosom. Asian countries, big and small alike, are far more interested in doing business with the West than with Russia. Even the DPRK, the world's most totalitarian state, looks to Washington not Moscow, while Iran appears to value cooperation with Russia in very specific areas only, such as the nuclear industry.

Third, the larger the alleged Asian consensus, the more unwieldy it becomes. Together, its putative members amount to considerably less than the sum of their parts. Through our Western lens, we overestimate the unity within organizations such as the SCO or ASEAN, and underestimate the competing interests and jealousies that undermine their effectiveness. In focusing on Russia's assertive behavior in its European neighborhood, we ignore the myriad of rivalries across Asia—between Russia and China in Central Asia; China and India across the board; China and Japan in East Asia; India and Pakistan; Iran and the Arab Middle East. In this disordered pluralistic environment,[26] the notion of an emerging anti-Western consensus is nonsensical.

Meanwhile, the United States remains at the forefront of global affairs, notwithstanding its trials over the past decade. This is not only a function of a more internationalist administration in the White House but also longer term "facts on the ground." The global economic downturn is said to herald the irrevocable decline of the West. Yet it has also highlighted that there is *no alternative to* the United States as long as China and India remain decades away from completing their modernization. Bandwagoning behind an anti-Western consensus makes no sense at all because there is no "Eastern alternative," least of all for Russia, but also for China, India, and other Asian countries. Instead, there is a global system, characterized by growing interdependency, and which over time will evolve naturally—and gradually—in response to changing international realities. We are indeed witnessing a shift in global power to the East, but it is far slower and more uneven than many suppose.

Counterintuitive though it may seem, the West has a genuine stake in a more active and effective Russian engagement in Asia. A successful Russia would be one that focuses on economic cooperation rather than indulging in futile geopolitical games; that is influential in key areas such as counter-terrorism and WMD counterproliferation; that has developed constructive ties with major Asian countries (Japan and India, as well as China) and multilateral institutions; and that is a serious contributor to Eurasian security and prosperity. The problem for the West today is that Russia has achieved none of these things. This not only deprives us of its important contribution on a host of vital issues but also generates considerable frustration and resentment in Moscow. In these unpromising circumstances, it is hardly surprising that some Russian decision makers believe that the only way to make an impact in Asia is to play the part of regional and global spoiler.

The challenge for policy makers everywhere is to deal with the world as it is, not as they might hope—or fear—to see it. For Moscow, notions such as the BRICs and a "new world order" cannot form the basis of effective decision making because they bear so little relation to reality. If Russia is ever to develop a successful eastern dimension, then it must be on the basis of pragmatic, unsentimental, and non-ideological engagement. Equally, it would be absurd for the United States or the major European powers to construct policy in response to a nonexistent authoritarian alliance, or to counter Russian objectives merely because they emanate from Moscow. Just as Russia needs to develop a more positive, less geopolitical agenda in Asia, so America and Europe should look to engage it—in Asia as well as Europe—in meeting real rather than imaginary challenges.

Notes

1. Dmitri Trenin, *Integratsiya i identichnost: Rossiya kak "novy zapad,"* (Moscow: Evropa, 2006), 169–70.
2. Robert Kagan, *The Return of History and the End of Dreams* (London: Atlantic Books, 2008), 53, 71–74.
3. Bobo Lo, *Axis of Convenience: Moscow, Beijing, and the New Geopolitics* (Washington, DC: Brookings and Chatham House, 2008), 18–19.
4. This reached a peak in 2006, with some two million Russian visitors to China and 900,000 Chinese visitors to Russia.
5. As a result of the "unequal" treaties of Aigun (1858), Peking (1860), and Tarbagatai (1864), the Russian Empire acquired around one-and-a-half million square kilometers of Chinese territory, including the southern part of the present-day Russian Far East.

6. Samuel P. Huntington, *The Clash of Civilizations and the Remaking of World Order* (London: Touchstone Books, 1998), 139.
7. The original phrase is "while Russia is in Asia, it is not of Asia." See F. Kazemzadeh, review of *Russia and Asia: Essays on the Influence of Russia on the Asian People*, ed. W. S. Vucinich, *Journal of Modern History* 47, no. 1 (March 1974): 173.
8. The government of Kyrgyzstan has, on two separate occasions, indicated its intention to close the U.S. base at Manas. Both times, Washington has managed to stave off closure by significantly increasing the rent for the base. Following the latest revolution in April 2010, there is speculation that the new interim government may revisit the agreement, although the situation remains very unclear.
9. Yevgeny Primakov first broached the idea of a Moscow-Beijing-New Delhi axis during a visit to India in December 1998.
10. The phrase "responsible stakeholder" was first coined by Robert Zoellick in September 2005 in relation to China.
11. This dismissive attitude has been reinforced by the circumstances of the global financial crisis, which showed Russia to be the worst-performing of the G-20 economies in 2009. The word in Beijing and Shanghai is of "BICs, not BRICs." Author's conversations in Beijing and Shanghai, 2009.
12. More recently, there have been signs that Moscow's patience is wearing thin. In May 2010, Russia and China approved tougher UN sanctions against Iran. The sanctions, although limited, may signal a new and more difficult phase in the relationship.
13. Mongolia is especially rich in mineral deposits (copper, molybdenum, uranium, gold, and silver), an area in which Russian mining companies have considerable experience.
14. Under the 1945 Yalta agreement between Stalin, Roosevelt, and Churchill, the Soviet Union agreed to enter the war against Japan within three months of the end of the war in Europe. In return for fulfilling this commitment, it regained Sakhalin and acquired the Kurile islands, including the southernmost island, which had never been under Russian rule. Since then, Russia and Japan have disputed the sovereignty of what Moscow calls the South Kuriles, and Tokyo, the Northern Territories.
15. During Putin's visit to Pyongyang in July 2000, Kim Jong-Il undertook to discontinue the DPRK's nuclear weapons program. He claimed subsequently that he had been "joking."
16. Charles Krauthammer, "The Unipolar Moment," *Foreign Affairs* 70, no. 1 (Winter 1990/1991).
17. Although Beijing's reaction has generally been muted, its concerns have emerged from time to time, notably following Putin's endorsement of U.S. bases in central

Asia. See Yevgeny Primakov, *Russian Crossroads: Toward the New Millennium* (New Haven: Yale University Press, 2004), 71.

18. Comments by Chinese interlocutors, Beijing and Shanghai, May 2009.
19. See Ross Terrill, *The New Chinese Empire—and What It Means for the United States* (New York: Basic Books, 2004), 67–72.
20. The Chinese are flattered by the prestige that the G-2 idea confers on them. However, they worry they might be called on to fulfill responsibilities for which they are not ready, and that would prove a distraction from urgent tasks of domestic modernization.
21. Among the major economies, Russia has arguably been the greatest casualty of the global financial crisis. GDP growth in 2009 was -7.9 percent, compared to China's +8.7 percent.
22. Mikhail Gorbachev, *Perestroika: New Thinking for Our Country and the World* (London: Collins, 1987).
23. A twenty-year oil-for-loan agreement between China National Petroleum Company (CNPC) and Rosneft and Transneft has been interpreted by some as evidence that Russia is finally getting serious about energy cooperation with China. It is worth noting, though, that a similar oil-for-loan agreement was reached in 2004 between CNPC and Rosneft, but came under increasing strain as a result of the boom in oil prices. Rosneft first secured a renegotiation of the original agreement, then advised CNPC that it would not extend the arrangement beyond 2010. Although the collapse in oil prices following the global economic downturn led to a change of heart, it remains to be seen how resilient the new agreement will be.
24. See Kagan, *Return of History*; also John Kampfner, *Freedom for Sale: How We Made Money and Lost Our Liberty* (London: Simon and Schuster, 2009).
25. If Russia does have an authoritarian tradition, as many suggest, then it is homegrown. It certainly predates the Mongol invasion.
26. Lo, *Axis of Convenience*, 170–72.

CHAPTER FOURTEEN

Russia and the Newly Independent States of Central Asia: Relations Transformed

Rustem Zhangozha

Translated by Siriol Hugh-Jones

Setting Up "The Problem"

This chapter is devoted to an analysis of the new kind of relations developing between Russia and the post-Soviet countries of Central Asia. Fifteen states emerged from the collapse of the Soviet Union, among them five in Central Asia—Kazakhstan, Uzbekistan, Tajikistan, Kyrgyzstan, and Turkmenistan. Even a quick look at the literature shows that most of the research carried out on the countries of Central Asia has been done by non-Central Asian researchers who base their findings on what they observe from outside.[1] This paves the way for an opportunity for more detailed comparative analysis, a reconstruction of the complex symptoms and features of the relations the Central Asian countries have with each other in the context of the development of relations with Russia as seen "from within" Central Asia.

It remains an indisputable fact that global politics, history, culture, and value systems (at least in modern and contemporary history) have been viewed by generations of Central Asian populations through the prism of the Russian position toward them. Even today, this view of the world is unchanged, largely due to information flow inertia but also in no small part as a result of the considerable media resources and technology that Russia continues to direct toward the region. It is for this reason that, when trying to analyze the domestic politics of Central Asian countries, we have to interpret them in the context of Russian influence as the dominant factor. This is so whether the local elites, and in particular radical nationalists, like it or not.

Ever since they first arrived in Central Asia, the Soviets resolutely set about destroying the traditional hierarchy of local societies. Those who were similar to Soviet Russia in terms of class were promoted to the top of the power pyramid. The criteria for upward mobility within society and the political cadres were no longer a relatively good education and high level of culture as developed over generations, but devotion to the Bolshevist regime.

Another axis of Bolshevist power in the region became the two changes of alphabet (initially, Arabic script was replaced with the Latin script and Cyrillic was introduced later, in 1939). This meant that previous written sources were no longer accessible, and cultural and historical continuity was no longer an issue. Under these conditions, when the regional culture was placed "out of bounds" of the accepted culture and lost its legitimacy, the question of cultural heritage and continuity ceased to exist even for the local population. Persuaded en masse that their society and culture were invalid, their only option was to adapt to the new reality and rules of existence.

Russia's Historical Involvement in Central Asia

Whatever the miscalculations of Kremlin ideologues' domestic policies, under the influence of Russia Central Asia was given an enormous push toward Westernizing its way of life and modernizing its infrastructure. With the adoption of the Russian language, the region's national cultures gained access to world culture and advancements in science and production. Over the years of Soviet rule, educational institutions were set up in the republics of Central Asia in which the teaching was geared toward European standards. In a relatively short period, these republics saw the foundation of universities and national academies of science to which qualified scientists and teachers were sent from Russia's academic centers and universities. Given its significant potential resources, production facilities were set up in the region (although most of them were fairly basic refining facilities) as a result of which industrial development followed and consequently a domestic working class. Reforms were carried out to modernize agricultural production, and connections were established between sectors for the creation of a unified production, farming, and retail complex both regionally and throughout the Soviet Union.

All these radical changes were constructive in nature and facilitated a sharp rise in the modernization of the Central Asian Soviet republics. A still stronger impetus for their industry, economy, and agriculture came about as a result of the evacuation of industrial enterprises (with their skilled workers) from the western regions of the Soviet Union during World War II and the enormous campaign to develop virgin and fallow land and industrialize the national economies of the Central Asian republics.

These developments (which were also the subject of intensive propaganda through the local media) created a positive attitude toward Russia as the source and promoter of world culture. As a result of profound structural changes, the population and, primarily, the intelligentsia of the Central Asian "civilized" region began to think of itself as an integral part of a larger Soviet country and therefore did not—except for a few small, relatively uninfluential groups of human rights activists—support a departure from the USSR. The most radical demands made of Moscow came down to the right to study their own history and culture based on their intrinsic features and traditions without being constrained by Kremlin ideology and to widen the context in which native languages were used. Compliance with these demands would not have involved any sort of compromise on the part of Russia. On the contrary, it would have reinforced its authority as the country that brought to the region the civilizing achievements of world culture and enabled their implementation in local conditions.

The forced exit, in 1991, from a once-united country left the fledgling states of the region outside the cultural habitat they were already used to. For its nascent nation states, this unexpected independence came as a major and, judging from the current state of their national economies, education, and security systems, comprehensive threat of their marginalization as full members of the global community and the international political structure.

Central Asia

GEOPOLITICS AND POLITICAL ECONOMY

The Belovezhskie Accords, signed on December 8, 1991, by the heads of the three Slavic republics, established the Commonwealth of Independent States (CIS) and officially marked the end of the USSR. A few days later, Nursultan Nazarbaev and the other Central Asian leaders declared themselves ready to join the new union. However, their appeal was ignored by the initiators of the USSR's collapse. The mayor of Moscow, Yuri Luzhkov, venomously described the CIS as a "union of three Russian fur hats and five Tartar skullcaps." During the extraordinary special summit that followed in Ashgabat, the region's leaders endeavored to develop a common line in response to the altercation that had occurred. However, since the Kremlin had completely ignored this meeting, no coherent position was achieved, apart from mutual promises to give each other every possible support.

The collapse of the USSR was a transformational event for the region, yet its effect was to leave the geopolitical format of Central Asia unchanged. Rather unexpectedly for them, the five former Soviet republics acquired sovereignty but the Soviet borders to the south and the east remained closed.

When China decided to open its western borders it did so on its own terms. First, it initiated the introduction of a normative legal basis with the creation of a regional collective security organization (initially, the "Shanghai Five," which then became the Shanghai Cooperation Organization—the SCO—in 1997). This organization provided that citizens and residents of the signatory states were categorically banned from participating in any kind of separatist propaganda aimed at relations with Xinjiang.

Next, the regional borders southwest of Central Asia were suddenly opened, thanks to the United States, which was restricting Taliban advances into the region. For the first time since the 1930s, there was the prospect of an unrestricted exchange of trade and information over a border that had previously been firmly shut, and the use of Afghanistan as a way of establishing links with Pakistan and India and other states on the shores of the Indian Ocean.[2]

The region's internal stratification was clearly divided into three different geographic zones: agricultural—the towns and oases; nomadic—the steppe area; and mountain-nomadic—the mountain regions; these were the historical homelands of nations that were radically different both in their economic and social structure and in their psychological and behavioral stereotypes. Nomadic cattle herders preferred flat to vertical forms of social organization. Those living in densely populated oasis towns were organized along the strict lines of demarcation that are a feature of complex hierarchical systems. The "hill peoples," particularly the Pamirs and Pashtuns, developed cultures that emphasized their group identity through religious, ethnocultural, and sociopolitical relations with the hostile environment around them.

For all the region's cultural, political, geographical, and linguistic variety there are two respects in which it can be regarded as homogenous: its natural resources, and the incontrovertible fact that greater Central Asia occupies a crucial geopolitical position between major players in international politics that surround the region.

Questions about the definition of borders and the status of Central Asia are not new: as early as 1904 this issue was defined as the region's dominant feature in the high-profile lecture "The Geographical Pivot of History" given by the British geographer Halford John Mackinder at London's Royal Geographical Society.[3] In the context of this issue the very real question arises of what criteria should be used to measure the degree to which this region is part of the periphery or the "heartland" referred to by Mackinder. Many indicators could be used to examine this, but undoubtedly the most promising is that linked to political control.

At a second meeting of Central Asia's heads of state in Tashkent (in summer 1992) a representative from Azerbaijan was also present as an observer. At neither of these meetings was the idea of creating a Turkestan Federation (or Confederation) touched upon. The parties restricted themselves to signing a series of important international economic and cultural agreements, thereby indirectly confirming the comment of an anonymous observer's that "the nations of Central Asia sleep under the same blanket but dream different dreams." However, the prospect of creating an international association of the Turkic-speaking peoples of Central Asia—a call also coming at this time from the Association of Turkic Nations, which had held its own conference in Almaty in December 1991—was unreservedly welcomed and supported by the region's national intelligentsias.[4]

Proof of this is the fact that its three closest southern neighbors, Turkey, Iran, and Pakistan, began actively infiltrating Central Asia's markets, which were promising and extensive, though not well organized. These countries understood that, having offered assistance to the "brothers emerging from Soviet captivity into freedom," they could expect to occupy privileged positions when it came to the development and subsequent sharing of the region's significant natural resources; to be market leaders for goods and services, while at the same time lobbying for their interests at all levels of government in the newly formed countries. It was for these reasons that they actively participated in the implementation of the major project proposed by Nursultan Nazerbaev to create a Trans-Asian rail link and road following the ancient Silk Road.

Perhaps that was also why, a little later, the region was visited by a series of official and well-meaning visitors, Margaret Thatcher, James Baker, Turgut

Özal, Ali Akbar Velayati, and, hot on their heels, other leaders of the international community. China became noticeably more active. On the one hand, it was afraid (with some cause) that the new region would have a bad influence on the Turkic-speaking population of Eastern Turkestan, which includes the Xinjiang Uyghur Autonomous Region. On the other, it was afraid of ending up "at the back of the line" when various lucrative economic agreements with the countries of the "Central Asian Klondike" were parceled out. These promised considerable political dividends as well as further geopolitical prospects.

In this "market of supply and demand" it was impossible to ignore the still-powerful figure of Russia, which, having recognized the wasted opportunity of a "Slavic union" and the clear failure of its European overtures, did not want to lose control of its former empire, particularly as a significant share of its human resources remained in the region, together with an established manufacturing and communications infrastructure.

Of course, Russia has by no means exhausted its potential for effective maneuvering: for the Central Asian countries the presence of Russia could act as a counterbalance to the potential dangers of expansion on the part of both China and the "Muslim brothers." Within the region, Kyrgyzstan and in particular Tajikistan are interested in a union with Russia. They both have good reason to fear territorial encroachment from Uzbekistan, whose population is expanding and spilling over its state borders. As far as Kazakhstan is concerned, ethnically, almost half its people are Russian-speakers, so it simply has no choice but to engage in a policy of compromise and complementarity with Russia.

Russia endeavors to institutionalize its relations with the countries of Central Asia through the creation, at its own initiative, of commercial, political, economic, and military structures. But organizations such as the CIS, the Collective Security Treaty Organization (CSTO), and the Eurasian Economic Community (EurAsEC) are not yet yielding the necessary results. It would seem that in the years these organizations have existed, their effectiveness has yet to match their aims. The numerous projects set out in the many documents adopted at summits between participating members remain unrealized "good intentions." In the real practice of relations between the CIS countries and members of the CSTO and EurAsEC themselves, so many problems and disagreements have accumulated that they look less like good, reliable business partners and more like fractious neighbors suspicious of any and every move the others make.

In a word, taking into account the contraction of the different political and economic interests of the most diverse participants in these "Central Asian intrigues," one might conclude that the fragile equilibrium that exists today is almost bound to break, and that Zbigniew Brzezinski's description of the region as the "Central Asian Balkans" could become a tragic reality in the foreseeable future.[5]

Should the region become part of the new global market with consequential improvements to its social system and economy, this would give its population a genuine feeling of affluence and social stability (though not as much as they might have liked). But this would render it a relatively passive object of international politics, bearing the brunt of political and economic pressures linked to the interests of major transnational financial and industrial groups in the region's natural resources. On the other hand, the creation of a new regional, strategically unified formation would involve an approach to nation-state development that is the diametric opposite of that.

Central Asian Economic Integration

The strategically misguided economic development model adopted by the countries of Central Asia, which is oriented toward the export of natural resources instead of the development of their own manufacturing (either of essentials or of technology) to replace imports intended for domestic consumer markets, has resulted in a predictable crisis that coincided with the global financial crash. The latter has meant that the domestic crisis in these countries has been several times worse than that experienced by other countries. The combination of reduced exports and higher prices for imported goods has exacerbated the problem of maintaining the balance of payments in these countries, and this has forced their governments to seek loans from abroad (secured by the high profits of exporters of natural mineral resources.)

The extent to which manufacturing may be relocated is limited, and there is fierce competition among developing countries for the right to become the new manufacturing location for well-known consumer brands. This situation is pushing the post-Soviet countries toward deliberate economic integration, which would give them additional leverage in competing with countries that are dealing alone with their economic problems. The Central Asian countries have distinct advantages: impressive mineral and hydrocarbon resources; a plentiful, relatively skilled workforce who all speak the same language; a relatively large consumer market; and a convenient geopolitical location within the "contact zone" of the Eurasian continent. All these factors, together with the astute use of tax rate mechanisms by the governments of these countries; existing transport, communications, and logistics infrastructure; and existing business links have given the region genuine tangible opportunities, making it attractive to investors.[6]

By pooling their efforts to create effective environmental protections and develop mechanisms for rigorous compliance with legal norms and independent control, these countries of the post-Soviet space may be able to substantially reduce the threats from their Western partners acting to restrict the development of more advanced production facilities in the region and the potential environmental threats associated with the location of manufacturing facilities there.

When looking at the geopolitical situation in Central Asia we need to bear in mind that a measured program and consistent action on the part of Russia could become the essential counterbalance both sides need to prevent territorial and demographic expansion by ethnic Chinese into the region. Equally promising is the increase in constructive engagement aimed at working out the best way for Russia and the countries of the region to develop toward liberalizing and integrating their national economies and domestic policies. Russia's measured and constructive policies in relation to this strategically important region will assist the recovery both of its own economy and those of the region's states, as well as improve the international authority of post-Soviet states in the eyes of the world, making them more attractive to investors.[7]

However, in practice it is clear that Russia's foreign policy is dominated not by strategic but by short-term interests. It seems that Russia does not make the most of its residual ability to influence the modern generation of the region's population.

Central Asian Security

As far as Russia itself is concerned, a major threat to its security comes from its "soft underbelly" (given that Russia has no secure borders with Central Asia and therefore with Afghanistan and the "hot spot" of Western China, Xinjiang) and from closely interconnected organized criminal gangs of radical terrorists and drug traffickers who have a virtually clear transit corridor from northern Afghanistan into Tajikistan, Kyrgyzstan, and the Fergana Valley. The territory of Uzbekistan is protected from such threats by only the minefields on its borders with Kyrgyzstan and Tajikistan. Just how effective these minefields are in the fight against terrorism was shown by the incursions into Batken (in July 1999) and the events in Andijan (of May 2005), when terrorists infiltrated Uzbek territory without resistance. None of the national armies existing in Central Asia can guarantee that this terrorist traffic will be contained in the Fergana Valley or that, once it grows, it will not come down on Russia like an avalanche.

China is also subject to this threat. As a countermeasure, it imposes strict controls on its external border and moves its confines to the immediate source of the threat (e.g., by dividing Indian Kashmir with Pakistan) while implementing a rail project through the potential area of military engagement—from China into Kyrgyzstan and Tajikistan.

One of the main problems for Uzbekistan and Kazakhstan involves "cross-border water sources." Since the late 1990s China has begun to take water from the Cherny Irtysh and Ili rivers, thereby threatening not just Kazakhstan but the whole ecosystem of that geopolitical region, of which Russia is part, with an environmental catastrophe. If one adds to that the fact that over the last few decades Kazakhstan's water resources have fallen by twenty billion cubic meters and that this process is gaining pace, then the threat of reduced amounts of fresh water reaching Kazakhstan becomes increasingly immediate.

When analyzing bilateral relations between Kazakhstan and China as typical of developing countries with inadequate experience in diplomatic negotiations, one should note that the multivectored foreign policy announced by Central Asian governments is in practice implemented by way of an ad hoc reaction to existing threats. From the economic perspective, it is clear that the economic model adopted by the countries of Central Asia, primarily oriented toward the export of mineral resources, has become a problem.[8]

Russia's Military Interest in the Region

It seems that Russia is only just beginning to wake up to existing international reality, although the situation corresponds with what the twentieth century's most successful political analyst, Lenin, described as: "Yesterday was too early, tomorrow will be too late."

In 2005 political experts and Kyrgyzstan leaders (President Kurmanbek Bakiev, parliamentary speaker Omurbek Tekebaev, and Prime Minister Feliz Kulov) repeatedly assured Russian envoys that they supported the maintenance of a Russian military base in the city of Osh. At that time, the base in Osh was still in acceptable condition, and there was nothing to stop it from being kept as an antiterrorist center. But the representatives from the Kyrgyzstani side were unable to convince Russia's leaders of the need to retain the base, and military strategists from the Russian Federation's general staff were unable to decide which ministry should finance the military base at Osh and so closed it down.

On August 1, 2009, in the course of an informal summit between member states of the CSTO, the administration of newly re-elected President Bakiev agreed to allow Russia to position military bases on its territory (the battalion displaced from the Osh base is evidence of the purely symbolic nature of the military presence there, capable only of perimeter defense).[9] The political dividends for Russia, were it to locate military bases in Kyrgyzstan, are linked to its maintaining a presence there, and therefore control and influence over the region's internal politics, as well as over Central Asia's southeastern region. However, the economic benefit for Russia is not obvious: the right to station an isolated battalion of soldiers in return for $2 billion in permanent loans can hardly be described as a successful investment.

Furthermore, the Kyrgyzstan government is proposing that the Russian battalion's base be located not in Osh, in the strategically important central zone of the Fergana valley, but in the mountainous Batken region, where the battalion will effectively be isolated. Another obvious drawback to the existing prospects for a Russian military base in the south of the country is that it will not counterbalance the major U.S. "Gansi" air base (which uses the runway at the Manas civilian airport), located on the other side of the mountain range in the north of the country close to Bishkek, or be able to closely coordinate its actions with the Russian military base located twenty kilometers from the Kyrgyzstani capital—in Kant.

The major factor affecting these agreements is that Uzbekistan strongly objected to having a Russian military base situated right next to its border. On July 23, 2009, Uzbekistan's Ministry of Foreign Affairs announced that Tashkent supported the creation by the CSTO of the Collective Rapid Reaction Force (KSOR, founded in February 2009) only in order to repel "foreign aggression" and not for the resolution of so-called frozen conflicts in the post-Soviet space or deployments in the course of any internal conflict within the borders of member states. The ministry's official statement contained a comment to the effect that "KSOR should not become an instrument for resolving controversial questions either just within the CSTO or throughout the CIS." The announcement also noted that "every CSTO member is capable of resolving its own internal conflicts and problems by its own efforts without the involvement of any armed forces from abroad." It also emphasized that any decision to use the KSOR mechanism should be based on "absolute compliance with the principle of consensus."[10]

According to Uzbekistan's authorities, any deployment of even a token cohort of Russian troops in southern Kyrgyzstan as opposed to the north (Kant) threatens the national interests of Uzbekistan. The section that follows is an attempt to understand the logic behind such a vehement protest from Tashkent.

Traditionally, three regions of southern and western Kyrgyzstan, bordering Uzbekistan, are home to a large and expanding Uzbek diaspora: in the Jalal-Abad region they account for up to 40 percent of the population, in the Osh region up to 60 percent, and in the Batken region up to 10 percent. In a number of border regions these "minorities" account for up to 90 percent of the population. However, despite their prominent position in the demographic structure of Kyrgyzstan (800,000 of the country's population of five million), Uzbeks are virtually unrepresented in the organs of power and do not have equal rights with those from whom the country takes its name—the Kyrgyz. The situation is similar in the neighboring Fergana Valley in the Khujent region of Tajikistan with its predominantly Uzbek population.[11]

There is considerable agrarian overpopulation in the neighboring regions of Uzbekistan (in a number of cases the average per capita share of land under cultivation is 0.2 hundredths of a hectare), and in Uzbekistan as a whole; it is therefore clear that the cross-border regions of Kyrgyzstan, particularly those already settled by Uzbeks—first and foremost, the Osh section of the Fergana Valley—are a natural destination for demographic expansion.

One aspect of the threat to the territorial integrity of Kyrgyzstan is that in Central Asia's current political and legal climate, there is no premise taking place within the law for a change in the ethnic balance in the country's southern regions—and this will influence its administrative policy. In the meantime, specifically as a result of the low representation of ethnic Uzbeks in the country's administrative bodies, the Islamic underclass in Kyrgyzstan is increasingly actively organizing itself along ethnic lines.

It is easy to foresee that the problem of the constitutional status and equal rights of Kyrgyzstan's Uzbek population will very soon become a central issue in the bilateral relations between the countries. That is why Uzbekistan does not want to see in Kyrgyzstan either the collective forces of the CSTO, which would force the Uzbek minority (in reality the regional majority) to "make peace," or even a small number of Russian soldiers at a military base. The real role of the Russian peacekeepers in Abkhazia, South Ossetia, and Transdniester does not inspire any trust in them on the part of Tashkent and Uzbek political commentators.[12]

The Russian Ministry of Foreign Affairs may have been trying to avoid a "diplomatic misunderstanding" with Tashkent when it announced that the location of the base "had not yet been finalized" and was the "subject of further discussions with partners both in Kyrgyzstan and within the framework of the CSTO as a whole" and that Russia "had a number of different options for the location of the base."[13]

Uzbekistan wasted no time in replying. As announced by the Russian Federation's Ministry of Foreign Affairs: "In recent weeks Uzbekistan's determination to have American troops return to its territory was only going to be strengthened by Russia's plans to build its own military base in Kyrgyzstan." "The Uzbek side does not see it as necessary or sensible for an additional cohort of Russian military forces to be located in southern Kyrgyzstan," commented the Uzbeck Ministry of Foreign Affairs in response to the news.[14]

The state borders of the former Soviet republics were "carved out" more or less arbitrarily, completely ignoring the porousness of the boundaries and the mosaic-like distribution of ethnic groups throughout those areas of Central Asia where there is support for a reversion to earlier borderlines. At the very outset of the border demarcation process, which occurred as a result of the breakup of the Soviet Union, various Russian politicians (Alexandr Solzhenitsyn, Gavril Popov, Vladimir Zhirinovsky, Yuri Luzhkov, Konstantin Zatulin, and others) posed the question of what they claimed was, for Russia, the unequal border division with Kazakhstan, northern Kazakhstan having a large proportion of ethnic Russians, and the Crimea, which was included in Ukraine. Thus the newly formed post-Soviet countries cannot realistically hope that the mutual territorial claims they have against each other will not be shared by all the Central Asian states.

In this situation, one should not ignore the, as yet, purely hypothetical consideration that they will seek to realize their territorial claims against each other via local armed conflicts, seeking support from the Russian military formations acting under the auspices of KSOR. And although such a scenario in the potential development of the region would, from the very outset, be destructive for all involved, it cannot be completely ruled out.

Central Asia as a Source of Energy for China

Commenting on draft legislation adopted for a Kazakhstan-China gas pipeline, Kazakhstan's minister of energy and mineral resources, Sauat Mynbayev, explained: "The main purpose of the agreement is the development of long-term cooperation in the transportation of gas produced in Turkmenistan and Kazakhstan via new gas pipelines through Kazakhstan and China."[15] Construction began in July 2008 and by autumn 2009 had already cost more than $4 billion.[16] The total estimated cost of the project is approximately $7.5 billion, financed through loans, most of which will come from the China Development Bank, with the China National Petroleum Corporation (CNPC) providing a repayment guarantee for the construction period. Once construction is complete, delivery contracts will take the place of the repayment guarantee. PetroChina, which will be the consignor of deliveries, has taken these obligations on itself.

The gas line is divided into two phases. The delivery capacity of the first is forty billion cubic meters and will run from the Kazakhstan-Uzbekistan border to Kazakhstan's Chinese border. The second phase of the gas pipeline—Beyneu-Bozoy-Kyzylorda-Shymkent—has a capacity of ten billion cubic meters. The Kazakhstan section will begin at Kazakhstan's border with Uzbekistan, run 650 kilometers to the east through Kazakhstan and end at its border with China near the Khorgos frontier post.[17]

The Kazakhstan-China gas pipeline is part of an enormous project to build a "Central Asian" pipeline in the form of a specialized, extended branch system for the transportation of natural gas outside the region. For Astana, Kazakhstan's capital, this is the first export pipeline to allow its gas to reach foreign markets other than via Russia.

Proven and estimated reserves of natural gas, taking into account discoveries of new fields on Kazakhstan's Caspian shelf, make up about 3.3 trillion cubic meters, while potential resources reach 6–8 trillion cubic meters if

Caspian offshore fields are taken into account. By the end of 2010 Kazakhstan plans to increase natural gas production volumes by over 150 percent to around 45 billion cubic meters.[18]

Based on the results of the first half of 2009, China, previously the ninth largest investor in Kazakhstan, jumped to pole position. Cash flows from the PRC over those six months more than tripled (compared with the first six months of 2008) to reach $4.9 billion. As of June 30, 2009, Chinese investment in the sector amounted to $4.8 billion (58.9 percent of total foreign investment in the industry).

China has also invested $2.1 billion (10.2 percent) in the mining industry, $401 million (6 percent) in retail, and $432.6 million (1.1 percent) in financial services. But it should be noted that these funds were invested in the construction of infrastructure for the fuel and energy industry.[19] At the beginning of 2008 an equal joint venture, the "Asian Gas Pipeline," was set up for the construction of the China-Central Asia gas pipeline. The cost of the project is $20 billion, of which $6.5 billion will be spent on the Kazakhstan section. This project requires equally significant investment by China in the construction sector.[20]

A significant aspect of Chinese investment is that most of the financial awards are credits and loans (92 percent). Thus, Kazakhstan's total foreign debt to China in 2008 (which, at about $4 billion, had quadrupled as of June 30, 2009) almost doubled to reach $7.3 billion. This placed China after the Netherlands, the United States, and the UK as the fourth largest of Kazakhstan's country-creditors.

In Kazakhstan it is thought that the debt owed to its eastern neighbor will soon treble. As Karim Massimov, prime minister of the Republic of Kazakhstan noted: "Agreements have been reached with our foreign partners on the attraction from China of additional investments for the implementation of joint projects totaling $13 billion. In total, the government wishes to borrow about $23 billion from overseas. So far, there is no doubt that we shall pay back these debts. The question is whether China will be satisfied with material resources (and their monetary equivalent) or whether it will demand more."[21]

China's interest in investing such large amounts in Kazakhstan's economy is obvious: it is trying to broaden the extent and geography of its presence in Kazakhstan and, eventually, throughout the Central Asian region. Beijing is also banking on gaining freer access to Central Asia's mineral resources, primarily hydrocarbon deposits in the west (in Turkmenistan, Kazakhstan, and

Uzbekistan) and, in the southeast, uranium deposits (in Kazakhstan, Uzbekistan, Tajikistan, and Kyrgyzstan).[22]

At the end of 2008 there were more than 480 Chinese-Kazakhstani joint ventures operating on the basis of cross-border trade and in the oil and gas industry, while the volume of Chinese investment in the Republic of Kazakhstan was no less than $8.5 billion. In 2009–10, the volume of Chinese loans could exceed $10 billion. Thus China is actively taking advantage of the global crisis to reinforce its position as a major financial donor to Kazakhstan.[23]

The present situation evidently perfectly suits Astana, given that cooperation with China allows the country to reduce its dependence both on Western companies as a source of investment and on Russia's monopoly influence on the transit of unrefined hydrocarbons to global markets.

Russia's Energy Interest in Central Asia

Against the background of Turkmenistan's intensive cultivation of links with foreign states and countries, cooperation between Russia and Turkmenistan in the oil and gas sector starts to look rather more modest. Initial difficulties occurred in March 2009 when, during a visit to Moscow by the president of Turkmenistan, negotiations between the two countries on the construction of an "East-West" gas pipeline were concluded without any tangible results; a little later Ashgabat announced that it would be holding an international financial tender for this project. Later, in April 2009, there was an incident on the "Central Asia–Center" (CAC) gas pipeline, for which Turkmenistan blamed Russia. Russia, however, saw no need to put forward any convincing justification in its defense, thereby completely ignoring Turkmenistan's pretensions to being an independent state not only with economic obligations to other partners but also rights it is entitled to assert as an independent actor with its own foreign policy interests. One way or another, the shift in the economic and trade balance is evidence that Turkmenistan is increasingly reluctant to see Russia as a reliable, priority foreign partner in the oil and gas sector. It may well be that, in the series of moves it made following the incident on the CAC pipeline, Turkmenistan was also pursuing its aim of demonstrating its strengthened political will in terms of reducing its dependence on Russia, thereby increasing foreign competition around hydrocarbon resources and their transport routes. As a result, whereas in 2007 Gazprom anticipated it would invest about $2 billion in gas projects in Turkmenistan by 2010, it is now increasingly evident that there is little likelihood of major investment from Russia. It seems obvious that the future nature of Russia's and Russian companies' presence in Turkmenistan's oil and gas industry will be dictated not by political declarations and promises but by the concrete steps taken by the Russian Federation to maintain and reinforce its position.[24]

Should future cooperation continue to be limited to the purchase of Turkmenistan gas and its transportation, then the Russian position in Turkmenistan's oil and gas sector will at best remain at current levels, but even that is not absolutely clear. Much will depend on whether Ashgabat is able dramatically to increase hydrocarbon production levels and conduct a balanced energy policy. Moscow's interests are also a factor here.

Volumes of gas deliveries to or toward Russia are unlikely to expand in the short term, and given the evident drop in gas exports from Russia to Europe they are likely to remain relatively low (lower than before the global financial crisis)—at about 20 billion cubic meters per annum or possibly even lower.

As a result of the global financial crisis and the fall in demand for hydrocarbons, including gas, it does not make economic sense for Russia to increase the volumes of natural gas it purchases from Turkmenistan at market prices agreed to back in 2008. In this connection it seems to be no coincidence that Moscow is so far in no hurry (at least until it is able to make new agreements at a gas price more acceptable to it) to recommence deliveries of Turkmenistan gas, which were halted after the incident on the CAC pipeline in April 2009.

It is extremely difficult to predict what will happen with gas deliveries in the longer term and, in particular, to talk of any significant growth (compared with pre-crisis levels) in gas export volumes from Turkmenistan to/in the direction of Russia. The following issues are crucial: (1) whether Turkmenistan has adequate gas resources; (2) what the prices are for Turkmenistan's gas; (3) what the existing and planned pipeline capacity is, including in the direction of Russia; and (4) whether Ashgabat actively looks for new markets for its natural gas.

In a scenario favorable to Russia in the medium term (but probably not before 2020), potential volumes of gas exports from Turkmenistan to/in the direction of Russia could, in theory, reach 70–80 billion cubic meters per annum. However, that could happen only if an extremely complicated set of factors coincides. These primarily include the factors listed above but also depend on the constructive resolution of the project under which Russia, Kazakhstan, and Turkmenistan are to build and bring a Caspian oil pipeline into operation and rebuild the CAC pipeline, to permit Ashgabat's full compliance with its export obligations to its main partners—Russia (under the 2003 agreement), China (between 30 and 40 billion cubic meters per annum), Iran (10–15 billion cubic meters a year), and potentially even to participants in the Nabucco pipeline project (assuming it, including its Caspian section, gets built).[25] Given that it is unlikely that these factors will coincide, the current levels given in the optimistic scenario above should be seen as hypothetical rather than realistic. One might even anticipate a different scenario in which no oil deliveries to/in the direction of Russia will be made in the short term or, most likely, in the long term either.

Throughout the first decade of the twenty-first century, Turkmenistan has consistently produced about ten million tons of oil per annum and exported (primarily to its neighbors) between seven and eight million tons. Unless large new oil fields are discovered in Turkmenistan, production and export levels of the "black gold" will in the short term remain close to the present level and will be of no particular interest to Russia. In the medium term (up to 2020) oil production volumes in Turkmenistan could grow by about 1.5–2 times, thereby reaching 15–20 million tons, in which case exports could grow to 10–15 million tons per annum. It is difficult to foresee what proportion of such volumes would be produced and exported by Russian companies. Even taking into account the potential for Russian participation in the development of oil fields, it is unlikely that the black gold that resulted would be exported to/in the direction of Russia: it would be much more lucrative to refine the oil and/or supply it to countries that are not as geographically remote from Turkmenistan as Russia is, for example, to Uzbekistan, Tajikistan, and Kyrgyzstan.[26]

SMALLER IRRITANTS—THE ROGUN DAM

Among the local problems linked to the Russia factor in Central Asia is that of Russia's participation in projects to complete construction on the Rogun Dam hydroelectric power station (on the Vakhsh River in Tajikistan), the launch of which threatens to bring to a head a conflict between Uzbekistan and Tajikistan. The controversy might directly affect the level of bilateral, currently rather tepid, relations between the two countries as it will potentially increase the shortage of vital water resources for Uzbekistan.

There has been virtually no progress on the question of the construction of the power station in two decades. For Tajikistan the project is extremely important as the country suffers from a chronic shortage of electricity. The weakest link in completion of construction of the power station is financing. The capital, Dushanbe, has not received the investment promised from Russia, and its budget is inadequate to finance such an enormous project; potential overseas investors regard such a huge construction project with some skepticism.

The West offered Dushanbe a series of alternatives, for example, a network of small energy facilities, but the country's government was not interested. Tajikistan is attempting to obtain support and financing from Iran and, possibly, Turkey. Iran is expressing interest in participation in the project, hence the West's concern not only in connection with the as yet uncalculated environmental consequences of the launch but also with the fact that Iran will thereby acquire still greater influence in Tajikistan—and thereby in Central Asia as a whole. This is all the more important because Iran now occupies second place by volume of investment in the economy of Tajikistan and does not hide its intention to use and expand its influence throughout Central Asia.

The absence of a legislative base governing water use is a separate issue. The fact that a whole series of controversial issues linked with the distribution of fresh water flowing from Tajikistan and Kyrgyzstan into the valleys of Uzbekistan and Kazakhstan have not yet been legally settled could—taking into account their fundamental importance to agriculture and the population's very physical survival—escalate into an open military confrontation between these countries.

Furthermore, there is no simple answer to the question of whether Tajikistan, if the necessary investment for completion of the Rogun Dam hydroelectric power station means that construction recommences, will be able to implement this project on its own and can be relied upon to pay dividends to its investors. Ever since the breakup of the Soviet Union, Russia has been Tajikistan's only partner. But recently, relations between the two countries have significantly deteriorated. In an obvious attempt to underline its independence, Tajikistan's president Emomali Rakhmon announced that in the construction of the power station, Tajikistan would work with Moscow only on equal terms. Otherwise, he intends to refuse partnership with Moscow and rely on the country's own resources or find other partners.

Most countries are wary of this issue, as they understand it affects the interests of countries located farther down the Vakhsh River—the main fresh water supply into the valleys of Central Asia. For that reason, there is no evidence of any concrete intentions on the part of Europe, China, or India in this respect.

At the initiative of the Tajikistani government, it was planned that in 2009 $150 million would be invested from the national budget in equipment for the power station. The question is where the funds will come from. The law recently adopted by the country's parliament, which provides that the Rogun Dam hydroelectric power station cannot be privatized, has, in the opinion of many, finally put pay to the project's prospects from the viewpoint of potential investors. The World Bank, on which the Tajikistan government was relying for support, has adopted a cautious position.[27]

CENTRAL ASIANS IN RUSSIA

A more acute and vexatious question, at least as far as regional public opinion is concerned, is that no one has been held accountable for the deaths and physical abuse of hundreds of Central Asians within Russia.[28] Extremely negative fallout from the unlawful deaths of emigrants from Central Asia into Russia could find expression in tit-for-tat actions on the part of families and friends of the guest worker victims against the region's Russian-speakers. Worse still, guest workers who have lost hope of being given any protection by the Russian law-enforcement agencies may be forced to organize resistance groups for their own protection. Of course, these groups will act outside the Russian legal boundaries, which, not to beat about the bush, could bring about an avalanche of criminal offences around racial segregation.[29]

We are deliberately ignoring here the issues linked with the phenomenon of Russian Islam, which, as a result of demographic and migratory processes, is consistently increasing in influence. There is no doubt that the problem of political Islam, both within Russia and in Central Asia, is an extremely pressing issue and deserves specific multidisciplinary research. However, its analysis is outside the scope of our subject. Nevertheless, it seems appropriate to identify one aspect of the problem as the inevitable proliferation of contacts between Islamic movements in Central Asia and Russian Muslims in the North Caucasus and the Volga region, which will occur in the near future. The nature and direction these contacts take will largely determine many substantive aspects of relations between Russia and Central Asia.

In Place of a Conclusion

If we look at the complex of problems examined in this chapter, both those within Central Asia and those affecting its relations with Russia (in the context of a comprehensive civilization process), the crux lies in the fact that the integration process is being dictated by the development of a comprehensive cultural-historical matrix for the Eurasian space. On that basis, there are more grounds for optimism linked to a mutual rapprochement between Russia and the countries of Central Asia than for pessimism.

One needs only to examine the multifaceted causes and effects that make up the integration process between Russia and the countries of Central Asia in the single dimension of the short-term interests of one or another political group to see that nothing is simple. But it is nevertheless clear that the determining factor of Russia's strategic development and that of the countries of Central Asia is the process of their integration.

Unfortunately, a significant section of modern Russian society and its political elites, insisting on the priority of their own cultural traditions and value systems, are not yet ready (either psychologically or intellectually) to construct a new algorithm for the development of civilization. It seems obvious that an essential condition of a new architecture for the interstate commonwealth is the organic integration, to some extent, of the traditional values of the national cultures of the post-Soviet states into a culture of Central Eurasia.

Notes

1. See the in-depth research of Martha Brill Olcott and Alexey Malashenko. See also Vladimir Paramonov, "Analitiko-progroznaya rabota na postsovetskom prostranstve: zatyanuvshiisya period intellektualnoi spyachki" [An analytical forecast for the post-Soviet space: an extended period of intellectual torpor], http://viperson.ru/wind.php?ID=519203; Dosym Satpaev, "Mify i realii regionalnoy integratsii" [Myths and realities of regional integration], *Exclusive.kz* no. 11 (80) (November 2008); Svetlana Glinkina, "Chto mozhet oznachat programma Vostochnoe partnerstvo dlya Rossii?" [What might the Eastern Partnership program mean for Russia?], www.eurasianhome.org.

org/xml/t/expert.xml?lang=ru&nic=expert&pid; Georgy Sitnyansky, "Mirovoi demokraticheskii protsess i stepnaya traditsiya" [The global democratic process and the tradition of the steppe], *Aziya i Afrika segodnya* [Asia and Africa today] (1996): 14–19; "Etnokonfessionalnaya situatsiya v Kazakhstane i Kirgizii i natsionalnaya bezopasnost Rossii" [The ethno-religious situation in Kazakhstan and Kirghizia and Russian national security], in *Tsentralnaya Aziya* [Central Asia] (1997), 73–79; Georgy Sitnyansky, "Krest ili polumesyats? Kirghiziya pered vyborom very" [Cross or Crescent? Kirghiziya faced with a choice of faith], in *Etnos i religiya* [Ethnicity and religion] (Moscow: 1998); Georgy Sitnyansky, "Otkuda iskhodit ugroza edinstvu Rossii" [Where does the threat to Russian unity come from?], in *Aziya i Afrika sevodnya* [Asia and Africa today], no. 12 (1997): 36–39; Georgy Sitnyansky, "Pervye sredi ravnykh" [First among equals], *NG—Sodruzhestvo* [IS—Commonwealth], September 27, 2004; and Sergey Antonov, "Neoimperskaya politika Rossii i Tsentralnaya Aziya" [Russia's neo-imperialist policy and Central Asia], http://www.geokz.tv/article.php?aid=8363.
2. See http://www.kurs.kz/index.php?s=default&mode=pages&page=505.
3. See http://www.advantour.com/rus/central-asia/index.htm.
4. See Y. Shokamanov, *Tendentsii chelovecheskogo razvitiya v Kazakhstane* [Trends in human development in Kazakhstan] (Almaty, Kazakhstan: Statistics Agency of the Republic of Kazakhstan, 2001), 348, http://www.ukgu.kz/cgi-bin/.../cgiirbis_32.exe?; and Rustem Zhanguzhin, "Novye nezavisimye gosudarstva Tsentralnoy Azii v sisteme mezhdunarodnykh otnoshenii" [The new independent states of Central Asia in the system of international relations] (Kiev: 2004), 363–80.
5. Zbigniew Brzezinski, "Velikaya shakhmatnaya doska" [*The Grand Chessboard*] (Moscow: Mezhdunarodnaya otnosheniya, 1998), 149–51.
6. See Rosbalt, "PROON: Stranam Tsentralnoy Azii sleduyet bolee tesno sotrudnichat" [UNDP: Central Asian countries should collaborate more closely], December 7, 2005, http://www.rosbalt.ru/2005/12/07/237186.html.
7. See Alexey Krymin, "Demograficheskaya situatsiya v Uzbekistane" [The demographic situation in Uzbekistan], http://www.cainfo.ru/article/opinions/529.
There are between 5,092,000 and 7,289,000 people in Tajikistan. See *Wikipedia*, http://ru.wikipedia.org/wiki/; Lyudmila Sokolova, "Tajikistan: Demografichesya situatsiya i migratsiya naselenie" [Tajikistan: the demographic situation and population migration], in *Sovremennye etnopoliticheskie protsessy i migrattsionnaya situatsiya v Tsentralnoy Azii* [Current ethno-political processes and the migration situation in Central Asia] (Moscow: 1998), 205–15There are between 4,257,000 and 5,276,000 people in Kyrgyzstan. See "Ethnodemograficheskie protsessy i voprosy etnologii

Kyrgyzskoi Respubliki" [Ethnodemographic processes and ethnology issues in the Kyrgyz Republic], http://bankrabot.com/work/work_74820.html. In Turkmenistan there are about 6 million people. See http://www.demographia.ru/articles_N/index.html?idR=33&idArt=1111.

8. See www.polit.ru/news/2009/11/17/kazahstan_china_gaz.popup.html.
9. See Rian.ru, "Uchebnyi voennyi tsentr v Kirgizii budet otkryt dlya vsekh uchastnikov ODKB" [Military training centre in Kyrghizia will be open to all CSTO members], August 1, 2009, http://www.rian.ru/defense_safety/20090801/179391724.html;http://www.easttime.ru/analitic/1/4/452.html.
10. See http://www.centrasia.ru/news.php?st=1249902000.
11. See Farkhod Tolipov, "Teoria i praktika regionalnoi integratsii v Tsentralnoy Azii" [Theory and practice of regional integration in Central Asia], March 2, 2005, http://www.analitika.org/article.php?story=20050302061032204; Maral Salykzhanov, http://inosmikzcul.canalblog.com/; http://www.centrasia.ru/cnt.php; Andrei Dudnik, "Regionalyniy rasklad Tsentralnoi Azii na zavtrashnii den" [The regional breakdown of Central Asia tomorrow]; http://www.centrasia.ru/news.php?st=1249028580; and http://www.centrasia.ru/news.php?st=124990200.
12. See Modest Kolerov, "Osh-2: pochemu Uzbekistan ne khochet voennogo prisustviya Rossii na Yuge Kirgizii" [Osh-2: why Uzbekistan does not want Russia's military presence in Southern Kyrghizia], August 5, 2009, http://www.regnum.ru/news/1193389.html; Bakhadyr Musaeev, "Narod Uzbekistana privetstvoval by sozdanie v Ferganskoy doline rossiiskikh Ovoshchnykh Baz vmesto Voennykh" [The people of Uzbekistan would welcome the creation in the Fergana Valley of vegetables instead of military bases], http://www.centrasia.ru/news.php; S. Buntman, "Rastsenki bezopasnosti" [Evaluating security], http://www.echo.msk.ru/blog/buntman/610870-echo/; Alexander Shustov, "Yuzhno-kirgizskii brosok Rossii" [Russia's pitch for southern Kyrghizia], August 11, 2009, http://www.centrasia.ru/news.php?st=1249982940; A. V. Sokolov, "Russian Peacekeeping Forces in the Post-Soviet Area" in *Restructuring the Global Military Sector*, vol. 1, *New Wars*, ed. Mary Kaldor and Basker Vashee (London: Pinter, 1997).
13. See http://russian.irib.ir/index.php?option=com_content&task=view&id=24859&Itemid=143.
14. See http://www.centralasiaonline.com/ru/articles/090808_military_base_nws/.
15. See http://www.kazenergy.com/content/view/7106/64/lang,ru.
16. See http://www.kaztransgas.kz/article/61.
17. Ibid.
18. See http://www.gazpromquestions.ru/?id=38.

19. Novosti-Kazakhstan press agency, November 17, 2009.
20. See http://www.nationalbank.kz/?uid=0E24CA44-2219-B830.
21. See *Kazakhstan Today*, October 19, 2009.
22. See http://www.zakon.kz/85812-ao-bank-razvitija-kazakhstana.html.
23. See http://www.kurs.kz/index.php?s=default&mode=pages&page=505.
24. See http://www.energoinform.org/normatives/powerstrategy.aspx.
25. See http://www.ia-centr.ru/archive/public_detailsd5e8.html?id=34.
26. V. Paramonov, A. Strokov, and O. Stolpovskii, "Rossiiskoe neftegazovoe prisustvie v Turkmenistane: osnovnye problem i riski" [Russia's oil and gas presence in Turkmenistan: the basic problems, forecasts, and risks], http://ca-portal.ru/index.php.
27. A. Nakimdzhanov, "Smozhet li Tajikistan izbezhat zavisimosti v postroike Rogunskoi GES?" [Can Tajikistan avoid dependence in the construction of the Rosun Dam hydro-electric power station?], http://www.easttime.ru/news/1/10/1840.html.
28. See, in particular, http://www.vz.ru/politics/2009/8/21/319917.html; http://www.newsru.com/russia/05jul2005/students.html/; http://www.newsru.com/crime/12dec2008/nazichindecapitmb.html/; and http://www.newsru.com/russia/10apr2009/nazy.html.
29. See, in particular, http://www.newsru.com/russia/05jul2005/students.html/; and http://www.newsru.com/crime/12dec2008/nazichindecapitmb.html/.

CHAPTER FIFTEEN

Of Power and Greatness

Dmitri Trenin

The breakup of the Soviet Union, which happened suddenly and unexpectedly for most of its subjects as well as outsiders, finally closed the books on the historical Russian empire. It also signified the end of Soviet Russia as an ideological power, and an all-around military superpower, which constituted important trappings of the very last—Soviet—edition of Russian imperialism.[1] This is not the place to discuss whether the USSR was doomed from the start of perestroika, or whether it might have been preserved by more competent policies, supported, for example, by higher oil prices. The point of departure of this chapter is that Russia's *post-Communist* transformation included a major element of post-imperial—let's call it *post-Soviet*—adjustment. It is not that this fact was overlooked two decades ago: it could not have been. Rather, the imperial dismantlement was welcomed, acknowledged, and—taken for granted. Yet, it is this imperial legacy, including Russia's self-image and the mind-set of its elites and the public, that sets Russia apart from virtually all other former Communist countries that embarked on transformation. Whereas its former satellites and borderlands wholeheartedly embraced integration into the West, Russia was at first lukewarm about this, then ambivalent, and finally sought to reassert itself as a great power. "Great powers do not integrate," Foreign Minister Igor Ivanov told a senior Ukrainian diplomat in 2002.[2] Paying less than full attention to this difference distorts the assessment of Russia's recent record and its future prospects.

This chapter attempts to analyze the significance of exiting from an empire, as part of the transformational agenda, and the complexities of the process. It takes stock of Russia's achievements and failures in redesigning its new place and role in the world. It also seeks to put Russia into a broader international historical context and compares its experience with that of some other ex-imperial powers. This comparison should add to the understanding of the challenges facing the Russians today as they proceed to reinvent or at least reimagine their country yet again. Finally, the chapter explores the potential for an international role for Russia that is commensurate with its promise and its aspirations—and thus rewarding—and is useful for the rest of the global community.

Empire to Great Power

Outwardly, the *geopolitical catastrophe* of 1991—to use Vladimir Putin's phrase[3]—was far from complete. The Soviet Union did come apart at its seams, but the Russian Federation, contrary to many expectations, did not follow suit. Within it, both ethnically Russian and non-Russian lands stayed together in the great upheaval. Only Chechnya tried separatism in earnest, but it was eventually hauled back at a great cost to all involved and with excruciating pain. The rest of the North Caucasus, having watched the Chechen experience next door, stayed put. Tatarstan and Bashkortostan briefly toyed with the idea of full sovereignty, but in the end opted for an association, which has since been increasingly diluted. De-populated and underdeveloped, but resource-rich, Siberia, the crown jewel of the Russian empire, remained Russian. So, *l'empire est morte, vive l'empire*?

Well, not exactly. It is not simply that three layers of the empire are gone: the far-flung outposts of "non-capitalist orientation" in the Third World; the "socialist community" bloc in Eastern Europe and its affiliates in Mongolia, Vietnam, Laos, and Cuba; and finally, the inner circle of borderland Soviet republics. Each layer represented a specific aspiration in Moscow and a special function that went with it. Third World clients reflected both an early ideological ambition to supplant global capitalism with a communist socio-economic and political model, and a Cold War global competition for influence. With Communist internationalism dead, and Russia out of the race for primacy with the United States, this is gone for good. The second layer, particularly in Central Europe, originated largely out of strategic necessity; served as both a forward position and a protective buffer; and was abandoned as useless and too costly with the end of the Cold War confrontation. The former Soviet allies' subsequent integration into the European and Atlantic institutions has left Russia not only without a forward operating base (no regrets about it in Moscow) but also without a buffer vis-à-vis the core West, which created a sense of vulnerability within the Russian elite. It is the third layer, a diverse group of former Soviet republics and old imperial provinces, that turned out to be of utmost importance.

There, Ukraine, of course, was absolutely crucial. It was the Ukrainian referendum of December 1, 1991, that ended any illusions of a "more perfect union" to succeed the USSR. Zbigniew Brzezinski was basically right: without Ukraine, no Russian empire was possible.[4] In this respect, those who saw the post-Soviet Commonwealth of Independent States (CIS) as Russia's "third empire" misread the pointers.[5] The December 8, 1991, Belovezh agreement, which dismantled the USSR, founded the CIS not as its successor in disguise but as both a funeral committee for the great deceased and as a foster parent for its offspring. It was the Ukrainian president Leonid Kravchuk who coined the phrase about a "civilized divorce." This phrase had long been disputed in Russia, but eventually Putin concurred, although without citing the original source.[6]

What was even more important than the decision of Ukrainian voters was the evaporation of the imperial élan from the collective Russian mind. It should never be forgotten that it was the Russian elites who dealt the truly shattering blow to the USSR, by claiming sovereignty in June 1990 for the Russian Soviet republic, and by electing a separate Russian president in June 1991. The Ukrainians were thus responsible only for the coup de grâce. Having "liberated themselves" from the "imperial baggage," the Russians have been alternatively treating the former borderlands with benign neglect and trying to throw their weight around: no longer Big Brother, just Mr. Big. They continued to see themselves as a *great power*. What Russia stopped being was an *empire*: no more mystique; no more mission; no more sacrifice. The imperial mission accomplished, Russia thought itself free from the burden. From now on, they would seek to gain an advantage, and shun too much responsibility.

Thus, while the Russian empire died, unlamented, the great power in Russia lived on. It rested on a still sufficiently broad and solid territorial base. Russia's 1991 borders have often been called artificial, and not only by Russian nationalists. Most borders in the world, of course, are man-made.

Russia's present ones, however, are not unprecedented. They are strikingly similar to the boundaries of the tsardom of Muscovy around 1650, that is, before the "union with Ukraine" and the Baltic conquests of Peter the Great. They are—pre-imperial. True, pre-Petrine Russia included a number of territories that had been conquered, like Kazan or Astrakhan, or colonized, as Siberia all the way to the Pacific. Yet, the many ethnics living in that vast territory have been largely assimilated. Today, they keep their distinct cultures, their religion, and even their territorial homelands, organized now as republics of the Russian Federation; but they have generally accepted their status within Russia.

A brief comparison with Serbia/Yugoslavia is in order here. Where the Yugoslav People's Army fought for the continued existence of the Yugoslav federation, the Soviet Armed Forces accepted not only the dissolution of the USSR but their own disintegration: dozens of divisions deployed in 1991 in Ukraine and Belarus seamlessly formed the national defense establishments of those countries; the weapons holdings in Turkmenistan and even in Chechnya were turned over to the local authorities; and so on. Where Serbian politicians led by Slobodan Milosevic proclaimed the goal of reuniting all ethnic brethren within a Greater Serbia, Russian elites led by Boris Yeltsin accepted new borders that left some 25 million ethnic Russians in what came to be known as the "near abroad." Unlike Bosnian Serb leaders Radovan Karadzic and Ratko Mladic, Crimea's irredentist leader Yuri Meshkov was left out in the cold by the Kremlin.

It was precisely the Crimea, only transferred to Soviet Ukraine from the Russian republic as recently as 1954, that was the one area most Russians felt strongly about. However, Yeltsin was determined to avoid an armed conflict with Ukraine, which still held a fraction of former Soviet nuclear forces in its territory. Russia's acceptance of Crimea as part of Ukraine paved the way to de-nuclearization of the second-biggest former Soviet republic: an exercise of political responsibility and statesmanship on both sides.[7]

To summarize: having ceased to be a world empire, Russia remained a continental great power. The distinction is subtle, but crucial. Today Moscow does not control foreign governments; its sphere of influence could be said to include South Ossetia and, to a lesser extent, Abkhazia. Its military forces remain in a few foreign outposts, from Transnistria to Tajikistan, but their scale, mission, and capabilities cannot be compared with erstwhile Soviet deployments. The CIS did not and could not become Russia's third empire—after tsarist and Soviet. The principal reason for this was the exhaustion by the late 1980s of the Russian imperial spirit. The transition from an empire to a great power was not an obvious one. For almost three centuries, the two were inextricably linked. For some time during the 1990s, there was a fear in Russia of losing the great power status alongside the imperial one. Domestically, that would have meant disintegration and chaos; in foreign policy terms, a loss of independence and inevitable subjugation by one or several foreign countries. When he became foreign minister in 1996, Evgenii Primakov famously proclaimed that Russia has been, is, and will be a great power![8] This became a rallying point for the Russian elites. Virtually everyone chimed in. What was less clear was what it meant to be a "great power" in the new era.

What It Means to Be Great

The official thinking on that score has witnessed an interesting evolution, which, at the turn of the 2010s, is still proceeding. Yeltsin and Kozyrev; Gaidar and Chubais; Primakov and Chernomyrdin; Putin and Medvedev not only had differing—and at times confused—concepts of "great power," but their own thinking on the issue changed throughout their government careers. Distilling that thinking is not an easy task. Yet, doing that is indispensable for understanding the prime source of Russia's international ambitions and orientations after the loss of its empire. For that, the meaning that its leadership attaches to the notion of "great power" is key.

One obvious quality of a great power is its strategic independence. During the brief liberal internationalist period—roughly, Boris Yeltsin's first term and Andrei Kozyrev's stint as foreign minister[9]—Russia considered itself to be part of the Western world. To be sure, it regarded itself as a great power, but was ready to treat "common Western interests" as its own—and was not quite sure what special national interests it now had. In reality, while Russia at that time retained the freedom of action and was never "standing on its knees," as it was claimed later,[10] it was heavily dependent on the West and looked to it for guidance. In a revealing 1993 conversation with former U.S. president Richard Nixon, Andrei Kozyrev left the impression with his interlocutor that post-Soviet Russia would embrace general U.S./Western interests as its own. Nixon, ever the geopolitician, was bewildered.[11]

It makes sense to compare Russia's post-1991 predicament with that of post–World War II Britain and France. Unlike Britain, Russia never succeeded in forming a special relationship with the United States. During his 1992 visit to Washington, Yeltsin made a plea for an alliance with the United States only to be told by George H. W. Bush that, with the global confrontation over, there was no need for such an alliance. The NATO alliance, however, was left in place, and, while Moscow's former satellites were invited to join, Russia itself was told not to bother. This produced a lot of bad blood on the Russian side. In their eyes, NATO enlargement became a symbol of both Western exploitation of Russia's weakness and a breach of faith vis-à-vis Moscow.[12]

Unlike France, Russia did not have a European option where its leadership in integration would replace the trauma of the imperial collapse. Prime minister Viktor Chernomyrdin's public statements about Russia's wish to join the European Union betrayed profound lack of knowledge about the EU.[13] The Russian government talked, of course, about re- or new integration among ex-Soviet republics, but post-Soviet "integration" throughout the 1990s and much of the 2000s was largely a sham. Moscow itself hardly believed its own formal assertion of the priority status it notionally was giving to ties with the former republics.

Unlike postwar West Germany, Russia adamantly rejected being considered a loser in the Cold War. It was also not placed under foreign military occupation, protected on the outside and allowed to enjoy the *Wirtschaftswunder* inside. On the contrary, its GDP contracted by about one-half, and did not recover its 1990 level until 2007, after which it slumped again. If anything, Russia was akin to post–World War I Weimar Germany: reduced in both size and status but still big and potentially powerful, saddled with suspicion, if not guilt, for its Soviet-era behavior, unhappy and unanchored.

The West's disappointment with Russia, which culminated in its abandonment in despair following the 1998 financial default, was more than matched by Russia's disappointment with the West, which had refused to adopt its once formidable, and now malleable, adversary. Almost miraculously, however, the window of opportunity opened again, in the wake of the 9/11 terrorist attacks, when Vladimir Putin sought strategic alignment with the West on a global scale. This moment lasted barely more than a year and disappeared with the Bush administration's cold-shouldering of Russia and Washington's heavy focus on Iraq and the greater Middle East.

Thus, integration *into* the West—on a "French model," as some Russians viewed it,[14] in the 1990s, and then *with* the West—in the form of an "alliance with the Alliance,"[15] in the early 2000s, became lost opportunities. Spurned, as an unrequited lover, Russia in the mid-2000s turned to reasserting its great powerdom as a default position.[16] By definition, a great power did not take orders from anyone. Russia, Putin claimed, would no longer be under the thumb of the United States. According to the official Putin-era concept, it "rose from its knees." It had preserved its nuclear weapons and was gaining a new usable instrument: energy. Against the background of the rapidly soaring oil price, some even called it a weapon.[17]

From then on, the boosted great-power mentality blocked, or at least placed severe restrictions on, any further integrationist effort: great powers do not integrate themselves, though they could integrate others. In Russia's case, ironically, *neither* was actually possible. Since 2003, Moscow's resumed attempts at economic integration with other CIS states, such as the Single Economic Space,[18] were inconsistent, hampered by Russia's own weakness, and constrained by its CIS partners' desire for more independence. As to occasional neoimperialist talk among the Russian elites, it was still all "on the cheap."

Ostensibly a firebrand, but essentially a steam-valve controller, Vladimir Zhirinovsky characterized this better than anyone. Rather than fomenting irredentism, he reduced it to *sound and fury*, and thus neutralized it. Words substituted for action. Emotions were put onto a treadmill. Troubled souls could vent their feelings and relieve themselves, but apart from a few ruffled feathers, everything remained in place.

At the top, there was neither money nor strong will for irredentism; at the bottom, the popular slogan was "Russia for the (ethnic) Russians," anti-immigrant and, while reprehensible, essentially defensive. The basic meaning of great power in the Russian minds, then, was its *own* independence, rather than others' dependence on it.

As great power trappings go, it comes after independence in this enumeration, but it might as well come ahead of it: great powers are domestically sovereign. If they are democracies, these are sovereign nations. If they are autocracies, these are regimes impervious to outside pressure. Post-Soviet Russia, with its mild authoritarian regime, enjoying the consent of the governed, falls into the latter category, where domestic independence means full sovereignty for the ruling elite. They are truly above law and moral conventions. The experience of the 1990s, when the Russian federal budget lived from one IMF handout to another, when Moscow audiences listened to foreign lecturers, and foreign advisers had easy access to top Russian bureaucrats, is not fondly remembered by the ruling groups of the 2000s. Putin's objective was to make the ruling regime safe from foreign pressure—and free from outside support—and to place it firmly on continuing popular assent, procured by a combination of effective policies. The massive inflow of oil and gas revenue in the mid-2000s made this largely possible. Foreigners were told to mind their own business, and domestic critics were disqualified as a "fifth column" of the West "scavenging at foreign embassies," in Putin's own words.[19] It is a combination of strategic and domestic independence that formed the substance of the much-quoted formula of *sovereign democracy*. Since democracy requires political participation, of which there is not much in today's Russia, the reality is more like *sovereign bureaucracy*.[20]

The notion of a great power, however, also has a meaning beyond the country's national borders. Like the king on stage, a great power, Russian traditionalists think, is played by the crowd of clients and supplicants. In the realpolitik-grounded view of the Russian leadership, the world is composed of a handful of truly sovereign great powers—America, China, and now again (after the interlude of the 1990s) Russia—and their respective "spheres of influence." It is in the nature of global politics, the Russian leaders and their advisers believe, that great powers should compete over these spaces, so as to extend their sway and establish authority. From this perspective, regional primacy is both natural and stabilizing; universal primacy is both an illusion and a threat.

In this competition, Russia's post-Soviet posture was essentially revisionist: Moscow militated against the U.S. "unipolar moment" and the "new world order" it established in the wake of the Cold War's end. Russia itself considered its own policies wholly defensive. Besides advancing multipolarity—a form of global oligarchy that would bar anyone's global predominance—Russia has been trying to regain soft dominance—but not control—in the former Soviet (i.e., imperial) space. The Russian leaders did not aspire to full control of that space, à la Lenin, at the close of the Russian Civil War; or in the manner of Stalin, before, during, and after World War II. Where Stalin's foreign minister Vyacheslav Molotov congratulated himself with having helped restore the "just" borders of the state,[21] Russia's current foreign minister Sergei Lavrov speaks about the "civilizational unity" that ties Russia and its near neighbors, whose formal sovereignty Russia nevertheless does not formally dispute—with the important exception of Georgia's borders.[22]

From that perspective, it is the United States that is seen as a poacher and intruder, who has crossed all imaginable borders, as Putin stated in his 2007 Munich speech.[23] What business, the Kremlin was heard asking at the close of the George W. Bush administration, does the United States have in Ukraine, Georgia, and Central Asia other than to expand its sphere of influence and pin down Russia, constrain and diminish it? Why does the U.S. Sixth Fleet frequent the waters of the Black Sea? Why, of all things, NATO enlargement in the absence of a threat to the West from Russia? To counter U.S. moves and to irritate Washington, Moscow has recently been using Venezuela and the other "Bolivarian" states—Nicaragua, Bolivia, Ecuador—to send one message to Washington: Get off my back!

This countervailing tactic, as the last example shows, means going beyond the "natural" area of Russian activism and carries the risk of re-entering global competition with a very powerful rival, which puts Moscow at a clear disadvantage. Russia, however, refuses to accept the rank of a middle power with merely a regional role. It sees itself as a global actor, playing in the major leagues.

This is a hugely important point: to be a great power means to be a co-ruler of the world. Both Mikhail Gorbachev in his final years in power as the last Soviet leader and Boris Yeltsin in his early years as Russia's first president envisaged something like a benign U.S.-Russian co-hegemony. This was not to be. In the later thinking of the Kremlin, the global anarchy prevailing after the end of the bipolar era can best be structured as a global oligarchy, a.k.a. multipolarity. This is not an analytical conclusion, but an active posture. Multipolarity is the antithesis of unipolarity, or U.S. global dominance. Moscow started its campaign against it in the mid-1990s—symbolized by Yevgeny Primakov's replacement of Andrey Kozyrev as foreign minister, and has been more vocal than any of its fellow travelers, including Beijing and Paris. True, the official Russian rhetoric is less strident than that of Presidents Mahmoud Ahmadinejad or Hugo Chávez, but these figures are occasionally seen in Moscow as tactical allies in resisting U.S. global hegemony—much as the late Saddam Hussein and Slobodan Milosevic were in the past. Meanwhile, the real post–Cold War G-2 began forming between the United States and China.

Since the days of Peter the Great, Russia sought to be a great power in Europe, a status it finally achieved as a result of victory over Napoleon. It then was a key member of the Holy Alliance, which maintained order in

Europe. From the Russian perspective, being one of a half-dozen mightiest powers to jointly manage the world is a natural aspiration. Moscow's preferred, if not ideal model is still the United Nations Security Council, with its supreme authority in the matters of war and peace and its all-important veto right enjoyed by the five permanent members, including Russia. When the Cold War ended, and the forty-year paralysis of the United Nations was over, Moscow hoped that a revitalized UN would be the heart of a new global order. In Europe, Moscow proposed that the Conference on Security and Cooperation in Europe be reformed into an organization with its own UN-style Security Council for Europe. These expectations turned out to be illusions. Instead, Russia had to live with the "unipolar moment"—and fight it.

After the end of the Cold War, Russia sought membership in the exclusive group of industrialized democracies, which became the G-8 when it joined in 1998. This was a hard-won badge of equality with the United States and the leading Western powers. This formal equality, however, did not lead to integration. Even though it appreciated the G-8 membership as a status symbol, Russia could not fully associate itself with the West—which, for its part, did not see Russia as being "one of us," and occasionally threatened it with excommunication. Importantly and symbolically, Russia was not invited to join the financial core of the club, which remained G-7 right up to the 2008 economic crisis. The crisis has produced a group much more germane to the economic and political realities of the early twenty-first-century world than either G-7 or G-8: G-20! True to form, Russia embraced the new club and sought to demonstrate its active posture there.

Thus, Russia seeks multiple and partially overlapping memberships: in the "home" post-imperial clubs it naturally dominates (CIS); exclusive Western/global clubs (such as the G-8 and the G-20); exclusive non-Western global clubs (such as BRIC, for Brazil-Russia-India-China, the leading emerging economies); and non-Western regional clubs (like the Shanghai Cooperation Organization, where Russia is a de facto co-chair, alongside China). As a country straddling Europe and Asia, Russia seeks to register its presence in broad groupings like the Organization for Security and Cooperation in Europe (OSCE), which it hoped, in the 1990s, would supplant NATO; and the Asia-Pacific Economic Cooperation (APEC) grouping, which Russia joined in 1999. It took pride in hosting global and regional summits: the G-8 in 2006; BRIC in 2009; and the forthcoming APEC in 2012.

Russia, however, shows relatively less interest in rules-based organizations with dozens of members without veto rights, such as the OSCE, the Council of Europe, APEC, the WTO, the OECD, or the UN General Assembly, for that matter. There, Russia wants to gain membership, so as to ensure that these organizations do not act against Russian interests. It seeks to retain freedom of maneuver by staying away from the OPEC and is being cautious about its gas equivalent, where Russia would have a major role, but whose discipline might constrain it.

What is striking about this analysis of Russian government views and practices is that it lays bare a fundamental distinction between an empire and a great power. Empires, for all the coercion they necessarily entail, do produce some public goods, in the name of a special mission. Great powers can be at least equally brutish and oppressive, but they are essentially selfish creatures. The great debate in Russia on the national interest, which, in 1992, signaled the transition to the post-imperial condition, eventually evolved into a concept of national egoism.

A Critique of Russia's Contemporary Foreign Policy

Managing imperial decline is always a very risky business. Managing a lighting-speed plunge from the position of a superpower to that of a supplicant is almost impossible. And managing that with a minimal loss of life is incredible. Yet, Russia has been able to end a war (in Afghanistan); withdraw from a number of Third World outposts; allow a series of peaceful—"velvet"—revolutions in Central and Eastern Europe; and permit the reunification of Germany—within NATO. It also disbanded the Warsaw Pact; concluded an agreement halving strategic nuclear weapons and pledged to withdraw a force of three quarters of a million men strong from Europe and Mongolia; let the three Baltic republics opt out of the Soviet Union, with no strings attached; and, finally, dismantled the Soviet Union itself, undoing the many ties running hundreds of years back.

Any criticism of Russia's foreign policy—including this author's—needs to take account of these unparalleled acts of voluntary self-limitation. Clearly, the Russian leadership was acting under the pressure of circumstances, but its actions hugely benefited other nations and ensured that the process of change was peaceful and orderly. It is neither correct nor fair to ignore Russian benevolence when discussing the revolutions in Eastern Europe, the fall of the Berlin Wall, the end of the Cold War, or the independence of the new states that emerged out of the Soviet Union. Walesa and Kohl, Bush and Baker, Ukraine's Rukh and the Baltic Popular Fronts all played their roles. The decisive factors were Gorbachev and Yeltsin and the Russian elites they represented.[24]

It also needs to be added that Russia's foreign policy was not evolving in a vacuum. In the early 1990s, more than ever before—or after, for that matter—it looked to the West for leadership and guidance. It got neither. It wanted to belong—and was told to first go through a transformation no one had ever seen or knew how to carry out. It craved equality, only to be told about the new balance of power. It recognized the Soviet debt, so as to be a good international citizen, and asked for a new Marshall Plan. It was commended on the former, and was given assistance packages that turned out to be among the least effective in world financial history. It was lectured on a variety of issues, but the only lessons it really learned were taught by the teachers' own actions, not their sermons.

Russia redesigning itself as a great power—after the collapse of both its empire and its dreams of Western integration—was not only inevitable but also stabilizing. It allowed the Russian leadership to regain some balance and a modicum of orientation in the rapidly changing world. The qualities of a great power, such as strategic independence, domestic sovereignty, free pursuit of interests abroad, and full participation in global governance, represent genuine values in international relations. Russia's problem is not that it embraced all those, but that it adopted a model of foreign policy that focused too much on traditional geopolitics.

Of course, Russian leaders understood their country's technological backwardness, the deteriorating quality and quantity of human resources there, and a general lack of appeal. They knew that whether or not Russia was a great power, it was far from being a *great country*. They did not probably believe all the international ratings that placed Russia closer to the bottom of most "good" lists, and nearer the top of many "bad" ones. They even ordered some indigenous Russian ratings to set the record straight. Yet, their gut reaction was to disparage their own seemingly naïve ideas about international relations, and adopt a no-nonsense realpolitik approach as a true compass in world affairs.

The crude version of realpolitik, now in use at the Kremlin, leads to problems. If Russia insists on using raw power criteria for international relations, it logically has to accept its own essential inequality vis-à-vis those whom it regards as no more than equals: America, China, the European Union. This produces a conundrum: Russia does not accept a junior position vis-à-vis its principal counterparts, but is fully conscious of their material superiority. When Russian leaders, true to their elevated self-image, try to imitate U.S. behavior, which they subconsciously accept as a gold standard of contemporary power politics, they immediately see the difference.[25] In particular, Russia has a big problem with its concept of spheres of interest, which, due to the notion of "spheres," which betrays lingering territorial thinking, is indistinguishable from spheres of influence. Moreover, even legitimate interests pushed too far cease to be legitimate.

To deal with these obvious problems, some of which have existed ever since Russia entered the European political system, it had to learn to punch well above its weight. In the early eighteenth century, Peter the Great set out to build a modern army and founded Russia's navy. To compensate for the country's technological backwardness and inferior education levels, Peter and his successors could rely on imported technology; administrative, industrial, and military expertise; and the superior manpower resources of Russia. He succeeded, but his success demanded mobilization measures very harsh even by the terms of his time.

Resource mobilization was traditionally achieved by means of a high degree of political centralism. Russian absolutism, autocracy, and, finally, Communist totalitarianism allowed the country's rulers to use whatever was needed in pursuit of their geopolitical goals. Peter, for instance, had the church bells confiscated to be melted down to produce cannons—he was free to do it, having abolished the patriarchy and sending a military officer to preside over the church's synod. Stalin, of course, had built a command economy that, when the war came, produced enough arms and materiel to ensure that the Red Army defeated the Nazi Wehrmacht. In the post-industrial age, however, mobilization capacity has become less crucial than capacity to innovate, which calls for political, economic, and societal structures very different from authoritarian government with a militarized economy and an obedient and docile population.

After World War II, and especially during the 1970s and 1980s, the clear emphasis on the arms industry to compensate for general economic weakness was taken ad absurdum, when the Soviet civilian economy was reduced to being an appendage of the military industrial complex. As a result, the Soviet

Armed Forces, for example, had more tanks than the rest of the world combined. The impossible burden this represented was among the key drivers of Gorbachev's early decision to seek disarmament agreements with the United States. Several decades later, the once-mighty military industrial complex is history. Russia has lost advance positions in a number of traditional areas and has not developed new capacities in producing state-of-the-art arms and equipment.

Thus, it is no wonder that in the post-Soviet period, Moscow has had to rely on its nuclear arsenal to make up for its increasing conventional military weakness. In one of his last statements as president, Yeltsin admonished Bill Clinton "never to forget, not for a minute, not for a second," that Russia was a nuclear superpower. Nuclear arsenals, however, have been notoriously difficult to operationalize. Under Yeltsin's successor, Vladimir Putin, energy power emerged as a usable policy instrument. Energy abundance was also thought to be a compensation for the nonperformance and decline of the Russian manufacturing industry. However, the actual practice of shutting off the valve to put pressure on Ukraine to pay up, as in 2006 and again in 2009, has led to Gazprom and Russia damaging their reputation as a reliable energy supplier to the European Union.

Finally, Russia sought to increase its leverage vis-à-vis the West by means of building tactical alignments with the West's adversaries. The original idea was that Moscow would be able to act as an intermediary between the international community and the particularly tough customers once known as "rogue regimes." The Russian leadership, never forgetting its roots and experience, hoped to play a unique role of interpreter-cum-facilitator. Moscow's efforts throughout the 1990s and the early 2000s to mediate between the West and leaders like Slobodan Milosevic, Kim Jong Il, and Saddam Hussein turned out to be unsuccessful. As Russia's relations with the United States worsened, it stopped mediating and started embracing such anti-American figures as Venezuela's Chàvez. The payoff from these embraces, however, is dubious. Supporting Chàvez and his Bolivarian friends is financially costly, but could also become politically dangerous in case of some military adventure involving Russian-supplied arms.

It appears that the Russian elites are afflicted by status-mania. At one level, this is based on the conviction that Russia will either be a great power, or it won't be. The fear of chaos and disintegration is supported by historical reminiscences, most recently those of the late 1980s and early 1990s. This affliction, however, has rational roots as well. International status is something the Russian leaders offer to the Russian people as proof of their able leadership, to compensate for the deficiencies or failures of domestic policies and, more importantly, as justification for the harshness of the domestic regime. Faced with the superior might of an essentially adversarial West, Russia, they argue, has no choice but to accept the "unity of command." In totalitarian times, ideas such as "a besieged fortress" were in abundant supply. In the wake of the terrorist attack at Beslan and the Orange Revolution in Ukraine, preoccupation with security led to a harder line both at home and abroad. Although, with respect to contemporary Russia, the notion of a "national security state" is a serious exaggeration, the excessive focus on international status and domestic regime security hampers efforts at modernization. This leaves less room for a useful international role—except in terms of balancing the world hegemon under the rubric of asymmetrical and conflict-prone multipolarity. Other roles are clearly secondary.

Is There a Realistic Alternative to Realpolitik?

It looks as if Russia has exited the twentieth century through two doors at the same time. As a result, it has espoused a worldview that is a curious combination of nineteenth-century realpolitik and twenty-first-century postmodern, globalized attitudes. No doubt, the revival of realpolitik had everything to do with the bitter experience with Gorbachev's "new political thinking." The ideas that the "new thinkers" sought to implement—a balance of interests instead of a balance of forces; a world without nuclear weapons; a common European home and universal human values—started to fade even while Gorbachev was still in power. The fall of the Berlin Wall was still a happy moment, but the Gulf War already offered the contours of a new world order, with its "unipolar moment," leading to the bombings of Yugoslavia and the invasion of Iraq. The official Russian reaction to it was encapsulated in a Putin phrase: "The weak get beaten." Moscow's resistance to NATO's eastern enlargement turned into a symbol of its rejection of U.S. hegemony. However, at the same time Russia could not afford confrontation with the West and was increasingly dependent on it economically and financially: it did join the world economy, but as a raw materials producer par excellence. Russian companies are investing in NATO countries, and Moscow is insisting on visa-free movement between Russia and the EU countries, most of whom are also NATO members. No wonder this leads to schizophrenia. Yet, there is an alternative to the narrow, the outdated, and the incongruous in Russia's foreign policy making.

The concept of right as might—which has certainly been partially inherited by the twenty-first century—needs to be expanded through the notion of right as responsibility. In the twenty-first century, the power of attraction definitely trumps that of coercion. This is a direct result of the changing nature of power. Military power still matters, but it is no longer supreme. Suffice it to refer to the U.S. experiences in Iraq and Afghanistan: routing Saddam Hussein or the Taliban was relatively easy; managing the post-victory conditions in either place turned out to be anything but. The hearts and minds are key, and not only in occupied territories. The advent of soft power is as much a feature of the twenty-first century as the discovery of nuclear power, which shaped the second half of the twentieth. Thus, Russia will have to adapt its hard power to the necessities of the new age and learn to master its soft power, while ensuring the right mix of the two. This will not be easy.

The key to modernizing Russia's foreign policy is embracing all-around modernization of the country as the paramount goal also in international affairs. In other words, foreign relations need to be viewed, above all, as a resource for domestic modernization. Other interests and needs must be subordinated to that overriding priority. Russian elites need to realize not merely that only a great country can be a great power, but that without modernization Russia will fall even farther behind its neighbors and become a backward periphery, a raw materials appendage of both Europe *and* East Asia. In the end, if that trend continues, the very notion of Russia as a great power will be inevitably exposed as a sham. Then, Russia's disintegration would likely become a matter of time.

In practical terms, this calls for self-liberation from the obsession with Washington's presumed "hidden agenda" of diminishing and destroying Russia, dropping the idea of a historical revenge for the "loss of the Cold War," and getting rid of primitive anti-Americanism, which is distorting the worldview of Russian elites. Unless their minds become enlightened, and their energies focused on a positive agenda, proclaimed modernization will inevitably turn to mobilization, which will drive Russia down, instead of helping it on the way up.

Another important insight for the Russian leaders should be that Russia will be unable to modernize on its own. Even if they tried it, mobilization will not work—as it did in the 1930s. Globalization offers a range of opportunities, which should be seized. Accession to the World Trade Organization, forming regional customs unions, or continent-wide free trade areas have to be seen largely through the prism of activating incentives for the country's economic development. Russia's distant but important goal has to be joining the Organization of Economic Cooperation and Development, which, if achieved, will crown its modernization success.

Globalism, of course, is not a substitute for integration. True, the path to modernity that Moscow's erstwhile satellites in the Warsaw Pact and COMECON and the Baltic provinces used to join Europe is not, for a number of reasons—not least the elite's great power mentality—practical for Russia. However, Russia cannot afford isolation either. Moscow will have to devise a strategy of *non-institutional* integration with the developed world.

The European Union, due to its geographic proximity and the essential unity of European civilization, of which Russia is part, is Moscow's most important partner. The four spaces of EU-Russia collaboration, agreed in 2005 and largely neglected since, represent a road map of Russia's transformation. These should be expanded through economic integration, of which the most important element is genuine energy partnership. Like the European Coal and Steel Community, which led to the formation of the EEC in the 1950s, a European Energy Partnership could pave the way to a Russia economically integrated with the EU. There is a need for a new or modified Energy Charter to which Russia can accede. Russia's eventual entry into the WTO would pave the way to creating a pan-European economic area, reaching all the way to the Pacific and to the edges of Central Asia.

Such a degree of economic integration demands appropriate security guarantees. What is needed is a genuine security community, a demilitarized environment in the Euro-Atlantic area. In practical terms, one needs to deal with Moscow's concerns regarding Washington's intentions vis-à-vis Russia, and with Russia's neighbors' concerns with respect to what Moscow wants. Such a security community will not be the result of a single treaty. Rather, it has a chance to emerge from a process of mutual confidence building, leading to the establishment of trust across Europe and the Atlantic. This trust will not only allow North America, Europe, and Russia to build a common security space, or a zone of stable peace where wars and military conflicts are safely excluded among member-states, but to form genuine family relations among the three branches of European civilization: West-Central European, East European/Russian, and American.

This confidence building can be realized through a number of specific steps. Top of the list is dealing with the twin obsessions: Russia's with presumably hostile American intentions, and Central and Eastern European countries' with Russian allegedly evil intentions. Both are baseless in reality but still deeply rooted in the respective psyches. On the former, the United States needs to take the lead; on the latter, the Russian Federation.

A true game-changer in the first case could be a genuine offer by the United States to Russia to construct a joint missile defense system, with European participation. This would allow for a strategic breakthrough: from continued mutual assured destruction, even if at lower levels, to strategic collaboration. Another crucial step would be turning the NATO-Russia Council into a central mechanism for discussing, and eventually deciding, all important security issues in the Euro-Atlantic area. This would include, in particular, cooperation on solving the outstanding frozen conflicts. The case of Transdniester is the easiest of these difficult tasks, and could become a pilot project for successful U.S.-European-Russian-Ukrainian interaction. With the United States, France, and Russia as co-chairs of the Minsk group on Nagorno-Karabakh, their even-handedness and unity of purpose can help the Armenians and Azeris toward an eventual agreement, which, of course, is theirs to make. The South Caucasus is also an area where Turkey has a useful role to play, including in Abkhazia, whose final status needs to be decided by the international community as a whole, as does the status of South Ossetia—and Kosovo, for that matter.

Russia needs to start dismantling the mistrust it encounters in the neighboring countries. Particularly in the absence of diplomatic relations, contact and dialogue with Georgian political and public figures about the future of Russo-Georgian relations is essential. Restoring and expanding trade and transport links is in mutual interest, but it is also an enabler of productive political dialogue. Whatever the attitudes in Moscow to President Saakashvili, a cold war with Georgia serves no useful purpose. Abkhazia and especially Ossetia are difficult issues, but reconciliation with Georgia needs to be a goal of Moscow's policy in the South Caucasus, with clear implications for Russian-EU and Russian-U.S. relations.

Seen from Russia, Europe cannot start on the Oder or Elbe rivers. The historical lands between Russia and Germany require considerably more attention and good will from Moscow. The Russian leadership needs to work actively to impress on the Poles and the Balts, above all, but also on others in Central and Eastern Europe that modern Russia treats them not as runaway serfs or servants, but as good neighbors. The difficult and often painful issues from the past need to be dealt with by means of respecting the humanity of the innocent victims, whoever they are, and working toward greater understanding of the historical experience through the opening of archives and joint drafting of history school books.

Getting Russo-Ukrainian relations right will be immensely important but also particularly difficult. Yet, freedom of choice remains the fundamental principle, which has to be honored by all, East and West. Russians, for their part, will need to realize that no matter how close the ties between the two peoples and countries are, Ukraine will remain independent of the Russian Federation, even as it seeks closer relations with the European Union. Attitude toward Ukraine's independence will remain a touchstone of Russia's post-imperial transformation.

As for the European Union, it will need to embrace a broader concept of Europe to include not only the six Eastern Partnership countries but also Russia and possibly Kazakhstan. The long-term goal could be a pan-European Economic Area, built on the basis of free trade agreements with the neighboring countries. The ambitious idea of a political union between Europe and Russia reaches beyond the limits of the present discussion. However, progressive economic integration; thickening human ties—which would be boosted by easing and eventually dropping the visa regime; and emerging political cooperation are paving the way in that very direction.

There are several caveats in this approach.

One is that, while proceeding along the path of non-institutional integration, Russia should abandon some of the habits of a great power. It will preserve its sovereignty, but should not seek to construct a binary Europe (Euro-Asian Economic Community [EurAsEC]+Collective Security Treaty Organization [CSTO] vs EU+NATO). This will probably be made easier by the reluctance of Moscow's nominal allies and partners, including Belarus, to be seen trailing in the wake of Russian foreign and security policy.

Russia will have pride in its own rich legacy, but it should find a way toward historic reconciliation with the countries of Central and Eastern Europe that still bear grudges against imperial and Soviet policies and practices. While Russia is right to point out to the divisiveness of the NATO enlargement issue in Ukraine and the unresolved conflicts that create problems for Georgia's accession, it has to accept the sovereign right of all countries to seek membership in security institutions of their choice. The only limitations here are the ones with the roots in the countries concerned, such as Ukrainian people's reluctance to join NATO, and the configuration of Georgia's borders.

Another caveat is that Russia needs to learn to produce global public goods. It has a major role to play in a number of areas of utmost importance: combating extremism in the Muslim world; preventing nuclear weapons proliferation; dealing with climate change—to name but a few.

Russia has a sizeable Muslim element within its own borders. The end of hostilities in Chechnya notwithstanding, the North Caucasus has become a fertile ground for extremism, terrorism, and banditry. To combat it, Russia would have to change the dysfunctional feudal pattern of imperial rule in the tiny but restless ethnic enclaves stretching from the Caspian to the Black Sea. More regional development assistance under conditions of more competent and transparent government; more pluralism to ensure more representation of diverse interests; an enlightened Muslim clergy to combine the modernization drive with the values of Islam; a professional police, security, and military force to deal with maintenance of law and order: all of these appear to be the principal instruments for a positive policy in the North Caucasus. In some respects, such as Islam-friendly modernization, representation, and accountability, or religious tolerance, other Muslim-majority regions of Russia, such as Tatarstan and Bashkortostan, can lead the way.

In Central Asia, which lies just south of Russia's borders, Moscow has a responsibility to help maintain security, ensure general political stability, and promote economic and social development in the region. Close economic integration with Kazakhstan, Moscow's principal partner there, is a key instrument to achieve these goals. Others would include the Collective Security Treaty Organization to combat extremism and terrorism, drug trafficking, and illegal migration; and to maintain certain domestic political standards and friendly relations among its member-states. The Euro-Asian Economic Community would focus on promoting trade, economic, and societal development in the region. Working along with China within the Shanghai Cooperation Organization (SCO) would also help advancing those objectives.

In Afghanistan, Russia will certainly not join in the U.S./NATO military effort. However, it has been assisting it by making its transit routes available to the Allies. In the longer term, it can help promote national reconciliation and economic reconstruction. Russians can help train Afghan military and police officers. Moscow has knowledge and experience to contribute to an interethnic balance in Afghanistan. It can help create a positive atmosphere around Afghanistan, in particular through its co-leadership in the SCO, which also includes China and the Central Asia states, and (as observers) Afghanistan, Iran, Pakistan, India, and also Mongolia. Finally, Russia has a major stake in stemming the drug flow from Afghanistan, and will cooperate with NATO and its own allies in the CSTO to reduce the drug threat.

Russia has an outstanding role to play in preventing further spread of nuclear weapons. As a member of the Six-Party Talks on the North Korean nuclear issue, it is part of a common effort designed to cap and roll back Pyongyang's nuclear program. As a member of another six-party effort to avert Iran's acquisition of nuclear weapons, it has an even greater role to play. Playing that role will not be easy. Rather than opposing U.S. policies of sanctions and dismissing U.S./Israeli military threats against Iran, or, conversely, toying with the idea of "swapping" Iran for some geopolitical "prize" in the post-Soviet space, Russia needs to engage with the United States and Europe in forging a common strategy vis-à-vis Iran, while at the same time using its contacts in Tehran—and also in Jerusalem and Beijing—to help ensure the success of such a strategy.

The goal of the Iran strategy would be to reach an agreement whereby: (1) Iran forswears its nuclear weapons ambitions while pursuing a peaceful nuclear program, complete with a full nuclear cycle, under very close, intrusive monitoring by the IAEA; (2) the United States and Iran restore diplomatic relations; (3) Iran and Iraq join the Gulf Cooperation Council to form an inclusive security arrangement in the region; and (4) Iran joins the WTO and fully reintegrates into the world economy.

On climate-related issues, Russia's major contribution would be raising the energy efficiency of its economy. Russia has also a major responsibility for preserving its vast taiga forests and its sweet water reserves, such as Lake Baikal. The melting of the Arctic icecap, while allowing Russia to expand its North Sea route shipping linking Europe and East Asia and to explore the resources of the Arctic shelf, increases its responsibility for protecting the environment and for peaceful resolution of territorial/exploration rights disputes. In the multipolar world of the twenty-first century, Russia will need to acquire the habits of multilateralism.

Great to Good

A security community does not have to be a values community. Russia is not a democracy today. Its transformation will take time to produce modern values among the country's population and, more specifically, within its moneyed elite and the political class. Yet, neither greatness nor power is any longer possible without a moral standing. If Russia wants to play a leading, or simply a significant positive role, the vaunted pragmatism of its early 2000s foreign policy and the pervasive cynicism—and brutality—of Russian daily life will have to yield to a framework of basic values and moral principles. Indeed, this is the same requirement as for Russia's domestic transformation: it will get nowhere unless underpinned by some basic values.

In this respect, Russia could place special emphasis on promoting a few principles on the world arena: justice for all, religious and ethnic tolerance, and support for international law. The concept of justice could complement that of legality.[26] Muslim–Orthodox Christian relations in Tatarstan could be a model for religious tolerance elsewhere in Europe. Moscow's insistence—for instance, at the UN Security Council level—on observing international law could enhance the stability of the world system as a whole. To make those roles credible, Russia has to match the principles it may wish to uphold internationally with its own domestic practices, and, of course, its behavior abroad. Thus, there is a rich potential to be explored in moving from great to good.

This chapter does not touch upon what it would take to bring about the changes discussed in it. In the author's view, these need not result from a political revolution. An upheaval is more likely to throw Russia back than to push it forward. Expecting some "other Russia" to take over from the "usurpers" is naïve. The 1917 lesson is that the elites need to think beyond their immediate interests and be able to collaborate for the common good. What is missing in today's Russia is just this—common cause, a res publica. The conservative modernization that the leaders of United Russia are talking about today would only make sense as a way to avert a destructive upheaval at home and marginalization abroad, not an effort to conserve the socioeconomic and political realities of contemporary Russia.

The task before Russia is extremely difficult, and the challenges are formidable. To many outsiders, Russia is already dead, beyond salvation. This is a premature judgment. Given the cumulative experience of the twentieth century, and the stresses of the last twenty years, Russians are not doing too badly, for now. It will be the next decade or two that will be decisive. Will corruption be checked or will it finish off the country? Will Russians stay atomized, or will they reach out to one another to form a civic nation? Will this nation establish its sovereignty, and constitute a democracy, or will it stay passive and allow the unaccountable elite to rule over it, in bitter irony, in the name of sovereign democracy? The stakes are incredibly high, and although there is still enough talent in place to turn things around, there is no guarantee of success.

Notes

1. As used here, "empire" and hence "imperialism" are not derogatory terms, but terms denoting a certain type of state organization and state policy.
2. As recalled by Olexandr Chaliy, then Ukraine's first deputy foreign minister, in a conversation on February 7, 2010.
3. Vladimir Putin, "Annual Message to the Federal Assembly of the Russian Federation" (Moscow, April 25, 2005), http://eng.kremlin.ru/speeches/2005/04/25/2031_type70029type82912_87086.shtml.
4. Zbigniew Brzezinski, *The Great Chessboard: American Primacy and Its Geostrategic Imperatives* (New York: Basic Books, 1999), 46.
5. For example, see Dmitri Furman, "SNG—poslednyaya forma Rossiyskoy imperii" [The CIS is the last form of the Russian Empire], in *Posle imperii* [After the empire], ed. Igor Klyamkin (Moscow: Liberal Mission Foundation, 2007), 80.
6. Vladimir Putin's comment at a press conference following the Russo-Armenian talks in Yerevan, March 25, 2005, http://eng.kremlin.ru/speeches/2005/03/25/2234_type82914type82915_85953.shtml.
7. Yegor Gaidar, *Gibel' imperii. Uroki dlya sovremennoy Rossii* [Death of an empire. Lessons for modern Russia] (Moscow: ROSSPEN, 2007).
8. Yevgenii Primakov, "Mezhdunarodnye otnosheniya na poroge 21-go veka: problemy I perspektivy" [International relations on the eve of the twenty-first century: problems and prospects], *Mezhdunarodnaya Zhizn*, no. 10 (1996): 3–13.
9. Yeltsin's first term ran from 1991 to 1996, and Kozyrev was foreign minister from 1990 to 1996.

10. "Rising from the knees" became a refrain with many pro-Kremlin commentators in the second half of the 2000s.
11. As reported by Dimitri Simes in his book, *After the Collapse* (New York: Simon and Schuster, 1999), 19.
12. The issue was not, as some authors (notably, Mark Kramer) correctly point out, that Mikhail Gorbachev had never been given assurances as to the non-expansion of NATO membership beyond its Cold War boundaries. The Russians thought they had unilaterally wound down the confrontation, dissolved their empire, and embraced Western values. They expected, in turn, to be embraced by the West. What they saw instead was the expansion of the Cold War military alliance toward their borders. Their conclusions about why this was happening were often wrong, but their concerns were genuinely felt. See Mark Kramer, "The Myth of a No-NATO-Enlargement Pledge to Russia," *Washington Quarterly* (April 2009): 39–60.
13. For a reference to Viktor Chernomyrdin's comment, see Konstantin Smirnov and Vladislav Dorofeev, "Skazano: ES!" *Kommersant-Vlast*, July 29, 1997, http://www.kommersant.ru/doc.aspx?DocsID=13702.
14. Vyacheslav Nikonov made that argument in the mid-1990s. See his *Epokha peremen. Rossiys 90-kh glazami konservatora* [Collected articles. The nineties through the eyes of a conservative] (Moscow: 1999).
15. To use the phrase coined by Alexander Vershbow, U.S. Ambassador to Russia in the early 2000s. See *Kommersant*, "NATO budet delit'sya," November 21, 2001, http://www.kommersant.ru/doc.aspx?DocsID=295303.
16. For the author's extensive analysis, see Dmitri Trenin, "Russia Leaves the West," *Foreign Affairs*, July/August 2006.
17. See, for example, Vitaly Panyushkin and Mikhail Zygar, *Gazprom. Novoye russkoye oruzhie* (Moscow: Zakharov, 2008).
18. An idea broached in 2004 with the aim of integrating Ukraine economically with Russia, alongside Kazakhstan and Belarus. It lost whatever meaning it might have had after Ukraine's Orange Revolution in late 2004.
19. Putin's comments were reported by *Rossiyskaya gazeta* on November 22, 2007, http://www.rg.ru/2007/11/22/putin-forum.html.
20. See Derluguian, chap. 3 in this volume.
21. Molotov's quote as reported by Felix Chuev, *Sorok besed s Molotovym. Iz dnevnika Feliksa Chueva* [Forty interviews with Molotov. From the diary of Felix Chuev] (Moscow: Terra, 1991).
22. Sergei Lavrov, "Russian Foreign Policy and a New Quality of the Geopolitical Situation," *Diplomatic Yearbook* 2008, http://www.mid.ru/brp_4.nsf/e78a48070f128a7b4325

6999005bcbb3/19e7b14202191e4ac3257525003e5de7?OpenDocument.

23. Putin's speech at the Munich Security Conference, February 10, 2007, http://eng.kremlin.ru/speeches/2007/02/10/0138_type82912type82914type82917type84779_118123.shtml.

24. Today, while many Russians are ambivalent about Gorbachev's legacy as far as Russian interests are involved, they see him as a true hero of Germany, and possibly of other countries formerly dominated by the Soviet Union. See, for example, Dmitri Medevedev's interview in *Der Spiegel*, November 7, 2009, http://eng.kremlin.ru/speeches/2009/11/07/1230_type82916_222598.shtml.

25. We need only consider Russia's military operation against Georgia in 2008, following Tbilissi's attack on South Ossetia, which was modeled on NATO's 1999 intervention in Kosovo; or the recognition of Kosovo, on the one hand, and of Abkhazia and South Ossetia, on the other.

26. To illustrate the point, it is worth comparing the Russian director Nikita Mikhalkov's film 12 with the original, *Twelve Angry Men*, directed by Sydney Lumet.

AFTERWORD

Russia and the West: Toward Understanding

Vladimir I. Yakunin

This chapter is about *Russia in crisis*.

The author himself comes from this Russian reality and, together with 150 million people close to him, finds himself negotiating the eddies of Russia's chaos. Yet at the same time he bears the burden of responsibility for many incidences of destruction and transition—"both professionally and personally." This chapter was not easy to write. Every sentence provoked memories and gave rise to many unanswered questions.

For us, the subject of Russia and the West is extremely current. It is essential that Russia understand itself through the prism of the West in order to recognize what is happening to us, the historical choices and challenges we face, and the options for our future as a country and a nation. This subject has an immediate effect on the fate of everyone in Russia and on the entire "post-Soviet" space.

This same subject is topical in the West, too. These days, Western historians and philosophers systematize their knowledge of the West with the help of "Russia as a mirror." After all, Russia was the West's ethnicizing *significant other*, and European national and civilizational self-perception largely rejected the image of Russia and the Russians.

We need to define Russia's civilizational identity. Without for the moment getting into the structural nuances of the civilizational matrix (more of this later), this afterword examines the question of whether Russia is part of that entity known as "the West" or "Western civilization." Opinions on this vary. I shall set out the conclusions in favor of the position I share myself, which can be summarized as follows: Russia developed as an alternative (to the Western) *Christian Orthodox civilization*. On the main issues of existence it never offered different solutions to those of the West and thus became its existential partner and opponent—however much the Russian state and elite periodically endeavored to avoid that.

There has long been tension between the West and Russia. This is unavoidable in relations between two different civilizations, one of which, the West, is extremely dynamic. It is unthinkable without expansion—hence the West's achievements: Charlemagne's conquests; the great geographic discoveries and building of colonial empires in Asia, Africa, America, and Australia; the emergence of an unorthodox type of economy, the aim of which was the persistent expansion of wealth (capitalism); and the creation of new ways of learning, the aim of which was the persistent acquisition of knowledge (science). All these were unique attributes of a unique civilization. We study all this but cannot transform ourselves from one moment to the next, like the fairy-tale frog-prince.

Some in the West refute the thesis of Russia's civilizational autonomy. Alain Besançon writes that we either consider Russia has simply "fallen behind" Europe or accept that we are dealing with a "distortion" of Europe. Besançon claims that the choice of one of these two points of view has immediate practical results; on it depends the policies that the European West will adopt in relation to Russia.[1]

Part of the Russian "elite," ingrained with Eurocentrism, accepts this explanation. But this image, which our radical pro-Western liberals endeavor to create of "Russia as a Europe that has lost its way," only leads to a schism in Russian society, a figurative and geographic drama within the national consciousness that substantially complicates the huge "molecular" work of Russia's nations in creating a modern pattern of dealings between Russia and the West. There is no need to pour oil on the fire from the West as well.

But Europe, too, has not generally considered that Russia "belongs" to it, and this applies even to those thinkers who respect Russia as a civilization. They have acknowledged its fundamental difference from the West. Oswald Spengler wrote:

> Up to now I have refrained from mentioning Russia—intentionally, for with Russia it is not a question of different peoples but of different worlds.... The distinctions between Russian and Western spirit cannot be drawn too sharply. As deep a cleavage as there is between the spirit, religion, politics, and economics of England, Germany, America, and France, when compared with Russia these nations suddenly appear as a unified world. It is easy to be deceived by some inhabitants of Russia who reflect strong Western influence. The true Russian is just as inwardly alien to us as a Roman in the Age of Kings or a Chinese long before Confucius would be if they were suddenly to appear among us. The Russians have been aware of this every time they have drawn a line of demarcation between "Mother Russia" and "Europe."[2]

This is a critically important factor. In order to be a member of the "European family of nations," that family itself has to recognize you as one of them. It is not a question of paying your money and taking a seat. It is not that kind of theater. Even if Russians' self-denial proved to be of indubitable benefit to them, it is not viable simply because of the iron curtain that separates the West itself from us and which is much stronger than Stalin's. At the time of the breakup of the USSR in 1991, the West obviously did not consider Soviet Russia as part of Western civilization.

For our purposes, an important document is the article by the Czech writer Milan Kundera, "The Stolen West or a Farewell Bow to Culture," published in 1984.[3] Kundera accused the West of making a deal with Russia and giving up part of Europe to be torn to shreds by barbarous non-Europeans. What was more, Kundera, who regards the USSR as the "organic" embodiment of "Russian traits," was accusing not the USSR but Russia of barbarity. Kundera was a Cold War warrior, but why did this article have such resonance? It was because it coincided with the ideas of the Western elite.

In theory, this question is not new. I agree here with Immanuel Wallerstein's approach, in which a single, planetary world system was formed in the "long sixteenth century" made up of the "core" (the countries of the West), the "semiperiphery" (which includes Russia), and the "periphery." It is impossible to change a country's position in this structure (to move, for example, from the semiperiphery to the core). Consequently, Russia is not part of the Western system and is doomed to the semiperiphery. This conclusion was refuted by Russia (not with any pretension of joining the "motherland"), but for us the very fact of Russia's exclusion from the West is important.

Historically, prior to the development of a single world-system space, there were a number of localized world systems that matched the existence of "civilizations." The unification of the civilizational centers with the civilizational peripheries produced "global empires." In practice, each of these civilizations, including Russia, historically promoted its own imperial model.

Then emerged the model of a single form of world organization in which the West, as the victor and architect of the "new world order," occupied the center and exploited the rest of the world. All other countries structured themselves around it. Regional states in the new world order can be broken down into four groups: (1) "oil republics," providing the West with oil and other raw materials; (2) "banana republics," providing the West with food; (3) "republics of contrasts," financing the West by exploiting their people through the purchase of Western goods with a large share of added value and, above all provided with no global currency; and (4) "assembly plant countries," carrying out the function of industrial suppliers to the West.

Thus, the world system that exists today is neocolonial in nature. World colonialism did not disappear with the collapse of the English and French colonial systems but assumed a new format, a new embodiment. The main mechanism of its support nowadays is not so much military might as more integration into the single financial system and the parasitical dollar pyramid.

In Soviet times Russia broke loose from this world system and the "Socialist camp" formed around it, which began to take shape as an independent world system (a bipolar world). At the end of the twentieth century the Socialist camp entered crisis and broke up. Mankind is currently going through a period of the "restructuring" of the system of world organization that has engendered an intense "dialogue of civilizations." However, we see no indications in this process of Russia being included with the West as part of the "motherland."

Russia as Civilization

How should we regard the system of cultures and civilizations objectively, having "freed ourselves" from the pull of the Eurocentrist intellectual apparatus? How can Russia and the West be viewed "from above" on the civilizational world map as materially different entities (despite many similarities)? These questions lie at the heart of the problem of why it is sometimes so difficult to understand one another but so easy to be suspicious of each other.

The nineteenth-century Russian poet Fyodor Tyutchev said: "You cannot understand Russia using your head; you cannot apply the same standard."[4] But after all, every nation and country has its own unique profile, not just Russia. There, we have arrived at the key word—*profile*. What sort of profile? Why are we not always able, like Kipling's character Mowgli, to say to others "We be of one blood, ye and I!"[5]? Because we *are* different, and our differences are subject to empirical exposure. And in order to exist we proceed from the key formula: "We are different but equal as human beings."

Differences between nations and countries arose historically. They are reinforced by culture, faith, traditions, languages, and attitudes. There are those who think it possible to learn a language at the drop of a hat, to change one's faith, and to use mass manipulation to force traditions and attitudes to change so that those who are regarded as "second class" may join the "first class" community. In contemporary Russia certain radical reformers genuinely hope this will happen. The clearest illustration of what this will lead to is demographic. Our research shows that rises in mortality, reductions in the birth rate, and falling life expectancy are caused less by lower standards of living (the material factor) than by the attempt to destroy Russians' and their community's mental, cultural, and philosophical bases, along with Russia's spiritual values and its multinational and multiconfessional civilization, which has existed for thousands of years.

Nations, states, and civilizations have developed for centuries under their own unique conditions. They either survived or disappeared from history. Ways and means of survival were reinforced in memory, skills, traditions, and approaches; in ways of life, culture, and law; in the structure of the state, the organization of labor, government, the rules of community life. That is how different (with the operative word being "different") civilizations were born. But what was shared was the fact that the experience they accrued and reinforced as part of their identity was of the same kind: it was the *experience of success*.

It is clear that nations and civilizations maximize their success only when they use their own formulae for success. Of course, the social nature of mankind leads to intercultural exchange, a sharing of knowledge and experience, a certain universalization of the formula for life. It is worth carrying out a mental experiment and asking oneself what will happen once mankind is completely able to meet its needs in terms of food, energy, water, and mineral and biological resources? Will the unique success formulae of different nations—and the nations themselves—remain? Or will we reach such a homogeneous state that civilizations will converge, faiths will draw closer, indeed, the whole of humanity will simply unite with its Creator? The logic of the mental experiment forces us to acknowledge that this is all probable. But when could all this happen? The same logic indicates that it will take hundreds, thousands, tens and hundreds of thousands of years.

For the moment we remain different. But the differences are a key to civilizational, national, and country success. So, how do we measure the success we are talking about? What is it: Gross domestic product? Labor productivity? The size of the budget? The health of the nation? Supremacy in education and innovation? Military might? It has been suggested (at Davos) that indexes be developed of global competitiveness or democratic development or other indicators reflecting ways in which humans typically manage their lives. But there is not yet a single, universal, balanced index of individual countries' success.

All countries, not just Russia, need to find criteria—for development, for state and social decision making and actions, for government—that would offer objective indicators of success. But in terms of the choice of a way of life and one or another country's path toward development, can individual indicators such as democracy, competitiveness, innovation, and the like be convincing when taken out of their multifaceted context? Probably not. It is precisely this lack of agreement that is largely responsible for the differences of opinion between Russia and NATO, Russia and the United States, and so on, despite the fact that both sides genuinely strive to remove discrepancies, to understand each other, and to work together.

Instead, we are forever being told to follow external advice. One of the arguments here is that Russian civilization is a replica of European or Western civilization, that the success formulae for Russia are the same as for Western civilization. In the example of demography we have already demonstrated that this is, to a catastrophic extent, not the case. But there is also the general challenge that, once solved, would show why we are different and why the formulae for success are also different for every nation, country, and civilization. We formulate this challenge as finding the *value profile* of civilizational identity, which can be measured and compared for different countries. A quantitative measure is required, apart from vague discussions of whether Russians are European or Asian. We also need criteria. It seems to us that there is such a measure, and moreover, in the course of finding it, we will encounter the identical problem of the *universal idea* of the progress of mankind, and a further challenge—how to combine religious ideas on the nature of the world and man with concepts of rational knowledge and science.

For instance, no one in Russia is opposed to democracy, but the sanctity of the authoritarian and paternalist principles are much more pronounced within the Russian people than in Europeans or Americans. That is why the system of government, branded as authoritarian by those who have not fully investigated it, takes on a different nature in Russia; paradoxically, this may promote that very democracy considerably better than would the copying of electoral models traditional in the West. After all, is it likely that someone in the West would come up with all the ruses and stunts that lobbyists in contemporary Russia use to abuse democracy and make money for their own shady purposes? No, those tricks are Russian. The West has its own. So, what are we arguing about—democracy or the quality of the stunts?

Of the same ilk are demands for the immediate formation in Russia of a civil society, the same as in the West. But civil society is no simple matter. The West toiled long and hard over its construction. We are doing what we can, but Russian civil society is as yet imperfect. But after all, isn't the main thing to be moving in the right direction? The West's civil society, as a structured band of individuals, is bound together by the fulcrum of private ownership—and revolves around this fulcrum. But the quintessence of ownership is private ownership by an individual. Descartes depicted the separation of the spirit and the body,[6] but then Descartes had never been to Russia! What can *we* do if the Marxists failed to completely root out communality and national values in Russia!

Russia and the West: Differences and Similarities

What sort of historical horizon is necessary and adequate for sensible examinations of contemporary Russia? Our discussion will rely on the well-documented history of the nineteenth century, post-reform modernization, and the ageing of Russia's historical choice as a civilization. There is also the catastrophe of the Russian Revolution, forced industrialization, the Great Patriotic War (World War II), and the "long today"—the Cold War involving the defeat and liquidation of the USSR and the systemic crisis of the 1990s, with "Project Putin" as the way of overcoming it.

Let us take a look at the main stages in the formation of modern Russia. People think of themselves as a nation only in comparison with other nations (the *others*), primarily those that have the greatest influence on their fate. Ever since the sixteenth century the main others for the Russians became the Western nations and Western civilization as a whole. The reverse was also true.

Russia's attitude toward the West was one of keen attention, and it adopted many of the West's ideas and much of its technology and social institutions. As far as the relationship with the West was concerned, there was ongoing debate among Russians themselves, and long-term conflicts arose that even spawned two philosophical movements—the Westernizers and the Slavophiles.

We shall not avoid difficult issues; discussing them helps us to understand the present. An important aspect of Russians' self-awareness was Western *Russophobia*, which emerged as a developed ideology in the second half of the sixteenth century. One of the first sources of Russophobia was the image of the Slavs of Rus as religious apostates. Among a series of enlightened Westerners and in Russia itself the spiritual link between Rus and Byzantium was regarded as the reason for Russians' "intellectual immaturity." Pyotr Chaadaev, an early Russian philosopher, wrote: "Blaming our fate, we turned to the wretched, and by these [Western] nations much despised, Byzantium for the moral code which should have been the basis of our upbringing."[7]

The key idea of modern Russophobia was expressed in artistic form by Karl Marx, who said that Muscovy had grown up and been educated in the vicious and miserable school of Mongolian slavery; that it had won its strength by becoming "a virtuoso in the arts of slavery"; and that even after its liberation, Muscovy as conqueror continued to play its traditional slavelike role having become the master. He wrote that, in order to become the master of the West, Russia needed "to become civilized...by remaining a slave, i.e., having given Russians that external veneer of civilization which would prepare them for an acceptance of the technology of Western nations, without infecting them with [those nations'] ideas."[8]

Marx applied this surprisingly controversial cliché for years on end: "There is only one alternative left for Europe: either Asiatic barbarism under Muscovite leadership will descend upon her head like an avalanche, or she must restore Poland, thus placing between herself and Asia twenty million heroes."[9] How up-to-date that sounds!

The paradox is that this cliché is the only bit of Marxism that the European elite seems to have retained. Incidentally, nowadays, fearful of China's rise in the East, this same elite has moved on from Marx to Rousseau, who predicted that "Russia will never really be civilized.... The Russian empire would like to subjugate Europe and will find itself subjugated. The Tartars, its subjects or neighbors, will become its masters—and ours."[10] Is it not about time we got rid of this Eurocentric delusion? It is striking that during World War II exactly the same judgments were made about Russia.

Consequently, the West's "Cold War" against the USSR assumed a messianic, quasi-religious nature. In it, the enemy was referred to as the "evil empire" and victory as the "end of history." The founder of neoliberalism, Leo Strauss, defined the aim of this war as "the complete victory of the town over the country or of the West over the East." This messianism was not aimed at a bright future; it was brimming with absolute pessimism. Strauss explained the idea of the supposed victory of the West: "The completion of history is the beginning of the decline of Europe, of the West, and therewith, since all other cultures have been absorbed into the West, the beginning of the decline of mankind. There is no future for mankind." Thus, the destruction of the "evil empire" was regarded as the end of this world and of mankind. From this proceed the mystical utopias of the new world order, globalization, the search for a new global evil, and the readdressing of the traditional norms of international law and morality on which the world has stood for the last three centuries.

In the West today there are many who criticize the conservatism of Russia's current leaders with their primary emphasis on "order," and who hold up the example of the Sturm und Drang period under Yeltsin, who destroyed the "evil empire." It would be sensible for them, at least in theory, to try out this Sturm on themselves. We remember how the Western press applauded the tanks firing on the Russian parliament in October 1993—CNN had broadcast the shooting live to the world. What a sight! But this applause was a cold shower for the whole of Russian society, including the "social base" of Yeltsin himself. Russian citizens had not expected such behavior from those they regarded as shield bearers of democracy and law. That was why they took a step back toward the *siloviki* and Putin; they had grown up.

Here is the thesis I would like to propound: In our joint interests we need to carry out a sober assessment of the potential for dialogue between Russia and the West, and to find a way of overcoming the inertia of those processes that in the 1990s led to a mutual cooling off. We need to rationalize those formations that have already become established in the post-Soviet period and that could otherwise create a more profound alienation (without its being more evident or more dramatic) than in the Cold War years.

Russia's Philosophical Identity

In times of deep crisis, such as the Russian Revolution or the destruction of the USSR, what is involved is not isolated political and social conflicts but their merger into one large system of *civilizational* crisis; this does not lend itself to explanation in personal terms. It takes over the whole of society; no one is immune; it presents each of us with "eternal" questions. In this chapter I am trying to deal with the main question of what has brought about the current state of Russia. I believe that for Western readers the media have created a different impression of the makeup of the factors that determine Russia's fate. I won't argue but ask that my voice be heard.

During the perestroika era we used to say that it was after the Russian Revolution, the turning point at the beginning of the twentieth century, that we "fell out of civilization." This marked the beginning of a world revolution of non-industrialized countries endeavoring to avoid being drawn into the periphery of Western capitalism. We cannot ignore this global historical event—it gave rise to the current world order.

Over the two centuries prior to this revolution Russia had set itself up as a self-sufficient, localized civilization that was described from different viewpoints by Marx and Spengler, Toynbee and Sorokin, Kundera and Huntington. Russian classical literature described both its different facets and its general atmosphere. I would re-emphasize that the West was the mirror to this—the "significant other" for the Russia and Eurasia of the eighteenth to twentieth centuries.

Pushkin expressed the general thought in terms of Russians' ethics and aesthetics, while "slices" of the whole were explored by writers familiar to twentieth-century Europe. Even today there are those who think of Tolstoy as "the mirror of the Russian revolution,"[11] Dostoevsky as the "mirror of a bad conscience," Chekhov as the "mirror of the Russian intelligentsia" before the storm, and Gorky and Blok as prophets of the new world. We have to look through this prism and at the significance of the current moment. "God is not in might but in right" was the old Russian formula. And Russia's crises were always caused by doubts and searches for a new truth.

Behind this stands a fact that official Soviet ideology kept quiet: Russian civilization was developed under conditions of the *religious manifestation of the spirit*.

The German theologian Romano Guardini wrote about "religious susceptibility": "By this we mean not belief in the Christian Revelation or the determination to live a life conforming to it but the immediate contact with the religious content of things, when a person is carried along by the secret current of the world, an ability which has existed in all times and among all peoples. But this means that a man of the 'new era' does not just lose faith in the Christian Revelation; his natural religious organ begins to atrophy and the world becomes for him a profane reality."[12]

In this sense Russians have not yet become people of the "new era." Of course, mastering the skills of rational scientific thought, mass scientific education, and the modernization of the economy and way of life have led to a weakening of traditional religious belief, reinforced by religious skepticism. But in Russia (except during the Soviet period) there have never been systematic cultural and political attempts at rooting out the "natural religious organ"; it is enjoying a revival even in post-Soviet Russia.

The Russian Revolution was itself a movement based on profound religious feeling (one could even talk of the heresy of *Soviet millennialism*). The bourgeoisie and proletariat were abstractions, the content of which were completely different from what they were in the West—"proletariat" was understood as the *Russian people*, while "bourgeoisie" was understood as the *descendants of Cain*.

Among religious thinkers were many of the activists who participated in the creation of Soviet culture—Bryusov and Yesenin, Kluyev and Platonov, Vernadsky and Tsiolkovsky. A leading heretic and idolater was Maxim Gorky. In his article on his striving for a new way, the Israeli historian Mikhail Agursky writes that "the religious roots of Bolshevism as a movement of the people go back to the complete negation by a significant part of the Russian nation of the existing world as a world of injustice and to a dream of the creation of a new 'deified' world. Gorky more than anyone else expressed the religious roots of Bolshevism, its *Promethean theomachy*."[13]

John Maynard Keynes, having worked in Russia in the 1920s, wrote (in 1925): "Leninism is a strange combination of two things which Europeans have kept for some centuries in different compartments of the soul—religion and business.... One feels that here is the laboratory of life."[14]

N. A. Berdyaev, in the book *Self-knowledge (an attempt at a philosophical autobiography)*,[15] wrote: "We had none of the individualism characteristic of European history and European humanism, although for us what was characteristic was the acute formulation of the problem of the clash of the individual with global harmony (Belinsky, Dostoevsky). But collectivism is in the Russian national makeup—Left and Right, in Russian religious and social movements, in the type of Russian Christianity." During the Russian revolution the Bolsheviks received widespread support because they (there are those who always see this as a paradox) were the more moderate, more pragmatic force.

The German writer and philosopher Hermann Hesse, in his research into the meaning of Dostoevsky's images (1925), provided this definition of the peculiarity of the Russian spirit: it is "conscience, the ability of a person to face God." He explains his thought as follows: "This conscience has nothing in common with morality, with the law, it may be in the most terrible, mortal discord with them and nevertheless it is endlessly strong, it is stronger than stagnation, stronger than greed, stronger than vanity."[16]

This is the problem the Russian government encountered when undertaking its reform: this *other* Russian conscience is *endlessly strong*. It cannot be easy for a government to deal with this conscience, to crush it with its self-interest, law, and mercantilism. For this reason it has to tread carefully and cannot always obey the orders of the International Monetary Fund and liberal opposition; sometimes it even has to disappoint its respected Western friends and high-ranking partners with its apparent "authoritarianism" and "lack of democracy."

Russian authorities are criticized for "dragging their feet"—but they are gradually reforming the political system while retaining the relics of paternalism. A new image has grown up of a petrified state incapable of reform. It is easy to create such an image—you just take a certain feature and behave as if it expresses the country's entire cultural and civilizational profile. Thus Besançon writes that "Throughout the seventy years of communist rule Soviet Russia was infatuated with the wish to 'catch up with and overtake' the West; it ended with it building a 'noncapitalist' state, meaning, among other things, a 'non-European' and 'ultra-Russian' state."[17]

Let us assume that this is the case. But does that necessarily mean that a non-European and ultra-Russian state cannot become a capitalist one—in its own way, that is, while preserving its cultural identity? Yes, the kinds of societies, states, and governments in Russia are in some way distinct from those of the West. One can sum up the main metaphors of Russian society and contemporary Western society as follows: *society as a family* versus *society as a market*. But at the same time, even in Russian society there were, are, and will continue to be *market* structures, just as in Western society there are *family* structures. Different societies are dynamic and resilient at the same time—they are complicated, evolving systems.

A *political* order is built, and determines the type of government, based on perceptions of humanity and those ties that bind people into a society. With the ideal of the family as the model, society will produce a so-called paternalist state. Here the relations between the government and its subjects in the *hierarchy* are based on the relations of a father and his children. It is clear that perceptions of freedom and mutual rights and obligations here are different from those of the government in a Western society, the role of which is reduced to the functions of a policeman at a marketplace (the government is the "night watchman," a service government).

At the moment, in the transition period, the Russian Federation's nationhood has not yet been established; it contains many "hybrid" forms; it can be glimpsed behind numerous features of Russia's traditional nationhood albeit in a much modernized form. Soviet power was an idiocratic government for a traditional society. Berdyaev even wrote, almost with distaste: "The socialist state is not a secular state; it is a sacral state.... It resembles an authoritarian, theocratic state.... Preservers of the messianic 'idea' of the proletariat are a particular hierarchy—the communist party."[18]

Over the years the sacral component of the Soviet state has weakened, moving from messianic belief in world revolution to the "cult of Stalin" linked with the idea of strengthening *one's own* country and rejecting Trotsky's permanent revolution. D. E. Furman wrote that "the principal conveyors of these trends clearly emerged from the depths of a bureaucracy which, firstly, inherited many elements of a traditional Christian consciousness and, secondly, wants not stormy revolution but its own secure position."

Thus, who will accuse the current Russian government that grew out of the USSR—Trotsky's grandchildren, the heralds of new revolutions? Of what will they accuse those in the government who have "emerged from the depths of bureaucracy"—of preferring storms to a secure position, both for its citizens and the country itself? It is strange to hear these accusations from adherents of a society based on the rule of law.

After the conclusion of the postwar reconstruction period, the Soviet government in actual fact became increasingly open and less ideological. Let us take a sober look at the dynamic of the changes and compare the forms of society and government at four stages of the system in place right up to the destruction of the USSR:

- the "mobilization" (Stalinism) of the prewar and war years (the 1930s and 1940s);
- Khrushchev's "thaw" (1953–64);
- the calm ("stagnation") of the Brezhnev period (1965–84);
- Gorbachev's perestroika (1985–91).

Can one call stagnant a state that has carried out root-and-branch institutional reform every fifteen years or so? Who needs permanent revolution in such a difficult country? Who wants endless upheavals similar to the troubled 1990s? Who would wish such trauma upon their own country?

The political order that has begun to develop since 2000 with the election of Vladimir Putin as president was necessary for the fulfillment of extraordinary tasks—reinstating the "vertical" of state government destroyed in the 1990s and the country's coherence; healing, as far as possible, the cultural trauma suffered by the population; overcoming the demographic crisis, taking the first steps toward reviving the economy, and alleviating the mass poverty that had arisen in the 1990s; curbing rampant criminality. In essence the challenge was to put the country through intensive care (to adopt the language used earlier referring to Russia's capacity for survival). What is more, these tasks were by no means all that needed to be accomplished urgently. This turning point explains the strengthening of the state's legitimacy and Putin's electoral success. To ignore this is to demonstrate extraordinary indifference to the mass suffering that Russia's population endured in the 1990s. Humanists in Europe can count, after us, the cost of Russian reforms in human lives. For this you need to add, beginning with 1991, the number of people who died unnecessarily (a relatively long-term trend), those not born, and the number of (actual) human lives that Russia lost from the artificial reduction in life expectancy. The number is shocking—twenty-eight million people!

But even in the face of indifference to such Russocentric facts, it is strange not to appreciate the significance of the social stability that was ensured in a nuclear power thanks to the measures given above. Moreover, the stability of a country such as Russia is not just of national value. Rational-thinking people both in Europe and the United States should have an interest in it.

Russia succeeded in achieving something the politicians of the 1990s had not banked on—the Russian Federation was not divided into opposing classes. "New Russians" stood out like nobility among the particular "small nation." The sociocultural archetypes of the majority of the Russian population turned out to be firm, and to date the radicalizing, multiparty-system society that was spoken of in the 1990s remains unbuilt. It was supposed that a system of such parties would divide society into classes by social interests. This did not happen, and the parties that emerged in the course of a temporary displacement of the intelligentsia toward the ranks of the social democrats and liberalism declined.

The inertia of paternalism played a stabilizing role—the building of power on the basis of confrontation between parties was viewed with mistrust. In 1995 an extensive survey showed that

> both the old and the new ideological mode encourage a good half of respondents to tend toward an acknowledgement of the incompatibility of the domestic form of social order with "western democracy." A comparison of two tests separated by an eventful year and a half (the tests were carried out in June 1993 and October 1994) shows that what we have here is not just an indicator of the public mood but an arrangement akin to a canon of Russians' social awareness. This is not an average but a genuinely universal situation, divisible—in varying proportions—by the relative and absolute majority in practically all categories of respondents observed.[19]

In our enlightened and pragmatic era the heads of the "progressive section of humanity" were turned by *economocentrism*. The market became the measure of all things.

Nowadays, in Russia (which is going through a prolonged crisis) we are beginning to better understand that world-outlook matrix, which brings together the ways our nations organize their lives and their approaches to community life. This organization has withstood a series of the severest tests. But even where certain important structures are destroyed or damaged, the way Russia is built has allowed society and culture to be preserved in the extreme conditions of social poverty that the post-Soviet nations experienced in the 1990s. This is no trivial matter.

In the process of overcoming the crisis in Russia, valuable practical models and social forms were discovered that were used in the way people organized themselves, in the creation of "molecular" and a wide variety of networks of mutual help and support. Friedrich von Hayek, the ideological founder of contemporary neoliberalism, wrote that "nationwide solidarity with a universal ethical code or with a single system of values covertly present in any economic plan was a thing unknown in a free society and had to be created from zero."[20]

Thus, in the West, in the opinion of neoliberalist philosophers, "nationwide solidarity" had been reduced to "zero" and now it had to be "created from zero." In Russia the "nationwide solidarity with a universal ethical code" about which von Hayek wrote has existed and continues to exist. Surely there is no need to reduce it to zero? If we take a look at the entire post-Soviet space we see a huge variety of experience of solidarity in a modern industrial society. In 2000, the average purchasing power of a wage package amounted in Ukraine to 27 percent of the 1990 level and in Tajikistan to 7 percent. It is interesting to imagine what would have happened to social stability and the preservation of cultural norms in Europe or the United States had there been such a drop in public prosperity. Such stability required a particular interaction between the government and society, for which the primary criterion was the imperative of surviving in one piece, not adherence to the ideological norms of a well-fed, prosperous society. And this was despite sharp conflicts within both the government and society.

Do those nations that today enjoy a high level of prosperity not need to be aware of such experience? And is it not odd that, at the very time when in Russia and other post-Soviet republics there has been interaction that has allowed a series of difficult obstacles in our unsettled progress to be overcome, many Western academics and commentators have subjected our countries' "regimes" to the most severe, uncompromising criticism? The collapse of Russia or Tajikistan is hardly likely to benefit the West!

Since this book is dedicated also to the "progressive section of humanity," we need to mention something about Russia in terms of the *economy*. What I am going to say will elicit surprise and antipathy in some Western colleagues, and I do not know whether I can explain it: The contemporary market is incompatible with common sense, but the Russian population is loathe to dispense with common sense completely. That is the problem!

I begin with a distinction of principle between the Russian economy and Western capitalism, which seems to have been forgotten. It lies in the long-term removal of huge resources from the colonies, which was a condition of the development of the modern-day West. The investments made on the back of these assets created conditions for rapid growth, which in the twentieth century meant the West was able, as the leader in science and technology, to charge the rest of the world for its intellectual property and charge on world currency emissions (the dollar and now the euro).

A replication of the Western economic system would not permit Russia to retain the status of a civilization—neither the USSR nor contemporary Russia has had, has, or will have access to foreign labor. Our research has shown that, for example, the motivation for individual labor productivity of a Russian worker and a European is categorically different. The material factor has a greater influence on the European and less on the Russian, while it is clear that social prestige as a motivating factor works in reverse.

Environmental conditions also explain why the dynamic and forms of Russia's economic development have differed from those in the West. Fernand Braudel raised the—enormous in economic history—subject of space being the "primary enemy."[21] Due to the size of its territory and low population density, transport costs in Russia as a share of the price of a product were 50 percent at the end of the nineteenth century, and in foreign trade transport costs were six times higher than in the United States. On Russia's domestic market trade was always "long distance." No wonder that this alone sharply increased the role of self-sufficiency and meant that the national economy had to be organized differently from those of western Europe. In particular, this was why both the government and the business community in tsarist Russia acknowledged the need for large-scale *economic planning* ten years before the revolution.

Let us take the climatic conditions—which are immune to totalitarianism and to democracy. In fourteenth-century England and France, fields were plowed three or four times a year and in the eighteenth century up to seven times. This improved the structure of the soil and removed the weeds. The longest that fields were left unplowed was two months. Livestock were able to graze virtually throughout the year, and the biological richness of the meadows meant large numbers of livestock could be kept, which in turn provided plenty of fertilizer for the plowed fields. In the central belt of Russia the fallow period, during which it is impossible to carry out any work, lasts seven months.

Braudel sets out information on harvest levels in the West. In France between 1319 and 1327 wheat harvests yielded between 12 and 17 hundredweight per hectare. In western Europe, in general, harvests grew between the thirteenth and nineteenth centuries from five to ten times what was sown. In Russia at the turn of the nineteenth century the harvest was 2.4 times what was sown. This was *four times* lower than in Western Europe. This difference, which was the basis of the West's "own" wealth (i.e., acquired not from the colonies but from its own land), accrued *year after year for a thousand years*. If one mentally weighs the size of this advantage, then the Russian plowman must be given his due for his feats.

In these conditions capitalism was inconceivable. The economy could be based only on serfdom, on communal farming, and then on collective and state farms. Today, in the course of attempts to introduce small farming, we are beginning to understand this not in theory but in practice.

In 1992, in a genuine attempt to follow the doctrine of liberalizing and moving to a market economy, the Russian government abolished cooperatives and state farms, and parceled out the land to their workers. As a result, the volume of agricultural production in 1999 was 37 percent of the 1990 level. By the beginning of 2009, of twelve million investors only 400,000 (3 percent) had officially acquired ownership of their land. In 2008 farmers produced 8.5 percent of the total agricultural production while occupying 19.9 percent of Russia's total area under cultivation—and that was with maximum effort on their part. The direct labor costs in the production of a liter of milk grew 7.5 times in the case of small farmers compared with Soviet enterprises.

Ideologies aside, one has to accept that the radical exchange of the established system for the Western pattern has led to profound crisis and chaos. It is appropriate here to remember the warning of Claude Lévi-Strauss. Having studied the West's contacts with other cultures, he wrote that it was difficult to imagine how one civilization could adopt the way of life of another without renouncing its own identity. He said that in practice, this could lead to only two results: either disorganization and the collapse of one of the systems—or an original synthesis leading, however, to the emergence of a third system incompatible with the other two.[22]

It is this synthesis in which the Russian government, business, and the whole society are now engaged. This task is much more difficult than it seems to certain of our enthusiasts and to Western experts with their textbooks. Such problems, caused by attempts to radically change Russia's institutions and ways of life by following templates that work well in the West, have dogged our reforms at every step. The state cannot afford to ignore these lessons. Already there has been too much wasted effort.

Clearly, a market economy requires that money, land, and labor be converted into products. Land we dealt with earlier, the money market has pushed us into the current crisis, and the labor market has been marked by general confusion. In the 1990s people sometimes worked for six months without pay, despite all the laws of the market. They gave their labor not as a *commodity* but as an item of value to society. They asked for wages not on the grounds of "payment for goods" but so that they could survive. Protest demonstrations did not feature accusations characteristic of a cheated market trader: "You have stolen my goods! Now you need to pay for them." On the contrary, workers and teachers demanded to be paid "or else we have nothing to feed our children!" These are arguments based on fairness; but as Adam Smith and David Ricardo emphasized, a seller's basic needs, and fairness and compassion still more so, are categories that do not lend themselves to the market.

Take, for example, one of the most fundamental features of a civilized identity—*anthropology*, the "human model." It is impossible to build an economy in confrontation with this factor. If we desire success and not civil war, albeit a "cold" one, only compromises and a careful synthesis are appropriate here. Weber describes in detail the problems of this kind, which arose during the establishment of capitalism in Europe.[23] We see them in Russia too—and want to solve them by following Weber's wise directions and the lessons of successful capitalists rather than inveterate ideologues.

People are constantly trying to convince us that "Russians are not good workers" because they have modest demands. One such ideologue writes that "Russians are lazy because they do not know how to live. Many companies have found that Russian employees, particularly low-level employees, decline salary rises where these do not entail more intensive work. Employees are prepared to put up with a low standard of living as long as they are left in peace. Academics, consultants, and company leaders are debating how widespread this attitude to labor is among Russians and what to do about it."

But this type of modesty is an invaluable cultural resource for Russia, a phenomenon studied exhaustively by several generations of anthropologists. With it, Russians have mastered enormous territory and made it a part of the sum of human knowledge, have carried out forced industrialization, have created a whole science with its own style, and have turned their country into the second superpower. These were their demands, for the sake of which they worked with unprecedented intensity and efficiency. Again, we see that "Man does not live by bread alone." It was neither Stalin nor Putin who said that.

Over the twenty years of reform the public attitude toward the money-grubbing embodied in "big business" in Russia has remained unchanged. This attitude is so negative that sociologists struggle to measure it. A qualitative conclusion from a Russia-wide public opinion poll in 2003 was that "the attitude of respondents to big business is largely that the majority of those polled effectively reject its right to exist."[24] Of those polled, 70–75 percent were convinced that it is only possible to "earn big money" by breaking the law.

The synthesis of Russia's culture with private ownership is a large and difficult problem, and its solution is hampered most by politicians demanding that it be cut like a Gordian knot. In Russia the urge to acquire property was blameworthy, and Weber saw this as the main obstacle to the development of capitalism. Berdyaev notes an important feature: "Russian judgments about ownership and theft are determined not by the attitude to ownership as a social institution but by the attitude to people.... This is also linked to Russian opposition to the bourgeoisie and Russian rejection of the bourgeois world.... For Russia the fact that we have never had, and never will have, any significant and influential bourgeois ideology greatly distinguishes us from the West." If that is the case then it would be silly to force the issue. We need a social agreement taking the cultural restrictions into account.

The acceptance or not of the civilizational peculiarities of the Russian economy regarding the market economy of the West periodically becomes, in Russia, the subject of intense debate and greatly influences the development of events. The pressure of Eurocentrism on Russia's educated classes has on more than one occasion led to both heads of government and the intelligentsia, which opposes it, refusing to allow the domestic economy to find its own way and choosing instead to imitate Western structures. As a rule, this has led to enormous delays in or the failure of reforms and to serious ideological and social conflicts.

Today the narrowness of this view is striking. In the 1930s Arnold Toynbee suggested in *A Study of History* that the thesis of world unification on the basis of the Western economic system as the natural outcome of a single and uninterrupted process of the development of human history leads to the most blatant distortion of the facts and a striking contraction of the historical horizon.[25]

Conclusions

In the West, Russia is criticized for being slow to assimilate the values of the market and of democracy. But humanity is resilient only if it preserves its variety, and we are searching for the types of institutions that would achieve a balance between and reconcile very disparate values. We acknowledge that we have not yet found such institutions, and Russia today is an ailing civilization. This is not the first time in history this has happened, nor will it be the last.

In the new era Russia has on more than one occasion "fallen ill" earlier and/or more seriously than its Western neighbors and has then provided the "serum" for vaccinations, saving them through the benefit of her experience. Not for the first time Russia has succumbed to exaggerated illusions regarding the possibility of directly applying Western institutions to itself. During the first revolution this only led to the reinforcement of contradictions. Weber warned the Russian leaders at the time (1906): "It is highly ridiculous to see any connection between the high capitalism of today—as it is now being imported into Russia and as it exists in America—with democracy or with freedom in any sense of these words."[26]

Today, Russia keeps being reminded that democracy is the unique essence of "European culture" and it should copy it exactly. The majority who supported Vladimir Putin are dismissed as "nostalgic" or even "reactionary," and there is no desire to investigate why this majority supported the move from Yeltsinism. Do the norms of rational thought not require the search for rational reasons for such conservatism? Here we shall put forward just three indicators out of hundreds of similar ones to illustrate the extremely rational, even pragmatic bases for such support.

The first involves the fact that the retreat from the radicalism of the 1990s partially alleviated the cultural trauma and removed the shock of the social shake-up caused by the extreme impoverishment of the majority of the population between 1992 and 1999. This had an immediate effect on demography—mortality fell and the birth rate began to rise (see fig. 16.1).

From the very first steps by Putin's government in 1999 the economy, which at the beginning of the 1990s was subjected to the most profound crisis, began to revive. Figure 16.2 shows the dynamics of industrial production (in real terms, i.e., uninfluenced by oil prices). This growth was only interrupted by the crisis of 2008.

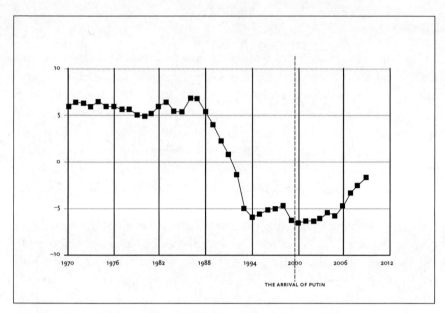

Figure 16.1 Natural growth (losses) among Russia's population (per 1,000)

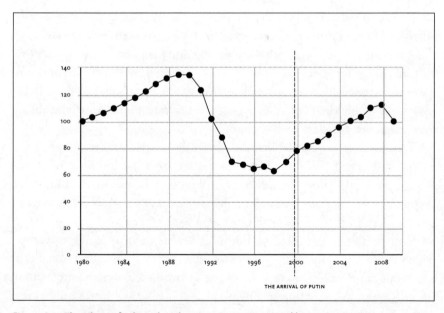

Figure 16.2 The volume of industrial production in Russia in comparable prices, 1980 = 100

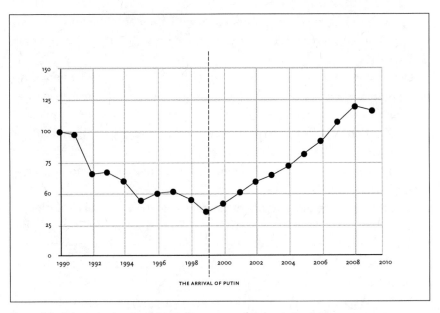

Figure 16.3 Indexes showing the average real-term wages of workers in Russia, 1990 = 100

Finally, with Putin's arrival the vector of social policy changed. This was manifest in the simplest, most comprehensible way—reliable growth in real-term wages right up to the crisis of 2008 (see fig. 16.3).

It is therefore natural for there to be nothing strange about public support for Putin and his policies. On the contrary, it would be strange if these policies provoked dissatisfaction. In fact, it is departures from these policies that give rise to dissatisfaction. But these departures are the consequences of numerous unresolved issues and necessary compromises.

I would like to draw attention to the following circumstances discussed in the Western media. The public crisis phase that Russia has been living through for the last twenty years, just like the illness of the USSR during the "incubation" period of this crisis, has given Russians and all the post-Soviet nations greater new knowledge of people and society, the government and the economy, the national and the social. Our crisis is the consequence of the interweaving, in unfavorable conditions, of the contradictions of a traditional society undergoing forced modernization with the contradictions of rapid urbanization and the intrusion of the postmodern into this syncretized cultural milieu.

There is much in this unusual system that we are only just beginning to understand, having encountered the consequences of ignorance in our, at times, unfortunate experience. Soviet society was not ready for these processes. They are not described in the textbooks of Marxism, liberalism, or anthropology. But are our neighbors in the West and the East, who have not yet experienced such crises, really so much better equipped with knowledge and understanding?

It would be in the general interest to help us systematize this knowledge, formulate it, and make it globally available. But the inertia of Russophobic dogma and stereotypes stands in the way. It is sad to see the aplomb with which many ideologues give naïve, clichéd explanations for the phenomena we are observing in our crisis society, those "strange attractions" born out of our chaos. We hear the banal advice given in the genuine conviction that nothing is easier to understand than the illness of an organism "similar to Burkina Faso but with rockets." (Of course, I am not referring to the authors of this volume.)

But however ailing Russia may be today, her foundations as a civilization have withstood the ordeal this time too. Russia's potential is great—as history has shown on more than one occasion. Russia still has the ability to get along with other cultures and nations, and to find a means of mutually beneficial cooperation. The efforts of certain politicians, who have not yet "removed their Cold War fatigues," to take advantage of Russia's current situation to "finish off," rob, or degrade her are shortsighted and unfair. I am certain that in the future this will serve no purpose for the overwhelming majority of the population both in the West and in the East.

Wisdom, kindness, and farsightedness have no geographic restrictions. They are either there—or they are not.

Notes

1. A. Besançon, "Rossija – evropejskaja strana?" [Is Russia a European country?], *Otechestvennyje zapiski*, no. 5 (2004): 246–66.
2. O. Spengler, "Pessimism? Pessimism li eto? Den'gi i mashina. Filosofija liriki. Prusskaja ideja i socialism" [Pessimism?: Is that pessimism? Money and technics. Philosophy of lyrics. Prussianism and socialism], in *Prusskaja ideja i socialism* [Prussianism and socialism], ed. O. Spengler, trans. G. D. Gurvich (Moscow: Kraft+, 2003), 249–50. See also http://rusk.ru/st.php?idar=19439.
3. *Granta*, no. 11 (1984). See http://magazines.russ.ru/nlo/2001/52/mill-pr.html.
4. F. Tyutchev, *Polnoje sobranije stikhotvorenij* [Complete set of poems] (Leningrad: Sovetskij pisatel', 1987), 2:165.
5. R. Kipling, *Maugli* [Mowgli] Kaliningrad: Amber Tale, 1998).
6. R. Descartes, *Sochinenija v 2 t.* [Works in 2 volumes], ed. V.V. Sokolov (Moscow: Mysl', 1989), vol. 1.
7. P. Chaadayev, "Filosoficheskije pisma" [Philosophical letters], in *Rossija glazami russkogo. Chaadajev, Leontjev, Solovjov*, ed. A. Zamaleev (St. Petersburg, 1991), 30.
8. K. Marx, "Razoblachenije diplomaticheskoj istorii XVIII veka" [The revelations of the diplomatic history of the 18th century], in K. Marx, *Sochinenija* [Works], 2nd ed., ed. F. Engels (Moscow, 1960), 16:205.
9. K. Marx, "Rech' na pol'skom mitinge v Londone 22 janvarja 1867 g" [Speech at the Polish meeting in London, January 22, 1867], *Glos Wolny*, no. 130 (1867); *Le Socialism*, no. 18 (1908).
10. J. J. Rousseau, *Traktaty: Perevody* [Collected Writings: Translations], ed. V. S. Alexeev-Popov, Y. M. Lotman, N. A. Poltoratsky, and A. D. Hajutin (Moscow: AN SSSR, 1969).
11. V. Lenin, *Tolstoy kak zerkalo russkoj revoljutsii* [Leo Tolstoy as the mirror of the Russian revolution] (Moscow: Politizdat, 1980).
12. R. Guardini, "Konets novogo vremeny" [The End of the Modern World], *Voprosy filosofii*, no. 4 (1990): 123–67.
13. M. Agursky, *Ideologija natsional-bolshevisma* [Ideology of National Bolshevism] (Paris: YMCA Press, 1980).
14. J. Keynes, *Short View on Russia* (London: Hogarth Press, 1925). See also J. Keynes, *Begly vzgljad na Rossiju* [Short View on Russia], trans. E. Lavrk, http://www.ecsocman.edu.ru/data/441/927/1216/19Kejns_Beglyj_vzglyad.pdf.
15. N. Berdyaev, *Samopoznanije* (Opyt filosofskoj avtobiografii) [Self-knowledge (an attempt at a philosophical autobiography)] (Paris: YMCA-press, 1949).

16. Hermann Hesse, "Hermann Hesse on Dostoevsky" (essay, Bern, 1925, first published in *Vossische Zeitung*, March, 1925).
17. A. Besançon, "Rossija – evropejskaja strana?" [Is Russia a European country?], *Otechestvennyje zapiski*, no. 5 (2004): 264.
18. N. Berdyaev, "Filosofija neravenstva. Pis'mo devjatoje. O socialisme" [The philosophy of inequality. Letter nine. On socialism], in N. Berdyaev, *Sobranije sochinenij* [Collected works] (Paris: YMCA-Press, 1990), 4:176–202.
19. "Ekonomicheskije i sotsialnyje peremeny: monitoring obschestvennogo mnenija" [Economic and social changes: survey of the public opinion], Moscow, no. 2 (1995).
20. F. Hayek, *Doroga k rabstvu* [The Road to Serfdom] (Moscow: Novoje izdatel'stvo, 2005), 158. See http://www.inliberty.ru/assets/files/hayek_road_to_serfdom.pdf.
21. F. Braudel, *Shto takoje Frantsija? Kn. 1. Prostranstvo i istorija* [The Identity of France, vol. 1, History and Environment] (Moscow: Izd-vo im. Sabashnikovykh, 1994).
22. C. Lévi-Strauss, *Antropologia estructural: Mito, sociedad, humanidades* (Mexico: Siglo XXI Eds., 1990).
23. M. Weber, *Izbrannyje proizvedenija* [Selected works], ed. Y.N. Davydova (Moscow: Progress, 1990).
24. Fond "Obschestvennoje mnenije," Vserossijsky opros gorodskogo i sel'skogo naselenija. Rossijane o krupnom bisnesse [Foundation "Public opinion," All-Russian public opinion poll. Russians on big business], July 2003. See http://content.mail.ru/arch/2207/321483.html.
25. A. Toynbee, *Postizhenije istorii* [A Study of History], trans. A.P. Ogurtsov (Moscow: Progress, 1991).
26. M. Weber, "K polozheniju burzhuaznoj demokratii v Rossii" [On the conditions of bourgeois democracy in Russia], in *Politicheskaja nauka. Rossija: opyt revoljutsij i sovremennost'* (Moscow: INION, 1998), 5–121.

Contributors

OLEG ATKOV is general secretary of the World Public Forum "Dialogue of Civilizations," vice president of Joint Stock Company "Russian Railways," and professor at Russian State Medical University.

CRAIG CALHOUN is president of the Social Science Research Council and University Professor of the Social Sciences at New York University. His most recent book is *Nations Matter: Culture, History, and the Cosmopolitan Dream* (Routledge, 2007). He is also the editor of *Robert K. Merton: Sociology of Science and Sociology as Science* (Columbia University Press, 2010).

TIMOTHY J. COLTON is chair of the Department of Government at Harvard University and author of *Yeltsin: A Life* (Basic Books, 2008).

GEORGI DERLUGUIAN is a historical sociologist at Northwestern University. His monograph *Bourdieu's Secret Admirer in the Caucasus* (University of Chicago Press, 2005) was recognized by the American Sociological Association as among the best books in political sociology for 2005.

PIOTR DUTKIEWICZ is professor and director of the Centre for Governance and Public Management at Carleton University in Ottawa, Canada, and former director of the Institute of European and Russian Studies.

MIKHAIL K. GORSHKOV is professor and director of the Institute of Sociology at the Russian Academy of Sciences.

LEONID GRIGORIEV is senior researcher at the Institute of World Economy and International Relations (IMEMO), Russian Academy of Sciences, and dean of the Management Department at International University.

NUR KIRABAEV is professor of philosophy at Moscow State University and vice rector of the Peoples' Friendship University of Russia.

ANDREW C. KUCHINS is senior fellow and director of the Russia and Eurasia Program at the Center for Strategic and International Studies in Washington, D.C.

BOBO LO is an independent scholar and consultant. His recent publications include *Axis of Convenience: Moscow, Beijing and the New Geopolitics* (Brookings and Chatham House, 2008) and *Vladimir Putin and the Evolution of Russian Foreign Policy* (Blackwell and Chatham House, 2003).

RODERIC LYNE was British ambassador to the Russian Federation from 2000 to 2004 and now works as a consultant, company director, writer, and lecturer on matters relating to Russia.

VLADIMIR POPOV is senior economic affairs officer for the UN Department of Economic and Social Affairs (DESA) and professor at the New Economic School in Moscow.

ALEXANDER RAHR is professor and head of the Berthold Beitz Center at the German Council on Foreign Relations in Berlin. He was formerly a senior analyst for the Radio Liberty Research Institute in Munich and consultant to the RAND Corporation.

RICHARD SAKWA is professor of Russian and European politics at the University of Kent and an associate fellow of the Russia and Eurasia Program at the Royal Institute of International Affairs, Chatham House.

DMITRI TRENIN is director of the Carnegie Moscow Center and author of numerous books on Russian foreign and security policy and international relations in Eurasia.

GUZEL ULUMBEKOVA is chairman of the board of the Association of Medical Societies for Quality (ASMOK), Russia.

VLADIMIR I. YAKUNIN is founding president of the World Public Forum "Dialogue of Civilizations" and president of Joint Stock Company "Russian Railways."

RUSTEM ZHANGOZHA is professor and lead research fellow at the Institute of World Economy and International Relations, National Academy of Sciences of Ukraine.

Index

Abkhazia, 305, 308, 394, 431n25; international community and status of, 424; recognition refused to independence of, 369, 370, 373; in Russian sphere of influence, 410. *See also* Georgia; Russian–Georgian War (August 2008)

ABM (Anti-Ballistic Missile) Treaty, 303, 332, 335, 372

Abramovich, Roman, 111n23

Academy of Sciences, 229, 238, 241

administrative regime, 4, 87, 108

Afanasiev, M., 201

Afghanistan, 282, 309, 332, 338, 370; Asian policies of Russia and, 356; Central Asian links with Indian Ocean region, 386; deteriorating security situation in, 337; drug trafficking from, 323, 324, 346, 391, 427; initial U.S. military success in, 333, 335, 348, 422; Northern Distribution Network (NDN), 344–46, 352n33; Russian strategic position on, 345–46, 352n34, 368, 371, 390; in Shanghai Cooperation Organization (SCO), 427; Soviet war in, 282, 295, 368, 417; state-building failure in, 317; U.S./NATO–Russian cooperation and, 312, 323–24, 334–35, 344–46, 426–27. *See also* Taliban

Africa, xiii, 56, 67, 68, 295; Cold War and, 282; colonization of, 66; developmental state in, 25; economic growth in, 41; rulers' term limits in, 141n22; Western colonial empires in, 434

agriculture, 52, 83, 98, 122, 449–50

Agursky, Mikhail, 443

Ahmadinejad, Mahmoud, 365, 415

A Just Russia party, 229

Albania, GDP in, 42

alcoholism, 63, 251–52

Alexander II, Emperor, 2

Algeria, 101, 276, 322

Anderson, Perry, 20

Andropov, Yuri, 3

anthropology, 451, 456

Arctic region, 10, 32, 282, 317, 427

463

Armenia, 42, 43, 276, 309, 424
arms control, 129, 273, 303, 332, 335, 339–41. *See also specific treaties*
ASEAN (Association of Southeast Asian Nations), 369, 379
Asia, xiii, 34, 301, 322, 324; American presence in, 355; economic crisis (1997), 337; evolution of Russian thinking about, 358–60; geopolitics and, xiv, 360–64; management of "difficult states" in, 366–68; multilateralism in, 368–70; resurgence of, 75; Russian expansion into, 6, 353; Russia's place within, 354, 357; Siberian gas fields and, 318; strategic partnerships in, 364–66; subregions of, 356; understandings of Asia and "Asianness," 357–58; way forward for Russian policy in, 376–78; Western colonial empires in, 434; Western reaction to Russia's engagement with, 378–80. *See also* Central Asia; East Asia; Eurasia; South Asia
"Asian values," 66, 67
Asia-Pacific Economic Cooperation (APEC), 369, 416, 417
Aslund, Anders, 10
Association of Turkic Nations, 387
Atkov, Oleg, 5
Australia, 67, 434
Austria, 75
authoritarianism, 12, 73, 289, 333, 444; democracy and, 92, 117, 439; index of political rights and, 49; law and order ensured by, 56; liberalism and, 29; quality of institutions and, 68; reversion to, 66; in Russian history, 288; state's ambiguous relationship to, 13; strong, 55, 56

Azerbaijan, 342, 365, 387; European "common neighborhood" and, 373; European Union (EU) and, 309; GDP in, 42, 43; Nagorno-Karabakh conflict and, 424

Baker, James, 387, 418
Bakiyev, Kurmanbek, 345, 392
Baku-Tbilisi, Ceyhan (BTC) pipeline, 316
Balkans, 56, 282, 285, 295, 297
Baltic republics, 81, 128, 275, 282; departure from Soviet Union, 417; in European Union (EU), 304; NATO membership for, 311, 335; neo–Cold War policy of, 306; Russian reconciliation with, 425; U.S. influence in, 368
Bashkhortostan, 15, 426
Basmanny justice, 89
Belarus, 55, 57, 70n6, 282, 319, 410; European "common neighborhood" and, 373; European Union (EU) and, 304, 309; GDP in, 42, 43; Human Development Index, 49; independence of, 289; reluctance to follow Russian foreign policy, 425; Russian reunification with, 306; strong authoritarianism in, 56; U.S. influence in, 368
Belinsky, Vissarion, 444
Belovzhskie Accords, 385, 409
Berdyaev, N. A., 443–44, 445, 452
Berezovsky, Boris, 21
Berlin-Paris-Moscow axis, 306, 311, 313
Berlin Wall, fall of, 271, 417–18, 421
Besançon, Alain, 434, 444
Beslan hostage crisis, 98, 334, 335, 421
Bichler, Shimshon, 22
Biden, Joe, 337, 350n17

billionaires, number of, 17, 44, 46, 192
birthrate: decrease in, 246, 249, 260, 437; increase in, 19, 453, 454
Bismarck, Otto von, 77
Blok, Alexander, 442
Bolivia, 415
Bologna Process, 231, 232–33, 239–42, 243
Bolsheviks/Bolshevism, 87, 94, 443, 444. *See also* Russian Revolution (1917)
Bonapartism, 95
Bosnia, 42
Botswana, 66
brain drain, xiv
Braudel, Fernand, 449
Brazil, xiii, 39n49, 41, 46, 363
Brezhnev, Leonid, 15, 79, 139n7, 203, 275, 446
BRIC (Brazil, Russia, India, China), 27, 279, 365, 380, 416; diplomacy of, 363; instrumentalism in Russian foreign policy and, 372; summits of, 375, 376–77
Britain (UK), 4, 118, 276, 279; climate and agriculture in, 449; Cold War and, 272–74; colonial empire of, 436; oriental studies in, 358; Russian relations with, 294–95; special relationship with United States, 411–12
Brown, Gordon, 343
Bryusov, Valery, 443
Brzezinski, Zbigniew, 389, 409
budget deficits, 18, 57
Bulgaria, 42, 304
bureaucracy/bureaucrats, 4, 200, 204, 219; autonomous, 12–13; big business and, 18; Bolshevik, 77; Christian consciousness and, 445; elites in competition with, 206; hegemonic, 23; inefficiency of, 84; liberal-technocrats and, 102; modernization and, 31; Muscovite, 75; oligarchs and, 20; private business and, 199; Putin and, 138; sovereign bureaucracy, 74; of Soviet Union, 15; in state companies, 203
Bush, George H. W. (Bush I), administration of, 328, 329, 330, 331, 332, 412
Bush, George W. (Bush II), administration of, 303, 312, 327, 415, 418; Iranian nuclear program and, 341; missile deployments in Europe and, 343; peak of U.S. power during, 348; Russia's resurgence under Putin and, 331–37
business elites, 192, 198, 203, 206; characteristics of, 196; middle class and, 215; state role in economy and, 195; in tsarist Russia, 191
businesses, small, 208, 212, 215, 221
Byzantium, 440

Canada, 4, 10, 46, 67
capital, xiv, 63, 192; accumulation of, 19, 20, 22, 26, 81–82; foreign, 137; human capital, 65, 66, 217; modernization and, 221
capitalism, 73, 119, 373, 452; agriculture and, 450; authoritarian, 378; of continental Europe, 80; democracy and, 453; establishment of in Europe, 451; nascent, 145, 146; non-industrialized countries and, 442; organized crime and, 19; Soviet ambition to supplant, 408; state capitalism, 181, 217; transition from communism, xi; Western colonialism and, 448–49; Western dynamism and, 434; without capital, 23; world system of, xiii, xiv

Caspian Sea region, 282, 316; ethnic enclaves in, 426; Northern Distribution Network (NDN), 344; oil and gas resources in, 306, 317, 399

Caucasus (Transcaucasus) region, 120, 182, 282, 295; energy pipelines across, 316; European Union (EU) and, 304; German–Russian relations and, 312; Islamic movements of Central Asia and, 401; Russia's traditional leverage over, 305; terrorism and banditry in, 426; Turkey's role in, 424; U.S. influence in, 368. *See also* Russian–Georgian War (August 2008)

Central Asia, xv, 6, 83, 282, 402; American influence in, 362; Central Asians living in Russia, 401; China's influence in, 361, 362, 370, 375–76, 390, 391; decision making in, 359; economic integration of, 389–90; energy interest of Russia in, 397–99; as energy source for China, 395–97; ethnic-based patronage networks, 96; as European outpost, 353; gas pipelines/resources, 309, 316, 318; geopolitics in, xiv, 385–89; independence after Soviet collapse, 383; Islamic extremism in, 367; Northern Distribution Network (NDN), 344; reassertion of Russian influence in, 352n34, 353, 363, 368; Russia's historical involvement in, 384–85; Russia's military interest in, 391–95; security in, 390–91, 426; strength of Russian ties with, 356; U.S. influence in, 415; U.S. military bases in, 323, 332, 349n8

Central Europe, 15, 204, 424; Cold War legacy and, 275; democratic regimes in, 55, 56; elites in, 211; ethnic wars avoided in, 81; former COMECON countries of, 194; GDP in, 43; missile defense system in, 303, 309; pace of transformation in, 284; Soviet occupation of, 276

Chaadaev, Pyotr, 440

Chancellor, Richard, 73, 74

Charlemagne, 434

Chávez, Hugo, 415, 420

Chechnya, xv, 82, 410; attempt to leave Russian Federation, 15, 408; human rights abuses in, 306; Islamic extremism in, 302; "purges" in, 19; Putin and, 120, 122; wars in, 89, 205, 329, 333, 334, 367

Chekhov, Anton, 42

Cheney, Dick, 287, 328, 332

Chernomyrdin, Viktor, 411, 412

China, xiii, 41, 52, 279, 332; Caspian region and, 306; Central Asia and, 362, 390, 391, 395–97; Cold War and, 273; corruption in, 45; "crony communism" in, 103; economic growth in, 41; energy consumption by, 316; evolutionary path of, 214; GDP growth, 39n49; geopolitics and, xiv, 361–63; German trade with, 313; globalization and, xvi; gradual reforms in, 55; G-2 relationship with United States, 374, 382n20, 415; Human Development Index, 49; human rights in, 90, 287; institutional trajectory and history of, 67; Iranian nuclear program and, 343; Japan's relations with, 276; Korean Six-Party Talks and, 367; Ming dynasty, 75; murder rate, 46; nuclear arms control and, 340; rise of, 282, 296, 347, 355, 378, 440–41; Shanghai Cooperation Organization (SCO) and, 370,

386, 426; Siberian energy imports, 318; as strategic partner of United States, 303; strong authoritarianism in, 56, 62. *See also* Sino-Russian relations

China National Petroleum Corporation (CNPC), 382n23, 395

Christianity, Orthodox. *See* Orthodox Church/Christianity

Christianity, Western, xiii

Chubais, Anatoly, 411

Churchill, Winston, 381n14

CIS (Commonwealth of Independent States), 10, 55, 304, 305, 316, 388, 393; Collective Security Pact Organization (CSPO) of, 324; democratic political systems in, 56; establishment of, 385–86, 409; Russian domination in, 416; Single Economic Space, 413; as "third empire," 409, 410–11

citizens/citizenship, 2, 39n50, 95, 287

civilizations, 434–35, 436–39, 449, 450

civil liberties, 28, 39n50, 178

civil society, xvi, 29, 81, 128, 145; autonomy of, 103; democracy and, 212; development of, 90; differences between Russia and West, 439; elites and, 213, 214; feebleness of, 152; modernization and, 211; para-constitutionalism and, 98; "sovereign democracy" and, 106; weak, 207, 217, 219, 281

Civil War, Russian, 14, 197, 223n9, 414

class conflicts, 80, 83, 443

clientelism, 95

climate/climate change, 78, 289, 308, 449

Clinton, Bill, administration of, 296–97, 327, 332, 420; "alliance with Russian reform," 328, 331; frustration with Yeltsin policies, 329–30

coalitions, social, 34

Cold War, 84, 90, 271, 272, 456; burdensome legacy of, 274–75; experience of, 272–74; isolationism and, 359; legacy of, 287; lexicon of, 296; as messianic Western crusade, 441; new members of NATO/EU and, 306; renewal of, 320, 330; Russian identity and, 435; Russia's place in Europe and, 308; "small," 308; Third World and, 408; USSR/Russia as loser of, 303, 412, 422, 439

Cold War, end of, 284, 295, 301, 302, 307; Asian multilateral institutions and, 369; Russia's loss of buffer with West, 408–9; "unipolar moment" of United States and, 414; U.S. policy toward Russia after, 327

Collective Security Treaty Organization (CSTO), 324, 345, 368, 369, 370, 388; binary Europe and, 425; Collective Rapid Reaction Force (KSOR), 392–93, 395; ethnic conflicts in Central Asia and, 394; terrorism and drug trafficking combated by, 426, 427

Colombia, 46

colonialism, 66, 68, 436

"color" revolutions, 82, 204, 335, 347. *See also* Orange Revolution (Ukraine)

Colton, Timothy, 5

COMECON countries, 52, 194, 369, 423

communism, xvii, 94, 274, 373; catching up with West as goal of, 444; challenge to reelection of Yeltsin, 101; control of information and, 289; "crony communism" in China, 103; dissolution of, 87, 104, 137; fall of, 245; resource

mobilization and, 419; Russia's Asian territory and, 353; threat of "communist revenge," 199; transition to capitalism, xi, xiv; Westernization and, 67
Communist Party, Soviet, 91, 117, 204, 222n6, 226, 445
Communist Party of the Russian Federation (KPRF), 82, 229
Comprehensive Test-Ban Treaty (CTBT), 341
"Concept of the Long-Term Socioeconomic Development of the Russian Federation," 122
conservatism, 29, 30, 73, 79, 87, 453
constitution, Russian, 89, 96; para-constitutionalism and, 97–100; powers of presidency, 119–20; presidential powers in, 129, 135; terms limits on presidential tenure, 123–24, 131
Constitutional Court, 138, 143n51
constitutional state, 87, 88, 89, 91; administrative regime and, 92; democracy paradox and, 101; as normative state, 108
consumption/consumers, 2, 14, 83, 146, 221
containment policy, 290, 291, 305, 306, 309. *See also* Cold War
contracts, enforcement of, 54, 55, 56
Conventional Forces in Europe (CFE) Treaty, 303, 320
corporations, multinational, 74
corruption, 41, 71n14, 84, 120, 152, 429; anti-corruption initiatives, 136; as burden on Russia, 137; comparison of Russia and China, 45; democracy and, 178; education system and, 242–43, 290; as failure of Putin regime, 123; in health care system, 266; Medvedev's condemnation of, 107; metacorruption, 101; middle class and, 216; Ministry of the Interior reforms and, 3; modernization and, 1, 213, 219, 220; organized crime and, xv; public anger at, 289–90; in Soviet Union, 44; weak state and, 21; Western institutions seens as enablers of, 331
Costa Rica, 17
Council of Europe, 287, 288, 320, 417
Council of Ministers, 134
Cowan, M. P., 24
Cox, Robert W., 101–2
crime, 41, 47; in China, 67; curbed under Putin, 446; decrease in, 16; organized crime (mafias), xv, 18, 19, 82, 101, 313; in Soviet Union, 46; transnational, 377
Crimea, 394, 410
Croatia, GDP in, 42
Cuba, 17, 48, 290, 408
Cuban missile crisis, 272, 275
culture, xiii, 289, 294, 357
Czech Republic, 17, 306; GDP in, 42; missile defense system in, 309, 336, 342–43

Dagestan, 15
Dahrendorf, Ralf, 90
Day in the Life of an Oprichnik, A (Sorokin), 74
debt, 15, 17, 18
de-industrialization, 11, 19, 27, 48
democracy/democratization, 1, 57, 83, 107, 277; after Stalin's death, 78; "anarcho-democracy," 95; authoritarianism combined with, 92, 117; commodification of, 19, 28; constitutional, 108, 118; constraints on, 19; "cosmopolitan democracy," xvi; democracy index, 57,

468 Index

58–59; democratic evolutionism, 89–91, 100, 103–8; depoliticization and paradox of, 100–102; elites and, 212; EU expansion and, 304; failed, 88–89; German–Russian relations and, 313; illiberal, 56, 68; incomplete, 145; index of political rights and, 49; in India, 374; Kantian democratic peace, 328; liberal, 12, 87, 92, 109; "managed," 122; middle class and, 194; para-politics and, 99; promoted in U.S. foreign policy, 335; prospect of Russian integration into EU and, 283; Putin's attitude toward, 28–29; quality institutions and, 66; Russian identity and, 148, 150, 447; Russians' view of, 147, 174–75, 176, 178–79, 179; in Soviet Union, 74; state's ambiguous relationship to, 13; victory of, 15, 44; Yeltsin and, 9. *See also* "sovereign democracy"

Deng Xiaoping, 125, 126
depoliticization, 100–102, 105
Deripaska, Oleg, 111n23, 129–30
Derluguian, Georgi, 4
Desert Storm, Operation, 329
developing countries, 15, 41, 70n8; abnormal, 44; normal, 44, 50, 67
developmental state, 12, 20, 25, 26, 29, 30–34
diamonds, 11, 48
dictatorship, 115, 140n11
diseases, xviii, 250, 251, 261, 267
distortions, pre-transition, 51, 52, 54, 57, 58–59, 60
Dostoevsky, Fyodor, 442, 444
dot.com bubble, 331
drug abuse, 251, 252
drug trafficking, 324, 346, 390–91, 426, 427

Dubin, Boris, 217
Dugin, Alexander, xiv
Duma, State (parliament), 100, 120, 121, 122, 124, 129; confrontation with Yeltsin, 41, 88–89, 228; education committee, 235, 236; political elites in, 192; presidency and, 135; public attitudes toward, 175, 176, 177; Public Chamber and, 98
Durnovo, P. N., 191
Dutkiewicz, Piotr, 4
Duverger, Maurice, 127
Dzherzhinsky, Felix, 277

East Asia, 35, 65, 77, 347, 368; American military presence in, 362; community/collectivist institutions in, 68; democracy in, 56; developmental-state model and, 30; economic growth in, 63; Sino-Japanese rivalry in, 379
Easter, Gerald, 103
Eastern Europe (EE), 10, 52, 54, 195, 424; Cold War legacy and, 275, 276; economies of, 41; elites in, 211; EU expansion into, 304; geopolitics and, xiii; German economy and, 313–14; murder rate, 46; pace of transformation in, 284; revolutions of 1980s in, 204, 417; role of state in, 26; Russia–EU relations in, 293–94; Soviet Union and, 79, 276; strong institutions in, 62
economic/financial crisis, xviii, 10, 27, 83, 336; Asian (1997), 337; Central Asia and, 389; confidence in obedience and, 23; currency reserves of Russia and, 317; developmental state and, 25; education system and, 235; energy exports and, 319; EU-Russian relations and, 323;

financial collapse in Russia (1998), 202, 206, 331; Gref plan and, 122; health care and, 261–62; modernization and, xv, 216, 219; oil prices and, 12; political parties and, 185; Russia hit hard by, 1, 382n21; Russian public opinion and, 184; unpredictable global environment and, 33; U.S.–China relations and, 374; Western decline associated with, 379

economics, xii, xiv, xvi, 102–3, 205, 359

economists, xv, 2, 34, 83

economy, xii, 30, 145–46, 448–49; centrally planned economy (CPE), 52, 55, 60, 63, 181; evolution since end of Soviet era, 4; gradual transition, 51, 53; growth of, xi, 18; mixed, 181; oil and gas exports, 11; raw materials dependency, 152, 291; recession of 1990s, 14–15. *See also* shadow economy; shock therapy

Ecuador, 415

education, 5, 19, 69, 98, 180; access to, 28; Bologna Process and vocational education, 239–42; middle-class intelligentsia and, 208; modernization and, 242–43; as "national project," 122; post-Soviet philosophy of, 227–36; pros and cons of mass higher education, 236–39; social inequalities and, 170; in Soviet Union, 225–27, 236, 242; standard-of-living measurements and, 162, 162, 165, 170

Egypt, 68

elections, 25, 28, 39n48, 56, 128; democracy paradox and, 101; free and fair, 101, 106, 175; under Gorbachev, 91; new evolutionism in practice, 104–5; para-politics and, 99; political parties as main actors in, 96; Putin's reelection (2004), 121;

regional, 135–36, 185; Russo-Western tensions and, 301; U.S. influence and, 329

elites, 2, 89, 116; Communist, 191; composition of, 5, 191, 192–93; as consumers, 97; corporate, xvi; democracy and, 106, 428; emergence of, 193–201; great-power status of Russia and, 411; imperial mission abandoned by, 409; intellectual, 192, 193, 205–6, 208–12, 214; Japan admired by, 366; middle class and, 207–12; military, 192–93, 196; modernization and, 213–21; regional, 105, 195, 198, 203; religious, 192, 193, 195, 196; Russian identity and, 434; of Russia's neighboring states, 305; Soviet, 195; Stalinist terror and, 76, 195; structure of, 201–7; tsarist, 191; Yeltsin and, 101. *See also* business elites; political elites

emigration, 208, 209, 224n19, 278

energy/energy exports, xiv, 1, 11, 280; power of energy sector, 27; Russia's great-power status and, 305; as Russia's link with Europe, 315–19. *See also* gas, natural; oil and oil prices

environment, xviii, 427

Estonia, 42, 43, 55, 70n6, 128

etatization, 9, 35n1

ethnicity, 22, 149, 294; assimilated ethnics, 410; conflicts in Central Asia and, 393–94; ethnic tolerance, 428

Eurasia, xiv, 131, 337, 373, 402, 442; Central Asian economic integration, 390; "color" revolutions in, 335; "imitation democracies" in, 92; security in, 355, 380

Eurasian Economic Community (EurAsEC), 369, 370, 388, 425, 426

Eurasianism, xiv
Eurocentrism, 347, 434, 436, 441, 452
Europe, xvi, 77, 347, 355; declining hegemony of, xii, xiii; Gorbachev's proposal to, 80; three branches of European civilization, 424; world economic crisis and, 1. *See also* Central Europe; Eastern Europe; Western Europe
Europe, Russia's place in, 6, 34, 73, 272, 274, 290, 298; "Asian-ness" of Russia and, 357; energy as link, 315–19; European rejection of Russian image, 433; Germany as Russia's advocate, 310–15; modernization partnership with West and, 324; resource mobilization and, 419; Russia and Europe as separate civilizations, 435; Russia as raw materials appendage of Europe, 422; as unanswered question of Cold War, 308
European Economic Community (EEC), 53, 288, 315, 423
European Union (EU), 13, 251, 419; birthrates in, 248; dependence on Russian gas imports, 307, 316, 318, 319; energy pipelines and, 315–16, 420; former Soviet republics and, 309; GDP in, 41; German–Russian "special" relationship and, 310, 314; historical reunification of West and, 304; life expectancy in, 247; as model for Russia, 30, 34; mortality rate in, 247–48; prospects for Russian integration into, 183, 283–84, 285, 312, 323, 412; prospects for Russia's integration into, 423; Russia's relations with, 5, 271, 296, 304–8, 359, 378; strategic disagreement with Russia, 282; "strategic partnership" with Russia, 297; tensions in former Soviet area and, 293; as trading partner of Russia, 302, 357–58; Ukraine and, 293–94, 425
EU-Russia Partnership and Cooperation Agreement, 271, 277, 284, 322
"evil empire," 273, 441
exchange rates, 57, 69

Fabian Society, 24
factions/factionalism, 96, 101, 105, 108
fascism, 98
Federal Assembly, 107, 124
federalism, 109, 128, 145
Federal Security Service (FSB), 177, 178
Federation Council, 124, 141n17, 176, 177
FIGs (Financial Industrial Groups), 21, 36n22
financial crisis. *See* economic/financial crisis
Finland, 11, 49
Fish, Stephen, 89
Fissile Material Cut-off Treaty (FMCT), 341
Forbes magazine, 17, 44, 130
Ford, Henry, 77
foreign policy, Russian, 5–6, 34, 105, 204; "Asianization" of, 353, 355, 370–76, 378; contradictory goals of, 305; critique of, 417–21; Eastern dimension of, 353–54; energy resources of Russia and, 303; geopolitics and, 361, 376; public opinion and, 182; Russian identity and, 147; strategic partnerships in Asia, 364–66, 377
foreign policy, U.S. *See* U.S.–Russian relations
former Soviet Union (FSU), 41, 44, 54, 57; ethnic Russians living in, 283; European

Union (EU) and, 309; GDP change in, 43; mass politics in, 106; NATO membership for states of, 286; poor initial conditions for transition in, 60; Russian policy toward republics of, 333; semi-presidentialism in, 128; transformational recession in, 55; transplanted Western institutions in, 68; weak democracy in, 56. *See also* post-Soviet space; Soviet Union (USSR)

Fradkov, Mikhail, 128

France, 132, 249, 252, 276, 279, 411; climate and agriculture in, 449; colonial empire of, 436; oriental studies in, 358; post-imperial, 412

Freedom House, 49, 71n14

free press, 9–10

Friedrich the Great, 76

fuel prices, 11, 48

Fukuyama, Francis, 283

Furman, Dimitry, 92, 445

Gaidar, Yegor, 329, 411

Gaman-Golutvina, O. V., 192, 193

gas, natural, 22, 309; Central Asia–Center (CAC) pipeline, 397–99; German–Russian relations and, 312–13; Kazakhstan–China pipeline, 395–96; prices/price control, 32, 68; Russia as top producer of, 317, 355; Russian economy dependent on, 11

Gazeta.ru Web site, 106, 133

Gazprom, 37n28, 38n33, 315, 319, 420; in Central Asia, 397–98; as motor of Russian economy, 128

GDP (Gross Domestic Product), 2, 235, 261, 280; of BRIC countries, 39n49; comparison with United States, 331; decline in, 69, 200, 216, 280; economic recession and, 41, 42–43; education spending as percentage of, 229, 233; energy sector, 317; foreign debt as percentage, 18; of Germany, 412; health care spending and, 253, 254, 257, 264; Human Development Index and, 48; medical research and, 265; oil and gas sector, 11, 37n33; as per-capita percentage of U.S. level, 62; ratio to net investment, 52, 71n14; recession of 1990s and, 14, 58–59, 61; Russia's growth potential, 279; shadow economy and, 15; variations in dynamics of, 57, 58–59

gender, 22

"Geographical Pivot of History, The" (Mackinder), 387

geography, 289, 294, 355; Asian territory of Russia, 354, 357; of Central Asia, 386; Russia's relation to Western world and, 434; "spheres of influence" and, 304

geopolitics, 74, 75, 79, 375, 419; Afghanistan problem and, 324; Asian policies and, 360–64; in Central Asia, xiv, 385–89; expansion of territorial states, 75; NATO expansion and, 308; overextended power of United States, 336; pseudomultilateralism and, 369; rapprochement, 91; renunciation of, 377, 379; return of, xii–xiv; Russia's autonomy and, 90; tsarist Russia and, 76

Georgia, 129, 276, 320, 347; borders of, 414, 426; democracy in, 287; European "common neighborhood" and, 373; European Union (EU) and, 304, 309; GDP in, 42, 43; NATO and, 303, 426;

prospect of Russian reconciliation with, 424; renewed conflict with Russia as prospect, 292; Rose Revolution ("color" revolution), 82, 286; Russian forces in, 293; separatist regions of, 305, 308; U.S. influence in, 415. *See also* Abkhazia; Ossetia, South; Russian–Georgian War (August 2008)

Germany, 4, 279; democracy in, 90; East Germany (GDR), 310, 313; geopolitics and, xiii; Nazi regime, 276; number of billionaires, 17, 44; postwar transformation of, 284; reunification of, 311, 329, 417; "special" relationship with Russia, 309–15; Weimar Republic, 100, 412; West Germany, 310, 412

Gini coefficient, 44, 45

globalization, xvi, 2, 38n43, 183, 318, 423

"Go, Russia!" (Medvedev), 106–8, 133, 134; modernization and, 281; on pace of change, 136–37; on relations with West, 271, 291

Goldgeier, James, 328, 329, 330

Google, xiv

Gorbachev, Mikhail, 15, 84, 91, 133, 283; disarmament agreements with United States, 420; elites under, 203, 418; end of Cold War and, 273; failure of reforms, 5, 81; German reunification and, 310–11, 312, 329; great-power status of Russia and, 415; modernization and, 2; NATO expansion and, 430n12; "new thinking" concept, 376, 421; U.S. foreign policy and, 328–29. *See also* perestroika

Gore, Al, 331

Gorky, Maxim, 442, 443

Gorshkov, Mikhail, 5

governance, xvi, 3, 13, 24. *See also* power; state, the

Gramsci, Antonio, 92

Great Depression, xvii, 337

great power, Russia as, 14, 151, 201, 219, 278–79; Asian policies and, 376; critique of Russian foreign policy, 417–21; delusion of normative convergence and, 373–74; energy exports and, 305, 315; legacy of Russian empire, 407, 408–11; meaning of greatness, 411–17; realpolitik and its alternatives, 421–27; relations with Asia and, 359–60; relations with West and, 285; "triple transformation" of, 327; World War II victory and, 306

Greece, 15, 44, 288

Gref, German, 122

Grigoriev, Leonid, 5

growth diagnostics, 65

G-7 (G-8) countries, 284, 295, 309, 311, 312, 416

G-20 countries, 296, 377, 381n11, 416

Guardini, Romano, 443

Gudkov, Lev, 217

gulag, 104, 276

Gulf Cooperation Council, 427

Gulf War, 421

Gustavus Adolphus, 76

Hale, Henry, 97

Hamas, election of, 101

Hanson, Philip, 102

Hart–Hagel report, 338

Hausmann, R., 65

Havel, Vaclav, 290

Hayek, Friedrich von, 448

health/health care, xvii, 5, 19, 44, 69, 98,

245–46; access to, 28, 262; basic factors in health status of Russians, 251–54; challenges and expectations for, 260–63; demographics and, 246–51; middle class and, 208; as "national project," 122; occupational health, 251, 253–54; private insurance companies, 256; regulation and management of, 259–60, 263; social inequalities and, 170; standard-of-living measurements and, 154, 164, 166, 168; strategy directions for, 263–68; system structure and resources, 254–60. *See also* birthrate; life expectancy; mortality rate

Hegel, G.W.F., 24, 152
Hesse, Herman, 444
Himmler, Heinrich, 277
history, end of, 283, 441
Hitler, Adolf, 276, 277, 306
Hong Kong, 56
housing, 98, 122, 159, 171, 289
Hu Jintao, 130, 364
Human Development Index, 48, 49
human rights, xv, 89, 90, 175, 286; in Chechnya, 306; genuine guarantees of, 178; German–Russian relations and, 313, 315; U.S. foreign policy and, 332; "values" argument and, 287
Hungary, 17, 42
Huntington, Samuel, 360, 442
Hussein, Saddam, 329, 415, 420, 422
hyperinflation, xv, 82

identity, 97, 146, 152; civilizational, 433–35, 438, 450; foreign policy and, 147; philosophical, 442–47; relations with West and, 277; Russia between East and West, 358, 360, 363, 371; Russia's quest for, 148–51; World War II and, 306
ideology, 22, 23, 24, 79; in Cold War, 275; communist, 197; democracy as legitimating ideology, 99; dogmatism, 227; "ideological disciplines" in Soviet education, 228, 229; intellectual elite and, 208; of Putin regime, 28, 29; social sciences elites and, 210
IMF (International Monetary Fund), xv, xviii, 183, 284, 413, 444
immigration, 249–50
import/export licenses, 21
import substitution, 56
incomes and income inequalities, 14, 41, 44, 68, 121; in China, 67; of elites, 220; monthly average among different strata, 158, 159; Russians' attitudes toward, 147, 170; stability of incomes, 28; standard-of-living measurements and, 154, 159–62, 160, 161
India, xiii, 15, 41, 44, 347, 356, 377; China's relations with, 363, 379; community/collectivist institutions in, 68; economic growth in, 41; GDP growth, 39n49; Kashmir and, 391; Pakistan as rival of, 367, 379; rise of, 378; Russia's relations with, 365, 366, 372, 373; in Shanghai Cooperation Organization (SCO), 427; Soviet strategic relationship with, 367; tension with Pakistan, 363
Indonesia, 17, 25, 280, 362, 376
industrialization, xvii, 288, 439; in Central Asia, 385; over-industrialization, 52; re-industrialization, 35; of Soviet Union, 78; World War II and, 78
industrial output/production, 12, 52; decline in, 10; dynamics in real terms,

453, 454; health conditions and, 253–54; reduction during recession, 52, 53
inflation (consumer price index), 18, 51, 57, 58–59
infrastructure, 65, 66, 69, 263, 265
INF (Intermediate-Range Nuclear Forces) Treaty, 340
innovation, xiv, 38n46, 107, 185, 215; "bottom-up" modernization and, 211; as buzzword, 279; modernization and, 220, 221; sporadic and unique nature of, 75; technological, 2, 27, 34
Inozemtsev, Vladislav, 34
Institute of Contemporary Development (INSOR), 106, 219, 220
Institute of Sociology, Russian Academy of Sciences (IS RAS), 146, 153, 169, 172, 175, 181, 182
institutional collapse, 51, 54, 56, 67, 68
intellectuals/intelligentsia, xi, xii, 30, 73, 74; elites and, 195, 196, 208; Eurocentrism and, 452; marginalization of, 82; modernization and, 76–77; perestroika and, 79; political leaning of, 447; privatization and, 199; professional elites, 204; public sphere and, 99; as rank of middle class, 217; in Soviet Union, 153; Stalinism and, 78
intelligence services, 204, 205
Interior, Ministry of the, 3, 18
Internet, 121, 129, 221, 243
investment, 52, 53, 54, 68–69
Iran, xiii, 68, 294, 353, 363, 379; Asian policies of Russia and, 364; Central Asia and, 387, 400; gas pipelines/reserves, 316, 318; missile defense and, 342–44; nuclear program, 303, 317, 337, 373, 427; as regional power, 376; Rogun Dam (Tajikistan) and, 400; Russian military support for, 301; in Safavi period, 75; in Shanghai Cooperation Organization (SCO), 427; Sino-Russian relations and, 374; strategic partnership with Russia, 364, 365; theocracy in, 374; UN sanctions against, 346, 381n12; U.S.–Russian relations and, 341–42, 377, 427
Iraq, 296, 317, 322, 412, 427
Iraq war, 297, 337, 421; Berlin-Paris-Moscow axis and, 311, 312; initial U.S. military success, 333, 335, 348, 422; Russian opposition to, 306, 334
Ireland, 275–76
irrendentism, 81, 410, 413
Islamic extremism, 302, 303, 362, 367
Islam/Islamic world, xiii, 372, 401, 426
Israel, 11, 46, 49, 344, 427
Italy, 15, 44, 252
Ivanov, Igor, 407
Ivanov, Sergei, 104
Ivan the Terrible, 74, 75, 76, 77

Jackson-Vanik amendment, 347
Japan, 49, 276, 302, 347, 377; China's relations with, 363; democratization of, 66; developmental state in, 25; economic growth rate, 62, 63, 64; GDP in, 41; geopolitics and, xiv; as major Asian power, 356; Meiji Restoration, 76; murder rate, 46; number of billionaires, 17; postwar transformation of, 284; Russia's territorial dispute with, 363, 366–67, 373, 381n14; U.S. alliance with, 362, 366, 375; world economic crisis and, 1
Joint-Stock Company "Russian Railways"

(JSC "RZD"), 256, 263
journalists, 16, 99, 134, 136
justice/juridical system, 104, 109, 122, 129, 428; independence of, 277; lack of justice, 152; pretrial detention for economic offenses, 136; public trust in, 175, 177
Just Russia party, 104

Kaliningrad enclave, 306
Kant, Immanuel, 152
Kapuscinski, Ryszard, 9
Karadzic, Radovan, 410
Karimov, Islam, 336, 349n8
Kasparov, Garry, 105
Kas'yanov, Mikhail, 124, 128
Kazakhstan, 287, 323, 399, 425; border demarcation with Russia, 394; China's economic ties to, 395–97; economic integration with Russia, 426; emergence from Soviet collapse, 383; GDP in, 42; geopolitics and, 362; Northern Distribution Network (NDN) and, 344, 345; Russian-speakers in, 388; water resources, 391
Keynes, John Maynard, 443
Keynesian economics, xvi
KGB (Soviet state security police), 10, 82, 126, 133, 275, 276, 333
Khodorkovsky, Mikhail, 89, 122, 222n6, 276, 333
Khrushchev, Nikita, 74, 139n7, 197, 275; de-Stalinization under, 276; "thaw" of, 74, 446
Kim Jong Il, 420
King of the Mountain: The Nature of Political Leadership (Ludwig), 115
Kirabaev, Nur, 5

Kissinger, Henry, 339
Kluyev, Nikolai, 443
knowledge economy/industry, 1, 239
Kohl, Helmut, 311, 313, 314, 418
Kolodko, W., 54
Komsomol entrepreneurs, 198, 213, 222n6
Korea, North (DPRK), 294, 366, 367, 379, 427
Korea, South (Republic of Korea), 15, 17, 44, 49, 377; developmental state in, 25; economic growth fate, 63, 64; Japan's relations with, 276; trade with Russia, 11; U.S. alliance with, 362, 375
Korean Six-Party Talks, 367, 369, 370, 427
Kosovo, 308, 330, 331, 431n25; independence of, 336; international community and status of, 424; U.S. military success in, 333
Kosygin, Aleksei, 139n7
Kozak Plan, 305
Kozyrev, Andrei, 302, 411, 415
Krastev, Ivan, 13
Krauthammer, Charles, 369
Kravchuk, Leonid, 409
Kryshtanovskaya, Olga, 198, 206
Kuchins, Andrew, 6
Kudrin, Finance Minister, 281
Kulov, Feliz, 392
Kundera, Milan, 435, 442
Kurbsky, Andrei, 74
Kurginyan, Sergei, 99
Kursk submarine, sinking of, 17
Kyoto Protocol, 322
Kyrgyzstan, 42, 43, 347, 349n8, 368; China's economic interest in, 397; desire for union with Russia, 388; drug trafficking into, 391; emergence from Soviet

collapse, 383; ethnic Uzbeks in, 393–94; Russian military base at Osh, 392, 393; in Shanghai Cooperation Organization (SCO), 370; U.S. military base at Manas, 345, 362, 381n8, 392

land distribution, 65
Lane, David, 149
language, xiii, 149, 357, 384, 385
Laos, 408
Latin America, xvi, 41, 56, 67; Cold War and, 282; Soviet/Russian comparison to, 65, 200, 207; weak middle class in, 194
Latvia, 42, 43, 128
Lavrov, Sergei, 282, 287, 414
law, 4, 22, 54; constitutional, 99; electoral, 12; international, 283, 428; legal reform, 193; "telephone law," 89
law, rule of, 68, 277; capitalism and, 217; as concern of Medvedev, 138; European Union (EU) and, 288; law enforcement agencies and, 292; rule-of-law index, 56, 57, 58–59, 70n8; Russo-Western tensions and, 301
law and order, 44, 54, 289; collapse of state institutions and, 55; democracy and, 56; German–Russian relations and, 313, 314
leadership: in post-communist transition, 118–20; of Putin–Medvedev tandem, 127–32; Russian terms for, 118, 126, 129; search for model of, 117–18; term limits on presidential tenure, 123; web of, 115–17
League of Nations, 24
Ledyaev, V., 201
Lee Kwan Yew, 125, 126
Leftwich, Adrian, 25

Lenin, Vladimir, 24, 118, 378, 391, 414
Lermontov, Mikhail, 77
Levada, Yuri, 194
Lévi-Strauss, Claude, 450
Liberal-Democratic Party of Russia (LDPR), 229
liberalism, 28, 289, 456; authoritarianism and, 29; "Leninist liberals," 105; in U.S. foreign policy, 328
liberalization, economic, 14, 28; in China, 67; endogeneity problem and, 60; gradual, 62; speed of, 51, 54, 60; Yeltsin and, 50
life expectancy, xvii, 17, 44, 47, 248–49, 437; artificial reduction in crisis of 1990s, 446; in demographic forecasts, 261; health care policy and, 257, 263; mortality rate and, 48; Russia compared with EU countries, 247, 247
Limonov, Eduard, 28
List, Friedrich, 23
Lithuania, 42, 43, 128, 320
Litvinenko, Alexander, 276
Lo, Bobo, 6
"loans for shares" auctions, 15, 16, 21, 329
Lomonosov Moscow State University, 227, 231
Louis XIV, 76
Lüdendorff, Erich, 77
Ludwig, Arnold M., 115
Luzhkov, Yuri, 385, 394
Lyne, Roderic, 6

Macedonia, 42
Machiavelli, Niccolò, 117
Mackinder, Sir Halford, xiii–xiv, 387
macrosociology, 74

mafias. *See* crime
Makarychev, Andrey S., 102, 103
Malaysia, 25
Malthusian growth regime, 66, 67
Mao Tse-tung, 276
Margelov, Mikhail, 272
marginalization, 2, 28, 32, 219
Marx, Karl, 24, 77, 440, 441, 442
Marxism, 13, 209, 439, 440, 456
Massimov, Karim, 396
Mauritius, 17, 46, 66
McFaul, Michael, 272, 328, 329, 330
media, 1, 12, 28, 106, 181; freedom of, 36, 89; intellectual elite and, 214; modernization and, 213; Putin's restrictions on independence of, 333; state control and, 13, 121; Western, 455
Medvedev, Dmitry, 25, 84, 142n26; Afghanistan transport routes and, 345; anti-alcohol campaign, 253; constitutional state and, 93–94; crisis of regime, 12; democratic evolutionism and, 106; European security and, 293; goal of integration with global economy, 318; inaugurated as president, 336; as leader, 117, 133; on legacy of history, 292; on "legal nihilism," 88, 133; modernization and, 135; national projects and, 126; nuclear arms control and, 339, 342, 344; political personality of, 105; popularity of, 35n7; on "privileged interests" of Russia, 282; prospects for democracy and, 137; reform program, 108; on relations with West, 271, 319; "reset" of Russo-Western relations and, 309. *See also* "Go, Russia!" (Medvedev); Putin–Medvedev tandem

Memorial for Human Rights and Historical Association, 104, 277
MENA (Middle East and North Africa), 66, 68
Merkel, Angela, 309, 313
Meshkov, Yuri, 410
Mexico, 46
middle classes, 5, 31, 73; characteristics of, 164–66, 166–67, 168–69, 169; civil society and, 213, 214; composition of, 202; elites and, 194, 195, 202, 207–12; emergence of, 147; identification with, 153, 165; modernization and, 33, 201, 216, 221; privatization and, 198; proletarians as nascent middle class, 78–79; *raznochintsy*, 76–77; Russian Revolution and, 195, 197; strength of, 194; transformation recession (1990s) and, 200; upper level of, 169–70
Middle East, xiv, 41, 282, 317; Arab–Iranian rivalry in, 379; community institutions in, 66; greater, 324, 347, 412; identity as subregion, 356; peace settlement in, 324
migration, illegal, 308, 426
military forces: defense spending, 15; demographic crisis and, 246; elites and, 202, 204; idea of Russian "greatness" and, 279; modernization of, 185; of Muscovy, 75; post-communist transition and, xi; public trust in, 177, 178; recovery of, 205; Russian bases in Central Asia, 393–95; sovereignty and, 29; withdrawal of Soviet forces, 410, 417
military-industrial complex, 192, 205, 206, 209, 217, 419
"Millennium Manifesto" (Gref), 121, 122, 151

Mills, C. Wright, 206
Milosevic, Slobodan, 410, 415, 420
Milov, Vladimir, 10
minimum wage, 155
mining/mineral products, 11, 26, 48, 181
Minsk group on Nagorno-Karabakh, 424
Mironov, Sergei, 124
missile defense systems, 303, 309, 334, 336, 342–44
Mladic, Ratko, 410
modernity, 27, 76
modernization, xi, xv, 4, 20, 38n46, 50, 92; accelerated, 27; bureaucratic versus intellectual, 199, 211; Cold War and, 273; conservative, 3, 30, 32–33, 428; deep, 30, 33; education and, 225, 236, 242–43; elites in fight for, 213–21; etatization and, 9, 35n1; European Union (EU) and, 307; false starts, 74; as fashionable topic, 27, 279; Islam and, 426; leadership and, 115; marginalization as alternative to, 2, 28; meanings of, xvii; metapolitics and, 102; of military forces, 185; nationalism in relation to, xii; pace of, 291; of Peter the Great, 94, 292; public support for, 216; quality of institutions and, 4; resource mobilization and, 419, 422–23; Russian tradition of, 75–77; Russia's roots in European civilization and, 324; of Siberia, 314, 322; of Soviet Central Asia, 384; stages of, 116; Stalinist, 78, 197, 292; strategic decline of Russia and, 348; supporters and opponents of, 218, 281; terror and, 74, 76; top-down, 2, 211, 215, 216, 217, 220
Moldova, 282, 305, 373; European Union (EU) and, 309; GDP in, 42, 43;
semi-presidentialism in, 128
Molotov, Vyacheslav, 414
monetarism, xvi
Mongol complex, 358, 440
Mongolia, 364, 366, 381n13, 408; GDP in, 42; Russian forces withdrawn from, 417; in Shanghai Cooperation Organization (SCO), 427
monopolies, 26, 82, 128
Monroe Doctrine, 283
Montenegro, 42
mortality rate, 246, 247–49; alcohol consumption and, 252; decrease in, 16, 50, 453, 454; health care spending and, 257, 258; increase in, 47, 63, 437; infant, 247, 263; life expectancy and, 48; morbidity and, 250–51
multilateralism, 337, 368–70, 427
murder rate, 18–19, 46–47, 47, 50, 63, 67
Muscovy, 75, 117, 410, 440

Nabucco pipeline, 309, 316, 399
NAFTA (North American Free Trade Agreement), 53
Napoleon I, Russian victory over, 415
national interest, 126, 194, 195, 213, 329
nationalism, xi, xv, 278, 289; borders of Russia and, 409; in Central Asia, 383; globalization and, xvi; modernization in relation to, xii; right-wing, 100
national security. *See* security
National System of Political Economy (List), 23
NATO (North Atlantic Treaty Organization), 271, 283, 288, 295, 319, 422, 438; in Afghanistan, 282, 309; Eastern European countries in, 302; German

reunification and, 417; Iraq war and, 296; Kosovo war and, 331; missile defense in Central Europe and, 342; NATO–Russia Council, 344, 424; "New Strategic Concept" of, 293, 344; prospect of Russia joining, 284, 285, 312, 323; sovereignty pooled by members of, 297; viewed as adversary of Russia, 182, 272; World War II victory celebration in Moscow and, 347; Yugoslavia bombed by, 276, 286, 421

NATO enlargement, 285–86, 292, 301, 334, 339, 430n12; absence of Russian threat and, 415; Berlin-Paris-Moscow axis and, 313; "China card" in energy disputes and, 366; Clinton administration and, 330; as exploitation of Russia's weakness, 412; geopolitics and, 308; rejection of U.S. hegemony in resistance to, 421; Russian fear of "encirclement" and, 323; second round of, 332, 335; Ukraine and Georgia, 303, 425–26; United States blamed for, 311; U.S.–Russian relations and, 336

natural resources, xiii, 73, 376, 377, 389
natural sciences, 197, 205, 209, 210, 226
Nazarbaev, Nursultan, 385, 387
Nazism, 276
"near abroad," 282, 356, 410
Nemtsov, A., 252
Nemtsov, Boris, 10
neocontainment, 290
neoliberalism, xv, 80, 101, 441, 448
neopatrimonialism, 81
"New Russians," 447
Nicaragua, 415
Nicholas II, Tsar, 2

Nigeria, 44, 141n22
Nitzan, Jonathan, 22
Nixon, Richard, 273, 411
NKVD (Soviet secret police), 276
Nobel Prize winners, 44
nomenklatura, 78, 80, 81, 224n18; new, 214; replaced with new elites, 198, 199; rules for recruitment into, 197
Nonproliferation Treaty (NPT), 341
Nord Stream pipeline, 309
"Normal Country, A: Russia after Communism" (Schleifer and Triesman), 41
North Africa, 66, 317
Norway, 322, 346–47
Nunn, Sam, 339

Obama, Barack, administration of, 6, 130, 286, 327, 328; Afghanistan war and, 344–46; nuclear arms control and, 339–44; "reset button" and, 337–38, 372; visit to Moscow (2009), 271, 272, 290, 345
Obrazovanie (Education) national project, 230
OECD (Organization for Economic Cooperation and Development), 212, 252, 259, 417; health care and, 266; mortality rate in countries of, 257, 258; Russia as nonmember of, 320; Russia's goal of joining, 423; Russia's lag behind, 280
oil and oil prices, 9, 10, 22, 25, 382n23; decline in, 11–12, 69; economic dependency on, 11; economic growth/recovery and, 68, 333; hikes of 1970s, 52; oil as weapon, 413; "oil republics," 436; peak (July 2008), 336; price control, 32; Putin's political fortunes and, 121;

recovery of, 31; rise after 1998 crash, 279; Russia as top oil producer, 317, 355; Russian "greatness" and, 278; world economic crisis and, 280

Old Believers, 76

oligarchs, xv, 16, 24, 91, 111n23, 198; bureaucrats opposed to, 207; conflict with Russian government, 17–18, 25; financial crisis (1998) and, 206; loyalty to Putin, 123; number of billionaires, 17, 44; political economy of dualism and, 103; politics and, 21–22; privatization of state property and, 89; Putin's crackdown on, 122; state power structure and, 20; state property acquired by, 14; as threat to constitutional state, 101; Yeltsin and, 82, 119

OPEC (Organization of Petroleum Exporting Countries), 318, 417

oprichnina terror (1560s), 74

Orange Revolution (Ukraine), 122, 286, 305, 334, 421, 430n18. *See also* "color" revolutions

Organization for Security and Co-operation in Europe (OSCE), 320, 323, 416, 417

Organization of Islamic Conference (OIC), 369

oriental studies, 226, 358

Orthodox Church/Christianity, xiii, xvii, 73, 444; church elites, 192, 193, 195–97, 202–5; Muslim relations with, 428; public trust in church, 177; Russia's civilizational identity and, 434; Slavophilism and, 358; Western values rejected by, 278

Ossetia, South, 9, 182, 205, 305, 308; Georgian attack on, 182, 431; international community and status of, 424; recognition refused to independence of, 369, 370, 373; Russian forces in, 394; in Russian sphere of influence, 410. *See also* Georgia; Russian–Georgian War (August 2008)

Ostpolitik (eastern policy), German, 310, 311

Our Home is Russia, 229

Özal, Turgut, 387–88

Pakistan, 344, 363, 367, 376; Central Asia and, 387; enmity with India, 367, 379; Kashmir and, 391; in Shanghai Cooperation Organization (SCO), 427

Palestine, 101

Pappe, Y., 206

para-constitutionalism, 97–100

Paris Charter (1990), 320

parliament. *See* Duma, State (parliament)

parties, political, 29, 33, 74, 96, 109, 128; bureaucracy and, 12; class divisions and, 447; dualism and, 104; education policy and, 229; formation of new parties, 135; organizational bases of, 97; Russians' attitudes toward, 175, 176, 177

patents, 241

patriotism, 151, 208

Pavlovsky, Gleb, 25

peasants, 74, 76, 78

perestroika, 49, 74, 79–80, 84, 103–4, 407, 442; democracy and, 174; education system and, 226–27; elites and, 191; leadership web and, 118–19; Medvedev's modernization compared to, 321; Western suspicion of, 273

Perry, William, 339

Peter the Great, 2, 76, 77, 139n7; Academy of Sciences and, 238; Baltic conquests of, 410; great-power status of Russia and, 415; modernization of, 292; resource mobilization of, 419; state-society relations and, 94
petrodollars, 18, 32, 79, 83, 122, 333
Philippines, 362
Pipes, Richard, 150
Platonov, Andrei, 443
Poland, 275, 306, 322, 440; GDP in, 42; missile defense system in, 309, 336, 342, 343; NATO membership for, 302; Poland-Lithuania, 75; Russian reconciliation with, 321, 346, 425
police/law enforcement, 3, 205; public distrust of, 175, 177; rule of law and, 292; secret, 77, 78
Politburo, 118
political economy, 20, 22, 102–3, 149, 228, 385–89
political elites, 192, 196, 198, 199, 202–3, 213, 214
political rights index, 49, 50
politics, 101, 178; economics and, xii, xiv, 102–3; evolution since end of Soviet era, 4; metapolitics, 102; para-politics, 99–100, 105, 107; political leadership and personalties, 5; Russians' interest in, 179–81, 180; social reproduction and, xiv–xviii; trusteeship and, 27
Politkovskaya, Anna, 276, 334
pollution, 253, 254, 262
Popov, Gavril, 394
Popov, Vladimir, 4, 11, 16
population size, 246, 454
populism, macro-economic, 56, 57

Portugal, 15, 44, 280, 288
post-Soviet space, 281–86, 293, 347; Central Asian economic integration, 390; energy routes through, 315; EU "neighboring policy" and, 304; frozen conflicts in, 293, 306, 392–93, 424; geopolitical rivalries in, 306, 310, 311; NATO expansion into, 323; Russian reintegration model for, 305; secession rights in, 308; social solidarity in, 448. *See also* former Soviet Union (FSU)
poverty, 18, 27, 308, 446; borderline of, 154, 155, 157, 158, 159, 163; features of poverty in Russia, 156–58; measurement of, 154–55, 155; middle class reduced to, 200; preservation of Russian society and, 447
power, 116, 377; balance of, 332, 336, 360; as confidence in obedience, 23; hard and soft, 422; philosophy of, 25; vertical of, 22, 29, 178, 333, 446
presidency (executive power), 24, 95, 119–20, 135; American, 116, 127; divided, 131–32; public trust in, 177, 178
Presidential Council for the Implementation of the National Projects, 97–98
press, freedom of the, 174, 176
price controls, 54
Primakov, Yevgeny, 230, 411, 415
Priority National Project (PNP) "Health," 249, 253
privatization, 2, 16, 28; elites and, 198–99, 203, 207–8, 211; financial elite and, 201; of government, 18; grab-and-run, 81; of the state, 18, 19, 21, 22, 89, 149; voucher privatization, 15, 20
productivity, xvi, 68, 449; capital, 63; Soviet average annual productivity, 65; Total

Factor Productivity (TFP), 62, 63
progressivism, 30, 33
property ownership, 159–61, 160, 166, 167, 199, 224n20; concentration of, 198; distribution of, 170, 171; negative attitudes toward, 170; Russian opposition to bourgeoisie and, 452; social inequalities and, 170–71
property rights, 21, 54, 55, 56, 147; elites and, 193, 220; intellectual, 241–42; undermining of, 89
Prussia, 76
Public Chamber, 97, 98
public opinion, 19, 452; levels of trust in institutions, 175, 177, 178; on relations with West, 182–83, 272; values and, 287–88
public sphere, 99
Pushkin, Alexander, 442
Putin, Vladimir, xv, 18, 84, 409; administrative regime and, 93; American influence in Central Asia and, 362; authoritarianism of, 73, 89, 333, 335; Bush II administration and, 331–37; constitutional coup of, 10; "Conversations," 129, 131, 133; crisis of regime, 12; democracy and, 28–29, 88, 121; on demographic crisis, 245; as dictator, 32; on "dictatorship of law," 88; education policy and, 230; election of (2000), 446; elites under, 203, 207; on European values, 286; former Soviet republics and, 306; German–Russian relations and, 311–12, 313, 315; ideology of regime, 28, 29; India and, 365; KGB background, 10, 133, 333; "Millennium Manifesto" and, 121, 122, 151; missile deployments in Central Europe opposed by, 342; modernization and, 74; nuclear arms control and, 40; oil revenue and, 200; oligarchs and, 19; para-politics and, 99; personality cult of, 10; political economy of Russia and, 22, 23; political process and, 101, 102; popularity of, 12, 35n7, 50–51, 123, 124–25, 453; post-presidential role of, 123–27; presidential term limits and, 123–24, 131, 141n22; on relations with West, 284, 302, 357, 358, 359, 413; restoration of the state and, 19–20, 82–83, 120–23, 334; Russia as global player and, 301; Russian identity and, 151; *siloviki* and, 95, 105, 123; on Soviet collapse, 408; strategic alignment with West sought by, 412; trusteeship idea and, 22, 24, 26; on U.S.–Russian relations, 272
Putin–Medvedev tandem, 50, 127–32, 138; dual state and, 105; as novelty in leadership, 115; possibility of political divergence within, 132–37; public approval rating of, 51; Russian public opinion and, 185

Al-Qaeda, 282

Rahr, Alexander, 6
Rakhmon, Emomali, 400
Rathenau, Walter, 77
Reagan, Ronald, 273–74
realpolitik, 287, 294, 418, 421
recession, transformational (1990s), 14, 41, 51; causes of, 52; collapse of state institutions and, 55; end of, 57; inevitability of, 60; loss of middle class in, 200; reduction of industrial output, 54. *See*

also economic/financial crisis
regions, governors/leaders of, 18, 81, 82, 101; election of, 290; modernization and, 218; public trust in, 177, 178; Putin and, 121
regions, Russian, 12, 15, 141n17, 174; developmental opportunities for, 27; elections in, 104–5, 185; health care system in, 254–55, 256, 265; population statistics in, 248–49; Putin's visits to, 129
religion, xvii, 22, 180, 289, 294, 357, 410
rents, 28, 96
reproduction, social, xii, xiv–xviii
research and development (R&D), 11, 49, 69, 136, 265
"resourcialization," 11, 48
retirement age, 260, 261
Ricardo, David, 451
Rice, Condoleezza, 331–32
Rodrik, Dani, 65
Romania, 42, 306
Roosevelt, Franklin D., 337, 381n14
Rosstat (Russian Federal Statistics Service), 246, 253, 254, 260
Rousseau, Jean-Jacques, 441
RTS index, 11
ruble, 17, 155, 280, 377
Rumsfeld, Donald, 332
Rus, Kievan, 357, 440
Russia, tsarist (imperial), 6–7, 12, 75–76, 77, 80, 139n7; constitutional-monarchy period, 105; control of information in, 289; eastward expansion of Russia and, 353; elites of, 191, 195; tsar as sovereign, 118
Russian Far East (RFE), 353, 380n5; relations with China and, 359, 361, 366; U.S. network of alliances in Asia and, 362; vulnerability of, 354
Russian Federation (RF), 130, 149, 198, 257, 424, 447; education system, 227, 228, 230, 233, 237; endurance of, 408; Europe and, 274; health statistics, 245–51; Kosovo war and, 330; lifestyles and health status, 251–53; military spending, 205; nationhood of, 445; republics of, 410; Ukraine and, 425; Western institutions' links with, 284
Russian–Georgian War (August 2008), 308, 309; Georgia's attack on South Ossetia, 182, 431; German–Russian relations and, 314; Kosovo NATO intervention as model for, 431n25; NATO–Russia ties suspended after, 344; prospect of renewed Cold War and, 320; U.S.–Russian relations and, 336, 337, 338. *See also* Abkhazia; Ossetia, South
Russian language, 149, 384, 388, 401
Russian Orthodox Church. *See* Orthodox Church/Christianity
Russian Revolution (1917), 14, 29, 67, 77, 93, 191; as catastrophe, 439; as model for non-industrialized countries, 442; religious dimension of, 443; split among elites and, 195; state power and, 94; World War I and, 289. *See also* Bolsheviks/Bolshevism; communism; Soviet Union (USSR)
Russians, 5, 12, 278; attitude toward work, 451; capitalist businesses founded by, xiv; democracy supported by, 29, 39n50, 174; expectations of, 23; in former Soviet republics, 283, 394, 410; identity and values, 146–47, 172, 173, 174, 180–81; income

levels among, 154–55, 155; national identity and, 148–51; "New Russians," 447; perceptions of crisis (2009), 151; rights and freedoms of, 10; West viewed by, 289, 358
Russophobia, Western, 440, 456
Rutskoi, Alexander, 143n40, 284

Saakashvili, Mikhail, 305, 424
Sachs, Jeffrey, xv
Sadovnichii, V. A., 227
Safaraliev, G., 236
Safranchuk, Ivan, 291
Saint-Simon, Henri de, 24
St. Petersburg State University, 231
Sakwa, Richard, 4, 29
Sarkozy, Nicolas, 343
Saudi Arabia, 287
Schleifer, Andrew, 41
Schmidt, Helmut, 310
Schmitt, Carl, 100
Schröder, Gerhard, 312–13, 314
Schumpeter, Peter, 23, 76
sciences, 5, 197, 434; in Central Asia, 384; education and, 231, 232, 237, 238–39, 243; Nobel Prize winners, 44; professional elites from, 204, 205, 208–9; research, 31; Soviet education system and, 227; West as leader in, 449. *See also* natural sciences
Scowcroft, Brent, 329
security, 294, 303, 358; geopolitics in tension with, 362; national security, xviii, 128, 267, 308; nuclear, 338, 339–42; security apparatus, xii, 87, 120, 204, 275
Seers, Dudley, 26
Self-knowledge (Berdyaev), 443–44

Semashko, N., 255, 256
semi-presidentialism, 127–28, 131
September 11, 2001 (9/11), attacks, 311, 332, 336, 412
Serbia, 42, 410
serfdom, 450
"seven bankers," 16
shadow economy, 15, 44, 46, 54, 71n14, 241
Shah of Shahs (Kapuscinski), 9
Shanghai Cooperation Organization (SCO), 356, 368, 369, 370, 379, 426; establishment of, 386; NATO cooperation with, 309, 324; Russia as co-chair of, 416, 427
Shenton, Robert, 24, 38n36
Shevardnadze, Eduard, 305
shock therapy, xv, 51, 52, 55, 89, 149
Shultz, George, 339
Shuvalov, Igor, 143n45, 280–81
Siberia, 302, 410; as crown jewel of Russian empire, 408; as European outpost in Asia, 353; gas fields of, 318; modernization of, 314, 322; prison camps in, 122; universities, 231
siloviki, 95, 102, 105, 111n23, 441; end of Putin's presidency and, 124; modernization and, 201, 217, 218; popular support for, 175; Putin's elite coalition and, 123
Singapore, 25, 125, 362
Singer, Hans, 26
Sino-Russian relations, 5, 6, 296, 353, 382n23; diplomatic rapprochement, 359; geopolitics in Asia and, 361; instrumentalism in Russian foreign policy and, 372; Iran and, 381n12; rivalry in Central Asia, 379; Russia as Western power and, 374; Sinocentric bias in Asia policies,

371, 375–76; as strategic partnership, 364–65, 366, 368–69; trade relations, 11. *See also* China

Slavophiles, 278, 358, 440

Slavs, eastern, 149

Slovakia, 42, 70n6, 304

Slovenia, 42, 332

Smith, Adam, 23, 451

smoking, as health factor, 251, 252

Smolin, O., 235

Sobchak, Anatolii, 120, 126

Sochi Declaration, 338

Social Chamber, 24

socialism, 24, 221

social sciences, xi, xii, 197; elites of, 205, 209–10; Marxist, 209; Soviet education system and, 226

sociology, 116, 145, 148, 152, 209

Solzhenitsyn, Alexander, 394

Sorokin, Vladimir, 74, 442

SORT (Strategic Offensive Reductions Treaty), 335, 340, 372

South Africa, xiii, 46

South America, xiii, 66

South Asia, 66, 68, 355, 368

"sovereign democracy," 29, 73, 103, 111n23, 429; civil society and, 106; great-power status of Russia and, 414; Surkov as ideologue of, 123, 334

"sovereignization," 4

sovereignty, 14, 15, 73, 287, 429; in European Union (EU), 285, 297; globalization and, 38n43; of Kosovo, 308; Putin's emphasis on, 22; Russia–EU relations and, 307; tsar as sovereign leader, 118; of Ukraine, 294

Soviet Union (USSR), xvi, 109, 298, 369, 449, 455; as abnormal developing country, 44; Afghanistan war, 282, 295, 368, 417; agriculture in, 450; annual average productivity, 65; armed forces of, 410, 419–20; Central Asia in, 384–85; Cold War and, 272–74, 281–82; crime in, 46; economy of, 11, 48, 64; education system, 225–27, 236, 242; elections in, 91; elites of, 195, 196, 207, 209, 210; generation born at end of, 202, 221; health care system, 255, 259, 265, 269n11; India's strategic relationship with, 367; inflation in, 57; labor camps, 47; leadership in, 118–19; level of corruption in, 15, 44; as military superpower, 296; modernizaton and, 273; as normal developing country, 49–50; as "organic" embodiment of Russian traits, 435; political economy of collapse, 80–82; post-Soviet attitudes toward Soviet era, 174; Putin's regime in relation to, 12; resurrection of, 10; Russian civilization and, 442–43; scientific establishment, xvii; shadow economy in, 15; socialist bloc and, 408; terror in, 77–78; Total Factor Productivity (TFP) in, 62–63, 64; transition to democracy, 198; in World War II, 78. *See also* Bolsheviks/Bolshevism; communism; former Soviet Union (FSU); Russian Revolution (1917)

Soviet Union, collapse of, xi, xv, 46, 152, 227, 255, 277; armed forces' acceptance of, 410; Central Asia and, 383, 386; debate about reasons for, 311; as end of Russian imperialism, 407; new states born from, 283, 383, 394, 418; U.S.–Russia security cooperation and, 334–35

Spain, 75, 81, 223n9, 284, 288
speech, freedom of, 19, 174, 176
Spengler, Oswald, 434–35, 442
spheres of influence, 304, 305, 338, 410, 414, 415, 419
spy scandals, 332
stability/stabilization, xi, xii, 2, 147, 150, 184; Asia compared with Europe, 360; of Brezhnev period, 79; in Central Asia, 389, 426; demographic crisis and, 246; economic, xv, xvi, xviii, 221; elites and, 197, 202, 215; erosion of U.S. power and, 348; freedom exchanged for, 19; hegemonic, 20; of leadership, 18; macroeconomic, 16; modernization and, 13; oil revenues as basis of, 200; Putin and, 96; social solidarity and, 448; stability-stagnation phase, 13, 32; trusteeship and, 27
Stalin, Joseph, 2, 47, 76, 77; cult of, 78, 118, 140n8, 445; modernization of, 292; post-Soviet Russian views of, 277; state power and, 94; suspicion of foreigners, 275; terror under, 334; Western view of, 306; World War II and, 276, 414, 419; Yalta agreement and, 381n14
Stalinism, 77–78, 79, 126, 191–92, 446; elites and, 195; Medvedev's condemnation of, 136; purges under, 118; Russian textbooks and, 277; whitewashing of, 133
standard of living (consumer opportunities), 153–55, 159, 188n19; of low-income Russians, 158–64; of middle classes, 165–66, 166–67, 168
START (Strategic Arms Reduction Treaty), 321, 339–40, 377
state, the, xv, 14–15, 219; collapse of institutions in 1980s–1990s, 51, 55; definition of, 16; dual state, 87–88, 91–94, 96, 98; economic stability and, xvi; media and power of, 13; mixed economy and, 181; modernization and, 4, 216; monopolies, 82; privatization of, 18, 19, 21, 22; property sold off, 15, 21; restoration of, 19–20, 27, 334; Russians' attitudes toward power of, 174, 181; society and, 94; as traditional dominant institution in Russia, 4; traditional functions of, 54. *See also* constitutional state; developmental state
State Council, 97, 236
State Duma. *See* Duma
"Stolen West or a Farewell Blow to Culture, The" (Kundera), 435
Stolypin, Pyotr, 2
strategic partnerships, 364–66, 377
Strauss, Leo, 441
Study of History, A (Toynbee), 452
subsidies, 15, 53, 54
suicide rate, 16, 19, 46, 47, 50, 63
Sultygov, Abdul-Khakim, 126
Surkov, Vladislav, 111n23, 123, 134–35, 334
Svanidze, Nikolai and Marina, 134, 136
Sweden, 76, 309
Syria, 301

Taiwan, 25, 63, 64
Tajikistan, 370, 410; China's economic interest in, 397; desire for union with Russia, 388; drug trafficking into, 391; emergence from Soviet collapse, 383; ethnic Uzbeks in, 393; GDP in, 42, 43; purchasing power of wage in, 448; Rogun Dam hydroelectric power station, 399–401

Talbott, Strobe, 327
Taliban, 282, 323, 332, 334–35; routed by U.S. forces, 422; as threat to stability in Central Asia, 362, 386. *See also* Afghanistan
Tatarstan, 408, 426, 428
taxes, 21, 29, 136; on big and small businesses, 212; education system and, 235; health care spending and, 264, 270n16; inheritance tax, 201; regions and federal budget, 15; state monopoly on collection of, 16
technocracy/technocrats, 80, 103, 108; depoliticization and, 100, 105; liberal-technocrats, 95, 102, 111n23; Soviet nomenklatura, 81
technology, xvii, 31, 79, 185, 389; conservative modernization and, 32; diversified economy and, 291; education and, 230, 243; elites and, 197; health care system and, 255, 262; innovation and, 27, 239; investment in, xi; modernization and, 221; nanotechnology, 239; Russia as civilization and, 440; Russia's backwardness in, 133; Soviet education system and, 226; transfer from West, 315; Western, 303, 449
Tekebaev, Omurbek, 392
television, 22, 25, 142n33; public trust in, 177; state control of, 13, 23
terrorism, xv, 120, 308; in Central Asia, 391; East–West coalitions against, 309, 321; in North Caucasus, 426. *See also* Beslan hostage crisis; September 11, 2001 (9/11), attacks
Thailand, 17, 362
Thatcher, Margaret, 283, 387

Third Reich, 78
Third World, 41, 79, 80, 408, 417
Tilly, Charles, 89
Time of Troubles, 16, 334
Titov, German, 272
Tolstoy, Lev, 442
Total Factor Productivity (TFP), 62–63, 64
totalitarianism, 74, 78, 116, 379, 419, 421
Toynbee, Arnold, 442, 452
trade, terms of, 52
trade unions, 175, 177, 184, 185
Transdniester republic (Transnistria), 305, 394, 410, 424
travel abroad, 169, 174, 176
Trenin, Dmitri, 6–7
Triesman, Daniel, 41
Trotsky, Leon, 445
trusteeship, 20, 22, 26, 27, 38n36; League of Nations' institution of, 24; move away from, 34
tsars. *See* Russia, tsarist (imperial)
Tsiolkovsky, Konstantin, 443
Tucker, Robert, 94
Turkestan Federation (Confederation), 387
Turkey, xiii, 41, 68, 276; Caucasus region and, 424; Central Asia and, 387, 400; European Union (EU) and, 288; Ottoman, 75; Rogun Dam (Tajikistan) and, 400
Turkmenistan, 42, 141n22, 318, 322, 410; China's economic interest in, 396; emergence from Soviet collapse, 383; energy cooperation with China, 362; gas pipeline project with Russia, 397–99; Northern Distribution Network (NDN) and, 345
Tyutchev, Fyodor, 437

Ukraine, 4, 37n28, 129, 282, 319, 323, 418; Crimea as territory of, 394, 410; depoliticization of energy relations with Russia, 321; divided executive in, 132; European "common neighborhood" and, 373; European Union (EU) and, 304, 305, 307, 309; famine in, 276; gas conflict with Russia, 307, 309, 316, 420; GDP in, 42, 43; Human Development Index, 49; independence of, 289; Orthodox Church in, 205; prospect of NATO membership, 303, 305, 425–26; purchasing power of wage in, 448; relations with EU and Russia, 293–94, 425; Russian empire and, 409; union with Russia, 410; U.S. influence in, 368, 415. *See also* Orange Revolution (Ukraine)

Ulumbekova, Guzel, 5

unemployment, 18

Union of Right Forces, 229

United Civi Front (OGF), 105

United Nations (UN), 230, 283, 323, 368; Cold War paralysis of, 416; Framework Convention on Climate Change, 322; General Assembly, 417; Iranian nuclear program and, 341, 343, 346, 381n12; Security Council, 283, 323, 341, 343, 416, 428

United Russia party, 29–30, 97, 104, 105, 123, 229; conservative modernization and, 428; in Duma elections, 126–27; electoral laws favoring, 122; as majority in the Duma, 135, 141n17; origins of, 121–22; Putin as leader of, 126, 127, 129, 138

United States, xvi, 4, 67; balance of world power and, 282; China's relations with, 372, 374; collapse of Soviet Union and, 311; constitution of, 130; constraints on power of, 279; declining hegemony of, xii–xiii, xviii; economic crisis and, 184; fertility rate in, 249; GDP in, 41; geopolitics in Asia and, 361–63; German trade with, 313; Iran sanctions and, 427; Iraq war and, 306; Korean Six-Party Talks and, 367; life expectancy in, 44; military presence in Asia, 362, 368; murder rate, 46; new NATO/EU members and, 306; number of billionaires, 17; presidency in, 116, 127, 130; Russian public's attitude toward, 182; Siberian energy imports, 318; trade with Russia, 11; unipolar dominance of, 327, 331, 334, 336, 414

Unity bloc, 120, 122

urbanization, 262, 456

U.S.–Russian relations, 296, 297, 327–28; Afghanistan and, 344–46; American foreign policy of 1990s, 328–31; arms control negotiations, 129; Bush II administration and, 331–37; crises and revivals in, 377; geopolitical rivalry, 310; as global problematic partnership, 368; imaginary curtain and, 272; long view of, 347–48; nuclear security and nonproliferation issues, 339–44; Obama administration's "reset button," 5–6, 337–38, 346–47, 372; in Putin's first term, 302–3; strategic alliance as prospect, 332

Uzbekistan, 55, 57, 70n6, 318, 345–46, 349n8; China's economic interest in, 397; emergence from Soviet collapse, 383; expanding population of, 388, 393; GDP in, 42, 43; geopolitics and, 362; Northern Distribution Network (NDN) and,

344, 345; opposition to Russian military base in Kyrgyzstan, 393, 394; Rogun Dam, 399, 400; strong authoritarianism in, 56; terrorist infiltration into, 391; uprising (2005) in, 336

Valdai Discussion Club, 37n28, 112n47, 125, 143n37
Velasco, A., 65
Velayati, Ali Akbar, 388
Venezuela, 10, 15, 44, 301, 322, 415
Vernadsky, Vladimir, 443
Vietnam, 52, 55, 56, 408
Virtual Gulag Museum, 104
visa barriers, dismantling of, 322
voucher privatization, 15, 20, 198
VTsIOM (Russian Public Opinion Research Center), 236

Walesa, Lech, 290, 418
Wallerstein, Immanuel, 39n50, 435
Warsaw Pact, 271, 283, 286, 304, 423; disbanding of, 417; German–Russian relations and, 312
water supplies, 377, 427; geopolitics of Central Asia and, 391; Rogun Dam (Tajikistan) and, 399–401; Russian health care system and, 253, 262
Wealth of Nations, The (Smith), 23
Weber, Max, 77, 451, 452, 453
West, the, xviii, 6, 73, 75; arms race with, 79; Asian–Russian engagement and, 355, 378–80; civilizational identity of Russia and, 438; Cold War and, 273, 274, 281–82; democratic model of, 9; as disunited entity, 301, 306, 311, 312; economic crisis and, 184, 379; education system, 228, 229; energy alliance with Russia, 316–17, 318–19, 322; exclusion of Russia from, 435; former Communist countries integrated into, 407; "new world order" and, 436; philosophical identity of Russia and, 442–47; public attitude in Russia toward, 182–83; Russia as part of, 411, 434; Russia as significant other of, 433, 442; Russian national identity and, 148, 357; secretiveness of Russian society and, 145; similarities and differences with Russia, 439–42; standard of living in, 154; strategic disagreement with Russia, 282–86; "values" argument with Russia, 286–88
Western Europe, 10, 77, 122, 278; balance of world power and, 282; in Cold War, 272; murder rate, 46; standard of living, 290; as technological rich space, 302
Westernizers, 73, 278, 440
Westphalian system, 287
White, Gordon, 38n43
Wilson, Andrew, 99
Witte, Sergei, 24
WMD (weapons of mass destruction), 355, 377, 379
workers/working class (proletariat), xvi, 74, 77, 83, 153; average real-term wages, 455; marginalization of, 82; in post-Stalinist USSR, 78
World Bank, 17, 401
World Health Organization (WHO), 251, 252, 263
World Trade Organization (WTO), 13, 183
World War I (Great War), xiii, 14, 197, 288–89
World War II, xiii, 192, 197, 303, 385, 414,

441; drop in industrial output during, 14; German–Russian reconciliation after, 310; as Great Patriotic War, 276, 279, 439; Russian and Western perceptions of, 276, 306–7; Russia's third modernization and, 78; Soviet victory in, 419

WTO (World Trade Organization), 311, 320, 321, 347, 417; Iran and, 427; Russia's eventual entry into, 423

Xinjiang Uyghur Autonomous Region (China), 386, 388, 390

Yabloko (Russian United Democratic Party), 229
Yakovlev, Alexander, 277
Yalta agreement, 286, 306, 381n14
Yanukovich, Viktor, 305, 321
Yassin, Yevgeny, 2
Yeltsin, Boris, 9, 19, 123, 133; Bush I administration and, 328, 329, 330; Clinton administration and, 329–31; communist challenge to reelection of, 101; costly reforms under, 55; debacles under presidency of, 82; democracy and, 28; Duma (parliament) confrontation with, 228, 441; elites under, 203, 204, 418; former Soviet republics and, 306; German reunification and, 310–11, 312; great-power status of Russia and, 411, 415; India and, 365; as leader, 117, 119–20, 128; liberalization policies of, 50; modernization and, 93; national identity and, 148; new political order and, 87; nuclear forces of Russia and, 420; post-Soviet borders of Russia and, 410; privatization of the state and, 21; on prospect of Russia in NATO, 284; Putin appointed by, 120–21; regions and, 15; relations with West and, 301; shock therapy and, 119, 149; U.S.–Russian relations and, 412

Yesenin, Sergei, 443
Yugoslavia, 275, 276, 286, 329, 410, 421
Yukos oil company, 89, 103, 105, 306, 312, 333
Yurchak, Alexei, 94
Yushchenko, Viktor, 305

Zambia, 141n22
Zatulin, Konstantin, 394
Zernov, V., 235
Zhangozha, Rustem, 6
Zhirinovsky, Vladimir, 394, 413
Zlobin, Nikolai, 37
Zubkov, Viktor, 128